Fodor's

MAINE, VERMONT & NEW HAMPSHIRE

12th Edition

Fodor's Travel Publications New Y[illegible] [illegible]oronto, London, Sydney, Auckland
www.fodors.com

Excerpted from *Fodor's New England*

Be a Fodor's Correspondent

Your opinion matters. It matters to us. It matters to your fellow Fodor's travelers, too. And we'd like to hear it. In fact, we need to hear it.

When you share your experiences and opinions, you become an active member of the Fodor's community. That means we'll not only use your feedback to make our books better, but we'll publish your names and comments whenever possible. Throughout our guides, look for "Word of Mouth," excerpts of your unvarnished feedback.

Here's how you can help improve Fodor's for all of us.

Tell us when we're right. We rely on local writers to give you an insider's perspective. But our writers and staff editors—who are the best in the business—depend on you. Your positive feedback is a vote to renew our recommendations for the next edition.

Tell us when we're wrong. We're proud that we update most of our guides every year. But we're not perfect. Things change. Hotels cut services. Museums change hours. Charming cafés lose charm. If our writer didn't quite capture the essence of a place, tell us how you'd do it differently. If any of our descriptions are inaccurate or inadequate, we'll incorporate your changes in the next edition and will correct factual errors at fodors.com immediately.

Tell us what to include. You probably have had fantastic travel experiences that aren't yet in Fodor's. Why not share them with a community of like-minded travelers? Maybe you chanced upon a beach or bistro or B&B that you don't want to keep to yourself. Tell us why we should include it. And share your discoveries and experiences with everyone directly at fodors.com. Your input may lead us to add a new listing or highlight a place we cover with a "Highly Recommended" star or with our highest rating, "Fodor's Choice."

Give us your opinion instantly at our feedback center at www.fodors.com/feedback. You may also e-mail editors@fodors.com with the subject line "Maine,Vermont & New Hampshire" Editor." Or send your nominations, comments, and complaints by mail to "Maine, Vermont & New Hampshire" Editor, Fodor's, 1745 Broadway, New York, NY 10019.

You and travelers like you are the heart of the Fodor's community. Make our community richer by sharing your experiences. Be a Fodor's correspondent.

Happy traveling!

Tim Jarrell, Publisher

FODOR'S MAINE, VERMONT & NEW HAMPSHIRE

Editors: Cate Starmer, Carolyn Galgano

Editorial Contributors: Josh McIlvain, Debbie Harmsen
Writers: Neva Allen, Stephen Allen, John Blodgett, Bethany Cassin Beckerlegge, Sascha de Gersdorff, Amanda Knorr, Susan MacCallum-Whitcomb, Michael Nalepa, Brigid Sweeney, Linh Tran, Mary Ruoff, George Semler, Sarah Stebbins, and Michael de Zayas

Production Editor: Jennifer DePrima
Maps & Illustrations: Mark Stroud and David Lindroth, *cartographers;* Bob Blake, Rebecca Baer, *map editors;* William Wu, *information graphics*
Design: Fabrizio La Rocca, *creative director*; Guido Caroti, Siobhan O'Hare, *art directors*; Tina Malaney, Chie Ushio, Ann McBride, Nora Rosansky, Jessica Walsh, *designers*; Melanie Marin, *senior picture editor*
Cover Photo: (Grafton, Vermont): Chad Ehlers/photolibrary.com
Production Manager: Amanda Bullock

COPYRIGHT

12th Edition

ISBN 978-1-4000-0464-5

ISSN 1073-6581

SPECIAL SALES

This book is available at special discounts for bulk purchases for sales promotions or premiums. Special editions, including personalized covers, excerpts of existing books, and corporate imprints, can be created in large quantities for special needs. For more information, write to Special Markets/Premium Sales, 1745 Broadway, MD 6-2, New York, New York 10019, or e-mail specialmarkets@randomhouse.com.

AN IMPORTANT TIP & AN INVITATION

Although all prices, opening times, and other details in this book are based on information supplied to us at press time, changes occur all the time in the travel world, and Fodor's cannot accept responsibility for facts that become outdated or for inadvertent errors or omissions. So **always confirm information when it matters,** especially if you're making a detour to visit a specific place. Your experiences—positive and negative—matter to us. If we have missed or misstated something, **please write to us.** We follow up on all suggestions. Contact the Maine, Vermont & New Hampshire editor at editors@fodors.com or c/o Fodor's at 1745 Broadway, New York, NY 10019.

PRINTED IN CHINA

10 9 8 7 6 5 4 3 2 1

CONTENTS

MAPS

ABOUT THIS BOOK

Our Ratings

Sometimes you find terrific travel experiences and sometimes they just find you. But usually the burden is on you to select the right combination of experiences. That's where our ratings come in.

As travelers we've all discovered places whose worthiness is obvious. And sometimes a place is so wonderful that superlatives don't do it justice: you just have to see for yourself. These sights, properties, and experiences get our highest rating, **Fodor's Choice,** indicated by orange stars throughout this book.

Black stars highlight sights and properties we deem **Highly Recommended,** places that our writers, editors, and readers praise again and again for consistency and excellence.

By default, there's another category: any place we include in this book is by definition worth your time, unless we say otherwise. And we will.

Disagree with any of our choices? Care to nominate a place or suggest that we rate one more highly? Visit our feedback center at www.fodors.com/feedback.

Budget Well

Hotel and restaurant price categories from ¢ to $$$$ are defined in the opening pages of each chapter. For attractions, we always give standard adult admission fees; reductions are usually available for children, students, and senior citizens. Want to pay with plastic? **AE, D, DC, MC, V** following restaurant and hotel listings indicate if American Express, Discover, Diners Club, MasterCard, and Visa are accepted.

Restaurants

Unless we state otherwise, restaurants are open for lunch and dinner daily. We mention dress only when there's a specific requirement and reservations only when they're essential or not accepted—it's always best to book ahead.

Hotels

Hotels have private bath, phone, TV, and air-conditioning and operate on the European Plan (a.k.a. EP, meaning without meals), unless we specify that they use the Continental Plan (CP, with a continental breakfast), Breakfast Plan (BP, with a full breakfast), or Modified American Plan (MAP, with breakfast and dinner), Full American Plan (FAP, with all means), or are all-inclusive (AI, with all meals and most activities). We always list facilities but not whether you'll be charged an extra fee to use them, so when pricing accommodations, find out what's included.

Listings

- ★ Fodor's Choice
- ★ Highly recommended
- Physical address
- Directions or Map coordinates
- Mailing address
- Telephone
- Fax
- On the Web
- E-mail
- Admission fee
- Open/closed times
- Metro stations
- Credit cards

Hotels & Restaurants

- Hotel
- Number of rooms
- Facilities
- Meal plans
- Restaurant
- Reservations
- Dress code
- Smoking
- BYOB

Outdoors

- Golf
- Camping

Other

- Family-friendly
- See also
- Branch address
- Take note

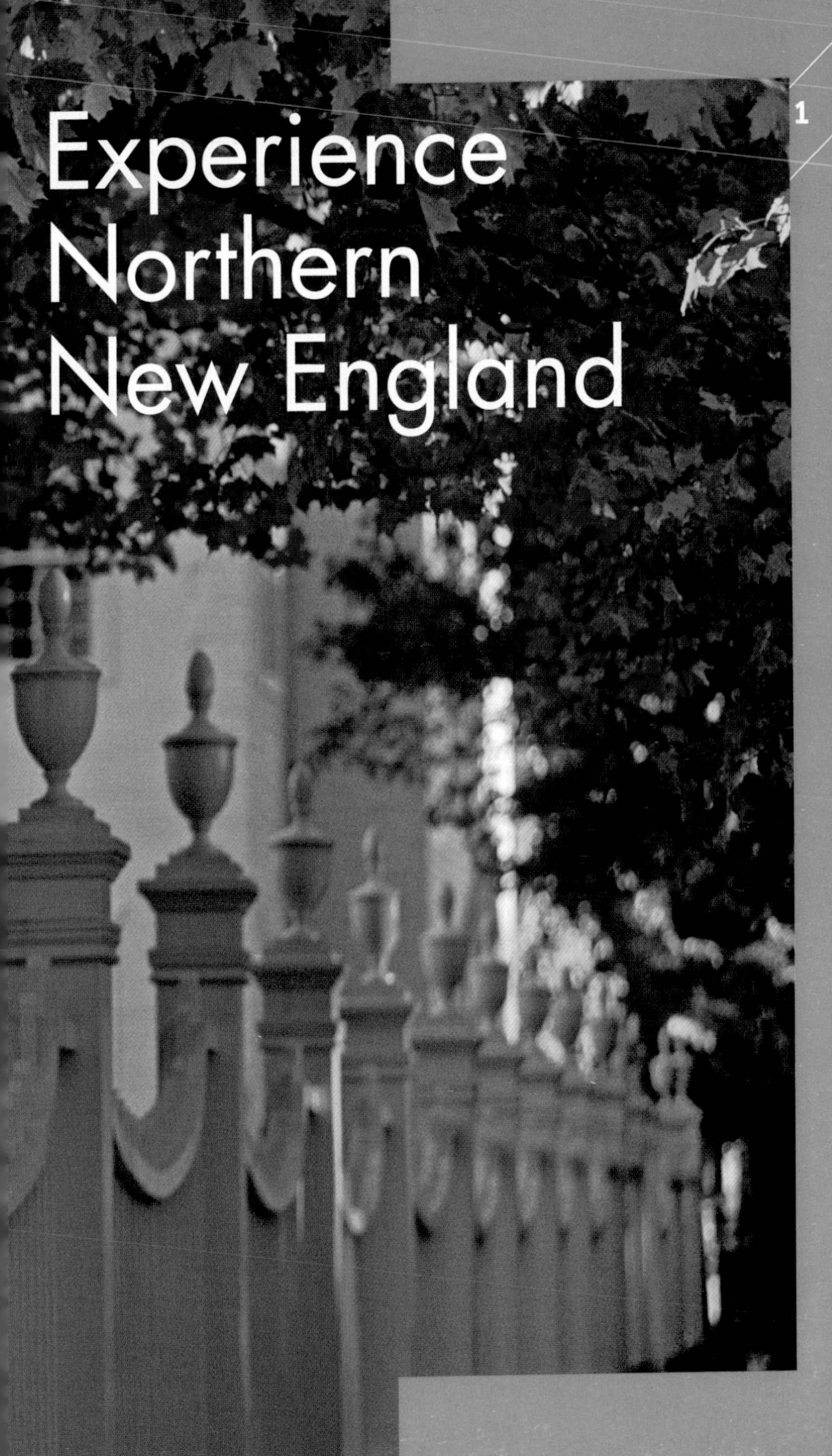

Experience Northern New England

1

WHAT'S WHERE

The following numbers refer to chapters.

2 Vermont. Southern Vermont has farms, freshly starched New England towns, quiet back roads, bustling ski resorts, and strip-mall sprawl. Central Vermont's trademarks include famed marble quarries, and large dairy herds and pastures that create the quilted patchwork of the Champlain Valley. The heart of the area is the wilderness of the Green Mountain National Forest. Both the state's largest city (Burlington) and the nation's smallest state capital (Montpelier) are in northern Vermont, as are some of the most rural and remote areas of New England. With Montréal only an hour from the border, the Canadian influence is strong here.

3 New Hampshire. Portsmouth, the star of New Hampshire's 18-mi coastline, has great shopping, restaurants, music, and theater, as well as one of the best historic districts in the nation. The Lakes Region, rich in historic landmarks, also has good restaurants, several golf courses, hiking trails, and antiques shops. People come to the White Mountains to hike and climb, to photograph the dramatic vistas and the vibrant foliage, and to ski. Western and central New Hampshire have managed to

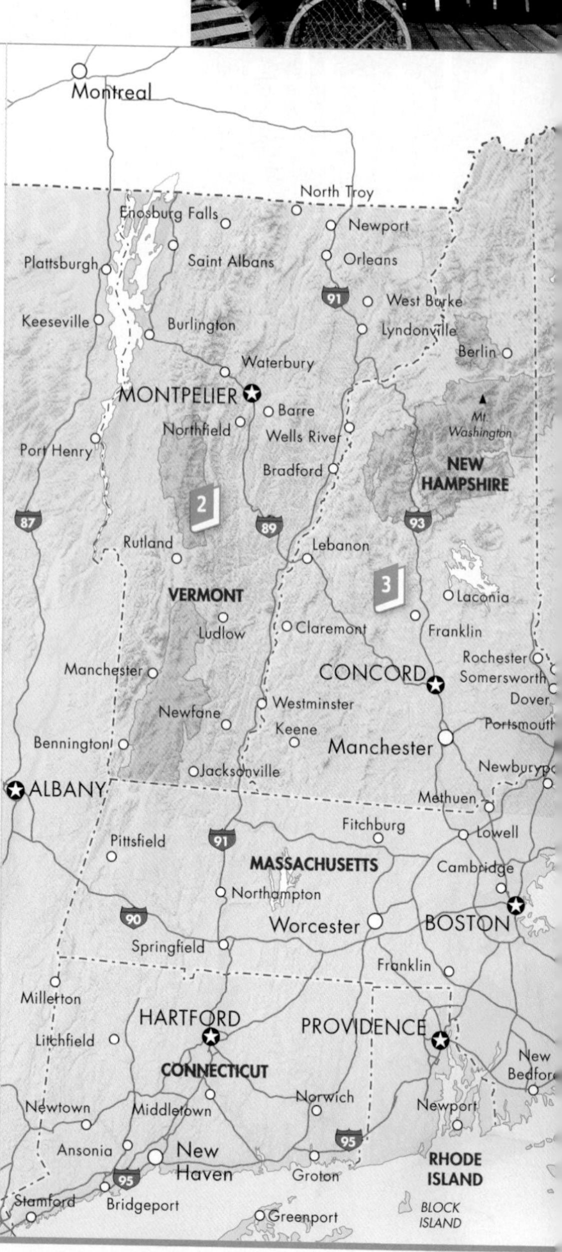

keep the waterslides and the outlet malls at bay. The lures here include Lake Sunapee, the charming college town of Hanover, and Mt. Monadnock, the second-most-climbed mountain in the world.

4 Inland Maine. Maine is by far the largest state in all of New England. At its extremes it measures 300 mi by 200 mi; all other New England states could fit within its perimeter. The Western Lakes and vast North Woods regions attract skiers, hikers, campers, anglers, and other outdoors enthusiasts.

5 Coastal Maine. Classic townscapes, rocky shorelines punctuated by sandy beaches, and picturesque downtowns draw vacationing New Englanders to Maine like a magnet. Maine's southernmost coastal towns are too overdeveloped to give you the rugged, Down East experience, but the Kennebunks will: classic townscapes, rocky shorelines punctuated by sandy beaches, quaint downtown districts. Purists hold that the Maine Coast begins at Penobscot Bay, where the vistas over the water are wider and bluer, the shore a jumble of granite boulders. East of the bay is Acadia National Park, with waterfront Bar Harbor being the park's main gateway town, for both motorists and cruise ship passengers.

NORTHERN NEW ENGLAND PLANNER

When to Go

Northern New England is a largely year-round destination, with winter popular with skiers, summer a draw for families and beach lovers, and fall a delight to those who love the bursts of autumnal color. Spring can also be a great time, with sugar shacks transforming maple sap into all sorts of tasty things and lilacs scenting the air. But, take note that you'll probably want to avoid rural areas during mud season (April) and black-fly season (mid-May to mid-June).

Average Temperatures

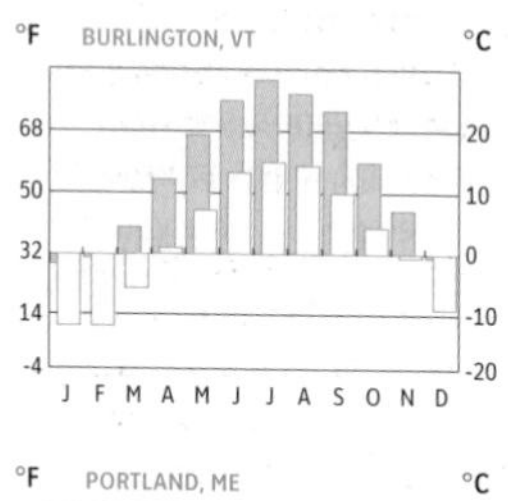

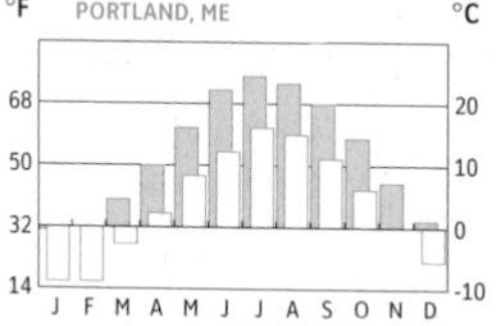

Getting Here

Most travelers visiting New England head for a major gateway, such as Boston or Manchester, New Hampshire, and then rent a car to explore the region. The New England states form a fairly compact region, with few important destinations more than six hours apart by car.

Air Travel: Boston's Logan Airport is one of the nation's most important domestic and international airports, with direct flights arriving from all over North America and across the globe. New England's other major airports receive few international flights (mostly from Canada) but do offer a wide range of direct domestic flights to East Coast and Midwest destinations, and to a lesser extent to the western United States. Times from U.S. destinations are similar, if slightly shorter, to Albany and Hartford, assuming you can find direct flights.

Airports: The main gateway to New England is Boston's Logan International Airport (BOS), the region's largest. Manchester Boston Regional Airport (MHT), about an hour north of Boston in New Hampshire, is another major airport. Additional New England airports served by major carriers include Portland International Jetport (PWM) in Maine and Burlington International Airport (BTV) in Vermont. Other airports are in Albany, New York (ALB, near Vermont), and Bangor, Maine (BGR).

Train Travel: Amtrak offers frequent daily service along its Northeast Corridor route from Washington, Philadelphia, and New York to Boston. Amtrak's high-speed *Acela* trains link Boston and Washington, with a stop at Penn Station in New York and other communities along the way. The *Downeaster* connects Boston with Portland, Maine, with stops in coastal New Hampshire.

Other Amtrak services include the *Vermonter* between Washington, D.C., and St. Albans, Vermont, and the *Ethan Allen Express* between New York and Rutland, Vermont. These trains run on a daily basis. To avoid last-minute confusion, allow 15 to 30 minutes to make train connections.

1

Getting Around

Car Travel: New England is best explored by car. Areas in the interior are largely without heavy traffic and congestion, and parking is consistently easy to find, even in cities. Coastal New England is considerably more congested, and parking can be hard to find in resort towns along the coast. Still, a car is typically the best way to get around even on the coast (though you may want to park it at your hotel and use it as little as possible, exploring on foot, on a bike, or by local transit and cabs once you arrive). In the interior, public transportation options are more limited and a car is almost necessary. Morning and evening rush-hour traffic isn't usually much of a problem, except in larger cities and along the coast. Note that Interstate 95 is a toll highway throughout New England, and Interstate 90 (it's the Massachusetts Turnpike) is a toll road throughout Massachusetts. If you rent a car at Logan International Airport, allow plenty of time to return it—as much as 60 minutes to be comfortable.

See the Getting Here and Around section in the planner at the beginning of each chapter and Travel Smart Maine, Vermont & New Hampshire for more information on transportation.

Boat Travel: Ferry routes provide access to many islands off the Maine Coast. In addition, ferries cross Lake Champlain between Vermont and upstate New York. International service between Portland and Bar Harbor, Maine, and Yarmouth, Nova Scotia, is also available. With the exception of the Lake Champlain ferries—which are first-come, first-served—car reservations are always advisable.

Travel Times

From Boston to	By Air	By Car	By Bus	By Train
Acadia National Park, ME	1 hour	5 hours	not applicable	not applicable
Burlington, VT	no direct flight	3½ hours	4½–5 hours	8¾ hours
New York, NY	¾–1 hour	4 hours	4½–7 hours	3½–4¼ hours
Portland, ME	no direct flight	2 hours	2¼ hours	2½ hours

Online Resources

Check out the official home page of each New England state for information on state government, as well as for links to state agencies with information on doing business, working, studying, living, and traveling in these areas. GORP is a terrific general resource for just about every kind of recreational activity; just click on the state link under "Destinations" and you'll be flooded with links to myriad topics, from wildlife refuges to ski trips to backpacking advice.

Yankee, New England's premier regional magazine, also publishes an informative travel Web site. Another great Web resource is Visit New England.

Online Info **GORP** (*www.gorp.com*). **Visit New England** (*www.visitnewengland.com*). ***Yankee Magazine*** (*www.yankeemagazine.com/travel*).

Visitor Info **Maine Office of Tourism** (*888/624–6345* *www.visitmaine.com*). **State of New Hampshire Division of Travel and Tourism Development** (*800/386–4664 or 603/271–2665* *www.visitnh.gov*). **Vermont Department of Tourism and Marketing** (*802/828–3237, 800/837–6668 brochures* *www.vermontvacation.com*).

MAINE, VERMONT & NEW HAMPSHIRE TOP ATTRACTIONS

Acadia National Park

(A) The first national park established east of the Mississippi River is the wonder of the Maine Coast. In the warmer months, take a drive around Mount Desert Island's 20-mi Park Loop Road to indulge in spectacular views of the mountains and the sea. Head to the top of Cadillac Mountain for amazing 360-degree views; bike the scenic 45-mi carriage-road system; or go on a park ranger–led boat trip in search of porpoises, seals, and seabirds. Adorable Bar Harbor is the park's gateway town.

Appalachian Trail

(B) The 2,160-mi Appalachian Trail, running from Springer Mountain, Georgia, to Katahdin, Maine, cuts through New Hampshire, Vermont, and Maine. Though the trail is best known as a weeks-long endurance test for expert hikers, many short stretches can be walked in a few hours. "AT" terrain in Maine and New Hampshire can be quite challenging.

Baxter State Park

(C) Baxter State Park's 200,000 acres contain numerous lakes and streams, plus Mt. Katahdin, Maine's tallest peak and the northern terminus of the Appalachian Trail. Offering frequent sightings of moose, white-tailed deer, and black bear, the remote park provides a wilderness experience not found elsewhere in New England.

Green Mountains

(D) Vermont takes its nickname (the Green Mountain State) and its actual name (*verts monts* is "green mountains" in French) from this 250-mi-long mountain range that forms the spine of the state. Part of the Appalachian Mountains, the Green Mountains are a wild paradise filled with rugged hiking trails (most notably the Long Trail and the Appalachian Trail), unspoiled forests, quaint towns, and some of the East Coast's best ski resorts.

Lake Winnipesaukee

(E) As fun to fish as it is to pronounce, the largest (and longest) lake in New Hampshire is home to three species of trout, bass, bluegill, and more. The 72-square-mi lake also contains more than 250 islands, beaches, arcades, water parks, and countless other fun family diversions. In summer, Winnipesaukee buzzes with activity as travelers flock to resort towns like Wolfeboro, Weirs Beach, and Meredith.

Maine Coast

(F) Maine's coast would stretch for thousands of miles if you could pull it straight. The Southern Coast is the most visited section, but don't let that stop you from heading farther "Down East" (Maine-speak for "up the coast"). Despite the cold North Atlantic waters, beachgoers enjoy miles of rocky beaches, with sweeping views of lighthouses, forested islands, and the wide-open sea.

Mt. Washington

(G) New England's highest mountain, this New Hampshire peak has been scaled by many a car (as the bumper stickers will attest). You can also take a cog railway to the top or, if you're an intrepid hiker, navigate a maze of trails. The weather station here recorded a wind gust of 231 MPH in April 1934—the highest wind speed ever recorded at a surface station—and the average temperature at the summit is below freezing.

Portland Head Light

(H) The towering white stone lighthouse stands over the keeper's house, a white home with a red roof. Besides a harbor view, its park has walking paths, picnic facilities, and wide, grassy expanses perfect for flying a kite in the gusty ocean winds. This iconic Maine lighthouse is in Cape Elizabeth's Fort Williams Park.

TOP EXPERIENCES

Peep a Leaf

Tourist season in most of New England is concentrated in late spring and summer, but a resurgence happens in September and October, when leaf peepers from all corners descend by the car- and busload to see the leaves turn red, yellow, orange, and all shades in between. Foliage season can be fragile and unpredictable—temperature, winds, latitude, and rain all influence when the leaves turn and how long they remain on the trees—but that makes the season even more precious.

Comb a Beach

Whether sandy or rocky, New England beaches can be filled with flotsam and jetsam. Anything from crab traps unmoored by heavy waves to colored sea glass worn smooth by the water to lost jewelry and the like can appear at your feet. Also common are shells of sea urchins, clams, and other bivalves that gulls have dropped to crack open and eat the tender insides. During certain times of the year sand dollars of all sizes and colors are plentiful—you may even find one still whole.

Hit the Slopes

Though the mountain snow in New England is not as legendary as the powder out West (and, in fact, can be downright unpleasant when packed snow becomes crusty ice), skiing is quite popular here. Vermont has several ski areas, with Killington being the largest resort in the Northeast: its 200 trails span seven mountains. New Hampshire's White Mountains also cater to snow-sport lovers, while Sunday River and Sugarloaf in Maine are perennial favorites with advanced intermediate and expert skiers. Beginners (and lift-ticket bargain hunters) can choose from a number of small but fun hills throughout Northern New England.

Eat a Maine Lobster

Maine lobsters are world renowned, and available throughout New England, but without a doubt the best place to eat them is near the waters of origin. Lobster meat is sweet, especially the claws, and most agree that simple preparation is the best way to go: steamed and eaten with drawn butter or pulled into chunks and placed in a hot dog bun with a leaf of lettuce and the barest amount of mayonnaise—the famous New England lobster roll.

Rise and Shine at a B&B

New England's distinct architecture, much of it originating in the 18th and 19th centuries, has resulted in beautiful buildings of all shapes and sizes, many of which have been restored as bed-and-breakfasts. These inns typify the cozy, down-home, and historic feel of New England, and are an ideal lodging choice. This is especially true when the weather is cold, and the warm ambience of many of these inns more than justifies the slightly higher prices you'll pay here versus a hotel.

Watch a Whale

The deep, cold waters of the North Atlantic serve as feeding grounds and migration routes for a variety of whales, including the fin, the humpback, the occasional blue, and the endangered right whales. Maine's Southern Coast and Mid-Coast regions are the best places to hop aboard a whale-watching boat to motor 10 mi or more off the coast.

Fair Thee Well

New Englanders love their fairs and festivals. Maine-iacs celebrate the moose, clam, lobster, and blueberry, and a fair highlights organic farmers and their products. Maple sugar and maple syrup are feted in Vermont, while "live free or die" New Hampshire honors American

independence. Many rural communities throughout New England hold agricultural fairs in late August and September.

Find the Perfect Souvenir

Artists and craftspeople abound in New England, meaning that finding the perfect souvenir of your vacation will be an enjoyable hunt. Whether you choose a watercolor of a picturesque fishing village, a riotously colorful piece of hand-painted pottery, or a handcrafted piece of jewelry, you'll be supporting the local economy while taking a little piece of the region home with you.

Get Up Close and Personal with Nature

New England might be known for its flashy foliage in fall and spectacular slopes in winter, but the outdoors can delight the senses in all seasons. You can breathe in the ocean air as you drive along the Maine Coast. Alternatively, enjoy the fragrance of the mountains and forests while hiking along the Appalachian Trail. You may observe such animals as moose and bear. Close to the ocean there are numerous chances to see birds, seals, and whales.

Savor Sweet Stuff

Summer vacations in New England go hand in hand with sweet treats; it's difficult to visit without sampling homemade fudge at an old-fashioned candy store, or bringing home some saltwater taffy. Be sure to try a Maine specialty—the delectable whoopie pie (made from two chocolate circles of cake with vanilla cream filling in between). If you are visiting Maine when the tiny but succulent wild blueberry is in season, take every opportunity to savor this flavorful fruit, whether in pie, muffin, or pancake form. In Vermont, go on a factory tour at Ben & Jerry's and have a delicious cone afterward. You can even have dessert for breakfast when you top your pancakes with Vermont's legendary maple syrup.

Check out Lighthouses

Maine's long and jagged coastline is home to more than 60 lighthouses, perched high on rocky ledges or on the tips of wayward islands. Lighthouse enthusiasts and preservation groups restore and maintain many of them and often make them accessible to the public. Some of the state's more famous lights include Portland Head Light, immortalized in one of Edward Hopper's paintings; Two Lights, a few miles down the coast in Cape Elizabeth; and West Quoddy Head, on the easternmost tip of land in the United States.

Sail the Coast

The coastline of Northern New England is a sailor's paradise, complete with hidden coves, windswept islands, and picture-perfect harbors where you can pick up a mooring for the night. With nearly 3,500 mi of undulating, rocky shoreline, you could spend a lifetime of summers sailing the waters off the Maine Coast and never see it all. If you're not one of the lucky few with a sailboat to call your own, there are many companies that offer sailboat charters, whether for day or weeklong trips.

Get the First Sight of First Light

At 1,530 feet, Cadillac Mountain, in Maine's Acadia National Park, is the highest mountain on the New England Coast—so what better place to view the sunrise? Drive the winding and narrow 3.5-mi road to the summit before dawn, and you could be the first person in the United States to see the sun's rays. (Note that this depends on the time of year; sometimes the first sunrise is at West Quoddy Head Lighthouse in Lubec, Maine).

OUTDOOR ACTIVITIES

The Beach

Long, wide beaches edge the Maine and New Hampshire Coast. The waters are at their warmest in August, though they're cold even at the height of summer along much of Maine. Inland, small lake beaches abound, most notably in New Hampshire and Vermont. Though most hit these sandy getaways in summer, beaches can even be enjoyable in winter (for a stroll, not a swim), as you'll likely have the shore to yourself.

Many of the beaches have lifeguards on duty in season; some have picnic facilities, restrooms, changing facilities, and concession stands. Depending on the locale, you may need a parking sticker to use the lot.

Hampton Beach State Park, New Hampshire. The Granite State's ocean shore is short, but this state park along historic Route 1 takes full advantage of the space it has. In addition to swimming and fishing, there are campsites and an amphitheater with a band shell for fair-weather concerts.

Old Orchard Beach, Maine. Think Coney Island on a smaller scale. A ghost town in the off-season, the main drag fills with cruising cars and amblers of all ages come summer. There's a white-sand beach to be sure (lapped by cold North Atlantic waters), but many come to ride the Pirate Ship at Palace Playland, drop quarters at the arcade, and browse the multitude of trinket-and-T-shirts shops.

Reid State Park, Maine. Just east of Sheepscot Bay on Georgetown Island, oceanside Reid State Park, with its large dunes, is a beach bum's wonderland. The water is cold much of the year, but it's a beautiful and quiet place to spend some solitary time looking for sand dollars or climbing the rocks at low tide, exploring tidal pools. Great views can be had from the park's rocky Griffith Head.

Bicycling

Biking on a road through New England's countryside is an idyllic way to spend a day. Many ski resorts allow mountain bikes in summer.

Acadia National Park, Maine. At the heart of this popular park is the 45-mi network of historic carriage roads covered in crushed rock that bicyclists share only with equestrians and hikers. Sturdier riders can ascend the road to the top of Cadillac Mountain, but take caution: heavy traffic in the high season can make this a dangerous proposition. Biking in Maine is also scenic in and around Kennebunkport, Camden, Deer Isle, and the Schoodic Peninsula.

Killington Resort, Vermont. Following the lead of many ski resorts in the western United States, Killington allows fat-tire riders on many of its ski trails long after the snow has melted. Stunt riders can enjoy the jumps and bumps of the mountain bike park.

All Along the Coast. U.S. 1, Maine. The major road that travels along the Maine Coast is only a narrow two-lane highway for most of its route, but it is still one of the country's most historic highways. As a result, it's very popular in spring, summer, and fall with serious long-distance bike riders. Bicyclists should ride carefully and look out for motorists who may be trying to catch a glimpse of the sea.

Boating

Along many of New England's larger lakes, sailboats, rowboats, canoes, kayaks, and outboards are available for rent at local marinas. Sailboats are available for rent at a number of seacoast locations, but you may

be required to prove your seaworthiness. Lessons are frequently available.

Allagash Wilderness Waterway, Maine. This scenic and remote waterway—92 mi of lakes, ponds, rivers, and streams—is part of the 740-mi Northern Forest Canoe Trail, which floats through New York, Vermont, Québec, and New Hampshire as well as Maine.

Lake Champlain, Vermont. Called by some the Sixth Great Lake, 435-square-mi Lake Champlain is bordered by Vermont's Green Mountains to the east and the Adirondacks of New York to the west. Burlington, Vermont, is the state's largest lakeside city and a good bet for renting a boat—be it canoe, kayak, rowboat, skiff, or motorboat. Attractions include numerous islands and deep-blue water that's often brushed by New England breezes.

Golf

Golf caught on early in New England. The region has an ample supply of public and semiprivate courses, many of which are part of distinctive resorts or even ski areas. One dilemma facing golfers is keeping their eye on the ball instead of the scenery. The views are marvelous at Balsams Wilderness grand resort in Dixville Notch, New Hampshire, and also at the nearby course at the splendid old Mount Washington Hotel in Bretton Woods. During prime season, make sure you reserve ahead for tee times, particularly near urban areas and at resorts.

The Gleneagles Golf Course at the Equinox, Vermont. One of the stateliest lodging resorts in all of New England, the Equinox golf course is par-71 and 6,423 yards, and is especially alluring in fall when the trees that line the fairways explode in color. After golf, go to the 13,000-square-foot spa for some pampering. The resort is ringed by mountain splendor.

Samoset Resort on the Ocean, Maine. Few things match playing 18 holes on a championship course that's bordered by the North Atlantic. In Rockport, Maine, along Penobscot Bay, Samoset Resort's course is open from May through October. Book a room at the luxurious hotel here to make it a complete golf vacation.

Hiking

Probably the most famous trails in the region are the 273-mi Long Trail, which runs north–south through the center of Vermont, and the Maine–to–Georgia Appalachian Trail, which runs through New England on both private and public land. The Appalachian Mountain Club (AMC) maintains a system of staffed huts in New Hampshire's Presidential Range, with bunk space and meals available by reservation. State parks throughout the region afford good hiking.

Mt. Washington, New Hampshire. The cog railroad and the auto road to the summit are popular routes up New England's highest mountain, but for those with stamina and legs of steel it's one heck of a hike. There are a handful of trails to the top, the most popular beginning at Pinkham Notch Visitor Center. Be sure to dress in layers and have some warm clothing for the frequent winds toward the peak.

The Long Trail, Vermont. Following the main ridge of the Green Mountains from one end of Vermont to the other, this is the nation's oldest long-distance trail. In fact, some say it was the inspiration for the Appalachian Trail. Hardy hikers make a go of its 273-mi length, but day hikers can drop in and out at many places along the way.

QUINTESSENTIAL MAINE, VERMONT & NEW HAMPSHIRE

Artisans

Northern New England's independent artisans have built a thriving cottage industry. Some of the finest potters spin their wheels on the coast, and one-off, often whimsical jewelry is wrought in silver, pewter, and other metals. Modern furniture makers take classic simple New England designs, including those of the Shakers and Quakers, and refine them for buyers the world over who are willing to pay thousands for craftsmanship that has withstood the test of time. The varied landscapes throughout the three states have patiently sat for thousands of painters, whose canvases are sold in small shops and local museums. Visitors who come to Maine, Vermont, and New Hampshire to create their own art have plenty to paint or photograph. Photographers especially focus their lens on classic New England architecture, colorful lobster buoys, and the mighty windjammers.

The Coast

The coast of Maine and New Hampshire is both workplace and playground. Starting in the 17th century, boatbuilders sprang up in one town after another to support the shipping and fishing trades. Today, the boatyards are far fewer than in historical times, but shipping and especially fishing remain important to the economy on the coast and beyond. But it's not all work and no play—some of the classic wooden sailboats now serve cruise goers, and some fishermen have traded in their lobster boats for whale-watching vessels. Maine's Reid and Popham Beach state parks are a beachcomber's paradise, and the relatively chilly waters of the North Atlantic don't scare away swimmers come summertime.

If you want to get a sense of Northern New England culture, and indulge in some of its pleasures, start by familiarizing yourself with the rituals of daily life. Here are a few highlights of life in Maine, Vermont, and New Hampshire that you can sample with relative ease.

Fall Foliage

It's impossible to discuss Northern New England without mentioning that time of year when the region's deciduous trees explode in reds, yellows, oranges, and other rich hues. The season can be finicky, defined as much by the weather as it is by the species of trees—a single rainstorm can strip trees of their grandeur. But what happens in one region doesn't necessarily happen in another, and if you have the time you can follow the colors from one area to the next. Remember, you'll be competing with thousands of other like-minded leaf peepers, so be sure to book lodging early on for the hot spots. Your preparedness will pay off the first time you drive down a winding country road aflame in the bright sun of a crisp Northern New England autumn day.

Food, Glorious Food

Maine will forever be famous for its delectable lobsters, and Vermont equally known for its maple treats. But Maine lobster and Vermont Grade A maple syrup are just samples to whet your appetite. Dining in Northern New England is a feast for the gastronomist to behold, and it runs the gamut from the simply prepared to the most artistic of presentations; from blueberry pie just like Grandma used to make to slow-cooked Long Island duck with kumquat, stuffed profiterole, glazed carrots, and long pepper. Beyond lobsters, also delicious are the area's shellfish: shrimp, clams (little redneck is a perennial favorite), scallops, crab, and mussels. Chefs who grew up here may leave to learn their trade, but often return and enrich the dining scene; the region is known for attracting newcomers as well.

NORTHERN NEW ENGLAND TODAY

The People

The idea of the self-reliant, thrifty, and often stoic New England Yankee has taken on almost mythic proportions in American folklore, but in some parts of New England—especially in rural Maine, New Hampshire, and Vermont—there still is some truth to this image, which shouldn't come as a surprise. You need to be independent if you farm an isolated field, live in the middle of a vast forest, or work a fishing boat miles off the coast. Like any part of the country, there are stark differences between urban New Englanders and those you encounter outside the cities. Both, though, are usually fiercely proud of the region, its rugged beauty, and its contributions to the nation.

The Politics

Though they're often portrayed as a bunch of loony liberals, the political views of New Englanders are actually more complex. The region's representation in both the United States Senate and the House of Representatives is heavily Democratic, even in those states that elect a Republican governor. Voters in New Hampshire, which now hosts the nation's first primary each presidential election season, tend to lean conservative but with a distinctly libertarian slant, as do residents in many rural portions of New England. Four states that allow same-sex marriage are in New England (Massachusetts, Vermont, New Hampshire, and Connecticut).

The Economy

Long gone are the days since New England's shoe and textile industries sailed overseas, when many a mill town suffered blows to employment and self-image. In recent years, the unemployment rate has fallen below the national average. In Maine, the lobster-fishing industry, a main component of that state's economy, is in crisis. As lobster is viewed as an expensive delicacy, demand has decreased dramatically in tough times. Between 2005 and 2009 lobster prices dropped nearly $2 a pound, putting a financial squeeze on the industry as fuel costs have risen.

Exports are a major part of the modern New England economy, consisting heavily of computer and other electronics, chemicals, and specialized machinery. The service industries also are strong, especially in the insurance and financial sectors. Some towns are known for a particular export: Bath, Maine, has naval shipyards supplying the military with high-technology fighting ships; Barre, Vermont, quarries granite. Assorted foods produced include maple syrup, blueberries, lobster, and other seafood.

The Language

As people move around, the local accents have begun to blend, creating more of a general New England accent. (In fact, in some urban areas, you may not hear any accent.) Linguistic differences, however, are still evident in some places, especially close to the coast.

Maine has a Boston-like accent (lengthened vowels, dropped Rs in certain places) but with nuanced differences. True Mainers drop or soften their Rs—making their favorite dish "lobstah"; they also often accentuate the vowel, so a one-word syllable can be pronounced like two, meaning "here" may become "hee-yuh."

In New Hampshire the accent is not nearly as strong, but it comes out in certain words, like how locals pronounce their capital "Cahn-cuhd."

NORTHERN NEW ENGLAND WITH KIDS

New England is ideally suited for family vacations, offering historic sites, beaches, sports and recreation, outdoor adventures, and some of the most beautiful mountain and coastal scenery around. Places that are especially appealing to children are indicated by a rubber-duckie icon (🐤) in the margin.

Children's Museum of Maine, Portland, Maine. How can kids not enjoy a museum with an exhibit called Attack of the Bloodsuckers? Located in the heart of Portland's Arts District, this interactive facility has been voted the nation's 14th-best children's museum by *Child Magazine*. There's something scheduled most every day, and in summer special camps are available. A first-floor exhibit called Our Town includes a lobster boat, car repair shop, and supermarket—all for hands-on learning.

Hampton Beach, New Hampshire. This seaside diversion draws families to its almost Coney Island–like fun. Along the boardwalk, kids enjoy arcade games, parasailing, live music, and an annual children's festival. They can even learn how saltwater taffy is made.

Montshire Museum of Science, Norwich, Vermont. This interactive museum uses more than 60 hands-on exhibits to explore nature and technology. The building sits amid 110 acres of woodlands and nature trails. Live animals are on-site as well.

Shelburne Farms, Shelburne, Vermont. This working dairy farm is also an educational and cultural resource center. Visitors can watch artisans make the farm's famous cheddar cheese from the milk of more than 100 purebred and registered Brown Swiss cows, and a children's farmyard and walking trails round out the experience.

Southworth Planetarium, Portland, Maine. This University of Southern Maine facility offers classes such as night sky mythology and introductory astronomy. The 30-foot dome houses a star theater complete with lasers, digital sounds, and a star projector that displays more than 5,000 heavenly bodies.

Story Land, Glen, New Hampshire. This fantasyland theme park has been entertaining young children and their parents since 1954. The $24 per person admission (ages three and older) covers all 21 rides, which include the Flying Fish, Swan Boats, Antique Cars, and the Huff Puff and Whistle Railroad. When summer gets too hot, kids can enjoy the Oceans of Fun Sprayground.

Whale-watching, in Maine. Few things speak of the great, deep, blue unknown like a whale, and any sighting of these magnificent creatures is dramatic and not soon forgotten. The whale-watching season varies by tour skipper, but generally is contained between the months of April and October. A few companies to sign on with for spotting these mighty creatures are Cap'n Fish's Boat Trips in Boothbay Harbor, which has both whale- and puffin-watching adventures; Bar Harbor Whale Watching Co., offering three-hour excursions via catamaran; Old Port Mariner Fleet, based in Portland and also offering fishing trips; and Island Cruises, which departs from Head Harbour Wharf in Wilson's Beach and allows passengers to spot whales while aboard a lobster boat.

GREAT ITINERARIES

HIGHLIGHTS OF THE MAINE COAST

Much of the appeal of the Maine Coast lies in its geographical contrasts, from its long stretches of swimming and walking beaches in the south to the cliff-edged, rugged rocky coasts in the north. And not unlike the physical differences of the shoreline, each town along the way reveals a slightly different character. This sampler tour will provide you with a good taste of the Maine Coast.

Day 1: The Yorks

Start your trip in York Village with a leisurely stroll through the seven buildings of the Old York Historical Society, getting a glimpse of 18th-century life in this gentrified town. Spend time wandering amid the shops or walking the nature trails and beaches around York Harbor. There are several grand lodging options here, most with views of the harbor. If you prefer a livelier pace, continue on to York Beach, a haven for families with plenty of entertainment venues. Stop at Nubble Light for a seaside lunch or dinner.

Days 2 and 3: Ogunquit

For well over a century, Ogunquit has been a favorite vacation spot for those looking to combine the natural beauty of the ocean with a sophisticated environment. Take a morning walk along the Marginal Way to see the waves crashing on the rocks. In Perkins Cove, have lunch, stroll the shopping areas, or sign on with a lobster boat cruise to learn about Maine's most important fishery—the state's lobster industry supplies more than 90% of the world's lobster intake. See the extraordinary collection at the Ogunquit Museum of American Art, take in a performance at one of the several theater venues, or just spend time on the beach.

Day 4: The Kennebunks

Head north to the Kennebunks, allowing at least two hours to wander through the shops and historic homes of Dock Square in Kennebunkport. This is an ideal place to rent a bike and amble around the backstreets, head out on Ocean Avenue to view the large mansions, or ride to one of the several beaches to relax awhile.

Days 5 and 6: Portland

You can easily spend several days in Maine's largest city, exploring its historic neighborhoods, shopping and eating in the Old Port, or visiting one of several excellent museums. A brief side trip to Cape Elizabeth takes you to Portland Head Light, Maine's first lighthouse, which was commissioned by George Washington in 1790. The lighthouse is on the grounds of Fort Williams Park and is an excellent place to bring a picnic. Be sure to spend some time wandering the ample grounds. There are also excellent walking trails (and views) at nearby Two Lights State Park. If you want to take a boat tour while in Portland, get a ticket for Casco Bay Lines and see some of the islands that dot the bay.

Day 7: Bath to Camden

Head north from Portland to Bath, Maine's shipbuilding capital, and tour the Maine Maritime Museum or have lunch on the waterfront. Shop at boutiques and antiques shops, or view the plentitude of beautiful homes. Continue on U.S. 1 north, through the towns of Wiscasset and Damariscotta, where you may find yourself pulling over frequently for outdoor flea markets or intriguing antiques shops.

Days 8 and 9: Camden

Camden is the picture-perfect image of a seaside tourist town: hundreds of boats bobbing in the harbor, immaculately kept antique homes, streets lined with boutiques and specialty stores, and restaurants serving lobster at every turn. The modest (by Maine standards, anyway) hills of nearby Mt. Battie offer good hiking and a great spot from which to picnic and view the surrounding area. Camden is one of the hubs for the beloved and historic windjammer fleet—there is no better way to see the area than from the deck of one of these graceful beauties. If you're an art lover, save some time for Rockland's Farnsworth Art Museum and the Wyeth Center.

Days 10 and 11: Mount Desert Island and Acadia National Park

From Camden, continue north along U.S. 1, letting your interests dictate where you stop (or head south to explore the Blue Hill peninsula). Once you arrive on Mount Desert Island, you can choose to stay in Bar Harbor, the busiest village in the area, or in the quieter Southwest Harbor area; either way, the splendor of the mountains and the sea surround you. If you have more time, several days can easily be spent exploring Acadia National Park, boating or kayaking in the surrounding waters, and simply enjoying the stunning panorama.

A CELEBRATION

Picture this: one scarlet maple offset by the stark white spire of a country church, a whole hillside of brilliant foliage foregrounded by a vintage barn or perhaps a covered bridge that straddles a cobalt river. Such iconic scenes have launched a thousand postcards and turned New England into the ultimate fall destination for leaf peepers.

OF COLOR

By Susan MacCallum-Whitcomb

Mother Nature, of course, puts on an annual autumn performance elsewhere, but this one is a showstopper. Like the landscape, the mix of deciduous (leaf-shedding) trees is remarkably varied here and creates a broader than usual palette. New England's abundant evergreens lend contrast, making the display even more vivid. Every September and October, leaf peepers arrive to cruise along country lanes, join outdoor adventures, or simply stroll on town greens.

Did you know the brilliant shades actually lurk in the leaves all year long? Leaves contain three pigments. The green chlorophyll, so dominant in summer that it obscures the red anthocyanins and orangey-yellow carotenoids, decreases in fall and reveals a crayon box of color.

Above, Vermont's Green Mountains are multicolored in the fall (and often white in winter).

PREDICTING THE PEAK

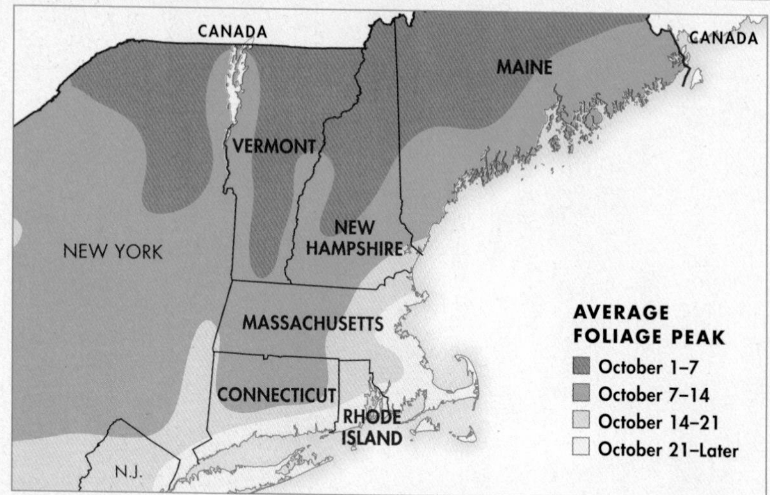

LOCATION

Pinning down precisely when colors will appear remains an inexact science, although location plays a major role. Typically, the transformation begins in the highest and northernmost parts of New England in mid-September, then moves steadily into lower altitudes and southern sectors throughout October.

For trip planning, think in terms of regions rather than states. In Maine (a huge state that runs north–south) leaf color can peak anytime from the fourth week of September to the third week of October, depending on the locale.

ROOM AT THE INN?

Accommodations fill quickly in autumn. Vermont's top lodgings sell out months in advance for the first half of October. So book early and expect a two-night minimum stay requirement. If you can't find a quaint inn, try basing yourself at a B&B or off-season ski resort. Also, be prepared for some sticker shock; you can save if you travel midweek.

WEATHER

Early September weather is another deciding factor. From the foliage aficionado's perspective, the ideal scenario is calm, temperate days capped by nights that are cool but still above freezing. If the weather is too warm, it delays the onset of the season. If it's too dry or windy, they shrivel up or blow off.

COLOR CHECK RESOURCES

Curious about current conditions? In season, each state maintains a dedicated Web site reporting on foliage conditions. Weather Channel has peak viewing maps and Foliage Network uses a network of spotters to chart changes.

- **Foliage Network:** 🌐 *www.foliagenetwork.com*
- **Maine:** ☎ *888/624-6345* 🌐 *www.mainefoliage.com*
- **New Hampshire:** ☎ *800/258-3608* 🌐 *www.visitnh.gov*
- **Vermont:** ☎ *800/837-6668* 🌐 *www.foliage-vermont.com*
- **Weather Channel:** 🌐 *www.weather.com*

TOP TREES FOR COLOR

A AMERICAN BEECH. This tree's smooth, steel-gray trunk is crowned with gold, copper, and bronze-tinted leaves in autumn, giving it a metallic sheen. Though the elliptical leaves sometimes hang on all winter, its "fruit" goes fast because beechnuts are a popular snack for birds, squirrels, and even bears.

B NORTHERN RED OAK. The upside of oaks is that they retain their fall shading until late in the season—the downside is that, for most species, that color is a boring brown. Happily, the northern red isn't like other members of the oak family. Its elongated, flame-shaped leaves turn fiery crimson and incandescent orange.

C QUAKING ASPEN. Eyes and ears both prove useful when identifying this aspen. Look for small, ovate leaves that usually become almost flaxen. Or listen for the leaves' quake: a sound, audible in even a gentle breeze, which the U.S. Forest Service likens to that made by "thousands of fluttering butterfly wings."

D SUGAR MAPLE. The leaf of the largest North American maple species is so lovely that Canada put it on its national flag. Each generally has five multi-pointed lobes—plus enough anthocyanin to produce a deep red color. The tree itself produces plentiful sap and is the cornerstone of New England's syrup industry.

E WHITE ASH. This tall tree typically grows to between 65 to 100 feet. Baseball enthusiasts admire the wood (which is used to craft bats); while foliage fans admire the compound leaves, each consisting of five to nine slightly serrated, tapering leaflets. They range in hue from burgundy and purple to amber.

F WHITE BIRCH. A papery, light, bright bark makes this slender hardwood easily recognizable. Centuries ago, Native Americans used birch wood to make everything from canoes to medicinal teas. Today's photographers know the bark also makes great pictures since it provides a sharp contrast to the tree's vibrant yellow leaves.

FALL FOLIAGE ITINERARY

In fall, northern New England's dense forests explode into reds, oranges, yellows, and purples. This itinerary works its way south and west from west-central Maine into northwestern Vermont. ⇨ For local drives perfect for an afternoon, also see our Fall Foliage Drive Spotlights in Chapters 2 (Vermont), 3 (New Hampshire), and 4 (Inland Maine).

DAYS 1 AND 2

WESTERN LAKES AND MOUNTAINS: MAINE

The Rangley Lakes Region in west-central Maine is a concentrated area of sparkling lakes and mountainous terrain, with peaks covered in flaming foliage. Some of Maine's taller mountains are here, and the lakes make for a nice foreground in photographs. Drive south toward the Rumford and Bethel regions and you run into even more mountains, including a couple of the state's premier ski areas and a section of White Mountain National Forest.

DAYS 3 AND 4

WHITE MOUNTAINS AND LAKES REGION: NEW HAMPSHIRE

In New Hampshire, I–93 narrows as it winds through craggy Franconia Notch. The sinuous Kancamagus Highway passes through the mountains to Conway. In Center Harbor, in the Lakes Region, you can ride the MS *Mount Washington* for views of the Lake Winnipesaukee shoreline, or ascend to Moultonborough's Castle in the Clouds for a falcon's-eye look at the colors.

DAY 5

NORTHEAST KINGDOM: VERMONT

After a side trip along Lake Willoughby, explore St. Johnsbury, where the Fairbanks Museum and the St. Johnsbury Athenaeum reveal Victorian tastes in art and natural-history collecting. In Peacham, stock up for a picnic at the Peacham Store.

DAYS 6 AND 7

BURLINGTON AREA: VERMONT

The north country's palette unfolds in Newport, where the blue waters of Lake Memphremagog reflect the foliage. In Burlington, the elms will be turning colors on the University of Vermont campus. Take a ferry ride across Lake Champlain for great views of Vermont's Green Mountains and New York's Adirondacks. After visiting the resort town of Stowe, continue beneath the cliffs of Smugglers' Notch.

THE MOOSE IS LOOSE!

⚠ Take "Moose Crossing" signs seriously because things won't end well if you hit an animal that stands six feet tall and weighs 1,200 pounds. Some 40,000 reside in northern New England. To search out these ungainly creatures in the wild, consider an organized moose safari in northern New Hampshire or Maine.

Vermont

WORD OF MOUTH

"I spend the rest of the year looking forward to [autumn in Vermont]. There is nowhere else on earth I'd rather be in October. We do get lots of visitors this time of year (I love to look for the out-of-state license plates when I am out peeping at leaves—they always outnumber the Vermont plates)."

—patomech

WELCOME TO VERMONT

TOP REASONS TO GO

★ **Small-town charm:** Vermont rolls out a seemingly never-ending supply of tiny, charming towns made of steeples, general stores, village squares, red barns, and B&Bs.

★ **Ski resorts:** The East's best skiing takes place in uncrowded, modern facilities, with great views and lots and lots of fresh snow.

★ **Fall foliage:** Perhaps the most vivid colors in North America wave from the trees in September and October, when the whole state is ablaze.

★ **Gorgeous landscapes:** This sparsely populated, heavily forested state is an ideal place to find peace and quiet amid the mountains and valleys.

★ **Tasty and healthy eats:** The state's great soil and focus on local farming and ingredients yields great cheeses, dairies, orchards, vineyards, local food resources, and restaurants.

1 Southern Vermont. Most people's introduction to the state is southern Vermont, accessible by car from New York and Boston. Like elsewhere across the state, you'll find unspoiled towns, romantic B&Bs, rural farms, and pristine forests. There are two notable exceptions: sophisticated little Manchester has upscale shopping, and independent Brattleboro is a hippie outpost and environmentally conscious town.

2 Central Vermont. Similar to southern Vermont in character and geography, central Vermont's star is Stowe, the quintessential ski town east of the Mississippi. Warren, Waitsfield, and Middlebury are among its charming small towns.

3 Northern Vermont. The northernmost part of the state is a place of contrasts. Burlington, on Vermont's "West Coast," is the state's most populous city at around 60,000 residents; it's an environmentally sensitive, crunchy, laid-back college town. To the east, the landscape becomes desolate, with natural beauty and almost no significant population, making the Northeast Kingdom a refuge for nature lovers and aficionados of wide open northern beauty.

GETTING ORIENTED

Vermont can be divided into three regions. The southern part of the state, flanked by Bennington on the west and Brattleboro on the east, played an important role in Vermont's Revolutionary War–era drive to independence (yes, there was once a Republic of Vermont) and its eventual statehood. The central part is characterized by rugged mountains and the gently rolling dairy lands near Lake Champlain. Northern Vermont is home to the state's capital, Montpelier, and its largest city, Burlington, as well as its most rural area, the Northeast Kingdom. The Green Mountains run from north to south up the center of the state; this central spinal corridor is unpopulated, protected national forest.

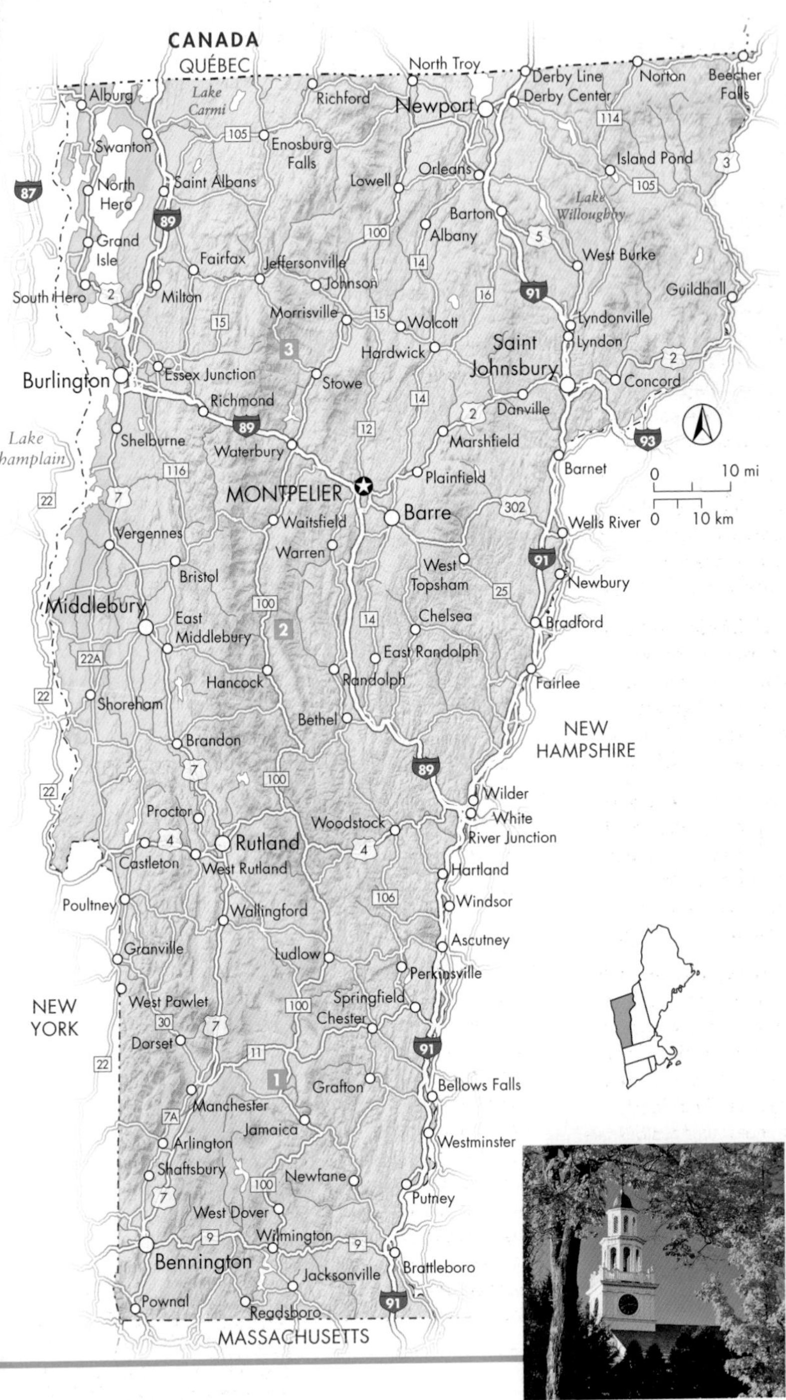
CANADA
QUÉBEC
Lake Carmi
Alburg
Swanton
North Hero
Grand Isle
South Hero
Saint Albans
Enosburg Falls
Richford
North Troy
Newport
Derby Line
Derby Center
Norton
Beecher Falls
Island Pond
Lake Willoughby
Orleans
Lowell
Barton
Albany
West Burke
Guildhall
Fairfax
Milton
Jeffersonville
Johnson
Morrisville
Wolcott
Hardwick
Lyndonville
Lyndon
Saint Johnsbury
Concord
Burlington
Essex Junction
Richmond
Stowe
Danville
Marshfield
Lake Champlain
Shelburne
Waterbury
Barnet
Plainfield
MONTPELIER
Barre
Waitsfield
Warren
Wells River
Vergennes
Bristol
West Topsham
Newbury
Middlebury
East Middlebury
Chelsea
Bradford
East Randolph
Randolph
Hancock
Shoreham
Fairlee
Bethel
Brandon
NEW HAMPSHIRE
Proctor
Wilder
White River Junction
Woodstock
Rutland
Castleton
West Rutland
Hartland
Poultney
Windsor
Wallingford
Granville
Ascutney
Ludlow
Perkinsville
West Pawlet
Springfield
Chester
NEW YORK
Dorset
Grafton
Bellows Falls
Manchester
Jamaica
Arlington
Westminster
Shaftsbury
Newfane
Putney
West Dover
Wilmington
Bennington
Brattleboro
Jacksonville
Pownal
Readsboro
MASSACHUSETTS
0 10 mi
0 10 km

VERMONT PLANNER

When to Go

In summer, the state is lush and green, although in winter, the hills and towns are blanketed with snow and skiers travel from around the East Coast to challenge Vermont's peaks. Fall is one of the most amazing times to come. If you have never seen a kaleidoscope of autumn colors, a trip to Vermont is worth braving the slow-moving traffic and paying the extra money for fall lodging. The only time things really slow down is during "mud" season—otherwise known as late spring. Even innkeepers have told guests to come another time. Activities in the Champlain Islands come essentially to a halt in the winter, except for ice fishing and snowmobiling. Two of the state's biggest attractions, Shelburne Farms and the Shelburne Museum, are closed mid-October through April. Otherwise, though everything looks completely different depending on the season, Vermont is open all year.

Getting Here and Around

Air Travel: Continental, Delta, JetBlue, United, and US Airways fly into Burlington International Airport. Rutland State Airport has daily service to and from Boston on US Airways Express.

Boat Travel: Lake Champlain Ferries (☎ *802/864–9804* 🌐 *www.lakechamplainferries.com*) operates three ferry crossing routes between the lake's Vermont and New York shores: Grand Isle–Plattsburgh, NY; Burlington–Port Kent, NY; and Charlotte–Essex, NY.

Car Travel: Vermont is divided by a mountainous north–south middle, with a main highway on either side: scenic Route 7 on the western side and Interstate 91 (which begins in New Haven and runs through Hartford, central Massachussets, and along the Connecticut River in Vermont to the Canadian border) on the east. Interstate 89 runs from New Hampshire across central Vermont from White River Junction to Burlington and up to the Canadian border. For current road conditions, call 800/429–7623.

Train Travel: Amtrak (☎ *800/872–7245* 🌐 *www.amtrak.com*) has daytime service linking Washington, D.C., with Brattleboro, Bellows Falls, White River Junction, Montpelier, Waterbury, Essex Junction, and St. Albans via its Vermonter line. Amtrak's Ethan Allen Express connects New York City with Fair Haven and Rutland.

Planning Your Time

There are many ways to take advantage of Vermont's beauty: skiing or hiking its mountains, biking or driving its back roads, fishing or sailing its waters, shopping for local products, visiting its museums and sights, or simply finding the perfect inn and never leaving the front porch.

Distances are relatively short, yet the mountains and many back roads will slow a traveler's pace. You can see a representative north–south section of Vermont in a few days; if you have up to a week, you can hit the highlights. Note that many inns have two-night-minimum stays on weekends and holidays.

About the Restaurants

Everything that makes Vermont good and wholesome is distilled in its eateries, making the regional cuisine much more defined than neighboring states. With an almost political intensity, farmers and chefs have banded together to insist on utilizing Vermont's wonderful bounty. Especially in summer, the produce and meats are impeccable. Many of the state's restaurants belong to the Vermont Fresh Network (🌐 *www.vermontfresh.net*), a partnership that encourages chefs to create menus from local produce.

Great chefs are coming to Vermont for the quality of life, and the New England Culinary Institute is a recruiting ground for new talent. Seasonal menus use local fresh herbs and vegetables along with native game. Look for imaginative approaches to native New England foods such as maple syrup (Vermont is the largest U.S. producer), dairy products (especially cheese), native fruits and berries, "new Vermont" products such as salsa and salad dressings, and venison, quail, pheasant, and other game.

Your chances of finding a table for dinner vary with the season: lengthy waits are common at peak times (a reservation is always advisable); the slow months are April and November. Some of the best dining is at country inns.

About the Hotels

Vermont's only large chain hotels are in Burlington and Rutland. Elsewhere it's just quaint inns, B&Bs, and small motels. The many lovely and sometimes quite luxurious inns and B&Bs provide what many people consider the quintessential Vermont lodging experience. Most areas have traditional base ski condos; at these you sacrifice charm for ski-and-stay deals and proximity to the lifts. Rates are highest during foliage season, from late September to mid-October, and lowest in late spring and November, although many properties close during these times. Winter is high season at Vermont's ski resorts.

WHAT IT COSTS

	¢	$	$$	$$$	$$$$
Restaurants	under $10	$10–$16	$17–$24	$25–$35	over $35
Hotels	under $100	$100–$149	$150–$199	$200–$250	over $250

Restaurant prices are based on the median main course price at dinner. Hotel prices are for two people in a standard double room in high season, excluding service and tax. Some inns add a 15%–18% service charge. (Vermont has a 9% hotel tax.)

Outdoor Activities

Biking: Vermont, especially the often deserted roads of the Northeast Kingdom, is great bicycle-touring country. Many companies lead weekend tours and weeklong trips throughout the state. If you'd like to go it on your own, most chambers of commerce have brochures highlighting good cycling routes in their area.

Canoeing and Kayaking: Getting on Vermont's many rivers and lakes is a great way to experience nature. Outfitters can be found almost anywhere there's water.

Fishing: Central Vermont is the heart of the state's warm-water lake and pond fishing area. Lake Champlain, stocked annually with salmon and lake trout, has become the state's ice-fishing capital.

Hiking: Vermont is an ideal state for hiking—80% of the state is forest, and trails are everywhere. The Appalachian Trail runs the length of the state. In fact, it was the first portion of the trail to be completed, and in Vermont it is called the Long Trail. Many bookstores in the state have numerous volumes dedicated to local hiking.

Skiing: The Green Mountains run through the middle of Vermont like a bumpy spine, visible from almost every point in the state; generous accumulations of snow make them an ideal site for skiing. Route 100 is also known as Skier's Highway, passing by 13 of the state's ski areas.

VERMONT FALL FOLIAGE DRIVE

Eighty percent of Vermont is forested, and since cities are few and far between, the interior of Vermont is a rural playground for leaf peepers and widely considered to have the most intense range of foliage colors anywhere on the continent. The few distractions from the dark reds and yellow, oranges and russets—the tiny towns and hamlets—are as pristine as nature itself.

Begin this drive in Manchester Village, along the old-fashioned, well-to-do homes lining Main Street, and drive south to Arlington, North Bennington, and Old Bennington. Stop first just a mile south along 7A at **Hildene**, the Lincoln family home. The 412 acres of explorable grounds here are ablaze with color, and the views over the Battenkill Valley are as good as any you can find anywhere. Continue south another mile along 7A to **Equinox Nursery**, where you can pick your own pumpkin from a huge patch, try delicious apple cider and cider doughnuts, and take in the stunning countryside. A few more miles south along 7A is the small town of Arlington.

BEST TIME TO GO

Late September and early October are the times to go, with the southern area peaking about a week later than the north. Remember to book hotels in advance. The state has a Fall Foliage Hotline and an online interactive map (☎ *800/VERMONT* 🌐 *www.foliage-vermont.com*).

PLANNING YOUR TIME

The drive from Manchester to Bennington outlined here is just 30 minutes, but a relaxed day is best to take in all the sights. You'll want to allot one to two hours for Hildene, and less than an hour for each of the other stops.

From 7A in Arlington, you can take two adventurous and stunning detours. One is pure foliage: follow 313 west a few miles to the New York state border for more beautiful views Or head east a mile to East Arlington where delightful shops await you, including **Grist Mill Antiques**, which is set right above a wonderfully cascading brook. (You can continue even farther east from this spot to Kelly Stand Road leading into the Green Mountains; this is a little-known route that can't be beat.) Back on 7A South in Arlington, stop at the **Cheese House**, the delightfully cheesy roadside attraction.

Farther south into Shaftsbury is **Clearbrook Farm**, a brilliant place for cider and fresh produce and pumpkins. Robert Frost spent much of his life in South Shaftsbury, and you can learn about his life at his former home, the **Stone House.** From South Shaftsbury take Route 67 through North Bennington and continue on to Route 67A in Old Bennington. Go up the 306-foot-high **Bennington Battle Monument** to survey the seasonal views across four states. Back down from the clouds, walk a few serene blocks to the cemetery of the **Old First Church**, where Robert Frost is buried, and contemplate his autumnal poem, "Nothing Gold Can Stay."

NEED A BREAK?

Equinox Nursery (✉ *1158 Main St. [7A], Manchester* ☎ *802/362-2610* 🌐 *www.equinoxvalleynursery.com* ⏲ *Apr.–Dec., Mon.–Sat. 8–5, Sun. 9–4*) carries fresh produce, seasonal snacks, and is full of family-friendly fall activities—a corn maze, pumpkin golf (mini played with small pumpkins and croquet mallets), hay rides, and pumpkin carving.

Set on more than 20 acres, **Clearbrook Farm** (✉ *47 Hidden Valley Rd., Manchester* ☎ *802/442-4273* 🌐 *www.clearbrookfarm.com* ⏲ *May–Aug., daily 9–6; Sept.–Oct., daily 10–6*) sells their own organic produce, in addition to baked goods and other seasonal treats.

Get your Vermont cheddar fix at the **Cheese House** (✉ *5187 Rt. 7A, Arlington* ☎ *802/375-9033* 🌐 *www.thevermontcheesehouse.com*), which also sells maple syrup and other local products and gifts.

Updated by Michael de Zayas

Vermont is an entire state of hidden treasures and unspoiled scenery. Wander anywhere in the state—80% is forest—and you'll travel a pristine countryside dotted with farms and framed by mountains. Tiny towns with church steeples, village greens, and clapboard Colonial-era houses are perfect for exploring.

In summer, clear lakes and streams make great swimming and fishing. In fall, the leaves have their last hurrah, painting the mountainsides a stunning show of yellow, gold, red, and orange. In winter, Vermont's ski resorts are the prime enticement. Almost anywhere you go, any time of year, it will make you smile and reach for your camera.

Sprawl has no place here. Highways are devoid of billboards by law, and on some roads cows still stop traffic twice a day en route to and from the pasture. In spring, sap boils in sugarhouses, some built generations ago, and up the road a chef trained at the New England Culinary Institute in Montpelier might use the resulting maple syrup to glaze a pork tenderloin.

It's the landscape, for the most part, that attracts people to Vermont. The rolling hills belie the rugged terrain underneath the green canopy of forest growth. In summer, clear lakes and streams provide ample opportunities for swimming, boating, and fishing; the hills attract hikers and mountain bikers. The more than 14,000 mi of roads, many of them only intermittently traveled by cars, are great for biking. Vermont has the best ski resorts in the eastern United States, centered along the spine of the Green Mountains north to south. The traditional heart of skiing is the town of Stowe.

Vermont may seem locked in time, but technological sophistication appears where you least expect it: wireless Internet access in a 19th-century farmhouse-turned-inn and cell phone coverage from the state's highest peaks. Like an old farmhouse under renovation, Vermont's historic exterior is still the main attraction.

SOUTHERN VERMONT

Cross into the Green Mountain State from Massachusetts on Interstate 91, and you might feel as if you've entered a new country. There isn't a town in sight. What you see are forested hills punctuated by rolling pastures. When you reach Brattleboro, no fast-food joints or strip malls line the exits to signal your arrival at southeastern Vermont's gateway city. En route to downtown, you pass by Victorian-era homes on tree-lined streets. From Brattleboro, you can cross over the spine of the Green Mountains toward Bennington and Manchester.

The state's southwest corner is the southern terminus of the Green Mountain National Forest, dotted with lakes, threaded with trails and old forest roads, and home to three big ski resorts: Bromley, Stratton and Mount Snow.

The towns are listed in counterclockwise order in this section, beginning in the east in Brattleboro, then traveling west along Route 9 toward Bennington, then north to Manchester and Weston and south along scenic Routes 100 and 30 back to Townshend and Newfane.

BRATTLEBORO

60 mi south of White River Junction.

Brattleboro has drawn political activists and earnest counterculturists since the 1960s. Today, the city of 12,000 is still politically and culturally active, making it Vermont's hippest outside of Burlington.

GETTING HERE AND AROUND

Brattleboro is near the intersection of Route 9, the principal east–west highway also known as the Molly Stark Trail, and Interstate 91. For downtown, use Exit 2 from Interstate 91.

ESSENTIALS

Visitor Information **Brattleboro Area Chamber of Commerce** (✉ *180 Main St.* ☎ *802/254-4565 or 877/254-4565* 🌐 *www.brattleborochamber.org*).

EXPLORING

Brattleboro Museum and Art Center. Downtown is the hub of Brattleboro's art scene, with this museum in historic Union Station at the forefront. It presents changing exhibits created by locally, nationally, and internationally renowned artists. ✉ *10 Vernon St.* ☎ *802/257–0124* 🌐 *www.brattleboromuseum.org* 🎟 *$6, free 1st Fri. each month 5–8:30* ⏲ *Thurs.–Mon. 11–5, 1st Fri. each month 11–8:30.*

SPORTS AND THE OUTDOORS

BIKING **Brattleboro Bicycle Shop** (✉ *165 Main St.* ☎ *802/254–8644* 🌐 *www.bratbike.com*) rents and repairs hybrid bikes.

CANOEING **Vermont Canoe Touring Center** (✉ *451 Putney Rd.* ☎ *802/257–5008*) rents canoes and kayaks.

SHOPPING

★ **Brattleboro Books** (✉ *106 Main St.* ☎ *802/257–7044*) boasts more than 75,000 used books and is a great source for local goings-on.

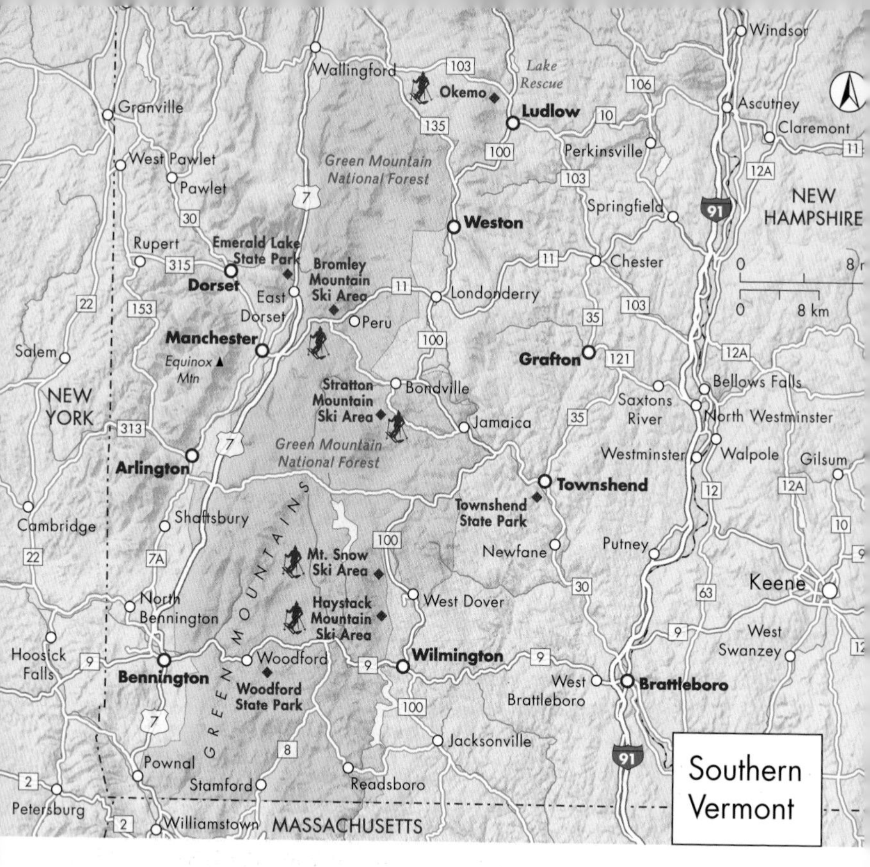

ART **Gallery in the Woods** (✉ *143 Main St.* ☎ *802/257–4777* 🌐 *www.galleryinthewoods.com*) sells art, jewelry, and glassware from around the world. To get a sense of the vibrant works being produced by young local artists, head to the back of the **Turn it Up** record shop to find **Through the Music** (✉ *2 Elliot St.* ☎ *802/779–3188* 🌐 *www.turnitup.com*), an otherwise easy-to-miss gallery. The excellent contemporary art spans genres from painting to pottery. **Vermont Artisan Designs** (✉ *106 Main St.* ☎ *802/257–7044* 🌐 *www.vtartisans.com*) displays ceramics, glass, wood, clothing, jewelry, and furniture from more than 300 artists.

OFF THE BEATEN PATH

Putney. Nine miles upriver, this small town, with a population of just over 2,000, is the country cousin of bustling Brattleboro and is a haven for writers, artists, and craftspeople. There are dozens of pottery studios to visit and a few orchards. In 2009, a fire burned down the world-class general store that had served as the heart of the community, but there is talk of rebuilding. Watch wool being spun into yarn at the **Green Mountain Spinnery** (✉ *7 Brickyard La., off I–91, Exit 4* ☎ *802/387–4528 or 800/321–9665* 🌐 *www.spinnery.com*). The factory shop, which is open daily all year, sells yarn, knitting accessories, and patterns. Tours are conducted at 1:30 on the first and third Tuesday of the month. **Harlow's Sugar House** (✉ *563 Bellows Falls Rd., Putney* ☎ *802/387–5852* 🌐 *www.vermontsugar.com*), 2 mi north of Putney, has a working cider mill and sugarhouse, as well as seasonal apple and berry picking. The family has been sugaring on this farm since 1927. You can buy cider, maple syrup, and other items in the gift shop.

NIGHTLIFE AND THE ARTS

ARTS Brattleboro has an evening gallery walk on the first Friday of each month from 5:30 to 8:30.

NIGHTLIFE **Latchis Theater** (✉ *50 Main St.* ☎ *802/246–1500* 🌐 *latchis.com*) hosts art exhibits when movies aren't playing. It's worth walking in just to check out the hand-painted murals of Greek mythology.

QUICK BITES

The gathering spot in town for coffee and conversation is Mocha Joe's (✉ *82 Main St.* ☎ *802/257-7794*), which takes great care in sourcing beans from places like Kenya, Ethiopia, and Guatemala. This is ground zero for Brattleboro's contemporary bohemian spirit.

WHERE TO EAT

¢–$ AMERICAN ✕ **Brattleboro Food Co-op.** This is one of the best foodie stops in the state to stock up on Vermont's finest artisanal products. Its charms include different grades of maple syrup served from tap. Pick up a pre-made sandwich or order a plate of curry chicken at the deli counter, then eat it in this busy market's small sitting area. Natural and organic is the focus, with everything from tofu sandwiches to beef *satay* (skewered grilled meat). The delicatessen is connected to a natural-foods market and serves breakfast. ✉ *2 Main St.* ☎ *802/257–0236* 🌐 *www.brattleborofoodcoop.com* ▭ *MC, V.*

$$–$$$ ITALIAN ✕ **Max's.** Pasta creations at this trendy place include artichoke-mascarpone ravioli and Tuscan-style cauliflower with linguine. Complementing this *nuovo* Italian menu are eclectic entrées such as mahimahi in parchment and lavender tea–smoked salmon. Sunday brunch is both traditional and adventurous, with everything from eggs to curry rice kedgeree. ✉ *889 Putney Rd.* ☎ *802/254–7747* ▭ *MC, V* ⊗ *No dinner Mon. Closed Tues.*

$$–$$$ STEAKHOUSE ★ ✕ **Peter Havens.** In a town better known for tofu than toniness, this chic little bistro knows just what to do with a filet mignon: serve it with Roquefort walnut butter. One room is painted a warm red, another in sage; both are punctuated by copies of Fernando Botero paintings, creating a look that is one of the most sophisticated in the state. Try the house-cured gravlax made with lemon vodka or the fresh seasonal seafood, which even includes a spring fling with soft-shell crabs. The wine list is superb. ✉ *32 Elliot St.* ☎ *802/257–3333* 🌐 *www.peterhavens.com* ▭ *AE, MC, V* ⊗ *Closed Sun. and Mon. No lunch.*

$$$$ ECLECTIC Fodor's Choice ★ ✕ **T.J. Buckley's.** It's easy to miss this tiny restaurant, but it's worth seeking out as the most romantic little eatery in Vermont. Open the doors to the sleek black 1920s diner and enter what amounts to a very intimate theater, with a mere 18 seats for the show. The stage is an open kitchen, the flames a few feet away, and working under the whisper of vocal jazz and candlelight is the star of the show: Michael Fuller, the dashing owner and sole chef, who has been at the helm for 25 years. The contemporary menu is conveyed verbally each day and is based on locally available ingredients. It's dinner theater for culinary fans, a romantic triumph. ✉ *132 Elliot St.* ☎ *802/257–4922* ✍ *Reservations essential* ▭ *No credit cards* ⊗ *Closed Mon. and Tues. No lunch.*

¢–$ SOUTHERN ✕ **Top of the Hill Grill.** Hickory-smoked ribs, beef brisket, apple-smoked turkey, and pulled pork are a few of the favorites at this barbecue outside town. Larger parties can opt for "family-style" dinners, and homemade pecan pie is the dessert of choice. You can sit indoors in the informal dining room with big windows, but the best seats are outdoors at picnic tables overlooking the West River. ✉ *632 Putney Rd.* ☎ *802/258–9178* 🌐 *www.topofthehillgrill.com* ▭ *No credit cards* ⊗ *Closed Nov.–mid-Apr.*

BILLBOARDS AND VERMONT

Did you know that there are no billboards in Vermont? The state banned them in 1967 (similar laws exist in Maine, Alaska, and Hawaii), and the last one came down in 1975, so when you look out your window, you see trees and other scenic sights, not advertisements. (It may make playing the Alphabet Game with your child a bit difficult.)

WHERE TO STAY

$$$ **Forty Putney Road.** Engaging hosts Tim and Amy Brady run this French-style manse and have restored some of its more interesting original features (like nickel-plated bathroom fixtures) and added new ones (like flat-screen TVs). They've made sure that it's full of thoughtful and comforting details, such as the mini-fridge stocked with complimentary soda, water, granola bars, and chips. Other indoor and outdoor treats include a hot tub, a billiard table, and the neighboring Retreat Meadows, a bird sanctuary that has good hiking trails. There's no restaurant, but a decent pub menu and wine are offered. **Pros:** caring hosts; clean, remodeled rooms. **Cons:** short walk into town; rates vary and spike during busy periods. ✉ *192 Putney Rd.* ☎ *802/254–6268 or 800/941–2413* 🌐 *www.fortyputneyroad.com* *5 rooms, 1 suite* *In-room: DVD, Wi-Fi. In-hotel: room service, bar, laundry service, Wi-Fi hotspot, no kids under 12* ▭ *AE, D, MC, V* *BP.*

$$ Fodor's Choice ★ **Hickory Ridge House.** If you're looking for a relaxing country getaway, this 1808 Federal-style mansion, a former sheep farm set on a wide meadow, is a sure bet. The historic redbrick house has a sturdy comfort that distinguishes it from daintier inns. Owners Gillian and Dennis Pettit, along with their dogs Jack and Gracie, bring an English touch to it all. Most rooms have Rumford fireplaces and canopy beds; all have fine linens. A separate two-bedroom cottage has a full kitchen. Thousands of acres of nature preserve surround the property's 8 acres of cleared meadow, making it great for hiking and cross-country skiing. **Pros:** peaceful, scenic property; terrific house; great breakfast; quintessential B&B experience. **Cons:** can be expensive. ✉ *53 Hickory Ridge Rd., 11 mi north of Brattleboro, Putney* ☎ *802/387–5709 or 800/380–9218* 🌐 *www.hickoryridgehouse.com* *6 rooms, 1 cottage* *In-room: DVD, Wi-Fi. In-hotel: Internet terminal, Wi-Fi hotspot, some pets allowed* ▭ *MC, V* *BP.*

$ **Latchis Hotel.** To stay in the heart of town at a low rate, you can do no better than the Latchis. The three-story art deco landmark is run by a nonprofit group dedicated to preserving and restoring the 1938 building. Rooms are not lavish, but they are clean and functional, with original sinks and tiling in the bathrooms. Most overlook Main Street,

The rolling green hills of Putney are home to many organic farm operations.

with New Hampshire's mountains in the background. The lobby has original and notably colorful terrazzo floors. Downstairs you can catch a movie under the impressive zodiac ceiling of the Latchis Theater or eat at the Flat St. Brew Pub ($–$$). **Pros:** heart-of-town location; good value. **Cons:** clean but dull furnishings; less personality than area B&Bs. *⊠ 50 Main St. ☎ 802/254–6300 or 800/798–6301 ⊕ www.latchis.com ⇨ 30 rooms, 3 suites ♁ In-room: refrigerator, Wi-Fi. In-hotel: Wi-Fi hotspot ▭ AE, MC, V ¦◎¦ CP.*

WILMINGTON

18 mi west of Brattleboro.

The village of Wilmington, with its classic Main Street lined with 18th- and 19th-century buildings, anchors the Mount Snow Valley. Most of the valley's lodging and dining establishments, however, line Route 100, which travels 5 mi north to West Dover and Mount Snow, where skiers flock on winter weekends. The area abounds with cultural activity year-round, from concerts to art exhibits.

GETTING HERE AND AROUND

Wilmington is at the junction of Routes 9 and 100. West Dover and Mount Snow are a few miles to the north along Route 100.

ESSENTIALS

Visitor Information **Mount Snow Valley Chamber of Commerce** (*⊠ 21 W. Main St. ☎ 802/464–8092 or 877/887–6884 ⊕ www.visitvermont.com*).

CLOSE UP

Vermont Maple Syrup

Vermont is one of the country's smallest states, but it's the largest producer of maple syrup. A visit to a maple farm is a great way to learn all about sugaring, the process of taking maple tree sap and making syrup. Sap is stored in a sugar maple tree's roots in the winter, and in the spring when conditions are just right, the sap runs up and is capable of being tapped. Tapping season takes place in March and April, which is when all maple in the state is produced.

Maple sap is collected in buckets.

One of the best parts of visiting a maple farm is getting to taste the four grades of syrup. As the sugaring season goes on and days get warmer, the sap becomes progressively darker and stronger flavored. Color, clarity and flavor define the four grades of syrup. Is one grade better than another? Nope. It's just a question of taste. Sap drawn early in the season produces the lightest color, and has the most delicate flavor: this is called Vermont Fancy. Vermont Grade A Medium Amber has a mellow flavor. Vermont Grade A Dark Amber is much more robust, and Vermont Grade B is the most flavorful, making it often the favorite of first-time tasters.

Is one syrup better than another? Can you actually tell the difference? You'd need an exceptionally nuanced palate to discern between one Vermont syrup and another, but aesthetics can alter taste, and authenticity counts. So when visiting a maple farm, make sure that this is a place that actually makes its own syrup, as opposed to just bottling or selling someone else's.

Sugarhouses are located throughout the state, but there's no better introduction to Vermont mapling than a visit to **Morse Farm Sugarworks** (🌐 *www.morsefarm.com*) in Montpelier, Vermont. Burr Morse's family has been mapling for more than 200 years, longer than anyone else in the state. Attractions here include a free tour of a sugar house, tastings, and an outdoor museum and woodshed theater. If you're traveling with children, **Jed's Maple Products** (🌐 *www.jedsmaple.com*), far in the Northeast Kingdom is a good option as owners Steve and Amy Wheeler take kids into the woods to show how to tap trees. Always call ahead if you're planning a visit.

There are approximately 50 maple farms that are free and open all year to the public. The official industry Web site for **Vermont Maple Syrup** (🌐 *www.vermontmaple.org*)is a great resource that has a map of maple farms that host tours, a directory of producers open year-round, and a list of places you can order maple by mail. In addition, you can learn about the Annual Maple Open House weekend, which is when sugarhouses throughout the state open their doors to the public.

—Michael de Zayas

During the spring sugaring season, water is boiled off the maple sap to concentrate the syrup's flavor.

EXPLORING

Adams Farm. At this working farm you can collect fresh eggs from the chicken coop, feed a rabbit, milk a goat, ride a tractor or a pony, and jump in the hay—plus run through the corn maze in summer and take sleigh rides in winter. The indoor livestock barn is open Wednesday through Sunday, November to mid-June; an outdoor version is open daily the rest of the year. The farm store sells more than 200 handmade quilts and sweaters. ✉ *15 Higley Hill Rd., 3 mi north of Wilmington, off Rte. 100* ☎ *802/464–3762* 🌐 *www.adamsfamilyfarm.com* *$6.96–$14.95* ⏲ *Wed.–Sun. 10–5.*

Southern Vermont Natural History Museum. This museum, 5 mi east of Wilmington on Route 9, houses one of New England's largest collections of mounted birds, including three extinct birds and a complete collection of mammals native to the Northeast. The museum also has live hawk and owl exhibits. ✉ *7599 Rte. 9* ☎ *802/464–0048* *$5* ⏲ *June–late Oct., daily 10–5; late Oct.–May, most weekends 10–4, call ahead.*

SPORTS AND THE OUTDOORS

BOATING **Green Mountain Flagship Company** (✉ *389 Rte. 9, 2 mi west of Wilmington* ☎ *802/464–2975* 🌐 *www.greenmountainflagship.com*) rents canoes, kayaks, and sailboats from May to late October on Lake Whitingham.

SKI AREA The closest major ski area to all of the Northeast's big cities, **Mount Snow Resort** (✉ *400 Mountain Rd., Mount Snow* ☎ *802/464–3333; 802/464–2151 snow conditions; 800/245–7669 lodging* 🌐 *www.mountsnow.com*), is also one of the state's premier family resorts and has a full roster of year-round activities. The almost 800-acre facility encompasses a hotel, 10 condo developments, an 18-hole golf course, a health club and spa, 45 mi of mountain-biking trails, and an extensive network of hiking trails.

Mount Snow prides itself on its 101 snowmaking fan guns, which let it open earlier than any ski area in the state. More than half of the 107 trails down its 1,700-foot vertical summit are intermediate, wide, and sunny. There are four major downhill areas. The main mountain is mostly beginners' slopes, especially toward the bottom, while the north face includes the majority of the expert terrain. Corinthia used to be a separate ski mountain, but is now connected with a mix of trail levels. The south face, Sunbrook, has wide, sunny trails. The trails are served by 19 lifts, including three high-speed quads. Snowmaking covers 85% of the terrain. There are 98 acres of glades. The ski school's instruction program is designed to help skiers of all ages and abilities. Mount Snow also has five terrain parks of different skill levels and a 400-foot half-pipe with 18-foot walls. Skiing programs start with the Cub Camp, designed for kids age 3. Snow Camp teaches kids 4 to 6, and Mountain Camp and Mountain Riders are for kids 7 to 14; there's also a well-organized child-care center.

WHO WAS MOLLY STARK?

In the heart of Wilmington, to the side of Crafts Inn (built by Stanford White in 1902) is a sculpture in honor of Molly Stark, the wife of Revolutionary War general John Stark. The general was said to have roused his troops in the Battle of Bennington, vowing victory over the British: "They are ours, or this night Molly Stark sleeps a widow!" He lived, and the victory path across Vermont, now Route 9, is called the Molly Stark Trail.

Two cross-country ski centers near Mount Snow provide more than 68 mi of varied terrain. **Timber Creek** (✉ *R1 Tomber Creek Rd., at Rte. 100, north of Mount Snow, West Dover* ☎ *802/464–0999* 🌐 *www.timbercreekxc.com*) is appealingly small, with 9 mi of groomed loops and equipment rentals. The groomed trails at the **White House of Wilmington** (✉ *178 Rte. 9* ☎ *802/464–2135* 🌐 *www.whitehouseinn.com*) cover 30 mi; you can rent Nordic gear and snowshoes there.

SNOWMOBILE TOURS **High Country Tours** (✉ *Mount Snow base lodge, Rte. 100, West Dover* ☎ *802/464–2108* 🌐 *www.high-country-tours.com*) runs one-hour, two-hour, and half-day snowmobile tours from two locations: one near Mount Snow, the other west of Wilmington in Searsburg.

SHOPPING

Downtown Wilmington is lined with unique shops and galleries. **Quaigh Design Centre** (✉ *11 W. Main St. [Rte. 9]* ☎ *802/464–2780*) sells great pottery and artwork from Britain and New England—including works by Vermont woodcut artists Sabra Field and Mary Azarian—and Scottish woolens. **Young and Constantin Gallery** (✉ *10 S. Main St.* ☎ *802/464–2515*) sells handblown glassware, ceramics, handmade jewelry, and art from local and nationally known artisans.

THE ARTS

A year-round roster of music, theater, film, and fine art is presented at the **Memorial Hall Center for the Arts** (✉ *14 W. Main St.* ☎ *802/464–8411* 🌐 *www.memhall.org*).

WHERE TO EAT

¢–$ DINER

Dot's Restaurant. Look for the classic red neon sign (one of only a handful still permitted in Vermont) at the main corner in downtown Wilmington: Dot's is a local landmark. A photo inside depicts the interior in the early 1940s—except for the soda fountain, all else is identical, from the long counter with swivel chairs to the fireplace in the back. This friendly place is packed with locals and skiers; the menu includes chicken *cordon bleu* (chicken stuffed with ham and cheese, then breaded and fried) and homemade roast beef. Berry berry pancakes are de rigeur for breakfast, which starts at 5:30 AM, and a bowl of turkey chili is perfect for lunch. A second location is in West Dover. ✉ *3 W. Main St.* ☎ *802/464–7284* 🌐 *www.dotsofvermont.com* ▭ *MC, V.*

$$$–$$$$ CONTINENTAL Fodor's Choice ★

Inn at Sawmill Farm. No other restaurant in Vermont aims as high with its haute Continental food, wine, and service as the restaurant at Sawmill. Order a beer and the bottle is served chilled in a small ice bucket, as if it were champagne. This reverent service and deference to potables come from the top: chef-owner Brill Williams passionately cares for his 17,000-bottle cellar, the biggest restaurant collection in the state. Try the potato-crusted fish of the day served in beurre blanc or grilled loin of venison. Gourmands of Mount Snow, this is your place, even if it can be a touch pretentious. ✉ *7 Crosstown Rd., at Rte. 100, West Dover* 📫 *Box 367* ☎ *802/464–8131 or 800/493–1133* 🌐 *www.theinnatsawmillfarm.com* ▭ *AE, D, MC, V* ⊗ *Closed early Apr.–late May. No lunch.*

WHERE TO STAY

$$–$$$

Deerhill Inn. Though the exterior of this inn leaves something to be desired, the interior makes up for it. The common living room features a large stone fireplace and works by local artists hang on the walls. Guest rooms are cozy and adorned with English floral linens; balcony rooms are more spacious. Chef-owner Michael Allen heads the wonderful dining room ($$$$)—one of the best in town. **Pros:** great restaurant; nicely renovated rooms. **Cons:** unimpressive building exterior; must drive to town and resort. ✉ *14 Valley View Rd., West Dover* 📫 *Box 136, West Dover 05356* ☎ *802/464–3100 or 800/993–3379* 🌐 *www.deerhill.com* *12 rooms, 2 suites* ⊗ *Closed weekdays in Apr. and Nov.* *In-room: no phone, no a/c, DVD (some), no TV (some), Wi-Fi. In-hotel: restaurant, bar, pool, Internet terminal, Wi-Fi hotspot, no kids under 12* ▭ *AE, MC, V* *BP, MAP.*

$$$$

Grand Summit Hotel. The 200-room base lodge at Mount Snow is an easy choice for skiers who don't care about anything but getting on the slopes as quickly as possible. Package deals with lift tickets can save you here. The lobby has the look of a traditional ski lodge, with a big center fireplace, but the overall feel is that of an efficient, new hotel. Rooms are clean and fairly basic. A big outdoor heated pool sits beside two hot tubs at the base of the slopes. In summer guests enjoy the property golf and tennis courts. **Pros:** easy ski access; modern property. **Cons:** somewhat bland decor in rooms; not a historic option. ✉ *1 Mount Snow Rd., West Dover* ☎ *800/451–4211* 🌐 *www.mountsnow.com/grandsummit.html* *104 rooms, 96 suites* *In-room: kitchen (some), refrigerator (some), DVD (some), Wi-Fi. In-hotel: 2 restaurants, bar, golf course,*

OUTDOOR OUTFITTERS AND INFORMATION

BIKING

Vermont Bicycle Touring (✉ *Monkton Rd., Bristol* ☎ *802/453–4811 or 800/245–3868* 🌐 *www.vbt.com*) leads numerous tours in the state. **P.O.M.G. Bike Tours of Vermont** (✉ *Richmond Box 1080,* ☎ *802/434–2270 or 888/635–2453* 🌐 *www.pomgbike.com*) leads weekend and five-day bike tours.

CANOEING AND KAYAKING

Umiak Outdoor Outfitters (✉ *849 S. Main St., Stowe* ☎ *802/253–2317* 🌐 *www.umiak.com*) has day excursions and customized overnight trips. **BattenKill Canoe** (✉ *6328 Rte. 7A, Sunderland* ☎ *802/362–2800 or 800/421–5268* 🌐 *www.battenkill.com*) organizes canoe tours (some are inn-to-inn) and fishing trips. **True North Kayak Tours** (✉ *25 Nash Pl., Burlington* ☎ *802/860–1910* 🌐 *www.vermontkayak.com*) operates a guided tour of Lake Champlain and a natural-history tour; the company also customizes multiday trips and coordinates special trips for kids.

FISHING

For information about fishing, including licenses, call the **Vermont Fish and Wildlife Department** (☎ *802/241–3700* 🌐 *www.vtfishandwildlife.com*).

HIKING

The **Green Mountain Club** (✉ *4711 Waterbury-Stowe Rd. [Rte. 100], Waterbury Center* ☎ *802/244–7037* 🌐 *www.greenmountainclub.org*) publishes hiking maps and guides. The club also manages the Long Trail.

SKIING

For skiing information, contact **Ski Vermont/Vermont Ski Areas Association** (✉ *26 State St., Box 368, Montpelier* ☎ *802/223–2439* 🌐 *www.skivermont.com*).

SPORT TOURS

Country Inns Along the Trail (📫 *Box 59, Montgomery 05470* ☎ *802/326–2072 or 800/838–3301* 🌐 *www.inntoinn.com*) arranges self-guided hiking, skiing, and biking trips from inn to inn in Vermont.

tennis courts, pool, gym, spa, children's programs (ages 4–14), laundry service, Internet terminal, Wi-Fi hotspot ▭ *AE, D, MC, V.*

$$$$ **Inn at Sawmill Farm.** Full of character and charm, this inn in a converted barn has common rooms elegantly accented with English chintzes, antiques, and Oriental rugs. Each of the guest rooms—in the main inn or in cottages scattered on the property's 22 acres—is individually decorated, and many have sitting areas and fireplaces. Dinner in the formal dining room, as well as a full breakfast, is included in the price of a stay. **Pros:** spacious grounds; attentive service. **Cons:** overload of floral prints in some rooms; room size varies. ✉ *7 Crosstown Rd., at Rte 100, West Dover* 📫 *Box 367* ☎ *802/464–8131 or 800/493–1133* 🌐 *www.theinnatsawmillfarm.com* *21 rooms* *In-room: no phone, no TV. In-hotel: restaurant, tennis court, pool* ▭ *AE, D, MC, V* ⊙ *Closed early-Apr.–late May* 🍽 *BP, MAP.*

$$ **White House of Wilmington.** It's hard to miss this 1915 Federal-style mansion standing imposingly atop a high hill off Route 9 east of Wilmington. Grand balconies and the main balustraded terrace overlook the hill. A grand staircase leads to rooms with antique bathrooms and brass

wall sconces; some rooms have fireplaces and lofts. There is a cross-country ski touring and snowshoeing center on-site along with 7 mi of groomed trails; tubes are also provided for the great hill. A small indoor pool is formed from an old coal bin and surrounded by hand-painted murals of Roman bath scenes. The restaurant ($$$$) has an extensive wine list and undeniably romantic dining in the Mahogany Room. **Pros:** great for kids and families; intriguing, big, old-fashioned property; intimate dining. **Cons:** not in town, so you have to drive to everything. ✉ *178 Rte. 9, Wilmington* ☎ *802/464–2135 or 800/541–2135* 🌐 *www.whitehouseinn.com* *24 rooms, 1 cottage* *In-room: no phone, no a/c (some), no TV, Wi-Fi (some). In-hotel: restaurant, bar, pools, laundry service, Internet terminal, Wi-Fi hotspot* *AE, D, MC, V* *BP.*

2

BENNINGTON

21 mi west of Wilmington.

Bennington is the commercial focus of Vermont's southwest corner. It's really three towns in one: Downtown Bennington, Old Bennington, and North Bennington. Downtown Bennington has retained much of the industrial character it developed in the 19th century, when paper mills, gristmills, and potteries formed the city's economic base.

GETTING HERE AND AROUND

The heart of modern Bennington is at the intersection of U.S. 7 and Route 9. Old Bennington is a couple of miles west on Route 9, at Monument Avenue. North Bennington is a few miles north on Rte 67A.

ESSENTIALS

Visitor Information **Bennington Area Chamber of Commerce** (✉ *100 Veterans Memorial Dr. [U.S. 7]* ☎ *802/447–3311 or 800/229–0252* 🌐 *www.bennington.com*).

EXPLORING

TOP ATTRACTIONS

Bennington Battle Monument. This 306-foot stone obelisk—with an elevator to the top—commemorates General John Stark's victory over the British, who attempted to capture Bennington's stockpile of supplies. Inside the monument you can learn all about the battle, which took place near Walloomsac Heights in New York state on August 16, 1777, and helped bring about the surrender of the British commander "Gentleman Johnny" Burgoyne two months later. The summit provides commanding views of the Massachusetts Berkshires, the New York Adirondacks, and the Vermont Green Mountains. ✉ *15 Monument Circle, Old Bennington* ☎ *802/447–0550* *$2* *Mid-Apr.–Oct., daily 9–5.*

Bennington Museum. The rich collections at this museum include military artifacts, early tools, dolls, toys, and the Bennington Flag, one of the oldest of the Stars and Stripes in existence. One room is devoted to early Bennington pottery, and two rooms cover the history of American glass (fine Tiffany specimens are on display). The museum displays the largest public collection of the work of Grandma Moses (1860–1961), the popular self-taught artist who lived and painted in the area. ✉ *75 Main St. (Rte.*

The poet Robert Frost is buried in Bennington at the Old First Church, "Vermont's Colonial Shrine."

9), Old Bennington ☎ *802/447–1571* 🌐 *www.benningtonmuseum.com* 🎟 *$9* ⏲ *Nov.–Aug., Thurs.–Tues. 10–5; Sept. and Oct., daily 10–5.*

North Bennington. North of Old Bennington is this village, home to Bennington College, lovely mansions, Lake Paran, three covered bridges, and a wonderful old train depot. Contemporary stone sculpture and white-frame neo-Colonial dorms surrounded by acres of cornfields punctuate the green meadows of the placid campus of **Bennington College** (✉ *Rte. 67A off U.S. 7 [look for stone entrance gate]* ☎ *802/442–5401* 🌐 *www.bennington.edu*). The architecturally significant **Park-McCullough House** (✉ *1 Park St., at West St.* ☎ *802/442–5441* 🌐 *www.parkmccullough.org* 🎟 *$8* ⏲ *Mid-May–mid-Oct., daily 10–4; last tour at 3*) is a 35-room classic French Empire–style mansion, built in 1865 and furnished with period pieces. Several restored flower gardens grace the landscaped grounds, and a stable houses a collection of antique carriages. Call for details on the summer concert series.

Robert Frost Stone House Museum. A few miles north along Route 7A is the town of Shaftsbury. It was here that Frost came in 1920 "to plant a new Garden of Eden with a thousand apple trees of some unforbidden variety." The museum tells the story of the nine years (1920–29) Frost spent living in the house with his wife and four children. (He passed the 1930s in a house up the road in Shaftsbury, now owned by a Hollywood movie producer.) It was here that he penned "Stopping by Woods on a Snowy Evening" and published two books of poems. Seven of the Frost family's original 80 acres can be wandered. Among the apple boughs you just might find inspiration of your own. ✉ *75*

Main St. (Rte. 9), Shaftsbury ☎ *802/447–6200* 🌐 *www.frostfriends.org* 🎫 *$5* ⏲ *May–Nov.; Tues.–Sun. 10–5.*

2

WORTH NOTING

West of downtown, **Old Bennington** is a National Register Historic District centered along the axis of Monument Avenue and well endowed with stately Colonial and Victorian mansions. Here, at the Catamount Tavern (now a private home north of Church Street), Ethan Allen organized the Green Mountain Boys, who helped capture Fort Ticonderoga in 1775.

Old First Church. In the graveyard of this church, the tombstone of the poet Robert Frost proclaims, "I had a lover's quarrel with the world." ✉ *1 Church La., at Monument Ave., Old Bennington.*

SPORTS AND THE OUTDOORS

Lake Shaftsbury State Park (✉ *Rte. 7A, 10½ mi north of Bennington* ☎ *802/375–9978* 🌐 *www.vtstateparks.com/htm/shaftsbury.cfm*) has a swimming beach, nature trails, boat and canoe rentals, and a snack bar. **Woodford State Park** (✉ *Rte. 9, 10 mi east of Bennington* ☎ *802/447–7169* 🌐 *www.vtstateparks.com/htm/woodford.cfm*) has an activities center on Adams Reservoir, playground, boat and canoe rentals, and nature trails.

SHOPPING

The **Apple Barn and Country Bake Shop** (✉ *604 Rte. 7S., 1½ mi south of downtown Bennington* ☎ *802/447–7780* 🌐 *theapplebarn.com*) sells home-baked goodies, fresh cider, Vermont cheeses, maple syrup, and apples! Thirty varieties are grown in its orchards. You can pick berries here too, making it a fun family stop. You can watch them making cider donuts at the bakery and café on weekends most of the year. The showroom at the **Bennington Potters Yard** (✉ *324 County St.* ☎ *802/447–7531 or 800/205–8033* 🌐 *www.benningtonpotters.com*) stocks first-quality pottery and seconds from the famed Bennington Potters. Take a free tour on weekdays from 10 to 3 when the potters are working, or follow a self-guided tour around the yard.

BOOKS **Now & Then Books** (✉ *439 Main St.* ☎ *802/442–5566* 🌐 *www.nowandthenbooksvt.com*) is a great used bookstore in an upstairs shop with nearly 50,000 volumes in stock. **The Bennington Bookshop** (✉ *467 Main St.* ☎ *802/442–5050*) sells new books and gifts and has free Wi-Fi.

THE ARTS

The **Bennington Center for the Arts** (✉ *44 Gypsy La.* ☎ *802/442–7158* 🌐 *www.benningtoncenterforthearts.org*) hosts cultural events, including exhibitions by local and national artists. The on-site **Oldcastle Theatre Co.** (☎ *802/447–0564* 🌐 *www.oldcastletheatreco.or/*) hosts fine regional theater from May through October. The **Basement Music Series** (✉ *29 Sage St., North Bennington* ☎ *802/442–5549* 🌐 *www.vtartxchange.org*), run by the nonprofit Vermont Arts Exchange, is a funky basement cabaret venue in an old factory building. Purchase tickets in advance for the best contemporary music performances in town.

WHERE TO EAT

¢ AMERICAN ✕ **Blue Benn Diner**. Breakfast is served all day in this authentic diner, where the eats include turkey hash and breakfast burritos with scrambled eggs, sausage, and chilies, plus pancakes of all imaginable varieties.

The menu lists many vegetarian selections. Lines may be long, especially on weekends: locals and tourists alike can't stay away. ✉ *314 North St.* ☎ *802/442–5140* ✍ *Reservations not accepted* ▭ *No credit cards.*

$$–$$$ CONTINENTAL ✕ **Four Chimneys Inn.** It's a treat just to walk up the long path to this classic Old Bennington mansion, the most refined setting around. The dining room is a discreet, quiet room lit by candles and a gas fireplace. Chef Pete Jaenecke creates a sophisticated seasonal menu. If you're lucky, it might include hand-crafted *agnolotti* (ravioli) pasta filled with Angus beef, braised in port with a shallot confit and cherry ragout and topped with a local blue cheese, or maybe the poached salmon in a lemon-dill beurre blanc sauce. ✉ *21 West Rd. (Rte. 9), Old Bennington* ☎ *802/447–3500* 🌐 *www.fourchimneys.com* ✍ *Reservations essential* ▭ *AE, D, MC, V* ⏲ *No lunch. Closed Tues. and Wed.*

$–$$ ECLECTIC ★ ✕ **Pangaea Lounge.** Don't let the dusty old storefront and scuffed-up floor fool you. Bennington's in-the-know crowd comes here before anywhere else for affordable comfort food and an excellent bar. Directly next door is Pangaea, the restaurant's fancier twin, which is somewhat overpriced and not as intimate. At the helm at the corner bar is Jason, an impressive mixologist. The eclectic pub fare includes such dishes as pot roast chimichangas, Cobb salad with Danish blue cheese, salmon burgers, and seared pork loin with a potato croquette. On weekends in warmer months, follow the crowd out back to the deck. ✉ *3 Prospect St., 3 mi north of Bennington, North Bennington* ☎ *802/442–4466* ▭ *AE, MC, V* ⏲ *No lunch.*

WHERE TO STAY

¢–$ ★ **Eddington House.** You can thank Patti Eddington for maintaining this three-bedroom house, the best value in all of Vermont. You get a spotless and updated room in a house you can't help but feel is your own. Patti lives in an attached barn, giving you all the privacy you need, but homemade desserts and wine are always out on the counter. The house is in the heart of North Bennington, across the street from a market and two restaurants. One room has a four-poster bed with a lovely old tub, separate shower, and great light; there's also one suite. Ask about the excellent dinner package. **Pros:** budget prices for great B&B; privacy and gentle service. **Cons:** slightly off usual tourist track; only three rooms so it fills up fast. ✉ *21 Main St., North Bennington* ☎ *802/442–1551* 🌐 *www.eddingtonhouseinn.com* *3 rooms* *In-room: no phone, no TV (some), Wi-Fi. In-hotel: Wi-Fi hotspot, some pets allowed, no kids under 12* ▭ *AE, MC, V* *BP.*

$$–$$$ Fodor's Choice ★ **Four Chimneys Inn.** This is the quintessential Old Bennington mansion and one of the best inns in Vermont. The three-story 1915 neo-Georgian looks out over a substantial lawn and a wonderful old stone wall. On the second floor, rooms 1, 3, and 11 have great bay windows and fireplaces. One has a chandelier hung over a hot tub, reproduction antique washstands, and a flat-screen TV cleverly concealed by a painting. All rooms are light and bright. Owner and innkeeper Lynn Green's careful attention keeps the property in high style. Two cottages in back (a two-story brick former icehouse and a former carriage house) overlook a pond. **Pros:** stately mansion that's extremely well kept; formal dining; very clean, spacious, renovated rooms. **Cons:** common room/

bar closes early. ✉ *21 West Rd. (Rte. 9), Old Bennington* ☎ *802/447–3500* 🌐 *www.fourchimneys.com* *9 rooms, 2 suites* *In-room: DVD, Internet, Wi-Fi. In-hotel: restaurant, bar, bicycles, laundry service, Wi-Fi hotspot, no kids under 5* *AE, D, MC, V* *BP.*

ARLINGTON

15 mi north of Bennington.

Smaller than Bennington and more down to earth than upper-crust Manchester to the north, Arlington exudes a certain Rockwellian folksiness, and it should. Illustrator Norman Rockwell lived here from 1939 to 1953, and many of his neighbors served as models for his portraits of small-town life.

GETTING HERE AND AROUND

Arlington is at the intersection of Routes 313 and 7A. Take 313 west to reach West Arlington.

EXPLORING

The endearing town of **East Arlington** (✉ *1 mi east of Arlington on East Arlington Rd.*) sits on the shore of Roaring Brook, east of Arlington. An 18th-century gristmill is now home to a fine antiques shop, one of a few in town, and other fun shops, including a fudge and teddy bear store.

A covered bridge leads to the quaint town green of **West Arlington** (✉ *West of Arlington on Rte. 313 W*), where Norman Rockwell once lived. River Road runs along the south side of the Battenkill River, a scenic drive. If you continue west along Route 313, you'll come to the Wayside General Store, a real charmer, where you can pick up sandwiches and chat with locals. The store is frequently mentioned (anonymously) in the Vermont columns written by Christopher Kimball, editor of *Cooks Illustrated.*

SPORTS AND THE OUTDOORS

★ **BattenKill Canoe** (✉ *6328 Rte. 7A, Sunderland* ☎ *802/362–2800 or 800/421–5268* 🌐 *www.battenkill.com*) rents canoes for trips along the Battenkill River, which runs directly behind the shop. If you're hooked, they also run bigger white-water trips as well as inn-to-inn tours.

SHOPPING

ANTIQUES More than 70 dealers display their wares at **East Arlington Antiques Center** (✉ *1152 East Arlington Rd., East Arlington* ☎ *802/375–6144*) , which is in a converted 1930s movie theater. Among the finds is one of the country's best stoneware collections. Manager Jon Maynard is a charmer. Fodor's Choice ★ **Gristmill Antiques** (✉ *316 Old Mill Rd., East Arlington* ☎ *802/375–2500*) is a beautiful two-floor shop in a historic mill that looks out over Roaring Brook.

The Village Peddler (✉ *261 Old Mill Rd., East Arlington* ☎ *802/375–6037* *www.villagepeddlervt.com*) has a "chocolatorium" chocolate museum where you can learn all about chocolate. It sells fudge and other candies and has a large collection of teddy bears for sale. From December to March, it's closed on Tuesdays and Wednesdays.

NIGHTLIFE AND THE ARTS

The **Friday Night Fireside Music Series** (✉ *River Rd., West Arlington* ☎ *802/375–6516*) in the cozy tavern at the West Mountain Inn features great live music acts every other Friday evening from November through May for a $10 cover.

WHERE TO STAY

$$–$$$ **Arlington Inn.** Greek Revival columns at this 1848 home lend it an imposing presence in the middle of town, but the atmosphere is friendly and old-fashioned. Rooms are dainty and Victorian, dressed heavily in florals, and spread among the main inn, parsonage, and carriage house. Landscaping includes a garden, gazebo, pond, and waterfall. The inn runs one of the most respected restaurants in town, and its little old bar is one of the most wonderful in the state. **Pros:** heart-of-town location; friendly atmosphere. **Cons:** rooms are dated; expensive dining. ✉ *Rte. 7A* ☎ *802/375–6532 or 800/443–9442* 🌐 *www.arlingtoninn.com* *13 rooms, 5 suites* *In-room: Wi-Fi. In-hotel: restaurant, bar, Wi-Fi hotspot* *AE, D, MC, V* *BP, MAP.*

$–$$ **Hill Farm Inn.** Simple cottages and the best views in the Manchester area make this former dairy farm a winner. You can roam a mile of riverfront along the Battenkill and pet friendly goats, sheep, chickens, and a lazy pig named Blossom. The main inn, from 1830, has a large wraparound porch with sweeping views of Mt. Equinox. Rooms here and in the separate 1790 guesthouse aren't modern, but they're clean and comfortable, furnished with sturdy antiques and even a spinning wheel in the upstairs hallway. If you're here spring through fall, try the charming one- and two-bedroom cabins scattered on the lawn, which offer privacy and a wonderful feeling of freedom in this glorious setting. **Pros:** lovely open meadow setting; farm animals on-site; cabins offer privacy and fun. **Cons:** rooms are quite simple, not luxurious. ✉ *458 Hill Farm Rd., off Rte. 7A, Sunderland* ☎ *802/375–2269 or 800/882–2545* 🌐 *www.hillfarminn.com* *6 rooms, 5 suites, 4 cabins* *In-room: no a/c (some), kitchen (some), refrigerator (some), Wi-Fi (some). In-hotel: Wi-Fi hotspot* *AE, D, MC, V* *BP.*

$$$–$$$$ Fodor's Choice ★ **West Mountain Inn.** This 1810 farmhouse sits on 150 acres on the side of a mountain, offering plenty of hiking trails and easy access to the Battenkill River, where you can canoe or go tubing. In winter you can sled down a former ski slope or borrow the inn's snowshoes or cross-country skis. In summer, blithe innkeeper Amie Emmons lines the front yard with Adirondack chairs that overlook the mountains. A kids' room is filled with games and videos; there are also resident alpacas and a golden retriever. As the house is a patchwork of additions and gables, rooms have eccentric configurations; though they are not flawless, they are comfortable and have great views and interesting sitting areas. The onsite restaurant is well-respected, with dishes that focus on organic and locally grown vegetables and meats. **Pros:** mountainside location; great for families; lots of outdoor activities. **Cons:** slightly outdated bedding and carpets; not luxurious. ✉ *1 River Rd., Arlington* ☎ *802/375–6516* 🌐 *www.westmountaininn.com* *16 rooms, 6 suites* *In-room: no phone, no TV. In-hotel: restaurant, bar, water sports, bicycles, laundry service* *AE, D, MC, V* *BP, MAP.*

MANCHESTER

★ *9 mi northeast of Arlington.*

Well-to-do Manchester has been a popular summer retreat since the mid-19th century, when city dwellers traveled north to take in the cool clean air at the foot of 3,816-foot Mt. Equinox. Manchester Village's tree-shaded marble sidewalks and stately old homes—Main Street here could hardly be more picture perfect—reflect the luxurious resort lifestyle of more than a century ago. A mile north on 7A, Manchester Center is the commercial twin to Colonial Manchester Village, as well as where you'll find the town's famed upscale factory outlets doing business in attractive faux-Colonial shops.

Manchester Village also houses the world headquarters of Orvis, the outdoor goods brand that began here in the 19th century and has greatly influenced the town ever since. Its complex includes a fly-fishing school with lessons in its casting ponds and the Battenkill River.

GETTING HERE AND AROUND

Manchester is the main town for the ski resorts of Stratton and Bromley and is roughly 15 minutes from either on Routes 11 and 30. It's 15 minutes north of Arlington, 30 minutes north of Bennington and south of Rutland on Routes 7 and 7A. Take 7A for a more scenic drive.

ESSENTIALS

Visitor Information Chamber of Commerce, Manchester and the Mountains (✉ *5046 Main St.* ☎ *802/362–2100 or 800/362–4144* 🌐 *www.manchestervermont.net*). **Green Mountain National Forest Visitor Center** (✉ *2538 Rte. 30* ☎ *802/362–2307* 🌐 *www.fs.fed.us/r9/gmfl* ⏲ *Weekdays 8–4:30*).

EXPLORING

American Museum of Fly Fishing. This museum houses the world's largest collection of angling art and angling-related objects. Rotating exhibitions draw from a permanent collection of more than 1,500 rods, 800 reels, 30,000 flies, and the tackle of notables like Winslow Homer, Bing Crosby, and Jimmy Carter. Every August the museum organizes a fly-fishing festival with kids' activities and vendors selling antique equipment. ✉ *4070 Main St. (Rte. 7A)* ☎ *802/362–3300* 🌐 *www.amff.com* 🎟 *$5* ⏲ *Jan.–May, Nov., and Dec., Tues.–Sat 10–4; June–Oct., Tues.–Sun. 10–4.*

Fodor's Choice ★ **Hildene.** The Lincoln Family Home is a twofold treat, providing historical insight into the life of the Lincolns while escorting you through the lavish Manchester life of the 1900s. Abraham had only one son who survived to adulthood, Robert Todd Lincoln, who served as secretary of war and head of the Pullman Company. Robert bought the beautifully preserved 412-acre estate and built a 24-room mansion where he and his descendants lived from 1905–75. The entire grounds are open for exploration—you can hike, picnic, and ski; see the astronomical observatory; loll in beautiful gardens; and walk through the sturdy Georgian Revival house, which holds the family's original furniture, books, and possessions. One of three surviving stovepipe hats owned by Abraham, a Lincoln Bible, a gorgeously restored Pullman car, and

The formal gardens and mansion at Robert Todd Lincoln's Hildene are a far cry from his father's log cabin.

Robert's Harvard University yearbook are among the treasures you'll find. When the 1,000-pipe aeolian organ is played, the music reverberates as though from the mansion's very bones.

Rising from a 10-acre meadow, the new Hildene Farm opens in 2010. The agriculture center is built in a traditional style—post-and-beam construction of timber felled and milled on the estate—and as an exemplar of renewable energy, from the closed-loop cord wood heating system to the solar panels covering the roof. A herd of goats and informative farming displays recall the Lincolns' use of this land. Best of all, you can watch goat cheese being made and take some home.

The highlight, though, may be the elaborate formal gardens: in June a thousand peonies bloom. When snow conditions permit, you can cross-country ski and snowshoe on the property. Robert's carriage house now houses the gorgeous museum store and visitor center—the nicest of its kind in the state—that showcases, among other things, a live bee exhibit and Mary Todd Lincoln's 1928 vintage Franklin car. Allow half a day for exploring Hildene. ✉ *1005 Hildene Rd., at Rte. 7A* ☎ *802/362–1788* 🌐 *www.hildene.org* 🎫 *Tour $13, grounds pass $5* 🕘 *Daily 9:30–4:30.*

Southern Vermont Arts Center. Rotating exhibits and a permanent collection of more than 700 pieces of 19th- and 20th-century American art are showcased at this 12,500-square-foot museum. The original building, a graceful Georgian mansion set on 407 acres, is the frequent site of concerts, performances, and film screenings. In summer and fall, a pleasant restaurant with magnificent views serves lunch. ✉ *West Rd.* ☎ *802/362–1405* 🌐 *www.svac.org* 🎫 *$8* 🕘 *Tues.–Sat. 10–5, Sun. noon–5.*

2

SPORTS AND THE OUTDOORS

BIKING **Battenkill Sports** (✉ *1240 Depot St. [U.S. 7, Exit 4]* ☎ *802/362–2734 or 800/340–2734* 🌐 *www.battenkillsports.com*) rents, sells, and repairs bikes and provides maps and route suggestions.

FISHING **Battenkill Anglers** (✉ *6204 Main St., Manchester* ☎ *802/379–1444*) teaches the art and science of fly-fishing in both private and group lessons. **Orvis Fly-Fishing School** (✉ *6204 Rte. 7A, Manchester Center* ☎ *802/362–4604 or 866/531–6213* 🌐 *www.orvis.com/schools*) is nationally renowned. The company opened a new building just for the fly school across the street from its flagship store in 2009. Courses are offered mid-April to mid-October, ranging from two-hour pond trips with casting lessons and fishing with private instructors to three-day advanced classes on the Battenkill.

HIKING There are bountiful hiking trails in the Green Mountain National Forest. Shorter hikes begin at the Equinox Resort, which owns about 1,000 acres of forest and has a great trail system open to the public.

One of the most popular segments of Vermont's **Long Trail** (🌐 *www.greenmountainclub.org*) starts from a parking lot on Route 11/30 five minutes out of town and goes to the top of Bromley Mountain. The strenous 6-mi round-trip takes about four hours. A moderate four-hour hike starts off Manchester East Road and ends at Vermont's most impressive cataract, **Lye Brook Falls.**

The **Mountain Goat** (✉ *4886 Main St.* ☎ *802/362–5159* 🌐 *mountaingoat.com*) sells hiking and backpacking equipment and rents snowshoes and cross-country and Telemark skis.

ICE-SKATING The Olympic-size indoor **Riley Rink** (✉ *410 Hunter Park Rd.* ☎ *802/362–0150* 🌐 *www.rileyrink.com*) has rentals and a concession stand.

SHOPPING

★ In Manchester Village, **Frog Hollow at Equinox** (✉ *3566 Main St. [Rte. 7A]* ☎ *802/362–3321*) is a nonprofit collective that sells such contemporary works as jewelry, glassware, and home furnishings from Vermont artisans. **Long Ago and Far Away** (✉ *Green Mountain Village Shops, 4963 Main St.* ☎ *802/362–3435* 🌐 *www.longagoandfaraway.com*) specializes in fine indigenous artwork, including Inuit stone sculpture. The large **Tilting at Windmills Gallery** (✉ *24 Highland Ave.* ☎ *802/362–3022* 🌐 *www.tilting.com*) displays and sells the paintings and sculpture of nationally known artists.

Fodor's Choice ★ **Northshire Bookstore** (✉ *4869 Main St.* ☎ *802/362–2200 or 800/437–3700* 🌐 *www.northshire.com*) is the heart of Manchester Center, adored by visitors and residents for its ambience, selection, and service. Up the central black iron staircase is a second floor dedicated to children's books, toys, and clothes. Connected to the bookstore is the Spiral Press Café, where you can sit for a grilled pesto-chicken sandwich or a latte and scone. **■ TIP→ Adding to the gravitational draw is the Wi-Fi connection and the visitor information booth open Wednesday–Sunday 1–5.**

★ The two-story, lodge-like **Orvis Flagship Store** (✉ *4200 Rte. 7A* ☎ *802/362–3750* 🌐 *www.orvis.com/*) has a trout pond as well as the company's latest clothing and accessories. It's a required shopping destination for many visitors—the Orvis name is pure Manchester. Spread out across Manchester Center, **Manchester Designer Outlets** (✉ *U.S. 7 and Rte. 11/30* ☎ *802/362–3736 or 800/955–7467* 🌐 *www.manchesterdesigneroutlets.com*) is the most upscale collection of stores in northern New England—and every store is a discount outlet! Adding to the allure, town ordinances decree the look of the shops be in tune with the surrounding historic homes, making these the most attractive and decidedly Colonial-looking outlets you'll ever see. In 2009, Kate Spade and Kenneth Cole added their names to the long list of upscale clothiers who call Manchester home. Among them are Michael Kors, Betsey Johnson, Ann Taylor, Tumi, Escada, Armani, Coach, Polo Ralph Lauren, Brooks Brothers, and Theory. There are also less expensive brand outlets like Pacsun, Gap, and Banana Republic.

NIGHTLIFE AND THE ARTS

Fodor's Choice ★ Near Bromley Mountain, **Johnny Seesaw's** (✉ *3574 Rte. 11* ☎ *802/824–5533* 🌐 *www.jseesaw.com*) is a classic rustic ski lodge with two huge fireplaces and a relaxed attitude. There's live music on weekends and an excellent "comfort food" menu. It's closed April through Memorial Day. The **Falcon Bar** (✉ *3567 Main St. [Rte. 7A]* ☎ *802/362–4700* 🌐 *www.equinoxresort.com*) at the Equinox resort opened in 2008 and instantly became a Manchester classic. The bar has a sophisticated indoor setting with music on weekends, or you can take in the wonderful outdoor deck. In winter the place to be is under the heating lamps surrounding the giant Vermont slate fire pit. The **Perfect Wife** (✉ *2594 Depot St. [Rte. 11/30]* ☎ *802/362–2817* 🌐 *www.perfectwife.com*) is decidedly more local, with music three to four nights a week.

WHERE TO EAT

$$$ FRENCH ✕ **Bistro Henry.** The active presence of chef-owner Henry Bronson accounts for the continual popularity of this friendly place that's about $5 per dish cheaper than the other good restaurants in town. The menu works off a bistro foundation, with a peppery steak au poivre and a medium rare duck breast served with a crispy leg, and mixes things up with eclectic dishes like seared tuna with wasabi and soy; crab cakes in a Cajun rémoulade; and a delicious scallop dish with Thai coconut curry and purple sticky rice. The wine list is extensive, and Dina Bronson's desserts are memorable—indulge in the "gooey chocolate cake," a great molten treat paired with a homemade malt ice cream. ✉ *1942 Rte. 11/30, 3 mi east of Manchester Center* ☎ *802/362–4982* 🌐 *www.bistrohenry.com* 💳 *AE, D, DC, MC, V* ⊗ *Closed Mon. No lunch.*

$$$$ CONTINENTAL ✕ **Chantecleer.** There is something wonderful about eating by candlelight in an old barn. Chantecleer's dining rooms (in winter ask to sit by the great fieldstone fireplace) are wonderfully romantic, even with a collection of roosters atop the wooden beams. The menu leans toward the Continental with starters like a fine escargot glazed with Pernod in a hazelnut and parsley butter. Crowd pleasers include Colorado rack of lamb and whole Dover sole filleted tableside. A recipe from the chef's Swiss hometown makes a winning dessert: Basel Rathaus Torte, a delicious hazelnut layer cake. ✉ *8 Reed Farm La., off Rte. 7A, 3½ mi north of Manchester, East Dorset* ☎ *802/362–1616* 🌐 *www.chantecleerrestaurant.com* ✍ *Res-*

Manchester Designer Outlets' Colonial-style architecture helps blend upscale discount shopping with the surrounding town.

ervations essential ▭ *AE, DC, MC, V* ⊙ *Closed Nov. and Apr.–mid-May. Closed Mon. and Tues. No lunch.*

$$$$ STEAKHOUSE ✕ **Chop House.** Walk to the very back room of the Equinox resort's Marsh Tavern, past a velvet curtain, and you'll have entered a different eatery—a wonderful, very expensive steakhouse called the Chop House. It opened in 2009, but you can't claim to be the first here—the marble above the fireplace is chiseled L. L. ORVIS 1832 (and way before he claimed the spot the Green Mountain Boys gathered here to plan their resistance). Today, you'll yield to USDA Prime aged corn- or grass-fed beef broiled at 1,700 degrees and finished with herb butter. The New York strip, 32-oz rib eye, 16-oz milk-fed veal chops, filet mignon, lamb, and seafood are delicious, a must for deep-pocketed lovers of steaks and seafood. ✉ *3567 Main St.* ☎ 802/362–4700 ⊕ *www.equinoxresort.com* ▭ *AE, D, DC, MC, V.*

$ PIZZA ✕ **Depot 62 Cafe.** The best pizzas in town are topped with terrific fresh ingredients and served in the middle of a high-end antiques showroom, making this restaurant a local secret worth knowing about. The wood-fired oven yields masterful results—like the arugula pizza, a beehive of fresh greens atop a thin-crust base. This a great place for lunch or an inexpensive but satisfying dinner. Sit on your own or at the long communal table. ✉ *505 Depot St.* ☎ *802/366–8181* ▭ *MC, V.*

$$$ FRENCH ✕ **Mistral's.** This classic French restaurant is tucked in a grotto off Route 11/30 on the climb to Bromley Mountain. The two dining rooms are perched over the Bromley Brook, and at night lights magically illuminate a small waterfall. Ask for a window table. Specialties include Chateaubriand béarnaise and rack of lamb with rosemary for two.

Chef Dana Markey's crispy sweetbreads with porcini mushrooms are a favorite. ✉ *10 Toll Gate Rd.* ☎ *802/362–1779* ▭ *AE, DC, MC, V* ⏲ *Closed Wed. No lunch.*

$ ECLECTIC ✗ **Perfect Wife.** Owner-chef Amy Chamberlain, the self-proclaimed aspiring flawless spouse, creates freestyle cuisine like turkey schnitzel and grilled venison with a caramelized shallot and dried cranberry demi-glace. There are two entrances to the restaurant, and we recommend the hilltop tavern, which looks over the more formal dining room below. The tavern is one of the livelier local spots in town, with live music on weekends and a pub menu with burgers, potpies in winter, and Vermont microbrews on tap. ✉ *2594 Depot St. (Rte. 11/30), 2½ mi east of Manchester Center* ☎ *802/362–2817* 🌐 *www.perfectwife.com* ▭ *AE, D, MC, V* ⏲ *Closed Sun. No lunch.*

$$$ AMERICAN ✗ **The Reluctant Panther.** The dining room at this luxurious inn is a large, modern space, where dark wood and high ceilings meld into a kind of nouveau Vermont aesthetic. The food is indulgent and rich as well as very expensive, making this a special-occasion kind of place. The dinner menu includes maple-rubbed Vermont lamb, scallops, and a duet of Long Island duck breast and confit of leg cannelloni. In the warmer months, sit outside on the lovely landscaped patio. ✉ *1 West Rd.* ☎ *800/822–2331* 🌐 *www.reluctantpanther.com* ▭ *AE, D, DC, MC, V* ⏲ *No lunch. Jan.–Apr. closed weekdays.*

WHERE TO STAY

$$$$ Fodor's Choice ★ **The Equinox.** The Equinox defines the geographic center and historic heart of Manchester Village and has been *the* fancy hotel in town—and in the state—since the 18th century. A head-to-toe renovation in 2008 re-elevated the property to the lofty tier befitting its white, two-story Doric columns and bellhops uniformed in jodhpurs and knee-high argyle socks. Rooms have huge flat-screen TVs, leather chairs, two-tone cream wallpaper, plush-top mattresses, and marble bathrooms with granite sinks. If you crave Colonial, the brown 1811 House across the street is part of the resort. If you've got big bucks, ask for a room in the Charles Orvis Inn next door, which has hot tubs and private porches. The spa is the best in southern Vermont; the concierge will arrange falconry, fishing, or shooting lessons; the resort's golf course is across the street; and there's a new wine bar in addition to three good dining choices. **Pros:** heart-of-town location; full-service hotel; great golf and spa. **Cons:** big-hotel feeling; overrun by New Yorkers on weekends. ✉ *3567 Main St. (Rte. 7A)* ☎ *802/362–4700 or 888/367–7625* 🌐 *www.equinoxresort.com* *164 rooms, 29 suites* *In-room: kitchen (some), refrigerator (some), Wi-Fi. In-hotel: 3 restaurants, bar, golf course, tennis courts, pool, spa, laundry service, Wi-Fi hotspot* ▭ *AE, D, DC, MC, V.*

$$$–$$$$ **Wilburton Inn.** A few miles south of Manchester and overlooking the Battenkill Valley from a hilltop all its own, this turn-of-the-century complex is centered on a Tudor mansion with 11 bedrooms and suites and richly paneled common rooms containing part of the owners' vast art collection. Besides the main inn, five guest buildings are spread over the grounds, dotted with more owner-created sculpture. Rooms at the Wilburton vary greatly in condition, so choose carefully. The dining room is an elegant affair, with a menu to match—entrées might include

poached Maine lobster with gnocchi or a roasted antelope chop with bordelaise sauce. One note: weddings take place here most summer weekends. **Pros:** beautiful setting with easy access to Manchester; fine dining. **Cons:** rooms in main inn, especially, need updating; limited indoor facilities. ✉ *257 River Rd.* ☎ *802/362–2500 or 800/648–4944* 🌐 *www.wilburton.com* *30 rooms, 4 suites* *In-hotel: restaurant, tennis courts, pool* *AE, MC, V* *BP.*

DORSET

★ *7 mi north of Manchester.*

Lying at the foot of many mountains and with a village green surrounded by white clapboard homes and inns, Dorset has a solid claim to the title of Vermont's most picture-perfect town. The town has just 2,000 residents but two of the state's best and oldest general stores.

The country's first commercial marble quarry was opened here in 1785. Dozens followed suit, providing the marble for the main research branch of the New York City Public Library and many Fifth Avenue mansions, among other notable landmarks, as well as the sidewalks here and in Manchester. A remarkable private home made entirely of marble can be seen on Dorset West Road, a beautiful residential road west of the town green. The marble Dorset Church on the green features two Tiffany stained-glass windows.

EXPLORING

Fodor's Choice ★ **Dorset Quarry.** On hot summer days the sight of dozens of families jumping, swimming, and basking in the sun around this massive swimming hole makes it one of the most wholesome and picturesque recreational spots in the United States. First mined in 1785, this is the oldest marble quarry in the United States. The popular area visible from Route 30 is actually just the lower quarry, and footpaths lead to the quiet upper quarry. ✉ *Rte. 30, 1 mi south of Dorset green* ☎ *No phone* *Free.*

★ **Merck Forest and Farmland Center.** This 3,100-acre farm and forest is a nonprofit educational center with 30 mi of nature trails for hiking, cross-country skiing, snowshoeing, and horseback riding. You can visit the farm, which grows organic fruits and vegetables (and purchase them at the farm stand), and check out the pasture-raised horses, cows, sheep, pigs, and chickens. There are also remote cabins and tent sites for rental. ✉ *3270 Rte. 315, Rupert* ☎ *802/394–7836* 🌐 *www.merckforest.org* *Free* *Daily, dawn–dusk.*

SPORTS AND THE OUTDOORS

Emerald Lake State Park (✉ *U.S. 7, East Dorset* ☎ *802/362–1655* 🌐 *www.vtstateparks.com/htm/emerald.cfm* *$3*) has a small beach, a marked nature trail, an on-site naturalist, boat rentals, and a snack bar.

SHOPPING

The **Dorset Union Store** (✉ *Dorset Green* ☎ *802/867–4400* 🌐 *www.dorsetunionstore.com*) first opened in 1816 as a village co-op. Today this privately owned general store makes good prepared dinners, has a big wine selection, rents DVDs, and sells food and gifts. The **H. N. Williams General Store** (✉ *2732 Rte. 30* ☎ *802/867–5353* 🌐 *www.*

hnwilliams.com) is the most authentic and comprehensive general store in the state. It was started in 1840 by William Williams and has been run by the same family for six generations. This is one of those unique places where you can buy both maple syrup and ammo and catch up on posted town announcements. A farmers' market (🌐 *www.dorsetfarmersmarket.com*) is held outside on Sundays in summer.

THE ARTS

Dorset is home to a prestigious summer theater troupe that presents the annual Dorset Theater Festival. Plays are held in a wonderful converted pre-Revolutionary barn, the **Dorset Playhouse** (✉ *104 Cheney Rd., off town green* ☎ *802/867–2223 or 802/867–5777* 🌐 *www.dorsetplayers.org/*), which the playhouse also hosts a community group in winter.

WHERE TO EAT

$–$$ AMERICAN ✕ **Dorset Inn Dining Room.** Since 1796, the inn that houses this restaurant has been continuously operating, and even today you can count on three meals a day, every day of the year. The comfortable tavern, which serves the same menu as the more formal dining room, is popular with locals, and Patrick, the amiable veteran bartender, will make you feel at home. The menu highlights ingredients from local farms served by chef Thom Simonetti. Popular choices include yam fritters served in maple syrup and a lightly breaded chicken breast saltimbocca, stuffed with prosciutto and mozzarella. ✉ *8 Church St., Dorset Green at Rte. 30* ☎ *802/867–5500* 🌐 *www.dorsetinn.com* ▭ *AE, MC, V.*

$$$ ECLECTIC ★ ✕ **West View Farm.** Chef-owner Raymond Chen was the lead line cook at New York City's Mercer Kitchen under Jean-Georges Vongerichten before opening this local ingredient–friendly restaurant. You'll find traditional floral wallpaper and soft classical music, but that's where the similarities to Dorset's other eateries end. Chen's dishes are skillful and practiced, starting with an *amuse-bouche* such as *brandade* (salt cod) over pesto. French influences are evident in the sautéed mushrooms and mascarpone ravioli in white truffle oil. Asian notes are evident, too, as in the lemongrass ginger soup with shiitake mushrooms that's ladled over grilled shrimp. A tavern serves enticing, inexpensive small dishes. ✉ *2928 Rte. 30* ☎ *802/867–5715 or 800/769–4903* 🌐 *www.westviewfarm.com* ▭ *AE, MC, V* ⊗ *Closed Tues. and Wed.*

WHERE TO STAY

$–$$ **Inn at West View Farm.** Although these rooms could use a little attention, they offer an inexpensive way to stay in an old farmhouse with comfortable common rooms—along with easy access to an amazing dining room. The white clapboard farmhouse is part of a former 1870 dairy farm. A deck in back looks out at the smaller farm buildings that dot the 5-acre yard. Rooms display imperfections, like an occasional stain or crack, and the carpeting could use an update, but they are very clean, and the furniture and wallpaper satisfy the Colonial farmhouse urge. **Pros:** great restaurant; good value. **Cons:** rooms aren't perfectly maintained. ✉ *2928 Rte. 30* ☎ *802/867–5715* 🌐 *www.innatwestviewfarm.com* *9 rooms, 1 suite* *In-room: Wi-Fi. In-hotel: restaurant, bar, laundry service, Wi-Fi hotspot, no kids under 10* ▭ *AE, MC, V* *BP.*

$$–$$$ **Squire House.** There are three rooms for rent in this big house that combines modern comforts and antique fixtures on a wonderfully quiet road. And there's enough space and quiet, with three big common rooms, that it can feel like home. The house was built in 1918 and was designed with 9-foot ceilings and great light throughout. Rooms are newly carpeted and spotless. Owners Gay and Roger Squire are rightly proud of their breakfasts served in a richly paneled dining room. Roger is a flute player and enjoys the company of other musicians, who get a 10% discount. **Pros:** big estate feels like your own; well-maintained. **Cons:** bathrooms less exciting than rooms; no credit cards. ✉ *3395 Dorset West Rd.* ☎ *802/867–0281* 🌐 *www.squirehouse.com* *2 rooms, 1 suite* *In-room: no phone, refrigerator (some), DVD (some), no TV (some), Wi-Fi. In-hotel: laundry service, Wi-Fi hotspot, no kids under 14* *No credit cards* *BP.*

STRATTON

26 mi southeast of Dorset.

Stratton is really Stratton Mountain Resort—a mountaintop ski resort with a self-contained "town center" of shops, restaurants, and lodgings clustered at the base of the slopes. When the snow melts, golf, tennis, and a host of other summer activities are big attractions, but the ski village remains quiet. For those arriving from the north along Route 30, Bondville is the town at the base of the mountain. At the junction of Routes 30 and 100 is the tiny Vermont village of Jamaica, with its own cluster of inns and restaurants on the east side of the mountain.

GETTING HERE AND AROUND

From Manchester or Route 7, follow Route 11/30 east until they split. Route 11 continues past Bromley ski mountain while Route 30 turns south 10 minutes toward Bondville, the town closest to Stratton Mountain.

SPORTS AND THE OUTDOORS

SKI AREAS About 20 minutes from Stratton, **Bromley** (✉ *Rte. 11, Peru* ☎ *802/824–5522 or 800/865–4786* 🌐 *www.bromley.com*) is a favorite with families. The 43 trails are evenly divided between beginner, intermediate, and expert. The resort runs a child-care center for kids ages 6 weeks to 4 years and hosts children's programs for ages 3–12. An added bonus: the trails face south, making for glorious spring skiing and warm winter days.

★ About 30 minutes from Manchester, sophisticated, exclusive **Stratton Mountain** (✉ *5 Village Rd., Bondville. Turn off Rte. 30 and go 4 mi up access road* ☎ *802/297–2200; 802/297–4211 snow conditions; 800/787–2886 lodging* 🌐 *www.stratton.com*) draws affluent families and young professionals from the New York–southern Connecticut corridor. An entire village, with a covered parking structure for 700 cars, is at the base of the mountain. Activities are afoot year-round. Stratton has 15 outdoor tennis courts, 27 holes of golf, a climbing wall, horseback riding, hiking accessed by a gondola to the summit, and instructional programs in tennis and golf. The sports center, open year-round, has two indoor tennis courts, three racquetball courts, a 25-meter indoor swimming pool, a hot tub, a steam room, a fitness facility with Nautilus equipment, and a restaurant. Adjacent to the base lodge are a condo-hotel, restaurants, and about 25 shops lining a pedestrian mall.

In terms of downhill skiing, Stratton prides itself on its immaculate grooming, making it excellent for cruising. The lower part of the mountain is beginner to low-intermediate, served by several chairlifts. The upper mountain is served by several high-speed quads and a 12-passenger gondola. Down the face are the expert trails, and on either side are intermediate cruising runs with a smattering of wide beginner slopes. The third sector, the Sun Bowl, is off to one side with two high-speed, six-passenger lifts and two expert trails, a full base lodge, and plenty of intermediate terrain. Snowmaking covers 95% of the slopes. Every March, Stratton hosts the U.S. Open Snowboarding championships; its snowboard park has a 380-foot half-pipe. A Ski Learning Park provides its own Park Packages for novice skiers. In all, Stratton has 15 lifts that service 92 trails and 90 acres of glades. There is a ski school for children ages 4–12. The resort also has more than 18 mi of cross-country skiing and the Sun Bowl Nordic center. An on-site day-care center takes children from 6 weeks to 5 years old for indoor activities and outdoor excursions.

NIGHTLIFE AND THE ARTS

Popular **Mulligan's** (✉ *Stratton Village Sq. 11B, Mountain Rd., Bondville* ☎ *802/297–9293*) hosts bands or DJs in the late afternoon and on weekends in winter. ★ Year-round, the **Red Fox Inn** (✉ *103 Winhall Hollow Rd., Bondville* ☎ *802/297–2488* 🌐 *www.redfoxinn.com*) is the best après-ski nightlife spot in southern Vermont. It hosts Irish music Wednesday night; an open mike Thursday night; and rock and roll at other times.

WHERE TO EAT

$$$ AMERICAN

✕ **Red Fox Inn.** This two-level converted barn has the best nightlife in southern Vermont and a fun dining room to boot. The restaurant has been here since 1979, but you'd believe since 1900. The upper level is the dining room—the big A-frame has wagon wheels and a carriage suspended from the ceiling. Settle in near the huge fireplace for rack of lamb, free-range chicken, or penne à la vodka. Downstairs is the tavern where there's Irish music, half-price Guinness, and fish-and-chips on Wednesday. Other nights there might be live music, karaoke, or video bowling. The bar operates daily year-round. ✉ *103 Winhall Hollow Rd., Bondville* ☎ *802/297–2488* 🌐 *www.redfoxinn.com* ▭ *AE, MC, V* ⊙ *No lunch. Closed Mon.–Wed. June–Oct.*

$$$$ CONTEMPORARY Fodor's Choice ★

✕ **Three Mountain Inn.** If you're in the Stratton area and can splurge on an expensive meal, don't miss dinner at this charming inn. The prix-fixe meal includes *amuse-bouche*, starter, salad, entrée, and dessert for $55, plus the best restaurant bread in Vermont, a homemade herb focaccia. A starter might be baked Malpeque oysters with a chorizo and fennel jam; entrées include grilled swordfish with toasted couscous and a mint cucumber sauce. Each dining room has a fireplace, and common areas have terrific original wall and ceiling beams, making the restaurant a romantic winner. ✉ *3732 Rte. 30/100, Jamaica* ☎ *802/874–4140* 🌐 *www.threemountaininn.com* ▭ *AE, D, MC, V* ⊙ *No dinner Mon. and Tues.*

2

WHERE TO STAY

$$ **Long Trail House.** Directly across the street from Stratton's ski village, this fairly new condo complex is one of the best choices close to the slopes. Units have fully equipped kitchens with ovens and dishwashers. The studios are an excellent value; they come with Murphy beds that fold out into the living room area for additional sleepers. **Pros:** across from skiing; good rates available; outdoor heated pool. **Cons:** room decor varies; two-night stay required on weekends. ✉ *1 Stratton Mtn. Rd., Bondville* ☎ *802/297–2200 or 800/787–2886* ⊕ *www.stratton.com* *100 units* *In-room: safe (some), kitchen, DVD (some). In-hotel: pool, laundry facilities* ▭ *AE, D, DC, MC, V.*

$$–$$$ **Red Fox Inn.** Stay here for great mid-week rates (50% off Sunday through Thursday) and relaxed, no-frills accommodations off the noisy mountain. Tom and Cindy Logan's "white house," an early 1800s farmhouse, is in an open meadow 4 mi from Stratton and 8 mi from Bromley. The feeling here is warm and cozy, with original wood floors and simple furnishings. Downstairs rooms have bay windows; upstairs rooms are smaller. **Pros:** great nightlife and food next door; real local hosts; secluded. **Cons:** a drive to ski areas; weekends overpriced. ✉ *103 Winhall Hollow Rd., Bondville* ☎ *802/297–2488* ⊕ *www.redfoxinn.com* *8 rooms, 1 suite* *In-room: no phone, no a/c, no TV, Wi-Fi. In-hotel: restaurant, bar, Wi-Fi hotspot* ▭ *AE, MC, V.*

$$$–$$$$ Fodor's Choice ★ **Three Mountain Inn.** A 1780s tavern, this romantic inn in downtown Jamaica (10 mi northeast of Stratton) feels authentically Colonial, from the wide paneling to the low ceilings. Comfortable and intimate rooms are appointed with a blend of historic and modern furnishings, including featherbeds. Most rooms have fireplaces and mountain views, and three have private decks. Owners Ed and Jennifer Dorta-Duque attend to your stay and oversee truly enchanting dinners. **Pros:** charming, authentic, romantic, small-town B&B; well-kept rooms; great dinners. **Cons:** can be expensive. ✉ *3732 Rte. 30/100, Jamaica* ☎ *802/874–4140* ⊕ *www.threemountaininn.com* *14 rooms, 1 suite* *In-room: DVD (some), no TV (some), Wi-Fi. In-hotel: restaurant, bar, pool, bicycles, laundry service, Internet terminal, Wi-Fi hotspot, some pets allowed, no kids under 12* ▭ *AE, D, MC, V* *BP.*

WESTON

17 mi north of Stratton.

Best known for the Vermont Country Store, Weston was one of the first Vermont towns to discover its own intrinsic loveliness—and marketability. With its summer theater, classic town green with a Victorian bandstand, and an assortment of shops, the little village really lives up to its vaunted image.

SHOPPING

For paintings, prints, and sculptures by Vermont artists and craftspeople, go to the **Todd Gallery** (✉ *614 Main St.* ☎ *802/824–5606* ⊕ *www.toddgallery.com*), open Thursday–Monday, 10–5. ★ The **Vermont Country Store** (✉ *657 Main St. [Rte. 100]* ☎ *802/824–3184* ⊕ *www.vermontcountrystore.com*) is an old-fashioned emporium selling all manner of items. The store was first opened in 1946 and is still run by the Orton family, though it has become something of an empire, with a large catalog and online business. One room is set aside for Vermont Common Crackers and bins of fudge and other candy. In others you'll find nearly forgotten items such as Lilac Vegetol aftershave and horehound drops, as well as practical items such as sturdy outdoor clothing and even typewriters. Nostalgia-evoking implements dangle from the store's walls and rafters. (There's another store on Route 103 in Rockingham.)

THE ARTS

In July and August, the **Kinhaven Music School** (✉ *354 Lawrence Hill Rd.* ☎ *802/824–4332* 🌐 *www.kinhaven.org*) stages free student classical music concerts on Friday at 4 and Sunday at 2:30. Faculty concerts are Saturday at 8 PM.

The members of the **Weston Playhouse** (✉ *703 Main St., Village Green, off Rte. 100* ☎ *802/824–5288* 🌐 *www.westonplayhouse.org*), the oldest professional theater in Vermont, produce Broadway plays, musicals, and other works. Their season runs from late June to early September.

WHERE TO STAY

$$$ **Inn at Weston.** Highlighting the country elegance of this 1848 inn, a short walk from the town green, is innkeeper Bob Aldrich's collection of 500 orchid species—rare and beautiful specimens surround the dining table in the gazebo, and others enrich the indoors. Rooms in the inn, carriage house, and Coleman House (across the street) are comfortably appointed, and some have fireplaces. The restaurant ($$$; closed Monday) serves contemporary regional cuisine amid candlelight. Vermont cheddar cheese and Granny Smith–apple omelets are popular choices for breakfast. **Pros:** great rooms; terrific town location. **Cons:** top-end rooms are expensive. ✉ *160 Main St. (Rte. 100), Box 66* ☎ *802/824–6789* 🌐 *www.innweston.com* *13 rooms* *In-room: no TV (some), Wi-Fi. In-hotel: restaurant, bar, Wi-Fi hotspot, no kids under 12* *AE, DC, MC, V* *BP.*

LUDLOW

9 mi northeast of Weston.

Ludlow was once a nondescript factory town that just happened to have a small ski area—Okemo. Today, that ski area is one of Vermont's largest and most popular resorts, and downtown Ludlow is a collection of restored buildings with shops and restaurants.

SPORTS AND THE OUTDOORS

SKI AREAS Once only a faint blip on skiers' radar, **Ascutney** (✉ *Rte. 44, Brownsville* ☎ *802/484–7711 or 800/243–0011* 🌐 *www.ascutney.com*) has remade itself into a bona fide destination. The 56 trails on an 1,800-foot vertical drop are served by six lifts, including a high-speed quad chairlift accessing double-diamond terrain near the summit. Day care is available for children ages 6 weeks to 6 years, with learn-to-ski programs for toddlers and up. On Saturday from 5 to 8 PM, children ages 4–12 can join Cheddar's Happy Hour and movie night.

Family-owned since 1982 and still run by Tim and Diane Mueller, **Okemo Mountain Resort** (✉ *77 Okemo Ridge Rd.* ☎ *802/228–4041; 802/228–5222*

You never know what you'll find at a rambling general store like Weston's Vermont Country Store.

snow conditions; 800/786–5366 lodging 🌐 *www.okemo.com*) has evolved into a major year-round resort, now with two base areas. Known for its wide, well-groomed trails, it's a favorite among intermediates. Jackson Gore, a second base village north of Ludlow off Route 103, has an inn, restaurants, a child-care center, and shops. The resort offers numerous ski and snowboarding packages. There's also ice skating at the Ice House, a covered, open-air rink open 10–9 daily in the winter. The Spring House, next to the entrance of Jackson Gore Inn, has a great kids' pool with slides, a racquetball court, fitness center, and sauna. The yoga and Pilates studio has classes a few times a week. A day pass is $12.

At 2,200 feet, Okemo has the highest vertical drop of any resort in southern Vermont. The beginner trails extend above both base areas, with more challenging terrain higher on the mountains. Intermediate trails are the theme here, but experts will find steep trails and glades at Jackson Gore and on the South Face. Of the 113 trails, 42% have an intermediate rating, 33% are rated novice, and 25% are rated for experts. They are served by an efficient system of 18 lifts, including nine quads, three triple chairlifts, and six surface lifts; 95% of the trails are covered by snowmaking. Okemo has four terrain parks for skiers and snowboarders, including one for beginners; two 400-foot-long Superpipes, and a mini half-pipe.

For cross-country skiing, the **Okemo Valley Nordic Center** (✉ *Fox La.* ☎ *802/228–1396*) has 16 mi of groomed cross-country trails and 6 mi of dedicated snowshoe trails and rents equipment.

If you're looking for non-snow-related activities, you can play basketball and tennis at the Ice House next to Jackson Gore Inn or perfect your swing at the 18-hole, par-70, 6,400-yard, Heathland-style course at the Okemo Valley Golf Club. Seven target greens, four outdoor putting greens, a golf academy, an indoor putting green, swing stations, and a simulator provide plenty of ways to improve your game year-round. The newer, off-site 9-hole **Tater Hill Golf Course** (✉ *6802 Popple Dungeon Rd., Windham, 22 mi south of Ludlow* ☎ *802/875–2517*) has a pro shop, putting green, and a driving range.

WHERE TO EAT

$–$$ ITALIAN ✕ **Cappuccino's**. This locals' place in town serves mostly Italian fare. Pasta dishes include Pasta Pink, which is loaded with crabmeat and shrimp in a sherry cream tomato sauce, and Pasta Balsamic, with chicken and tomatoes. While it's a year-after-year favorite for Ludlow residents, it can make a romantic après-ski dinner spot. ✉ *41 Depot St.* ☎ *802/228–7566* 🌐 *www.cappuccinosrestaurant.com* ▭ *MC, V* ⊙ *Closed Mon. No lunch.*

$$–$$$ AMERICAN ✕ **Coleman Brook Tavern**. Slopeside at the Jackson Gore Inn, Colebrook is the fanciest and most expensive of Okemo's 19 places to eat, but it's not formal—you'll find ski-boot-wearing diners crowding the tables at lunch. Big wing chairs and large banquettes line window bays. Ask to sit in the Wine Room, a separate section where tables are surrounded by the noteworthy collection of wines. Start with a pound of clams steamed in butter, garlic, white wine, and fresh herbs. Then move on to the sesame seed–crusted ahi tuna served over green-tea soba noodles in a ginger-miso broth. The s'mores dessert is cooked with a tabletop "campfire." ✉ *111 Jackson Gore Rd., Okemo* ☎ *802/228–1435* ▭ *AE, D, DC, MC, V.*

¢–$ PIZZA ✕ **Goodman's American Pie**. This pizzeria has the best wood-fired oven pizza in town. It also has character to spare—sit in chairs from old ski lifts and order from a counter that was once a purple VW bus. Though it's on Main Street, it's set back and kind of hidden—you may consider it your Ludlow secret. Locals and Okemo regulars already in the know stop by to design their own pizza from 25 ingredients; there is also a section of six specials. The Rip Curl has mozzarella, Asiago, ricotta, chicken, fresh garlic, and fresh tomatoes. Slices are available. Arcade games are in the back. ✉ *106 Main St.* ☎ *802/228–4271* ▭ *No credit cards* ⊙ *Closed Wed.*

$–$$ ECLECTIC ✕ **Harry's**. The local favorite when you want to eat a little out of town, this casual roadside restaurant 5 mi northwest of Ludlow has a number of international influences. Traditional contemporary entrées such as pork tenderloin are at one end of the menu and Mexican dishes at the other. The large and tasty burrito, made with fresh cilantro and black beans, is one of the best bargains around. Chef-owner Trip Pearce also owns the equally popular Little Harry's in Rutland. ✉ *3621 Rte. 103, Mount Holly* ☎ *802/259–2996* 🌐 *www.harryscafe.com* ▭ *AE, MC, V* ⊙ *Closed Mon. and Tues. No lunch.*

$$$ ECLECTIC Fodor's Choice ★ ✕ **Inn at Weathersfield Dining Room**. This is Vermont's best restaurant, hidden 15 mi east of Ludlow, a culinary gem inside an 18th-century countryside inn. A chalkboard in the foyer lists the area farms that grow the food you'll eat here on any given night, and it's no gimmick: chef Jason Tostrup (a former sous chef at Thomas Keller's Bouchon in Napa Valley, and a veteran of New York's Vong, Daniel, and Jean Georges) is passionate about local ingredients. Its farm-to-table cuisine is created with

a sophistication that many less principled restaurants lack. A daily five-course "Verterra" prix-fixe menu ($65) might feature stuffed local quail in a cider-soy glaze or local "humanely raised" veal served two ways. Service is excellent, and the wine list is large and reasonably priced. If it's summer, savor the patio. ✉ *1342 Rte. 106, Perkinsville* ☎ *802/263–9217* 🌐 *www.innatweathersfield.com* ▭ *AE, D, MC, V* ⏲ *No lunch. Closed Mon. and Tues. and Apr. and beginning of Nov.*

WHERE TO STAY

$$–$$$ **Inn at Water's Edge.** Want to ski but resent the busy Ludlow and Okemo scene? You'll find a happy middle ground at this inn 5 mi north of town. Former Long Islanders Bruce and Tina Verdrager converted their old ski house and barns into this comfortably refined haven. The centerpiece of the relaxed common areas is a huge 1850 English bar, with comfortable banquettes, a big double-sided fireplace, and a billiards table. Rooms are standard Victorian affairs, clean and nice, but uninspiring compared to the grounds and setting. Although most guests come for skiing, golf and spa packages are also available, and in summer the inn's dock has two canoes and a small sailboat on charming Echo Lake. **Pros:** bucolic setting on a lakefront; interesting, big house. **Cons:** ordinary B&B rooms. ✉ *45 Kingdom Rd.* ☎ *802/228–8134 or 888/706–9736* 🌐 *www.innatwatersedge.com* *9 rooms, 2 suites* *In-room: no phone, no TV, Wi-Fi. In-hotel: restaurant, room service, bar, water sports, laundry service, Internet terminal, Wi-Fi hotspot, no kids under 12* ▭ *AE, MC, V* *BP, MAP.*

$$ ★ **Inn at Weathersfield.** Once you discover the food and charming rooms at Weathersfield, you won't want to go home. This is the kind of great B&B where relaxation rules—there's not much to do besides seasonal sports like hiking and cross-country skiing or watch *something* from the DVD collection. The 1972 house set way back from the road on 21 acres has 12 rustic but very comfortable rooms, nearly all with fireplaces. Owners Jane and Dave Sandelman have created a sanctuary—there's nothing fancy here, but everything is perfectly comfortable, from the wood floors to the stone fire pit on the back deck. **Pros:** dynamite restaurant and tavern; comfy, relaxed inn; quiet. **Cons:** 15-mi drive from the Okemo slopes. ✉ *1342 Rte. 106, Perkinsville* ☎ *802/263–9217* 🌐 *www.innatweathersfield.com* *12 rooms* *In-room: no phone (some), no a/c (some), safe (some), kitchen (some), refrigerator (some), DVD (some), no TV (some), Internet (some), Wi-Fi (some). In-hotel: restaurant, bar, laundry service, Wi-Fi hotspot* ▭ *AE, D, MC, V* *BP* ⏲ *Closed first two weeks in Nov.*

$$$$ **Jackson Gore Inn.** This slope-side base lodge is the place to stay if your aim is convenience to Okemo's slopes. The resort includes three restaurants and a martini bar ($12 a pop, but generous sizes), plus an arcade. You can use the Spring House health center, which includes a fitness center, a racquetball court, hot tubs, a sauna, and great kids' pools with slides. Right next to the original Jackson Gore structure are the newer annexes, Adams House, and Bixby House, which feature whirlpool tubs and slightly more contemporary furnishings. Most units have full kitchen facilities. Besides Jackson Gore, Okemo offers 145 other condo units all across the mountain. **Pros:** ski-in, ski-out at base of mountain; good for families. **Cons:** chaotic and noisy on weekends; expensive. ✉ *77 Okemo Ridge Rd., off Rte. 103* ☎ *802/228–1400 or 800/786–5366* 🌐 *www.*

CLOSE UP

Vermont Artisanal Cheese

Hankering for some good cheddar during your time in Vermont? Would you like that aged one year, two years, three years; clothbound or smoked? Or perhaps instead you'd like an expertly crafted raw goat's milk tomme or some just-made sheep's ricotta?

Vermont is the artisanal cheese capital of the country, with over 40 creameries (and growing fast) that are open to the public—carefully churning out hundreds of different cheeses. Many creameries are "farmstead" operations, meaning that the animals that provide the milk are on site where their milk is made into cheese. If you eat enough cheese during your time in the state, you may be able to differentiate between the many types of milk (cow, goat, sheep, or even water buffalo), as well as make associations between the geography and climate of where you are and the taste of the cheese you eat.

This is one of the reasons why taking a walk around a dairy is a great idea: you can see the process in action, from grazing to aging to eating. Almost all dairies welcome visitors, though it's universally recommended that you call ahead to plan your visit. At **Shelburne Farms** (🌐 *www.shelburnefarms.org*), a chalkboard stands in the cheesemaking facility and notes which part of the complex cheese-making process visitors can witness at various times throughout the day. **Vermont Butter & Cheese** (🌐 *www.butterandcheese.net*), one of the leaders of the artisanal cheese movement, invites curious cheese aficionados to visit their 4,000 square-foot creamery where gem-like goat cheeses such as Bonne Bouche—a perfectly balanced, cloud-like cheese—are made Monday through Friday. Consider **Bardwell Farm** (🌐 *www.considerbardwellfarm.com*)in West

Vermont sheep's milk cheese.

Pawlet was the first cheese cooperative in the state, founded in 1864, and today, a new generation of cheesemakers make nine goat and cow milk cheeses on-site, including the bright, nutty, and exceptionally delicious Pawlet. Visit their Web site for information regarding cheesemaking workshops and classes offered at the farm. For a taste of the classic Vermont cheddar, head to **Cabot Creamery** (🌐 *www.cabotcheese.coop*)and take a tour of the factory and see how the many varieties of cheddars are made.

If you can't get yourself to a creamery for a visit, don't fret: almost every general store, grocery, or gourmet food shop carries at least a couple of delicious Vermont cheeses, the most common being Cabot and Grafton cheddars, plus usually something from a cheesemaking operation particularly close by. **The Vermont Cheese Council** has developed the **Vermont Cheese Trail**, a map of 38 creameries with contact information for each (🌐 *www.VTcheese.com*).

If you're a real cheese lover, definitely plan your trip to Vermont around the state's world-class food event, the annual **Vermont Cheesemakers Festival** (🌐 *www.vtcheesefest.com*)at Shelburne Farms—each summer approximately 50 cheesemakers gather to sell and sample their various cheeses.

—Michael de Zayas

okemo.com ⇨ *263 rooms* ♙ *In-room: kitchen (some), refrigerator, DVD, Wi-Fi. In-hotel: 3 restaurants, bar, golf courses, tennis courts, pools, gym, spa, children's programs (ages 2–12), laundry facilities, Internet terminal, Wi-Fi hotspot, some pets allowed* ▭ *AE, MC, V* 🍽 *EP, BP.*

GRAFTON

★ *8 mi south of Chester.*

Out-of-the-way Grafton is as much a historical museum as a town. During its heyday, citizens grazed some 10,000 sheep and spun their wool into sturdy yarn for locally woven fabric. When the market for wool declined, so did Grafton. Then in 1963, the Windham Foundation—Vermont's second-largest private foundation—commenced the town's rehabilitation. Not only was the Old Tavern preserved, but so were many other commercial and residential structures in the village center.

EXPLORING

The **Historical Society Museum** (✉ *10 Main St. [Rte. 121]* ☎ *802/843–2584* 🌐 *www.graftonhistory.org* 🎟 *$3* ⏲ *Memorial Day–Columbus Day, weekends and holidays 10–noon and 2–4*) documents the town's history with exhibits that change yearly.

SHOPPING

Gallery North Star (✉ *151 Townshend Rd.* ☎ *802/843–2465* 🌐 *www.gnsgrafton.com*) exhibits the oils, watercolors, lithographs, and sculptures of Vermont-based artists. Sample the best of Vermont cheddar at the **Grafton Village Cheese Company** (✉ *533 Townshend Rd.* ☎ *802/843–2221* 🌐 *www.graftonvillagecheese.com*).

WHERE TO STAY

$$$–$$$$ ★ 🏨 **Old Tavern at Grafton.** This 1801 classic is one of the oldest operating inns in the country and still one of Vermont's greatest lodging assets. While the rooms could use a designer's touch without forgoing a link to the past, legitimately memorable pleasures are to be had lingering on the porches, in the authentically Colonial common rooms, and with a book by the fire in the old fashioned library—at once rustic, comfy, and elegant. In the main building, with its wraparound porches sheltered by two-story white columns, are 11 guest rooms; the rest are dispersed among six other close-by buildings. Two dining rooms ($$$)—one with formal Georgian furniture, the other with rustic paneling and low beams—serve American fare. You'll also get access to the unusual guests-only bar at the Phelps Barn. The inn runs the nearby Grafton Ponds Cross-Country Ski Center. **Pros:** classic Vermont inn and tavern; professionally run; appealing common areas. **Cons:** rooms are attractive but not stellar. ✉ *92 Main St. (Rte. 121)* ☎ *802/843–2231 or 800/843–1801* 🌐 *www.oldtavern.com* ⇨ *39 rooms, 7 suites* ♙ *In-room: no a/c (some), no TV, Wi-Fi. In-hotel: 2 restaurants, bar, tennis court, bicycles, Internet terminal, Wi-Fi hotspot* ▭ *AE, MC, V* ⏲ *Closed mid-Apr.* 🍽 *BP.*

TOWNSHEND

9 mi south of Grafton.

One of a string of attractive villages along the banks of the West River, Townshend embodies the Vermont ideal of a lovely town green presided over by a gracefully proportioned church spire. The spire belongs to the 1790 Congregational Meeting House, one of the state's oldest houses of worship. North on Route 30 is the Scott Bridge (closed to traffic), the state's longest single-span covered bridge.

OFF THE BEATEN PATH

With a village green surrounded by pristine white buildings, **Newfane**, 6 mi southeast of Townshend, is sometimes described as the quintessential New England small town. The 1839 First Congregational Church and the Windham County Court House, with 17 green-shuttered windows and a rounded cupola, are often open. The building with the four-pointed spire is Union Hall, built in 1832.

SPORTS AND THE OUTDOORS

At **Townshend State Park** (✉ *Rte. 30 N* ☎ *802/365–7500* 🌐 *www.vtstateparks.com/htm/townshend.cfm*) you'll find a sandy beach on the West River and a trail that parallels the river for 2½ mi, topping out on Bald Mountain Dam. Up the dam, the trail follows switchbacks literally carved into the stone apron.

SHOPPING

The **Big Black Bear Shop** (✉ *Rte. 30, 3/4¾ mi north of town, Newfane* ☎ *802/365–4160 or 888/758–2327* 🌐 *www.bigblackbear.com*) at Mary Meyer Stuffed Toys Factory, the state's oldest stuffed toy company, offers discounts of up to 70% on stuffed animals of all sizes. The **Newfane Country Store** (✉ *Rte. 30, Newfane* ☎ *802/365–7916* 🌐 *www.newfanecountrystore.com*) carries homemade fudge and other Vermont foods, gifts, crafts, and many quilts—which can also be custom ordered.

WHERE TO EAT

¢ AMERICAN — ✕ **Townshend Dam Diner.** Folks come from miles around to enjoy traditional fare such as Mom's meat loaf, chili, and roast beef croquettes, as well as Townshend-raised bison burgers and creative daily specials. Breakfast, served all day every day, includes such tasty treats as raspberry chocolate-chip walnut pancakes and homemade French toast. You can sit at any of the collection of 1930s enamel-top tables or in the big swivel-chairs at the U-shaped counter. The diner is a few miles northwest of the village on Route 30. ✉ *5929 Rte. 30, West Townshend* ☎ *802/874–4107* ▭ *No credit cards* ⏲ *Closed Tues.*

$$$ CONTINENTAL — ✕ **Windham Hill Inn.** This remote inn is a fine choice for a romantic fancy dinner. Chef Graham Gill heads up the Frog Pond dining room (don't worry; there are no frogs' legs on the menu). Start with a spiced Vermont quail, served with hand-rolled pappardelle and a wild mushroom ragout. Entrées include a fig-and-balsamic-glazed seared duck breast served with roasted pear and garden Swiss chard and a *cipollini* onion and fingerling potato sauté. There's a remarkably large wine list. A four-course prix fixe is $60. ✉ *311 Lawrence Dr., West Townshend* ☎ *802/874–4080* ✍ *Reservations essential* 🌐 *www.windhamhill.com* ▭ *AE, D, MC, V.*

WHERE TO STAY

¢ **Boardman House.** This handsome Greek-Revival home on the town green combines modern comfort with the relaxed charm of a 19th-century farmhouse. It also happens to be one of the cheapest stays in Vermont. The uncluttered guest rooms are furnished with Shaker-style furniture, colorful duvets, and paintings. Both the breakfast room and front hall have trompe-l'oeil floors. **Pros:** inexpensive; perfect village green location. **Cons:** no phone and cell-phone reception is bad. ✉ *On the green* ☎ *802/365–4086* *4 rooms, 1 suite* *In-room: no phone, no TV, Wi-Fi. In-hotel: Wi-Fi hotspot, no kids under 5* *No credit cards* *BP.*

$$$ ★ **Four Columns Inn.** Rooms and suites in this white-columned, 1834 Greek-Revival mansion were designed for luxurious romantic getaways. The inn is right in the heart of town on the lovely Newfane green, giving you the quintessential Vermont village experience. Some of the suites have cathedral ceilings; all have gas fireplaces and double whirlpool baths, and one has a 12-head spa shower. The elegant restaurant ($$$–$$$$; closed Tuesday) serves new American cuisine. There's also a tavern with a nice selection of artisanal beers. Come here for a serene getaway, as tiny Newfane is adorable but quiet. **Pros:** great rooms; center of town location. **Cons:** little area entertainment in town. ✉ *On the green, 6 mi southeast of Townshend, Newfane* *Box 278, 05345* ☎ *802/365–7713 or 800/787–6633* *www.fourcolumnsinn.com* *6 rooms, 9 suites* *In-room: no TV (some), Wi-Fi. In-hotel: restaurant, bar, pool, laundry service, Internet terminal, Wi-Fi hotspot, some pets allowed* *AE, DC, MC, V* *BP.*

$$–$$$ ★ **Windham Hill Inn.** As there's not too much to do nearby, you might find yourself sitting by a fire or swimming in the outdoor pool at this calm, quiet retreat, and that's a good thing. The 165 hillside acres have magnificent views of the West River Valley and are perfect for real relaxing. Period antiques, Oriental carpets, and locally made furniture are hallmarks of the 1825 brick farmhouse. The white barn annex has a great rough-hewn parlor that leads to the rooms, most of which have fireplaces. The Marion Goodfellow room has a staircase up to a cozy private cupola with 360-degree views. **Pros:** quiet getaway; good food; lovely setting. **Cons:** rural location makes entertainment not an option; spotty cell service; expensive dinners. ✉ *311 Lawrence Dr., West Townshend* ☎ *802/874–4080 or 800/944–4080* *www.windhamhill.com* *21 rooms* *In-hotel: restaurant, bar, tennis court, pool, laundry service, Internet terminal, no kids under 12* *AE, D, MC, V* *BP.*

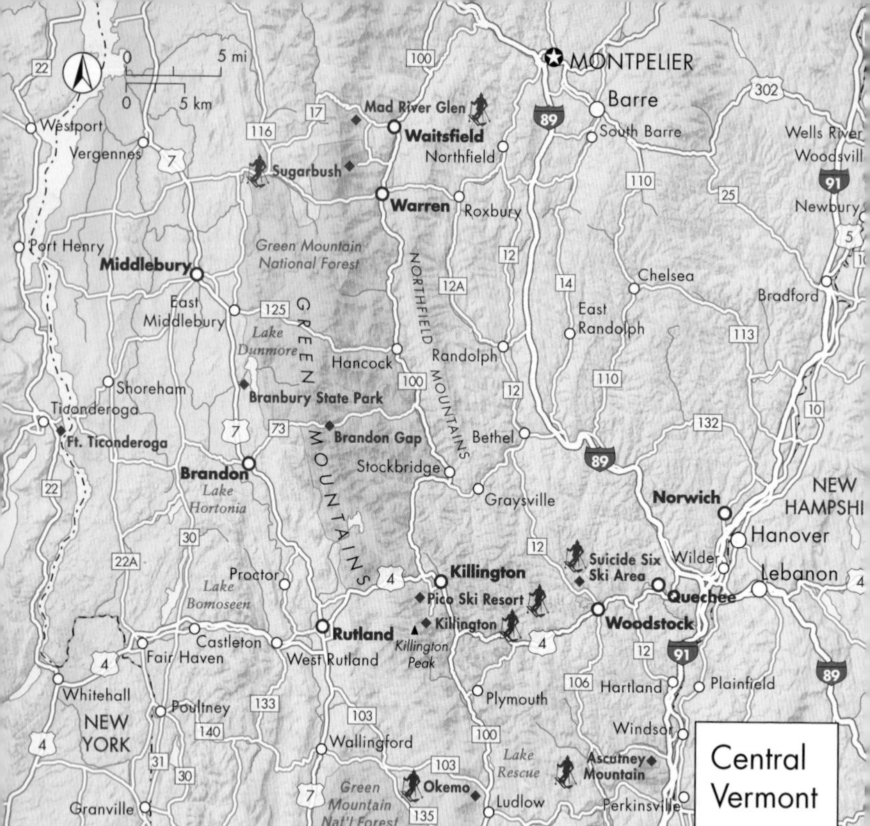

CENTRAL VERMONT

Central Vermont's economy once centered on marble quarrying and mills. But today, as in much of the rest of the state, tourism drives the economic engine. The center of the dynamo is Killington, the East's largest downhill resort, but central Vermont has more to discover than high-speed chairlifts and slope-side condos. The old mills of Quechee and Middlebury are now home to restaurants and shops, giving wonderful views of the waterfalls that once powered the mill turbines. Woodstock has upscale shops and a national historic park. Away from these settlements, the protected (except for occasional logging) lands of the Green Mountain National Forest are laced with hiking trails.

Our coverage of towns begins with Norwich, on U.S. 5 near Interstate 91 at the state's eastern edge, winds west toward U.S. 7, then continues north to Middlebury before heading over the spine of the Green Mountains to Waitsfield.

2

NORWICH

6 mi north of White River Junction.

On the shores of the Connecticut River, Norwich boasts beautifully maintained 18th- and 19th-century homes set about a handsome green. Norwich is the Vermont sister to sophisticated Hanover, New Hampshire, over the river.

GETTING HERE AND AROUND

Most attractions are off Interstate 91; the town sits a mile to the west.

EXPLORING

★ **Montshire Museum of Science.** Numerous hands-on exhibits here explore nature and technology. Kids can make giant bubbles, watch fish and turtles swim in giant aquariums, explore wind, and wander a maze of outdoor trails by the river. An ideal destination for a rainy day, this is one of the finest museums in New England. *1 Montshire Rd. 802/649–2200 www.montshire.org $10 Daily 10–5.*

SHOPPING

★ Are you a baker? **King Arthur Flour Baker's Store** (*135 Rte. 5 S 802/649–3881 or 800/827–6836 www.bakerscatalogue.com Mon.–Sat. 8:30–6, Sun. 8:30–4*) is a must-see for those who love bread. The shelves are stocked with all the ingredients and tools in the company's *Baker's Catalogue,* including flours, mixes, and local jams and syrups. The bakery has a viewing area where you can watch products being made, and you can buy baked goods or sandwiches. A separate education center has evening and weekend classes and weeklong baking packages.

QUECHEE

11 mi southwest of Norwich, 6 mi west of White River Junction.

A historic mill town, Quechee sits just upriver from its namesake gorge, an impressive 165-foot-deep canyon cut by the Ottauquechee River. Most people view the gorge from U.S. 4. To escape the crowds, hike along the gorge or scramble down one of several trails to the river.

ESSENTIALS

Visitor Information Quechee Chamber of Commerce (*1789 Quechee St. 802/295–7900 or 800/295–5451 www.quechee.com*).

EXPLORING

Simon Pearce. The main attraction in the village is this glassblowing factory, which an Irish glassmaker by the same name set up in 1981 in a restored woolen mill by a waterfall. Water power still drives the factory's furnace. Visitors may take a free self-guided tour of the factory floor and see the glassblowers at work. The store in the mill sells contemporary glass and ceramic tableware and home furnishings, such as glass lamps and clocks. Seconds and discontinued items are reduced 25%. A fine restaurant here uses the Simon Pearce glassware and is justly popular. *The Mill, 1760 Main St. 802/295–2711 www.simonpearce.com Store daily 9–9; glassblowing Tues.–Sat. 9–9, Sun. and Mon. 9–5.*

Vermont Institute of Natural Science (VINS) Nature Center. Next to Quechee Gorge, this science center has 17 raptor exhibits, including bald eagles, peregrine falcons, and owls. All the caged birds have been found injured and are unable to survive in the wild. Predators of the Sky, a 30-minute live bird program, starts daily at 11, 1, and 3:30. ✉ *6565 Woodstock Rd. (Rte. 4)* ☎ *802/359–5000* 🌐 *www.vinsweb.org* 🎟 *$8* ⏲ *May–Oct., daily 10–5; Nov.–Apr., daily 10–4.*

SPORTS AND THE OUTDOORS

FISHING

The **Vermont Fly Fishing School/Wilderness Trails** (✉ *1119 Main St.* ☎ *802/295–7620*) leads workshops, rents fishing gear and mountain bikes, and arranges canoe and kayak trips. In winter, the company conducts cross-country and snowshoe treks.

POLO

Quechee Polo Club (✉ *Dewey's Mill Rd., ½ mi north of U.S. 4* ☎ *802/295–7152*) draws hundreds of spectators on summer Saturdays to its matches near the Quechee Gorge. Admission is $8 per carload.

SHOPPING

ANTIQUES AND CRAFTS

The 40 dealers at the **Hartland Antiques Center** (✉ *U.S. 4* ☎ *802/457–4745*) stock furniture, paper items, china, glass, and collectibles. More than 350 dealers sell their wares at the **Quechee Gorge Village** (✉ *573 Woodstock Rd., off U.S. 4* ☎ *802/295–1550 or 800/438–5565* 🌐 *www.quecheegorge.com*), an antiques and crafts mall in an immense reconstructed barn that also houses a country store and a classic diner. A merry-go-round and a small-scale working railroad operate when weather permits.

CLOTHING AND MORE

Scotland by the Yard (✉ *8828 Woodstock Rd. [U.S. 4]* ☎ *802/295–5351 or 800/295–5351* 🌐 *www.scotlandbytheyard.com*) sells all things Scottish, from kilts to Harris tweed jackets and tartan ties.

WINE

Ottauquechee Valley Winery (✉ *5967 Woodstock Rd. [U.S. 4]* ☎ *802/295–9463*), in a historic 1870s barn complex, has a tasting room and sells fruit wines, such as apple and blueberry.

WHERE TO EAT AND STAY

$$–$$$ AMERICAN Fodor's Choice ★

✕ **Simon Pearce.** Candlelight, sparkling glassware from the studio downstairs, exposed brick, and large windows overlooking the falls of the roaring Ottauquechee River create an ideal setting for contemporary American cuisine. The food is widely considered to be worthy of a pilgrimage. Sesame-seared tuna with noodle cakes and wasabi as well as roast duck with mango chutney sauce are house specialties; the wine cellar holds several hundred vintages. The lunch menu might include a roasted duck quesadilla or Mediterranean lamb burger. ✉ *The Mill, 1760 Main St.* ☎ *802/295–1470* 🌐 *www.simonpearce.com* 💳 *AE, D, DC, MC, V* *Reservations not accepted.*

$$–$$$

Parker House. This beautiful 1857 house on the National Historic Register was once home to the mill owner who ran the textile mill next door (which is now Simon Pearce). Rooms are bright and clean with queen and king beds. Walter and Joseph are the names of the two cute rooms that face the river in back. Downstairs is an attractive bar area and a good French restaurant ($$$) with a menu that changes nightly. **Pros:** in-town; riverfront location; spacious, cute rooms. **Cons:** no yard. ✉ *1792 Main St.* ☎ *802/295–6077* 🌐 *www.theparkerhouseinn.com* *7 rooms, 1 suite* *In-room: no TV, Wi-Fi. In-hotel: restaurant, room*

Simon Pearce is a glass gallery and restaurant, both powered by hydroelectricity from Quechee falls.

service, bar, laundry service, Internet terminal, Wi-Fi hotspot, some pets allowed ▭ *AE, MC, V* 🍽 *BP.*

$–$$ **Quechee Inn at Marshland Farm.** Each room in this handsomely restored 1793 country home has Queen Anne–style furnishings and period antiques. From the old barn, the inn runs bike and canoe rentals, a fly-fishing school, and kayak and canoe trips. Eleven miles of cross-country and hiking trails are on the property, and you also have privileges at the Quechee Club, a private golf, tennis, and ski club. The dining room's ($$–$$$) creative entrées include shellfish bouillabaisse and rack of lamb with green peppercorn pesto. **Pros:** historic; spacious property. **Cons:** bathrooms are dated. ✉ *Main St.* ☎ *802/295–3133 or 800/235–3133* 🌐 *www.quecheeinn.com* *22 rooms, 3 suites* *In-room: Wi-Fi. In-hotel: restaurant, bar, water sports, bicycles, Wi-Fi hotspot* ▭ *AE, D, DC, MC, V* 🍽 *BP.*

WOODSTOCK

★ *4 mi west of Quechee.*

Woodstock is a Currier & Ives print come to life. Well-maintained Federal-style houses surround the tree-lined village green, which is not far from a covered bridge. The town owes much of its pristine appearance to the Rockefeller family's interest in historic preservation and land conservation and to native George Perkins Marsh, a congressman, diplomat, and conservationist who wrote the pioneering book *Man and Nature* (1864) about humanity's use and abuse of the land. Only busy U.S. 4 detracts from the town's quaintness.

ESSENTIALS

Visitor Information **Woodstock Area Chamber of Commerce** (✉ *18 Central St.* ☎ *802/457–3555 or 888/496–6378* 🌐 *www.woodstockvt.com*).

EXPLORING

Billings Farm and Museum. Founded by Frederick Billings in 1871 as a model dairy farm, this is one of the oldest dairy farms in the country and sits on the property that was the childhood home of George Perkins Marsh. Concerned about the loss of New England's forests to overgrazing, Billings planted thousands of trees and put into practice Marsh's conservationist farming ideas. Exhibits in the reconstructed Queen Anne farmhouse, school, general store, workshop, and former Marsh homestead demonstrate the lives and skills of early Vermont settlers. ✉ *5302 River Rd. (Rte. 12, ½ mi north of Woodstock)* ☎ *802/457–2355* 🌐 *www.billingsfarm.org* 🎟 *$11* ⏲ *May–late Oct., daily 10–5; call for winter holiday and weekend schedules.*

Marsh-Billings-Rockefeller National Historical Park. This 555-acre park is Vermont's only national park and the nation's first to focus on natural resource conservation and stewardship. The pristine and stunning park encompasses the forest lands planned by Frederick Billings according to Marsh's principles, as well as Frederick Billings's mansion, gardens, and carriage roads. The entire property was the gift of Laurance S. Rockefeller, who lived here with his late wife, Mary, Billings's granddaughter. You can learn more at the visitor center, tour the residential complex with a guide every hour on the hour, and explore the 20 mi of trails and old carriage roads that climb Mt. Tom. ✉ *54 Elm St.* ☎ *802/457–3368 Ext. 22* 🌐 *www.nps.gov/mabi* 🎟 *Tour $6* ⏲ *May–Oct., mansion and garden tours 10–5; grounds daily dawn–dusk.*

OFF THE BEATEN PATH

Plymouth Notch Historic District. U.S. president Calvin Coolidge was born and buried in Plymouth Notch, a town that shares his character: low-key and quiet. The perfectly preserved 19th-century buildings resemble nothing so much as a Vermont town frozen in time. In addition to the homestead—where "Silent Cal" was sworn in by his father as president at 2:47 AM on August 3, 1923, after the sudden death of President Warren G. Harding—there is a visitor center, a general store once run by Coolidge's father (a room above it was used as the summer White House), a cheese factory, two large barns displaying agricultural equipment, and a one-room schoolhouse. Coolidge's grave is in the cemetery across Route 100A. ✉ *Rte. 100A, 6 mi south of U.S. 4, 1 mi east of Rte. 100* ☎ *802/672–3773* 🌐 *www.historicvermont.org/coolidge* ⏲ *Late May–mid-Oct., daily 9:30–5.*

SPORTS AND THE OUTDOORS

BIKING **The Start House** (✉ *28 Central St.* ☎ *802/457–3377* 🌐 *www.thestarthouseskiandbike.com*) rents, sells, and services bikes and skis and distributes a free touring map for biking.

GOLF Robert Trent Jones Sr. designed the 18-hole, 6,000-yard, par-70 course at **Woodstock Country Club** (✉ *14 The Green* ☎ *802/457–6674* 🌐 *www.woodstockinn.com*), which is run by the Woodstock Inn. Green fees are $70 weekdays, $95 weekends.

The upscale Woodstock area is known as Vermont's horse country.

HORSEBACK RIDING **Kedron Valley Stables** (✉ *Rte. 106 S, South Woodstock* ☎ *802/457–1480 or 800/225–6301* 🌐 *www.kedron.com*) conducts one-hour guided trail rides and horse-drawn sleigh and wagon rides.

SHOPPING

ART In downtown Woodstock, **Stephen Huneck Studio** (✉ *49 Central St.* ☎ *802/457–3206*) invites canines and humans to visit the artist's gallery, filled with whimsical animal carvings, prints, and furniture.

CLOTHING ★ **Who Is Sylvia?** (✉ *26 Central St.* ☎ *802/457–1110*), in the old firehouse, sells vintage clothing and antique linens, lace, and jewelry.

FOOD The **Woodstock Farmers' Market** (✉ *468 Woodstock Rd., U.S. 4* ☎ *802/457–3658* 🌐 *www.woodstockfarmersmarket.com*) is a year-round buffet of local produce, fresh fish, and excellent sandwiches and pastries. The maple-walnut scones go fast every morning except Monday, when the market is closed. Take the Taftsville covered bridge off Route 4 east of town to **Sugarbush Farm Inc.** (✉ *591 Sugarbush Farm Rd.* ☎ *802/457–1757 or 800/281–1757* 🌐 *www.sugarbushfarm.com*), where you'll learn how maple sugar is made and get to taste as much syrup as you'd like. The farm also makes excellent cheeses and is open 10 to 5 year-round. East of town, the **Taftsville Country Store** (✉ *404 Woodstock Rd. U.S. 4], Taftsville* ☎ *802/457–1135 or 800/854–0013* 🌐 *www.taftsville.com*) sells a wide selection of Vermont cheeses, moderately priced wines, and Vermont specialty foods.

WHERE TO EAT

$–$$ ECLECTIC ★ ✕ **Barnard Inn.** The dining room in this 1796 brick farmhouse breathes 18th century, but the food is decidedly 21st century. Former San Francisco restaurant chef-owners Will Dodson and Ruth Schimmelpfennig create inventive four-course prix-fixe menus with delicacies such as beef carpaccio and pan-seared escolar in lemon-and-caper herb butter. In the back is a local favorite, Max's Tavern, which serves upscale pub fare such as beef with Gorgonzola mashed potatoes and panfried trout with almond *beurre noisette* (browned butter). ✉ *5518 Rte. 12, 8 mi north of Woodstock, Barnard* ☎ *802/234–9961* 🌐 *www.barnardinnrestaurant.com* 💳 *AE, MC, V* ⊗ *Closed Sun. and Mon. No lunch* ✍ *Reservations essential.*

$ CAFÉ ✕ **Keeper's Café.** Creative, moderately priced fare draws customers from all over the region to this café. Chef Eli Morse's menus include such light dishes as pancetta salad and fresh corn soup and such elaborate entrées as herb garlic roast chicken with a sherry caper sauce. Blackboard specials change daily. Housed inside a former general store, the small dining room feels relaxed, with locals table-hopping to chat with friends. ✉ *3685 Rte. 106, 12 mi south of Woodstock, Reading* ☎ *802/484–9090* 💳 *AE, MC, V* ⊗ *Closed Sun. and Mon. No lunch.*

$$ ITALIAN Fodor's Choice ★ ✕ **Pane e Saluto.** Don't let the size fool you—meals at this little upstairs restaurant are exciting and memorable, thanks to young couple Deirdre Heekin and Caleb Barker. Hip contemporary decor, an intimately small space, and Heekin's discreetly passionate front-of-house direction all come together to complement the Barker's slow-food-inspired passion for flavorful, local and farm-raised dishes. Try *ragu d'agnello e maiale* (spaghetti with an *abruzzese* ragu from roasted pork and lamb) followed by *cotechino e lenticche* (a garlic sausage with lentils). You might expect such an *osteria* in Berkeley or Brooklyn, but this tiny spot pumps life into the blood of old Woodstock. Ask about the culinary tours the team leads each year in Italy. ✉ *61 Central St.* ☎ *802/457–4882* 🌐 *www.osteriapaneesalute.com* 💳 *AE, MC, V* ⊗ *Closed Tues. and Wed. and Apr. and Nov. No lunch.*

$–$$ FRENCH ★ ✕ **Prince & the Pauper.** Modern French and American fare with a Vermont accent is the focus of this candlelit Colonial restaurant off the Woodstock green. The grilled duck breast might have an Asian five-spice sauce, and lamb and pork sausage in puff pastry comes with a honey-mustard sauce. A three-course prix-fixe menu is available for $48; a less-expensive bistro menu can be ordered from in the lounge. ✉ *24 Elm St.* ☎ *802/457–1818* 🌐 *www.princeandpauper.com* 💳 *AE, D, MC, V* ⊗ *No lunch.*

WHERE TO STAY

$$$$ **Fan House.** Do you have an elusive dream, one that hankers for an authentic home in the heart of a very small, quaint Vermont town? Take the one-minute walk from the perfect general store in Barnard to this 1840 white Colonial, and here it is. The three rooms put together by Sara Widness—who happens to be an expert on luxury travel—are cozy, comfortable, and avoid romantic clichés. The rooms are simply adorned with tapestries, antique rugs, claw-foot tubs, comfy sofas, and old bed frames guarding soft linens and a mountain of pillows. The living room hearth, the old wood stove in the kitchen, and the library nook create a real sense of home. **Pros:** center of old town; homey comforts;

good library. **Cons:** upstairs rooms can be cool in winter. ✉ *6296 Rte. 12 N* ✆ *Box 294, 05031* ☎ *802/234–6704* 🌐 *www.thefanhouse.com* *3 rooms* *In-room: no phone, no TV. In-hotel: Internet terminal, no kids under 12* ▭ *No credit cards* ⊗ *Closed Apr.* 🍽 *BP.*

$$–$$$ **Kedron Valley Inn.** You're likely to fall in love at the first sight of this 1828 three-story brick building that forms the centerpiece of this quiet, elegant retreat. This and another 19th-century building along with a motel-style 1968 log lodge make up this inn on 15 acres. Many of the rooms have a fireplace or a Franklin stove, and some have private decks or terraces. The motel units boast country antiques and reproductions. A big spring-fed pond has a white sand beach with toys for kids. In the restaurant ($$$), the chef creates French masterpieces such as fillet of Norwegian salmon stuffed with herb seafood mousse in puff pastry. **Pros:** good food; quiet setting. **Cons:** 5 mi south of Woodstock. ✉ *10671 South Rd. (Rte. 106), South Woodstock* ☎ *802/457–1473 or 800/836–1193* 🌐 *www.kedronvalleyinn.com* *21 rooms, 6 suites* *In-room: no phone, no a/c (some). In-hotel: restaurant, bar, Internet terminal, some pets allowed* ▭ *AE, MC, V* ⊗ *Closed Apr.* 🍽 *BP.*

$$ **Shire Riverview Motel.** Some rooms in this immaculate motel have decks—and almost all have views—overlooking the Ottauquechee River. Rooms are simple, a step above usual motel fare, with four-poster beds and wing chairs; two rooms have hot tubs, and the suite has a full kitchen. Complimentary coffee is served each morning; in summer sip it on the riverfront veranda. The real key here is walking distance to the green and all shops. **Pros:** inexpensive access to the heart of Woodstock; views. **Cons:** dull rooms; unexciting exterior. ✉ *46 Pleasant St.* ☎ *802/457–2211* 🌐 *www.shiremotel.com* *42 rooms, 1 suite* *In-room: kitchen (some), refrigerator* ▭ *AE, D, MC, V.*

$$$$ Fodor's Choice ★ **Twin Farms.** Let's just get it out: Twin Farms is the best lodging choice in Vermont. Some even say it's the best small property in the country. And if you can afford it—stays begin at well over $1,000 a night—you'll want to experience it. Three rooms are in the beautiful main building, which was once home to writer Sinclair Lewis. The rest are individual cottages, secluded among 300 acres. Each incredible room and cottage is furnished with a blend of high art (Jasper Johns, Milton Avery, Cy Twombly), gorgeous folk art, and furniture that goes beyond comfortable sophistication. The food may be the best in Vermont. The service—suave, relaxed—definitely is. Prices include all meals, alcohol, and activities; there's a good spa, a pub within a big game room, and a private ski hill. **Pros:** impeccable service; stunning rooms; sensational meals. **Cons:** astronomical prices; must drive to town/Woodstock. ✉ *1 Stage Rd., Barnard* ☎ *802/234–9999* 🌐 *www.twinfarms.com* *3 rooms, 10 cottages* *In-room: DVD, Wi-Fi. In-hotel: restaurant, room service, bars, tennis courts, pools, gym, spa, water sports, bicycles, laundry service, Internet terminal, Wi-Fi hotspot, no kids under 12* ▭ *AE, D, DC, MC, V* ⊗ *Closed Apr.* 🍽 *AI.*

$$$ Fodor's Choice ★ **Woodstock Inn and Resort.** If this is your first time in Woodstock and you want to feel like you're in the middle of it all, stay here. Set back far from the main road but still on the town's gorgeous green, the Inn is the town's beating heart. You'll feel that right away when looking at the main fireplace, set immediately through the front doors, which burns

impressive 3-foot logs. Rooms are contemporary and luxurious, with huge flat-screen TVs, sleek furniture, and great bathrooms done in simple subway tiles. The resort also owns and gives you access to Suicide Six ski mountain and the Woodstock Golf Club. **Pros:** exciting, big property; contemporary furnishings; professionally run. **Cons:** can lack intimacy. ✉ *14 The Green (U.S. 4)* ☎ *802/457–1100 or 800/448–7900* 🌐 *www.woodstockinn.com* *135 rooms, 7 suites* *In-room: safe, refrigerator, Internet, Wi-Fi (some). In-hotel: 2 restaurants, room service, bar, golf course, tennis courts, pools, gym, bicycles, laundry service, Internet terminal* 💳 *AE, D, MC, V* 🍴 *BP.*

KILLINGTON

15 mi east of Rutland.

With only a gas station, post office, motel, and a few shops at the intersection of Routes 4 and 100, it's difficult to tell that the East's largest ski resort is nearby. The village of Killington is characterized by unfortunate strip development along the access road to the ski resort. But the 360-degree views atop Killington Peak, accessible by the resort's gondola, make it worth the drive.

SPORTS AND THE OUTDOORS

BIKING **True Wheels Bike Shop** (✉ *2886 Killington Rd.* ☎ *802/422–3234*) sells and rents bicycles and has information on local routes.

FISHING Kent Pond in **Gifford Woods State Park** (✉ *Rte. 100, ½ mi north of U.S. 4* ☎ *802/775–5354* 🌐 *www.vtstateparks.com/htm/gifford.cfm*) is a terrific fishing spot.

GOLF At its namesake resort, **Killington Golf Course** (✉ *4763 Killington Rd.* ☎ *802/422–6700*) has a challenging 18-hole, par-72 course. Green fees are $69 midweek and $79 weekends inclusive of carts. Twilight rates are slightly cheaper.

★ "Megamountain," "Beast of the East," and plain "huge" are apt descriptions of **Killington** (✉ *4763 Killington Rd.* ☎ *802/422–6200; 802/422–3261 snow conditions; 800/621–6867 lodging* 🌐 *www.killington.com*). The American Skiing Company operates Killington and its neighbor, **Pico**, and over the past several years has improved lifts and snowmaking capabilities. Thanks to its extensive snowmaking system, the resort typically opens in October, and the lifts often run into May. Après-ski activities are plentiful and have been rated the best in the East by national ski magazines. With a single call to Killington's hotline or a visit to its Web site, skiers can plan an entire vacation: choose accommodations, book air or railroad transportation, and arrange for rental equipment and ski lessons. Killington ticket holders can also ski at Pico: a shuttle connects the two areas.

The Killington–Pico complex has a host of activities, including an alpine slide, a golf course, two waterslides, a skateboard park, and a swimming pool. The resort rents mountain bikes and advises hikers. The K-1 Express Gondola takes you up the mountain to Vermont's second-highest summit.

In terms of downhill skiing, it would probably take several weeks to test all 200 trails on the seven mountains of the Killington complex, even though all except Pico interconnect. About 70% of the 1,182 acres of skiing terrain can be covered with machine-made snow. Transporting skiers to the peaks of this complex are 32 lifts, including 2 gondolas, 12 quads (including 6 high-speed express quads), 6 triples, and a Magic Carpet. The K-1 Express Gondola goes to the area's highest elevation, 4,241-foot Killington Peak. The Skyeship Gondola starts on U.S. 4, far below Killington's main base lodge, and savvy skiers park here to avoid the more crowded access road. After picking up more passengers at a mid-station, the Skyeship tops out on Skye Peak. Although Killington has a vertical drop of 3,050 feet, only gentle trails—Juggernaut and Great Eastern—go from top to bottom. The skiing includes everything from Outer Limits, the East's steepest and longest mogul trail, to 6½-mi Great Eastern. In the Fusion Zones, underbrush and low branches have been cleared to provide tree skiing. Killington's Superpipe is one of the best rated in the East. Instruction programs are available for youngsters ages 3–8; those 6–12 can join an all-day program.

When weekend hordes hit Killington, the locals head to **Pico** (✉ *51 Alpine Dr. [Rte. 4], Killington* ☎ *802/422–6200 or 866/667–7426* 🌐 *www.picomountain.com*). One of Killington's "seven peaks," Pico is physically separated from its parent resort. The 50 trails range from elevator-shaft steep to challenging intermediate trails near the summit, with easier terrain near the bottom of the mountain's 2,000-foot vertical. The learning slope is separated from the upper mountain, so hotshots won't bomb through it. The lower express quad can get crowded, but the upper one rarely has a line.

CROSS-COUNTRY SKIING

Mountain Top Inn and Resort (✉ *195 Mountaintop Rd., Chittenden* ☎ *802/483–6089 or 800/445–2100* 🌐 *www.mountaintopinn.com*) has 50 mi of hilly trails groomed for Nordic skiing, 37 mi of which can be used for skate skiing. You can also enjoy snowshoeing, dogsledding, ice skating, and snowmobile and sleigh rides. In the summer there's horseback riding, fishing, hiking, biking, and water sports.

NIGHTLIFE AND THE ARTS

On weekends, listen to live music and sip draft Guinness at the **Inn at Long Trail** (✉ *U.S. 4* ☎ *802/775–7181* 🌐 *www.innatlongtrail.com*). **Taboo** (✉ *2841 Killington Rd.* ☎ *802/422–9885*) serves all-you-can-eat pizza on Monday nights in winter, and $3 Long Trail pints on Sunday. It's open year-round. During ski season, the **Pickle Barrel Night Club** (✉ *1741 Killington Rd.* ☎ *802/422–3035* 🌐 *www.picklebarrelnightclub.com*) has a band every happy hour on Friday and Saturday. After 8, the crowd moves downstairs for dancing, sometimes to big-name bands.Twentysomethings prefer to dance at the **Wobbly Barn** (✉ *2229 Killington Rd.* ☎ *802/422–6171* 🌐 *www.wobblybarn.com*), open only during ski season.

WHERE TO EAT AND STAY

$$$$ CONTINENTAL ★

✕ **Hemingway's.** Chef-owner Ted Fondulas has kept Hemingway's an enduringly respected restaurant in the state since 1982 and the fine-dining favorite for Killington skiers. Among the house specialties are the cream of garlic soup and a seasonal kaleidoscope of dishes. Native baby pheasant with local chanterelles or seared scallops with truffles and caramelized onions are just two entrées that might appear on the menu. Diners can opt for the prix-fixe, three- to six-course menu or the wine-tasting menu. Request seating in either the formal vaulted dining room, the intimate wine cellar, or the garden room. ✉ *4988 U.S. 4* ☎ *802/422–3886* 🌐 *www.hemingwaysrestaurant.com* ✍ *Reservations essential* ▭ *AE, D, DC, MC, V* ⏲ *Closed Mon. and Tues., early Nov., and mid-Apr.–mid-May. No lunch.*

$$ **Birch Ridge Inn.** A slate-covered carriageway about a mile from Killington base stations leads to one of the area's most popular off-mountain stays, a former executive retreat in two renovated A-frames. Rooms range in style from Colonial and Shaker to Mission, and all have a sitting area with a TV hidden behind artwork—in one room, a dollhouse rotates up to reveal it. Six rooms have gas fireplaces, and four have whirlpool baths. In the intimate slate-floored dining room ($$$; closed Monday and Tuesday), choose either a four-course prix-fixe dinner or order à la carte. **Pros:** quirky; well maintained. **Cons:** oddly furnished; older building style. ✉ *37 Butler Rd.* ☎ *802/422–4293 or 800/435–8566* 🌐 *www.birchridge.com* *10 rooms* *In-room: no a/c (some), Wi-Fi. In-hotel: restaurant, bar, Wi-Fi hotspot, no kids under 12* ▭ *AE, D, MC, V* ⏲ *Closed May* *BP, MAP.*

$$$$ **Woods Resort & Spa.** These clustered upscale two- and three-bedroom town houses stand in wooded lots along a winding road leading to the spa. Most units have master baths with saunas and two-person whirlpool tubs. Vaulted ceilings in the living rooms give an open, airy feel. The resort has a private shuttle to the ski area. **Pros:** contemporary facility; clean, spacious rooms; lots of room choices. **Cons:** lacks traditional Vermont feeling. ✉ *53 Woods La.* ☎ *802/422–3139 or 800/642–1147* 🌐 *www.woodsresortandspa.com* *107 units* *In-room: no a/c, kitchen, Wi-Fi. In-hotel: tennis courts, pool, gym, spa, laundry facilities, some pets allowed* ▭ *AE, MC, V.*

RUTLAND

15 mi southwest of Killington, 32 mi south of Middlebury.

On and around U.S. 7 in Rutland are strips of shopping centers and a seemingly endless row of traffic lights—very un-Vermont. Two blocks west, however, stand the mansions of the marble magnates. Preservation work has uncovered white and verde marble facades; the stonework harkens back to the days when marble ruled Vermont's second-largest city outside of Burlington county. The county farmers' market is held in Depot Park Saturdays 9–2.

ESSENTIALS

Visitor Information **Rutland Region Chamber of Commerce** (✉ *256 N. Main St.* ☎ *802/773–2747 or 800/756–8880* 🌐 *www.rutlandvermont.com*).

EXPLORING

Chaffee Art Center. The beautiful former mansion of the local Paramount Theatre's founder, this arts center exhibits the work of more than 200 Vermont artists. ✉ *16 S. Main St.* ☎ *802/775–0356* 🌐 *www.chaffeeartcenter.org* *Free* ⏲ *Tues.–Sat. 10–5, Sun. noon–4.*

New England Maple Museum and Gift Shop. Maple syrup is Vermont's signature product, and this museum north of Rutland explains the history and process of turning maple sap into syrup with murals, diorama exhibits, and a slide show. If you don't get a chance to visit a sugarhouse, this is a fine place to sample the four different grades and pick up some souvenirs. ✉ *4578 U.S. 7, Pittsford, 9 mi south of Brandon* ☎ *802/483–9414* 🌐 *www.maplemuseum.com* 🎟 *Museum $2.50* 🕐 *Late May–Oct., daily 8:30–5:30; Nov., Dec., and mid-Mar.–late May, daily 10–4.*

Paramount Theatre. The highlight of downtown is this 700-seat, turn-of-the-20th-century gilded playhouse, designed in the spirit of a Victorian opera house. The gorgeous, fully renovated theater holds over a thousand people and is home to music, theater and a film series highlighting its past as a 1930s motion picture theater. ✉ *36 Center St.* ☎ *802/775–0570* 🌐 *www.paramountvt.org.*

Vermont Marble Exhibit. North of Rutland, this monument to marble highlights one of the main industries in this region and illustrates marble's many industrial and artistic applications. The hall of presidents has a carved bust of each U.S. president, and in the marble chapel is a replica of Leonardo da Vinci's *Last Supper.* Elsewhere you can watch a sculptor-in-residence shape the stone into finished works of art, compare marbles from around the world, and check out the Vermont Marble Company's original "stone library." Factory seconds and foreign and domestic marble items are for sale. A short walk away is the original marble quarry in Proctor. Marble from here became part of the U.S. Supreme Court building and the New York Public Library. ✉ *52 Main St., 4 mi north of Rutland, off Rte. 3, Proctor* ☎ *802/459–2300 or 800/427–1396* 🌐 *www.vermont-marble.com* 🎟 *$7* 🕐 *Mid-May–Oct., daily 9–5:30.*

Wilson Castle. As you drive a long country road just outside Rutland, the opulent vision of this 32-room mansion will surprise you. Completed in 1867, it was built over the course of eight years by a Vermonter who married a British aristocrat. The current owner, Blossom Wilson Davine Ladabouche, still owns the property and makes her summer home in the old servants' quarters. Within the mansion are 84 stained-glass windows (one inset with 32 Australian opals), hand-painted Italian frescos, and 13 fireplaces. It's magnificently furnished with European and Asian objets d'art. ✉ *W. Proctor Rd., Proctor* ☎ *802/773–3284* 🌐 *www.wilsoncastle.com* 🎟 *$9.50* 🕐 *Late May–mid-Oct., daily 9–6, last tour at 5.*

SPORTS AND THE OUTDOORS

BOATING Rent pontoon boats, speedboats, waterskiing boats, Wave Runners, and water toys at **Lake Bomoseen Marina** (✉ *145 Creek Rd., off Rte. 4A, 1½ mi west of Castleton* ☎ *802/265–4611*).

HIKING **Deer's Leap** (✉ *Starts at the Inn at Long Trail on Rte. 4 west of Rutland*) is a 3-mi round-trip hike to a great view overlooking Sherburne Gap and Pico Peak. **Mountain Travelers** (✉ *147 Rte. 4 E* ☎ *802/775–0814*) sells hiking maps and guidebooks, gives advice on local hikes, rents kayaks, and sells sporting equipment.

DID YOU KNOW?

The pastoral image of Vermont is very much rooted in reality. Co-ops provide many small working farms the chance to compete with larger organizations. You may even recognize your favorite brand of milk.

WHERE TO EAT AND STAY

¢–$ ECLECTIC **Little Harry's.** Locals have packed this restaurant ever since chef-owners Trip (Harry) Pearce and Jack Mangan brought Vermont cheddar ravioli and lamb lo mein to downtown Rutland in 1997. (It's the "little" to the bigger Harry's near Ludlow.) The 17 tabletops are adorned with laminated photos of the regulars. For big appetites on small budgets, the pad thai and the burrito are huge meals for under $8. *121 West St. 802/747–4848 MC, V No lunch.*

$$ **Inn at Rutland.** If you love B&Bs and are tired of Rutland's chain motels, this stately 1889 Victorian mansion on Main Street is a welcome sight. Large plate-glass windows illuminate the entryway, library, and sitting room. A large table dominates the dining room, which has hand-tooled leather wainscoting. Upstairs, the rooms have antiques; two rooms have private porches and whirlpool tubs. **Pros:** solid, non-motel choice. **Cons:** unexciting rooms. *70 N. Main St. 802/773–0575 or 800/808–0575 www.innatrutland.com 8 rooms In-room: Wi-Fi. In-hotel: restaurant, Internet terminal, Wi-Fi hotspot AE, D, MC, V.*

BRANDON

15 mi northwest of Rutland.

Thanks to an active artists' guild, Brandon is making a name for itself. In 2003 the Brandon Artists Guild, led by American folk artist Warren Kimble, auctioned 40 life-size fiberglass pigs painted by local artists. The "Really Really Pig Show" raised money for the guild (as well as other organizations) and brought fame to this once overlooked community. Since then the guild has taken on birdhouses, rocking chairs, artists' palettes, cats and dogs, and, in 2009, "Starring Brandon," which featured ornamented star-shaped frames spread throughout town.

ESSENTIALS

Visitor Information Brandon Visitor Center (*4 Grove St. [Rte. 7 at 73 W], 802/247–6401 brandon.org*).

EXPLORING

Stephen A. Douglas Museum. The famous early American statesman was born in Brandon in this house in 1813. He left 20 years later to establish himself as a lawyer, becoming a three-time U.S. senator and arguing more cases before the U.S. Supreme Court than anyone else. This museum, which opened in 2009, recounts the early Douglas years, early Brandon history, and the anti-slavery movement in Vermont—the first state to abolish it. *4 Grove St., at U.S. 7 802/247–6401 brandon.org/douglasbirthplace Free Daily 9–5.*

★ **The Inside Scoop and Antiques by the Falls.** A husband-and-wife team runs these two separate and equally fun-loving businesses under one roof: a colorful ice cream stand and penny candy store and an antiques store filled floor to ceiling with Americana. *22 Park St., East Brandon 802/247–6600.*

2

SPORTS AND THE OUTDOORS

The **Moosalamoo Association** (☏ *800/448–0707*) manages, protects, and provides stewardship for more than 20,000 acres of the Green Mountain National Forest, northeast of Brandon. More than 60 mi of trails take hikers, mountain bikers, and cross-country skiers through some of Vermont's most gorgeous mountain terrain. Attractions include Branbury State Park, on the shores of Lake Dunmore; secluded Silver Lake; and sections of both the Long Trail and Catamount Trail (the latter is a Massachusetts-to-Québec ski trail). The Blueberry Hill Inn has direct public access to trails.

GOLF **Neshobe Golf Club** (✉ *224 Town Farm Rd., Rte. 73 east of Brandon* ☏ *802/247–3611* 🌐 *www.neshobe.com*) has 18 holes of par-72 golf on a bent-grass course totaling nearly 6,500 yards. Green fee is $38–$42. The Green Mountain views are terrific. Several local inns offer golf packages.

HIKING For great views from a vertigo-inducing cliff, hike up the Long Trail to **Mt. Horrid**. The steep, hour-long hike starts at the top of Brandon Gap (about 8 mi east of Brandon on Route 73). A large turnout on Route 53 marks a moderate trail to the **Falls of Lana**. West of Brandon, four trails—two short ones of less than 1 mi each and two longer ones—lead to the abandoned Revolutionary War fortifications at **Mt. Independence**. To reach them, take the first left turn off Route 73 west of Orwell and go right at the fork. The road will turn to gravel and fork again; take a sharp left-hand turn toward a small marina. The parking lot is on the left at the top of the hill.

WHERE TO EAT AND STAY

$–$$ **CAFÉ** ✕ **Café Provence**. Robert Barral, a former Chicago Four Seasons chef and 16-year director of the New England Culinary Institute, graces Brandon with this delicious informal eatery named after his birthplace. One story above the main street, the café with hints of Provence—flowered seat cushions and dried-flower window valences—specializes in eclectic farm-fresh dishes. Goat-cheese cake with mesclun greens, braised veal cheeks and caramelized endive, and a portobello pizza from the restaurant's hearth oven are just a few of the choices. Breakfast offerings include buttery pastries, eggs Benedict, and breakfast pizza, and outdoor seating can be had under large umbrellas. ✉ *11 Center St.* ☏ *802/247–9997* 🌐 *www.cafeprovencevt.com* 💳 *MC, V.*

$$–$$$ **Fodor's Choice** ★ **Blueberry Hill Inn**. In the Green Mountain National Forest, 5½ mi off a mountain pass on a dirt road, you'll find this secluded inn with its lush gardens and a pond with a wood-fired sauna on its bank. Many rooms have views of the mountains; all are furnished with antiques and quilts. The restaurant ($$$$) prepares a four-course prix-fixe menu nightly, with dishes such as venison fillet with cherry sauce. This is a very popular place for weddings. The grounds are gorgeous, and there's lots to do if you're into nature: biking, hiking, and a cross-country ski center with 43 mi of trails. **Pros:** peaceful setting within the national forest; terrific property with lots to do; great food. **Cons:** forest setting not for those who want to be near town. ✉ *1307 Goshen–Ripton Rd., Goshen* ☏ *802/247–6735 or 800/448–0707* 🌐 *www.blueberryhillinn.com* *12 rooms* *In-room: no phone, no a/c, no TV, Wi-Fi. In-hotel: restaurant, bicycles, Internet terminal, Wi-Fi hotspot, some pets allowed* 💳 *AE, MC, V* *MAP.*

MIDDLEBURY

★ *17 mi north of Brandon, 34 mi south of Burlington.*

In the late 1800s Middlebury was the largest Vermont community west of the Green Mountains, an industrial center of river-powered wool and grain mills. This is Robert Frost country: Vermont's late poet laureate spent 23 summers at a farm east of Middlebury. Still a cultural and economic hub amid the Champlain Valley's serene pastoral patchwork, the town and countryside invite a day of exploration.

EXPLORING

Middlebury College. Founded in 1800, Middlebury College was conceived as a more godly alternative to the worldly University of Vermont but has no religious affiliation today. In the middle of town, the early-19th-century stone buildings contrast provocatively with the postmodern architecture of the Center for the Arts and the sports center. Music, theater, and dance performances take place throughout the year at the **Wright Memorial Theatre** and **Center for the Arts.** ✉ *38 College St.* ☎ *802/443–5000* 🌐 *www.middlebury.edu.*

Robert Frost Interpretive Trail. About 10 mi east of town on Route 125 (1 mi west of Middlebury College's Bread Loaf campus), this easy ¾-mi trail winds through quiet woodland. Plaques along the way bear quotations from Frost's poems. A picnic area is across the road from the trailhead.

UVM Morgan Horse Farm. The Morgan horse—Vermont's official state animal—has an even temper, stamina, and slightly truncated legs in proportion to its body. The University of Vermont's Morgan Horse Farm, about 2½ mi west of Middlebury, is a breeding and training center where in summer you can tour the stables and paddocks. ✉ *74 Battell Dr., off Morgan Horse Farm Rd. (follow signs off Rte. 23), Weybridge* ☎ *802/388–2011* 🎟 *$4* ⏲ *May–Oct., daily 9–4.*

Vermont Folklife Center. In the Masonic Hall, exhibits include photography, antiques, folk paintings, manuscripts, and other artifacts and contemporary works that examine facets of Vermont life. ✉ *3 Court St.* ☎ *802/388–4964* 🎟 *Donations accepted* ⏲ *Gallery May–Dec., Tues.–Sat. 11–4.*

Vermont State Craft Center/Frog Hollow. More than a crafts store, this arts center mounts changing exhibitions and displays exquisite works in wood, glass, metal, clay, and fiber by more than 250 Vermont artisans. The center, which overlooks Otter Creek, sponsors classes taught by some of those artists. Burlington and Manchester also have centers. ✉ *1 Mill St.* ☎ *802/388–3177* 🌐 *www.froghollow.org* ⏲ *Call for hrs.*

OFF THE BEATEN PATH

Fort Ticonderoga Ferry. Established in 1759, the Fort Ti cable ferry crosses Lake Champlain between Shoreham and Fort Ticonderoga, New York, at one of the oldest ferry crossings in North America. The trip takes seven minutes. ✉ *4675 Rte. 74 W, 18 mi southwest of Middlebury, 9 mi south of Brandon, Shoreham* ☎ *802/897–7999* 🎟 *Cars, pickups, and vans with driver and passenger $8; bicycles $2; pedestrians $1* ⏲ *May–last Sun. of Oct., daily 8–5:45.*

2

SHOPPING

ART **Historic Marble Works** (✉ *2 Maple St.* ☎ *802/388–3701*), a renovated marble manufacturing facility, is a collection of unique shops set amid quarrying equipment and factory buildings. One of them, **Danforth Pewter** (☎ *802/388–0098* 🌐 *www.danforthpewter.com*), sells handcrafted pewter vases, lamps, and tableware.

WHERE TO EAT

$ PIZZA ★ ✕ **American Flatbread–Rutland**. On weekends this is the most happening spot in town, and no wonder: the pizza is extraordinary, and the attitude is pure Vermont. Wood-fired clay domes create masterful thin crusts from organically grown wheat. Besides the innovative, delicious pizzas, try an organic mesclun salad tossed in the house raspberry-ginger vinaigrette. If you love pizza and haven't been here, you're in for a treat. There are also locations in Waitsfield and Burlington. ✉ *137 Maple St., at the Marble Works* ☎ *802/388–3300* 🌐 *www.americanflatbread.com* ✍ *Reservations not accepted* ▭ *MC, V* ⊙ *Closed Sun. and Mon. No lunch.*

$$–$$$ ECLECTIC Fodor's Choice ★ ✕ **Mary's at Baldwin Creek**. People drive from the far reaches of Vermont to eat at this restaurant just beyond the charming, little-known town of Bristol, 13 mi northeast of Middlebury. If you care about food, you'll be in awe of chef-owner Douglas Mack's credentials: for starters, he founded the Vermont Fresh Network (🌐 *www.vermontfresh.net*). Membership in this group, which promotes the use of farm-fresh ingredients, is now a hallmark of any respectable restaurant in the state. Plan time to visit the huge vegetable gardens that surround this beautiful property. A slow approach to locally grown foods finds life here with hearty fare like summer lasagna, a prime showcase for the flavors of the veggies grown 50 feet from your table, and Mack's near-legendary garlic soup, a creamy year-round staple that seems genetically engineered to please. Desserts are hit or miss. ✉ *1869 Rte. 116, Bristol* ☎ *802/453–2432* 🌐 *www.innatbaldwincreek.com* ▭ *MC, V* ⊙ *Closed Mon. and Tues. No lunch.*

$$–$$$ ECLECTIC ✕ **Storm Café**. There is no setting in town quite like the deck overlooking the Otter Creek Falls at one end of the long footbridge over the creek. Even if you're not here in summer, the eclectic ever-changing menu at this small restaurant in the old Frog Hollow Mill makes it worth a visit any time of year. "Stormy" Jamaican jerk–seasoned pork tenderloin and melt-in-your-mouth desserts like an apricot soufflé are favorites. ✉ *3 Mill St.* ☎ *802/388–1063* 🌐 *www.thestormcafe.com* ▭ *MC, V.*

WHERE TO STAY

$–$$ **Swift House Inn**. The 1824 Georgian home of a 19th-century governor showcases white-panel wainscoting, mahogany furnishings, and marble fireplaces. The stellar rooms—most with Oriental rugs and nine with fireplaces—have period reproductions such as canopy beds, curtains with swags, and claw-foot tubs. Some bathrooms have double whirlpool tubs. Rooms in the attractive Gatehouse suffer from street noise but are charming and a solid value. The seven-room carriage house has more expensive rooms with wood fireplaces and king-size beds. **Pros:** attractive, spacious, well-kept rooms; professionally run. **Cons:** near to but not quite in the heart of town. ✉ *25 Stewart La.* ☎ *802/388–9925* *www.swifthouseinn.com* *20 rooms* *In-room: DVD (some), Wi-Fi. In-hotel: restaurant, room service, bar, laundry service, Wi-Fi hotspot, some pets allowed* *AE, D, DC, MC, V* *BP.*

WAITSFIELD AND WARREN

32 mi northeast (Waitsfield) and 25 mi east (Warren) of Middlebury.

Skiers discovered the high peaks overlooking the pastoral Mad River Valley in the 1940s. Now the valley and its two towns, Waitsfield and Warren, attract the hip, the adventurous, and the low-key. Warren is tiny and adorable, with a general store that attracts tour buses. The gently carved ridges cradling the valley and the swell of pastures and fields lining the river seem to keep notions of ski-resort sprawl at bay. With a map from the Sugarbush Chamber of Commerce you can investigate back roads off Route 100 that have exhilarating valley views.

ESSENTIALS

Visitor Information **Sugarbush Chamber of Commerce** (*Rte. 100* *802/496–3409 or 800/828–4748* *www.madrivervalley.com*).

SPORTS AND THE OUTDOORS

OUTFITTER **Clearwater Sports** (*4147 Main St. [Rte. 100], Waitsfield* *802/496–2708* *clearwatersports.com*) rents canoes, kayaks, tubing, and camping equipment and leads guided river trips and white-water instruction in the warm months; in winter, the store leads snowshoe and backcountry ski tours and rents Telemark equipment, snowshoes, and one-person Mad River Rocket sleds.

GOLF Great views and challenging play are the trademarks of the Robert Trent Jones–designed 18-hole mountain course at **Sugarbush Resort** (*1091 Golf Course Rd., Warren* *802/583–6725* *www.sugarbushgolf.com*). The green fees run from $48 to $100.

SLEIGH RIDES **Mountain Valley Farm** (*1719 Common Rd., Waitsfield* *802/496–9255* *mountainvalleyfarm.com*) offers horse-drawn carriage and sleigh rides with reservations.

SKI AREAS **Blueberry Lake Cross-Country Ski Area** (*424 Plunkton Rd., East Warren* *802/496–6687* *www.blueberrylakeskivt.com*) has 18 mi of trails through thickly wooded glades.

The hundreds of shareholders who own **Mad River Glen** (*Rte. 17* *802/496–3551; 802/496–2001 snow conditions; 800/850–6742 cooperative office* *www.madriverglen.com*) are dedicated, knowledgeable skiers devoted to keeping skiing what it used to be—a pristine alpine experience. Mad River's unkempt aura attracts rugged individualists looking for less-polished terrain: the area was developed in the late 1940s and has changed relatively little since then. It remains one of only three resorts in the country that ban snowboarding.

Mad River is steep, with natural slopes that follow the mountain's fall lines. The terrain changes constantly on the 45 interconnected trails, of which 30% are beginner, 30% are intermediate, and 40% are expert. Intermediate and novice terrain is regularly groomed. Five lifts—including the world's last surviving single chairlift—service the mountain's 2,037-

Sheep's cheese is just one of the many food products that contribute to great fresh local meals in Vermont.

foot vertical drop. Most of Mad River's trails are covered only by natural snow. The kids' ski school runs classes for little ones ages 4 to 12. The nursery is for infants to 6-year-olds; reservations are recommended.

Known as the capital of free-heel skiing, Mad River Glen sponsors Telemark programs throughout the season. Every March, the North America Telemark Organization (NATO) Festival attracts up to 1,400 visitors. Snowshoeing is also an option. There is a $5 fee to use the snowshoe trails, and rentals are available.

Sugarbush (✉ *Sugarbush Access Rd., accessible from Rte. 100 or 17* 📭 *Box 350, Warren 05674* ☎ *802/583–6300; 802/583–7669 snow conditions; 800/537–8427 lodging* 🌐 *www.sugarbush.com*) has remade itself as a true skier's mountain, with steep, natural snow glades and fall-line drops. Not as rough around the edges as Mad River Glen, Sugarbush also has well-groomed intermediate and beginner terrain. A computer-controlled system for snowmaking has increased coverage to nearly 70%. At the base of the mountain are condominiums, restaurants, shops, bars, and a sports center.

Sugarbush is two distinct, connected mountain complexes connected by the Slide Brook Express quad. Lincoln Peak, with a vertical of 2,400 feet, is known for formidable steeps, especially on Castlerock. Mount Ellen has more beginner runs near the bottom, with steep fall-line pitches on the upper half of the 2,650 vertical feet. There are 115 trails in all: 23% beginner, 48% intermediate, 29% expert. The resort has 18 lifts: seven quads (including four high-speed versions), three triples, four doubles, and four surface lifts. There's half- and full-day instruction available for children ages 4–12, ski/day care for 3-year-olds, and supervised ski and ride programs for teens. Sugarbear Forest, a terrain garden, has fun bumps and jumps. The Sugarbush Day School accepts children ages 6 weeks to 6 years.

SHOPPING

All Things Bright and Beautiful (✉ *27 Bridge St., Waitsfield* ☎ *802/496–3997*) is a 12-room Victorian house jammed to the rafters with stuffed animals of all shapes, sizes, and colors as well as folk art, prints, and collectibles. One of the rooms is a coffee and ice-cream shop. **Cabin Fever Quilts** (✉ *4276 Main St. No. 1 [Rte. 100], Waitsfield* ☎ *802/496–2287* 🌐 *www.cabinfeverquiltsvt.com*), inside a converted old church, sells fine handmade quilts.

NIGHTLIFE AND THE ARTS

NIGHTLIFE The Back Room at **Chez Henri** (✉ *Lincoln Peak base area, Sugarbush Village, Warren* ☎ *802/583–2600*) has a pool table and is the place to go après-ski. Live bands play most weekends at **Purple Moon Pub** (✉ *6163 Main St. [Rte. 100], Waitsfield* ☎ *802/496–3422* 🌐 *www.purplemoonpub.com*).

★ In the basement of the Pitcher Inn, **Tracks** (✉ *275 Main St., Warren* ☎ *802/493–6350* 🌐 *www.pitcherinn.com*) is a public bar run by the Relais & Châteaux property. It has billiards, darts, a really fun shuffleboard game played on a long table with sawdust, a full tavern menu, and a giant moose head.

ARTS The **Green Mountain Cultural Center** (✉ *Inn at the Round Barn Farm, 1661 E. Warren Rd.* ☎ *802/496–7722* 🌐 *www.theroundbarn.com*) hosts concerts, art exhibits, and educational workshops. The **Valley Players** (✉ *4254 Main St. [Rte. 100], Waitsfield* ☎ *802/496–9612* 🌐 *www.valleyplayers.com*) present musicals, dramas, follies, and more.

WHERE TO EAT

$ PIZZA Fodor's Choice ★ ✕ **American Flatbread–Waitsfield**. Is this the best pizza experience in the world? It just may be. In summer, dining takes place outside around fire pits in the beautiful valley, a setting and meal not to be forgotten. The secret is in the love, but some clues to the magic are in the organically grown flour and vegetables and the wood-fired clay ovens. The "new Vermont sausage" is Waitsfield pork in a maple-fennel sausage baked with sundried tomatoes, caramelized onions, cheese, and herbs; it's a dream, as are the more traditional pizzas. As a restaurant, it's open only Friday and Saturday evenings, but the retail bakery is open Monday–Thursday 7:30 AM–8 PM; if you're here during that time anything in the oven is yours for $10. This is the original American Flatbread location—plan your trip around it. ✉ *46 Lareau Rd., off Rte. 100, Waitsfield* ☎ *802/496–8856* *Reservations not accepted* ▭ *MC, V* 🌐 *www.americanflatbread.com* ⏲ *Closed Sun.*

$$$–$$$$ ECLECTIC ✕ **Common Man**. A local institution since 1972, this restaurant is in a big 1800s barn with hand-hewn rafters and crystal chandeliers hanging from the beams. That's the Common Man for you: fancy and après-ski at once. Bottles of Moët & Chandon signed by the customers who ordered them sit atop the beams. The eclectic New American cuisine highlights locally grown produce and meats. The menu might include an appetizer of sautéed sweetbreads and apples, a salad of organic field greens, and entrées ranging from fish stew in tomato and saffron broth

to grilled venison or sautéed and confited rabbit. Dinner is served by candlelight. Couples sit by the big fireplace. ✉ *3209 German Flats Rd., Warren* ☎ *802/583–2800* 🌐 *www.commonmanrestaurant.com* ▭ *AE, DC, MC, V* ⊙ *Closed Mon. mid-Apr.–mid-Dec. No lunch.*

¢–$ CAFÉ ✕ **The Green Cup.** You can count on products and ingredients from the community at this local favorite. Chef-owner Jason Galiano is famed for his egg specialties, making this the best place around for breakfast (served every day except Wednesday) or just to hang out with a cup of coffee—there's free Wi-Fi. Jason's sister Sarina works front of house and preps orders. Egg specials, soups, and pastries are all made from scratch. Dinner plates are designed to be shared on Sunday and Monday nights, filling a void in the area, when most restaurants are closed. ✉ *40 Bridge St., Waitsfield* ☎ *802/496–4963* 🌐 *www.greencupvermont.com* ▭ *MC, V* ⊙ *No dinner Tues.–Sat.*

WHERE TO STAY

$$ ★ **Inn at the Round Barn Farm.** A Shaker-style round barn (one of only five in Vermont) is the physical hallmark of this B&B, but what you'll remember when you leave is how comfortable a stay here is. In winter, you toss your shoes under a bench when you come in and put on a pair of slippers from a big basket. There's magic in that gesture, breaking down barriers between guests and giving you permission to kick back. You'll feel like a kid in the downstairs rec room with its TV, games, and billiard table. The guest rooms, inside the 1806 farmhouse, have eyelet-trimmed sheets, elaborate four-poster beds, richly colored wallpapers, and brass wall lamps for easy bedtime reading. Many have fireplaces and whirlpool tubs. Cooper, the inn dog, is your guide—literally—as you snowshoe or hike the miles of trails on this beautiful property filled with gardens and sculpture. Plan a winter trip around one of the moonlit snowshoe walks, which terminate with hot chocolate in an old cabin. **Pros:** great trails, gardens, and rooms; nice breakfast; unique architecture. **Cons:** no restaurant. ✉ *1661 E. Warren Rd., Waitsfield* ☎ *802/496–2276* 🌐 *www.theroundbarn.com* *11 rooms, 1 suite* *In-room: no TV, Wi-Fi. In-hotel: pool, Internet terminal, Wi-Fi hotspot, no kids under 15* ▭ *AE, D, MC, V* *BP.*

$$$$ Fodor's Choice ★ **Pitcher Inn.** Across from the justly famous Warren General Store is the elegant Pitcher Inn, Vermont's only Relais & Châteaux property. Ari Sadri, the hands-on manager, exudes an easygoing sophistication that makes staying here a delight. Each comfortable room has its own unusual and elaborate motif—which you'll either love or hate. The Mountain Room, for instance, is designed as a replica of a fire tower in the Green Mountains, with murals on some walls and others covered in stone and glass to resemble a mountain cliff. All the bathrooms, however, are wonderful, with rain showerheads and Anichini linens and superb toiletries. **Pros:** exceptional service; great bathrooms; fun pub; great location. **Cons:** many rooms can be considered kitschy or downright silly. ✉ *275 Main St., Warren* ☎ *802/496–6350 or 888/867–4824* 🌐 *www.pitcherinn.com* *9 rooms, 2 suites* *In-room: refrigerator (some), Wi-Fi. In-hotel: restaurant, bar, spa, water sports, bicycles, Internet terminal, Wi-Fi hotspot* ▭ *AE, MC, V* *BP.*

NORTHERN VERMONT

Vermont's northernmost region reveals the state's greatest contrasts. To the west, Burlington and its suburbs have grown so rapidly that rural wags now say that Burlington's greatest advantage is that it's "close to Vermont." The north country also harbors Vermont's tiny capital, Montpelier, and its highest mountain, Mt. Mansfield, site of the famous Stowe ski resort. To the northeast of Montpelier is a sparsely populated and heavily wooded territory that former Senator George Aiken dubbed the "Northeast Kingdom." It's the domain of loggers, farmers, and avid outdoors enthusiasts.

Our coverage of towns begins in the state capital, Montpelier, moves west toward Stowe and Burlington, then goes north through the Lake Champlain Islands, east along the boundary with Canada toward Jay Peak, and south into the heart of the Northeast Kingdom.

MONTPELIER

38 mi southeast of Burlington, 115 mi north of Brattleboro.

With only about 8,000 residents, little Montpelier is the country's smallest capital city. But it has a youthful energy—and certainly an independent spirit—that makes it seem almost as large as Burlington. The well-preserved downtown bustles with state and city workers walking to meetings or down the street to one of the coffee shops and good restaurants.

EXPLORING

★ **Morse Farm Maple Sugarworks.** With eight generations of sugaring, the Morses are the oldest maple family in existence, so you're sure to find an authentic maple farm experience here. Burr Morse heads up the operation now, along with his son Tom. You can see an earlier generation, Burr's father, Harry Morse, hamming it up in a hilarious video playing at the theater. More than 3,000 trees produce the syrup (sample all the grades), candy, cream, and sugar that's sold in their gift shop. ✉ *1168 County Rd.* ☎ *800/242–2740* 🌐 *www.morsefarm.com* 🎫 *Free.*

Vermont Museum. The Vermont Historical Society runs this engaging museum recounting more than 150 years of state history. The collection here was begun in 1838 and features all things Vermont, from a catamount (the now extinct Vermont cougar) to Ethan Allen's shoe buckles. The museum store has a great collection of books, prints, and gifts. ✉ *109 State St.* ☎ *802/828–2291* 🌐 *www.vermonthistory.org* 🎫 *$5* ⏲ *May–Oct., Tues.–Sat. 10–4.*

QUICK BITES

La Brioche Bakery (✉ *89 Main St.* ☎ *802/229–0443* 🌐 *www.necidining.com/la-brioche.com*) is a great downtown stop for breakfast and lunch. New England Culinary Institute students are up at 4 AM preparing breads for thankful locals. There's a great selection of soups, salads, and sandwiches.

★ **Vermont State House.** The regal, gold-domed capitol surrounded by forest is emblematic of this proud rural state. With the gleaming dome and columns of Barre granite 6 feet in diameter, the statehouse is home to the oldest legislative chambers in their original condition in the United

States. Half-hour tours take you through the governor's office and the house and senate chambers. The goddess of agriculture tops the gilded dome. Interior paintings and exhibits make much of Vermont's sterling Civil War record. ✉ *115 State St.* ☎ *802/828–2228* *Donations accepted* *Weekdays 8–4; tours July–mid-Oct., weekdays every ½ hr 10–3:30 (last tour at 3:30), Sat. 11–3 (last tour at 2:30).*

OFF THE BEATEN PATH

Rock of Ages Granite Quarry. The attractions here range from the awe-inspiring (the quarry resembles the Grand Canyon in miniature) to the mildly ghoulish (you can consult a directory of tombstone dealers throughout the country) to the whimsical (an outdoor granite bowling alley). You might recognize the sheer walls of the quarry from *Batman and Robin,* the film starring George Clooney and Arnold Schwarzenegger. At the crafts center, skilled artisans sculpt monuments; at the quarries themselves, 25-ton blocks of stone are cut from sheer 475-foot walls by workers who clearly earn their pay. ✉ *558 Graniteville Rd., Exit 6 off I–89, follow Rte. 63, 7 mi southeast of Montpelier, Graniteville* ☎ *802/476–3119* *www.rockofages.com* *Tour of active quarry $4, craftsman center and self-guided tour free* *Visitor center May–Oct., Mon.–Sat. 8:30–5, Sun. 10–5; narrated tour on Sat. (call for times).*

SHOPPING

Unique shops attract locals and tourists alike to Montpelier. For hip children's clothing made in Vermont, head to **Zutano** (✉ *79 Main St.* ☎ *802/223–2229* *www.zutano.com*).

WHERE TO EAT

$$ ECLECTIC ★ **Ariel's.** Well off the beaten path, this small restaurant overlooking a lake is worth the drive down a dirt road. Chef Lee Duberman prepares eclectic treats such as scallop, lobster, and shrimp ravioli in a ginger shiitake broth. Her husband, sommelier Ricard Fink, recommends selections from the wine cellar. The full menu is offered Friday and Saturday; a pub menu ($–$$) is served Wednesday, Thursday, and Sunday. ✉ *29 Stone Hill Rd., 8 mi south of Montpelier, Brookfield* ☎ *802/276–3939* *DC, MC, V* *Closed Nov. and Apr.; Mon. and Tues. May–Oct.; Mon.–Thurs. Dec.–Mar.* *www.arielsrestaurant.com.*

$$ AMERICAN **Main Street Grill and Bar.** Nearly everyone working here is a student at the New England Culinary Institute. Although this is a training ground, the quality and inventiveness are anything but beginner's luck. The menu changes daily, but clam chowder and Misty Knoll Farm free range chicken breast are reliable winners. The lounge downstairs has lighter fare, including a tapas menu. ✉ *118 Main St.* ☎ *802/223–3188* *www.necidining.com.com* *AE, D, DC, MC, V* *Closed Mon.*

$ AMERICAN **Restaurant Phoebe.** The best location on State Street, fresh ingredients, and young culinary-obsessed cooks have made this casual neighborhood place a big hit since it opened in 2006. Chef-owner Aaron Millon—a '97 New England Culinary Institute graduate—is committed to a "holistic cuisine" that stresses the freshest local ingredients. There's a chef's beef cut of the day, selected from the best local farms, the daily soups are great, and delicious breads are baked in-house. ✉ *52 State St.* ☎ *802/262–3500* *www.restaurantphoebe.com* *AE, MC, V* *Closed Mon. No lunch weekends.*

DID YOU KNOW?

Vermont actually means Green Mountains (*vert mont* in French). The Long Trail, Appalachian Trail, and many other hiking routes crisscross the namesake peaks, which are part of the Appalachian Mountain chain.

2

$ SOUTHERN **River Run Restaurant.** Mississippi-raised chef Jimmy Kennedy has brought outstanding Southern fare to northern Vermont. Fried catfish, hush puppies, collard greens, and whiskey cake are just a few of the surprises awaiting diners at this rustic, hip eatery with a full bar. Try the buttermilk biscuits at breakfast. ✉ *65 Main St., 10 mi east of Montpelier, Plainfield* ☎ *802/454–1246* 🌐 *www.riverrunbbq.com* ▭ *No credit cards* ⏲ *Closed Mon.–Wed. No dinner Sun.*

$ ITALIAN **Sarducci's.** Legislative lunches have been a lot more leisurely since Sarducci's came along to fill the trattoria void in Vermont's capital. These bright, cheerful rooms alongside the Winooski River are a local favorite for pizza fresh from wood-fired ovens, wonderfully textured homemade Italian breads, and imaginative pasta dishes such as pasta *pugliese,* which marries penne with basil, black olives, roasted eggplant, portobello mushrooms, and sun-dried tomatoes. ✉ *3 Main St.* ☎ *802/223–0229* 🌐 *www.sarduccis.com* ▭ *AE, MC, V* ⏲ *No lunch Sun.*

WHERE TO STAY

$–$$ **Inn at Montpelier.** There are two places in town to stay and this is the charming option—the other is a basic hotel across from the statehouse. This well-cared-for circa 1830 inn has antique four-poster beds and Windsor chairs. Outside the formal sitting room is a sensational wraparound Colonial-revival porch, perfect for reading a book or enjoying a drink from the inn's full bar and watching the townsfolk stroll by. Guests get use of a pantry and the common rooms. You can leave your car here and walk everywhere in town. **Pros:** beautiful home; relaxed central setting; amazing porch. **Cons:** some rooms are small. ✉ *147 Main St.* ☎ *802/223–2727* 🌐 *www.innatmontpelier.com* *19 rooms* *In-room: Wi-Fi. In-hotel: bar, laundry service* ▭ *AE, D, DC, MC, V* *CP.*

EN ROUTE

On your way to Stowe from Interstate 89, be sure to stop at **Ben & Jerry's Ice Cream Factory,** a must for ice-cream lovers. Ben Cohen and Jerry Greenfield began selling ice cream from a renovated gas station in Burlington in the 1970s. The tour only skims the surface of the behind-the-scenes goings-on at the plant—a flaw forgiven when the free samples are dished out. ✉ *1281 Waterbury-Stowe Rd. (Rte. 100), 1 mi north of I–89, Waterbury* ☎ *802/846–1500* 🌐 *www.benjerry.com* *Tour $3* ⏲ *Late Oct.–June, daily 10–6; July–mid-Aug., daily 9–9; mid-Aug.–late Oct., daily 9–7. Tours run every half hour.*

STOWE

Fodor's Choice ★

22 mi northwest of Montpelier, 36 mi east of Burlington.

Long before skiing came to Stowe in the 1930s, the rolling hills and valleys beneath Vermont's highest peak, the 4,395-foot Mt. Mansfield, attracted summer tourists looking for a reprieve from city heat. Most stayed at one of two inns in the village of Stowe. When skiing made the town a winter destination, the arriving skiers outnumbered the hotel beds, so locals took them in. This spirit of hospitality continues, and many of these homes are now lovely country inns. The village itself is tiny, just a few blocks of shops and restaurants clustered around a picture-perfect white church with a lofty steeple, but it serves as the

Northern Vermont
QUÉBEC
NEW YORK
NEW HAMPSHIRE
COLD HOLLOW MOUNTAINS
GREEN MOUNTAINS
Rouses Point
Champlain
Alburg
Chazy
Plattsburgh
Lake Champlain Islands
North Hero
North Hero State Park
Kill Kare State Park
Burton Island State Park
Grand Isle
Grand Isle State Park
Sand Bar State Park
South Hero
Lake Champlain
Port Kent
Willsboro Point
Essex
Westport
Swanton
Saint Albans
Highgate Center
Lake Carmi
Enosburg Falls
Richford
Montgomery
Jay Peak
Jay
North Troy
Lake Memphremagog
Newport
Derby Line
Norton
Beecher Falls
Colebrook
Seymour Lake
Island Pond
North Stratford
Orleans
Lowell
Westmore
Lake Willoughby
Albany
The Craftsburys
Caspian Lake
Greensboro
West Burke
Maidstone Lake
Burke Mountain
East Burke
Groveton
Guildhall
Lyndonville
Lyndon
0 10 mi
0 10 km
Fairfax
Cambridge
Jeffersonville
Milton
Hyde Park
Smugglers' Notch Resort
Morrisville
Wolcott
Hardwick
Stowe Mountain Resort
Jericho
Winooski
Burlington
Essex Junction
South Burlington
Stowe
Bolton Valley
Richmond
Shelburne
Shelburne Museum
Ben & Jerry's Ice Cream Factory
Waterbury
Montpelier
Rock of Ages Granite Quarry
Barre
Waitsfield
Marshfield
Mollys Falls Pond
Plainfield
Lake Groton
Danville
St. Johnsbury
Concord
Whitefield
Barnet
Lisbon
Wells River
223
133
105
114
78
2
9
87
89
104
36
108
242
100
91
v111
102
3
5
5A
14
16
15
128
7
vn12
22
116
17
302
93

anchor for Mountain Road, which leads north past restaurants, lodges, and shops on its way to Stowe's fabled slopes.

ESSENTIALS

Visitor Information **Stowe Area Association** (✉ *Main St., Box 1320, Stowe* ☎ *802/253–7321 or 877/467–8693* 🌐 *www.gostowe.com*).

2

EXPLORING

Gondola. Mt. Mansfield's "Chin" area is accessible by the eight-seat gondola. At the gondola's summit station isthe **Cliff House Restaurant** (☎ *802/253–3558 Ext. 237*), where lunch is served daily 11–3. ✉ *1 Mountain Rd., 8 mi off Rte. 100* ☎ *802/253–3000* 🎟 *Gondola $14* ⏲ *Mid-June–mid-Oct., daily 10–5; early Dec.–late Apr., daily 8–4; closed in Nov. and May.*

Mt. Mansfield. With its elongated summit ridge resembling the profile of a recumbent man's face, Mt. Mansfield has long attracted the adventurous. The mountain is ribboned with hiking and ski trails.

Trapp Family Lodge. Built by the von Trapp family, of *Sound of Music* fame, this Tyrolean lodge and its surrounding pastureland are the site of a popular outdoor music series in summer and an extensive cross-country ski-trail network in winter. A teahouse serves food and drinks. ✉ *1 Luce Hill Rd.* ☎ *802/253–8511 or 800/826–7000* 🌐 *www.trappfamily.com.*

Vermont Ski Museum. The state's skiing history is documented here with myriad exhibits. ✉ *1 Main St.* ☎ *802/253–9911* 🌐 *www.vermontskimuseum.org.*

SPORTS AND THE OUTDOORS

CANOEING AND KAYAKING **Umiak Outdoor Outfitters** (✉ *849 S. Main St. [Rte. 100], south of Stowe Village* ☎ *802/253–2317* 🌐 *www.umiak.com*) rents canoes and kayaks for day trips and leads overnight excursions. The store also operates a rental outpost at Lake Elmore State Park in Elmore, on the Winooski River off Route 2 in Waterbury, at North Beach in Burlington, and on the Lamoille River in Jeffersonville.

FISHING The **Fly Rod Shop** (✉ *2703 Waterbury Rd. [Rte. 100], 1½ mi south of Stowe* ☎ *802/253–7346 or 800/535–9763* 🌐 *www.flyrodshop.com*) provides a guiding service; gives fly-tying, casting, and rod-building classes in winter; rents fly tackle; and sells equipment, including classic and collectible firearms.

GOLF **Stowe Country Club** (✉ *1 Mountain Rd.* ☎ *802/253–4893*) has a scenic 18-hole, par-72 course; a driving range; and a putting green. Green fees are $45–$75; cart rental is $18.

HIKING Ascending **Mt. Mansfield** makes for a scenic day hike. Trails lead from Route 108 (Mountain Road) to the summit ridge, where they meet the north-to-south Long Trail. Views from the summit take in New Hampshire's White Mountains, New York's Adirondacks across Lake Champlain, and southern Québec. The Green Mountain Club publishes a trail guide.

ICE-SKATING **Jackson Arena** (✉ *1 Park St.* ☎ *802/253–6148*) is a public ice-skating rink, with skate rentals available.

SKI AREA ★ To be precise, the name of the village is Stowe and the name of the mountain is Mt. Mansfield, but to generations of skiers, the area, the complex, and the region are just plain Stowe. **Stowe Mountain Resort** (✉ *5781 Mountain Rd.* ☎ *802/253–3000; 802/253–3600 snow* *conditions; 800/253–4754 lodging* 🌐 *www.stowe.com*) is a classic that dates from the 1930s. Even today, the area's mystique attracts as many serious skiers as social ones. Improved snowmaking, new lifts, and free shuttle buses that gather skiers from lodges, inns, and motels along Mountain Road have added convenience to the Stowe experience. Yet the traditions remain: the Winter Carnival in January, the Sugar Slalom in April, ski weeks all winter. Three base lodges—including the luxurious Stowe Mountain Lodge that opened in 2008—provide the essentials, including two on-mountain restaurants.

The resort provides hiking, in-line skating, an alpine slide, gondola rides, and an 18-hole golf course. It also has 22 mi of groomed cross-country trails and 24 mi of backcountry trails. Four interconnecting cross-country ski areas have more than 90 mi of groomed trails within the town of Stowe.

Mt. Mansfield, with an elevation of 4,395 feet and a vertical drop of 2,360 feet, is one of the giants among eastern ski mountains. The mountain's symmetrical shape allows skiers of all abilities long, satisfying runs from the summit. The famous Front Four (National, Liftline, Starr, and Goat) are the intimidating centerpieces for tough, expert runs, yet there is plenty of mellow intermediate skiing, with 59% of the runs rated at that level and 116 trails total. One long beginner trail, the Toll Road Trail, is 3½ mi. Mansfield's satellite sector is a network of intermediate trails and one expert trail off a basin served by a gondola. Spruce Peak, separate from the main mountain, is a teaching hill and a pleasant experience for intermediates and beginners. In addition to the high-speed, eight-passenger gondola, Stowe has 11 lifts, including two quads, two triples, and five double chairlifts, plus one handle tow, to service its 48 trails. Night-skiing trails are accessed by the gondola. The resort has 73% snowmaking coverage. Snowboard facilities include a half-pipe and two terrain parks—one for beginners, at Spruce Peak, and one for experts, on the Mt. Mansfield side. Children's programs are headquartered at Spruce Peak, with ski-school programs for ages 4 to 12.

SHOPPING

In Stowe, Mountain Road is lined with shops from town up toward the ski area. North of Stowe, shops line Route 100 from Interstate 89. On Route 100 south toward Waterbury, between the cider mill and Ben & Jerry's, you can visit the **Cabot Cheese Annex Store** (✉ *3600 Waterbury-Stowe Rd. [Rte. 100], 2½ mi north of I–89* ☎ *802/244–6334*).

★ Watch apples pressed into cider at the **Cold Hollow Cider Mill** (✉ *Rte. 100, 3 mi north of I–89* ☎ *802/244–8771 or 800/327–7537*). The on-site store sells cider, baked goods, Vermont produce, and specialty foods. Sample all the cold cider you like; kids get free cider popsicles.

NIGHTLIFE AND THE ARTS

THE ARTS **Stowe Performing Arts** (☎ *802/253–7792* 🌐 *www.stowearts.com*) sponsors a series of classical and jazz concerts in July in the Trapp Family Lodge meadow. **Stowe Theater Guild** (✉ *67 Main St., Town Hall Theater* ☎ *802/253–3961 summer only* 🌐 *www.stowetheatre.com*) performs musicals in summer and plays in September.

Continued on page 113

LET IT SNOW

WINTER ACTIVITIES IN VERMONT

by Elise Coroneos

SKIING AND SNOWBOARDING IN VERMONT

Less than 5 mi from the Canadian border, Jay Peak is Vermont's northernmost ski resort.

Ever since America's first ski tow opened in a farmer's pasture near Woodstock in January 1934, skiers have headed en masse to Vermont in winter. Today, 20 alpine and 30 nordic ski areas range in size and are spread across the state, from Mount Snow in the south to Jay Peak near the Canadian border. The snowmaking equipment has also become more comprehensive over the years, with 70% of the trails in the state using man-made snow. Here are some of the best ski areas by various categories:

GREAT FOR KIDS **Smugglers' Notch, Okemo,** and **Bromley Mountain** all offer terrific kids' programs, with classes organized by age categories and by skill level. Kids as young as 3 (4 at some ski areas) can start learning. Child care, with activities like stories, singing, and arts and crafts, are available for those too young to ski; some ski areas, like Smuggler's Notch, offer babysitting with no minimum age daytime and evening.

BEST FOR BEGINNERS Beginner terrain makes up nearly half of the mountain at **Stratton,** where options include private and group lessons for first-timers. Also good are small but family-friendly **Ascutney** and **Bromley Mountains,** which both designate a third of their slopes for beginners.

EXPERT TERRAIN The slopes at **Jay Peak** and massive **Killington** are most notable for their steepness and pockets of glades. About 40% of the runs at these two resorts are advanced or expert. Due to its far north location, Jay Peak tends to get the most snow, making it ideal for those skilled in plowing through fresh powder. Another favorite with advanced skiers is Central Vermont's **Mad River Glen,** where many slopes are ungroomed (natural) and the motto is "Ski it if you can." In addition, **Sugarbush, Stowe,** and **Smugglers' Notch** are all revered for their challenging untamed side country.

Mount Mansfield is better known as Stowe.

Stratton Mountain clocktower

NIGHT SKIING Come late afternoon, **Bolton Valley** is hopping. That's because it's the only location in Vermont for night skiing. Ski and ride under the lights from 4 until 8 Wednesday through Saturday, followed by a later après-ski scene.

APRÈS-SKI The social scenes at **Killington, Sugarbush,** and **Stowe** are the most noteworthy (and crowded). Warm up after a day in the snow in Killington with all-you-can-eat pizza on Monday nights and daily happy hour specials at the Nightspot Outback, or stop by the always popular Wobbly Barn. For live music, try Chez Henri in Sugarbush or the Matterhorn Night Club in Stowe.

SNOWBOARDING Boarders (and some skiers) will love the latest features for freestyle tricks in Vermont. **Okemo** has a superpipe and five terrain parks, including a new gladed park with all-natural features; **Stratton** has a half pipe, rail garden, and four other parks. **Mount Snow's** Carinthia Peak is an all-terrain park–dedicated mountain, the only of its kind in the state. Head to **Killington** for Burton Stash, another beautiful all-natural features terrain park. Note that snowboarding is not allowed at skiing cooperative **Mad River Glen.**

CROSS-COUNTRY To experience the best of cross-country skiing in the state, simply follow the Catamount Trail, a 300-mi nordic route from southern Vermont to Canada. **The Trapp Family Lodge** in Stowe has 40 mi of groomed cross-country trails and 60 mi of back-country trails. Another top option is **The Mountain Top Inn & Resort,** just outside of Killington. Its Nordic Ski and Snowshoe Center provides instruction for newcomers, along with hot drinks and lunches when it is time to take a break and warm up.

TELEMARK Ungroomed snow and tree skiing are a natural fit with free-heel skiing at **Mad River Glen. Jay Peak** also has telemark rentals and instruction.

MOUNTAIN-RESORT TRIP PLANNER

TIMING

■ **Snow Season.** Winter sports time is typically from December to April, weather permitting. Holidays are the most crowded.

■ **March Madness.** Most of the season's snow tends to come in March, so that's the time to go if you want to ski on fresh, nature-made powder. To increase your odds, choose a ski area in the northern part of the state.

■ **Summer Scene.** During summertime, many ski resorts reinvent themselves as prime destinations for golfers and mountain bikers. Other summer visitors come to the mountains to enjoy hiking trails, climbing walls, aquatic centers, chairlift and horseback rides, or a variety of festivals.

■ **Avoid Long Lift Lines.** Try to hit the slopes early—many lifts start at 8 or 9 AM, with ticket windows opening a half-hour earlier. Then take a mid-morning break as lines start to get longer and head out again when others come in for lunch.

SAVINGS TIPS

■ **Choose a Condo.** Especially if you're planning to stay for a week, save money on food by opting for a condominium unit with a kitchen. You can shop at the supermarket and cook breakfast and dinner.

■ **Rent Smart.** Consider ski rental options in the villages rather than those at the mountain. Renting right at the ski area may be more convenient, but it may also cost more.

■ **Discount Lift Tickets.** Online tickets are often the least expensive; multi-day discounts and and ski-and-stay packages will also lower your costs. Good for those who can plan ahead, early-bird tickets often go on sale before the ski season even starts.

■ **Hit the Peaks Off-peak.** In order to secure the best deals at the most competitive rates, avoid booking during school holidays. Presidents Week in February is the busiest, because that's when Northeastern schools have their spring break.

Top left, Killington's six mountains make up the largest ski area in Vermont. Top right, Stratton has a Snowboard-cross course.

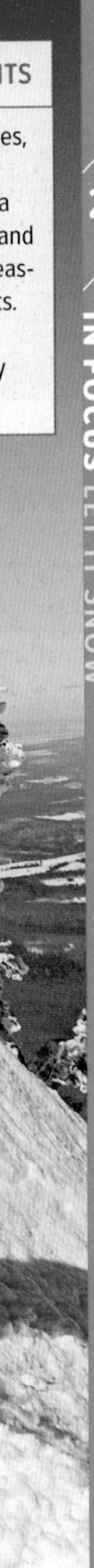

THINK WARM THOUGHTS

It can get cold on the slopes, so be prepared. Consider heated boots or purchase a pair each of inexpensive hand and feet warmers that fit easily in your gloves and boots. Helmets, which can also be rented, provide not only added safety but warmth.

VERMONT SKI AREAS BY THE NUMBERS

Okemo's wide slopes attract snowbirds to Ludlow in Central Vermont.

Numbers are a helpful way to compare mountains, but remember that each resort has a distinct personality. This list is composed of ski areas in Vermont with at least 100 skiable acres. For more information, see individual resort listings.

SKI AREA	Vertical Drop	Skiable Acres	# of Trails & Lifts	Terrain Type ●	■	◆/◆◆	Snowboarding Options
Ascutney Mountain	1,800	150	57/6	30%	40%	30%	Terrain park
Bolton Valley	1,704	165	64/6	27%	47%	26%	Terrain park
Bromley	1,334	177	45/10	35%	34%	31%	Terrain park
Burke Mountain	2,011	250	45/4	25%	45%	30%	Terrain park
Jay Peak	2,153	385	76/8	20%	40%	40%	Terrain park
Killington	3,050	752	141/22	29%	29%	42%	Terrain park, Half-pipe
Mad River Glen	2,037	115	45/5	30%	30%	40%	Snowboarding not allowed
Mount Snow	1,700	588	80/20	14%	73%	13%	Terrain park, Half-pipe
Okemo	2,200	632	119/19	32%	36%	32%	Terrain park, Superpipe, RossCross terrain cross park
Pico Mountain	1,967	214	50/7	20%	48%	32%	Triple Slope
Smugglers' Notch	2,610	310	78/8	19%	56%	25%	Terrain park
Stowe	2,360	485	116/13	16%	59%	25%	Terrain park, Half-pipe
Stratton	2,003	600	92/13	42%	31%	27%	Terrain park, Half-pipe, Snowboardcross course
Sugarbush	2,600	578	53/16	20%	45%	35%	Terrain park, Half-pipe

CONTACT THE EXPERTS

Ski Vermont (☎ *802/223-2439* 🌐 *www.skivermont.com*), a non-profit association in Montpelier, Vermont, and **Vermont Department of Tourism** (🌐 *www.vermontvacation.com*) are great resources for travelers planning a wintertime trip to Vermont.

KNOW YOUR SIGNS

On trail maps and the mountains, trails are rated and marked:

● Beginner

◆ Advanced

■ Intermediate

◆◆ Expert

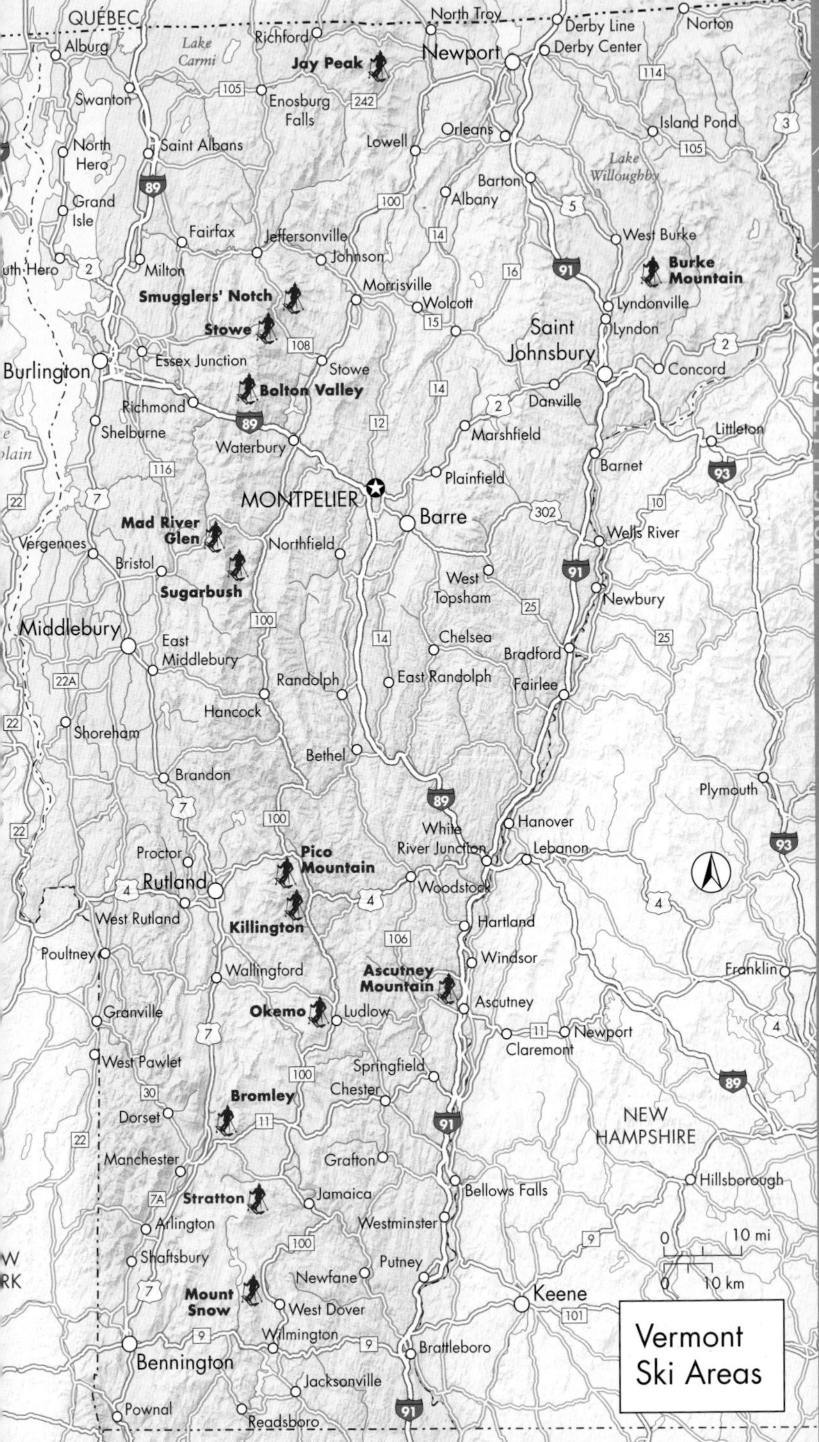
QUÉBEC
Alburg
Lake Carmi
Richford
Jay Peak
North Troy
Newport
Derby Line
Derby Center
Norton
Swanton
Enosburg Falls
Orleans
Island Pond
North Hero
Saint Albans
Lowell
Lake Willoughby
Grand Isle
Barton
Albany
Fairfax
Jeffersonville
Johnson
West Burke
Milton
Burke Mountain
Smugglers' Notch
Morrisville
Wolcott
Lyndonville
Stowe
Lyndon
Saint Johnsbury
Burlington
Essex Junction
Concord
Bolton Valley
Richmond
Danville
Shelburne
Marshfield
Littleton
Waterbury
Barnet
Plainfield
MONTPELIER
Barre
Mad River Glen
Vergennes
Northfield
Wells River
Bristol
Sugarbush
West Topsham
Newbury
Middlebury
East Middlebury
Chelsea
Bradford
Randolph
East Randolph
Fairlee
Hancock
Shoreham
Bethel
Brandon
Plymouth
Hanover
White River Junction
Lebanon
Proctor
Pico Mountain
Rutland
Woodstock
West Rutland
Killington
Hartland
Poultney
Windsor
Franklin
Wallingford
Ascutney Mountain
Ascutney
Okemo
Ludlow
Granville
Newport
Claremont
West Pawlet
Springfield
Bromley
Chester
Dorset
NEW HAMPSHIRE
Manchester
Grafton
Hillsborough
Stratton
Jamaica
Bellows Falls
Arlington
Westminster
Shaftsbury
Putney
Newfane
Mount Snow
Keene
West Dover
Wilmington
Bennington
Brattleboro
Jacksonville
Pownal
Readsboro
0 10 mi
0 10 km
Vermont Ski Areas

MORE WINTER FUN

A horse and sleigh ride in South Woodstock

DOG SLEDDING

Being pulled through the woods by a team of of up to eight adult Siberian Huskies, you might feel like you are a pioneer taking on the elements—or like you're in Alaska's Iditarod.

Pros: unique experience; kids love it.

Cons: dogs can be stubborn; pricey.

■ **Peacepups Dog Sledding** (☎ 802/888–7733 🌐 www.peacepupsdogsledding.com) at Lake Elmore, 15 miles from Stowe, offers two-hour day tours using a team of eight dogs. Choose between sitting back and riding inside a padded toboggan while your driver (and the dogs) do the work, or join in the driving using a two-person tandem sled. Either cost $120 per adult ($60 for kids under 12). Tours head out every Wednesday, Friday, Saturday, and Sunday at 10 AM, noon, and 2 PM from mid-December to the end of March, weather permitting.

■ Twilight dog sledding tours leave the **Stowe Mountain Resort** (☎ 802/253-3656 🌐 www.stowe.com) for one hour every Tuesday and Thursday. The cost is $150 for guests of the resort or $160 for nonguests. This is a sit-down ride inside a padded toboggan.

■ For a taste of how the professionals do it, head to Burke Mountain during **Vermont's Annual Dog Sled Dash** (🌐 www.sleddogdash.com). Usually held in February, the event is the largest of its kind in New England, with more than 100 teams entering for part of the $10,000 purse. Vacationers come to witness the event—put on some snowshoes and trek in to find the best vantage points. If you fancy your own dog-sledding skills, you can register online.

ICE SKATING

If you want outdoor activity but want to stay in one spot and not be outside for a long time—or not even outside at all, but just feel like you are—ice skating might be just your thing. In Vermont you can skate surrounded by the nearby snowcapped mountains or in the comfort of an indoor professional facility.

Pros: excellent activity for groups; easy access (venues are often close to your lodging); inexpensive.

Cons: can be crowded.

■ **The Ice Station at Okemo** (☎ 802/228–1406 🌐 www.okemo.com), near the Jackson Gore base, is a roof-covered natural ice rink with a warming area for those with comfort in mind. Open mid-December through April from 2 to 9 PM on weekdays and 10 AM to 9 PM on weekends. The cost is $4 for rink access plus $4 to rent skates.

■ Check out **Jay Peak's** (☎ 802/988–2611 🌐 www.jaypeakresort.com) new, $7 million full-size rink, which opened in 2010. At the time of this writing, prices were not yet set.

■ For the ultimate outdoor skating experience, head to **Lake Morey** in Fairlee, home to America's longest natural ice skating trail. From December to April, the lake freezes over and is groomed for ice skating, providing a magical 4-mi stretch of ice amid forested hillsides. It is maintained by the **Upper Valley Trails Alliance** (☎ 802/649–9075 🌐 www.uvtrails.org). Bring your own skates or find rentals at the nearby **Nordic Skater** (☎ 866/244–2570 🌐 www.nordicskater.com), which also runs outdoor skating workshops for $30.

Snowmobiling

Snowshoeing at Trapp Family Lodge

SLEDDING AND TUBING

Want down-the-mountain action but prefer not to ski or board? Tubing is offered at many Vermont ski areas with lifts to tow riders back up, or you can just ask the locals for the best sledding hills. Either way it is especially popular with kids: get ready to hear the question "Can we do it again?" multiple times.

Pros: fun for families and groups; cheaper than skiing.

Cons: rides can be bumpy; not for very young (and short) kids.

■ A standout is Stratton's **Coca Cola Tubing Park** (☎ 800/787–2886 🌐 www.stratton.com). Careen down any one of four lanes that stretch up to 750 feet long. Kids must be 5 years or older to ride. Open 4 to 8 PM Friday, 11 AM to 9 PM Saturday, and 11 AM to 3 PM Sunday. Tickets are $15 for one hour and $22 for two hours.

■ **Okemo** (☎ 866/706–5366 🌐 www.okemo.com) offers a tubing facility at its Jackson Gore base area as an après-ski activity from 3 to 6 PM on Friday and Saturday (hours may vary). Take a conveyor-style lift to the top of the hill and then ride down one of four groomed lanes. Tubes rent for $9 an hour. Kids must be at least 42 inches tall to ride.

■ For extra adventure, visitors at **Smugglers' Notch** (☎ 800/419–4615 🌐 www.smuggs.com) can try airboarding, which uses an inflated sled. First-timers must enroll in an two-hour clinic ($25), after which they can rent and ride for $20 (plus a valid lift ticket) from 2 to 4 PM. Riders must be at least 10 years old and 48 inches tall.

SLEIGH RIDES

Riding a sleigh in Vermont is not quite dashing through the snow on a one-horse open sleigh—the speed is gentle enough that you can sip hot cocoa on the ride, and the sleigh is big, so it usually takes two horses. But you will see Christmas-card-like settings as the sleigh takes you down trails lined with fir trees. Many farms and some resorts offer sleigh rides from December through April, weather permitting. When there is no snow on the ground, horse-drawn carriage rides may be available. The Woodstock area is known as Vermont's horse country, and many local stables have different types of riding options year-round.

Pros: great way to see scenery; fun group activity.

Cons: slow speed; not comfortable if it's windy or snowing hard.

■ The **Mountain Top Inn & Resort** (☎ 802/483–2311 🌐 www.mountaintopinn.com) just 11 mi from Killington, offers a Sleigh and Dinner Package for $150 for two adults (includes tax and gratuity). The sleigh ride through the resort's wooded trails followed by a three-course dinner is the perfect nightcap. Call for the regularly scheduled 30 minute rides starting at $25 per person, with discounts for children. Private rides are also available.

■ The **Kedron Valley Stables** (☎ 802/457–1480 🌐 www.kedron.com), in South Woodstock, runs hour-long sleigh rides for up to three people for $95, or for four to eight people for $115. For groups over eight, there's an extra charge of $14 per each additional person.

Okemo Resort

Tubing down Magic Mountain.

SNOWMOBILING

Travel a snow-covered highway through densely forested valleys, past snow-capped mountains, and into friendly villages—all without exerting your own energy. Thanks to the extensive trails administered through the state's VAST (Vermont Association of Snow Travellers) system, it's possible to see extensive back country normally beyond the realm of visitors. Snowmobiles usually hold two riders.

Pros: you can cover a lot of ground.

Cons: can be noisy; expensive; controversial because of environmental impact.

■ Snowmobile rentals are available at several ski areas, including **Killington** (☎ 802/422–2121 🌐 www.killingtonsnowmobiletours.com) and **Okemo** (☎ 800/328–8725 🌐 www.killingtonsnowmobiletours.com/okemo). Both have one-hour guided tours across groomed ski trails ($89 for one person, $119 for two). If you are feeling more adventurous, take the two-hour backcountry tour through 25 mi of the Calvin Coolidge State Forest ($144 for one person, $189 for two). Helmets and boots are included.

■ For an after-hours perspective, try night snowmobiling at **Smugglers' Notch Resort** (☎ 802/644–8851 🌐 www.smuggs.com) and **Stratton** (☎ 802/824–5399 🌐 www.stratton.com). Smugglers' evening tours depart daily on the hour from 5–8 PM from around mid-December to early April, weather permitting. Stratton night tours are available on Saturday nights and holiday nights at from 5–8:30 PM, with additional nights available upon request. The cost is $80 per snowmobile per hour.

SNOWSHOEING

Hikers wanting to explore nature in the winter can do so in depth thanks to snowshoes, which easily attach to your boots. Showshoeing allows you to get up close and personal with the surrounding wilderness. Tranquil trails are easy to find in the Green Mountain State; just avoid those shared with snowmobiles. Some alpine resorts now have networks of snowshoeing trails. Many places that rent cross-country ski gear, like the Trapp Family Lodge, also rent snowshoes. Poles help snowshoers stabilize, especially on uneven and steep terrain.

Pros: inexpensive; great exercise; easy to do (no lesson required).

Cons: small children might get worn out quickly; can be a lot of work; colder than cross-country skiing because you're not moving fast.

■ **Mount Olga Trail** (🌐 www.trails.com) is the most popular snowshoeing destination in Vermont. Located in Wilmington's Molly Stark State Park, the trail is 2.3 mi long. The hike is relatively easy, climaxing with a 360-degree view of southern Vermont and northern Massachusetts.

■ Northeast Vermont's **Kingdom Trails** (☎ 802/626–5862 🌐 www.kingdomtrails.org) is a network of more than 100 mi of trails used for snowshoeing (hiking and mountain biking in summer). A day pass is $10 for adults, $5 for kids ages 8–15, and free for kids 7 and under. Guests at East Burke's **Inn at Mountain View Farm** (☎ 800/572–4509, 🌐 www.innmtnview.com), the closest inn to the beginning of the trails, receive free access.

NIGHTLIFE The **Matterhorn Night Club** (⊠ *4969 Mountain Rd.* ☎ *802/253–8198* 🌐 *www.matterhornbar.com*) hosts live music and dancing Thursday–Saturday nights and has a separate martini bar. The **Rusty Nail** (⊠ *1190 Mountain Rd.* ☎ *802/253–6245* 🌐 *rustynailbar.com*) rocks to live music on weekends.

2

WHERE TO EAT

$$ ECLECTIC ★ ✕ **Hen of the Wood.** Ask any great chef in Vermont where they go to find a tremendous meal and Hen of the Wood will inevitably be near the top of their list. The setting is riveting: a converted 1835 grist mill beside a waterfall. Inside the underground level of the mill a sunken pit formerly housing the grindstone is now filled with tables, and uneven stone walls are dotted floor to ceiling with tiny candles—decidedly romantic. Sophisticated dishes showcase the abundance of local produce, meat, cheese, and more. A typical plate on the daily changing menu may feature sheep milk's gnocchi, a local farm pork loin, shortribs, grassfed ribeye, and a wild Alaskan halibut. This is a very near to perfect Vermont dining experience. On occasion chef Eric Warnstedt's less-is-more philosophy stretches a bit too far, resulting in an underseasoned plate. In the warmer months, beg for coveted patio table overlooking a dramatic series of falls. ⊠ *92 Stowe St., Waterbury* ☎ *802/244–7300* 🌐 *www.henofthewood.com* *Reservations essential* ▭ *AE, DC, MC, V* ⊙ *No lunch.*

$$–$$$ CONTINENTAL ✕ **Michael's on the Hill.** Swiss-born chef Michael Kloeti trained in Europe and New York before opening this dining establishment in a 19th-century farmhouse outside Stowe. In addition to à la carte options, Michael's four-course prix-fixe menus ($60) highlight European cuisine such as roasted rabbit with mirepoix or ravioli with braised autumn vegetables. There's live piano music weekends. ⊠ *4182 Stowe-Waterbury Rd. (Rte. 100), 6 mi south of Stowe, Waterbury Center* ☎ *802/244–7476* 🌐 *www.michaelsonthehill.com* ▭ *AE, DC, MC, V* ⊙ *Closed Tues. No lunch.*

¢ CAFÉ ✕ **Red Hen Baking Co.** While it's about 15 mi from Stowe, if you're a devotee of artisanal bakeries, it'd be a mistake to miss out on a trip to have lunch or breakfast here. Try the ham-and-cheese croissants, sticky buns, homemade soups, and sandwiches. Red Hen supplies bread to some of the state's best restaurants, including Hen of the Wood, and is open 7 AM to 6 PM daily. ⊠ *961 Rte. 2, Middlesex* ☎ *802/223–5200* 🌐 *www.redhenbaking.com* *Reservations not accepted* ▭ *MC, V* ⊙ *No dinner.*

WHERE TO STAY

$$–$$$ **Green Mountain Inn.** Welcoming guests since 1833, this classic redbrick inn is across from the landmark Community Church and gives you access to the buzz of downtown. Rooms in the main building and annex still feel like a country inn, with Early American furnishings. Newer buildings have luxury rooms and suites. The Whip Bar & Grill ($$–$$$) puts an interesting twist on comfort food, as in cheddar-cheese-and-apple-stuffed chicken, and the outdoor heated pool is open year-round. **Pros:** fun location; lively tavern. **Cons:** farther from skiing than other area hotels. ⊠ *18 Main St.* ☎ *802/253–7301 or 800/253–7302* 🌐 *www.greenmountaininn.com* *105 rooms* *In-room: kitchen (some), refrigerator (some), DVD (some), Wi-Fi. In-hotel: restaurant, bar, pool, gym, laundry service, Internet terminal, Wi-Fi hotspot* ▭ *AE, D, MC, V.*

> **WORD OF MOUTH**
>
> "Try the Green Mountain Inn. Luxury rooms are fabulous, and compared to other 'luxury' locations in Stowe you get more for a lot less." —wolfhound

$$$$ **Stone Hill Inn.** This is a contemporary B&B—built in 1998—where classical music plays in the halls. Each soundproof guest room has a king-size bed. Bathrooms have two-sink vanities and two-person whirlpools in front of two-sided fireplaces. (Can you tell it's oriented toward couples?) A pantry is stocked with complimentary snacks and drinks. Common areas include a sitting room and a game room, and the 10 acres of grounds are beautifully landscaped with gardens and waterfalls. The inn is high up Mountain Road not far from the ski resort. **Pros:** clean and new; very comfortable. **Cons:** very expensive; a bit stiff. ✉ *89 Houston Farm Rd.* ☎ *802/253–6282* 🌐 *www.stonehillinn.com* *9 rooms* *In-room: no phone, safe, DVD, Wi-Fi. In-hotel: laundry facilities, Internet terminal, Wi-Fi hotspot, no kids under 18* 💳 *AE, D, DC, MC, V* *BP.*

$ **Stowe Motel & Snowdrift.** This family-owned motel sits on 16 acres across the river from the Stowe recreation path. Accommodations range from one-room studios with small kitchenettes to modern two-bedroom fireplace suites. Late-model mountain bikes, kids' bikes, tricycles, bike trailers, and helmets are available to guests. A game room has Ping-Pong and a pool table. The motel is owned by Peter Ruschp, whose father, Sepp, founded the Mt. Mansfield ski school in 1936. **Pros:** cheap; complimentary bikes and games. **Cons:** basic, motel-style accommodations. ✉ *2043 Mountain Rd. (Rte. 108)* ☎ *802/253–7629 or 800/829–7629* 🌐 *www.stowemotel.com* *52 rooms, 4 suites* *In-room: kitchen (some), refrigerator. In-hotel: tennis court, pools, bicycles, Internet terminal, Wi-Fi hotspot, some pets allowed* 💳 *AE, D, MC, V* *CP.*

$$$$ Fodor's Choice ★ **Stowe Mountain Lodge.** At the base of Stowe's skiing mountain, this 2008 addition to the Stowe lodging scene would be king of the hill for location alone, but a luxury stay here includes ski lodge perks that transcend the competition. Rooms are rustic-meets-contemporary in configurations from studio-size to three-bedroom, many with outdoor terraces. Guests get complimentary access to a fleet of new Mercedes-Benz cars to explore town or drive up the mountain. There's a spa and salon; a massive fitness room; a private 18-hole, Bob Cupp–designed golf course; and a huge heated outdoor pool. A stay includes "wellness lodges" with oversize hot tubs and saunas. There's also a game room for kids, a Ralph Lauren shop, and a most contemporary-looking bar and restaurant. In winter, you can watch the skiers on the mountain from your room and—with gondolas at the doorstep—join them in no time at all. **Pros:** ski valet and perfect setting; great concierge; great bar; activities galore. **Cons:** no separate kids' pool. ✉ *5781 Mountain Rd.* ☎ *802/253–3560* 🌐 *www.stowemountainlodge.com* *139 rooms* *In-room: safe, kitchen (some), refrigerator (some), DVD (some), Wi-Fi. In-hotel: restaurant, room service, bar, golf course, tennis courts, pool, gym, spa, children's programs (ages 2–14), laundry service, Internet terminal, Wi-Fi hotspot, some pets allowed* 💳 *AE, D, DC, MC, V* *EP*

$$$ **Stoweflake Mountain Resort and Spa.** Stoweflake has a lot in common with Topnotch; these two properties have the best and biggest spas in the state (along with Stowe Mountain Lodge) and a contemporary, serious approach to rooms and service. Stoweflake probably has a slightly better spa, perhaps due to the fun of the Bingham hydrotherapy waterfall, a nice 12-foot rock formation cascading into a hot tub. Accommodations range from standard hotel rooms to luxurious suites with fireplaces, refrigerators, double sinks, and whirlpool tubs. One- to three-bedroom town houses sit on the resort's perimeter. The spa overlooks an herb and flower labyrinth and is connected to the fitness center via a faux covered bridge. Stoweflake also hosts Stowe's annual Hot Air Balloon Festival. **Pros:** great spa; excellent service. **Cons:** urban-style resort. ✉ *1746 Mountain Rd., Box 369* ☎ *802/253–7355* 🌐 *www.stoweflake.com* *94 rooms, 30 town houses* *In-room: kitchen (some), refrigerator, DVD, Internet, Wi-Fi (some). In-hotel: 2 restaurants, room service, bar, golf course, tennis courts, pools, gym, spa, bicycles, laundry service, Internet terminal, Wi-Fi hotspot* 💳 *AE, D, DC, MC, V.*

THE CRAFTSBURYS

27 mi northeast of Stowe.

The three villages of the Craftsburys—Craftsbury Common, Craftsbury, and East Craftsbury—are among Vermont's finest and oldest towns. Handsome white houses and barns, the requisite common, and terrific views make them well worth the drive. Craftsbury General Store in Craftsbury Village is a great place to stock up on picnic supplies and local information. The rolling farmland hints at the way Vermont used to be: the area's sheer distance from civilization and its rugged weather have kept most of the state's development farther south.

WHERE TO STAY

$$ **Craftsbury Outdoor Center.** If you think simplicity is bliss and love the outdoors, give this place a try. In winter it's a hub for cross-country skiing (50 mi of groomed trails). In summer there's a giant lake for swimming and boating (sculling and running camps are held here). Two two-story simple lodges have rooms with communal TV/library areas. Many share baths. The simplest rooms have two twin beds and a wooden peg to hang a towel. Meals are served buffet-style. Cabin D is a heavenly setup, three bedrooms right on the edge of the lake. **Pros:** outdoor focus; activities galore. **Cons:** many rooms have a shared bath; many are sparely furnished. ✉ *535 Lost Nation Rd., Craftsbury Common* ☎ *802/586–7767 or 800/729–7751* 🌐 *www.craftsbury.com* *49 rooms, 10 with bath; 4 cabins; 2 suites* *In-room: no phone, no a/c, kitchen (some), refrigerator (some), no TV, Wi-Fi (some). In-hotel: restaurant, tennis court, gym, water sports, bicycles, laundry facilities, Internet terminal, Wi-Fi hotspot, some pets allowed* 💳 *MC, V* *MAP.*

CLOSE UP

Spa Vacations

Vermont's destination spas have come a long way since its *au naturel* mineral springs attracted affluent 19th-century city dwellers looking to escape the heat, but the principle remains the same: a natural place to restore mind and body. There are three big spas in Stowe and one in Manchester.

The **Equinox Resort's Avanyu Spa** (✉ *3567 Rte. 7A, Manchester* ☎ *802/362–4700* 🌐 *equinox.rockresorts.com*), with mahogany doors and beadboard wainscoting, feels like a country estate. At one end is an NCAA-length indoor pool and outdoor hot tub; at the other end are the treatment rooms. The signature 80-minute Spirit of Vermont combines Reiki, reflexology, and massage. In the co-ed relaxation room, spa-goers can nestle into overstuffed chairs next to a two-sided fireplace made of Vermont gneiss. The locker rooms, with marble accents and pottery-bowl wash basins, steam rooms and saunas.

Fodor's Choice★ On of the largest spas in New England, **Spa at Stoweflake** (✉ *1746 Mountain Rd. [Rte. 108], Stowe* ☎ *802/760–1083 or 800/253–2232* 🌐 *www.stoweflake.com*) features a massaging hydrotherapeutic waterfall, a Hungarian mineral pool, 30 treatment rooms, a hair and nail salon, and 120 services, such as the Bingham Falls Renewal, named after a local waterfall. This treatment begins with a seasonal body scrub, rinsed off in a Vichy shower, followed by an aromatherapy oil massage. The spacious men's and women's sanctuaries have saunas, steam rooms, and Jacuzzis.

Spa at Topnotch (✉ *4000 Mountain Rd. [Rte. 108], Stowe* ☎ *802/253–8585* 🌐 *www.topnotchresort.com*) provides an aura of calm, with its birch wood doors and accents, natural light, and cool colors. Signature services include a Vermont wildflower or woodspice treatment, which includes a warm herb wrap, exfoliation, and massage. Locker areas are spacious, with saunas, steam rooms, and Jacuzzis. The spa also has a full-service salon.

The Spa and Wellness Center at Stowe Mountain Lodge (✉ *7412 Mountain Rd. [Rte. 108], Stowe* ☎ *802/253–3560* 🌐 *www.stowemountainlodge.com*) is a 21,000-square-foot facility that opened along with Stowe's newest resort in 2008. Similar to Stoweflake and Topnotch, this is a state-of-the-art facility with 19 treatment rooms. Besides the expected array of facials, scrubs, and massages, the spa offers contemporary services like fitness assessments sound therapy.

At Killington, the **Woods Resort and Spa** (✉ *53 Woods La., Killington* ☎ *802/422–3139* 🌐 *www.woodsresortandspa.com*) is a European spa within an upscale condo complex. At the resort's clubhouse, the spa has a 75-foot indoor pool, sauna, steam room, and weight room. Spa services include massages, hot stone therapies, facials, salt scrubs, maple-sugar polishes, and mud treatments.

Okemo's ski area has a very similar spa facility to Killington's at the **Jackson Gore Resort** (✉ *Okemo Ridge Rd., off Rte. 103, Ludlow* ☎ *802/228–1400* 🌐 *www.okemo.com*), with a slopeside outdoor heated pool, hot tubs, a sauna, steam rooms, a fitness center, and massages like Swedish, deep tissue, and hot stone.

2

JEFFERSONVILLE

36 mi west of Greensboro, 18 mi north of Stowe.

Jeffersonville is just over Smugglers' Notch from Stowe but miles away in feel and attitude. In summer, you can drive over the notch road as it curves precipitously around boulders that have fallen from the cliffs above, then pass open meadows and old farmhouses and sugar shacks on the way down to town. Below the notch, Smugglers' Notch Ski Resort is the hub of activity year-round. Downtown Jeffersonville, once home to an artists' colony, is quiet but has excellent dining and sophisticated art galleries.

EXPLORING

Boyden Valley Winery. West of Jeffersonville in Cambridge, this winery conducts tours and tastings and showcases an excellent selection of Vermont specialty products and local handicrafts, including fine furniture. Its Big Barn Red is satisfyingly full-bodied, and it makes a brilliant line of ice wines. The winery is open daily May to December 10–5 and January to April, Friday to Sunday 10–5. Tours at 11:30 and 1. ✉ *70 Rte. 104 at Rte. 15, Cambridge* ☎ *802/644–8151* 🌐 *boydenvalley.com.*

SPORTS AND THE OUTDOORS

KAYAKING **Green River Canoe & Kayak** (✉ *155 Sterling Ridge Dr., Jeffersonville* ☎ *802/644–8336 or 802/644–8714*), at the junction of Routes 15 and 108 behind Jana's Restaurant, rents canoes and kayaks on the Lamoille River and leads guided canoe trips to Boyden Valley Winery.

LLAMA RIDES **Applecheek Farm** (✉ *567 McFarlane Rd., Hyde Park* ☎ *802/888–4482*) runs daytime and evening (by lantern) hay and sleigh rides, llama treks, and farm tours. **Northern Vermont Llamas** (✉ *766 Lapland Rd., Waterville* ☎ *802/644–2257*) conducts half- and full-day treks from May through October along the cross-country ski trails of Smugglers' Notch. The llamas carry everything, including snacks and lunches. Advance reservations are essential.

SKI AREA ★ **Smugglers' Notch Resort** (✉ *4323 Rte. 108 S* ☎ *802/644–8851 or 800/451–8752* 🌐 *www.smuggs.com*) consistently wins accolades for its family programs. Its children's ski school is one of the best in the country—possibly *the* best—but skiers of all levels come here. Smugglers' was the first ski area in the East to designate a triple-black-diamond run—the Black Hole. All the essentials are available in the village at the base of the Morse Mountain lifts, including lodgings, restaurants, and several shops. Smugglers' has a full roster of summertime programs, including pools, complete with waterfalls and waterslides; the Giant Rapid River Ride (the longest water ride in the state); lawn games; mountain biking and hiking programs; and craft workshops for adults. The Treasures Child Care Center accepts children 6 weeks and older.

The self-contained village has outdoor ice skating and sleigh rides. The numerous snowshoeing programs include family walks and backcountry trips. SmuggsCentral has an indoor pool, hot tub, Funzone playground with slides and miniature golf, and a teen center, open from 5 PM until midnight. In terms of Nordic skiing, the area has 18 mi of groomed and tracked trails and 12 mi of snowshoe trails.

For downhill skiing, Smugglers' has three mountains. The highest, Madonna, with a vertical drop of 2,610 feet, is in the center and connects with a trail network to Sterling (1,500 feet vertical). The third mountain, Morse (1,150 feet vertical), is adjacent to Smugglers' "village" of shops, restaurants, and condos; it's connected to the other peaks by trails and a shuttle bus. The wild, craggy landscape lends a pristine wilderness feel to the skiing experience on the two higher mountains. The tops of each of the mountains have expert terrain—a couple of double-black diamonds (and the only triple-black-diamond trail in the east) make Madonna memorable. Intermediate trails fill the lower sections. Morse has many beginner and advanced beginner trails. Smugglers' 70 trails are served by eight lifts, including six chairs and two surface lifts. Top-to-bottom snowmaking on all three mountains allows for 62% coverage. There are four progression terrain parks, including one for early beginners. Night skiing and snowboarding classes are given at the new Learning and Fun Park.

Ski camps for kids ages 3–17 provide excellent instruction, plus movies, games, and other activities. Wednesday, Thursday, and Saturday are kids' nights at Treasures, with dinner and supervised activities for children ages 3–11.

SHOPPING

The **Green Apple Antique Center** (⊠ *60 Main St.* ☎ *802/644–2989*) has a good bakery in the back of the store. **Smugglers' Notch Antique Center** (⊠ *906 Rte. 108* ☎ *802/644–8321* 🌐 *smugglersnotchantiques.com*) sells antiques and collectibles from 60 dealers in a rambling barn.

CLOTHING — Fodor's Choice ★ **Johnson Woolen Mills** (⊠ *51 Lower Main St. E, 9 mi east of Jeffersonville, Johnson* ☎ *802/635–2271* 🌐 *www.johnsonwoolenmills.com*) is an authentic factory store with deals on woolen blankets, yard goods, and the famous Johnson outerwear.

CRAFTS — **Vermont Rug Makers** (⊠ *933 Rte. 100C, 10 mi east of Jeffersonville, East Johnson* ☎ *802/635–2434*) weaves imaginative rugs and tapestries from fabrics, wools, and exotic materials. Its International Gallery displays rugs and tapestries from around the world.

WHERE TO EAT AND STAY

$ AMERICAN — ✕ **158 Main.** It's worth the short drive from Smuggler's Notch to try the best and most popular restaurant in neighboring Jeffersonville. Menu selections range from sesame-seared yellowfin tuna with jasmine rice and wasabi to the locals' favorite breakfast, the "Two Eggs Basic," which comes with two eggs any style, homemade toast, and home fries for $3.18. Portions are big; prices are not. Sunday brunch is served 8 AM–2 PM. ⊠ *158 Main St.* ☎ *802/644–8100* 🌐 *www.158Main.com* ✍ *Reservations not accepted* ▭ *AE, DC, MC, V* ⊙ *Closed Mon. No dinner Sun.*

$$$$ Fodor's Choice ★ — **Smugglers' Notch Resort.** From watercolor workshops to giant water parks to weeklong camps for kids, this family resort has a plethora of activities. In winter, the main activity is skiing, but children's programs abound. Lodging is in clustered condominium complexes, with the condos set away from the resort center. Rates are packages for three, five, and seven nights and can include use of all resort amenities and lift tickets and ski lessons in season. **Pros:** great place for families and to

learn to ski. **Cons:** not a romantic getaway for couples. ✉ *4232 Rte. 108 S* ☎ *802/644–8851 or 800/451–8752* 🌐 *www.smuggs.com* *550 condominiums* *In-room: no a/c (some). In-hotel: 4 restaurants, bar, tennis courts, pools, children's programs (ages 3–17)* *AE, DC, MC, V.*

2

BURLINGTON

Fodor's Choice ★ *31 mi southwest of Jeffersonville, 76 mi south of Montreal, 349 mi north of New York City, 223 mi northwest of Boston.*

As you drive along Main Street toward downtown Burlington, it's easy to see why the city is so often called one of the most livable small cities in the United States. Downtown is filled with hip restaurants and nightclubs, art galleries, and the Church Street Marketplace—a bustling pedestrian mall with trendy shops, craft vendors, street performers, and sidewalk cafés. Just beyond, Lake Champlain shimmers beneath the towering Adirondacks on the New York shore. On the shores of the lake, Burlington's revitalized waterfront teems with outdoors enthusiasts who stroll along its recreation path and ply the waters in sailboats and motor craft in summer.

EXPLORING

★ **ECHO Leahy Center for Lake Champlain.** Part of the waterfront's revitalization, this aquarium and science center gives kids a chance to check out 100 hands-on, interactive wind and water exhibits and a sunken shipwreck. ✉ *1 College St.* ☎ *802/864–1848* 🌐 *www.echovermont.org* *$9* *Daily 10–5, Thurs. until 8.*

Ethan Allen Homestead. One of the earliest residents of the Intervale area was Ethan Allen, Vermont's Revolutionary-era guerrilla fighter, who remains a captivating figure. Exhibits at the on-site visitor center answer questions about his flamboyant life. The house holds such frontier hallmarks as rough saw-cut boards and an open hearth for cooking. A re-created Colonial kitchen garden resembles the one the Allens would have had. After the tour and multimedia presentation, you can stretch your legs on scenic trails along the Winooski River. ✉ *1 Ethan Allen Homestead, off Rte. 127, north of Burlington* ☎ *802/865–4556* 🌐 *www.ethanallenhomestead.org* *$5* *May–Oct., Mon.–Sat. 10–4, Sun. 1–4.*

University of Vermont. Crowning the hilltop above Burlington is the campus of the University of Vermont, known simply as UVM for the abbreviation of its Latin name, Universitas Viridis Montis—the University of the Green Mountains. With more than 10,000 students, UVM is the state's principal institution of higher learning. The most architecturally interesting buildings face the green, which has a statue of UVM founder Ira Allen, Ethan's brother. ✉ *85 South Prospect St.* ☎ *802/656–3131* 🌐 *www.uvm.edu.*

Magic Hat Brewery. Magic Hat is a leader in Vermont's microbrewery revolution. You can tour their brewery, which puts out 400 bottles a minute, and get free beer samples at their South Burlington spot (on Route 7, before Shelburne). Their Growler Bar has 30 beers on tap. ✉ *5 Bartlett Bay Rd., South Burlington* ☎ *802/658–2739* 🌐 *magichat.*

net *Free* *Open Mon.–Sat. 10–6, Sun. noon–5. Tours Thurs. and Fri. 3, 4, and 5; Sat. noon, 1, 2, and 3; Sun. 1:30.*

SPORTS AND THE OUTDOORS

BEACHES The **North Beaches** (*North Beach Park off North Ave.* *802/864–0123* *Leddy Beach, Leddy Park Rd. off North Ave.*) are on the northern edge of Burlington. Leddy Beach is a good spot for sailboarding.

BIKING Burlington's 10-mi Cycle the City loop runs along the waterfront, connecting several city parks and beaches. It also passes the Community Boathouse and runs within several blocks of downtown restaurants and shops. **North Star Sports** (*100 Main St.* *802/863–3832* *northstar-sports.net*) rents bicycles and provides maps of bicycle routes. **Ski Rack** (*85 Main St.* *802/658–3313 or 800/882–4530* *www.skirack.com*) rents and services bikes and provides maps.

BOATING **Burlington Community Boathouse** (*Foot of College St., Burlington Harbor* *802/865–3377*) rents 19-foot sailboats. **Shoreline Cruise's** *Spirit of Ethan Allen III*, a 500-passenger, three-level cruise vessel, has narrated cruises and dinner and sunset sailings with awesome views of the Adirondacks and Green Mountains. *Burlington Boat House, College and Battery Sts.* *802/862–8300* *www.soea.com* *$12* *Cruises late May–mid-Oct., daily 10–9.*

Waterfront Boat Rentals (*Foot of Maple St. on Perkins Pier, Burlington Harbor* *802/864–4858*) rents kayaks, canoes, rowboats, skiffs, and Boston whalers. Affordable sailing lessons are available.

SKI AREA About 25 mi from Burlington, **Bolton Valley Resort** (*4302 Bolton Valley Access Rd., Bolton* *802/434–3444 or 877/926–5866* *www.boltonvalley.com*) is a family favorite. In addition to 61 downhill ski trails (more than half rated for intermediates), Bolton has night skiing Wednesday–Saturday, 62 mi of cross-country and snowshoe trails, and a sports center.

OFF THE BEATEN PATH

Green Mountain Audubon Nature Center. This is a wonderful place to discover Vermont's outdoor wonders. The center's 300 acres of diverse habitats are a sanctuary for all things wild, and the 5 mi of trails provide an opportunity to explore the workings of differing natural communities. Events include dusk walks, wildflower and birding rambles, nature workshops, and educational activities for children and adults. The center is 18 mi southeast of Burlington. *255 Sherman Hollow Rd., Huntington* *802/434–3068* *Donations accepted* *Grounds daily dawn–dusk, center Mon.–Sat. 8–4.*

SHOPPING

CRAFTS In addition to its popular pottery, **Bennington Potters North** (*127 College St.* *802/863–2221 or 800/205–8033* *www.benningtonpotters.com*) stocks interesting gifts, glassware, furniture, and other housewares. **Vermont State Craft Center/Frog Hollow** (*85 Church St.* *802/863–6458* *www.froghollow.org*) is a nonprofit collective that sells contemporary and traditional crafts by more than 200 Vermont artisans.

MARKETS **Church Street Marketplace** (*2 Church St., Main St. to Pearl St.* *802/863–1648*), a pedestrian thoroughfare, is lined with boutiques, cafés, and street vendors.Look for bargains at the rapidly growing **Essex Outlet Fair**

(✉ *21 Essex Way, Junction of Rtes. 15 and 289, Essex* ☎ *802/878–2851* 🌐 *www.essexshoppes.com*), with such outlets as BCBG, Brooks Brothers, Polo Ralph Lauren, and Levi's, among others.

NIGHTLIFE AND THE ARTS

THE ARTS

The **Fire House Art Gallery** (✉ *135 Church St.* ☎ *802/865–7165* 🌐 *www.burlingtoncityarts.com*) exhibits works by local artists. **Flynn Theatre for the Performing Arts** (✉ *153 Main St.* ☎ *802/652–4500 information; 802/863–5966 tickets* 🌐 *www.flynncenter.org*), a grandiose old structure, is the cultural heart of Burlington; it schedules the Vermont Symphony Orchestra, theater, dance, big-name musicians, and lectures. **St. Michael's Playhouse** (✉ *1 Winooski Park St., Michael's College, Rte. 15, Colchester* ☎ *802/654–2281 box office; 802/654–2617 administrative office* 🌐 *www.smcvt.edu*) stages performances in the McCarthy Arts Center. The **Vermont Symphony Orchestra** (☎ *802/864–5741* 🌐 *www.vso.org*) performs throughout the state year-round and at the Flynn from October through May.

NIGHTLIFE

The music at **Club Metronome** (✉ *188 Main St.* ☎ *802/865–4563* 🌐 *www.clubmetronome.com*) ranges from cutting-edge sounds to funk, blues, and reggae. National and local musicians come to **Higher Ground** (✉ *1214 Williston Rd., South Burlington* ☎ *802/265–0777* 🌐 *www.highergroundmusic.com*). The band Phish got its start at **Nectar's** (✉ *188 Main St.* ☎ *802/658–4771* 🌐 *www.liveatnectars.com*), which is always jumping to the sounds of local bands and never charges a cover. **Ri Ra** (✉ *123 Church St.* ☎ *802/860–9401* 🌐 *www.rira.com*) hosts live entertainment with Irish flair. **Vermont Pub and Brewery** (✉ *144 College St.* ☎ *802/865–0500* 🌐 *www.vermontbrewery.com*) makes its own beer and fruit seltzers and is arguably the most popular spot in town. Folk musicians play here regularly.

WHERE TO EAT

¢–$ PIZZA Fodor's Choice ★

✕ **American Flatbread–Burlington Hearth.** It might be worth going to college in Burlington just to be able to gather with friends at this wildly popular and delicious organic pizza place. On weekends, it's standing room only (seating is first-come, first-served) as kids bustle for house-made brews. The wood-fired clay dome oven combines with all organic ingredients to create masterful results, like the Punctuated Equilibrium, which has kalamata olives, roasted red peppers, local goat cheese, fresh rosemary, red onions, mozzarella, and garlic. Here's to the college life! (There are also locations in Rutland and Waitsfield.) ✉ *115 St. Paul St.* ☎ *802/861–2999* 🌐 *www.americanflatbread.com.com* *Reservations not accepted* ▭ *MC, V.*

$$$–$$$$ AMERICAN Fodor's Choice ★

✕ **Butler's Restaurant and Tavern.** This restaurant at The Essex are staffed by instructors and second-year students at the New England Culinary Institute. The menu offers a range of excellent dishes, from porcini-dusted beef tenderloin in béarnaise sauce to a classic Reuben sandwich. The wine selection pulses with enthusiasm. Dishes can be hit or miss depending on who's cooking, but service is taken very seriously. There is a bounty of local draft beers. Expect only high-quality local ingredients. ✉ *70 Essex Way, Essex Junction* ☎ *802/878–1100* 🌐 *www.vtculinaryresort.com* ▭ *AE, D, DC, MC, V* ⊗ *No dinner Sun. in winter.*

$–$$ CHINESE **A Single Pebble.** The creative, authentic Asian selections served on the first floor of this residential row house include traditional clay-pot dishes as well as wok specialties, such as sesame catfish and kung pao chicken. The dry-fried green beans (sautéed with flecks of pork, black beans, preserved vegetables, and garlic) are a house specialty. All dishes can be made without meat. ✉ *133–135 Bank St.* ☎ *802/865–5200* 🌐 *www.asinglepebble.com* ▭ *AE, D, MC, V* ⏲ *No lunch weekends.*

$–$$ ITALIAN ★ **Trattoria Delia.** Didn't manage to rent that villa in Umbria this year? The next best thing, if your travels bring you to Burlington, is this superb Italian country eatery around the corner from City Hall Park. Game and fresh produce are the stars, as in wild boar braised in red wine, tomatoes, rosemary, and sage served on soft polenta. Wood-grilled items are a specialty. ✉ *152 St. Paul St.* ☎ *802/864–5253* 🌐 *www.trattoriadelia.com* ▭ *AE, D, DC, MC, V* ⏲ *No lunch.*

WHERE TO STAY

$$ **The Essex.** "Vermont's Culinary Resort" is a hotel and conference center about 10 mi from downtown Burlington, with two good restaurants run by the New England Culinary Institute. The best part of a stay here is access to cooking classes offered each day in professional test kitchens on site. Very comfortable Susan Sargent–designed rooms are adorned with her vibrant colors in everything from the wall paint to the pillow covers; 30 rooms have fireplaces. A 19,000-square-foot spa opened in 2009, along with an Orvis-endorsed fly-fishing pond. **Pros:** daily cooking classes; colorful rooms; free airport shuttle. **Cons:** odd location in suburb of Burlington. ✉ *70 Essex Way, off Rte. 289, Essex Junction* ☎ *802/878–1100 or 800/727–4295* 🌐 *www.vtculinaryresort.com* *60 rooms, 60 suites* *In-room: Wi-Fi. In-hotel: 2 restaurants, bar, golf course, tennis courts, pool, spa* ▭ *AE, D, MC, V.*

¢ **G. G. T. Tibet Inn.** This motel probably has the cheapest rates in all of Vermont—$49 for two people in winter and $59 to $69 in summer—but that's not the main attraction. The lure here is the friendly face and evident care of the motel's Tibetan owner, whose name is Kalsang G.G.T. (Yes, G.G.T. really is his real last name.) Buddhist prayer flags flap from the exterior. All rooms have a microwave, a refrigerator, and basic motel furnishings with a big TV. Kalsang's smile at check-in will bring you back. **Pros:** great price; locally owned. **Cons:** no high-speed Internet. ✉ *1860 Shelburne Rd., South Burlington* ☎ *802/863–7110* 🌐 *www.ggttibetinn.com* *21 rooms* *In-room: Internet. In-hotel: pool* ▭ *AE, D, MC, V.*

$ ★ **Willard Street Inn.** High in the historic hill section of Burlington, this ivy-covered grand house with an exterior marble staircase and English gardens incorporates elements of Queen Anne and Colonial/Georgian-Revival styles. The stately foyer, paneled in cherry, leads to a more formal sitting room with velvet drapes. The solarium is bright and sunny with marble floors, many plants, and big velvet couches for contemplating views of Lake Champlain. All the rooms have down comforters and phones; some have lake views and canopied beds. Orange French toast is among the breakfast favorites. **Pros:** lovely old mansion loaded with character and details; friendly attention; common room snacks. **Cons:** long walk to downtown. ✉ *349 S. Willard St.*

CLOSE UP

Vermont by Bike

Road biking in the Green Mountains.

Vermont has more than 14,000 mi of roads, and almost 80% of them are town roads that see little high-speed traffic, making them ideal for scenic bike rides. The state is also threaded with thousands of miles of dirt roads suitable for mountain biking. Although mountain-bike trails and old farm and logging roads wind through the Green Mountain State, most are on private property and are, therefore, not mapped. Several mountain-biking centers around the state have extensive trail networks (and maps) that will keep avid fat-tire fans happy for a few hours or a few days. To road bike in Vermont, you'll want a map and preferably a bicycle with at least 10 gears. The only roads that prohibit cycling are the four-lane highways and Routes 7 and 4 in Rutland.

TOP ROAD BIKING ROUTES:
To make a relatively easy 16-mi loop, begin at the blinker on U.S. 7 in **Shelburne** and follow Mt. Philo Road south to Hinesburg Road, then west to Charlotte. Lake Road, Orchard Road, and Mouth of River Road go past orchards and berry fields. Bostwick Road returns to U.S. 7.

In the heart of the central Green Mountains is a moderate 18-mi loop on Routes 4, 100, and 100A that passes Calvin Coolidge's home in **Plymouth Notch.**

West of **Rutland** is a beautiful 27-mi ride on Routes 140, 30, and 133 that passes swimming holes, then hugs the shore of Lake St. Catherine. Start in Middletown Springs.

A scenic 43-mi ride in the **Northeast Kingdom** passes through pleasant Peacham and the birches and maples of Groton State Forest. Start in Danville and follow Peacham Road, then Routes 302 and 232 and U.S. 2.

For a real test, try the 48-mi ride over **Middlebury and Brandon Gaps** on Routes 125 and 73, which connect via Routes 153 and 100.

Burlington's pedestrian-only Church Street Marketplace and the nearby shores of Lake Champlain are great for exploring.

☎ 802/651–8710 or 800/577–8712 ⊕ www.willardstreetinn.com ⇒ 14 rooms ♿ In-room: Wi-Fi. In-hotel: Internet terminal, Wi-Fi hotspot, no kids under 12 ▭ AE, D, MC, V 🍽 BP.

SHELBURNE

5 mi south of Burlington.

A few miles south of Burlington, the Champlain Valley gives way to fertile farmland, affording stunning views of the rugged Adirondacks across the lake. In the middle of this farmland is the village of Shelburne, chartered in the mid-18th century and partly a bedroom community for Burlington. It has a lively food scene, and the Shelburne Inn and Farms are worth at least a day of exploring.

GETTING HERE AND AROUND

Shelburne is south of Burlington after the town of South Burlington, notable for its very un-Vermont traffic and commercial and fast-food–franchised stretch of U.S. 7. It's easy to confuse Shelburne Farms—2 mi west of town on the lake, with Shelburne Museum, which is just south of town directly on Route 7, but you'll want to make time for both.

EXPLORING

Fodor's Choice ★

Shelburne Farms. Founded in the 1880s as a private estate for two very rich New Yorkers, this 1,400-acre farm is much more than an exquisite landscape: it's an educational and cultural resource center with, among other things, a working dairy farm, a Children's Farmyard (featuring with hands-on workshops throughout the day), daily viewings of various stages of the farm's famous cheese being made, and a bakery whose aroma of fresh bread and pastries is an olfactory treat. It's a brilliant place for parents to expose their kids to the dignity of farm work and the joys of compassionate animal husbandry—indeed, children and adults alike will get a kick out of hunting for eggs in the oversize coop and milking a cow. Frederick Law Olmsted, co-creator of New York's Central Park, designed the magnificent grounds overlooking Lake Champlain. If you fall in love with the scenery, arrange a romantic dinner at the lakefront mansion or spend the night. ⊠ *West of U.S. 7 at 1611 Harbor Rd.* ☎ *802/985–8686* 🌐 *www.shelburnefarms.org* 🎫 *Day pass $6, tour an additional $5* ⏲ *Visitor center and shop daily 10–5; tours mid-May–mid-Oct. (last tour at 3:30); walking trails daily 10–4, weather permitting.*

Fodor's Choice ★ **Shelburne Museum.** You can trace much of New England's history simply by wandering through the 45 acres and 37 buildings of this museum. The outstanding 80,000-object collection of Americana consists of 18th- and 19th-century period homes and furniture, fine and folk art, farm tools, more than 200 carriages and sleighs, John James Audubon prints, an old-fashioned jail, and even a private railroad car from the days of steam. The museum also has an assortment of duck decoys, an old stone cottage, a display of early toys, and the *Ticonderoga,* a side-wheel steamship, grounded amid lawn and trees. ⊠ *5555 Shelburne Rd. (U.S. 7)* ☎ *802/985–3346* 🌐 *www.shelburnemuseum.org* 🎫 *$18* ⏲ *May–Oct., daily 10–5.*

Shelburne Vineyard. South of Shelburn Museum on Route 7 you'll see rows of organically grown vines. Visit the attractive tasting room and learn how wine is made. ⊠ *6308 Shelburne Rd. (Rte. 7)* ☎ *802/985–8222* 🎫 *Free* 🌐 *www.shelburnevineyard.com.*

Vermont Teddy Bear Company. On the 25-minute tour of this fun-filled factory you'll hear more puns than you ever thought possible and learn how a few homemade bears, sold from a cart on Church Street, have turned into a multimillion-dollar business. A children's play tent is set up outdoors in summer, and you can wander the beautiful 57-acre property. ⊠ *6655 Shelburne Rd.* ☎ *802/985–3001* 🌐 *www.vermontteddybear.com* 🎫 *Tour $2* ⏲ *Tours Mon.–Sat. 9:30–5, Sun. 10:30–4; store daily 9–6.*

Shelburne Vineyard. South of Shelburn Museum on Route 7 you'll see rows of organically grown vines. Visit the attractive tasting room and learn how wine is made. ⊠ *6308 Shelburne Rd. (Rte. 7)* ☎ *802/985–8222* 🎫 *Free* 🌐 *www.shelburnevineyard.com*

SHOPPING

When you enter the **Shelburne Country Store** (⊠ *29 Falls Rd., Village Green off U.S. 7* ☎ *802/985–3657*), you'll step back in time. Walk past the potbellied stove and take in the aroma emanating from the fudge neatly piled behind huge antique glass cases. The store specializes in candles, weather vanes, glassware, and local foods.

WHERE TO EAT

$$–$$$ FRENCH ★ **Café Shelburne.** This popular restaurant serves creative French bistro cuisine. Specialties include sweetbreads with a port wine and mushroom sauce in puff pastry and homemade fettuccine with Vermont goat cheese. Desserts such as the sweet chocolate layered terrine and maple-syrup mousse with orange terrine are fabulous. *5573 Shelburne Rd. (U.S. 7) 802/985–3939 802/985–3939 www.cafeshelburne.com AE, MC, V Closed Sun. and Mon. No lunch.*

$$$ AMERICAN Fodor's Choice ★ **The Dining Room at the Inn at Shelburne Farms.** Dinner here will make you dream of F. Scott Fitzgerald. Piano wafts from the library, and you can carry a drink through the rooms of this 1880s mansion, gazing across a long lawn and formal gardens on the shore of dark Lake Champlain—you'll swear Jay Gatsby is about to come down the stairs. Count on just-grown ingredients that come from the market gardens as well as flavorful locally grown venison, beef, pork, and chicken. On weekends a spectacular spread of produce is set up next to a cocktail bar with fresh specialties. The dining room overlooks the lake shore, and Sunday brunch (not served in May) is the area's best. Breakfast is served as well. *1 Harbor Rd. 802/985–8498 www.shelburnefarms.org AE, MC, V Closed mid-May–mid-Oct.*

WHERE TO STAY

$$–$$$ Fodor's Choice ★ **Inn at Shelburne Farms.** It's hard not to feel a little bit like an aristocrat at this exquisite turn-of-the-20th-century Tudor-style inn, one of the most memorable properties in the country. What could easily be a museum with Do Not Touch signs posted everywhere is instead largely your private mansion. Perched at the edge of Lake Champlain, the grounds are vast. Kayak in the lake, laze on the many elegant porches, read the books in the library, or stroll through the elegantly manicured gardens. Views include the distant Adirondacks, as well as the sea of pastures and woods that make up the 1,400-acre working farm on which the mansion is situated. Each room is different, featuring various period wallpapers, high-end antiques, and other decorative touches without making you feel like a player in a costume drama. Teddy Roosevelt slept in the bed in Empire Room, which maintains the original furnishings. The dining room ($$$$) is open for three meals and is romance itself in the evening. **Pros:** stately lakefront setting in a fantastic historic mansion; great service; wonderful value; great restaurant. **Cons:** some may miss not having a TV in the room; closed in winter; must book far in advance. *1 Harbor Rd. 802/985–8498 www.shelburnefarms.org 24 rooms, 17 with bath; 2 cottages In-room: no a/c, no TV. In-hotel: restaurant, tennis court D, DC, MC, V Closed mid-Oct.–mid-May.*

VERGENNES

12 mi south of Shelburne.

Vermont's oldest city, founded in 1788, is also the third oldest in New England. The downtown area is a compact district of Victorian homes and public buildings. Main Street slopes down to Otter Creek Falls, where cannonballs were made during the War of 1812. The statue of

Shelburne Museum's many attractions include the Ticonderoga steamship and other pieces from New England's past.

Thomas MacDonough on the green immortalizes the victor of the Battle of Plattsburgh in 1814.

ESSENTIALS

Visitor Information **Addison County Chamber of Commerce** (✉ *2 Court St., Middlebury* ☎ *802/388–7951 or 800/733–8376* 🌐 *www.midvermont.com*).

OFF THE BEATEN PATH

Lake Champlain Maritime Museum. This museum documents centuries of activity on the historically significant lake. Climb aboard a replica of Benedict Arnold's Revolutionary War gunboat moored in the lake, learn about shipwrecks, and watch craftsmen work at traditional boatbuilding and blacksmithing. Among the exhibits are a nautical archaeology center, a conservation laboratory, and a restaurant. ✉ *Basin Harbor Rd., 7 mi west of Vergennes, Basin Harbor* ☎ *802/475–2022* 🌐 *www.lcmm.org* *$9* *May–mid-Oct., daily 10–5.*

SHOPPING

Dakin Farm (✉ *5797 Rte. 7, 5 mi north of Vergennes* ☎ *800/993–2546* 🌐 *www.dakinfarm.com*) sells cob-smoked ham, aged cheddar cheese, maple syrup made on-site, and other specialty foods. You can visit the ham smokehouse and watch the waxing and sealing of the cheeses.

WHERE TO EAT AND STAY

$–$$ ECLECTIC ✕ **Starry Night Café.** This chic restaurant is one of the hottest spots around, and it's increased in size to meet growing demand. Appetizers include house specials such as honey-chili glazed shrimp and gazpacho. Among the French-meets-Asian entrées are lobster-stuffed sole, pan-seared scallops, and grilled New York steak. ✉ *5371 Rte. 7, 5 mi north* *of Vergennes, Ferrisburg* ☎ *802/877–6316* 🌐 *www.starrynightcafe.com* ▭ *MC, V* ⊙ *Closed Mon. and Tues. No lunch.*

$$$$ Fodor's Choice ★ **Basin Harbor Club.** On 700 acres overlooking Lake Champlain, this ultimate family resort provides luxurious accommodations and a full roster of amenities, including an 18-hole golf course, boating (with a 40-foot tour boat), a 3,200-foot grass airstrip, and daylong children's programs. Some rooms in the guesthouses have fireplaces, decks, or porches. The rustic, camp-like cottages are charming and have one to three bedrooms. The restaurant menu ($–$$$) is classic American, the wine list excellent. Jackets and ties are required in common areas after 6 PM from late June through Labor Day. **Pros:** gorgeous lakeside property; activities galore. **Cons:** open only half the year. ✉ *48 Basin Harbor Rd.* ☎ *802/475–2311 or 800/622–4000* 🌐 *www.basinharbor.com* *36 rooms, 2 suites in 3 guesthouses, 77 cottages* *In-room: no a/c, no TV. In-hotel: 3 restaurants, golf course, tennis courts, pool, gym, bicycles, children's programs (ages 3–15), some pets allowed* ▭ *MC, V* ⊙ *Closed mid-Oct.–mid-May* *BP.*

LAKE CHAMPLAIN ISLANDS

43 mi north of Vergennes, 20 mi northwest of Shelburne, 15 mi northwest of Burlington.

Lake Champlain, which stretches more than 100 mi south from the Canadian border, forms the northern part of the boundary between New York and Vermont. Within it is an elongated archipelago composed of several islands—Isle La Motte, North Hero, Grand Isle, South Hero—and the Alburg Peninsula. With a temperate climate, the islands hold several apple orchards and are a center of water recreation in summer and ice fishing in winter. A scenic drive through the islands on U.S. 2 begins at Interstate 89 and travels north to Alburg Center; Route 78 takes you back to the mainland.

ESSENTIALS

Visitor Information Lake Champlain Regional Chamber of Commerce (✉ *60 Main St., Suite 100, Burlington* ☎ *802/863–3489 or 877/686–5253* 🌐 *www.vermont.org*). **Lake Champlain Islands Chamber of Commerce** (✉ *3537 Rte. 2, Suite 100, North Hero* ☎ *802/372–8400 or 800/262–5226* 🌐 *www.champlainislands.com*).

EXPLORING

Herrmann's Royal Lipizzan Stallions. These beautiful stallions, cousins of the noble white horses bred in Austria since the 16th century, perform intricate dressage maneuvers for delighted spectators for a brief period each summer on North Hero. These acrobatic horses are descendants of animals rescued from the turmoil of World War II by General George Patton and members of the Herrmann family. ✉ *U.S. 2, North Hero* ☎ *802/372–5683* *Barn visits free between performances, shows $17* ⊙ *Early July–late Aug., Thurs. and Fri. at 6 PM, weekends at 2:30 PM.*

Snow Farm Vineyard and Winery. Vermont's first vineyard and grape winery was started here in 1996; today it specializes in nontraditional botanical hybrid grapes to withstand the local climate. Take a self-guided tour, sip some samples in the tasting room, and picnic and listen to music at the free concerts on the lawn Thursday evenings mid-June through Labor Day. ✉ *190 W. Shore Rd., South Hero* ☎ *802/372–9463* *Free* *May–Dec., daily 10–5; tours May–Oct. at 11 and 2* 🌐 *snowfarm.com.*

St. Anne's Shrine. This spot marks the site where French soldiers and Jesuits put ashore in 1665 and built a fort, creating Vermont's first European settlement. The state's first Roman Catholic Mass was celebrated here on July 26, 1666. ✉ *92 St. Anne's Rd., Isle La Motte* ☎ *802/928–3362* *Free* *Mid-May–mid-Oct., daily 9–4.*

SPORTS AND THE OUTDOORS

On the mainland east of the Alburg Peninsula, **Missisquoi National Wildlife Refuge** (✉ *29 Tabor Rd., 36 mi north of Burlington, Swanton* ☎ *802/868–4781* 🌐 *missisquoi.fws.gov*) consists of 6,642 acres of federally protected wetlands, meadows, and woods. It's a beautiful area for bird-watching, canoeing, or walking nature trails. **Sand Bar State Park** (✉ *1215 U.S. 2, South Hero* ☎ *802/893–2825* 🌐 *www.vtstateparks.com/htm/sandbar.cfm* *$3.50* *Mid-May–early-Sept., daily dawn–dusk*) has one of Vermont's best swimming beaches.

BOATING **Apple Island Resort** (✉ *150 South St. [U.S. 2], South Hero* ☎ *802/372–5398*) rents sailboats, rowboats, canoes, kayaks, and motorboats. **Hero's Welcome** (✉ *3537 U.S. 2, North Hero* ☎ *802/372–4161 or 800/372–4376*) rents bikes, canoes, kayaks, and paddleboats.

WHERE TO STAY

$–$$ **North Hero House Inn and Restaurant.** This inn has four buildings right on Lake Champlain, including the 1891 Colonial-revival main house with nine guest rooms, the restaurant, a pub room, library, and sitting room. Many rooms have water views, and each possesses country furnishings and antiques. The beach is a popular spot for lake swimming in summer, and there are boat rentals nearby. The Homestead, Southwind, and Cove House have adjoining rooms that are good for families. Dinner ($$–$$$) is served in the informal glass greenhouse or Colonial-style dining room. **Pros:** relaxed vacation complex; superb lakefront setting. **Cons:** open just May to November. ✉ *U.S. 2, North Hero* ☎ *802/372–4732 or 888/525–3644* 🌐 *www.northherohouse.com* *26 rooms* *In-room: no a/c (some). In-hotel: restaurant, bar* *AE, MC, V* *CP* *Closed Dec.–Apr.*

$ **Ruthcliffe Lodge.** Good food and splendid scenery make this off-the-beaten-path motel directly on Lake Champlain a great value. If you're looking for a cheap, DIY summer place to take in the scenery, canoe the lake, or bicycle, this will do quite nicely. The lodge is on Isle La Motte—a rarely visited island. Rooms are very clean and simple: bed, dresser, night table, and stenciled wall border. Owner-chef Mark Infante specializes in Italian pasta, fish, and meat dishes ($$); there's alfresco seating that overlooks a lawn leading to the lakeshore. A full breakfast is included. **Pros:** inexpensive; serene setting; laid-back. **Cons:** rooms simple, not luxurious. ✉ *1002 Quarry Rd., Isle La Motte* ☎ *802/928–*

3200 🌐 www.ruthcliffe.com *7 rooms* *In-hotel: restaurant, bicycles* *MC, V* *BP* *Closed Columbus Day–mid-May.*

MONTGOMERY/JAY

32 mi east of St. Albans, 51 mi northeast of Burlington.

Montgomery is a small village near the Canadian border and Jay Peak ski resort. Amid the surrounding countryside are seven covered bridges.

OFF THE BEATEN PATH

Lake Memphremagog. Vermont's second-largest lake, Lake Memphremagog extends from Newport 33 mi north into Canada. Watch the sun set from the deck of the **East Side Restaurant** (✉ *47 Landingd St., Newport* ☎ *802/334–2340*), which serves excellent burgers and prime rib. Prouty Beach in Newport has camping facilities, tennis courts, and paddleboat and canoe rentals. ✉ *Veterans Ave.* ☎ *802/334–7951.*

SPORTS AND THE OUTDOORS

SKI AREA

Hazen's Notch Cross Country Ski Center and B&B (✉ *4850 Rte. 58* ☎ *802/326–4799*), delightfully remote at any time of the year, has 40 mi of marked and groomed trails and rents equipment and snowshoes.

★ Sticking up out of the flat farmland, **Jay Peak** (✉ *4850 Rte. 242, Jay* ☎ *802/988–2611; 800/451–4449 outside VT* 🌐 *www.jaypeakresort.com*) averages 355 inches of snow a year—more than any other Vermont ski area. Its proximity to Québec attracts Montréalers and discourages eastern seaboarders; hence, the prices are moderate and the lift lines shorter than at other resorts. The area is renowned for its glade skiing and powder.

Off-season, Jay Peak runs tram rides to the summit from mid-June through Labor Day and mid-September through Columbus Day ($10). The child-care center for youngsters ages 2–7 is open from 9 AM to 9 PM. If you're staying at Hotel Jay and Jay Peak Condominiums, you receive this nursery care free, as well as evening care and supervised dining at the hotel. Infant care is available on a fee basis with advanced reservations. In the winter, snowshoes can be rented, and guided walks are led by a naturalist. Telemark rentals and instruction are available.

Jay Peak has two interconnected mountains for downhill skiing, the highest reaching nearly 4,000 feet with a vertical drop of 2,153 feet. The smaller mountain has straight-fall-line, expert terrain that eases mid-mountain into an intermediate pitch. The main peak is served by Vermont's only tramway and transports skiers to meandering but challenging intermediate trails. Beginners should stick near the bottom on trails off the Metro lift. Weekdays at 9:30 AM and 1:30 PM, mountain ambassadors conduct a free tour. The area's 76 trails, including 21 glades and two chutes, are served by eight lifts, including the tram and the longest detachable quad in the East. The area also has two quads, a triple, and a double chairlift; one T-bar; and a moving carpet. Jay has 80% snowmaking coverage. The area also has four terrain parks, each rated for different abilities. There are ski-school programs for children ages 3–18.

2

SHOPPING

Trout River Store (✉ *91 Main St., Montgomery Center* ☎ *802/326–3058*), an old-time country store with an antique soda fountain, is a great place to stock up on picnic supplies, eat a hearty bowl of soup and an overstuffed sandwich, and check out local crafts.

WHERE TO STAY

$$$$ **Hotel Jay & Jay Peak Condominiums.** Centrally located in the ski resort's base area, the hotel and its simply furnished rooms are a favorite for families. Kids 13 and under stay and eat free, and during nonholiday times, they can ski free, too. Farther afield (but still mostly slope-side) are condominiums and town houses that range from studio to five-bedroom, with fireplaces, modern kitchens, and washer/dryers. Complimentary child care is provided to hotel and condo guests 9 AM–4 PM for kids ages 2–7. **Pros:** great for skiers and summer mountain adventurers. **Cons:** not an intimate, traditional Vermont stay. ✉ *4850 Rte. 242* ☎ *802/988–2611; 800/451–4449 outside VT* 🌐 *www.jaypeakresort.com* *48 rooms, 94 condominiums* *In-room: no a/c. In-hotel: restaurant, bar, tennis courts, pool* *AE, D, DC, MC, V* *MAP.*

$ **Inn on Trout River.** Guest rooms at this 100-year-old riverside inn sport a country-cottage style, and all have down quilts and flannel sheets in winter. Lemoine's Restaurant ($–$$) specializes in American and Continental fare. Try the raviolini stuffed with Vermont cheddar cheese and walnuts topped with pesto or the medallions of pork tenderloin in a maple syrup demi-glace. Hobo's Café ($$), also at the inn, serves simpler fare. **Pros:** traditional B&B. **Cons:** rooms heavy on the florals. ✉ *241 S. Main St., Montgomery Center* ☎ *802/326–4391 or 800/338–7049* 🌐 *www.troutinn.com* *9 rooms, 1 suite* *In-room: no a/c, no TV. In-hotel: restaurant, bar* *AE, DC, MC, V* *BP, MAP.*

EN ROUTE

Routes 14, 5, 58, and 100 make a scenic drive around the **Northeast Kingdom**, named for the remoteness and stalwart independence that have helped preserve its rural nature. You can extend the loop and head east on Route 105 to the city of Newport on Lake Memphremagog. Some of the most unspoiled areas in all Vermont are on the drive south from Newport on either U.S. 5 or Interstate 91 (the latter is faster, but the former is prettier).

LAKE WILLOUGHBY

30 mi southeast of Montgomery (summer route; 50 mi by winter route), 28 mi north of St. Johnsbury.

The cliffs of Mt. Pisgah and Mt. Hor drop to the edge of Lake Willoughby on opposite shores, giving this beautiful, deep, glacially carved lake a striking resemblance to a Norwegian fjord. The trails to the top of Mt. Pisgah reward hikers with glorious views.

EXPLORING

★ **Bread and Puppet Museum.** This ramshackle barn houses a surrealistic collection of props used by the world-renowned Bread and Puppet Theater. The troupe has been performing social and political commentary with the towering (they're supported by people on stilts), eerily expressive puppets for about 30 years and performs at the museum every Sunday June–August at 3. ✉ *753 Heights Rd. (Rte. 122), 1 mi east of Rte. 16, Glover* ☎ *802/525–3031* 🌐 *www.breadandpuppet.org* 🎫 *Donations accepted* ⏲ *June–Oct., daily 10–6.*

Cabot Creamery. The major cheese producer in the state, midway between Barre and St. Johnsbury, has a visitor center with an audiovisual presentation about the dairy and cheese industry. You can taste samples, purchase cheese and other Vermont products, and tour the plant. ✉ *2870 Main St. (Rte. 215), 3 mi north of U.S. 2, Cabot* ☎ *800/837–4261* 🌐 *www.cabotcheese.coop* 🎫 *$2* ⏲ *June–Oct., daily 9–5; Nov., Dec., and Feb.–May, Mon.–Sat. 9–4; Jan., Mon.–Sat. 10–4; call ahead to check cheese-making days.*

EAST BURKE

17 mi south of Lake Willoughby.

Once a sleepy village, East Burke is now the Northeast Kingdom's outdoor-activity hub. The Kingdom Trails attract thousands of mountain bikers in summer and fall. In winter, many trails are groomed for cross-country skiing.

ESSENTIALS

Visitor Information Kingdom Trails Association (📫 *Box 204, East Burke 05832* ☎ *802/626–0737* 🌐 *www.kingdomtrails.org*).

SPORTS AND THE OUTDOORS

Contact the Kingdom Trails Association for details and maps.

East Burke Sports (✉ *439 Rte. 114, East Burke* ☎ *802/626–3215* 🌐 *www.eastburkesports.com*) rents mountain bikes, kayaks, and skis, and provides guides for cycling, hiking, paddling, skiing, and snowshoeing. **Village Sport Shop** (✉ *511 Broad St., Lyndonville* ☎ *802/626–8448* 🌐 *www.villagesportshop.com*) rents bikes, canoes, kayaks, paddleboats, rollerblades, skis, and snowshoes.

SKI AREA About an hour's drive from Montpelier is **Burke Mountain** (✉ *1 Mountain Rd., East Burke* ☎ *802/626–3322* 🌐 *www.skiburke.com*). Racers stick to the Training Slope, served by its own poma lift. The other 44 trails and glades are a quiet playground.

WHERE TO EAT AND STAY

$–$$ AMERICAN ✕ **River Garden Café.** You can eat lunch, dinner, or brunch outdoors on the enclosed porch, on the patio amid perennial gardens, or inside this bright and cheerful café. The excellent fare includes lamb tenderloin, warm artichoke dip, bruschetta, pastas, and fresh fish, and the popular salad dressing is bottled for sale. ✉ *427 Rte. 114, East Burke* ☎ *802/626–3514* 🌐 *www.rivergardencafe.com* 💳 *AE, D, MC, V* ⏲ *Closed Mon. and Tues. Nov.–Apr.*

$$ 🏨 **Wildflower Inn.** The hilltop views are breathtaking at this rambling, family-oriented complex of old farm buildings on 570 acres. Guest rooms in the restored Federal-style main house and three other buildings are furnished with reproductions and contemporary furnishings. In summer, supervised day and evening programs engage the kids, allowing parents to explore the many nature trails on their own. You can play

DID YOU KNOW?

Long and skinny Lake Champlain is sometimes called the sixth Great Lake. Several small islands, like Grand Isle, are popular seasonal getaways in warm weather.

Catch a show and some social commentary at the Bread and Puppet theater in summer, or visit the museum year-round.

with farm animals at the petting barn, go biking, and play tennis and volleyball. In winter sleigh rides, snowshoeing, and cross-country skiing are popular. Junipers ($–$$; closed Sunday) serves comfort food such as meat loaf and lemon herb chicken and offers a kids' menu. **Pros:** mega kid-friendly nature resort; best of the Northeast Kingdom's expansiveness; relaxed. **Cons:** most rooms are simply furnished. ✉ *2059 Darling Hill Rd., 5 mi west of East Burke, Lyndonville* ☎ *802/626–8310 or 800/627–8310* 🌐 *www.wildflowerinn.com* *10 rooms, 13 suites, 1 cottage* *In-room: no a/c (some), kitchen (some), no TV. In-hotel: restaurant, tennis court, pool, children's programs (ages infant–17)* *MC, V* *Closed Apr. and Nov.* *BP.*

ST. JOHNSBURY

16 mi south of East Burke, 39 mi northeast of Montpelier.

St. Johnsbury, the southern gateway to the Northeast Kingdom, was chartered in 1786. But its identity was established after 1830, when Thaddeus Fairbanks invented the platform scale, a device that revolutionized weighing methods. The Fairbanks family's philanthropic efforts gave the city a strong cultural and architectural imprint. Today St. J, as the locals call it, is the friendly, adventure-sports-happy hub of the Northeast Kingdom.

EXPLORING

★ **Dog Mountain.** Artist Stephen Huneck is famous for his cheery folk art sculptures and paintings of dogs. Much more than an art gallery–gift shop, this deeply moving place is complete with a chapel where animal lovers can reflect on their deceased and living pets. Above all, this is a place to bring your dog: there is a swimming pond, an agility course, and hiking trails. ✉ *143 Parks Rd., off Spaulding Rd.* ☎ *800/449–2580* 🌐 *www.dogmt.com* 🎫 *Free* 🕙 *Daily 10–5.*

Fodor's Choice ★

Fairbanks Museum and Planetarium. This odd and deeply thrilling little museum displays the eccentric collection of Franklin Fairbanks, who surely had one of the most inquisitive minds in American history. He built this magnificent barrel-vaulted two-level gallery in 1889 just to house the specimens of plants, animals, mounted birds, mammals, reptiles, plants, and collections of folk art and dolls—and a seemingly unending variety of beautifully mounted curios—he had picked up around the world. The museum showcases over 175,000 items, but it's surprisingly easy to feast your eyes on everything here without getting a museum headache. There's also a popular 45-seat planetarium, the state's only public planetarium; as well the Eye on the Sky Weather Gallery, home to live NPR weather broadcasts. ✉ *1302 Main St.* ☎ *802/748–2372* 🌐 *www.fairbanksmuseum.org* 🎫 *Museum $6, planetarium $5* 🕙 *May–mid-Oct., Mon.–Sat. 9–5, Sun. 1–5; mid-Oct.–Apr., Tues.–Sat. 9–5, Sun. 1–5. Planetarium shows July and Aug., daily at 11 and 1:30; Sept.–June, weekends at 1:30.*

Fodor's Choice ★

St. Johnsbury Athenaeum. With its dark, rich paneling, polished Victorian woodwork, and ornate circular staircases, this building is both the town library (one of the nicest you're likely to ever come across) and one of the oldest art galleries in the country, housing more than 100 original works mainly of the Hudson River school. Albert Bierstadt's enormous (15 feet by 10 feet) *Domes of Yosemite* dominates the beautiful painting gallery. ✉ *1171 Main St.* ☎ *802/748–8291* 🌐 *www.stjathenaeum.org* 🎫 *Free* 🕙 *Mon. and Wed. 10–8; Tues., Thurs., and Fri. 10–5:30; Sat. 9:30–4.*

★ **Dog Mountain.** Artist Stephen Huneck is famous for his cheery folk art sculptures and paintings of dogs. Much more than an art gallery–gift shop, this deeply moving place is complete with a chapel where animal lovers can reflect on their deceased and living pets. Above all, this is a place to bring your dog: there is a swimming pond, an agility course, and hiking trails. ✉ *143 Parks Rd., off Spaulding Rd.* ☎ *800/449–2580* 🌐 *www.dogmt.com* 🎫 *Free* 🕙 *Daily 10–5.*

OFF THE BEATEN PATH

Peacham. Tiny Peacham, 10 mi southwest of St. Johnsbury, is on almost every tour group's list of "must-sees." With views extending to the White Mountains of New Hampshire and a white-steeple church, Peacham is perhaps the most photographed town in New England. The movie adaptation of *Ethan Frome,* starring Liam Neeson, was filmed here. One of the town's gathering spots, the **Peacham Store** (✉ *641 Bayley-Hazen Rd.* ☎ *802/592–3310* 🌐 *www.peacham.net*), sells specialty soups and stews. Next door, the **Peacham Corner Guild** sells local handcrafts.

WHERE TO STAY

$$$ ★ **Rabbit Hill Inn.** Few inns in New England have the word-of-mouth buzz that Rabbit Hill seems to earn from satisfied guests. Most of the spacious, elegant rooms have fireplaces, two-person whirlpool tubs, and

views of the Connecticut River and New Hampshire's White Mountains. The grounds have 10 acres of walking trails. The intimate candlelit dining room serves a three- or five-course prix-fixe dinner ($$$$) featuring contemporary new American and regional dishes such as grilled venison loin with cranberry-juniper orange glaze. Afternoon tea in the parlor, horseshoes, garden strolls—this inn is great for small pleasures. **Pros:** attractive, spacious rooms; lovely grounds; good food. **Cons:** might be too quiet a setting for some. ✉ *Rte. 18, 11 mi south of St. Johnsbury, Lower Waterford* ☎ *802/748–5168 or 800/762–8669* 🌐 *www.rabbithillinn.com* *19 rooms* *In-room: no TV. In-hotel: restaurant, bar, no kids under 14* 💳 *AE, D, MC, V* ⏲ *Closed 1st 3 wks in Apr., 1st 2 wks in Nov.* *BP, MAP.*

3

New Hampshire

WORD OF MOUTH

"A tiny bit south of Peterborough, at Rindge, we stopped at [JP Stephens] for a bowl of beef stew soup. We sat by a large picture window with a quintessential view over a little bridge covered with leaves leading to a little white cottage beside a pond reflecting both it and the surrounding autumn leaves. Perfect!"

—mazj

WELCOME TO NEW HAMPSHIRE

TOP REASONS TO GO

★ **The White Mountains:** Great for hiking and skiing, these rugged, dramatic peaks and notches are unforgettable.

★ **Lake Winnipesaukee:** Water parks, arcades, boat cruises, and classic summer camps make for a family fun summer.

★ **Fall Foliage:** Head to the Kancamagus Highway in the fall for one of America's best drives or seek out a lesser-known route that's just as stunning.

★ **Portsmouth:** Less than an hour from Boston, this great American city has coastline allure, colorful Colonial architecture, and the right amount of energy.

★ **Pristine Towns:** Jaffrey Center, Walpole, Tamworth, Center Sandwich, and Jackson are among the most charming tiny villages in New England.

1 The Seacoast. You can find historical sites, hopping bars, beaches, whale-watching, and deep-sea fishing all packed in along New Hampshire's 18 mi of coastline. Hampton Beach is the center of summertime activities, while Portsmouth is a hub of nightlife, dining, and Colonial history.

2 Lakes Region. Throughout central New Hampshire are lakes and more lakes. The largest, Lake Winnipesaukee, has 240 mi of coastline and attracts all sorts of water sports enthusiasts, but there are many more secluded and quiet lakes with enchanting B&Bs where relaxation is the main activity.

3 The White Mountains. Skiing, snowshoeing, and snowboarding in the winter; hiking, biking, and riding scenic railways in the summer—the Whites, as locals call their mountains, have plenty of natural wonders within a stone's throw from the roads, but other spots call for lung-busting hikes. Mount Washington, the tallest mountain in the Northeast, can be conquered by trail, train, or car.

4 Dartmouth-Lake Sunapee. Quiet villages can be found throughout the region. Many of them are barely removed from Colonial times, but some thrive as centers of arts and education and are filled with quaint shops. Hanover, the home of 240-year-old Dartmouth College, retains that true New England college town feel, with ivy-draped buildings and cobblestone walkways. Lake Sunapee is a wonderful place to swim, fish, or enjoy a cruise.

5 The Monadnocks and Merrimack Valley. The southwest region of the Granite State exemplifies both the vanguards of new technology economic activity—the cities of Manchester and Nashua—and the values of old New England in the hills surrounding Mt. Monadnock. High-tech firms have set up shop in old brick factory buildings while small towns still celebrate tradition and history.

GETTING ORIENTED

Although New Hampshire has three interstates running through it (I–95, I–93, and I–89), most of its regions are accessible only on smaller roads. From Boston or Portland, Maine, I–95 provides the best access to Portsmouth and the beaches along the coast, though many people like to drive along Route 1A, which parallels the coast. North of Portsmouth, Route 16 leads to the White Mountains, whose precipitous peaks seem to rise out of nowhere, and the lakes region, home to Lake Winnipesaukee. From there I–93 cuts north toward Franconia and Littleton and south into Concord, Manchester, and Nashua. State roads east and north of I–93 lead to Dixville Notch, which casts the first vote in presidential elections, and the Connecticut Lakes. Following the Connecticut River takes you to Hanover, home of Dartmouth College, Claremont, Charleston, Walpole, and Keene. From Concord, travelers head west to reach the Monadnock Region.

NEW HAMPSHIRE PLANNER

When to Go

Summer and fall are the best times to visit most of New Hampshire. Winter is a great time to travel to the White Mountains, but most other tourist sites in the state, including the Portsmouth museums and many attractions in the Lakes Region, are closed due to snow and cold weather. In summer, people flock to beaches, mountain trails, and lake boat ramps. In the cities, festivals showcase music, theater, and crafts. Fall brings leaf-peepers, especially to the White Mountains and along the Kancamagus Highway (Route 112). Skiers and snowboarders take to the slopes in winter, when Christmas lights and carnivals brighten the long, dark nights. Spring's unpredictable weather—along with April's mud and late May's black flies—tends to deter visitors. Still, the season has its joys, not the least of which is the appearance of the state flower, the purple lilac, from mid-May to early June as well as colorful rhododendrons.

Getting Here and Around

Air Travel: Manchester Boston Regional Airport is the state's largest and has nonstop service to more than 20 cities. Boston's Logan Airport is within one to three hours of most places in New Hampshire as is Bradley International in Hartford, Connecticut.

Car Travel: New Hampshire is an easy drive north from Boston and serves as a good base for exploring northern New England. Many destinations are near major highways, so getting around by car is a great way to travel. Interstate 93 stretches from Boston to Littleton and on into neighboring Vermont. Interstate 89 will get you from Concord to Hanover and eventually to Burlington, Vermont. To the east, Interstate 95, which is a toll road, passes through southern New Hampshire's coastal area on its way from Massachusetts to Maine. Throughout the state are quiet back country lanes and winding roads that might take a little longer but can make for some of the best parts of the journey.

Speed limits on interstate and limited-access highways are usually 65 mph, except in heavily settled areas, where 55 mph is the norm. On state and U.S. routes, speed limits vary considerably. On any given stretch, the limit may be anywhere from 25 mph to 55 mph, so watch the signs carefully. Right turns on red lights are permitted unless otherwise indicated.

Train Travel: Amtrak (🌐 *www.amtrak.com*) runs its Downeaster service from Boston to Portland, Maine, with stops in Exeter, Durham, and Dover.

Planning Your Time

Some people come to New Hampshire to hike or ski the mountains, fish and sail the lakes, or cycle along the back roads. Others prefer to drive through scenic towns, visiting museums and shops. Although New Hampshire is a small state, roads curve around lakes and mountains, making distances longer than they appear. You can get a taste of the coast, lake, and mountain areas in three to five days; eight days gives you time to make a more complete loop.

About the Restaurants

New Hampshire prides itself on seafood—not just lobster but also salmon pie, steamed mussels, fried clams, and seared tuna. Across the state you'll find country taverns with upscale Continental and American menus, many of them embracing regional ingredients. Alongside a growing number of contemporary eateries are such state traditions as greasy-spoon diners, pizzerias, and pubs that serve hearty comfort fare. Reservations are almost never required, and dress is casual in nearly every eatery.

About the Hotels

In the mid-19th century, wealthy Bostonians retreated to imposing New Hampshire country homes in summer months. Grand hotels were built across the state, especially in the White Mountains, when the area competed with Saratoga Springs, Newport, and Bar Harbor to draw the nation's elite vacationers. Today a handful of these hotel-resorts survive, with their large cooking staffs and tradition of top-notch service. Many of the vacation houses have been converted into inns and B&Bs. The smallest have only a couple of rooms and are typically done in period style. The largest contain 30 or more rooms and suites and have in-room fireplaces and even hot tubs. You'll also find a great many well-kept, often family-owned motor lodges—particularly in the White Mountains and Lakes regions. In the ski areas expect the usual ski condos and lodges. In the Merrimack River valley, as well as along major highways, chain hotels and motels prevail. There are numerous campgrounds across the state, which accommodate RVs as well. The White Mountains provide an excellent base for camping and hiking.

WHAT IT COSTS

	¢	$	$$	$$$	$$$$
Restaurants	under $10	$10–$16	$17–$24	$25–$35	over $35
Hotels	under $100	$100–$149	$150–$199	$200–$250	over $250

Prices are per person, for a main course at dinner. Prices are for a standard double room during peak season and not including tax or gratuities. Some inns add a 15%–18% service charge.

Outdoor Activities

Hitting the trails by boot and ski, fishing, kayaking and canoeing, biking, or just plain old walking will undoubtedly be a part of your visit.

Biking: Many ski resorts in the White Mountains offer mountain biking opportunities, providing chairlift rides to the top and trails for all skill levels at the bottom. Some of the state's best road biking is along the Kancamagus Highway and around Lake Sunapee.

Hiking: For the more adventurous, hiking the trails in the White Mountains or along the Appalachian Trail, also known as the Long Trail, is their reason for visiting. For those more interested in less arduous treks, there are plenty of day hikes in the White Mountain National Forest and state parks such as Pisgah, the state's largest, in Cheshire County, the Crawford Notch and Franconia Notch state parks in the Whites, and Mt. Monadnock

Skiing: Ski areas abound in New Hampshire—try Mt. Sunapee, Waterville Valley, Loon Mountain, or Canon Mountain. For cross-country skiing, nothing beats Gunstock Mountain Resort, with 32 mi of trails, also open for snowshoeing. Or visit Franconia Village, which has 37 mi of cross-country trails.

3

NEW HAMPSHIRE FALL FOLIAGE DRIVE

With its quaint villages graced with green commons, white town halls, and covered bridges, southwestern New Hampshire is dominated by the imposing rocky summit of Mt. Monadnock and brilliant colors in fall. Kancamagus Highway is another classic foliage route, but for more solitude and less traffic, try this more accessible route that peaks a few weeks later than the state's far north.

The Granite State is the second most forested state in the nation; by Columbus Day, the colors of the leaves of its maple, birch, elm, oak, beech, and ash trees range from green to gold, purple to red, and orange to auburn. Routes 12, 101, 202, and 124 compose a loop around Mt. Monadnock, named for its solitary type of mountain. Start in Keene with a cup of coffee at Prime Roast; for New Hampshire–made products, take a walk on Main Street or detour west on Route 9 to reach **Stonewall Farm** for something more country.

BEST TIME TO GO

Early October is best time to view foliage in southern New Hampshire, but the time can vary by up to four weeks. Call or check online for daily leaf changes (🌐 *www.visitnh.gov* ☎ *800/258–3608*).

PLANNING YOUR TIME

Expect to travel about 55 mi. The journey can take up to a full day if you stop to explore along the way.

From Keene, travel east on Route 101 through Dublin and over Pack Monadnock, a 2,290-foot peak (not to be confused with the 3,165-foot Grand, or Mt. Monadnock). In quaint **Peterborough**, browse the local stores, whose attitude and selection matches the state's independent spirit.

Then turn south on Route 202, stopping at **Colls Farmstand** for some seasonal treats before reaching Jaffrey Village. Just west on 124, in historic Jaffrey Center, be sure to visit the **Meeting House Cemetery** on the common where author Willa Cather is buried. A side trip, 4 mi south on 202, leads to the majestic **Cathedral of the Pines** in Rindge, one of the best places in the region for foliage viewing because the evergreens offset the brilliant shades of red.

Heading west on 124, you can take Dublin Road to the main entrance of **Monadnock State Park** or continue along to the Old Toll Road parking area for one of the most popular routes up the mountain, the **Halfway House Trail**. All of the hiking trails have great views, including the area's many lakes. Continuing on 124 you come to Fitzwilliam and Route 12; turn north back to Keene or, if your legs still have energy left to burn, continue west to Troy for some dancing at **East Hill Farm**.

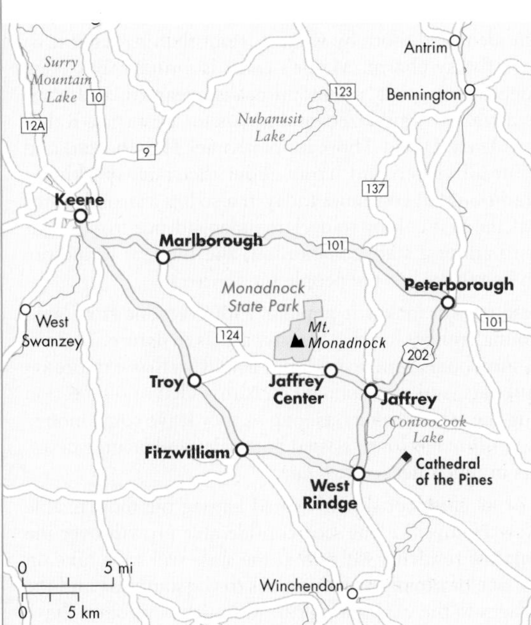

NEED A BREAK?

Stonewall Farm
(✉ *242 Chesterfield Rd., Keene* ☎ *603/357–7278* 🌐 *www.stonewallfarm.org* 🕒 *Grounds dusk–dawn. Learning center and gift shop weekdays 8:30–4:30. Farm stand May–Oct., daily 10–7*) is a nonprofit working farm that teaches visitors about the importance of agriculture. Fall activities for kids include horse-drawn hayrides and a pumpkin patch.

Colls Farmstand
(✉ *16 Colls Farm Rd., Jaffrey* ☎ *603/532–7540* 🌐 *www.collsfarmllc.com* 🕒 *Mon.–Sat. 9–6, Sun. 9–2*) carries maple syrup, jams, and other New Hampshire–made products.

East Hill Farm
(✉ *460 Monadnock St., Troy* ☎ *603/242–6495* 🌐 *www.east-hill-farm.com*) is a working farm and B&B that also offers country and square dancing several days of the week.

3

Updated by
Robert Audette

New Hampshire residents have often been called cantankerous, but beneath that crusty exterior is often hospitality and friendliness. The state's motto was coined by New Hampshire native General ;John Stark, who led the Colonial Army in its hard-fought battle of Bennington, Vermont, in 1777. "Live free or die; death is not the worst of evils," he said, in a letter written 20 years after the battle. The residents of the Granite State have taken "Live Free or Die" to heart, defining themselves by that principle for more than 200 years.

The state is often identified more by what it is not than by what it is. It lacks Vermont's folksy charm. Maine's coast is grander. But New Hampshire's independent spirit, mountain peaks, clear air, and sparkling lakes have attracted trailblazers and artists for centuries. Ralph Waldo Emerson, Henry David Thoreau, Nathaniel Hawthorne, and Louisa May Alcott all visited and wrote about the state, sparking a strong literary tradition that continues today. It also has a strong political history: it was the first colony to declare independence from Great Britain, the first to adopt a state constitution, and the first to require that constitution be referred to the people for approval.

The state's diverse terrain makes it popular with everyone from avid adventurers to young families looking for easy access to nature. You can hike, climb, ski, snowboard, snowshoe, and fish as well as explore on snowmobiles, sailboats, and mountain bikes. Natives have no objection to others enjoying the state's beauty as long as they leave some money behind. New Hampshire has long resisted both sales and income taxes, so tourism brings in much-needed revenue.

With a number of its cities consistently rated among the most livable in the nation, New Hampshire has seen considerable growth over the past decade. Longtime residents worry that the state will soon take on two personalities: one of rapidly growing cities to the southeast and the other of quiet villages to the west and north. Although newcomers have brought change, the independent nature of the people and the state's natural beauty remain constant.

THE SEACOAST

3

New Hampshire's 18-mi stretch of coastline packs in a wealth of scenery and diversions. The honky-tonk of Hampton Beach gets plenty of attention, good and bad, but first-timers are often surprised by the significant chunk of shoreline that remains pristine—especially through the town of Rye. This section begins in the regional hub, Portsmouth, cuts down the coast to the beaches, branches inland to the prep-school town of Exeter, and runs back up north through Dover, Durham (home of the University of New Hampshire), and Rochester. From here it's a short drive to the Lakes Region.

ESSENTIALS

Visitor Information **Seacoast New Hampshire** (🌐 *www.seacoastnh.com*).

PORTSMOUTH

★ *47 mi southeast of Concord; 50 mi southwest of Portland, Maine; 56 mi north of Boston.*

Settled in 1623 as Strawbery Banke, Portsmouth became a prosperous port before the Revolutionary War, and, like similarly wealthy Newport, Rhode Island, it harbored many Tory sympathizers throughout the campaign. Filled with grand residential architecture spanning the 18th through early 20th centuries, this city of 23,000 has many house museums, including the collection of 40-plus buildings that make up the Strawbery Banke Museum. With hip eateries, quirky shops, swank cocktail bars, respected theaters, and jumping live-music venues, this sheltered harbor city is a hot destination. Downtown, especially around elegant Market Square, buzzes with conviviality.

GETTING HERE AND AROUND

Interstate 95 and Route 1 run through Portsmouth. From the west take Route 101 and from the north take Route 16. Amtrak runs through Durham, which is a short drive to the coast. Once in Portsmouth, you can walk about the downtown, though you'll want a car for further attractions. COAST Trolley's downtown loop hits most of the city's historical sights during the summer.

ESSENTIALS

Bus and Trolley **COAST Bus** (☎ *603/743–5777* 🌐 *www.coastbus.org*).

Taxi **Anchor Taxi** (☎ *603/436–1888*). **Portsmouth Taxi** (☎ *603/431–6811*).

Visitor Information **Greater Portsmouth Chamber of Commerce** (✉ *500 Market St., Portsmouth* ☎ *603/436–3988* 🌐 *www.portsmouthchamber.org*).

EXPLORING

TOP ATTRACTIONS

John Paul Jones House. The yellow, hip-roof home was a boardinghouse when the Revolutionary War hero lived here while supervising shipbuilding for the Continental Navy. The 1758 structure, now the headquarters

of the Portsmouth Historical Society, displays furniture, costumes, glass, guns, portraits, and documents from the late 18th century. ✉ *43 Middle St.* ☎ *603/436–8420* 🌐 *www.portsmouthhistory.org* 🎟 *$5* ⏲ *June–Oct., Mon.–Sat. 10–4, Sun. noon–4.*

Port of Portsmouth Maritime Museum. The USS *Albacore,* built here in 1953, is docked at this museum in Albacore Park. You can board the prototype submarine, which was a floating laboratory designed to test an innovative hull design, dive brakes, and sonar systems for the Navy. The nearby Memorial Garden and its reflecting pool are dedicated to those who have lost their lives in submarine service. ✉ *600 Market St.* ☎ *603/436–3680* 🌐 *www.ussalbacore.org* 🎟 *$8* ⏲ *Daily 9:30–4:30.*

Redhook Ale Brewery. Tours here end with a beer tasting, but if you don't have time for the tour, stop in the Cataqua Public House to sample the fresh ales and have a bite to eat (open daily for lunch and dinner). The building is visible from the Spaulding Turnpike. ✉ *Pease International Tradeport, 35 Corporate Dr.* ☎ *603/430–8600* 🌐 *www.redhook.com* 🎟 *$1* ⏲ *See Web site for hours and tour info.*

★ **Strawbery Banke Museum.** The first English settlers named the area around today's Portsmouth for the wild strawberries along the shores of the Piscataqua River. The name survives in this 10-acre neighborhood, continuously occupied for more than 300 years and now doing

3

SIGHTSEEING TRAILS AND TROLLEYS

TRAILS

One of the best ways to learn about town history is the guided tour along the **Portsmouth Harbour Trail**, which passes more than 70 points of scenic and historical significance (✉ *Downtown, starting at Market Square* ☎ *603/427–2020 for guided tour* 🌐 *www.seacoastnh.com/harbourtrail* 🎫 *Guided tour $7* ⏲ *Highlights tour Thurs.–Sat., Mon. 10:30 AM, Sun. 1:30 PM. Twilight tour Thurs.–Sat. and Mon. 5:30 PM*). You can purchase a tour map ($2.50) at the information kiosk in Market Square, where guided tours start, at the chamber of commerce, and at several house museums. Guided walks are conducted late spring to early fall.

Important sites of African-American history are along the self-guided walk on the **Portsmouth Black Heritage Trail** (✉ *Downtown, starting at Prescott Park wharf* ☎ *603/431–2768* 🌐 *www.pbhtrail.org*). Included are the **New Hampshire Gazette Printing Office,** where skilled slave Primus Fowle operated the paper's printing press for some 50 years beginning in 1756, and the city's 1866 **Election Hall,** outside of which the city's black citizens held annual celebrations of the Emancipation Proclamation.

TROLLEYS

On the **Seacoast Trolley** (✉ *Departs from Market Sq. or from 14 locations en route* ☎ *603/431–6975* 🌐 *www.seacoasttrolley.com* 🎫 *$8*) guides conduct narrated tours of Portsmouth, Rye, and New Castle, with views of the New Hampshire coastline and area beaches. The 17-mi round-trip, which you can hop on and off of at several stops, runs from mid-June through Labor Day, 11 to 3.

Portsmouth is also served by the **Downtown Loop Coast Trolley** (✉ *Departs from Market Sq. every half hour* ☎ *603/743–5777* 🌐 *www.coastbus.org/downtown.html* 🎫 *50¢*), which makes numerous stops. Running from late June to late August, tours are narrated 90-minute round-trips through downtown and around the waterfront.

duty as an outdoor history museum, one of the largest in New England. The compound has 46 buildings dating from 1695 to 1820—some restored and furnished to a particular period, some used for exhibits, and some viewed from the outside only—as well as period gardens. Half the interior of the Drisco House, built in 1795, depicts its use as a dry-goods store in Colonial times, whereas the living room and kitchen are decorated as they were in the 1950s, showing how buildings were adapted over time. The Shapiro House has been restored to reflect the life of the Russian Jewish immigrant family who lived in the home in the early 1900s. Perhaps the most opulent house, done in decadent Victorian style, is the 1860 Goodwin Mansion, former home of Governor Ichabod Goodwin. ✉ *14 Hancock St.* ☎ *603/433–1100* 🌐 *www.strawberybanke.org* 🎫 *$15* ⏲ *May 1–Oct. 31, daily 10–5; special December tours.*

WORTH NOTING

Moffatt-Ladd House. The period interior of this 1763 home tells the story of Portsmouth's merchant class through portraits, letters, and furnishings. The Colonial-revival garden includes a horse chestnut tree planted by General William Whipple when he returned home after signing the Declaration of Independence in 1776. ✉ *154 Market St.* ☎ *603/436–8221* 🌐 *www.moffattladd.org* *Garden and house tour $6, garden only $2* ⏲ *Mid-June–mid-Oct., Mon.–Sat. 11–5, Sun. 1–5.*

QUICK BITES

Drop by Annabelle's Natural Ice Cream (✉ *49 Ceres St.* ☎ *603/436-3400* 🌐 *www.annabellesicecream.com*) for a dish of Ghirardelli chocolate chip or Almond Joy ice cream. Breaking New Grounds (✉ *14 Market Sq.* ☎ *603/436-9555*) is a big hangout in town and serves coffee, pastries, and gelato.

Wentworth-Coolidge Mansion Historic Site. A National Historic Landmark now part of Little Harbor State Park, this home site was originally the residence of Benning Wentworth, New Hampshire's first royal governor (1753–70). Notable among its period furnishings is the carved pine mantelpiece in the council chamber. Wentworth's imported lilac trees bloom each May. The visitor center stages lectures and exhibits and contains a gallery with changing exhibits. ✉ *375 Little Harbor Rd., near South Street Cemetery* ☎ *603/436–6607* 🌐 *www.nhstateparks.org/coolidge.html* *$7* ⏲ *June 17–Sept. 7, Wed.–Sun. 10–4; Sept. 12–Oct. 12, weekends 10–4.*

OFF THE BEATEN PATH

Though it consists of a single square mile of land, the small island of **New Castle**, 3 mi southeast from downtown via Route 1B, was once known as Great Island. The narrow roads and coastal lanes are lined with pre-Revolutionary houses, making for a beautiful drive or stroll. **Wentworth-by-the-Sea** (☎ *603/422–7322* 🌐 *www.wentworth.com*), the last of the state's great seaside resorts, towers over the southern end of New Castle on Route 1B. It was the site of the signing of the Russo-Japanese Treaty in 1905, when Russian and Japanese delegates stayed at the resort and signed an agreement ending the Russo-Japanese War that would win President Theodore Roosevelt a Nobel Peace Prize. The property was vacant for 20 years before it reopened as a luxury resort in 2003. **Also on New Castle, Ft. Constitution** (✉ *Wentworth St. off Rte. 1B, at the Coast Guard Station* ☎ *603/436–1552* 🌐 *www.nhstateparks.com/fortconstitution.html* *Free* ⏲ *Parking lot 8:30–dusk in summer, park itself is always open*) was built in 1631 and then rebuilt in 1666 as Ft. William and Mary, a British stronghold overlooking Portsmouth Harbor. The fort earned its fame in 1774, when patriots raided it in one of Revolutionary America's first overtly defiant acts against King George III. The rebels later used the captured munitions against the British at the Battle of Bunker Hill. Panels explain its history. Park at the dock and walk into the Coast Guard installation to the fort.

OFF THE BEATEN PATH

Isles of Shoals. Many of these nine small, rocky islands (eight at high tide) retain the earthy names—Hog and Smuttynose to cite but two—given them by transient 17th-century fishermen. A history of piracy, murder, and ghosts surrounds the archipelago, long populated by an independent lot who, according to one writer, hadn't the sense to winter on

Strawbery Banke Museum includes period gardens and 46 historic buildings.

the mainland. Not all the islands lie within the state's borders: after an ownership dispute, five went to Maine and four to New Hampshire.

Celia Thaxter, a native islander, romanticized these islands with her poetry in *Among the Isles of Shoals* (1873) and celebrated her garden in *An Island Garden* (1894; now reissued with the original color illustrations by Childe Hassam). In the late 19th century, **Appledore Island** became an offshore retreat for Thaxter's coterie of writers, musicians, and artists. The island is now used by the Marine Laboratory of Cornell University. **Star Island** contains a nondenominational conference center and is open for guided tours.

From late May to late October you can cruise of the Isles of Shoals or take a ferry to Star Island with **Isles of Shoals Steamship Company** (✉ *315 Market St.* ☎ *800/441–4620 or 603/431–5500* 🌐 *www.islesofshoals.com*).

SPORTS AND THE OUTDOORS

PARKS **Great Bay Estuarine Research Reserve.** Just inland from Portsmouth is one of southeastern New Hampshire's most precious assets. Amid its 4,471 acres of tidal waters, mudflats, and about 48 mi of inland shoreline, you can spot blue herons, ospreys, and snowy egrets, particularly during spring and fall migrations. Winter eagles also live here. The best public access is via the **Great Bay Discovery Center** (✉ *89 Depot Rd., off Rte. 33, Greenland* ☎ *603/778–0015* 🌐 *www.greatbay.org* ⏲ *May–Sept., Wed.–Sun. 10–4; Oct., weekends 10–4*). The facility has year-round interpretive programs, indoor and outdoor exhibits, a library and bookshop, and a 1,700-foot boardwalk as well as other trails through mudflats and upland forest.

A boat tour of Portsmouth Harbor is popular in warm weather, and a great introduction to the city's maritime heritage.

Prescott Park. Picnicking is popular at this waterfront park. A large formal garden with fountains is perfect for whiling away an afternoon. The park contains Point of Graves, Portsmouth's oldest burial ground, and two 17th-century warehouses. It's home to the annual **Prescott Park Arts Festival** (🌐 *www.prescottpark.org*). ✉ *Between Strawbery Banke Museum and the Piscataqua River* 🌐 *603/431–8748*.

Water Country. New Hampshire's largest water park has a river tube ride, large wave pool, white-water rapids, and 12 waterslides. ✉ *2300 Lafayette Rd.* ☎ *603/427–1112* 🌐 *www.watercountry.com* 🎟 *$36* ⏲ *Mid-June–Labor Day, hours vary.*

BOAT TOURS **Granite State Whale Watch** (✉ *Box 768, Rye Harbor State Marina, Rte. 1A, Rye* ☎ *603/964–5545 or 800/964–5545* 🌐 *www.granitestatewhalewatch.com* 🎟 *$31*) conducts naturalist-led whale-watching tours aboard the 150-passenger MV *Granite State* out of Rye Harbor State Marina from May to early October and narrated Isles of Shoals and fireworks cruises in July and August.

From May to October, **Portsmouth Harbor Cruises** (✉ *64 Ceres Str.* ☎ *603/436–8084 or 800/776–0915* 🌐 *www.portsmouthharbor.com*) operates tours of Portsmouth Harbor, foliage trips on the Cocheco River, and sunset cruises aboard the MV *Heritage*.

The **Isles of Shoals Steamship Co.** (✉ *Barker Wharf, 315 Market St.* ☎ *603/431–5500 or 800/441–4620* 🌐 *www.islesofshoals.com*) runs a three-hour Isles of Shoals, lighthouses, and Portsmouth Harbor cruise out of Portsmouth aboard the *Thomas Laighton*, a replica of a Victorian steamship, from April through December (twice daily in summer). Lunch and light snacks are available on board, or you can bring your own. There are also fall foliage cruises, narrated sunset cruises visiting five local lighthouses, and special holiday cruises.

One of the questions visitors to Portsmouth ask most frequently is whether they can tour the familiar red tugboats plying the waters of Piscataqua River and Portsmouth Harbor. Unfortunately, the answer is no, but you can get a firsthand look at Portsmouth's working waterfront aboard the **Tug Alley Too** (✉ *47 Bow St.* ☎ *603/430–9556 or 877/884–2553* 🌐 *www.tugboatalley.com*), a six-passenger replica. The 90-minute tours pass lighthouses, the Portsmouth Naval Shipyard, and Wentworth Marina. Tours are conducted daily from May through October and leave every two hours starting at 10 AM.

Explore the waters, sites, and sea life of the Piscataqua River Basin and the New Hampshire coastline on a guided kayak tour with **Portsmouth Kayak Adventure** (✉ *185 Wentworth Rd.* ☎ *603/559–1000* 🌐 *www.portsmouth.kayak.com*). Beginners are welcome (instruction is included). Tours are run daily from June through mid-October, at 10 and 2. Sunset tours take off at 6. If you'd rather pedal than drive, stop by **Portsmouth Rent & Ride** (✉ *958 Sagamore Ave.* ☎ *603/433–6777*) for equipment, maps, and suggested bike routes to Portsmouth sites, area beaches, and attractions. Guided two-hour tours of the seacoast area are also offered.

SHOPPING

Market Square, in the center of town, has gift and clothing boutiques, book and card shops, and exquisite crafts stores. **Nahcotta** (✉ *110 Congress St.* ☎ *603/433–1705* 🌐 *www.nahcotta.com*) is a wonderful contemporary art gallery and has a well-chosen selection of contemporary housewares, artist-crafted jewelry, and glassware. **Byrne & Carlson** (✉ *121 State St.* ☎ *888/559–9778* 🌐 *www.byrneandcarlson.com*) produces handmade chocolates in the European tradition. **N. W. Barrett** (✉ *53 Market St.* ☎ *603/431–4262* 🌐 *www.nwbarrett.com*) specializes in leather, jewelry, pottery, and other arts and crafts. It also sells furniture, including affordable steam-bent oak pieces and one-of-a-kind lamps and rocking chairs.

NIGHTLIFE AND THE ARTS

THE ARTS Seven galleries participate in the Art 'Round Town Reception, a gallery walk that takes place the first Friday of each month. Check out 🌐 *www.artroundtown.org* for more information. Beloved for its acoustics, the 1878 **Music Hall** (✉ *28 Chestnut St.* ☎ *603/436–2400; 603/436–9900 film line* 🌐 *www.themusichall.org*) brings the best touring events to the seacoast—from classical and pop concerts to dance and theater. The hall also hosts art-house film series. The **Prescott Park Arts Festival** (✉ *105 Marcy St.* ☎ *603/436–2848* 🌐 *www.prescottpark.org*) presents theater, dance, and musical events outdoors from June through August.

BARS **Two Ceres Street** (✉ *2 Ceres St.* ☎ *603/431–5967* 🌐 *www.twoceresstreet.com*) serves martinis such as the Lumberjack, with Maker's Mark and maple syrup, and the Hot and Dirty, with Grey Goose vodka, peperoncini, and olive juice. If vodka is your thing, you'll do no better than the book-lined English oak bar in **The Library Restaurant** (✉ *401 State St.* ☎ *603/431–5202* 🌐 *www.libraryrestaurant.com*), which has more than 120 brands of vodka and 96 kinds of martinis.

MUSIC Discover the local music scene at **The Red Door** (✉ *107 State St.* ☎ *603/373–6827* 🌐 *www.reddoorportsmouth.com*), which has a bar, a live music series, and DJs nightly. Indie music fans shouldn't miss Monday nights at 8 for the acclaimed live acts as part of the Hush Hush Sweet Harlot Music Series. The **Portsmouth Gas Light Co.** (✉ *64 Market St.* ☎ *603/430–9122* 🌐 *www.portsmouthgaslight.com*), a brick-oven pizzeria and restaurant, hosts local rock bands in its lounge, courtyard, and slick upstairs space. People come from Boston and Portland just to hang out at the **Press Room** (✉ *77 Daniel St.* ☎ *603/431–5186* 🌐 *www.pressroomnh.com*), which showcases folk, jazz, blues, and bluegrass performers.

WHERE TO EAT

$$ ECLECTIC ✕ **Blue Mermaid Island Grill.** This is a fun, colorful place for great fish, sandwiches, and quesadillas, as well as house-cut yucca chips. Specialties include plantain-encrusted cod topped with grilled mango vinaigrette and served with black-eyed pea–sweet potato hash, a sirloin with wild mushroom glaze, and braised short ribs with an island rub. In summer you can eat on a deck that overlooks the adorable Colonial homes of the Hill neighborhood. Live music includes soul, bluegrass, rock, and even yodeling Wednesday through Saturday. ✉ *409 The Hill* ☎ *603/427–2583* 🌐 *www.bluemermaid.com* 💳 *AE, D, DC, MC, V.*

¢–$ AMERICAN ★ ✕ **Friendly Toast.** The biggest and best breakfast in town (as well as lunch and dinner) is served at this funky, wildly colorful diner-style restaurant loaded with bric-a-brac. Almond Joy cakes (buttermilk pancakes, chocolate chips, coconut, and almonds), raspberry and orange French toast, and hefty omelets are favorites. Also enjoy the homemade breads and muffins. A late-night crowd gathers after the bars close; Friendly Toast is open 24 hours on weekends. ✉ *121 Congress St.* ☎ *603/430–2154* 🌐 *www.friendlytoast.net* 💳 *AE, D, MC, V.*

$$ SEAFOOD ✕ **Jumpin' Jay's.** A wildly popular downtown spot, this offbeat, dim-lighted eatery has a changing menu of fresh seafood from local fishermen and exotic locales such as New Zealand and Ecuador. Try the steamed Prince Edward Island mussels with a spicy lemongrass and saffron sauce, a Portuguese fisherman's stew, or the haddock piccata (served in a sauce of lemon, white wine, and capers). Singles like to gather at the central bar for dinner and furtive glances. ✉ *150 Congress St.* ☎ *603/766–3474* 🌐 *www.jumpinjays.com* 💳 *MC, V* ⏲ *No lunch.*

$$$ STEAKHOUSE ★ ✕ **Library Restaurant.** The Library is a former luxury hotel made over into a country library–themed restaurant. The 12-foot hand-painted dining room ceiling was constructed by the Pullman Car Woodworkers in 1889. Hand-carved Spanish mahogany paneling covers the walls, and the marble bar top used to be the check-in desk. Although the kitchen churns out light dishes such as crab cakes and barbecue shrimp, the mainstays are thick-cut steaks and chops. The crushed-peppercorn–encrusted steak is meat heaven. The English-style pub serves nearly 100 martinis made from vodkas such as Fris, Mezzaluna, Boomsma, and Thor's Hammer. Sunday brunch is also available. ✉ *401 State St.* ☎ *603/431–5202* 🌐 *www.libraryrestaurant.com* 💳 *AE, D, DC, MC, V.*

$$–$$$ SEAFOOD ★ ✕ **Pesce Blue.** Sleek, modern, and hip, this restaurant specializes in fresh seafood blended with simple Italian flavors. It's definitely industrial chic with its cinder-block walls, black industrial grid ceiling, wood

and chrome accents, and mosaic blue tiles. The menu changes daily but often includes a blackened salmon Caesar salad, fried anchovies, grilled jumbo prawns with sweet garlic custard, and a selection of local catches. There's patio dining in summer. ✉ *103 Congress St.* ☎ *603/430–7766* 🌐 *www.pescеblue.com* ▭ *AE, D, MC, V* ⏲ *Brunch Sat. and Sun.*

WHERE TO STAY

$$$ Fodor's Choice ★ **Governor's House.** Among Portsmouth's inns and small hotels, the Governor stands apart. Small, lavish, and quiet, this four-room B&B, a couple of blocks from the historic downtown area, is the perfect place for discerning couples. It was the home of Charles Dale, formerly the governor of New Hampshire, from 1930 to 1964. Frette linens made in Italy, down comforters, in-room Bose CD stereos with 300 CDs to choose from, high-speed Wi-Fi, a guest computer, in-room massages, complimentary wine, DVDs that include the last 60 Academy Award winners for Best Picture, and a deluxe Continental breakfast are among the extras at this 1917 Georgian Colonial. Ask innkeeper Bob Chaffee about the hand-painted bathroom tiles. Coffee, tea, and hot cocoa are available 24 hours a day. **Pros:** great rooms and home; free bicycle rental; great location. **Cons:** 15-minute bike ride to the beach. ✉ *32 Miller Ave.* ☎ *603/427–5140 or 866/427–5140* 🌐 *www.governors-house.com* *4 rooms* *In-room: no phone, refrigerator, DVD, Wi-Fi. In-hotel: tennis court, bicycles, laundry service, Internet terminal, Wi-Fi hotspot, no kids under 12* ▭ *D, MC, V* 🍴 *CP.*

$$ **Martin Hill Inn.** You may fall in love with this adorable yellow 1815 house surrounded by gardens once you see it from the street. It's a 10- to 15-minute walk from the historic district and the waterfront. The quiet rooms are furnished with antiques and decorated in formal Colonial or country-Victorian styles. The Greenhouse Suite has a solarium. You'll get to know your fellow travelers at breakfast served at 8:30 each morning at a common table. **Pros:** very clean; real antiques. **Cons:** not in historic district; early breakfast. ✉ *404 Islington St.* ☎ *603/436–2287* 🌐 *www.martinhillinn.com* *4 rooms, 3 suites* *In-room: no phone, no TV, Wi-Fi. In-hotel: Wi-Fi hotspot, no kids under 14* ▭ *MC, V* 🍴 *BP.*

$$$ Fodor's Choice ★ **Wentworth by the Sea.** What's not to love about this white colossus overlooking the sea on New Castle Island. The closest thing New Hampshire has to a Ritz-Carlton, Wentworth by the Sea has luxurious rooms and modern and opulent amenities including a good spa and an indoor heated pool. The coastline and island location are superb. Built in 1874 as a summer resort for East Coast socialites, wealthy patrons, and former presidents, the property reopened in spring 2003 after being rebuilt. All of the rooms have ocean and harbor views—the huge sunny suites, which have gas fireplaces, occupy a new building right on the water, facing the marina. Enjoy a lavish meal in the formal Wentworth Dining Room ($$$), or try the lighter tavern restaurant Roosevelt's Lounge ($$), and, in summer only, Latitudes ($$), a marina-front restaurant. **Pros:** great spa and restaurants; sense of history; oceanfront perch. **Cons:** not in downtown Portsmouth. ✉ *588 Wentworth Rd., New Castle* ☎ *603/422–7322 or 866/240–6313* 🌐 *www.wentworth.com* *127 rooms, 34 suites* *In-room: kitchen (some), DVD, Internet. In-hotel: 3 restaurants, room service, bars, tennis courts, pools, gym, spa, laundry service, concierge, Internet terminal, Wi-Fi hotspot, some pets allowed* ▭ *AE, D, DC, MC, V.*

Four of the nine rocky Isles of Shoals belong to New Hampshire, the other five belong to Maine.

RYE

8 mi south of Portsmouth.

On Route 1A as it winds south through Rye you'll pass a group of late-19th- and early-20th-century mansions known as **Millionaires' Row.** Because of the way the road curves, the drive south along this route is breathtaking. In 1623 the first Europeans established a settlement at Odiorne Point in what is now the largely undeveloped and picturesque town of Rye, making it the birthplace of New Hampshire. Today the area's main draws are a lovely state park, oceanfront beaches, and the views from Route 1A. Strict town laws have prohibited commercial development in Rye, creating a dramatic contrast with its frenetic neighbor Hampton Beach.

SPORTS AND THE OUTDOORS

★ **Odiorne Point State Park.** This site encompasses more than 330 acres of protected land, on the site where David Thompson established the first permanent European settlement in what is now New Hampshire. Several nature trails with interpretive panels describe the park's military history, and you can enjoy vistas of the nearby Isles of Shoals. The rocky shore's tidal pools shelter crabs, periwinkles, and sea anemones. Throughout the year, the **Seacoast Science Center** conducts guided walks and interpretive programs and has exhibits on the area's natural history. Displays trace the social history of Odiorne Point back to the Ice Age, and the tidal-pool touch tank and 1,000-gallon Gulf of Maine deepwater aquarium are popular with kids. Day camp is offered for grades K–8 throughout summer and during school vacations. Popular music concerts are held Thursday evenings in summer. ✉ *570 Ocean Blvd. (Rte. 1A), north of*

Wallis Sands, Rye Harbor State Beach ☏ *603/436–8043 science center; 603/436–1552 park* ⊕ *www.seacoastsciencecenter.org* ▣ *$5 science center, $4 park* ⊙ *Science center Apr.–Oct., daily 10–5; Nov.–Mar., Mon.–Sat. 10–5; park daily 8–dusk.*

Rye Airfield. If you've got active kids with you, consider spending the day at this extreme-sports park with an indoor in-line skate and skateboard arena and two BMX tracks. ✉ *U.S. 1* ☏ *603/964–2800* ⊕ *www.ryeairfield.com.*

3

BEACHES Good for swimming and sunning, **Jenness State Beach** (✉ *Route 1A* ☏ *603/436–1552* ⊕ *www.nhstateparks.com/jenness.html*) is a favorite with locals. The facilities include a bathhouse, lifeguards, and metered parking. **Wallis Sands State Beach** (✉ *Route 1A* ☏ *603/436–9404* ⊕ *www.nhstateparks.com/wallis.html* ▣ *$15 per car*) is a swimmers' beach with bright white sands, a bathhouse, and plenty of parking.

FISHING For a full- or half-day deep-sea angling charter, try **Atlantic Whale Watch Fleet** (✉ *Rye Harbor* ☏ *603/964–5220 or 800/942–5364* ⊕ *www.atlanticwhalewatch.com*).

WHERE TO EAT

$$–$$$ AMERICAN ★ **The Carriage House.** Walk across scenic Ocean Boulevard from Jenness Beach to this elegant cottage eatery that serves innovative dishes with a Continental flair. Standouts include crab cakes served with a spicy jalapeño sauce, penne *alla vodka* teeming with fresh seafood, creative Madras curries, and steak au poivre. Upstairs is a rough-hewn-wood–paneled tavern serving lighter fare. Savor a hot fudge–ice cream croissant for dessert. ✉ *2263 Ocean Blvd.* ☏ *603/964–8251* ⊕ *www.carriagehouserye.com* ▭ *AE, MC, V* ⊙ *No lunch.*

HAMPTON BEACH

8 mi south of Rye.

Hampton Beach, from Route 27 to where Route 1A crosses the causeway, is an authentic seaside amusement center—the domain of fried-dough stands, loud music, arcade games, palm readers, parasailing, and bronzed bodies. An estimated 150,000 people visit the town and its free public beach on the Fourth of July, and it draws plenty of people until late September, when things close up. The 3-mi boardwalk, where kids play games and see how saltwater taffy is made, looks like a leftover from the 1940s; in fact, the whole community remains remarkably free of modern franchises. Free outdoor concerts are held on many a summer evening, and once a week there's a fireworks display. Each August, locals hold a children's festival, and they celebrate the end of the season with a huge seafood feast on the weekend after Labor Day.

GETTING HERE AND AROUND

Interstate 95 is the fastest way to get to Hampton, but the town is best seen by driving on Route 1A, which follows the coast and offers access to a number of beaches. Route 1 is the quickest way to get around, but be prepared for strip malls and stoplights.

ESSENTIALS

Visitor Information **Hampton Area Chamber of Commerce** (✉ *1 Lafayette Rd., Hampton* ☎ *603/926–8718* 🌐 *www.hamptonchamber.com*).

SPORTS AND THE OUTDOORS

BEACHES **Hampton Beach State Park** (✉ *Rte. 1A* ☎ *603/926–3784* 🌐 *www.nhstateparks.com/hampton.html* 🎫 *$15 per car May–Oct., free Nov.–Apr.*) at the mouth of the Hampton River, is a quiet stretch of sand on the southwestern edge of town. It has picnic tables, a store (seasonal), and a bathhouse.

FISHING AND WHALE-WATCHING Several companies conduct whale-watching excursions as well as half-day, full-day, and nighttime cruises. Most leave from the Hampton State Pier on Route 1A. **Al Gauron Deep Sea Fishing** (✉ *State Pier* ☎ *603/926–2469* 🌐 *www.algauron.com*) maintains a fleet of three boats for whale-watching cruises and fishing charters. **Eastman Fishing Fleet** (✉ *River St., Seabrook* ☎ *603/474–3461* 🌐 *www.eastmansdocks.com*) offers whale-watching and fishing cruises, with evening and morning charters. **Smith & Gilmore Deep Sea** (✉ *State Pier* ☎ *603/926–3503 or 877/272–4005* 🌐 *www.smithandgilmore.com*) conducts deep-sea fishing expeditions and whale-watching trips.

NIGHTLIFE

Despite its name, the **Hampton Beach Casino Ballroom** (✉ *169 Ocean Blvd.* ☎ *603/929–4100* 🌐 *www.casinoballroom.com*) isn't a gambling establishment but a late-19th-century, 2,000-seat performance venue that has hosted everyone from Janis Joplin to Jerry Seinfeld, George Carlin, and B. B. King. Performances are scheduled weekly from April through October.

WHERE TO EAT AND STAY

$$$ AMERICAN ✕ **Ron's Landing at Rocky Bend.** Amid the motels lining Ocean Boulevard is this casually elegant restaurant. Try the sesame-seared ahi tuna with a pineapple, orange, and cucumber salsa for a starter. Good seafood entrées include the oven-roasted salmon with a hoisin glaze, a Frangelico cream sauce, slivered almonds, and sliced apple and the baked haddock stuffed with scallops and lobster and served with lemon-dill butter. From many tables you can enjoy a sweeping Atlantic view. Brunch is served Sundays, October to May. ✉ *379 Ocean Blvd.* ☎ *603/929–2122* 🌐 *www.ronslanding.com* 💳 *AE, D, DC, MC, V* ⏰ *Closed Mon. No lunch.*

$ 🏨 **Ashworth by the Sea.** You'll be surprised how contemporary this center-of-the-action, across-from-the-beach hotel is, especially after you see the classic old neon sign outside. Most rooms have decks, but request a beachside room for an ocean view; otherwise you'll look out onto the pool or street. The Sand Bar ($), on the roof deck between the hotel's two buildings, is a great place to watch the town's fireworks each Wednesday and have food and drinks. **Pros:** center-of-town location and across from beach; open all year. **Cons:** breakfast not included; very busy. ✉ *295 Ocean Blvd.* ☎ *603/926–6762 or 800/345–6736 www.ashworthhotel.com* *105 rooms* *In-room: Wi-Fi. In-hotel: 3 restaurants, room service, pool, laundry service, Wi-Fi hotspot* 💳 *AE, D, DC, MC, V.*

EN ROUTE At the 400-acre **Applecrest Farm Orchards** you can pick your own apples and berries or buy fresh fruit pies and cookies. Fall brings cider pressing, hayrides, pumpkins, and music on weekends. In winter a cross-country ski trail traverses the orchard. Author John Irving worked here as a teenager, his experiences inspiring the book *The Cider House Rules.* ✉ *133 Rte. 88, Hampton Falls* ☎ *603/926–3721* 🌐 *www.applecrest.com* ⏲ *May–Dec., daily 8–6.*

EXETER

3

★ *9 mi northwest of Hampton, 52 mi north of Boston, 47 mi southeast of Concord.*

In the center of Exeter, contemporary shops mix well with the esteemed Phillips Exeter Academy, which opened in 1783. During the Revolutionary War, Exeter was the state capital, and it was here amid intense patriotic fervor that the first state constitution and the first Declaration of Independence from Great Britain were put to paper. These days Exeter shares more in appearance and personality with Boston's blue-blooded satellite communities than the rest of New Hampshire—indeed, plenty of locals commute to Beantown. A handful of cheerful cafés and coffeehouses are clustered in the center of town.

GETTING HERE AND AROUND

Amtrak's Downeaster service stops here between Boston and Portland, Maine. On the road, it's 9 mi northwest of Hampton on Route 111. Route 101 is also a good way to get to Exeter from the east or west. The town itself is easy to walk around.

ESSENTIALS

Visitor Information **Exeter Area Chamber of Commerce** (✉ *24 Front St. #101, Exeter* ☎ *603/772–2411* 🌐 *www.exeterarea.org*).

EXPLORING

American Independence Museum. Adjacent to Phillips Exeter Academy in the Ladd-Gilman House, this museum celebrates the birth of the nation. The story unfolds during the course of a guided tour focusing on the Gilman family, who lived in the house during the Revolutionary era. See drafts of the U.S. Constitution and the first Purple Heart as well as letters and documents written by George Washington and the household furnishings of John Taylor Gilman, one of New Hampshire's early governors. In July the museum hosts the American Independence Festival. ✉ *1 Governor's La.* ☎ *603/772–2622* 🌐 *www.independencemuseum.org* 🎫 *$5* ⏲ *Mid-May–Oct., Wed.–Sat. 10–4 (last tour at 3).*

Phillips Exeter Academy. Above all else, the town is energized by the faculty and 1,000 high school students of the Phillips Exeter Academy. The grounds of the Academy's 129 buildings, open to the public, resemble an elite Ivy League university campus. The Louis Kahn–designed library contains the largest secondary-school book collection in the world. ✉ *20 Main St.* ☎ *603/772–4311* 🌐 *www.exeter.edu.*

SHOPPING

A Picture's Worth a Thousand Words (✉ *65 Water St.* ☎ *603/779–1991* 🌐 *www.apwatw.com*) stocks antique and contemporary prints, old maps, town histories, and rare books. Prestigious **Exeter Fine Crafts** (✉ *61 Water St.* ☎ *603/778–8282* 🌐 *www.exeterfinecrafts.com*) shows an impressive selection of juried pottery, paintings, jewelry, textiles, glassware, and other fine creations by some of northern New England's top artists.

WHERE TO EAT

¢ AMERICAN Fodor's Choice ★ **Loaf and Ladle.** There are three components to this extraordinary place: quality, price, and location. The name refers to homemade bread—more than 30 kinds—and soup—more than 100 varieties are offered on a rotating basis. A bowl of soup, which is a full meal, is $6.25, and it's hard to spend more than that here. Choose a chunk of anadama bread, made with cornmeal and molasses, to go with your soup, and take your meal to one of the two decks that hover over the Exeter River. It's simple and homey. *9 Water St. 603/778–8955 www.theloafandladle.com Reservations not accepted AE, D, DC, MC, V.*

$$–$$$ AMERICAN **Tavern at River's Edge.** A convivial downtown gathering spot on the Exeter River, this downstairs tavern pulls in parents of prep-school kids, University of New Hampshire (UNH) students, and suburban yuppies. It may be informal, but the kitchen turns out surprisingly sophisticated chow. Start with sautéed ragout of portobello and shiitake mushrooms, sun-dried tomatoes, roasted shallots, garlic, and Asiago cheese. Move on to New Zealand rack of lamb with rosemary-port demi-glace and minted risotto. In the bar, lighter fare is served daily 3–10. *163 Water St. 603/772–7393 www.tavernatriversedge.com AE, D, DC, MC, V No lunch.*

WHERE TO STAY

$$ ★ **The Exeter Inn.** This elegant brick Georgian-style inn on the Phillips Exeter Academy campus has been the choice of visiting parents since it opened in the 1930s. After a complete overhaul, completed in the spring of 2008, the place looks better than ever. Rooms have a clubby Ralph Lauren design, with striped wallpaper, 10-inch pillow-top mattresses, and flat-screen TVs. A lounge and restaurant serves three meals a day. **Pros:** contemporary, well-designed, clean rooms; near Academy. **Cons:** not close to town shops; you may not want to be on a prep-school campus. *90 Front St. 603/772–5901 or 800/782–8444 www.theexeterinn.com 41 rooms, 5 suites In-room: Wi-Fi. In-hotel: restaurant, room service, bar, gym, laundry service, Wi-Fi hotspot AE, D, DC, MC, V.*

$$ ★ **Inn by the Bandstand.** If you're visiting someone at the academy and want to stay in a B&B, we recommend this place in the heart of town. Rooms are individually furnished—to the extreme. Behind one door is floral Victorian. The Lakeheath Lodge room takes a rustic outdoorsy approach, with exposed ceiling beams and antlers over the brick fireplace and pine boughs strung over the headboard. Pillows are piled in profusion atop Ralph Lauren sheets. Character and comfort are constants in all rooms, including crystal decanters of sherry. It's one of the best B&Bs in the state. Breakfast is served at 8:30 only. **Pros:** perfect location in town; richly furnished rooms. **Cons:** early breakfast. *4 Front St. 603/772–6352 or 877/239–3837 www.innbythebandstand.com 7 rooms, 2 suites In-room: refrigerator, Wi-Fi. In-hotel: room service, Wi-Fi hotspot AE, D, MC, V BP.*

DURHAM

12 mi north of Exeter, 11 mi northwest of Portsmouth.

Settled in 1635 and the home of General John Sullivan, a Revolutionary War hero and three-time New Hampshire governor, Durham was where Sullivan and his band of rebel patriots stored the gunpowder they captured from Ft. William and Mary in New Castle. Easy access to Great Bay via the Oyster River made Durham a maritime hub in the 19th century. Among the lures today are the water, farms that welcome visitors, and the University of New Hampshire (UNH), which occupies much of the town's center.

GETTING HERE AND AROUND

By car, Durham can be reached on Route 108 from the north or south and Route 4 from Portsmouth from the east or Concord from the west. The Downeaster Amtrak train stops here between Boston and Portland, Maine. A good place to begin your exploration of Durham is at the art galleries on the campus of the University of New Hampshire.

ESSENTIALS

Visitor Information **University of New Hampshire** (☎ *603/862–1234* 🌐 *www.unh.edu*).

EXPLORING

Little Bay Buffalo Company. Visitors cannot roam this family-owned estate, but the 50 American bison ranging here are visible from an observation area and the parking lot. The store on the property sells bison-related gifts and top-quality bison meat. ✉ *50 Langley Rd.* ☎ *603/868–3300* ⏲ *Store Tues.–Sun. 10–5.*

SPORTS AND THE OUTDOORS

You can hike several trails or picnic at 130-acre **Wagon Hill Farm** (✉ *U.S. 4 across from Emery Farm* ☎ *No phone*), overlooking the Oyster River. The old farm wagon on the top of a hill is one of the most photographed sights in New England. Park next to the farmhouse and follow walking trails to the wagon and through the woods to the picnic area by the water. Sledding and cross-country skiing are winter activities.

SHOPPING

Emery Farm. In the same family for 11 generations, Emery Farm sells fruits and vegetables in summer (including pick-your-own raspberries, strawberries, and blueberries), pumpkins in fall, and Christmas trees in December. The farm shop carries breads, pies, and local crafts. Children can pet the resident goats and sheep and attend the storytelling events that are often held on Tuesday mornings in July and August. ✉ *135 Piscataqua Rd.* ☎ *603/742–8495* 🌐 *www.emeryfarm.com* ⏲ *Late Apr.–Dec., daily 9–6.*

NIGHTLIFE AND THE ARTS

THE ARTS The **Celebrity Series** (☎ *603/862–2290* 🌐 *www.unh.edu/celebrity*) at UNH brings music, theater, and dance to several venues. The **UNH Department of Theater and Dance** (✉ *Paul Creative Arts Center, 30 College Rd.* ☎ *603/862–2290* 🌐 *www.unh.edu/theatre-dance*) produces a variety of shows. UNH's **Whittemore Center Arena** (✉ *128 Main St.* ☎ *603/862–1379*

DID YOU KNOW?

Politics and patriotism have always been important to New Hampshire residents, whether it's Fourth of July celebrations, the earliest presidential primary elections, or the state's "Live Free or Die" motto.

CLOSE UP

New Hampshire Farmers' Markets

Winter squash is in season in New Hampshire from September to October.

One of the best and longest-running farmers' markets is the **Portsmouth Farmers' Market** (✉ *1 Junkins Ave., Portsmouth* ⏲ *May–early Nov., Sat. 8 AM–1 PM*), which features live music and regional treats, such as maple syrup and artisanal cheeses, in addition to bountiful produce. Don't miss the award-winning breads of the much-beloved bakery **Me & Ollie's** (🌐 *www.meandollies.com*). The market is part of the **Seacoast Growers Association** (🌐 *www. seacoastgrowers.org*), which also has weekly markets in Dover, Durham, Exeter, Hampton, and Kingston.

Just outside Manchester, the **Bedford Farmers' Market** (✉ *Benedictine Park, Wallace Rd., Bedford* 🌐 *bedford-farmersmarket.org* ⏲ *June–Oct., Tues. 3–6 PM*) has a particularly rich mix of local growers and food purveyors, selling seasonal jams, pasture-raised lamb and chicken, homemade treats for dogs and cats, goats' milk soaps and balms, and even New Hampshire wines from Jewell Towne Vineyard.

Lebanon Farmers' Market (✉ *Colburn ParkPark and Church Sts., Lebanon* 🌐 *www. lebanonfarmersmarket.org* ⏲ *Late May–late Sept., Thurs. 4–7 PM*) draws more than 30 vendors from throughout the northern Connecticut River valley. At the **Exit 20 Farmers' Market at Tanger Outlets** (✉ *I-93, Exit 20, Tanger Outlet shops* 🌐 *www. tangeroutlet.com* ⏲ *June–Sept., Wed. 3–6 PM*) you'll find folk art and country crafts in addition to food.

Established in 1632, **Tuttle's Red Barn** (✉ *151 Dover Point Rd., Dover* ☎ *603/742-4313* 🌐 *www. tuttlesredbarn.net*) is the oldest continuously functioning family farm in the country. The garden, farm, and gourmet shops are open daily year-round, and in season this is a terrific stop for sweet corn, tomatoes, berries, and greens.

—Andrew Collins

ⓦ *www.whittemorecenter.com*) hosts everything from Boston Pops concerts to home shows, plus college sports.

NIGHTLIFE Students and local yupsters head to the **Stone Church** (✉ *5 Granite St., Newmarket* ☎ *603/659–6321* ⓦ *www.thestonechurch.com*) —in an authentic 1835 former Methodist church—to listen to live rock, jazz, blues, and folk. The restaurant on the premises serves dinner Wednesday through Sunday.

WHERE TO EAT AND STAY

$$ SEAFOOD/ AMERICAN ★ ✕ **ffrost Sawyer Tavern.** That's not a typo, but an attempt to duplicate a quirk in obsolete spelling (the way capital letters used to be designated) of an old resident of this hilltop house. The eccentric stone basement tavern has its original beams, from which hang collections of mugs, hats, and—no way around it—bedpans. There's a terrific old bar. Choose from fine fare like pan-seared sea scallops or pecan-battered fried chicken breast; standards include burgers, pizza, and fish-and-chips. ✉ *17 Newmarket Rd.* ☎ *603/868–7800* ⓦ *www.threechimneysinn.com* ▭ *AE, D, MC, V.*

$$$ **Three Chimneys Inn.** This stately yellow structure has graced a hill overlooking the Oyster River since 1649. Rooms in the house and the 1795 barn are named after plants from the gardens and filled with Georgian- and Federal-style antiques and reproductions, canopy or four-poster beds with Edwardian drapes, and Oriental rugs; half have fireplaces.

There are two restaurants here: a formal dining room ($$$) and the ffrost Sawyer Tavern, quirky as the name implies. **Pros:** intimate inn experience; afternoon social hour. **Cons:** have to walk or drive into town. ✉ *17 Newmarket Rd.* ☎ *603/868–7800 or 888/399–9777* 🌐 *www.threechimneysinn.com* *23 rooms* *In-room: Wi-Fi. In-hotel: 2 restaurants, room service, bar, Wi-Fi hotspot, some pets allowed* ▭ *AE, D, MC, V* *BP.*

LAKES REGION

Lake Winnipesaukee, a Native American name for "smile of the great spirit," is the largest of the dozens of lakes scattered across the eastern half of central New Hampshire. With about 240 mi of shoreline of inlets and coves, it's the largest in the state. Some claim Winnipesaukee has an island for each day of the year—the total, though impressive, falls short: 274.

In contrast to Winnipesaukee, which bustles all summer long, is the more secluded Squam Lake. Its tranquility is no doubt what attracted the producers of *On Golden Pond*; several scenes of the Academy Award–winning film were shot here. Nearby Lake Wentworth is named for the state's first royal governor, who, in building his country manor here, established North America's first summer resort.

Well-preserved Colonial and 19th-century villages are among the region's many landmarks, and you'll find hiking trails, good antiques shops, and myriad water-oriented activities. This section begins at Wolfeboro and more or less circles Lake Winnipesaukee clockwise, with several side trips.

ESSENTIALS

Visitor Information Lakes Region Association (☎ *603/286–8008 or 800/60–LAKES* 🌐 *www.lakesregion.org*).

WOLFEBORO

40 mi northeast of Concord, 49 mi northwest of Portsmouth.

Quietly upscale and decidedly preppy Wolfeboro has been a resort since Royal Governor John Wentworth built his summer home on the shores of the lake in 1768. The town bills itself as the oldest summer resort in the country, and its center, bursting with tony boutiques, fringes Lake Winnipesaukee and sees about a tenfold population increase each summer. In 2007 French president Nicolas Sarkozy summered here. Mitt Romney is another summer resident. The century-old, white clapboard buildings of the Brewster Academy prep school bracket the town's southern end. Wolfeboro marches to a steady, relaxed beat, comfortable for all ages.

GETTING HERE AND AROUND

Enter on the west side of Lake Winnipesaukee on Route 28. Be prepared for lots of traffic in the summertime.

With 240 mi of shoreline, Lake Winnipesaukee is so much more than just the town of Wolfeboro.

ESSENTIALS

Visitor Information **Wolfeboro Chamber of Commerce** (☎ *603/569–2200* 🌐 *www.wolfeboro.com/chamber*).

EXPLORING

New Hampshire Boat Museum. Two miles northeast of downtown, this museum celebrates the Lakes Region's boating legacy with displays of vintage Chris-Crafts, Jersey Speed Skiffs, three-point hydroplanes, and other fine watercraft, along with model boats, antique engines, racing photography and trophies, and old-timey signs from marinas. ✉ *397 Center St.* ☎ *603/569–4554* 🌐 *www.nhbm.org* 🎫 *$5* ⏲ *Memorial Day–Columbus Day, Mon.–Sat. 10–4; Sun. noon–4.*

Wright Museum. Uniforms, vehicles, and other artifacts at this museum illustrate the contributions of those on the home front to the U.S. World War II effort. ✉ *77 Center St.* ☎ *603/569–1212* 🌐 *www.wrightmuseum.org* 🎫 *$6* ⏲ *May–Oct., Mon.–Sat. 10–4; Sun. noon–4; Feb.–Apr., Sun. noon–4.*

QUICK BITES

Brewster Academy students and summer folk converge upon groovy little Lydia's (✉ *33 N. Main St.* ☎ *603/569–3991*) for espresso, sandwiches, homemade soups, bagels, and desserts. Picking up pastries, cookies, freshly baked breads, and other sweets in the Yum Yum Shop (✉ *16 N. Main St.* ☎ *603/569–1919* 🌐 *www.yumyumshop.net*) has been a tradition since 1948—the butter-crunch cookies are highly addictive.

SPORTS AND THE OUTDOORS

BEACH **Wentworth State Beach** (✉ *Rte. 109* ☎ *603/569–3699* 🌐 *www.nhstateparks.com/wentworthbeach.html* 🎫 *$4*) has good swimming, fishing, picnicking areas, ball fields, and a bathhouse.

HIKING A short (¼-mi) hike to the 100-foot post-and-beam **Abenaki Tower**, followed by a more rigorous climb to the top, rewards you with a view of Lake Winnipesaukee and the Ossipee mountain range. The trailhead is on Route 109 in Tuftonboro.

WATER SPORTS Scuba divers can explore The Lady, the 125-foot-long cruise ship that sank in 30 feet of water off Glendale in 1895. **Dive Winnipesaukee Corp** (✉ *4 N. Main St.* ☎ *603/569–8080* 🌐 *www.divewinnipesaukee.com*) runs charters out to wrecks and offers rentals, repairs, scuba sales, and lessons in waterskiing.

SHOPPING

American Home Gallery (✉ *49 Center St., Wolfeboro Falls* ☎ *603/569–8989* 🌐 *www.juliefergus.com*) mixes an amazing array of antiques and housewares in with its architectural elements. You'll find an excellent regional-history section and plenty of children's titles at **Country Bookseller** (✉ *23A N. Main St.* ☎ *603/569–6030*), Wolfeboro's fine general-interest bookstore. The artisans at **Hampshire Pewter Company** (✉ *43 Mill St.* ☎ *603/569–4944 or 800/639–7704* 🌐 *www.hampshirepewter.com*) use 16th-century techniques to make pewter tableware and accessories. Come to shop or take a free tour Memorial Day through Columbus Day, weekdays at 10, 11, 1, 2, and 3.

WHERE TO EAT

$ ASIAN ✕ **East of Suez**. In a countrified lodge on the south side of town, this friendly restaurant serves creative pan-Asian cuisine, with an emphasis on Philippine fare, such as *lumpia* (pork-and-shrimp spring rolls with a sweet-and-sour fruit sauce) and *pancit canton* (panfried egg noodles with sautéed shrimp and pork and Asian vegetables with a sweet oyster sauce). You can also sample Thai red curries, Japanese tempura, and Korean-style flank steak. ✉ *775 S. Main St.* ☎ *603/569–1648* 🌐 *www.eastofsuez.com* 💳 *AE, MC, V* ⊗ *Closed Oct.–mid-May.*

$–$$ SEAFOOD ★ ✕ **Wolfetrap Grill and Raw Bar**. The seafood at this winsome shanty on Lake Winnipesaukee comes from the adjacent fish market. You'll find all your favorites here, including a clam boil for one that includes steamers, corn on the cob, onions, baked potatoes, sweet potatoes, sausage, and a hot dog. The raw bar serves oysters and clams on the half shell. ✉ *19 Bay St.* ☎ *603/569–1047* 🌐 *www.wolfetrap.com* 💳 *AE, D, MC, V* ⊗ *Closed Labor Day–Memorial Day.*

WHERE TO STAY

$$ ★ **Topsides B & B**. At this stylish retreat, refined rooms convey the allure of a particular region, from coastal France to Martha's Vineyard to British fox-hunting country. Lavish custom bedding, Persian rugs, marble dressers, and fresh flowers lend an eclectic sophistication to this pale-gray clapboard inn that's steps from downtown shops and restaurants. High-speed wireless, homemade bath amenities, and highly personalized attention complete the experience. **Pros:** great location; clean, simple rooms. **Cons:** Continental breakfast only. ✉ *209 S. Main St.* ☎ *603/569–3834*

OUTDOOR OUTFITTERS AND RESOURCES

BIKING

Bike the Whites (☎ *877/854-6535* ⊕ *www.bikethewhites.com*) organizes bike tours in New Hampshire and Vermont. **New England Hiking Holidays** (☎ *603/356-9696 or 800/869-0949* ⊕ *www.nehikingholidays.com*) arranges bicycling trips in the region.

HIKING

U.S. Forest Service (☎ *603/528-8721 or 877/444-6777* ⊕ *www.fs.fed.us/r9/forests/white_mountain*) or **Appalachian Mountain Club** (☎ *800/372-1758* ⊕ *www.outdoors.org*). **New England Hiking Holidays** (☎ *603/356-9696 or 800/869-0949* ⊕ *www.nehikingholidays.com*). **New Hampshire State Parks** (☎ *603/271-3556* ⊕ *www.nhstateparks.org*).

SKIING

Ski New Hampshire (*Box 10, North Woodstock, 03262* ☎ *603/745-9396 or 800/887-5464* ⊕ *www.skinh.com*).

⊕ *www.topsidesbb.com* *5 rooms* *In-room: Wi-Fi. In-hotel: Internet terminal, Wi-Fi hotspot, no kids under 12* *D, MC, V* *CP.*

$$–$$$ ★ **Wolfeboro Inn.** This 1812 inn has a commanding lakefront location and is a perennial favorite for those visiting Lake Winnipesaukee. Warm yourself up by the fieldstone fireplace in the guest area. Most rooms have nice outside light from big windows, and a number have terraces. The hotel has a tavern with four fireplaces and row upon row of pewter beer mugs, 1,900 in all, hanging from the ceiling. Renovations in 2008 spruced up the rooms in the original building, creating a boutiquey flavor. The owners have taken the same approach to classic old properties in Exeter and Concord. **Pros:** lakefront setting; interesting pub. **Cons:** availability sometimes limited due to weddings and corporate groups. ✉ *90 N. Main St.* *Box 1270, 03894* ☎ *603/569-3016 or 800/451-2389* ⊕ *www.wolfeboroinn.com* *41 rooms, 3 suites, 1 apartment* *In-room: Wi-Fi. In-hotel: restaurant, bar, Internet terminal, Wi-Fi hotspot* *AE, D, MC, V* *CP.*

ALTON BAY

10 mi southwest of Wolfeboro.

Lake Winnipesaukee's southern shore is alive with visitors from the moment the first flower blooms until the last maple sheds its leaves. Two mountain ridges hold 7 mi of the lake in Alton Bay, which is the name of both the inlet and the town at its tip. Cruise boats dock here, and small planes land year-round on the water and the ice. There's a dance pavilion, along with miniature golf, a public beach, and a Victorian-style bandstand.

EXPLORING

Mt. Major, 5 mi north of Alton Bay on Route 11, has a 2.5-mi trail up a series of challenging cliffs. At the top is a four-sided stone shelter built in 1925, but the reward is the spectacular view of Lake Winnipesaukee.

WHERE TO EAT

$$$$ AMERICAN ★ **Crystal Quail.** This four-table BYOB restaurant with seating for 12, inside an 18th-century farmhouse, is worth the drive for the sumptuous meals prepared by longtime proprietors Harold and Cynthia Huckaby, who use free-range meats and mostly organic produce and herbs in their cooking. The prix-fixe menu changes daily but might include saffron-garlic soup, a house pâté, mushroom and herb quail, or goose confit with apples and onions. *202 Pitman Rd., 12 mi south of Alton Bay, Center Barnstead 603/269–4151 www.crystalquail.com Reservations essential No credit cards BYOB Closed Mon. and Tues. No lunch.*

WEIRS BEACH

17 mi northwest of Alton Bay.

Weirs Beach is Lake Winnipesaukee's center for arcade activity. Anyone who loves souvenir shops, fireworks, waterslides, and hordes of children will feel right at home. Cruise boats also depart from here.

GETTING HERE AND AROUND

Weirs Beach is just north of Laconia and south of Meredith on Route 3.

EXPLORING

Funspot. The mothership of Lake Winnipesaukee's several family-oriented amusement parks, Funspot claims to be the largest arcade in the world, but it's much more than just a video-game room. Indeed, you can work your way through a miniature golf course, a driving range, an indoor golf simulator, 20 lanes of bowling, cash bingo, and more than 500 video games. Some outdoor attractions are closed in winter months. *Rte. 3, Weirs Beach 603/366–4377 www.funspotnh.com Mid-June–Labor Day, daily 9 AM–11 PM; Labor Day–mid-June, Sun.–Thurs. 10–10, Fri. and Sat. 10 AM–11 PM.*

Fodor's Choice ★ **MS *Mount Washington*.** This 230-foot boat makes 2½-hour scenic cruises of Lake Winnipesaukee from Weirs Beach from mid-May to late October, with stops in Wolfeboro, Alton Bay, Center Harbor, and Meredith (you can board at any of these). Evening cruises include live music and a buffet dinner and have nightly music themes, so check ahead to make sure it's music you like. The same company operates the MV *Sophie C.* ($22), which has been the area's floating post office for more than a century. The boat departs from Weirs Beach with mail and passengers and lets you see areas of the lake not accessible by larger ships. Additionally, you can ride the MV *Doris E.* ($22) on one- and two-hour scenic cruises of Meredith Bay and the lake islands throughout summer. *603/366–5531 or 888/843–6686 www.cruisenh.com $25 Day cruises, departures daily every few hours mid-June–late Oct. Special cruises, departure times vary.*

★ **Winnipesaukee Scenic Railroad.** The period cars of this railroad carry you along the lakeshore on one- or two-hour rides; boarding is at Weirs Beach or Meredith. Special trips that include dinner are also available, as are foliage trains in fall and special Santa trains in December. *U.S. 3, Weirs Beach 603/279–5253 or 603/745–2135 (Lincoln* *location)* ⊕ *www.hoborr.com* 🎫 *$14–$99* ⏲ *July–mid-Sept., daily; Memorial Day–late June and mid-Sept.–mid-Oct., weekends only. Call for hours.*

SPORTS AND THE OUTDOORS

BEACH AND BOATING **Ellacoya State Beach** (✉ *Rte. 11, Gilford* ☎ *603/293–7821* ⊕ *www.nhstateparks.com/ellacoya.html* 🎫 *$4* ⏲ *Mid-May–Labor Day*) covers just 600 feet along the southwestern shore of Lake Winnipesaukee. **Thurston's Marina** (✉ *18 Endicott St. N* ☎ *603/366–4811* ⊕ *www.thurstonsmarina.com*) rents watercraft such as pontoon boats and powerboats.

GOLF **Pheasant Ridge Golf Club** (✉ *140 Country Club Rd., Gilford* ☎ *603/524–7808* ⊕ *www.playgolfne.com*) has an 18-hole layout with great mountain views. Green fees range from $20 to $43.

SKI AREAS **Gunstock Mountain Resort.** High above Lake Winnipesaukee, this all-purpose recreation area, originally a WPA project, dates from 1937. In the past seven years, it has invested $10 million to increase snowmaking, options for beginning skiers, and amenities such as private ski lessons and slopeside dining. Thrill Hill, a snow-tubing park, has four runs, a lift service, and a 12-acre terrain park with jumps, rails, and tabletops for snowboarders looking for a challenge, and a racing program. The ski area has 53 trails, 21 open for night skiing, and 32 mi of cross-country and snowshoeing trails available. In summer enjoy the swimming pool, playground, hiking trails, mountain-bike rentals and trails, a skateboarding and blading park, guided horseback rides, pedal boats, and a campground. ✉ *719 Cherry Valley Rd., Gilford* ☎ *603/293–4341 or 800/486–7862* ⊕ *www.gunstock.com.*

SHOPPING

Pepi Herrmann Crystal (✉ *3 Waterford Pl.* ☎ *603/528–1020* ⊕ *www.handcut.com*) sells hand-cut crystal chandeliers and stemware. Take a tour and watch artists at work. Closed Monday.

NIGHTLIFE AND THE ARTS

The **New Hampshire Music Festival** (☎ *603/279–3300* ⊕ *www.nhmf.org*) presents award-winning orchestras from early July to mid-August; concerts occur at the Festival House on Symphony Lane in Center Harbor or at the Silver Cultural Arts Center on Main Street in Plymouth.

LACONIA

4 mi west of Gilford, 27 mi north of Concord.

The arrival in Laconia—then called Meredith Bridge—of the railroad in 1848 turned the once-sleepy hamlet into the Lakes Region's chief manufacturing hub. It acts today as the area's supply depot, a perfect role given its accessibility to both Winnisquam and Winnipesaukee lakes as well as Interstate 93. It also draws bikers from around the world for Laconia Motorcycle Week in June.

GETTING HERE AND AROUND

The best way to Laconia is on Route 3 or Route 11. Scenic rides from the south include Route 106 and Route 107.

EXPLORING

Belknap Mill. The oldest unaltered, brick-built textile mill in the United States (1823), Belknap Mill contains a knitting museum devoted to the textile industry and a year-round cultural center that sponsors concerts, workshops, exhibits, and a lecture series. ✉ *Mill Plaza, 25 Beacon St. E* ☎ *603/524–8813* 🌐 *www.belknapmill.org* 🎫 *Free* ⏲ *Weekdays 9–5.*

OFF THE BEATEN PATH

Canterbury Shaker Village. Shaker furniture and inventions are well regarded, and this National Historic Landmark helps illuminate the world of the people who created them. Established as a religious community in 1792, the village flourished in the 1800s and practiced equality of the sexes and races, common ownership, celibacy, and pacifism. The last member of the community passed away in 1992. Shakers invented such household items as the clothespin and the flat broom and were known for the simplicity and integrity of their designs. Engaging 90-minute tours pass through some of the 694-acre property's more than 25 restored buildings, many of them still with original Shaker furnishings, and crafts demonstrations take place daily. The Shaker Table restaurant ($$–$$$$) serves lunch daily and candlelight dinners Thursday–Sunday (reservations essential); the food blends contemporary and traditional Shaker recipes to delicious effect. A large shop sells fine Shaker reproductions. ✉ *288 Shaker Rd., 15 mi south of Laconia via Rte. 106, Canterbury* ☎ *603/783–9511 or 866/783–9511* 🌐 *www.shakers.org* 🎫 *$15, good for 2 consecutive days* ⏲ *Mid-May–Oct., daily 10–5; Apr., Nov., and Dec., weekends 10–4.*

SPORTS AND THE OUTDOORS

Bartlett Beach (✉ *Winnisquam Ave.*) has a playground and picnic area and no fee. **Opechee Park** (✉ *N. Main St.*) has dressing rooms, a baseball field, tennis courts, and picnic areas.

SHOPPING

The more than 50 stores at the **Tanger Outlet Center** (✉ *120 Laconia Rd., I–93 Exit 20, Tilton* ☎ *603/286–7880* 🌐 *www.tangeroutlet.com*) include Brooks Brothers, Eddie Bauer, Coach, and Mikasa.

WHERE TO STAY

$$ **Ferry Point House.** Four miles southwest of Laconia, this home across the street from Lake Winnisquam is a quiet retreat with easy access to a private boat house, rowboat, dock, and a small beach. Built in the 1800s as a summer retreat for the Pillsbury family of baking fame, this red Victorian farmhouse has superb views of the lake. White wicker furniture and hanging baskets of flowers grace the 60-foot veranda, and the gazebo by the water's edge is a pleasant place to lounge and listen for loons. The pretty rooms have Victorian-style wallpaper. **Pros:** affordable, lovely setting; parlor room has decanted sherry. **Cons:** best for relaxed do-it-yourselfers. ✉ *100 Lower Bay Rd., Sanbornton* ☎ *603/524–0087* 🌐 *www.ferrypointhouse.com* *9 rooms, 1 suite* *In-room: no phone, no a/c (some), no TV, Wi-Fi. In-hotel: water sports, Wi-Fi hotspot, no kids under 11* *No credit cards* *BP.*

What's your vessel of choice for exploring New Hampshire's Lakes Region: kayak, canoe, powerboat, or sailboat?

MEREDITH

11 mi north of Laconia.

Meredith is a favored spot for water-sports enthusiasts and anglers. Lodgers will love the luxurious beds at the Inns at Mill Falls, which is next to an old factory filled with gift and clothing shops. For a true taste of Meredith, take a walk down Main Street, just one block from busy Route 3, which is dotted with intimate coffee shops, salons and barber shops, family restaurants, redbrick buildings, antiques stores, and a gun shop. You can pick up area information at a kiosk across from the town docks. One caveat: on busy weekends, getting into town from the west can mean sitting in traffic for 30 minutes or more.

ESSENTIALS

Visitor Information **Meredith Area Chamber of Commerce** (☎ *877/279–6121* 🌐 *www.meredithcc.org*).

SPORTS AND THE OUTDOORS

Red Hill, a hiking trail on Bean Road off Route 25, northeast of Center Harbor and about 7 mi northeast of Meredith, really does turn red in autumn. The reward at the end of the route is a view of Squam Lake and the mountains.

BOATING Meredith is near the quaint village of Center Harbor, another boating hub that's in the middle of three bays at the northern end of Lake Winnipesaukee. **Meredith Marina** (✉ *2 Bayshore Dr.* ☎ *603/279–7921* 🌐 *www.meredithmarina.com*) rents powerboats. **Wild Meadow Canoes & Kayaks** (✉ *6 Whittier Way in Center Harbor* ☎ *603/253–7536 or 800/427–7536* 🌐 *www.wildmeadowcanoes.com*) has canoes and kayaks for rent.

SHOPPING

Annalee's Outlet Store (✉ *50 Reservoir Rd.* ☎ *603/270–6542* 🌐 *www.annalee.com* ⏲ *Daily 10–6*) sells, at a discount, the seasonal decorations and dolls of the Annalee company, famous for its felt dolls that Annalee Davis Thorndike began making here in 1933. More than 175 dealers operate out of the three-floor **Burlwood Antique Center** (✉ *194 U.S. 3* ☎ *603/279–6387* 🌐 *www.burlwood-antiques.com*), open May–October. **Keepsake Quilting & Country Pleasures** (✉ *Senters Market, Rte. 25B, Center Harbor, 5 mi northeast of Meredith* ☎ *603/253–4026 or 800/525–8086* 🌐 *www.keepsakequilting.com*), reputedly America's largest quilt shop, contains 5,000 bolts of fabric, hundreds of quilting books, and countless supplies, as well as handmade quilts.

★ The **League of New Hampshire Craftsmen** (✉ *279 U.S. 3* ☎ *603/279–7920* 🌐 *www.nhcrafts.org*) sells works by area artisans. It's next to the Inn at Church Landing. **Mill Falls Marketplace** (✉ *312 Daniel Webster Hwy.* ☎ *800/622–6455* 🌐 *www.millfalls.com*), part of the Inns at Mill Falls, contains shops with clothing, gifts, and books set around the old factory waterfall that runs through it. The **Old Print Barn** (✉ *343 Winona Rd., New Hampton* ☎ *603/279–6479*) carries rare prints—Currier & Ives, antique botanicals, and more—from around the world.

THE ARTS

The **Summer Theatre in Meredith Village** (✉ *One Laker La., Interlakes Auditorium, Rte. 25* ☎ *888/245–6374* 🌐 *www.interlakestheatre.com*) presents Broadway musicals during its 10-week season of summer stock.

WHERE TO EAT AND STAY

$$ AMERICAN ✕ **Lakehouse Grille.** With perhaps the best lake views of any restaurant in the region, this restaurant might be forgiven for ambitious dishes that fall short of being really good. Come here to be near the lake, especially in the convivial bar area, and you'll leave quite happy. The setting is an upscale lodge and is one of the Common Man restaurants. The best dishes are old reliables like steak, ribs, and pizza. Breakfast is served daily. ✉ *Church Landing, 281 Rte. 3* ☎ *603/279–5221* 🌐 *www.thecman.com* 💳 *AE, D, MC, V.*

$$ AMERICAN ✕ **Mame's.** This 1820s tavern, once the home of the village doctor, now contains a warren of dining rooms with exposed-brick walls, wooden beams, and wide-plank floors. Expect a wide variety of beef, seafood, and chicken plates, but don't be afraid to order the "Luncheon Nightmare," pumpernickel-rye bread topped with turkey, ham, broccoli, and bacon and baked in a cheese sauce. You can also find vegetarian dishes, burgers, sandwiches, and wonderful soups and salads on the menu. Save room for the bread pudding with apples and rum sauce. A cozy tavern upstairs features pub food. ✉ *8 Plymouth St.* ☎ *603/279–4631* 🌐 *www.mamesrestaurant.com* 💳 *AE, D, MC, V.*

$$$–$$$$ Fodor's Choice ★ 🏨 **Inns and Spa at Mill Falls.** There are four separate hotels here: two new properties are on the shore of Lake Winnipesaukee, one is connected to a 19th-century mill (now a lively shopping area) and its roaring falls, and the last has views overlooking the lake. The central Inn at Mill Falls, which adjoins an 18-shop market, has a pool and 54 spacious rooms. The lakefront Inn at Bay Point has 24 rooms—most with balconies, some

View simple yet functional furniture, architecture, and crafts at Canterbury Shaker Village.

with fireplaces. The 23 rooms at the lake-view Chase House at Mill Falls all have fireplaces; some have balconies. The star of the show is Church Landing, a dramatic lakefront lodge where most rooms have expansive decks with terrific water views. The Cascade Spa is one of the nicest in the state, with a heated pool that crosses from indoors to outdoors. **Pros:** many lodging choices and prices; lakefront rooms; fun environment. **Cons:** expensive; two buildings are not on lakefront. ✉ *312 Daniel Webster Hwy. (Rte 3), at Rte. 25* ☎ *603/279–7006 or 800/622–6455* 🌐 *www.millfalls.com* *156 rooms, 15suites* *In-room: refrigerator, Wi-Fi. In-hotel: 5 restaurants, room service, 4 bars, pools, gym, spa, water sports, Internet terminal, Wi-Fi hotspot* *AE, D, MC, V* *CP.*

HOLDERNESS

8 mi southeast of Plymouth; 8 mi northwest of Meredith.

Routes 25B and 25 lead to the prim small town of Holderness, between Squam and Little Squam lakes. *On Golden Pond,* starring Katharine Hepburn and Henry Fonda, was filmed on Squam, whose quiet beauty attracts nature lovers.

EXPLORING

Fodor's Choice ★ **Squam Lakes Natural Science Center.** Trails on this 200-acre property include a ¾-mi path that passes black bears, bobcats, otters, mountain lions, and other native wildlife in trailside enclosures. The "Up Close to Animals" series in July and August allows visitors to see a species at an educational presentation in an amphitheater. Children's activities include learning about bugs, watercolor painting of plants and animals, and wilderness survival skills. The boat ride is the best way to tour the lake: naturalists explain its science and describe the animals that make their home here, including fascinating stuff about the loon. ✉ *Rte. 113* ☎ *603/968–7194* 🌐 *www.nhnature.org* 🎟 *Center $13, boat tour $22, combination ticket $32* ⏲ *May–Oct., daily 9:30–4:30 (last entry at 3:30).*

WHERE TO EAT

$$$ AMERICAN ✕ **Manor on Golden Pond Restaurant.** Leaded glass panes and wood paneling set the decidedly romantic tone at this wonderful inn's dining rooms on a hill overlooking Squam Lake. The main dining room is in the manor's original billiard room and features woodwork from 1902. Two other dining rooms have very separate looks: one features white linen, fresh flowers, and candlelight; the other is in the style of a Parisian bistro. The menu changes weekly but might include lobster risotto, filet mignon, quail, or monkfish. Breakfast is also served. A fabulous seven-course tasting menu is $75. ✉ *31 Manor Dr., on the corner of Rte. 3 and Shepard Dr., Holderness* ☎ *603/968–3348* 🌐 *www.manorongoldenpond.com* *Reservations essential* 💳 *AE, D, MC, V.*

$–$$ AMERICAN ✕ **Walter's Basin.** A former bowling alley in the heart of Holderness makes an unlikely but charming setting for meals overlooking Little Squam Lake—local boaters dock right beneath the dining room. Among the specialties on this seafood-intensive menu are crostini with panfried rainbow trout. Burgers and sandwiches are served in the adjoining tavern. ✉ *15 Main St. (U.S. 3)* ☎ *603/968–4412* 💳 *D, MC, V* ⏲ *Call for winter schedule.*

WHERE TO STAY

$$$$ **Glynn House Inn.** Pam, Ingrid, and Glenn Heidenreich operate this upscale 1890s Queen Anne–style Victorian with a turret and wraparound porch and, next door, a handsome 1920s carriage house. Expect the best in New England B&B comforts: comfy beds, flat-screen TVs, free wine and hors d'oeuvres, and excellent service. All but one of the 13 rooms have fireplaces, and the eight suites all include double-whirlpool tubs. A multicourse breakfast is served in a Victorian dining room. Squam Lake is minutes away. **Pros:** luxurious; well run; social atmosphere. **Cons:** not much to do in town. ✉ *59 Highland St., Ashland* ☎ *603/968–3775 or 866/686–4362 www.glynnhouse.com* *5 rooms, 8 suites* *In-room: Wi-Fi. In-hotel: Wi-Fi hotspot, some pets allowed* 💳 *MC, V* *BP.*

$$ **Inn on Golden Pond.** Sweet-as-pie Bill and Bonnie Webb run this comfortable and informal B&B at a slight walk from the lake, to which they provide hiking trail maps. In the living room you'll see maps pinned with the origin of guests, who come from all over (especially New York City and Boston). Rooms have hardwood floors, braided rugs, comfortable reading chairs, and country quilt bedspreads and curtains. The homemade jam at breakfast is made from rhubarb grown on the property. **Pros:** friendly innkeepers; very clean rooms and common spaces. **Cons:** 5-minute walk to access lake; not luxurious. ✉ *Rte. 3* *Box 680, Holderness 03245* ☎ *603/968–7269* 🌐 *www.innongoldenpond.com* *6 rooms, 2 suites* *In-room: no phone, no TV, Wi-Fi. In-hotel: Internet terminal, Wi-Fi hotspot, no kids under 12* 💳 *AE, D, MC, V* *BP.*

$$$ **Fodor's Choice** ★ **The Manor on Golden Pond.** A name like that is a lot to live up to. Luckily, the Manor is the most charming inn in the Lakes Region. Stroll down to the beach for a dip in the lake or to take a canoe for a paddle. The house sits on a slight rise overlooking Squam Lake, and the grounds consist of 15 acres of towering pines and hardwood trees. Relax on the lawn in one of the Adirondack chairs, gazing out at the lake. Back in the stately inn, owners Brian and Mary Ellen Shields ensure comfort. Rooms carry out a British country theme, most with wood-burning fireplaces and more than half with double whirlpool tubs. Canopy beds, vintage blanket chests, and tartan fabrics fill the sumptuous bedchambers. The restaurant ($$$) is terrific, and the Three Cock Pub is endearing. There's a small spa, and afternoon tea is served in the library. **Pros:** wood fireplaces; comfy sitting rooms; great food; welcoming hosts. **Cons:** expensive. ☒ *U.S. 3 and Shepard Hill Rd.* ☎ *603/968–3348 or 800/545–2141* ⊕ *www.manorongoldenpond.com* *22 rooms, 2 suites, 1 cottage* *In-room: Wi-Fi. In-hotel: 2 restaurants, room service, bar, tennis court, pool, spa, laundry service, Internet terminal, Wi-Fi hotspot, no kids under 12* *AE, D, MC, V.*

CENTER SANDWICH

★ *12 mi northeast of Holderness on Route 103.*

With Squam Lake to the west and the Sandwich Mountains to the north, Center Sandwich claims one of the prettiest settings of any Lakes Region community. So appealing are the town and its views that John Greenleaf Whittier used the Bearcamp River as the inspiration for his poem "Sunset on the Bearcamp." The town attracts artisans—crafts shops abound among its clutch of charming 18th- and 19th-century buildings.

ESSENTIALS

Visitor Information **Squam Lakes Area Chamber of Commerce** (☎ *603/968–4494* ⊕ *www.squamlakschamber.com*). **The Sandwich Historical Society** (☎ *603/284–6269* ⊕ *www.sandwichhistorical.org*).

EXPLORING

Castle in the Clouds. This wonderful mountaintop estate was built in 1913–14 without nails. The elaborate mansion has 16 rooms, eight bathrooms, and doors made of lead. Owner Thomas Gustave Plant spent $7 million, the bulk of his fortune, on this project and died penniless in 1941. A tour includes the mansion and the Castle Springs spring water facility on this 5,200-acre property overlooking Lake Winnipesaukee; there's also hiking and pony and horseback rides. ☒ *Rte. 171, Moultonborough* ☎ *603/476–5900* ⊕ *www.castleintheclouds.org* *$12* *Mid-May–Oct. 24, daily 10–4:30.*

The **Loon Center** and **Frederick and Paula Anna Markus Wildlife Sanctuary** is the headquarters of the Loon Preservation Committee, an Audubon Society project. The loon, recognizable for its eerie calls and striking black-and-white coloring, resides on many New Hampshire lakes but is threatened by boat traffic, poor water quality, and habitat loss. Two trails wind through the 200-acre property; vantage points on the Loon Nest Trail overlook the spot resident loons sometimes occupy in late spring and summer. ✉ *183 Lee's Mills Rd.* ☎ *603/476–5666* 🌐 *www.loon.org* 🎟 *Free* ⏲ *Columbus Day–late June, Mon.–Sat. 9–5; July–Columbus Day, daily 9–5.*

SHOPPING

The **Old Country Store and Museum** (✉ *1011 Whittier Hwy., Moultonborough* ☎ *603/476–5750*) has been selling maple products, cheeses aged on-site, penny candy, and other items since 1781. Much of the equipment still used in the store is antique, and the museum (free) displays old farming and forging tools.

WHERE TO EAT

$$ AMERICAN ✕ **Corner House Inn.** This restaurant, in a converted barn adorned with local arts and crafts, serves classic American fare. Salads with local greens are a house specialty, but also try the chef's lobster-and-mushroom bisque or the shellfish sauté. Lunch and Sunday brunch are served, and on Thursday evenings there's storytelling. ✉ *22 Main St.* ☎ *603/284–6219* 🌐 *www.cornerhouseinn.com* 💳 *AE, MC, V* ⏲ *No lunch mid-June–mid-Oct.*

$$ AMERICAN ✕ **The Woodshed.** Farm implements and antiques hang on the walls of this enchanting 1860 barn. The fare is mostly traditional New England—prime rib, rack of lamb, marinated chicken—but with some surprises, such as Cajun-blackened pork tenderloin. Either way, the exceptionally fresh ingredients are sure to please. ✉ *128 Lee Rd., Moultonborough* ☎ *603/476–2311* 🌐 *www.thewoodshedrestaurant.com* 💳 *AE, D, DC, MC, V* ⏲ *Closed Mon. No lunch.*

TAMWORTH

13 mi east of Center Sandwich, 20 mi southwest of North Conway.

President Grover Cleveland summered in what remains a village of almost unreal quaintness—it's equally photogenic in verdant summer, during the fall foliage season, or under a blanket of winter snow. Cleveland's son, Francis, returned and founded the acclaimed Barnstormers Theatre in 1931, one of America's first summer theaters and one that continues to this day. Tamworth has a clutch of villages within its borders. At one of them—Chocorua—the view through the birches of Chocorua Lake has been so often photographed that you may experience déjà vu. Rising above the lake is Mount Chocorua (3,490 feet), which has many good hiking trails.

GETTING HERE AND AROUND

The five villages of Tamworth boast six churches, which are worth a half-day's casual drive to admire their white clabbered elegance. Downtown Tamworth is tiny and can be strolled in a few minutes, but you might linger in the hope to meet one of the town's many resident poets and artists.

EXPLORING

Remick Country Doctor Museum and Farm. For 99 years (1894–1993) Dr. Edwin Crafts Remick and his father provided medical services to the Tamworth area and operated a family farm. After the younger Remick died, these two houses were turned into the Remick Country Doctor

Museum and Farm. The exhibits focus on the life of a country doctor and on the activities of the still-working farm. You can tour the farm daily, and each season features a special activity such as maple syrup making or building without nails. The second floor of the house has been kept as it was when Remick passed away; it's a great way to see the life of a true Tamworth townsman. ✉ *58 Cleveland Hill Rd.* ☎ *603/323–7591 or 800/686–6117* 🌐 *www.remickmuseum.org* 🎟 *$3* ⏲ *Nov.–June, weekdays 10–4; July–Oct., Mon.–Sat. 10–4.*

3

SPORTS AND THE OUTDOORS

White Lake State Park. The 72-acre stand of native pitch pine here is a National Natural Landmark. The park has hiking trails, a sandy beach, trout fishing, canoe rentals, two camping areas, a picnic area, and swimming. ✉ *1632 White Mountain Hwy., Tamworth* ☎ *603/323–7350* 🌐 *www.nhstateparks.com/whitelake.html* 🎟 *$4* ⏲ *Late May–mid-June, weekends dawn–dusk; mid-June–early Sept., daily dawn–dusk.*

SHOPPING

The many rooms with themes—Christmas, bridal, and children's among them—at the **Chocorua Dam Ice Cream & Gift Shop** (✉ *Rte. 16, Chocorua* ☎ *603/323–8745*) contain handcrafted items. Don't forget to try the ice cream, coffee, or tea and scones.

THE ARTS

The **Arts Council of Tamworth** (☎ *603/323–8104* 🌐 *www.artstamworth.org*) produces concerts—soloists, string quartets, revues, children's programs—from September through June and an arts show in late July. **Barnstormers Summer Theatre** (✉ *Main St.* ☎ *603/323–8661* 🌐 *www.barnstormerstheatre.com*) has dramatic and comedic theater productions year-round.

WHERE TO EAT AND STAY

$ SEAFOOD ✕ **Jake's Seafood.** Oars and nautical trappings adorn the wood-paneled walls at this stop between West and Center Ossipee, about 8 mi southeast of Tamworth. The kitchen serves some of eastern New Hampshire's freshest and tastiest seafood, notably lobster pie, fried clams, and seafood casserole; other choices include steak, ribs, and chicken dishes. ✉ *2055 Rte. 16, West Ossipee* ☎ *603/539–2805* 🌐 *www.jakesseafoodco.com* 💳 *MC, V.*

$ SOUTHERN ★ ✕ **Yankee Smokehouse.** Need a rib fix? This down-home barbecue joint's logo depicting a happy pig foreshadows the gleeful enthusiasm with which patrons dive into the hefty sandwiches of sliced pork and smoked chicken and immense platters of baby back ribs and smoked sliced beef. Ample sides of slaw, beans, fries, and garlic toast complement the hearty fare. Even Southerners have been known to come away impressed. ✉ *Rtes. 16 and 25, about 5 mi southeast of Tamworth* ☎ *603/539–7427* 🌐 *www.yankeesmokehouse.com* 💳 *MC, V.*

$ ★ 🏨 **Lazy Dog Inn.** If you travel with your dog, you've just found your new favorite B&B. What began as a stagecoach stop has been operating as an inn almost continuously since 1845, and when Laura and Steven Sousa took over earlier this decade, they converted the inn to an über–doggie-friendly B&B. The barn became a "doggie lodge" with a number of runs, a canine lullaby CD plays, and the innkeepers care for the dogs during the day while guests explore the Lakes Region or the White Mountains. It's an exceptional niche, but it's not done at the expense of the rooms, which are the cleanest and best furnished within miles. The lodging rate includes dog care. **Pros:** mega–dog friendly; super clean. **Cons:** some rooms share bath; some people don't like dogs. ✉ *201 Rte. 16, Chocorua* ☎ *603/323–8350 or 888/323–8350* 🌐 *www.lazydoginn.com* *7 rooms, 3 with bath* *In-room: no phone, Wi-Fi. In-hotel: gym, Wi-Fi hotspot, some pets allowed, no kids under 14* *D, MC, V* *BP.*

THE WHITE MOUNTAINS

Sailors approaching East Coast harbors frequently mistake the pale peaks of the White Mountains—the highest range in the northeastern United States—for clouds. It was 1642 when explorer Darby Field could no longer contain his curiosity about one mountain in particular. He set off from his Exeter homestead and became the first European to climb what would later be called Mt. Washington. The 6,288-foot peak must have presented Field with formidable obstacles—its summit claims the highest wind velocity in the world ever recorded (231 MPH in 1934) and can see snow every month of the year.

Today an auto road and a cog railway lead to the top of Mt. Washington, and people come by the tens of thousands to hike and climb, photograph the vistas, and ski. The peak is part of the Presidential Range, whose peaks are named after early presidents, and part of the White Mountain National Forest, which has roughly 770,000 acres that extend from northern New Hampshire into southwestern Maine. Among the forest's scenic notches (deep mountain passes) are Pinkham, Kinsman, Franconia, and Crawford. From the notches lead trailheads for short hikes and multi-day adventures, which are also excellent spots for photographing the majestic White Mountains

This section of the guide begins in Waterville Valley, off Interstate 93, and continues to North Woodstock. It then follows portions of the White Mountains Trail, a 100-mi loop designated as a National Scenic and Cultural Byway.

ESSENTIALS

Visitor Information White Mountains Visitors Bureau (✉ *Kancamagus Hwy. [Rte. 112] at I–93, North Woodstock* ☎ *800/346–3687* 🌐 *www.whitemtn.org*). **White Mountain National Forest** (🌐 *www.fs.fed.us/r9/forests/white_mountain*).

WATERVILLE VALLEY

60 mi north of Concord.

The first visitors began arriving in Waterville Valley in 1835. A 10-mi cul-de-sac follows the Mad River and is surrounded by mountains. The valley was first a summer resort and then more of a ski area. Although it's now a year-round getaway, it still has a small-town charm. There are inns, condos, restaurants, shops, conference facilities, a grocery store, and a post office.

GETTING HERE AND AROUND

Depot Camp is a great starting point for hiking, snowshoeing, and cross-country skiing. In town, the Schuss bus has regular stops at the shops in Village Square, the lodges and condos, the Waterville Valley Conference Center, and the ski area. There's enough to do in this small village to keep outdoor enthusiasts busy for several days.

SPORTS AND THE OUTDOORS

The **White Mountain Athletic Club** (✉ *Rte. 49* ☎ *603/236–8303* 🌐 *www.wmacwv.com*) has tennis, racquetball, and squash as well as a 25-meter indoor pool, a jogging track, exercise equipment, whirlpools, saunas, steam rooms, and a games room. The club is free to guests of many area lodgings.

SKI AREA **Waterville Valley**. Former U.S. ski-team star Tom Corcoran designed this family-oriented resort. The lodgings and various amenities are about 1 mi from the slopes, but a shuttle renders a car unnecessary. This ski area has hosted more World Cup races than any other in the East, so most advanced skiers will be challenged. Most of the 52 trails are intermediate: straight down the fall line, wide, and agreeably long. A 7-acre tree-skiing area adds variety. One hundred percent snowmaking coverage ensures good skiing even when nature doesn't cooperate. The Waterville Valley cross-country network, with the ski center in the town square, has 65 mi of trails, about two thirds of which are groomed; the rest are backcountry. ✉ *1 Ski Area Rd.* 📫 *Box 540, 03215* ☎ *603/236–8311; 603/236–4144 snow conditions; 800/468–2553 lodging* 🌐 *www.waterville.com.*

WHERE TO STAY

$$$$ **Black Bear Lodge**. This family-friendly property has one-bedroom suites that sleep up to six and have full kitchens. Each of the 107 units is individually owned and decorated. Children's movies are shown at night in season, and there's bus service to the slopes. Guests can use the White Mountain Athletic Club. There's a small heated pool and hot tub. **Pros:** affordable. **Cons:** basic in its decor and services. ✉ *3 Village Rd.* 📫 *Box 357, 03215* ☎ *603/236–4501 or 800/349–2327* 🌐 *www.blackbearlodgenh.com* *107 suites* *In-room: no a/c (some), kitchen, Wi-Fi. In-hotel: pool, gym, Wi-Fi hotspot* *AE, D, MC, V.*

$$$$ **Golden Eagle Lodge**. Waterville's premier condominium property—with its steep roof punctuated by dozens of gabled dormers—recalls the grand hotels of an earlier era. Rooms are outfitted with upscale light-wood furniture and well-equipped kitchens; many have views of the surrounding peaks. Guests have access to the White Mountain Athletic Club. **Pros:** most reliable accommodation in town. **Cons:** somewhat bland architecture and decor. ✉ *28 Packard's Rd., Box 495* ☎ *603/236–4600 or 888/703–2453 www.goldeneaglelodge.com* *139 condominiums* *In-room: kitchen, Wi-Fi (fee). In-hotel: pool, laundry facilities, laundry service, Internet terminal, Wi-Fi hotspot (fee)* *AE, D, DC, MC, V.*

$$$$ **Snowy Owl Inn**. You're treated to afternoon wine and cheese in the atrium lobby, which has a three-story fieldstone fireplace and prints and watercolors of snowy owls. The fourth-floor bunk-bed lofts are ideal for families; first-floor rooms are suitable for couples seeking a quiet

getaway. Four restaurants are within walking distance. Guests have access to the White Mountain Athletic Club. **Pros:** affordable. **Cons:** bland. ✉ *4 Village Rd., Box 407* ☎ *603/236–8383 or 800/766–9969* 🌐 *www.snowyowlinn.com* *85 rooms* *In-room: kitchen (some), Wi-Fi. In-hotel: pools, gym, Internet terminal, Wi-Fi hotspot* *AE, D, DC, MC, V* *BP.*

LINCOLN/NORTH WOODSTOCK

64 mi north of Concord

These neighboring towns at the southwestern end of the White Mountains National Forest and one end of the Kancamagus Highway (Route 112) are a lively resort area, especially for Bostonian families who can make an easy day trip straight up Interstate 93 to Exit 32. Festivals, such as the New Hampshire Scottish Highland Games in mid-September, keep Lincoln swarming with people year-round. The town itself is not much of an attraction. Tiny North Woodstock maintains more of a village feel.

GETTING HERE AND AROUND

Lincoln and North Woodstock are places to spend a day shopping in their quaint shops, which are within easy walking distance of each other. It's a pleasant 1-mi stroll between the two towns. On Route 112, which connects the two villages, there is a state visitor center.

ESSENTIALS

Visitor Information Lincoln–Woodstock Chamber of Commerce (☎ *603/745–6621* 🌐 *www.lincolnwoodstock.com*).

EXPLORING

Clarke's Trading Post. This old-time amusement park is a kids' favorite and chock full of hokum. It consists of a bear show, half-hour train rides over a 1904 covered bridge, a museum of Americana inside an 1880s firehouse, a restored gas station filled with antique cars, and a replica of the Old Man of the Mountain that you can climb on. Tour guides tell tall tales and vendors sell popcorn, ice cream, pizza, and snacks. There's also a mammoth gift shop and a penny-candy store. ✉ *U.S. 3, off I–93 (Exit 33), North Lincoln* ☎ *603/745–8913* 🌐 *www.clarkstradingpost.com* *$12* *Memorial Day–Columbus Day, daily 9–5 (until 9 PM Sat. July 5–Aug. 16).*

FUN TOUR

A ride on the Hobo Railroad yields scenic views of the Pemigewasset River and the White Mountain National Forest. The narrated excursions take 80 minutes. ✉ ***Kancamagus Hwy. (Rte. 112), Lincoln*** ☎ ***603/745–2135*** 🌐 ***www.hoborr.com*** ***$10*** ***Late June–early Sept., daily; May–late June and early Sept.–Oct., weekends; call for schedule.***

The White Mountains
CANADA
QUÉBEC
MAINE
VERMONT
Highlands
Gorham
Mt. Madison
Mt. Adams
Mt. Jefferson
Mt. Clay
Mt. Washington Auto Road
Cog Railway
Observatory
Mount Washington
Mt. Washington State Park
Fabyan
Pinkham Notch
Crawford Notch
Crawford Notch State Park
WHITE MOUNTAINS
Story Land
Glen
Bartlett
Echo Lake State Park
North Conway
0 4mi
0 4 km
Pittsburg
First Connecticut Lake
Lake Francis
Beecher Falls
Aziscohos Lake
Wilsons Mills
Colebrook
Dixville Notch
Dixville Notch State Park
Errol
Upton
Umbagog Lake
0 8mi
0 8 km
Lake Willoughby
North Stratford
West Burke
Maidstone Lake
Groveton
Guildhall
West Milan
Milan
White Mountain Nat'l Forest
Lyndonville
Lyndon
Lancaster
Berlin
Concord
Jefferson
Gilead
See Detail Above
Gorham
Saint Johnsbury
Whitefield
Mount Adams
Littleton
Mt. Washington
Twin Mountain
Pinkham Notch
Barnet
Bethlehem
Fabyan
Wildcat
Bretton Woods
Franconia
North Chatham
Lisbon
Franconia Notch State Park
Black Mountain
Jackson
Wells River
Cannon Mt.
Story Land
Woodsville
White Mountain National Forest
Attitash Ski Area
Glen
Echo Lake State Park
Lincoln/North Woodstock
Loon Mountain
Kancamagus Hwy.
Bartlett
N. Conway
Newbury
Bear Notch Rd.
Cranmore Moutain
Lincoln
Fryeburg
White Mountain Nat'l Forest
Conway
Bradford
Waterville Valley
Waterville Valley
Mount Chocurua
TO HANOVER
TO CONCORD
TO SNOWVILLE, EAST MADISON
Conway Lake
257
3
2
16
302
26
102
105
114
5
91
110
93
113
116
112
25
10
49
118
153

SPORTS AND THE OUTDOORS

At **Whale's Tale Waterpark** (✉ *U.S. 3, off I–93 [Exit 33], North Lincoln* ☎ *603/745–8810* 🌐 *www.whalestalewaterpark.net* 🎫 *$25* ⏲ *Mid-June–Labor Day, daily 10–6*) you can float on an inner tube along a gentle river, careen down one of five waterslides, take a trip in a multipassenger tube, or body-surf in the large wave pool. Whale Harbor and Orca Park Play Island contain water activities for small children and toddlers.

At **Lost River Gorge in Kinsman Notch** (✉ *Kancamagus Hwy. [Rte. 112], 6 mi west of North Woodstock* ☎ *603/745–8720 or 800/346–3687* 🌐 *www.findlostriver.com* 🎫 *$14 adults, $10 children* ⏲ *See Web site for hours*) parents can enjoy the looks of wonder on their children's faces as they negotiate a wilderness of wooden boardwalks and stairs that snake up and down a granite gorge carved by the waters of the Lost River. Kids can also wiggle through a series of caves such as the Lemon Squeezer and pan for gems and fossils. A cafeteria, gift shop, and garden round out the amenities.

Pemi Valley Excursions (✉ *Main St., off I–93 [Exit 32], Lincoln* ☎ *603/745–2744* 🌐 *www.i93.com/pvsr*) offers a variety of recreational and scenic tours throughout the year. It's one of the best snowmobile outfitters in the region, offering one- to two-hour guided tours and half- and full-day snowmobile rentals. Spring through summer, you can ride horseback along wooded trails and along the Pemigewasset River, enjoy horse-drawn-carriage rides, and embark on moose-watching bus tours into the northernmost White Mountains.

SKI AREA **Loon Mountain.** Wide, straight, and consistent intermediate trails prevail at Loon, a modern resort on the western edge of the Kancamagus Highway (Route 112) and the Pemigewasset River. Beginner trails and slopes are set apart. In the winter of 2007–08 Loon opened up the South Peak, with new trails and an express quad. The most advanced among the 47 runs are grouped on the North Peak section, with 2,100 feet of vertical skiing, farther from the main mountain. Snowboarders have a half-pipe and their own park; an alpine garden with bumps and jumps provides thrills for skiers. In the base lodge and around the mountain are the usual food-service and lounge facilities. Day and night lift-served snow tubing is on the lower slopes. The touring center at Loon Mountain has 35 mi of cross-country trails, and there's ice-skating on an outdoor rink. ✉ *Kancamagus Hwy. (Rte. 112), Lincoln* ☎ *603/745–8111; 603/745–8100 snow conditions; 800/227–4191 lodging* 🌐 *www.loonmtn.com.*

NIGHTLIFE

Skiers head to the **Black Diamond Lounge** (✉ *60 Loon Mountain Rd.* ☎ *603/745–2244* 🌐 *www.mtnclub.com*) in the Mountain Club at the Loon Mountain resort. The **Olde Timbermill** (✉ *Mill at Loon Mountain, 167 Main St.* ☎ *603/745–3603*) has live dance music on weekends. The **North Country Center for the Arts** (*Papermill Theatre* ✉ *25 Mountain Brook Cir., Kancamagus Hwy. [Rte. 112], Lincoln* ☎ *603/745–6032; 603/745–2141 box office* 🌐 *www.papermilltheatre.org*) presents theater for children and adults and art exhibitions in July and August. The draws at the **Thunderbird Lounge** (✉ *Indian Head Resort, 664 U.S. 3, North Lincoln* ☎ *603/745–8000*) are nightly entertainment year-round and a large dance floor.

Continued on page 192

A WALK IN THE WOODS

Hiking the Appalachian Trail

By Melissa Kim

Tucked inside the nation's most densely populated corridor, a simple footpath in the wilderness stretches more than 2,100 miles, from Georgia to Maine. The Appalachian Trail passes through some of New England's most spectacular regions, and daytrippers can experience the area's beauty on a multitude of accessible, rewarding hikes.

Running along the spine of the Appalachian Mountains, the trail was fully blazed in 1937 and designed to connect anyone and everyone with nature. Within a day's drive of two-thirds of the U.S. population, it draws an estimated four million people every year. Through-hikers complete the whole trail in one daunting six-month season, but all ages and abilities can find renewal and perspective here in just a few hours. One-third of the AT passes through New England, and it's safe to say that the farther north you go, the harder the trail gets. New Hampshire and Maine challenge experienced hikers with windy, cold, and isolated peaks.

Top, hiking in New Hampshire's White Mountains. Above, autumn view of Profile Lake, Pemigewasset, NH.

ON THE TRAIL

New England's prime hiking season is in late summer and early fall, when the blaze of foliage viewed from a high peak is unparalleled. Popular trails see high crowds; if you seek solitude, try hiking at sunrise, a peaceful time that's good for wildlife viewing. You'll have to curb your enthusiasm in spring and early summer to avoid mud season in late April and black flies in May and June. With the right gear, attitude, and preparation, winter can also offer fine opportunities for hiking, snowshoeing, and cross-country skiing.

FOLLOW THE TRAIL

Most hiking trails are marked with blazes, blocks of colored paint on a tree or rock. The AT, and only the AT, is marked by vertical, rectangular 2- by 6-inch white blazes. Two blazes mark route changes; turn in the direction of the top blaze. At higher elevations, you might also see cairns, small piles of rocks carefully placed by trail rangers to show the way when a blaze might be obscured by snow or fog.

Scenic U.S. 302—and the AT—pass through Crawford Notch, a spectacular valley in New Hampshire's White Mountains.

Hikers gather outside Lakes of the Clouds Hut, near the peak of Mount Washington.

TRIP TIPS

WHAT TO WEAR: For clothes, layer with a breathable fabric like polypropylene, starting with a shirt, a fleece, and a wind- or water-resistant shell. Bring gloves, a hat, and a change of socks.

WHAT TO BRING: Carry plenty of water and lightweight high-energy food. Don't forget sunscreen and insect repellent. Bring a map and compass. Just in case: a basic first-aid kit, a flashlight or headlamp, whistle, multi-tool, and matches.

PLAN AHEAD: In your car, leave a change of clothing, especially dry socks and shoes, as well as extra water and food.

PLAY IT SAFE: Tell someone your hiking plan and take a hiking partner. Carry a rescue card with emergency contact information and allergy details.

BE PREPARED: Plan your route and check the weather forecast in advance.

REMEMBER YOUR BEGINNINGS: Look back at the trail especially at the trailhead and at tricky junctions. If you've got a digital camera, photograph trail maps posted at the trailhead or natural landmarks to help you find your way.

WHERE TO STAY

Day hikers looking to extend the adventure can also make the experience as hard or as soft as they choose. Through-hikers combine camping with overnight stays in primitive shelters, mountain huts, comfortable lodges, and resorts just off the trail.

Rustic cabins and lean-tos provide basic shelter in Maine's Baxter State Park. In Maine and New Hampshire, the Appalachian Mountain Club runs four-season lodges as well as a network of mountain huts for backcountry hikers. A hiker code of camaraderie and conviviality prevails in these huts. Experience a night and you might just find yourself dreaming of a through-hike.

FOR MORE INFORMATION

Appalachian Trail Conservancy
(www.appalachiantrail.org)

Appalachian National Scenic Trail
(www.nps.gov/appa)

Appalachian Mountain Club
(www.outdoors.org)

ANIMALS ALONG THE TRAIL

❶ Black bear

Black bears are the most common—and smallest—bear in North America. Clever and adaptable, these adroit mammals will eat whatever they can (though they are primarily vegetarian, favoring berries, grasses, roots, blossoms, and nuts). Not naturally aggressive, black bears usually make themselves scarce when they hear hikers. The largest New England populations are in New Hampshire and Maine.

❷ Moose

Spotting a moose in the wild is unforgettable: their massive size and serene gaze are truly humbling. Treasure the moment, then slowly back away. At more than six feet tall, weighing 750 to 1,000 pounds, a moose is not to be trifled with, particularly during rutting and calving seasons (fall and spring, respectively). Dusk and dawn are the best times to spot the iconic animal; you're most likely to see one in Maine, especially in and around ponds.

⚠ Black flies

Especially fierce in May and June, these pesky flies can upset the tranquility of a hike in the woods as they swarm your face and bite your neck. To ward them off, cover any exposed skin and wear light colors. You'll get some relief on a mountain peak; cold weather and high winds also keep them at bay.

❸ Bald eagles

Countless bird species can be seen and heard along the AT, but what could be more exciting than to catch a glimpse of our national bird as it bounces back from near extinction? Now it's not uncommon to see the majestic bald eagle with its tremendous wing span, white head feathers, and curved yellow beak. The white head and tail distinguish the bald from the golden eagle, a bit less rare but just as thrilling to see. Most of New England's bald eagles are in Maine, but they are now present—albeit in small numbers—in all six states.

WILDFLOWERS ALONG THE TRAIL

❹ Mountain laurel

The clusters of pink and white blooms of the mountain laurel look like bursts of fireworks. Up close, each one has the delicate detail of a lady's parasol. Blooms vary in color, from pure white to darker pink, and have different amounts of red markings. Connecticut's state flower, mountain laurel flourishes in rocky woods, blooming in May and June. Look for the shrub in southern New England; it's rare along the Appalachian trail in Vermont and Maine.

❺ Mountain avens

A member of the rose family, these showy yellow flowers abound in New Hampshire's White Mountains. You can't miss the large buttercup-like blooms on long green stems when they are in bloom from June through August. So common here, yet extremely rare: the only other place in the whole world where you can find mountain avens is on an island off the coast of Nova Scotia.

❻ Painted trillium

You might smell a trillium before you see it; these flowers have an unpleasant odor that may attract the flies that pollinate it. To identify this impressive flower, look for sets of three: three large pointed blue-green leaves, three sepals (small leaves beneath the petals), and three white petals with a brilliant magenta center. It can take four or five years for a trillium to produce one flower, which blooms in May and June in wet woodlands.

❼ Pink lady slippers

These delicate orchids can grow from 6 to 15 inches high and favor specific wet wooded areas in dappled sunlight. The slender stalk rises from a pair of green leaves, then bends a graceful neck to suspend the paper-thin pale pink closed flower. The slow-growing plant needs help from fungus and bees to survive and can live to be 20 years old. New Hampshire's state wildflower, the pink lady slipper blooms in June throughout New England.

● = Somewhat Common ● = Rare

CHOOSE YOUR DAY HIKE

MAINE

GULF HAGAS, Greenville
Difficult, 8-plus mi round-trip, 6–7 hours

This National Natural Landmark in the North Maine Woods is a spectacular sight for the adventurous day hiker. It involves a long drive on logging roads east from Greenville *(see Inland Maine section)* to a remote spot and a slippery, sometimes treacherous 8-mile hike around the rim of what's been dubbed Maine's Grand Canyon. Swimming in one of the sparkling pools under a 30-foot-high waterfall and admiring the views of cliffs, cascades, gorges, and chasms in this slate canyon, otherwise unthinkable in New England, will take your breath away.

TABLE ROCK, Bethel
Medium, 2.4 mi round-trip, 2 hours

Maine's Mahoosuc Range is thought to be one of the most difficult stretches of the entire AT, but north of Bethel at Grafton Notch State Park, day hikes range from easy walks in to cascading waterfalls to strenuous climbs up Old Speck's craggy peak. The Table Rock trail offers interesting sights—great views of the notch from the immense slab of granite that gives this trail its name, as well as one of the state's largest system of slab caves—narrow with tall openings unlike underground caves.

NEW HAMPSHIRE

ZEALAND TRAIL, Berlin
Easy, 5.6 mi round-trip, 3.5–4 hours

New Hampshire's Presidential range gets so much attention and traffic that sometimes the equally spectacular Pemigewasset Wilderness, just to its west, gets overlooked. Follow State Route 302 to the trailhead on Zealand Rd. near Bretton Woods. For an easy day hike to one of the Appalachian Mountain Club's excellent overnight huts, take the mostly flat Zealand Trail over bridges and past a beaver swamp to Zealand Pond. The last tenth of a mile is a steep ascent to the mountain retreat, where you might spot an AT through-hiker taking a well-deserved rest. (Most north-bound through-hikers reach this section around July or August.) In winter, you can get here by a lovely cross-country ski trip.

TRAIL NAMES

For through-hikers, doing the AT can be a life-altering experience. One of trail's most respected traditions is the taking of an alter ego: a trail name. Lightning Bolt: fast hiker. Pine Knot: tough as one. Bluebearee: because a bear got all her food on her very first night on the trail.

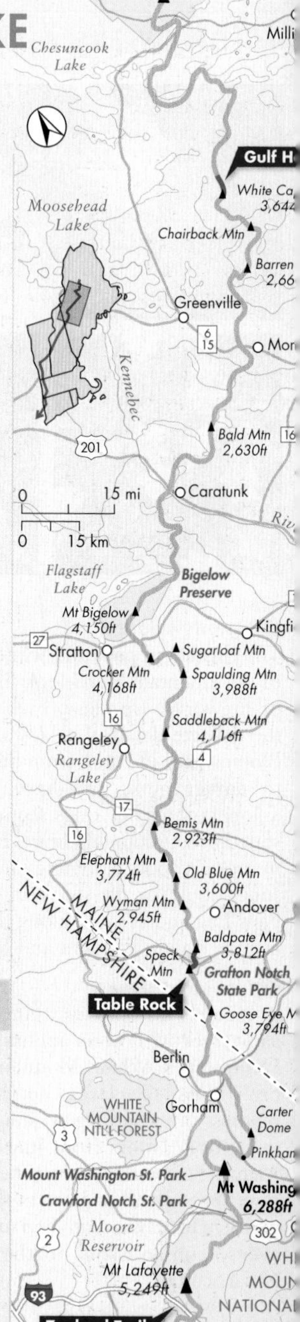

VERMONT

HARMON HILL, Bennington

Medium to difficult, 3.6 mi round-trip, 3–4 hours

This rugged hike in the Green Mountains goes south along the AT where it coincides with the Long Trail, Vermont's century-old "footpath in the wilderness." From the trailhead on Route 9 just east of Bennington, the first half mile or so is strenuous, with some rock and log staircases and hairpins. The payback is the sweeping view from the top; you'll see Mount Anthony, Bennington and its iconic war monument, and the rolling green hills of the Taconics to the west.

STRATTON MOUNTAIN, Stratton

Difficult, 6.6 mi round-trip, 5–6 hours

A steep and steady climb from the trailhead on Kelly Stand Rd. (between West Wardsboro and Arlington) up the 3,936-foot-high Stratton Mountain follows the AT and Long Trail through mixed forests. It's said that this peak is where Benton MacKaye conceived of the idea for the Appalachian Trail in 1921. An observation tower at the summit gives you a great 360-degree view of the Green Mountains. From July to October, you can park at Stratton resort and ride the gondola up (or down) and follow the .75-mi Fire Tower Trail to the southern true peak.

MASSACHUSETTS

MOUNT GREYLOCK, North Adams

Easy to difficult, 2 mi round-trip, less than 1 hour

There are many ways to experience Massachusetts's highest peak. From North Adams, follow Route 2 to the Notch Rd. trailheads. For a warm-up, try the Rounds Rock trail (Easy, 0.7 mi) for some spectacular views. Or drive up the 8-mi-long summit road and hike down the Robinson's Point trail (Difficult, 0.8 mi) for the best view of the Hopper, a glacial cirque that's home to an old-growth red spruce forest. At the summit, the impressive **Bascom Lodge**, built in the 1930s by the Civilian Conservation Corps, provides delicious meals and overnight stays (🌐 www.bascomlodge.net).

CONNECTICUT

LION'S HEAD, Salisbury

Medium, 4.6 mi round-trip, 3.5–4 hours

The AT's 52 miles in Connecticut take hikers up some modest mountains, including Lion's Head in Salisbury. From the trailhead on State Route 41, follow the white blazes of the AT for two easy miles, then take the blue-blazed Lion's Head Trail for a short, steep push over open ledges to the 1,738-foot summit with its commanding views of pastoral southern New England. Try this in summer when the mountain laurels—Connecticut's state flower—are in bloom.

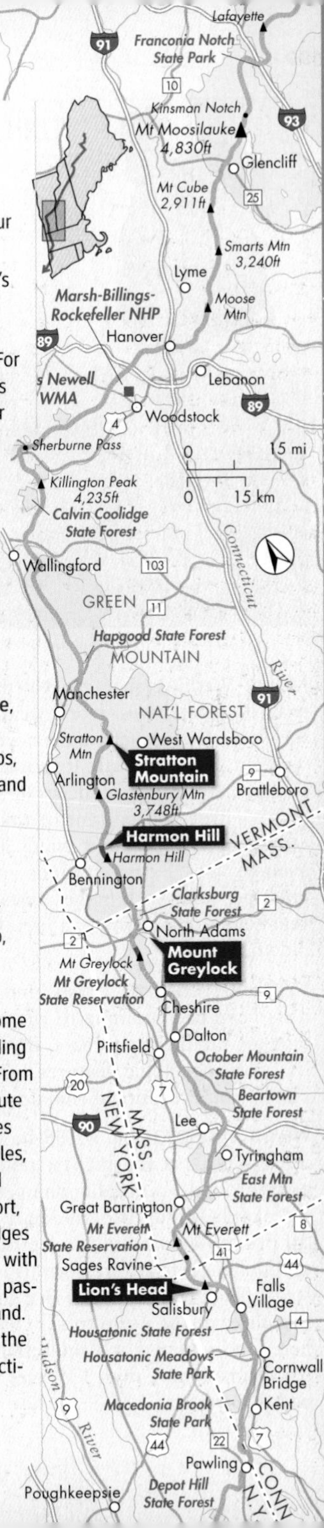

Lafayette
Franconia Notch State Park
Kinsman Notch
Mt Moosilauke 4,830ft
Glencliff
Mt Cube 2,911ft
Smarts Mtn 3,240ft
Lyme
Moose Mtn
Marsh-Billings-Rockefeller NHP
Hanover
Lebanon
Newell WMA
Woodstock
Sherburne Pass
0 15 mi
0 15 km
Killington Peak 4,235ft
Calvin Coolidge State Forest
Wallingford
GREEN MOUNTAIN NAT'L FOREST
Hapgood State Forest
Connecticut River
Manchester
Stratton Mtn
West Wardsboro
Stratton Mountain
Arlington
Glastenbury Mtn 3,748ft
Brattleboro
Harmon Hill
VERMONT
MASS.
Bennington
Clarksburg State Forest
North Adams
Mount Greylock
Mt Greylock
Mt Greylock State Reservation
Cheshire
Dalton
Pittsfield
October Mountain State Forest
Beartown State Forest
MASS.
NEW YORK
Lee
Tyringham
East Mtn State Forest
Great Barrington
Mt Everett State Reservation
Mt Everett
Sages Ravine
Lion's Head
Salisbury
Falls Village
Housatonic State Forest
Housatonic Meadows State Park
Cornwall Bridge
Hudson River
Macedonia Brook State Park
Kent
Pawling
CONN.
N.Y.
Depot Hill State Forest
Poughkeepsie

EXPERIENCE MOUNT WASHINGTON

Looking at Mt. Washington from Mt. Bond in the Pemigewasset Wilderness Area, New Hampshire.

Mount Washington is the Northeast's peak of superlatives: worst weather in the world, highest spot in the northeast, windiest place on Earth. It snows in the summer, there are avalanches in winter, and it's foggy 60 percent of the time. Strong 35-mile-per-hour winds are the average, and extreme winds of 100 miles per hour with higher gusts blow year-round. Here, you can literally get blown away.

Explorers, scientists, artists, and botanists have been coming to the mountain for hundreds of years, drawn by its unique geologic features, unusual plants, and exceptional climate.

WHY SO WINDY? The 6,288-foot-high treeless peak is the highest point for miles around, so nothing dampens the force of the wind. Also, the sharp vertical rise causes wind to accelerate. Dramatic changes in air pressure also cause strong, high winds. Add to that the fact that three major storm tracks converge here, and you've got a mountain that has claimed more than 135 lives in the past 150 years.

GOING UP THE MOUNTAIN

An ascent up Mount Washington is for experienced hikers who are prepared for severe, unpredictable weather. Even in summer, cold, wet, foggy, windy conditions prevail. The most popular route to the top is on the eastern face up the Tuckerman Ravine Trail. But countless trails offer plenty of moderate day hikes, like the Alpine Garden Trail, as an alternative to a summit attempt. Start at the Pinkham Notch Visitor Center on Route 16 to review your options.

BACKPACKING ON THE MOUNTAIN

Lakes of the Clouds Hut perches 5,050 feet up the southern shoulder, providing bunkrooms and meals in summer; reservations are required. On the eastern face, the **Hermit Lake Shelter Area** has shelters and tent platforms; to camp here you'll need a first-come, first-served permit from the Visitors Center. Both are operated by the **AMC** (☎ 603/466-2727; 🌐 www.outdoors.org).

NON-HIKING ALTERNATIVES

In the summer, the **Auto Road** (☏ 603/466-3988 🌐 www.mountwashingtonautoroad.com) and the **Cog Railway** (☏ 800/922-8825 🌐 www.thecog.com) present alternate ways up the mountain; both give you a real sense of the mountain's grandeur. In winter, a **Snow-Coach** (☏ 603/466-2333 🌐 www.greatglentrails.com) hauls visitors 4.5 miles up the Auto Road with an option to cross-country ski, telemark, or snowshoe back down.

WHERE TO EAT AND STAY

$ AMERICAN **Woodstock Inn, Station & Brewery.** If you like eateries loaded with character, don't miss these two restaurants inside the former Lincoln Railroad Station of the late 1800s. Down the hall is a great brewery and pub that serves 13 handcrafted brews and is decorated with old maps and memorabilia. You come here as much to mix with locals and enjoy the vibe as to eat. The menu is standard: pizza, quesadillas, wings, chicken, and seafood. *Exit 32, off I–93, North Woodstock* *603/745–3951* *www.woodstockinnnh.com* *AE, D, MC, V.*

$ **Indian Head Resort.** This is the place for families on a budget. The rooms are inexpensive and spacious, and there are lots of activities for children, including a stocked trout pond, ice cream socials, magicians, and kids' karaoke. For parents, a lounge features music and comedians on a nightly basis. The resort is also near kid-friendly attractions such as a water park, a trading post, and a scenic railroad. In the winter, skiers can hitch a ride on a free shuttle to Cannon or Loon Mountain ski areas. **Pros:** best place for kids at a great price. **Cons:** crowded and sometimes hard to get a reservation. *664 U.S. Route 3, 5 mi north of North Woodstock* *R.R. 1, Box 99, North Lincoln 03215* *603/745–8000 or 800/343–8000* *www.indianheadresort.com* *129 rooms, 99 cottages* *In-room: refrigerator, Wi-Fi. In-hotel: restaurant, room service, bar, tennis court, pools, gym, children's programs (all ages). Wi-Fi hotspot* *AE, D, DC, MC, V.*

$$$$ **Mountain Club on Loon.** If you want a ski-in, ski-out stay on Loon Mountain, this is your best and only option. A typical 1990s ski lodge with a stone fireplace in the lobby, outdoor heated hot tub, and a small game room, the Club isn't thrilling, but it's clean and modern. There are suites that sleep as many as 10, studios with Inova beds, and many units with full kitchens. All rooms are within walking distance of the lifts. There's also a full-service spa and a health club that has exercise classes. **Pros:** easy skiing access; clean, basic rooms; close to national forest. **Cons:** unexciting decor. *90 Loon Mountain, Kancamagus Hwy. (Rte. 112), Lincoln* *603/745–2244 or 800/229–7829* *www.mtnclub.com* *234 units* *In-room: kitchen (some). In-hotel: restaurant, bar, tennis courts, pool, gym, spa, laundry facilities, Wi-Fi hotspot* *AE, D, MC, V.*

FRANCONIA

16 mi northwest of Lincoln/North Woodstock on I–93.

Travelers have long passed through the White Mountains via Franconia Notch, and in the late 18th century a town evolved just to the north. It and the region's jagged rock formations and heavy coat of evergreens have stirred the imaginations of Washington Irving, Henry Wadsworth Longfellow, and Nathaniel Hawthorne, who penned a short story about the craggy cliff known as the Old Man of the Mountain. There is almost no town proper to speak of here, just a handful of stores, touched though it is by Interstate 93 (the Franconia Notch Parkway).

Four miles west of Franconia, Sugar Hill is a town of about 500 people. It's famous for its spectacular sunsets and views of the Franconia Mountains, best seen from Sunset Hill, where a row of grand hotels and mansions once stood.

GETTING HERE AND AROUND

Franconia is a small town with not much to offer tourists, but it is an access point for many ski areas and the villages of Sugar Hill, Easton, Bethlehem, Bretton Woods, Littleton, Lincoln, and North Woodstock, towns replete with white church steeples, general stores, country inns, and picturesque farms.

ESSENTIALS

Visitor InformationFranconia Notch Chamber of Commerce (☎ *603/823–9083* 🌐 *www.franconianotch.org*).

EXPLORING

Flume. This 800-foot-long chasm has narrow walls that cause an eerie echo from the gorge's running water. A wooden boardwalk and a series of stairways wind their way to the top of the falls that thunder down the gorge, followed by a 1-mi hike back to the visitor center. There's a gift shop, café, and dog walk on-site. ✉ *Franconia Notch Pkwy., Exit 34A* ☎ *603/745–8391* 🌐 *www.nhstateparks.com/franconia.html* 🎟 *$13 adults, $9 children, or a combined Cannon Mtn. Tram ride and Flume entrance for $24 adults, $18 children* ⏲ *Early May–late Oct., daily 9–5.*

Frost Place. Robert Frost's year-round home from 1915 to 1920 and his summer home for 19 years, this is where the poet soaked up the New England life. This place is imbued with the spirit of his work, down to the rusted mailbox in front that's painted R. FROST in simple lettering. Two rooms host occasional readings and contain memorabilia and signed editions of his books. Out back, you can follow short trails marked with lines from his poetry. A visit here will slow you down and remind you of the intense beauty of the surrounding countryside. *158 Ridge Rd.* ☎ *603/823–5510* 🌐 *www.frostplace.org* ⏲ *Check the Web site for readings and conference schedule.*

Old Man of the Mountain. This naturally formed profile in the rock high above Franconia Notch, a famous New Hampshire geological site, crumbled unexpectedly on May 3, 2003, from the strains of natural erosion. The iconic image had defined New Hampshire, and the Old Man's "death" stunned and saddened residents. You can still stop at the posted turnouts from Interstate 93 north- or southbound. In Franconia Notch State Park on the northbound side of the highway there is a pull-off; on the southbound side take Exit 34B and follow the signs. Another option is to go along the shore of Profile Lake for the best views of the mountain face. There's a small, free Old Man of the Mountain Museum administered by Franconia Notch State Park at the southbound viewing area (by the Cannon Mountain Tram parking area) open daily 9–5.

SPORTS AND THE OUTDOORS

SKI AREAS **Cannon Mountain**. The staff at this state-run facility in Franconia Notch State Park is attentive to skier services, family programs, snowmaking, and grooming. One of the nation's first ski areas, Cannon has 55 trails that present challenges rarely found in New Hampshire—for instance, the narrow, steep pitches off the peak of a 2,146-foot vertical rise. There are also two glade-skiing trails—Turnpike and Banshee—and a tubing park with lift service. Thirty-seven miles of cross-country trails are available to Nordic skiers. In summer, for $13 round-trip, the Cannon Mountain Aerial Tramway can transport you up 2,022 feet. It's an eight-minute ride to the top, where marked trails lead to an observation platform. The tram runs daily from mid-May through late October.

Franconia Village Cross-Country Ski Center. The cross-country ski center at the Franconia Inn has 39 mi of groomed trails and 40 mi of backcountry trails. One popular route leads to Bridal Veil Falls, a great spot for a picnic lunch. You can also enjoy horse-drawn sleigh rides and ice-skating on a lighted rink. ✉ *1300 Easton Rd.* ☎ *603/823–5542 or 800/473–5299* 🌐 *www.franconiainn.com.*

WHERE TO EAT AND STAY

¢ AMERICAN ★ ✕ **Polly's Pancake Parlor**. In the Dexter family for three generations, Polly's has been serving up pancakes, waffles, and French toast since the 1930s. Since then, smoked bacon and ham, sandwiches on homemade bread, desserts such as raspberry pie, delicious baked beans, and even gluten-free items have been added to the menu. Much of the food is made from grains ground on-site. Home mixes and maple syrup, cream, and sugar are for sale year-round. The restaurant closes for the cold season. ✉ *672 Rte. 117* ☎ *603/823–5575* 🌐 *www.pollyspancakeparlor.com* ▭ *AE, D, MC, V* ⊙ *Open 7–1. Closed mid-Oct.–mid-May. No dinner.*

$$ AMERICAN ✕ **Sugar Hill Inn**. This 1789 farmhouse is the fine-dining option in the area. Chef Val Fortin serves American fare such as peppercorn-crusted sirloin steak with grilled mushrooms and truffle oil and free-range duck breast with wild mushrooms, prosciutto, and chili-glazed scallops; the homemade desserts are always delicious. A four-course prix-fixe meal is $52. ✉ *116 Rte. 117* ☎ *603/823–5621* 🌐 *www.sugarhillinn.com* ✍ *Reservations essential* ▭ *AE, D, MC, V* ⊙ *Closed Tues. and Wed. No lunch.*

$$$ 🏨 **Franconia Inn**. At this 120-acre family-friendly resort, you can play tennis on four clay courts, swim in the outdoor heated pool or hot tub, mountain bike, and hike. The cross-country ski barn doubles as a horseback-riding center in the warm months. The white, three-story inn has unfussy country furnishings—you'll find canopy beds and country quilts in the rooms, most of which have period-style wallpapering or wood paneling. **Pros:** good for kids; amazing views; outdoor heated pool. **Cons:** may be too remote for some. ✉ *1300 Easton Rd.* ☎ *603/823–5542 or 800/473–5299* 🌐 *www.franconiainn.com* ⇨ *34 rooms, 3 suites, 2 2-bedroom cottages* ♂ *In-room: a/c, Wi-Fi. In-hotel: restaurant, bar, tennis courts, pool, bicycles, Wi-Fi hotspot* ▭ *AE, MC, V* ⊙ *Restaurant closed Apr. 1–15.*

$$$–$$$$ ★ **Sugar Hill Inn.** The nicest place in Franconia for a romantic retreat is the Sugar Hill Inn. The lawn's old carriage and the wraparound porch's wicker chairs put you in a nostalgic mood before you even enter this converted 1789 farmhouse. Many rooms and suites have hand-stenciled walls and views of the Franconia Mountains; some have gas fireplaces. Bette Davis visited friends in this house—the room with the best vistas is named after her. **Pros:** romantic, classic B&B; fine dinners. **Cons:** expensive. ✉ *116 Rte. 117* ☎ *603/823–5621 or 800/548–4748* 🌐 *www.sugarhillinn.com* *10 rooms, 4 suites* *In-room: no phone, a/c, DVD (some), no TV (some), Wi-Fi. In-hotel: restaurant, room service, bar, pool, Wi-Fi hotspot, kids on a case-by-case basis* *AE, D, MC, V* *BP, MAP.*

3

LITTLETON

7 mi north of Franconia and 86 mi north of Concord, on I–93.

One of northern New Hampshire's largest towns (this isn't saying much, mind you) is on a granite shelf along the Ammonoosuc River, whose swift current and drop of 235 feet enabled the community to flourish as a mill center in its early days. Later, the railroad came through, and Littleton grew into the region's commerce hub. In the minds of many, it's more a place to stock up on supplies than a bona fide destination, but few communities have worked harder at revitalization. Today, intriguing shops and eateries line the adorable Main Street, with its tidy 19th- and early-20th-century buildings that suggest a set in a Jimmy Stewart movie.

EXPLORING

Littleton Grist Mill. Stop by this restored 1798 mill just off Main Street on the Ammonoosuc River. It contains a small shop selling stone-ground flour products and a museum downstairs showcasing the original mill equipment. ✉ *18 Mill St.* ☎ *603/444–7478 or 888/284–7478* 🌐 *www.littletongristmill.com* *July–Dec., daily 10–5; Apr.–June, Wed.–Sat. 10:30–4, Sun. 10:30–3.*

OFF THE BEATEN PATH

Whitefield. Like Dixville Notch and Bretton Woods, Whitefield, 11 mi northeast of Littleton, became a prominent summer resort in the late 19th century, when wealthy industrialists flocked to the small village in a rolling valley between two precipitous promontories to golf, ski, play polo, and hobnob with each other. The sprawling, yellow clapboard Mountain View Hotel, which was established in 1865 and had grown to grand hotel status by the early 20th century, only to succumb to changing tourist habits and close by the 1980s, has been fully refurbished and is now open again as one of New England's grandest resort hotels. It's worth driving through the courtly Colonial center of town—Whitefield was settled in the early 1800s—and up Route 116 just beyond to see this magnificent structure atop a bluff overlooking the Presidentials.

Lancaster. About 8 mi north of Whitefield via U.S. 3, the affable seat of Coos County sits at the confluence of the Connecticut and Israel rivers, surrounded by low serrated peaks. Before becoming prosperous through commerce, Lancaster was an agricultural stronghold; at one time the only acceptable currency here was the bushel of wheat. It's still an intimate mountain town. Like Littleton, it has restored much of its main street, which now has a dapper mix of Victorian homes, funky artisan and antiques shops, and prim churches and civic buildings.

SHOPPING

Main Street and Union Street are filled with great little shops.

The **Village Book Store** (✉ *81 Main St.* ☎ *603/444–5263* 🌐 *www.booksmusictoys.com*) has a good selection of both nonfiction and fiction titles. **Potato Barn Antiques Center** (✉ *960 Lancaster Rd. [U.S. 3], 6 mi north of Lancaster, Northumberland* ☎ *603/636–2611* 🌐 *www.potatobarnantiques.com*) has several dealers under one roof—specialties include vintage farm tools, clothing, and costume jewelry.

QUICK BITES

Beside the Littleton Grist Mill, Miller's Café & Bakery (✉ *16 Mill St.* ☎ *603/444–2146* 🌐 *www.millerscafeandbakery.com* ⏲ *Closed Sun. and Mon.*) serves coffees, microbrews and wines, baked goods, sandwiches, and salads.

WHERE TO EAT AND STAY

$$ AMERICAN ★ ✕ **Tim-bir Alley.** This is a rare find in New Hampshire: an independent restaurant in a contemporary setting that's been around a long time (since 1983) and yet still takes its food seriously. If you're in town, don't miss it. Tim Carr's menu changes weekly and uses regional American ingredients in creative ways. Main dishes might include an eggplant pâté with feta cheese, red pepper, and a tomato-herb marmalade or a basil-and-olive-oil-flavored salmon with a spinach-Brie-pecan pesto. Save room for such desserts as white chocolate–coconut cheesecake. ✉ *7 Main St.* ☎ *603/444–6142* ▭ *No credit cards* ⏲ *Closed Mon. and Tues. No lunch.*

$ Fodor's Choice ★ **Thayers Inn.** This stately 1843 Greek-Revival hotel is the essence of Littleton. It's not a luxury hotel, and Thayers isn't out to impress the Joneses. The well-kept rooms are quaintly old-fashioned, with creaky floorboards, exposed pipes, steam radiators, high ceilings, and comfy wing chairs. So if you're traveling on a budget or just want an authentic northern town experience, this is a good choice. The Bailiwicks restaurant ($$$) has a martini bar with exposed oak beams and leather chairs. The lobster risotto and the homemade seafood cakes are delicious. **Pros:** one of the best values in New England. **Cons:** Continental breakfast only. ✉ *111 Main St.* ☎ *603/444–6469 or 800/634–8179* 🌐 *www.thayersinn.com* *22 rooms, 13 suites* *In-room: Wi-Fi. In-hotel: restaurant, bar, spa, Wi-Fi hotspot, some pets allowed* ▭ *AE, D, MC, V* *CP.*

BRETTON WOODS

14 mi southeast of Bethlehem; 28 mi northeast of Lincoln/Woodstock.

In the early 1900s private railcars brought the elite from New York and Philadelphia to the Mount Washington Hotel, the jewel of the White Mountains. A visit to the hotel, which was the site of the 1944 United Nations conference that created the International Monetary Fund and the International Bank for Reconstruction and Development (and the birth of many conspiracy theories), is not to be missed. The area is also known for its cog railway and Bretton Woods ski resort.

3

GETTING HERE AND AROUND

Bretton Woods is in the heart of the White Mountains on Route 302. A free shuttle helps get you around the various facilities at the resort. Helpful advice on how to enjoy your stay can be found at the concierge and activities desk in the main lobby of the Mount Washington Hotel.

EXPLORING

Fodor's Choice ★ In 1858 Sylvester Marsh petitioned the state legislature for permission to build a steam railway up Mt. Washington. A politico retorted that he'd have better luck building a railroad to the moon. But 11 years later, the **Mt. Washington Cog Railway** chugged its way up to the summit along a 3-mi track on the west side of the mountain, and today it's one of the state's most beloved attractions—a thrill in either direction. The train only runs in the summer, starting in May. A full trip ($59) is three hours with one hour at the summit. Trains depart at 11 AM and 2 PM. ✉ *U.S. 302, 6 mi northeast of Bretton Woods* ☎ *603/278–5404 or 800/922–8825* 🌐 *www.thecog.com* 🎟 *$59.*

SPORTS AND THE OUTDOORS

Fodor's Choice ★ **Bretton Woods.** Skiing with your family New Hampshire's largest ski area is one of the best family ski resorts in the country. It's also probably the best place in New England to learn to ski. (If it's your first time, get started at the free area serviced by a rope tow.) The views of Mt. Washington alone are worth the visit to Bretton Woods; the scenery is especially beautiful from the **Top of Quad restaurant,** which is open during ski season.

Trails appeal mostly to novice and intermediate skiers, including two magic carpet lifts for beginners. There are some steeper pitches near the top of the 1,500-foot vertical and glade skiing to occupy the experts in the family, as well as night skiing and snowboarding on weekends and holidays. Snowboarders enjoy the four terrain parks, including the all-natural Wild West Park and a half-pipe. A cross-country ski center has 62 mi of groomed and double-track trails, some of them lift-serviced. The Nordic Ski Center near the hotel offers access to 55 mi of cross-country trails and doubles as the golf clubhouse in summer.

Options for kids are plentiful. The Hobbit Ski and Snowboard School for ages 4–12 has full- and half-day instruction. Hobbit Ski and Snowplay program, for ages 3–5, is an introduction to skiing and fun on the snow. The ski area also offers an adaptive program for children and adults with disabilities. There are also organized activities in the nursery. The complimentary Kinderwoods Winter Playground has a sled carousel, igloos, and a zip line. Parents can buy an interchangeable family ticket that allows parents to take turns skiing while the other watches the kids—both passes come for the price of one.

A new addition is the year-round Canopy Tour, which has 10 zip lines, two sky bridges, and three rappel stations. Small groups, guided by experienced climbers and ski patrollers, leave every half hour. The tour, at $110, is one of the longest in the United States and is an exhilarating introduction to flora and fauna of the White Mountains and the history of the area. Kids are welcome but must weigh more than 70 lbs. ✉ *U.S. 302* ☎ *603/278–3320; 603/278–3333 weather conditions; 800/232–2972 information; 800/258–0330 lodging* 🌐 *www.brettonwoods.com.*

WHERE TO EAT

$$$ AMERICAN ✕ **The Bretton Arms Dining Room.** You're likely to have the best meal in the area at this intimate setting. Though the same executive chef oversees the Mount Washington Hotel dining room, the latter is immense, and the Bretton Arms is cozier. Three small interconnected rooms are separated by fireplaces. The menu is seasonal and might include Maine lobster tossed with fresh pasta and free-range Long Island duck breast; it also features locally sourced food. ✉ *U.S. 302* ☎ *603/278–1000* 🌐 *www.mtwashingtonresort.com* ▭ *AE, D, MC, V* ⏲ *No lunch.*

$$$ AMERICAN ★ ✕ **The Dining Room.** You'd be hard-pressed to find a larger or grander dining room in New Hampshire (only the Balsams can compare). The Mount Washington Hotel's enormous octagonal dining room, built in 1902, is adorned with Currier & Ives reproductions, Tiffany glass, chandeliers up the wazoo, massive windows that open to the Presidential Range, and a nightly musical trio. This may be the only restaurant in the state that requires a jacket (except in winter); if you forgot yours, they have about 30 you can borrow. Try seasonal dishes such as seared haddock and shrimp fricassee, lemon lobster ravioli with shrimp and scallops, or roast pork with onions and mushrooms. The Dining Room offers a "Gold Sash Dinner" at a chef's table with a customized menu and wine pairings. ✉ *In Mount Washington Hotel, U.S. 302* ☎ *603/278–1000* 🌐 *www.mtwashingtonresort.com* 👔 *Jacket required* ▭ *AE, D, MC, V.*

$–$$ AMERICAN ✕ **Fabyan's Station.** In 1890, 60 tourist trains a day passed through this station, now a casual restaurant. If you're looking for an easygoing meal, Fabyan's cooks up delicious clam chowder in a bread bowl and a 16-ounce T-bone grilled to perfection. Half the restaurant is a tavern with a long bar, and the other half serves sandwiches, fish, and steaks. There's a kids' menu, too, and a model train circles the dining room. ✉ *Rte. 302, 1 mi north of Bretton Woods ski area* ☎ *603/278–2222* ✍ *Reservations not accepted* ▭ *AE, D, MC, V.*

WHERE TO STAY

¢ ★ **The Lodge.** A stay at this inexpensive roadside motel run by Bretton Woods gives you free access to all of the resort facilities at Mount Washington Hotel, including the pools, gym, and arcade, which makes it a great deal. You can also use the free shuttle to the hotel and the ski area. The rooms are very clean and have private balconies that overlook

Bretton Woods is a year-round destination, and especially popular with families.

the Presidential Range. There's a small arcade, a great indoor pool, and a cute hearthside common area. **Pros:** cheap; free access to Mount Washington amenities; free ski shuttle. **Cons:** across street from resort amenities; Continental breakfast only. ✉ *U.S. 302* ☎ *603/278–1000 or 800/258–0330* 🌐 *www.mtwashington.com* *50 rooms* *In-room: Wi-Fi. In-hotel: restaurant, golf courses, tennis courts, pool, bicycles, children's programs (ages 4–12), laundry facilities, laundry service, Wi-Fi hotspot* *AE, D, MC, V* *CP.*

$$$ **Mount Washington Hotel.** The two most memorable sights in the White Mountains would have to be Mount Washington and the Mount Washington Hotel. Its grand scale and remarkable setting graced by the view of the Presidentials is astonishing. This 1902 resort has a 900-foot veranda and stately public rooms and glimmers with an early-20th-century ambience. It would take a full week to exhaust the recreational activities here: in winter try out the tubing, ice-skating, a great cross-country facility, a terrific downhill skiing complex, and dogsled and sleigh rides; in summer, you can enjoy horseback riding, carriage rides, fly-fishing, golf, mountain biking, and more. The Cave provides gin in a coffee cup and nightly entertainment in a former 1930s speakeasy. Kids will love the arcade, sweet shop, and playground, as well as a club with themed day and evening programs. The hotel also has a 25,000-square-foot spa and a renovated 18-hole Donald Ross golf course designed in 1915. Rooms have high ceilings and are furnished in a manner befitting the history and grandeur of this luxurious resort. The bathrooms are glorious, with white porcelain sinks and tubs and white tile. **Pros:** beautiful resort; loads of activities; free shuttle to skiing and activities. **Cons:** kids love to run around the hotel; Internet access expensive. ✉ *U.S. 302*

Fodor's Choice ★

The views of Mt. Washington and the Presidential range from the porch of Mt. Washington Hotel can't be beat.

☎ *603/278–1000* 🌐 *www.mtwashington.com* *177 rooms, 23 suites* *In-room: Internet, Wi-Fi (fee). In-hotel: 3 restaurants, room service, bars, golf course, tennis courts, pool, gym, spa, bicycles, children's programs (ages 4–12), laundry service, Internet terminal, Wi-Fi hotspot* *AE, D, MC, V* *BP, EP, MAP.*

$$$–$$$$ Fodor's Choice ★ **Notchland Inn.** Drop any cute house here and you couldn't but fall in love. Built in 1862 by Sam Bemis, America's grandfather of landscape photography, the house conveys mountain charm on a scale unmatched in New England. It's simply a legendary setting, in Crawford Notch, in the middle of the forest surrounded by the mountains. Innkeepers Les Schoof and Ed Butler have left wood-burning fireplaces in every room (17 in total in the house), have a big library, serve five-course meals, and give the range of the place to Abby and Crawford, their immense Bernese Mountain Dogs. **Pros:** middle-of-the-forest setting; marvelous house and common rooms; original fireplaces; good dinner. **Cons:** at 15 mi from the Bretton Woods ski area, will be too isolated for some; rooms could be better equipped (better bedding, for example). ✉ *2 Morey Rd., Hart's Location* ☎ *603/374–6131* 🌐 *www.notchland.com* *8 rooms, 5 suites, 3 cottages* *In-room: no phone, Wi-Fi. In-hotel: restaurant, Wi-Fi hotspot, some pets allowed, no kids under 12* *D, MC, V* *BP.*

EN ROUTE

Scenic U.S. 302 winds through the steep, wooded mountains on either side of spectacular Crawford Notch, southeast of Bretton Woods, and passes through **Crawford Notch State Park** (✉ *U.S. 302, Harts Location* ☎ *603/374–2272, 603/344–2272 campground* 🌐 *www.nhstateparks.com/crawford.html*), where you can picnic and take a short hike to Arethusa Falls or the Silver and Flume cascades. The park has a number of roadside photo opportunities. The visitor center has a gift shop and a cafeteria; **there's also a** campground.

BARTLETT

18 mi southeast of Bretton Woods.

With Bear Mountain to its south, Mt. Parker to its north, Mt. Cardigan to its west, and the Saco River to its east, Bartlett, incorporated in 1790, has an unforgettable setting. Lovely Bear Notch Road (closed in winter) has the only midpoint access to the Kancamagus Highway (Route 112). There isn't much town here (dining options are in Glen). It's best known for the Attitash Ski Resort, within walking distance.

3

SPORTS AND THE OUTDOORS

SKI AREA **Attitash Ski Resort.** Attitash, with a vertical drop of 1,760 feet, and Attitash Bear Peak, with a 1,450-foot vertical, have massive snowmaking operations and full-service base lodges. The bulk of the skiing and boarding is geared to intermediates and experts, with some steep pitches and glades. At 500 feet, the Ground Zero half-pipe is New England's longest. The Attitash Adventure Center has a rental shop, lessons desk, and children's programs. Attitash also has summer activities such as an alpine slide, guided horseback rides, and a scenic sky ride. ✉ *U.S. 302* *Box 308, 03812* ☎ *603/374–2368 or 800/233–7669* 🌐 *www.attitash.com.*

WHERE TO EAT

$$–$$$ ECLECTIC ✕ **Bernerhof Inn.** There are several options for dining at this inn. The Dining Room at the Bernerhof is the area's fine-dining choice, preparing traditional Swiss specialties such as fondue and Wiener schnitzel as well as hearty fare like herb-encrusted rack of lamb and veal Oscar (cutlets topped with crab meat, Bernaise sauce, and asparagus). The Black Bear pub pours microbrews and serves sandwiches and burgers as well as a very satisfying shepherd's pie. The CyBear Lounge serves afternoon appetizers you can snack on while checking your e-mail. ✉ *U.S. 302, Glen* ☎ *603/383–9132 or 800/828–3591* 🌐 *www.bernerhofinn.com* 💳 *AE, D, MC, V.*

$ SOUTHWESTERN ✕ **Margarita Grill.** Après-ski and hiking types congregate here in the dining room in cold weather and on the covered patio when it's warm for homemade salsas, wood-fired steaks, ribs, burgers, and a smattering of Tex-Mex and Southwestern specialties. Unwind with a margarita at bar after a day on the mountains. ✉ *78 U.S. 302, Glen* ☎ *603/383–6556* 🌐 *www.margaritagrillonline.com* 💳 *D, MC, V* ⏲ *No lunch weekdays.*

$–$$ AMERICAN ✕ **Red Parka Steakhouse and Pub.** This downtown Glen pub has been an institution for 37 years. A family-dining–oriented menu features an all-you-can-eat salad bar, baked stuffed shrimp, scallops, and hand-cut steaks. The barbecue sauce is made on-site, and beer is served in mason jars. Plan to spend some time reading the dozens and dozens of license plates that adorn the walls of the downstairs pub. ✉ *3 Station St., Glen* ☎ *603/383–4344* *www.redparkapub.com* *Reservations not accepted* 💳 *AE, D, MC, V.*

WHERE TO STAY

$-$$ **Attitash Mountain Village.** Across the street from the entrance to Attitash, you can't see this cluster of units from the road because they're in the pine trees (there are also a few slopeside condos), but they're there, along with hiking trails, a playground, a clay tennis court, two heated pools, an arcade, and a free stocked fishing pond. All in all it's a good deal for families on a budget who want to ski across the street. The accommodations are simple but serviceable, and there's a restaurant and a sports-style pub. **Pros:** simple, no-frills family place; playground. **Cons:** a bit run-down. *784 U.S. 302, Bartlett 603/374–6500 or 800/862–1600 www.attitashmtvillage.com 350 units In-room: no a/c (some), kitchen (some), refrigerator (some), DVD, Wi-Fi (some). In-hotel: restaurant, bar, tennis courts, pools, gym, laundry facilities, Internet terminal, Wi-Fi hotspot, some pets allowed AE, D, MC, V.*

$$ **Attitash Grand Summit Hotel & Conference Center.** This ski hotel is the choice for those who want ski-in, ski-out convenience. Accommodations include kitchenettes, video-game-equipped TVs, and stereos. Standard rooms have balconies. Crawford's Pub and Grille and Black Diamond Grill (breakfast and lunch) serve passable American fare and bar food ($–$$). **Pros:** ski-in, ski-out; nice pool and hot tubs; cheaper with ski package; full breakfast included. **Cons:** generally bland accommodations. *U.S. 302 Box 429 603/374–1900 or 800/223–7669 www.attitash.com 143 rooms In-room: kitchen (some), Wi-Fi. In-hotel: restaurants, bars, pool, gym, children's programs (ages 2–14), laundry facilities, Internet terminal, Wi-Fi hotspot AE, D, MC, V.*

JACKSON

★ *5 mi north of Glen.*

Just off Route 16 via a red covered bridge, Jackson has retained its storybook New England character. Art and antiques shopping, tennis, golf, fishing, and hiking to waterfalls are among the draws. When the snow falls, Jackson becomes the state's cross-country skiing capital. Four downhill ski areas are nearby. Hotels and B&Bs offer a ski shuttle. Visit Jackson Falls for a wonderful photo opportunity.

ESSENTIALS

Visitor Information Jackson Area Chamber of Commerce (*603/383–9356 www.jackson.com*).

EXPLORING

Story Land. That cluster of fluorescent buildings along Route 16 is a theme park with life-size storybook and nursery-rhyme characters. The 20 rides and five shows include a flume ride, Victorian-theme river-raft ride, farm tractor–inspired kiddie ride, pumpkin coach, variety show, and swan boats. In early spring, only parts of the park are open and admission is reduced to $16. *850 Rte. 16 603/383–4186 www.storylandnh.com $25 Mid-May–early Oct. Check Web site for dates and hours.*

SPORTS AND THE OUTDOORS

Nestlenook Estate and Resort (✉ *Dinsmore Rd.* ☎ *800/659–9443* 🌐 *www.nestlenookfarm.com*) maintains an outdoor ice-skating rink with rentals, music, and a bonfire. Snowshoeing and sleigh rides are other winter options; in summer you can fly-fish or ride in a horse-drawn carriage.

SKI AREAS **Black Mountain.** Friendly, informal Black Mountain has a warming southern exposure. The Family Passport allows two adults and two juniors to ski at discounted rates. Midweek rates ($29) are usually the lowest in Mt. Washington Valley. The 40 trails and glades on the 1,100-foot mountain are evenly divided among beginner, intermediate, and expert. There's a nursery for kids six months and up. Enjoy guided horseback riding in the summer. ✉ *1 Black Mountain Rd.* ☎ *800/698–4490; 800/475–4669 snow conditions* 🌐 *www.blackmt.com.*

★ **Jackson Ski Touring Foundation.** One of the nation's top four cross-country skiing areas, Jackson Ski Touring Foundation has 97 mi of trails. Many of the trails are groomed for regular cross-country and skate skiing. You can arrange lessons and rentals at the lodge, in the center of Jackson Village. ✉ *153 Main St., Jackson* ☎ *603/383–9355* 🌐 *www.jacksonxc.org.*

WHERE TO EAT

$–$$ AMERICAN ✕ **Red Fox Bar & Grille.** Some say this big family restaurant overlooking the Wentworth Golf Club gets its name from a wily fox with a penchant for stealing golf balls off the fairway. The wide-ranging menu has barbecued ribs and wood-fired pizzas as well as more refined dishes such as seared sea scallops with Grand Marnier sauce. The Sunday breakfast buffet is very popular. ✉ *49 Rte. 16* ☎ *603/383–4949* 🌐 *www.redfoxpub.com* ▭ *AE, D, MC, V* ⊙ *Lunch on Tues and Wed., summer only.*

$–$$ AMERICAN ★ ✕ **Thompson House Eatery.** One of the most innovative restaurants in generally staid northern New Hampshire, this eatery inside a rambling red farmhouse serves comfort food such as a wonderful meat loaf made with local beef, salads with in-season greens, maple scallops sautéed with a cream sauce, and a chocolate espresso pudding that will make your eyes roll with delight. ✉ *193 Main St.* ☎ *603/383–9341* 🌐 *www.thompsonhouseatery.com* ▭ *AE, D, MC, V* ⊙ *Lunch only on Tues. and Wed., late May–early Oct.*

$$$ AMERICAN Fodor's Choice ★ ✕ **Thorn Hill.** This famous inn serves up one of New England's most memorable meals. In warm months dine on the romantic porch, which overlooks the Presidential mountain range. The wine list is the state's most lauded, with 1,900 labels. The curated and changing "Top 50" list of reasonably priced bottles is a sure guide. Chef Peter Delmonte and pastry chef Brandon Gore create subtle and flavorful dishes such as a New York strip with chanterelle mushrooms and bordelaise sauce and salmon grilled with Mediterranean spices and served with hummus and cucumber *raita* (Indian yogurt sauce). The menu changes regularly and the once-a-month wine dinner is a favorite around the region. ✉ *42 Thorn Hill Rd.* ☎ *603/383–4242 or 800/289–8990* 🌐 *www.innatthornhill.com* ✍ *Reservations essential* ▭ *AE, D, MC, V* ⊙ *No lunch.*

WHERE TO STAY

$ **Christmas Farm Inn and Spa.** Despite its wintery name, this 1778 inn is an all-season retreat. Rooms in the main building and the saltbox next door are adorned with either Laura Ashley or Ralph Lauren fabrics. Other rooms are in a delightful old barn, in a sugarhouse, and in a few cottages about the wooded grounds. In the contemporary carriage house, which features private balconies, there's a great fireplace, and the 12 suites there have two-person whirlpool tubs and gas fireplaces. The inn's gardens are spectacular. **Pros:** kids welcome; nice indoor and outdoor pools. **Cons:** saltbox rooms could use improvement. ✉ *Rte. 16B, Box CC* ☎ *603/383–4313 or 800/443–5837* 🌐 *www.christmasfarminn.com* *22 rooms, 15 suites, 7 cottages* *In-room: Wi-Fi. In-hotel: restaurant, bar, pools, gym, spa, Wi-Fi hotspot* *AE, D, MC, V* *BP.*

$–$$ Fodor's Choice ★ **Inn at Jackson.** This B&B is impeccably maintained, charmingly furnished, and bright. The beautiful inn, a 1902 Victorian designed by Stanford White for the Baldwin family of piano fame, overlooks the village. The foyer's staircase is grand, but there's a remarkable relaxed and unpretentious ambience. Guest rooms have oversize windows; eight have fireplaces. The exceptional full breakfast may include anything from egg soufflé casserole to blueberry pancakes. **Pros:** super-clean rooms; great value; peaceful setting. **Cons:** third-floor rooms lack fireplaces. ✉ *12 Thorn Hill Rd., Box 822* ☎ *603/383–4321 or 800/289–8600* 🌐 *www.innatjackson.com* *14 rooms* *In-room: DVD, Wi-Fi. In-hotel: laundry service, Internet terminal, Wi-Fi hotspot, some pets allowed, no kids under 8* *AE, D, MC, V* *BP.*

$$$$ Fodor's Choice ★ **Inn at Thorn Hill.** This house, modeled after the 1891 Stanford White Victorian that burned down a decade ago, offers spacious rooms with a relaxed elegance. From a deck that overlooks the rolling hills around Jackson you can get your morning started with a summer breakfast of homemade muffins and bread, a tasty breakfast burrito with braised beef, or an exquisite eggs Florentine topped with spinach and Mornay sauce. A meal in the lounge might include house-cured and -smoked meats or a plate of artisan cheeses served with fruit chutney. Innkeepers Jim and Ibby Cooper are always on hand to spend time with guests, sipping wine and talking about local history. All of the rooms have cushy amenities: two-person Jacuzzis, fireplaces, and DVD players. The top units have steam showers, wet bars, and refrigerators. Cottages and rooms in the carriage house are less thrilling. A full spa provides a full range of beauty treatments and massages. Afternoon tea and a substantial full breakfast and dinner are included. **Pros:** great meals and service; romantic setting. **Cons:** small fee for Wi-Fi. ✉ *42 Thorn Hill Rd., Box A* ☎ *603/383–4242 or 800/289–8990* 🌐 *www.innatthornhill.com* *15 rooms, 7 suites, 3 cottages* *In-room: refrigerator (some), DVD (some), no TV (some), Wi-Fi. In-hotel: restaurant, room service, bar, pool, gym, spa, laundry service, Wi-Fi hotspot, no kids under 6* *AE, D, MC, V* *MAP.*

MT. WASHINGTON

★ *20 mi northwest of Jackson.*

GETTING HERE AND AROUND

Mt. Washington is the highest peak (6,288 feet) in the northeastern United States and the site of a weather station that recorded the world's highest winds, 231 MPH, in 1934. You can drive to the top, which climbs 4,600 feet in 7.5 mi, in the summer. A number of trailheads circle the mountain and the other peaks in the Presidential Range, but all of them are strenuous and for the hearty. For the best information on trails in the Presidents, visit *www.hikethewhites.com*. The Mt. Washington Cog Railway, which operates in the summer only, climbs 3,500 feet in 3 mi, at grades averaging 25%. (⇨ *Bretton Woods for information on the Mt. Washington Cog Railway.*)

3

ESSENTIALS

Visitor Information **Mount Washington Observatory** (*603/356–2137 www.mountwashington.org*). **White Mountain National Forest** (*71 White Mountain Dr., Clampton 603/536–6100 www.fs.fed.us/r9/white*).

EXPLORING

Mt. Washington Auto Road. Opened in 1861, this route begins at the Glen House, a gift shop and rest stop 15 mi north of Glen on Route 16, and winds its way up the east side of the mountain, ending at the top, a 7.5-mi and approximately half-hour drive later. At the summit is the Sherman Adams Summit Building, built in 1979 and containing a visitor center and a museum focusing on the mountain's geology and extreme weather conditions; you can stand in the glassed-in viewing area to hear the wind roar. The Mt. Washington Observatory is at the building's western end. Rules limit what cars may use the road. For instance, cars with automatic transmission must be able to shift down into first gear. A guided bus tour is available or you can reach the top along several rough hiking trails; those who hoof it can make the return trip via shuttle, tickets for which are sold at the Stage Office, at the summit at the end of the cog railway trestle. Remember that the temperature atop Mt. Washington will be much colder than down below—the average year-round is below freezing, and the average wind velocity is 35 mph. *Rte. 16, Pinkham Notch 603/466–3988 www.mountwashingtonautoroad.com Car and driver $23, each additional adult passenger $8 Check the Web site for hours of operation; closed late Oct.–mid-May.*

SnowCoaches. In winter, when the road is closed to private vehicles, you can opt to reach the top of Mt. Washington via a guided tour in one of the four-wheel-drive vehicles that leave from Great Glen Trails Outdoor Center, just south of Gorham, on a first-come, first-served basis. Great Glen's nine-passenger vans are refitted with snowmobile-like treads and can travel to just above the tree line. You have the option of cross-country skiing or snowshoeing down. *Rte. 16, Pinkham Notch 603/466–2333 www.greatglentrails.com $45 (includes all-day trail pass) Dec.–Mar., snow necessary, most days, beginning at 8:30.*

Reward your vehicle for tackling the auto road with the obligatory bumper sticker: "This Car Climbed Mt. Washington."

SPORTS AND THE OUTDOORS

Although not a town per se, scenic **Pinkham Notch** covers Mt. Washington's eastern side and has several ravines, including Tuckerman Ravine, famous for spring skiing. The Appalachian Mountain Club maintains a large visitor center here on Route 16 that provides information to hikers and travelers and has guided hikes, outdoor skills workshops, a cafeteria, lodging, regional topography displays, and an outdoors shop.

HIKING The **Appalachian Mountain Club Pinkham Notch Visitor Center** (✉ *Rte. 16, Box 298, Gorham* ☎ *603/466–2721; 603/466–2727 reservations* 🌐 *www.outdoors.org*) has lectures, workshops, slide shows, and outdoor skills instruction year-round. Accommodations include the adjacent Joe Dodge Lodge, the Highland Center at Crawford Notch with 100-plus beds and a 16-bed bunkhouse next to it, and the club's eight high-mountain huts spaced one day's hike from each other in the White Mountain National Forest portion of the Appalachian Trail. The huts provide meals and dorm-style lodging from June to late September or early October; the rest of the year they are self-service.

SKI AREAS **Great Glen Trails Outdoor Center.** Amenities at this fabulous lodge at the base of Mt. Washington include a huge ski-gear and sports shop, food court, climbing wall, observation deck, and fieldstone fireplace. In winter it's renowned for its dramatic 24-mi cross-country trail system. Some trails have snowmaking, and there's access to more than 1,100 acres of backcountry. It's even possible to ski or snowshoe the lower half of the Mt. Washington Auto Road. Trees shelter most of the trails, so Mt. Washington's infamous weather isn't such a concern. In summer it's the base from which hikers, mountain bikers, and trail runners can explore Mt. Washington. The center also has programs in canoeing, kayaking, and fly-fishing. ✉ *Rte. 16, Pinkham Notch* ☎ *603/466–2333* 🌐 *www.greatglentrails.com.*

Wildcat. Glade skiers favor Wildcat, with 28 acres of official tree skiing. The 47 runs include some stunning double-black-diamond trails. Skiers who can hold a wedge should check out the 2½-mi-long Polecat. Experts can zip down the Lynx. Views of Mt. Washington and Tuckerman Ravine are superb. The trails are classic New England—narrow and winding. Wildcat's expert runs deserve their designations and then some. Intermediates have mid-mountain to base trails, and beginners will find gentle terrain and a broad teaching slope. Snowboarders have several terrain parks and the run of the mountain. In summer you can go to the top on the four-passenger gondola ($15), ride a zip line, and hike the many well-kept trails. ✉ *Rte. 16, Jackson* ☎ *603/466–3326; 888/754–9453 snow conditions; 800/255–6439 lodging* 🌐 *www.skiwildcat.com.*

3

DIXVILLE NOTCH

63 mi north of Mt. Washington, 66 mi northeast of Littleton, 149 mi north of Concord.

Just 12 mi from the Canadian border, this tiny community is known for two things: the Balsams, one of New Hampshire's oldest and most celebrated resorts, and the fact that Dixville Notch and another New Hampshire community, Hart's Location, are the first election districts in the nation to vote in presidential general elections. When the 30 or so Dixville Notch voters file into the little Balsams meeting room on the eve of Election Day and cast their ballots at the stroke of midnight, they invariably make national news.

EXPLORING

One of the favorite pastimes in this area is spotting moose, those large, ungainly, yet elusive members of the deer family. Although you may catch sight of one or more yourself, **Northern Forest Moose Tours** (☎ *603/466–3103 or 877/986–6673* 🎫 *$25* 🕒 *May–Oct. Bus leaves at 6:30* PM) conducts bus tours of the region that have a 97% success rate for spotting moose.

OFF THE BEATEN PATH

Pittsburg. Well north of the White Mountains, in the Great North Woods, Pittsburg contains the four Connecticut Lakes and the springs that form the Connecticut River. The state's northern tip—a chunk of about 250 square mi—lies within the town's borders, the result of a dispute between the United States and Canada that began in 1832 and was resolved in 1842, when the international boundary was fixed. Remote though it is, this frontier town teems with hunters, boaters, fishermen, hikers, and photographers from early summer through winter. Especially in the colder months, moose sightings are common. The town has more than a dozen lodges and several informal eateries. It's about a 90-minute drive from Littleton and 40 minutes from Dixville Notch; add another 30 minutes to reach Fourth Connecticut Lake, nearly at the Canadian border. On your way, you pass the village of Stewartson, exactly midway between the Equator and the North Pole.

SPORTS AND THE OUTDOORS

Dixville Notch State Park (✉ *Rte. 26* ☎ *603/538–6707* 🌐 *www.nhstateparks.com/dixville.html*), in the northernmost notch of the White Mountains, has picnic areas, a waterfall, two mountain brooks, and hiking trails.

SKI AREA **Balsams.** Skiing was originally provided as an amenity for hotel guests at the Balsams, but the area has become popular with day-trippers as well. Slopes with names such as Sanguinary, Umbagog, and Magalloway may sound tough, but they're only moderately difficult. There are 16 trails and four glades for every skill level from the top of the 1,000-foot vertical. The Balsams has 47 mi of cross-country skiing, tracked and groomed for skating. Natural-history markers annotate some trails; you can also try Telemark and backcountry skiing, and there are 21 mi of snowshoeing trails. ✉ *1000 Cold Spring Rd.* ☎ *800/255–0600, 603/255–3951 snow conditions* 🌐 *www.thebalsams.com.*

WHERE TO EAT AND STAY

FRENCH Fodor's Choice ★ **Le Rendez Vous.** You might not expect to find an authentic French bakery and pastry shop in the small workaday village of Colebrook, 10 mi west of Dixville Notch, but Le Rendez Vous serves fabulous tarts and treats—the owners came here directly from Paris. Drop in to this quaint café—furnished with several tables and armchairs—for coffee, hand-dipped Belgian chocolates, croissants, a tremendous variety of fresh-baked breads, and all sorts of gourmet foods, from dried fruits and nuts to lentils, olive oils, and balsamic vinegar. ✉ *121 Main St., Colebrook* ☎ *603/237–5150* ▭ *AE, D, MC, V* ⊙ *Daily 9–5.*

$$$–$$$$ ★ **The Balsams.** Nestled in the pine groves of the North Woods since 1866, and thanks to relatively new management, this lavish grande dame resort has reversed its decline (it had been getting a little sloppy around the edges). The Balsams encompasses some 15,000 wooded acres—an area roughly the size of Manhattan. Even when the resort is filled to capacity (about 400 guests and 400 employees), it's still a remarkably solitary place. It draws families, golf enthusiasts, skiers, and others for a varied slate of activities from dancing to cooking demonstrations. Rooms are spacious, with large cedar-lined closets and ample dressers. Floral-print wallpaper, modern bathrooms, full-length mirrors, and reproduction antiques impart a dignified old-world grace. Most rooms have views overlooking the lake, gardens, and mountains; still, always inquire about the view when booking, as a handful afford less-promising vistas (the parking area, for example). In the dining room ($$$$; jacket and tie after 6 PM), sample a chilled strawberry soup spiked with Grand Marnier followed by broiled swordfish with white beans and lemon coulis. Rates include breakfast and dinner and unlimited use of the facilities. **Pros:** splendid grand resort; activities galore. **Cons:** grand scale limits intimacy; if no one were there it would be *The Shining*. ✉ *25 Rte. 26* ☎ *603/255–3400; 800/255–0600* 🌐 *www.thebalsams.com* *184 rooms, 20 suites* *In-room: no TV (some). In-hotel: 3 restaurants, room service, bar, golf courses, tennis courts, pool, gym, spa, bicycles, children's programs (ages 1–12), laundry service* ▭ *AE, D, MC, V* *FAP, MAP.*

$ **The Glen.** Each of this resort's seven cabins sits alone in the forest with private views of the First Connecticut Lake and cedar siding with decks that have Adirondack chairs to enjoy the bucolic view. Each cabin has efficiency kitchens and mini-refrigerators—not that you'll need either. Rates include hearty meals, served family-style, in the lodge restaurant. The lodge has three bedrooms, a common area adorned with the mounted heads of deer and moose, and a fireplace in the living room made of native stone. **Pros:** rustic; remote setting; charming lodge. **Cons:** remote; not luxurious. ✉ *118 Glen Rd., 1 mi off U.S. 3, Pittsburg* ☎ *603/538–6500 or 800/445–4536* 🌐 *www.theglen.org* *6 rooms, 9 cabins* *In-room: no phone, kitchen, no TV. In-hotel: restaurant* *No credit cards* ⏲ *Closed mid-Oct.–mid-May* *FAP.*

NORTH CONWAY

76 mi south of Dixville Notch; 7 mi south of Glen; 41 mi east of Lincoln/North Woodstock.

Before the arrival of the outlet stores, the town drew visitors for its inspiring scenery, ski resorts, and access to White Mountain National Forest. Today, however, the feeling of natural splendor is gone. Shopping is the big sport, and businesses line Route 16 for several miles. You'll get a close look at them because traffic slows to a crawl here. You can take scenic West Side Road from Conway to Intervale to circumvent the traffic and take in splendid views.

GETTING HERE AND AROUND

On Route 16/302 avoid the stores on the south side of town by parking near the fire station on Main Street and spend half a day visiting the unique shops and restaurants in this part of town. Taxis can get you around between Conway, North Conway, and Jackson.

ESSENTIALS

Taxi **Turtle Taxi** (☎ *603/356–7577* 🌐 *www.turtletaxi.net*). **Village Taxi** (☎ *603/356–3602* 🌐 *www.wmtransit.com*).

Visitor Information **North Country Chamber of Commerce** (☎ *603/237–8939 or 800/698–8939* 🌐 *www.northcountrychamber.org*).

EXPLORING

The **Conway Scenic Railroad** operates trips aboard vintage trains from historic North Conway Station. The Notch Train, through Crawford Notch to Crawford Depot (a 5-hour round-trip) or Fabyan Station (5½ hours), offers wonderful scenic views from the domed observation coach. The Valley Train provides views of Mt. Washington countryside on a 55-minute round trip to Conway or a 1¾-hour trip to Bartlett—lunch and dinner are served on some departures. The 1874 station displays lanterns, old tickets and timetables, and other railroad artifacts. Reserve your spot early during foliage season for the dining excursions. ✉ *38 Norcross Cir.* ☎ *603/356–5251 or 800/232–5251* 🌐 *www.conwayscenic.com* *$12–$70* ⏲ *Mid-Apr.–mid Dec; call for times.*

EXPLORING

Hartmann Model Railroad Museum. This building houses about 2,000 engines, more than 5,000 cars and coaches, and 14 operating layouts (from G to Z scales) in addition to a café, a crafts store, a hobby shop, and an outdoor miniature trains that you can sit on and ride.

✉ 15 Town Hall Rd. at Rte. 16 (U.S. 302), Intervale ☎ 603/356–9922 🌐 www.hartmannrr.com 🎟 $6 ⏲ Open daily 10–5. Closed Tues. June, Sept., and Oct. Closed Tues.–Thurs., Nov. 1–May 31.

Weather Discovery Center. The hands-on exhibits at this meteorological educational facility demonstrate how weather is monitored and how it affects us. The center is a collaboration between the National and Atmospheric Administration Forecast Systems lab and the Mt. Washington Observatory at the summit of Mt. Washington. *✉ 2779 Main St. ☎ 603/356–2137 🌐 www.mountwashington.org 🎟 $5 ⏲ May–Oct., daily 10–5; Nov.–Apr., Sat.–Mon. 10–5 (also open daily during school vacation mid-Feb.–early Mar.).*

SPORTS AND THE OUTDOORS

Echo Lake State Park. You needn't be a rock climber to catch views from the 700-foot White Horse and Cathedral ledges. From the top you'll see the entire valley, including Echo Lake, which offers fishing and swimming and on quiet days an excellent opportunity to shout for echoes. *✉ Off U.S 302 ☎ 603/271–3556 🌐 www.nhstateparks.com/echo.html 🎟 $4 ⏲ Late May–mid-June, weekends dawn–dusk; mid-June–early Sept., daily dawn–dusk.*

CANOEING AND KAYAKING

River outfitter **Saco Bound Canoe & Kayak** (*✉ 2561 E. Main St., Center Conway ☎ 603/447–2177 🌐 www.sacobound.com*) leads gentle canoeing expeditions, guided kayak trips, and white-water rafting on seven rivers and provides lessons, equipment, and transportation.

FISHING

North Country Angler (*✉ 2888 White Mountain Hwy. ☎ 603/356–6000 🌐 www.northcountryangler.com*) schedules intensive guided fly-fishing weekends throughout the region. It's one of the best tackle shops in the state.

SKI AREAS

Cranmore Mountain Resort. This downhill ski area has been a favorite of families since it began operating in 1938. Five glades have opened more skiable terrain. The 50 trails are well laid out and fun to ski. Most runs are naturally formed intermediates that weave in and out of glades. Beginners have several slopes and routes from the summit; experts must be content with a few short, steep pitches. In addition to the trails, snowboarders have a terrain park and a half-pipe. Night skiing is offered Thursday–Saturday and holidays. *✉ 1 Skimobile Rd., Box 1640, North Conway ☎ 603/356–5543; 603/356–8516 snow conditions; 800/786–6754 lodging 🌐 www.cranmore.com.*

King Pine Ski Area at Purity Spring Resort. Some 9 mi south of Conway, this family-run ski area has been going strong since the late 19th century. Some ski-and-stay packages include free skiing for midweek resort guests. King Pine's 16 gentle trails are ideal for beginner and intermediate skiers; experts won't be challenged except for a brief pitch on the Pitch Pine trail. There's tubing on weekend afternoons and night skiing and tubing on Friday and Saturday evenings, plus 9 mi of cross-country skiing. Indoors, you can enjoy a pool and fitness complex and go ice-skating. In summer the resort is a destination for waterskiing, kayaking, loon-watching, tennis, hiking, and other activities. *✉ 1251 Eaton Rd., East Madison ☎ 603/367–8896 or 800/373–3754 🌐 www.purityspring.com or www.kingpine.com.*

Sit back and enjoy the view on the Conway Scenic Railroad.

Forty miles of groomed cross-country trails weave through North Conway and the countryside along the **Mt. Washington Valley Ski Touring Association Network** (✉ *2079 Rte. 16/302, Intervale* ☎ *603/356–9920 or 800/282–5220* 🌐 *www.crosscountryskinh.com*).

SHOPPING

ANTIQUES **Richard Plusch Antiques** (✉ *2584 White Mountain Hwy.* ☎ *603/356–3333*) deals in period furniture and accessories, including glass, sterling silver, Oriental porcelains, rugs, and paintings.

CLOTHING More than 150 factory outlets—including L. L. Bean, Timberland, Pfaltzgraff, Lenox, Polo, Nike, Anne Klein, and Woolrich—line Route 16. A top pick for skiwear is **Joe Jones** (✉ *2709 Main St.* ☎ *603/356–9411* 🌐 *www.joejonessports.com*).

CRAFTS **Handcrafters Barn** (✉ *2473 White Mountain Hwy. [Main St./Rte. 16]* ☎ *603/356–8996* 🌐 *www.handcraftersbarn.com*) stocks the work of 350 area artists and artisans. The **League of New Hampshire Craftsmen** (✉ *2526 Main St.* ☎ *603/356–2441* 🌐 *www.nhcrafts.org*) carries the creations of the state's best artisans. **Zeb's General Store** (✉ *2675 Main St.* ☎ *603/356–9294 or 800/676–9294* 🌐 *www.zebs.com*) looks just like an old-fashioned country store and sells food items, crafts, and other products made in New England.

NIGHTLIFE

Horsefeather's (✉ *2679 White Mountain Hwy.* ☎ *603/356–6862* 🌐 *www.horsefeathers.com*), a restaurant and bar, often has rock, blues, and folk music, especially on weekends.

WHERE TO EAT

$–$$ AMERICAN ✕ **Delaney's Hole in the Wall.** This casual sports tavern displays its memorabilia such as autographed baseballs and an early photo of skiing at Tuckerman Ravine. Entrées range from fajitas to mussels and scallops sautéed with spiced sausage and Louisiana seasonings. Live music is featured on Wednesday nights. ✉ *2966 White Mountain Hwy. [Rte. 16], ¼ mi north of North Conway Village* ☎ *603/356–7776* 🌐 *www.delaneys.com* ▭ *AE, D, MC, V.*

$ AMERICAN ✕ **Muddy Moose.** This family restaurant buzzes with the noise of children. Its mac-and-cheese, blueberry-glazed ribs, burgers, and salads will satisfy kids and parents alike. A unique side dish of carrots with a hint of maple syrup is a pleasant surprise. The Muddy Moose Pie, made of ice cream, fudge, and crumbled Oreos, can feed a family of four. ✉ *2344 White Mountain Hwy.* ☎ *603/356–7696* 🌐 *www.muddymoose.com* ✍ *Reservations not accepted* ▭ *AE, D, MC, V.*

WHERE TO STAY

$$$–$$$$ **Buttonwood Inn.** A tranquil 6-acre oasis in this busy resort area, the Buttonwood is on Mt. Surprise, 2 mi northeast of North Conway Village. It's a peaceful retreat that lets you avoid the noise of downtown but still have access to area restaurants and shopping. Rooms in the 1820s farmhouse are furnished in Shaker style. Wide pine floors, quilts, and period stenciling add folksiness. Downstairs is the Mt. Surprise room, where a self-serve bar, library, board games, and a DVD library await you. **Pros:** good bedding and amenities; tranquil; clean. **Cons:** unexciting for those not wanting a remote getaway. ✉ *64 Mt. Surprise Rd.* 📫 *Box 1817, 03860* ☎ *603/356–2625 or 800/258–2625* 🌐 *www.buttonwoodinn.com* *9 rooms, 1 suite* *In-room: DVD (some), no TV (some). In-hotel: pool, Internet terminal, Wi-Fi hotspot* ▭ *AE, MC, V* *BP.*

$$–$$$ **Darby Field Inn.** After a day in the White Mountains, warm up by the fieldstone fireplace in the living room. Most rooms in this unpretentious 1826 farmhouse have mountain views; several have fireplaces. There are 10 mi of cross-country and hiking trails, as well as carriage rides and sleigh rides. The inn's dining room ($$$) prepares American fare. **Pros:** clean; romantic; remote. **Cons:** better for couples than families. ✉ *185 Chase Hill, Albany* ☎ *603/447–2181 or 800/426–4147* 🌐 *www.darbyfield.com* *11 rooms, 4 suites* *In-room: no phone, no a/c (some), DVD (some), no TV (some), Wi-Fi. In-hotel: restaurant, bar, pool, spa, Wi-Fi hotspot, no kids under 8* ▭ *AE, MC, V* ⊙ *Closed Apr.* *BP.*

$$$–$$$$ ★ **Snowvillage Inn**: Journalist Frank Simonds built the gambrel-roofed main house in 1916. To complement the tome-jammed bookshelves, guest rooms are named for famous authors; many have fireplaces. The nicest of the rooms, with 12 windows that look out over the Presidential Range, is a tribute to Robert Frost. Two additional buildings—the carriage house and the chimney house—also have libraries. The menu in the Sleigh Mill Grille ($$–$$$$; reservations essential) might include grilled rack of lamb with minted Mediterranean herbs and spices,

CLOSE UP

New Hampshire's Diners

Once named one of the country's "top 10 diners" by *USA Today*, the bustling **Red Arrow Diner** (✉ *61 Lowell St., Manchester* ☎ *603/626–1118* ✉ *63 Union Sq., Milford* ☎ *603/249–9222* 🌐 *www.redarrowdiner.com*) is open 24/7 and caters to politicos, students, artists, and regular Janes and Joes in the heart of the Granite State's largest city. The 1922 diner's daily "Blue Plate Specials" are served on actual blue plates, and you'll find such regular items as kielbasa and beans and house-brewed Arrow root beer and cream soda.

Up in the skiing and hiking haven of Lincoln, outdoorsy souls fuel up on hearty fare like banana-bread French toast and cherry pie à la mode at the cozy **Sunny Day Diner** (✉ *U.S. 3, just off I–93, Exit 33, Lincoln* ☎ *603/745–4833*), a handsomely restored building from the late 1950s. Travelers to the state's Lakes Region have long been familiar with the flashy pink exterior and neon signage of the **Tilt'n Diner** (✉ *61 Laconia Rd., Tilton* ☎ *603/286–2204* 🌐 *www.thecman.com*), a convivial 1950s-style restaurant that's known for its baked shepherd's pie and Southern breakfast—sausage gravy, biscuits, and baked beans with two eggs—served all day. On sunny days, dine at one of the picnic tables.

Dartmouth students and professors hobnob over stellar breakfast victuals at **Lou's Restaurant** (✉ *30 S. Main St., Hanover* ☎ *603/643–3321* 🌐 *www.lousrestaurant.net*), a cheap-and-cheerful storefront diner that serves up prodigious portions of corned-beef hash and eggs Benedict, as well as artfully decorated cupcakes and house-made donuts. Just beware of the long lines on weekend mornings. In the historic coastal city of Portsmouth, the **Friendly Toast** (✉ *121 Congress St., Portsmouth* ☎ *603/430–2154* 🌐 *www.thefriendlytoast.net*) might be the most vaunted breakfast spot in the state. Creative fare like Almond Joy pancakes (with coconut, chocolate chips, and almonds) and the "Flying Fish scramble" (eggs with smoked salmon, fresh dill, and cheddar) keep hungry bellies coming back again and again.

—Andrew Collins

Red Arrow Diner in Manchester.

sesame-encrusted yellow-fin tuna, or a medley pumpkin ravioli. The inn is also home to the White Mountain Cooking School, and overnight packages with cooking classes are available. You can hike easily up to beautiful Foss Mountain, directly from the inn. **Pros:** adorable property; fine dining. **Cons:** on the pricier side. ✉ *136 Stewart Rd., 6 mi southeast of Conway, Box 68, Snowville* ☎ *603/447–2818 or 800/447–4345* 🌐 *www.snowvillageinn.com* *18 rooms* *In-room: no TV. In-hotel: restaurant, no kids under 6* ▭ *AE, D, MC, V* 🍴 *BP, MAP.*

$$ **White Mountain Hotel and Resort.** West of the traffic of North Conway, the scenery becomes splendid. Rooms in this hotel at the base of Whitehorse Ledge have mountain views. Proximity to the White Mountain National Forest and Echo Lake State Park makes you feel farther away from the outlet malls than you actually are. There's a 9-hole golf course, and this area is great for biking. Three meals a day can be had at the at Ledges dining room ($$); there are also a tavern ($–$$) and a sumptuous brunch. Kids 18 and under stay free. **Pros:** scenic setting that's close to shopping; lots of activities. **Cons:** two-night-minimum summer weekends. ✉ *2560 West Side Rd., Box 1828* ☎ *800/533–6301* 🌐 *www.whitemountainhotel.com* *69 rooms, 11 suites* *In-room: refrigerator, DVD, Wi-Fi. In-hotel: 2 restaurants, room service, bar, golf course, tennis court, pool, gym, laundry facilities, laundry service, Wi-Fi hotspot* ▭ *AE, D, MC, V* 🍴 *BP, MAP.*

EN ROUTE

A great place to settle in to the White Mountains, take in one of the greatest panoramas of the mountains, and get visitor info is at the **Intervale Scenic Vista.** The stop, off Route 16 a few miles north of North Conway, is run by the DOT, has a helpful volunteer staff, features a wonderful large topographical map, and has terrific bathrooms.

KANCAMAGUS HIGHWAY

★ *36 mi between Conway and Lincoln/North Woodstock.*

Interstate 93 is the fastest way to the White Mountains, but it's hardly the most appealing. The section of Route 112 known as the Kancamagus Highway passes through some of the state's most unspoiled mountain scenery—it was one of the first roads in the nation to be designated a National Scenic Byway. The Kanc, as it's called by locals, is punctuated by overlooks and picnic areas, erupts into fiery color each fall, when photo-snapping drivers really slow things down. A number of campgrounds are off the highway. In bad weather, check with the White Mountains Visitors Bureau for road conditions.

SPORTS AND THE OUTDOORS

A couple of short hiking trails off the Kancamagus Highway (Route 112) yield great rewards with relatively little effort. The **Lincoln Woods Trail** starts from the large parking lot of the Lincoln Woods Visitor Center, 4 mi east of Lincoln. Here you can purchase the recreation pass ($5 per vehicle, good for seven consecutive days) needed to park in any of the White Mountain National Forest lots or overlooks; stopping briefly to take photos or to use the restrooms at the visitor center is permitted without a pass. The trail crosses a suspension bridge over the Pemigewasset River and follows an old railroad bed for 3 mi along the river. The parking and picnic area for **Sabbaday Falls**, about 15 mi west of Conway, is the trailhead for an easy ½-mi route to a multilevel cascade that plunges through two potholes and a flume.

DARTMOUTH–LAKE SUNAPEE

In the west-central part of the state, the towns around prestigious Dartmouth College and rippling Lake Sunapee vary from sleepy, old-fashioned outposts that haven't changed much in decades to bustling, sophisticated towns rife with cafés, art galleries, and boutiques. Among the latter, Hanover and New London are the area's main hubs, both of them increasingly popular as vacation destinations and with telecommuters seeking a quieter, more economical home base. Although distinct from the Lakes Region, greater Lake Sunapee looks like a miniature Lake Winnipesaukee, albeit with far less commercial development. For a great drive, follow the Lake Sunapee Scenic and Cultural Byway, which runs for about 25 mi from Georges Mills (a bit northwest of New London) down into Warner, tracing much of the Lake Sunapee shoreline. When you've tired of climbing and swimming and visiting the past, look for small studios of area artists. This part of the state, along with the even quieter Monadnock area to the south, has long been an informal artists' colony where people come to write, paint, and weave in solitude.

ESSENTIALS

Visitor Information Lake Sunapee Region Chamber of Commerce (☎ *603/526–6575 or 877/526–6575* 🌐 *www.sunapeevacations.com*).

NEW LONDON

16 mi northwest of Warner, 25 mi west of Tilton.

New London, the home of Colby-Sawyer College (1837), is a good base for exploring the Lake Sunapee region. A campus of stately Colonial-style buildings fronts the vibrant commercial district, where you'll find several cafés and boutiques.

GETTING HERE AND AROUND

From the south take Exit 11 on Interstate 93 to Crockett Corner and then north on Route 114. From the north take Exit 12 and travel south on Route 114. Mount Sunapee Ski Area offers a ski shuttle to and from many of the area hotels and B&Bs.

ESSENTIALS

Visitor and Ski Information Lake Sunapee Area Chamber of Commerce (☎ *603/526–6575* 🌐 *www.sunapeevacations.com*).

SPORTS AND THE OUTDOORS

A 3½-mi scenic auto road at **Rollins State Park** (✉ *Off Rte. 103, Main St., Warner* ☎ *603/456–3808* 🌐 *www.nhstateparks.com/rollins.html* 🎫 *$4*) snakes up the southern slope of Mt. Kearsarge, where you can hike a ½-mi trail to the summit. The road is closed mid-November through mid-June.

SHOPPING

Artisan's Workshop (✉ *Peter Christian's Tavern, 186 Main St.* ☎ *603/526–4227*) carries jewelry, glass, and other local handicrafts. Near New London in the tiny village of Elkins, **Mesa Home Factory Store** (✉ *11 Pleasant St.* ☎ *603/526–4497*) sells striking hand-painted dinnerware, hand-blown glassware, wrought-iron decorative arts, and other housewares at bargain prices.

THE ARTS

The **New London Barn Playhouse** (✉ *84 Main St.* ☎ *603/526–6710 or 800/633–2276* 🌐 *www.nlbarn.com*) presents Broadway-style and children's plays every summer in New Hampshire's oldest continuously operating theater.

WHERE TO EAT AND STAY

$–$$ AMERICAN

✕ **Four Corners Grille and Flying Goose Brew Pub.** With 12 handcrafted beers made with hops grown on-site, this inviting restaurant and pub is a hit with beer connoisseurs. Standouts include a shepherd's pie made with locally raised bison, paper-thin onion rings, fresh-cut steaks, and pretzel-covered chicken. The menu changes twice a year, in the summer and fall. Thursday evenings have live music. ✉ *40 Andover Rd., at the intersection of Rtes. 11 and 114* ☎ *603/526–6899* 🌐 *www.flyinggoose.com* 💳 *AE, D, MC, V.*

¢ CAFÉ Fodor's Choice ★ **Ellie's Café and Deli.** From its eggs Benedict to its oven-baked breakfast chimichanga to its pancakes with candied walnuts and crčme brulée French toast, the food at Ellie's is made for comfort and to fill you up. You can also linger over a cup of hot coffee in the rustic atmosphere of wood floors and exposed posts and beams. Lunch includes flatbread sandwiches or a veggie "tower," a baguette stuffed with portobello mushrooms, red onion, cucumber, and roasted red peppers. At the rear of the restaurant the Banks Gallery displays local art. ✉ *207 Main St.* ☎ *603/526–2488* 🌐 *www.elliescafeanddeli.com* ▭ *D, MC, V.*

$$–$$$ ★ **Inn at Pleasant Lake.** This 1790s inn lies across Pleasant Lake from majestic Mt. Kearsarge. Its spacious rooms have country antiques and modern bathrooms. The restaurant ($$$$; reservations essential) presents a prix-fixe menu that changes nightly but draws raves for such entrées as roasted rack of Australian lamb with a mushroom sauce and such desserts as fresh berries covered in a dark chocolate sauce. Afternoon tea and full breakfast are included. **Pros:** lakefront with a small beach; boating. **Cons:** away from town activities. ✉ *853 Pleasant St., Box 1030* ☎ *603/526–6271 or 800/626–4907* 🌐 *www.innatpleasantlake.com* *10 rooms* *In-room: no phone, no TV. In-hotel: restaurant, gym, beachfront* ▭ *MC, V* *BP.*

$–$$ **Follansbee Inn.** Built in 1840, this quintessential country inn on the shore of Kezar Lake is the kind of place that almost automatically turns strangers into friends. Next door to a quintessential white-clapboard church, it's a perfect fit in the 19th-century village of North Sutton. Each of the four suites and 13 rooms is filled with soft country quilts, and several overlook the water. In winter you can ice-fish, borrow the inn's snowshoes, or ski across the lake; in summer you can swim or boat from the inn's pier. A 3-mi walking trail circles the lake. **Pros:** relaxed lakefront setting; clean rooms. **Cons:** bar serves only wine and beer. ✉ *Rte. 114, North Sutton* ☎ *603/927–4221 or 800/626–4221* 🌐 *www.follansbeeinn.com* *17 rooms* *In-room: no phone, no a/c, no TV, Wi-Fi. In-hotel: bar, beachfront, bicycles* ▭ *MC, V* *BP.*

EN ROUTE

About midway between New London and Newbury on the west side of the lake, **Sunapee Harbor** is an old-fashioned, all-American summer resort community that feels like a miniature version of Wolfeboro, with a large marina, a handful of restaurants and shops on the water, a tidy village green with a gazebo, and a small museum in a Victorian stable run by the historical society. A plaque outside Wild Goose Country Store details some of Lake Sunapee's attributes—that it's one of the highest lakes in New Hampshire, at 1,091 feet above sea level, and one of the least polluted. An interpretive path runs along a short span of the Sugar River, the only outflow from Lake Sunapee, which winds for 18 mi to the Connecticut River.

3

NEWBURY

8 mi southwest of New London.

Newbury is on the edge of Mt. Sunapee State Park. The mountain, which rises to an elevation of nearly 3,000 feet, and the sparkling lake are the region's outdoor recreation centers. The popular League of New Hampshire Craftsmen's Fair, the nation's oldest crafts fair, is held at the base of Mt. Sunapee each August.

GETTING HERE AND AROUND

From New London, take 114 West to 103A South, which follows the eastern coast of Lake Sunapee to Newbury.

EXPLORING

Fells. John M. Hay, who served as private secretary to Abraham Lincoln and secretary of state for Presidents William McKinley and Theodore Roosevelt, built the Fells on Lake Sunapee as a summer home in 1890. House tours offer a glimpse of early-20th-century life on a New Hampshire estate. The grounds include a 100-foot-long perennial garden and a rock garden with a brook flowing through it. Miles of hiking trails can also be accessed from the estate. The building houses art and history exhibits and hosts educational programs for children all year. The estate is sometimes rented for weddings and other events. ✉ *456 Rte. 103A* ☎ *603/763–4789* 🌐 *www.thefells.org* 🎫 *$8* ⏲ *Labor Day–Columbus Day, daily 10–4; grounds open all year dawn–dusk.*

SPORTS AND THE OUTDOORS

BEACHES AND FISHING

Sunapee State Beach has picnic areas, a beach, and a bathhouse. You can rent canoes, too. ✉ *Rte. 103* ☎ *603/763–5561* 🌐 *www.nhstateparks.com/sunapeebeach.html* 🎫 *$4* ⏲ *Daily dawn–dusk.* **Lake Sunapee** has brook and lake trout, salmon, smallmouth bass, and pickerel.

BOAT TOURS

Narrated cruises aboard the **MV *Mt. Sunapee II*** (✉ *81 Main St., Sunapee Harbor* ☎ *603/938–6465* 🌐 *www.sunapeecruises.com*) provide a closer look at Lake Sunapee's history and mountain scenery and run from late May through mid-October, daily in summer and on weekends in spring and fall; the cost is $18. Dinner cruises are held on the **MV *Kearsarge*** (☎ *603/938–6465* 🌐 *www.mvkearsarge.com*) and leave from the dock at Sunapee Harbor, June through mid-October, Tuesday–Sunday evenings; the cost is $36 and includes a buffet dinner.

SKI AREA

Mount Sunapee. Although the resort is state-owned, it's managed by Vermont's Okemo Mountain Resort (in Ludlow). The agreement has allowed the influx of capital necessary for operating extensive lifts, snowmaking (97% coverage), and trail grooming. This mountain is 1,510 vertical feet and has 65 trails, mostly intermediate. Experts can take to a dozen slopes, including three nice double-black diamonds. Boarders have a 420-foot-long half-pipe and a terrain park with music. In summer, the Sunapee Express Quad zooms you to the summit. From here, it's just under a mile hike to Lake Solitude. Mountain bikers can use the lift to many trails, and an in-line skate park has beginner and advanced sections (plus equipment rentals). ✉ *Rte. 103, Box 2021* ☎ *603/763–3500; 603/763–4020 snow conditions; 877/687–8627 lodging* 🌐 *www.mtsunapee.com.*

SHOPPING

Overlooking Lake Sunapee's southern tip, **Outspokin' Bicycle and Sport** (✉ *4 Old Route 3, Sunapee Harbor* ☎ *603/763–9500* 🌐 *www.outspokin.com*) has a tremendous selection of biking, hiking, skateboarding, waterskiing, skiing, and snowboarding clothing and equipment. Right on the harbor in Sunapee village, on the marina, **Wild Goose Country Store** (✉ *77 Main St.* ☎ *603/763–5516*) carries quirky gifts, teddy bears, penny candy, pottery, and other engaging odds and ends.

WHERE TO STAY

$$–$$$ ★ **Sunapee Harbor Cottages.** This charming collection of six private cottages is within a stone's throw of Sunapee Harbor. Each unit sleeps five to eight people, making this a good deal for large groups and an extravagant pleasure for couples. All have gas fireplaces, porches, and a well-chosen mix of antiques and newer furnishings. Special winter rates are available for skiers visiting nearby Mt. Sunapee. **Pros:** attractive, spacious units. **Cons:** main house blocks view of the harbor. ✉ *4 Lake Ave., Sunapee Harbor* ☎ *603/763–5052 or 866/763–5052* 🌐 *www.sunapeeharborcottages.com* *6 cottages* *In-room: no a/c, kitchen, DVD, Wi-Fi* *MC, V.*

HANOVER

12 mi northwest of Enfield; 62 mi northwest of Concord.

Eleazer Wheelock founded Hanover's Dartmouth College in 1769 to educate the Abenaki "and other youth." When he arrived, the town consisted of about 20 families. The college and the town grew symbiotically, with Dartmouth becoming the northernmost Ivy League school. Hanover is still synonymous with Dartmouth, but it's also a respected medical and cultural center for the upper Connecticut River valley.

GETTING HERE AND AROUND

Lebanon Municipal Airport, near Dartmouth College, is served by US Airways Express from New York. By car, Interstate 91 North or Interstate 89 are the best ways to get to Lebanon, Hanover, and the surrounding area. Plan on spending a day visiting Hanover and to see all the sights on the Dartmouth campus.

Shops, mostly of the independent variety but with a few upscale chains sprinkled in, line Hanover's main street. The commercial district blends almost imperceptibly with the Dartmouth campus. West Lebanon, south of Hanover on the Vermont border, has many more shops.

ESSENTIALS

Airport **Lebanon Municipal Airport** (✉ *5 Airpark Rd., West Lebanon* ☎ *603/298–8878* 🌐 *www.flyleb.com*).

Taxi **Big Yellow Taxi** (☎ *603/643–8294* 🌐 *www.bigyellowtaxis.com*).

Visitor Information **Hanover Area Chamber of Commerce** (✉ *53 S. Main St., Suite 216, Hanover* ☎ *603/643–3115* 🌐 *www.hanoverchamber.org*).

DID YOU KNOW?

The Baker Memorial library was modeled after Independence Hall in Philadelphia. Today it is the heart of the Dartmouth College campus in Hanover.

EXPLORING

★ **Dartmouth College**. Robert Frost spent part of a brooding freshman semester at this Ivy League school before giving up college altogether. The buildings that cluster around the green include the **Baker Memorial Library,** which houses such literary treasures as 17th-century editions of William Shakespeare's works. The library is also well known for Mexican artist José Clemente Orozco's 3,000-square-foot murals that depict the story of civilization in the Americas. If the towering arcade at the entrance to the **Hopkins Center for the Arts** (☎ *603/646–2422* 🌐 *hop.dartmouth.edu*) appears familiar, it's probably because it resembles the project that architect Wallace K. Harrison completed just after designing it: New York City's Metropolitan Opera House at Lincoln Center. The complex includes a 900-seat theater for film showings and concerts, a 400-seat theater for plays, and a black-box theater for new plays. The Dartmouth Symphony Orchestra performs here, as does the Big Apple Circus. In addition to African, Peruvian, Oceanic, Asian, European, and American art, the **Hood Museum of Art** (✉ *Wheelock St.* ☎ *603/646–2808* 🌐 *www.hoodmuseum.dartmouth.edu* 🎟 *Free* ⏲ *Tues. and Thurs.–Sat. 10–5, Wed. 10–9, Sun. noon–5*) owns the Pablo Picasso painting *Guitar on a Table*, silver by Paul Revere, and a set of Assyrian reliefs from the 9th century BC. The range of contemporary works, including pieces by John Sloan, William Glackens, Mark Rothko, Fernand Léger, and Joan Miró, is particularly notable. Rivaling the collection is the museum's architecture: a series of austere, copper-roofed, redbrick buildings arranged around a courtyard. Free campus tours are available on request. ✉ *N. Main and Wentworth Sts.* ☎ *603/646–2900* 🌐 *www.dartmouth.edu.*

QUICK BITES

Take a respite from museum-hopping with a cup of espresso, a ham-and-cheese scone, or a freshly baked brownie at the Dirt Cowboy (✉ *7 S. Main St.* ☎ *603/643–1323* 🌐 *www.dirtcowboycafe.com*), a café across from the green and beside a used-book store. A local branch of a small Boston chain, The Wrap (✉ *35 S. Main St.* ☎ *603/643–0202*), occupies a slick basement space with comfy sofas and has a small patio to the side. Drop by for healthy burritos, wraps, soups (try the carrot-ginger), smoothies, and energy drinks.

★ **Enfield Shaker Museum**. In 1782, two Shaker brothers from Mount Lebanon, New York, arrived on Lake Mascoma's northeastern side, about 12 mi southeast of Hanover. Eventually, they formed Enfield, the ninth of 18 Shaker communities in the United States, and moved it to the lake's southern shore, where they erected more than 200 buildings. The Enfield Shaker Museum preserves the legacy of the Shakers, who numbered 330 members at the village's peak. By 1923, interest in the society had dwindled, and the last 10 members joined the Canterbury community, south of Laconia. A self-guided walking tour takes you through 13 of the remaining buildings, among them the Great Stone Dwelling (which served until recently as a hotel, the Shaker Inn) and an 1849 stone mill. Demonstrations of Shaker crafts techniques and numerous special events take place year-round. ✉ *447 NH Route 4A, Enfield* ☎ *603/632–4346* 🌐 *www.shakermuseum.org* 🎟 *$7.50* ⏲ *Mon.–Sat. 10–5, Sun. noon–5*

OFF THE BEATEN PATH

Upper Valley. From Hanover, you can make a 60-mi drive up Route 10 all the way to Littleton for a highly scenic tour of the upper Connecticut River valley. You'll have views of the river and Vermont's Green Mountains from many points. The road passes through groves of evergreens, over leafy ridges, and through delightful hamlets. Grab gourmet picnic provisions at the general store on Lyme's village common—probably the most pristine of any in the state—and stop at the bluff-top village green in historical Haverhill (28 mi north of Hanover) for a picnic amid the panorama of classic Georgian- and Federal-style mansions and faraway farmsteads. You can follow this scenic route all the way to the White Mountains region or loop back south from Haverhill—along Route 25 to Route 118 to U.S. 4 west—to Enfield, a drive of about 45 mi (75 minutes).

WHERE TO EAT

$$ AMERICAN

✕ **Canoe Club**. Bedecked with canoes, paddles, and classic Dartmouth paraphernalia, this festive spot presents live jazz and folk music most nights. The mood may be casual, but the kitchen presents rather imaginative food, including a memorable starter of a roasted beet medley with spiced chocolate sauce and orange glaze. Among the main courses, the seafood cioppino, with shrimp, scallops, onion, and sweet pepper, is a favorite. There's also a lighter, late-night menu. ✉ *27 S. Main St.* ☎ *603/643–9660* 🌐 *www.canoeclub.us* 💳 *AE, D, DC, MC, V.*

¢ AMERICAN ★

✕ **Lou's**. This is one of two places in town where students and locals really mix. After all, it's hard to resist. A Hanover tradition since 1948, this diner-cum-café-cum-bakery serves possibly the best breakfast in the valley—a plate of *migas* (eggs, cheddar, salsa, and guacamole mixed with tortilla chips) can fill you up for the better part of the day; blueberry-cranberry buttermilk pancakes also satisfy. Or grab a seat at the old-fashioned soda fountain and order an ice-cream sundae. ✉ *30 S. Main St.* ☎ *603/643–3321* 🌐 💳 *AE, MC, V* ⊗ *No dinner.*

ITALIAN $

✕ **Lui Lui**. The creatively topped thin-crust pizzas and huge pasta portions are only part of the draw at this chatter-filled eatery; the other is its dramatic setting inside a former power station on the Mascoma River. Pizza picks include the Tuscan (mozzarella topped with tomato and roasted garlic) and the grilled chicken with barbecue sauce. Pasta fans should dive into a bowl of linguine with homemade clam sauce. The owners also run Molly's Restaurant and Jesse's Tavern, which are nearby. *8 Glen Rd., West Lebanon* ☎ *603/298–7070* 🌐 *www.luilui.com* 💳 *AE, MC, V.*

$ ECLECTIC

✕ **Murphy's**. Students, visiting alums, and locals regularly descend upon this wildly popular pub, which has walls lined with shelves of old books. The varied menu features burgers and salads as well as meat loaf, crusted lamb sirloin, and eggplant filled with tofu. Check out the extensive beer list. ✉ *11 S. Main St.* ☎ *603/643–4075* 🌐 *www.murphysonthegreen.com* 💳 *AE, D, DC, MC, V.*

WHERE TO STAY

$$$–$$$$ ★

🏨 **Hanover Inn**. If you're in town for a Dartmouth event, you'll want to stay on the town's—and the college's—main square. Owned by Dartmouth, this sprawling, Georgian-style brick structure rises four white-trimmed stories. The original building was converted to a tavern

The Cornish–Windsor Bridge is the longest covered bridge in the United States, at 460 feet.

in 1780, and this expertly run inn, now greatly enlarged, has been operating ever since. Rooms have Colonial reproductions, Audubon prints, large sitting areas, and marble-accented bathrooms. The swank Zins Wine Bistro ($–$$) prepares lighter but innovative fare. **Pros:** center of campus and town; well managed. **Cons:** breakfast not included; overpriced. ✉ *The Green, 2 S. Main St., Box 151* ☎ *603/643–4300 or 800/443–7024* 🌐 *www.hanoverinn.com* *92 rooms, 23 suites* *In-room: Wi-Fi. In-hotel: restaurant, room service, bar, Internet terminal, Wi-Fi hotspot* *AE, D, DC, MC, V.*

$$$–$$$$ **Trumbull House.** The sunny guest rooms of this white Colonial-style house—on 16 acres on Hanover's outskirts—have king- or queen-size beds, writing desks, feather pillows, and other comfortable touches, as well as Wi-Fi. A romantic guesthouse has a private deck, whirlpool tub, refrigerator, and wet bar. Breakfast, with a choice of entrées, is served in the formal dining room or in front of the living room fireplace. Rates include the use of a nearby health club. **Pros:** quiet setting; lovely home; big breakfast. **Cons:** 5 mi east of town. ✉ *40 Etna Rd.* ☎ *603/643–2370 or 800/651–5141* 🌐 *www.trumbullhouse.com* *4 rooms, 1 suite, 1 cottage* *In-room: Wi-Fi. In-hotel: restaurant* *AE, D, DC, MC, V* *BP.*

CORNISH

22 mi south of Hanover.

Today Cornish is best known for its four covered bridges and for being the home of reclusive late author J. D. Salinger, but at the turn of the 20th century the village was known primarily as the home of the country's then most popular novelist, Winston Churchill (no relation to the British prime minister). His novel *Richard Carvell* sold more than a million copies. Churchill was such a celebrity that he hosted Teddy Roosevelt during the president's 1902 visit. At that time Cornish was an enclave of artistic talent. Painter Maxfield Parrish lived and worked here, and sculptor Augustus Saint-Gaudens set up his studio and created the heroic bronzes for which he is known.

GETTING HERE AND AROUND

About 5 mi west of town on Route 44, the Cornish-Windsor Bridge crosses the Connecticut River between New Hampshire and Vermont. The Blacksmith Shop covered bridge is 2 mi east of Route 12A on Town House Road, and the Dingleton Hill covered bridge is 1 mi east of Route 12A on Root Hill Road. Cornish itself is small enough to see in one morning.

EXPLORING

Cornish-Windsor Bridge. This 460-foot bridge, 1½ mi south of the Saint-Gaudens National Historic Site, connects New Hampshire to Vermont across the Connecticut River. It dates from 1866 and is the longest covered wooden bridge in the United States. The notice on the bridge reads: WALK YOUR HORSES OR PAY TWO DOLLAR FINE.

Fodor's Choice ★ **Saint-Gaudens National Historic Site.** Just south of Plainfield, where River Road rejoins Route 12A, a small lane leads to this historic site, where you can tour sculptor Augustus Saint-Gaudens's house, studio, gallery, and 150 acres of grounds and gardens. Scattered throughout are full-size casts of his works. The property has two hiking trails, the longer of which is the Blow-Me-Down Trail. Concerts are held every Sunday afternoon in July and August. The museum is about 1½ mi north of the Cornish-Windsor Bridge on Route 12A. ✉ *Off Rte. 12A* ☎ *603/675-2175* 🌐 *www.nps.gov/saga* 🎫 *$5, good for 7-day reentry* ⏲ *Buildings June–Oct., daily 9–4:30; grounds daily dawn–dusk.*

THE MONADNOCKS AND MERRIMACK VALLEY

Southwestern and south-central New Hampshire mix village charm with city hustle and bustle across two distinct regions. The Merrimack River valley has the state's largest and fastest-growing cities: Nashua, Manchester, and Concord. To the west, in the state's sleepy southwestern corner, is the Monadnock region, one of New Hampshire's least developed and most naturally stunning parts. Here you'll find plenty of hiking trails as well as peaceful hilltop hamlets that appear barely changed in the past two centuries. Mt. Monadnock, southern New Hampshire's largest peak, stands guard over the Monadnock region, which has more than 200 lakes and ponds. Rainbow trout, smallmouth and largemouth bass, and some northern pike swim in Chesterfield's Spofford Lake. Goose Pond, just north of Keene, holds smallmouth bass and white perch.

The towns are listed in counterclockwise order, beginning with Nashua and heading north to Manchester and Concord; then west to Charleston; south to Walpole; southwest to Keene and Jaffrey; and finally northeast to Peterborough.

NASHUA

98 mi south of Lincoln/North Woodstock; 48 mi northwest of Boston; 36 mi south of Concord; 50 mi southeast of Keene.

Once a prosperous manufacturing town that drew thousands of immigrant workers in the late 1800s and early 1900s, Nashua declined following World War II, as many factories shut down or moved to where labor was cheaper. Since the 1970s, however, the metro area has jumped in population, developing into a charming, old-fashioned community. Its low-key downtown has classic redbrick buildings along the Nashua River, a tributary of the Merrimack River. Though not visited by tourists as much as other communities in the region, Nashua (population 90,000) has some good restaurants and an engaging museum.

GETTING HERE AND AROUND

A good place to start exploring Nashua is at Main and High streets, where a number of fine restaurants and shops are located. Downtown Nashua has free Wi-Fi.

ESSENTIALS

Taxi **SK Taxi** (☎ *603/882–5155*). **D & E Taxi** (☎ *603/889–3999*).

WHERE TO EAT

$$ BISTRO Fodor's Choice ★ ✕ **Michael Timothy's Urban Bistro.** Part hip bistro, part jazzy wine bar Michael Timothy's is so popular that even foodies from Massachusetts drive here. The regularly changing menu might include stuffed pheasant with foie gras risotto and cranberry-clove jus or wood-grilled venison loin with port reduction, herb spaetzle, creamed morel mushrooms, and stewed lentils. Wood-fired pizzas are also a specialty—try the one topped with sirloin tips, caramelized onions, mushrooms, salami, sautéed spinach, and three cheeses. Sunday brunch is a big hit here. ✉ *212 Main St.* ☎ *603/595–9334* 🌐 *www.michaeltimothys.com* 💳 *AE, D, MC, V* ⏲ *Open for dinner at 3 Tues.–Sat.*

$$ ITALIAN ✕ **Villa Banca.** On the ground floor of a dramatic, turreted office building, this spot with high ceilings and tall windows specializes in traditional and contemporary Italian cooking. Start with Gorgonzola artichokes and move on to pasta Alfredo. The butternut squash ravioli is a sweet delight, and the macadamia nut–encrusted tilapia will satisfy the fish lover at your table. Note the exotic-martini menu, a big draw at happy hour. ✉ *194 Main St.* ☎ *603/598–0500* 🌐 *www.villabanca.com* 💳 *AE, D, DC, MC, V* ⏲ *No lunch Sun.*

MANCHESTER

18 mi north of Nashua, 53 mi north of Boston.

Manchester, with 108,000-plus residents, is New Hampshire's largest city. The town grew up around the Amoskeag Falls on the Merrimack River, which fueled small textile mills through the 1700s. By 1828, Boston investors had bought the rights to the Merrimack's water power and built the Amoskeag Mills, which became a testament to New England's manufacturing capabilities. In 1906 the mills employed 17,000 people and weekly churned out more than 4 million yards of cloth. This vast enterprise served as Manchester's entire economic base; when it closed in 1936, the town was devastated.

Today Manchester is mainly a banking and business center. The old mill buildings have been converted into warehouses, classrooms, restaurants, museums, and office space. The city has the state's major airport, as well as the Verizon Wireless Arena, which hosts minor-league hockey matches, concerts, and conventions.

GETTING HERE AND AROUND

Manchester Airport, the state's largest airport, has rapidly become a cost-effective, hassle-free alternative to Boston's Logan Airport, with nonstop service to more than 20 cities. Manchester can be hard to get around, but it offers a number of taxi services.

ESSENTIALS

Airport **Manchester Airport** (✉ *1 Airport Rd., Manchester* ☎ *603/624–6539* 🌐 *www.flymanchester.com*).

Taxi **Evergreen Limousine Airport Service** (☎ *603/624–0801* 🌐 *evergreenmata.com*). **Manchester Taxi** (☎ *603/623–2222*).

Visitor Information **Manchester Area Convention & Visitors Bureau** (✉ *889 Elm St., 3rd fl., Manchester* ☎ *603/666–6600* 🌐 *www.manchestercvb.com*).

EXPLORING

Fodor's Choice ★ **Amoskeag Mills.** There are miles of hallways in the brick buildings that comprise this former textile mill. To get a sense of what they are and what they meant to Manchester, there are two key museums. The **SEE Science Center** (☎ *603/669–0400* 🌐 *www.see-sciencecenter.org* 🎟 *$6* ⏲ *Weekdays 10–4, weekends 10–5*) is a hands-on science lab and children's museum with more than 70 exhibits. If you're in Manchester, child or adult, don't miss it. The world's largest permanent LEGO installation of regular-sized LEGOs is here, depicting the city's Amoskeag Millyard and the city of Manchester as it was in 1915. This mind-blowing exhibit is made up of 3 million LEGOs across 2,000 square feet. More important, the exhibit also conveys the massive size and importance of the mills, which ran a mile on each side of the Merrimack. Upstairs in the same building the **Millyard Museum** (☎ *603/622–7531* 🌐 *www.manchesterhistoric.org* 🎟 *$6* ⏲ *Wed.–Sat. 10–4*) has state-of-the-art exhibits that depict the region's history from when Native Americans lived alongside and fished the Merrimack River to the heyday of Amoskeag Mills. The interactive Discovery Gallery is geared toward

kids; there's also a lecture/concert hall and a large museum shop. ✉ *Mill No. 3, 200 Bedford St. (entrance at 255 Commercial St.).*

Fodor's Choice ★ **Currier Museum of Art.** A modern Sol LeWitt mural faces the original 1929 Italianate entrance to a permanent collection of European and American paintings, sculpture, and decorative arts from the 13th to the 20th century, including works by Edouard Monet, Picasso, Edward Hopper, Andrew Wyeth, and Georgia O'Keeffe. A major 2008 expansion more than doubled the gallery space and created a new shop, visitor entrance, café, and a winter garden. Also run by the Currier (tours depart from the museum) is the nearby Frank Lloyd Wright–designed Zimmerman House, built in 1950. Wright called this sparse, utterly functional living space "Usonian," an invented term used to describe 50 such middle-income homes he built with his vision of distinctly American architecture. It's New England's only Frank Lloyd Wright–designed residence open to the public. ✉ *150 Ash St.* ☎ *603/669–6144; 603/626–4158 Zimmerman House tours* 🌐 *www.currier.org* 🎟 *$10, free Sat. 10–noon; $18 Zimmerman House (reservations essential)* ⏲ *Sun., Mon., Wed., and Fri. 11–5; first Thurs. of every month 11–8; Sat. 10–5; call for Zimmerman House tour hrs.*

At the Currier Museum of Art, you can enjoy European and American classics, or visit a nearby Frank Lloyd Wright house.

NIGHTLIFE AND THE ARTS

THE ARTS The **Palace Theatre** (✉ *80 Hanover St.* ☎ *603/668–5588 box office* 🌐 *www.palacetheatre.org*) presents musicals and plays throughout the year. It also hosts the state's philharmonic and symphony orchestras and the Opera League of New Hampshire.

NIGHTLIFE **Club 313** (✉ *93 S. Maple St.* ☎ *603/628–6813* 🌐 *www.club313.net*) is New Hampshire's most popular disco for gays and lesbians. It's open Wednesday–Sunday.Revelers come from all over to drink at the **Yard** (✉ *1211 S. Mammoth Rd.* ☎ *603/623–3545* 🌐 *www.theyardrestaurant.com*), which is also a steak and seafood restaurant.

WHERE TO EAT

$–$$ AMERICAN ★ ✕ **Cotton.** Inside one of the old Amoskeag Mills buildings mod lighting and furnishings and a patio set in an arbor give this restaurant a swanky atmosphere. A blunt neon sign that reads FOOD belies its sophisticated menu. The kitchen specializes in putting a new spin on comfort food. Start with pan-seared crab cakes or the lemongrass chicken salad. The menu changes four times a year but might include 16-oz all-natural Delmonico steak or wood-grilled scallops as well as superb sweet-potato hash. For the past seven years Cotton's has been voted best martinis in New Hampshire by New Hampshire Magazine. ✉ *75 Arms St.* ☎ *603/622–5488* 🌐 *www.cottonfood.com* ▭ *AE, D, MC, V* ⊗ *No lunch weekends.*

¢–$ AMERICAN ★ ✕ **Jewell and the Beanstalk.** If you feel as if you just walked into a general store, that's because for many years that's just what this space was. It's been in the family for three generations, and meals made with items grown by urban farmers are standard fare as are homemade pies, cookies, and cakes. The cranberry chicken salad sandwich is delicious as is the roasted pork loin melt with sautéed apples and spinach. New Hampshire–made products are on sale at the café. ✉ *793 Somerville St.* ☎ *603/624–3709* 🌐 ▭ *AE, D, MC, V* ⊙ *No dinner except music night on Wed.*

¢ AMERICAN Fodor's Choice ★ ✕ **Red Arrow Diner.** This tiny diner is ground zero for presidential hopefuls in New Hampshire come primary season. The rest of the time, a mix of hipsters and oldsters, including comedian and Manchester native Adam Sandler, favor this neon-streaked, 24-hour greasy spoon, which has been going strong since 1922. Filling fare—platters of kielbasa, French toast, liver and onions, chicken Parmesan with spaghetti, and the diner's famous panfries—keeps patrons happy. Homemade sodas and éclairs round out the menu. Talk to "Santa," a long-time patron who sits at the end of the counter sipping coffee, about the history of the diner. ✉ *61 Lowell St.* ☎ *603/626–1118* 🌐 *redarrowdiner.com* ▭ *AE, D, MC, V.*

WHERE TO STAY

$$–$$$ **Ash Street Inn.** Because it's in an attractive residential neighborhood of striking Victorian homes, staying in this five-room B&B will give you the best face of Manchester. Every room in the historic sage-green 1885 house, run by Darlene and Eric Johnston, is painted a different color. There are good linens, and there's decanted brandy in the sitting room, which has the house's original stained glass. In the summer, a wraparound porch is a nice place to sit and enjoy a cooked-to-order breakfast, served on a flexible schedule. **Pros:** spotless newly decorated rooms; within walking distance of the Currier Museum. **Cons:** not a full-service hotel. ✉ *118 Ash St.* ☎ *603/668–9908* 🌐 *www.ashstreetinn.com* *5 rooms* *In-room: Wi-Fi. In-hotel: Wi-Fi hotspot, no kids under 12* ▭ *AE, D, MC, V* *BP.*

$$$–$$$$ ★ **Bedford Village Inn.** If you trade direct downtown access for a lovely manor outside of town, you'll be rewarded by the comforts of this beautiful and well-run property. The hayloft and milking rooms of this 1810 Federal farmstead, just a few miles southwest of Manchester, contain lavish suites with king-size four-poster beds, plus such modern perks as two phones and high-speed Wi-Fi. The restaurant ($$$$)—a warren of elegant dining rooms with fireplaces and wide pine floors—presents contemporary fare that might include a starter of organic Burgundy escargot followed by a roasted Gloucester monkfish. A five-course chef's tasting menu is available for $85. **Pros:** relaxing property just outside Manchester; exceptional grounds; great restaurant. **Cons:** outside of town. ✉ *2 Olde Bedford Way, Bedford* ☎ *603/472–2001 or 800/852–1166* 🌐 *www.bedfordvillageinn.com* *14 suites, 2 apartments* *In-room: DVD, Wi-Fi. In-hotel: restaurant, room service, bar, laundry service, Internet terminal, Wi-Fi hotspot* ▭ *AE, D, DC, MC, V.*

$–$$ **Radisson Manchester.** Of Manchester's many chain properties, the 12-story Radisson has the most central location—a short walk from Amoskeag Mills and great dining along Elm Street. Rooms are simple and clean, perfect for business travelers. Next door is the Center of New Hampshire conference center. Because of its busy location, this is the only hotel in the state where you have to pay for parking. **Pros:** central downtown location. **Cons:** fee for parking; unexciting chain hotel. ✉ *700 Elm St.* ☎ *603/625–1000 or 800/395–7046* 🌐 *www.radisson.*

com/manchesternh 244 *rooms, 6 suites* *In-room: Wi-Fi. In-hotel: 2 restaurants, room service, bar, pool, gym, laundry service, Internet terminal, Wi-Fi hotspot, parking (paid), some pets allowed* *AE, D, DC, MC, V.*

CONCORD

20 mi northwest of Manchester, 67 mi northwest of Boston, 46 mi northwest of Portsmouth.

New Hampshire's capital (population 42,000) is a quiet town that tends to the state's business but little else—the sidewalks roll up promptly at 6. Stop in town to get a glimpse of New Hampshire's State House, which is crowned by a gleaming gold, eagle-topped dome.

GETTING HERE AND AROUND

Taxis can help get you around town, though Main Street is easy to walk about. Event information can be found at *www.concord.com.*

ESSENTIALS

Taxi **Concord Cab** (*603/225–4222*).

Visitor Information **Concord Chamber of Commerce** (*40 Commercial St., Concord* *603/224–2508* *www.concordnhchamber.com*).

EXPLORING

The **Concord on Foot** walking trail winds through the historic district. Maps for the walk can be picked up at the Greater Concord **Chamber of Commerce** (*40 Commercial St.* *603/224–2508* *www.concordnhchamber.com*) or stores along the trail.

EXPLORING

Christa McAuliffe Planetarium. In a 40-foot dome theater, shows on the solar system, constellations, and space exploration abound. The planetarium was named for the Concord teacher who was killed in the Space Shuttle *Challenger* explosion in 1986. Children love seeing the tornado tubes, magnetic marbles, and other hands-on exhibits. Outside, explore the scale-model planet walk and the human sundial. *New Hampshire Technical Institute campus, 2 Institute Dr.* *603/271–7831* *www.starhop.com* *$9; $3 planetarium shows* *Mon.–Thurs. 10–5, Fri. 10–9, weeekends 10–5; call for show times and reservations.*

New Hampshire Historical Society. Steps from the state capitol, the society's museum is a great place to learn about the Concord coach, the stagecoach that was a popular mode of transportation before railroads. Rotating exhibitions may include New Hampshire quilts and their stories and historical protraits of residents. *6 Eagle Sq.* *603/228-6688* *www.nhhistory.org* *$5.50* *Tue.–Sat. 9:30–5, Sun. noon–5.*

Pierce Manse. Franklin Pierce lived in this Greek-Revival home before he moved to Washington to become the 14th U.S. president. He's buried nearby. *14 Horseshoe Pond La.* *603/225–4617* *www.politicallibrary.org* *$7* *Hours vary seasonally; check Web site.*

Fodor's Choice ★ **State House.** A self-guided tour of the neoclassical, gilt-domed statehouse, built in 1819, is a real treat. You get total access to the building and can even take a photo with the governor. This is the oldest capitol building in the nation in which the legislature uses its original chambers. In January and June you can watch the assemblies in action once a week: the 24 senators of the New Hampshire Senate (the fourth-smallest American lawmaking body) meet once a week. In a wild inversion, the state's representatives number 400—one representative per 3,000 residents, a ratio that is a world record. At the visitor center you'll see paraphernalia from decades of presidential primaries. ✉ *107 N. Main St.* ☎ *603/271–2154* 🌐 *www.ci.concord.nh.us/tourdest/statehs* 🎟 *Free* ⏲ *Weekdays 8–4:30.*

NIGHTLIFE AND THE ARTS

The **Capitol Center for the Arts** (✉ *44 S. Main St.* ☎ *603/225–1111* 🌐 *www.ccanh.com*) has been restored to reflect its Roaring '20s origins. It hosts touring Broadway shows, dance companies, and musical acts. The lounge at **Hermanos Cocina Mexicana** (✉ *11 Hills Ave.* ☎ *603/224–5669* 🌐 *www.hermanosmexican.com*) stages live jazz Sunday through Thursday nights.

SHOPPING

Capitol Craftsman Jewelers (✉ *16 N. Main St.* ☎ *603/224–6166* 🌐 *www.capitolcraftsman.com*) sells fine jewelry and handicrafts. The **League of New Hampshire Craftsmen** (✉ *36 N. Main St.* ☎ *603/228–8171* 🌐 *www.nhcrafts.org*) exhibits crafts in many media. **Mark Knipe Goldsmiths** (✉ *2 Capitol Plaza, Main St.* ☎ *603/224–2920* 🌐 *www.knipegold.com*) sets antique stones in rings, earrings, and pendants.

WHERE TO EAT AND STAY

¢–$ AMERICAN ★ ✕ **Arnie's Place.** If you need a reason to make the 1.5-mi detour from Interstate 93, then more than 50 kinds of homemade ice cream should do the trick. Try the toasted-coconut, raspberry, or vanilla flavors. The chocolate shakes are a real treat for chocoholics. The lemon freeze will give you an ice cream headache in no time, but it's worth it. A small dining room is available for dishes such as a barbecue platter (smoked on the premises), hamburgers, and hot dogs, but the five walk-up windows and picnic benches are the way to go. ✉ *164 Loudon Rd., Concord Heights* ☎ *603/228–3225* 💳 *MC, V* ⏲ *Closed Nov.–Jan.*

$ ECLECTIC ✕ **Barley House.** A lively, old-fashioned tavern practically across from the capitol building and usually buzzing with a mix of politicos, business folks, and tourists, the Barley House serves dependable chow: chorizo-sausage pizzas, burgers smothered with peppercorn-whiskey sauce and blue cheese, chicken potpies, Cuban sandwiches, beer-braised bratwurst, jambalaya, and Mediterranean chicken salad—it's an impressive melting pot of a menu. The bar turns out dozens of interesting beers, on tap and by the bottle, and there's also a decent wine list. It's open until 1 AM. ✉ *132 N. Main St.* ☎ *603/228–6363* 🌐 *www.thebarleyhouse.com* 💳 *AE, D, DC, MC, V* ⏲ *Closed Sun.*

¢–$ THAI ✕ **Siam Orchid.** This dark, attractive Thai restaurant with a colorful rickshaw gracing its dining room serves spicy and reasonably authentic Thai food. It draws a crowd from the capitol each day for lunch. Try the fiery broiled swordfish with shrimp curry sauce or the pine-nut chicken in an aromatic ginger sauce. There's a second location in Manchester. ✉ *158 N. Main St.* ☎ *603/228–3633* 🌐 *www.siamorchid.com* 💳 *AE, D, DC, MC, V* ⏲ *No lunch weekends.*

$$ **The Centennial**. This is the most contemporary hotel in New Hampshire, and it's home to Granite, the state's most contemporary restaurant ($$) and bar, making it a draw for the state's politicians and those doing business here. The modernity is unexpected, as this imposing brick-and-stone building was constructed in 1892 for widows of Civil War veterans, but the interior was renovated head-to-toe. Boutique furniture and contemporary art immediately set the tone in the lobby. Rooms have luxury linens, sleek carpet and furniture, and flat-screen TVs. Bathrooms have stone floors, granite countertops, and standalone showers. It's the state's first foray into a boutique-y, well-designed hotel, and it's a huge success. **Pros:** super contemporary and sleek hotel; very comfortable and clean rooms; great bar and restaurant. **Cons:** busy. ✉ *96 Pleasant St.* ☎ *603/227–9000 or 800/360–4839* 🌐 *www.thecentennialhotel.com* *27 rooms, 5 suites* *In-room: refrigerator, DVD, Wi-Fi. In-hotel: restaurant, room service, bar, gym, Internet terminal, Wi-Fi hotspot* 💳 *AE, D, DC, MC, V.*

CHARLESTOWN

Charlestown has the state's largest historic district. About 60 homes, handsome examples of Federal, Greek-Revival, and Gothic-Revival architecture, are clustered about the town center; 10 of them were built before 1800. Several merchants on the main street distribute brochures that describe an interesting walking tour of the district.

GETTING HERE AND AROUND

You can reach Charlestown from Interstate 91, but it's best to follow Route 12 North from Keene for a gorgeous scenic route. Walking about downtown Charlestown should take only 15 minutes of your day, but it's worth admiring the buildings in the town center. The Fort at No. 4 is less than 2 mi from downtown, north on Route 11.

EXPLORING

Fort at No. 4. In 1747, this fort was an outpost on the periphery of Colonial civilization. That year fewer than 50 militiamen at the fort withstood an attack by 400 French soldiers, ensuring that northern New England remained under British rule. Today, costumed interpreters at this living-history museum cook dinner over an open hearth and demonstrate weaving, gardening, and candle making. Each year the museum holds reenactments of militia musters and battles of the French and Indian War. ✉ *267 Springfield Rd., ½ mi north of Charlestown* ☎ *603/826–5700 or 888/367–8284* 🌐 *www.fortat4.org* *$8* *Early June–Oct., Wed.–Sun. 10–4:30.*

SPORTS AND THE OUTDOORS

On a bright, breezy day you might want to detour to the **Morningside Flight Park** (✉ *357 Morningside La., off Rte. 12/11, 5 mi north of Charlestown* ☎ *603/542–4416* 🌐 *www.flymorningside.com*), considered to be among the best flying areas in the country. Watch the bright colors of gliders as they take off from the 450-foot peak, or take hang-gliding lessons yourself.

WALPOLE

13 mi south of Charlestown.

Walpole possesses one of the state's most perfect town greens. Bordered by Elm and Washington streets, it's surrounded by homes built about 1790, when the townsfolk constructed a canal around the Great Falls of the Connecticut River and brought commerce and wealth to the area. The town now has 3,200 inhabitants, more than a dozen of whom are millionaires. Walpole is home to Florentine Films, Ken Burns's production company.

3

GETTING HERE AND AROUND

A short jaunt off of Route 12, north of Keene. The small downtown is especially photogenic.

OFF THE BEATEN PATH

Sugarhouses. Maple-sugar season occurs about the first week in March when days become warmer but nights are still frigid. A drive along maple-lined back roads reveals thousands of taps and buckets catching the labored flow of unrefined sap. Plumes of smoke rise from nearby sugarhouses, where "sugaring off," the process of boiling down this precious liquid, takes place. Many sugarhouses are open to the public; after a tour and demonstration, you can sample the syrup. **Bascom Maple Farm** (✉ *56 Sugarhouse Rd., Alstead* ☎ *603/835–6361* 🌐 *www.bascommaple.com*) has been family-run since 1853 and produces more maple than anyone in New England. Visit the 2,200-acre farm and get maple pecan pie and maple milk shakes. **Stuart & John's Sugar House & Pancake Restaurant** (✉ *19 Rte. 63, Westmoreland* ☎ *603/399–4486* 🌐 *www.stuartandjohnssugarhouse.com*) conducts a tour and sells syrup and maple gifts in a roadside barn. It also serves a memorable pancake breakfast weekends mid-February–April and mid-September–November.

SHOPPING

★ At **Boggy Meadow Farm** (✉ *13 Boggy Meadow La.* ☎ *603/756–3300 or 877/541–3953* 🌐 *www.boggymeadowfarm.com*) you can watch the cheese process unfold, from the 200 cows being milked to the finer process of cheese-making. The farmstead's raw-milk cheeses can be sampled and purchased in the store. It's worth a trip just to see the beautiful 400-acre farm.

WHERE TO EAT

$–$$ FRENCH Fodor's Choice ★

✕ **The Restaurant at L. A. Burdick Chocolate.** Famous candy maker Larry Burdick, who sells his artful hand-filled and hand-cut chocolates to top restaurants around the Northeast, is a Walpole resident. This restaurant has the easygoing sophistication of a Parisian café and may tempt you to linger over an incredibly rich hot chocolate. The Mediterranean-inspired menu utilizes fresh, often local ingredients and changes daily. Of course, dessert is a big treat here, featuring Burdick's tempting chocolates and pastries. For dinner, you might start with a selection of artisanal cheeses or reduction trio of pâtés, followed by a house beef stew or homemade sausages. ✉ *47 Main St.* ☎ *603/756–2882* 🌐 *www.burdickchocolate.com* 💳 *AE, D, MC, V* ⏲ *No dinner Sun. and Mon.*

KEENE

17 mi southeast of Walpole; 20 mi northeast of Brattleboro, Vermont; 56 mi southwest of Manchester.

Keene is the largest city in the state's southwest corner. Its rapidly gentrifying main street, with several engaging boutiques and cafés, is America's widest (132 feet). Each year, on the Saturday before Halloween, locals use the street to hold a Pumpkin Festival, where the small town competes with big cities such as Boston for the most jack o' lanterns in one place at one time.

ESSENTIALS

Visitor Information **Keene Chamber of Commerce** (✉ *48 Central Sq.* ☎ *603/352–1303* 🌐 *www.keenechamber.com*). **Monadnock Travel Council** (📫 *Box 358, Keene03431* ☎ *800/432–7864* 🌐 *www.monadnocktravel.com*).

EXPLORING

Keene State College. This hub of the local arts community is on the tree-lined main street and has a worthwhile art gallery and an art-house movie theater. **The Thorne-Sagendorph Art Gallery** (☎ *603/358–2720* 🌐 *www.keene.edu/tsag*) contains a permanent collection including works by George Rickey, Robert Mapplethorpe, and Vargian Bogosian and presents traveling exhibits. The **Putnam Theater** (☎ *603/358–2160* 🌐 *www.keene.edu/putnam*) shows foreign and art films. ✉ *229 Maint St.*

OFF THE BEATEN PATH

Chesterfield's Route 63. If you're in the mood for a country drive or bike ride, head west from Keene along Route 9 to Route 63 (about 11 mi) and turn left toward the hilltop town of Chesterfield. This is an especially rewarding journey at sunset, as from many points along the road you can see west out over the Connecticut River valley and into Vermont. The village center consists of little more than a handful of dignified granite buildings and a small general store. You can loop back to Keene via Route 119 east in Hinsdale and then Route 10 north—the entire journey is about 40 mi.

NIGHTLIFE AND THE ARTS

Elm City Brewing Co. (✉ *222 West St.* ☎ *603/355–3335* 🌐 *www.elmcitybrewing.com*), at the Colony Mill, serves light food and draws a mix of college students and young professionals. At Keene State College, the **Redfern Arts Center at Brickyard Pond** (✉ *229 Main St.* ☎ *603/358–2168* 🌐 *www.keene.edu/racbp*) has year-round music, theater, and dance performances in two theaters and a recital hall.

SHOPPING

★ **Colony Mill Marketplace** (✉ *222 West St.* ☎ *603/357–1240* 🌐 *www.colonymill.com*), an old mill building, holds 30-plus stores and boutiques such as the Toadstool Bookshop, which carries many children's and regional travel and history books, and Pocketful of Rye, a gift store. Also popular is Antiques at Colony Mill, which sells the wares of more than 120 dealers and has a food court.

DID YOU KNOW?

Keene's annual Pumpkin Festival includes over 25,000 carved jack-o-lanterns. At night, the pumpkins illuminate the streets with votive candles and the autumnal celebrations culminate in a fireworks display.

WHERE TO EAT AND STAY

$$–$$$ MEDITERRANEAN Fodor's Choice ★ ✕ **Luca's.** A deceptively simple storefront bistro overlooking Keene's graceful town square, Luca's dazzles with epicurean creations influenced by Italy, France, Greece, Spain, and North Africa. Enjoy sautéed shrimp with cilantro pesto and plum tomatoes, three-cheese ravioli with artichoke hearts, or grilled salmon marinated in cumin and coriander. For a real treat, ask Luca to surprise you with a sampler of items from his extensive menu, and don't forget to ask for the locally made gelato or sorbet for dessert. ✉ *10 Central Sq.* ☎ *603/358–3335* 🌐 *www.lucascafe.com* ▭ *AE, MC, V.*

$$–$$$ ★ **Chesterfield Inn.** Surrounded by gardens, the Chesterfield Inn sits above Route 9, the main road between Keene and Brattleboro, Vermont. Fine antiques and Colonial-style fabrics adorn the spacious guest quarters; 10 have fireplaces, and several have private decks or terraces that face the stunning perennial gardens and verdant Vermont hills. In the restaurant ($$) rosemary- and walnut-crusted rack of lamb, crab and papaya salad, and grilled spiced shrimp are among the highlights. **Pros:** attractive gardens; close to the Connecticut River. **Cons:** breakfast ends early. ✉ *20 Cross Rd., West Chesterfield* 📫 *Box 155, Chesterfield 03443* ☎ *603/256–3211 or 800/365–5515* 🌐 *www.chesterfieldinn.com* *13 rooms, 2 suites* *In-room: refrigerator, Wi-Fi. In-hotel: restaurant, Wi-Fi hotspot, some pets allowed* ▭ *AE, D, MC, V* 🍽 *BP.*

$ **E.F. Lane Hotel.** You can get a rare touch of urbanity in the sleepy Monadnocks in this upscale redbrick hotel in the middle of Main Street. The hotel was retrofitted in 2000 from the former Goodnow department store, a Keene landmark for more than 100 years. That accounts for some interesting room features, like a wall of exposed brick and 12-foot ceilings. Spacious rooms are furnished individually with reproduction Victorian antiques. "Chairman" suites have stairs that lead to an upper level and come with two bathrooms. There's live entertainment in the Chase Tavern Tuesday–Saturday. Ask for your free movie tickets and popcorn vouchers for the Colonial Theater across the street. **Pros:** spacious and comfortable rooms; center of town; free movie tickets. **Cons:** no gym. ✉ *30 Main St.* ☎ *603/357–7070 or 888/300–5056* 🌐 *www.eflane.com* *33 rooms, 7 suites* *In-room: refrigerator (some), Wi-Fi. In-hotel: restaurant, bar, Internet terminal, Wi-Fi hotspot, some pets allowed* ▭ *AE, D, MC, V* 🍽 *CP.*

$ **Inn at East Hill Farm.** If you have kids, and they like animals, meet bliss: a family resort with daylong kids' programs on a 170-acre 1830 farm overlooking Mt. Monadnock. Kids can start at 9 AM with milking the cows. Other activities include collecting eggs, horseback and pony riding, arts and crafts, storytelling, hiking, sledding, hay rides in summer, and horse-drawn sleigh rides in winter. You can feed sheep, donkeys, cows, rabbits, horses, chickens, goats, and ducks and play with Chloe the farm dog. Twice weekly in summer, trips are scheduled to a nearby lake for boating, waterskiing, and fishing. Rates include most activities and three meals in a camplike dining hall. Rooms are comfortable, not fancy, and some have fireplaces. The inn is 10 mi southeast of Keene off Route 124. **Pros:** rare agritourism and family resort; activities galore; beautiful setting. **Cons:** remote location; noisy mess-hall dining. ✉ *460*

Monadnock St., Troy ☎ 603/242–6495 or 800/242–6495 🌐 www.east-hill-farm.com 56 rooms In-room: no phone, no a/c (some), refrigerator, no TV (some), Wi-Fi. In-hotel: restaurant, tennis court, pools, children's programs (ages 2–18), laundry facilities, Wi-Fi hotspot, some pets allowed ▭ D, MC, V FAP.

JAFFREY CENTER

16 mi southeast of Keene.

Novelist Willa Cather came to Jaffrey Center in 1919 and stayed in the Shattuck Inn, which now stands empty on Old Meeting House Road. Not far from here, she pitched the tent in which she wrote several chapters of *My Ántonia*. She returned nearly every summer thereafter until her death and was buried in the Old Burying Ground, which also contains the remains of Amos Fortune, a former slave who bought his freedom in 1863 and moved to town when he was 71. Fortune, who was a tanner, also bought the freedom of his two wives. He died at the age of 91.

GETTING HERE AND AROUND

Jaffrey Center's historic district is on Route 124 and is home to a number of brick buildings. It should take less than an hour to view it in its entirety. Two miles east of town on Route 124 can be found the Old Burying Ground, which is behind the Meeting House.

ESSENTIALS

Visitor Information Jaffrey Chamber of Commerce (☎ *603/532–4549* 🌐 *www.jaffreychamber.com*).

EXPLORING

Cathedral of the Pines. This outdoor memorial pays tribute to Americans who have sacrificed their lives in service to their country. There's an inspiring view of Mt. Monadnock and Mt. Kearsarge from the Altar of the Nation, which is composed of rock from every U.S. state and territory. All faiths are welcome to hold services here; organ music for meditation is played at midday from Tuesday through Thursday in July and August. The Memorial Bell Tower, with a carillon of bells from around the world, is built of native stone. Norman Rockwell designed the bronze tablets over the four arches. Flower gardens, an indoor chapel, and a museum of military memorabilia share the hilltop. It's 8 mi southeast of Jaffrey Center. ✉ *10 Hale Hill Rd., off Rte. 119, Rindge* ☎ *603/899–3300 or 866/229–4520* 🌐 *www.cathedralofthepines.com* *Donations accepted* ⏲ *May–Oct., daily 9–5.*

SPORTS AND THE OUTDOORS

★ **Monadnock State Park.** The oft-quoted statistic about Mt. Monadnock is that it's America's most-climbed mountain—second in the world to Japan's Mt. Fuji. Whether this is true or not, locals agree that it's never lonely at the top. Some days, especially during foliage season, more than 400 people crowd its bald peak. Monadnock rises to 3,165 feet, and on a clear day the hazy Boston skyline is visible from its summit. The park maintains picnic grounds and a small campground (RVs welcome, but no hookups) with 28 sites. Five trailheads branch into more than two

Jaffrey Center is known for its historic buildings and its proximity to Mount Monadnock.

dozen trails of varying difficulty that wend their way to the top. Allow between three and four hours for any round-trip hike. A visitor center has free trail maps as well as exhibits documenting the mountain's history. In winter, you can cross-country ski along roughly 12 mi of groomed trails on the lower elevations of the mountain. ✉ *Off Rte. 124, 2½ mi north of Jaffrey Center* ☎ *603/532–8862* 🌐 *www.nhstateparks.com/monadnock.html* 🎟 *$4* ⏲ *Daily dawn–dusk* ☞ *No pets.*

Rhododendron State Park. More than 16 acres of wild rhododendrons bloom in mid-July at this park, which has the largest concentration of *Rhododendron maximum* north of the Allegheny Mountains. Bring a picnic lunch and sit in a nearby pine grove or follow the marked footpaths through the flowers. On your way here, be sure to pass through Fitzwilliam's well-preserved historic district of Colonial and Federal-style houses, which have appeared on thousands of postcards. ✉ *Rte. 119 W, off Rte. 12, 10 mi southwest of Jaffrey Center, Fitzwilliam* ☎ *603/239–8862* 🌐 *www.nhstateparks.com/rhodo.html* 🎟 *$4* ⏲ *May–Nov., daily 8–sunset.*

SHOPPING

You'll find about 35 dealers at **Bloomin' Antiques** (✉ *3 Templeton Turnpike, Fitzwilliam Center* ☎ *603/585–6688*). Meanwhile, **Fitzwilliam Antiques Centre** (✉ *13 Rte. 12, Fitzwilliam* ☎ *603/585–9092*) sells the goods of some 40 dealers.

THE ARTS

Amos Fortune Forum, near the Old Burying Ground, brings nationally known speakers to the 1773 meetinghouse on summer evenings. ✉ *Jaffrey Meetinghouse, Rt. 124* 🌐 *www.amosfortune.com.*

WHERE TO EAT AND STAY

$$ AMERICAN **JP Stephens.** An appealing choice either for lunch or dinner, this rustic-timbered dining room overlooks a small mill pond in Rindge, about 8 mi south of Jaffrey Center. The 1790 building used to house a sawmill, a gristmill, a forge, and a blacksmith. The sole meunière is delicate and flavorful and the apple brandy and walnut chicken is sweet and brazen. Try the pub cheese made with horseradish or the twice-baked potato. *377 U.S. 202, Rindge 603/899–3322 jpstephensrestaurant.com D, MC, V Closed Mon.*

$–$$ **Benjamin Prescott Inn.** Thanks to the dairy farm surrounding this 1853 Colonial house—with its stenciling and wide pine floors—you feel as though you're miles out in the country rather than just minutes from Jaffrey Center. A full breakfast of local eggs, homemade muffins, and blueberry pancakes with fruit and maple syrup prepares you for a day of antiquing or hiking. **Pros:** inexpensive; homey and comfortable. **Cons:** 2 mi east of town. *433 Turnpike Rd. (Rte. 124 E) 603/532–6637 or 888/950–6637 www.benjaminprescottinn.com 7 rooms, 3 suites In-room: no phone, no TV, Wi-Fi. In-hotel: Wi-Fi hotspot, no kids under 10 AE, MC, V BP.*

$ **The Monadnock Inn.** Rooms in this 1830s home are painted in lively lavenders, yellows, or peaches, a cheery presence in the heart of pristine Jaffrey Center, and a perfect place to get away from it all. Although full of period furnishings, they have a hip sensibility as well as high-thread-count bedding, fluffy towels, and fine toiletries. There's a good restaurant with an impressive Sunday brunch; indulge in the delightful banana bread French toast or any dish with fresh eggs from a local farm. For dinner, try the lobster mac and cheese or the New Hampshire veal schnitzel. **Pros:** well-lit rooms with lacy curtains; feels like grandma's house. **Cons:** limited amenities. *379 Main St., Box 484 603/532–7800 or 877/510–7019 www.themonadnock.com 9 rooms, 2 suites In-room: no phone, no a/c, DVD (some), no TV (some), Wi-Fi. In-hotel: restaurant, bar, Wi-Fi hotspot Dining room closed Tues. AE, D, DC, MC, V CP.*

$$$ **Woodbound Inn.** A favorite with families and outdoors enthusiasts, this 1819 farmhouse became an inn in 1892. It occupies 200 acres on the shores of Contoocook Lake. Accommodations are functional but clean and cheerful; they range from quirky rooms in the main inn to modern hotel-style rooms in the Edgewood building to cabins with fireplaces by the water. There's a 9-hole, golf course and lots of boating and fishing. **Pros:** relaxed, lakefront resort; new focus on food. **Cons:** older; simple furnishings. *247 Woodbound Rd., Rindge 603/532–8341 or 800/688–7770 www.woodboundinn.com 44 rooms, 39 with bath; 11 cabins In-room: refrigerator (some), no TV (some). In-hotel: restaurant, bar, golf course, tennis court, some pets allowed AE, MC, V BP, MAP.*

3

PETERBOROUGH

9 mi northeast of Jaffrey Center, 30 mi northwest of Nashua, on Route 101.

Thornton Wilder's play *Our Town* was based on Peterborough. The nation's first free public library opened here in 1833. The town, which was the first in the region to be incorporated (1760), is still a commercial and cultural hub.

GETTING HERE AND AROUND

Parking is just off Main Street, with shopping, coffee, and food all close by. Stand on the bridge and watch the roiling waters of the Nubanusit River on the north end of Main Street.

ESSENTIALS

Visitor Information **Greater Peterborough Chamber of Commerce** (☎ *603/924–7235* 🌐 *www.greater-peterborough-chamber.com*).

EXPLORING

Mariposa Museum. You can play instruments or try on costumes from around the world and indulge your cultural curiosity at this nonprofit museum dedicated to hands-on exploration of international folklore and folk art. The three-floor museum is inside a historic redbrick Baptist church, across from the Universalist church in the heart of town. The museum hosts a number of workshops and presentations on dance and arts and crafts. There's also a children's reading nook and a library. ✉ *26 Main St.* ☎ *603/924–4555* 🌐 *www.mariposamuseum.org* 🎟 *$5* ⏲ *July and Aug., daily 11–5; Sept.–June, Wed.–Sun. 11–5.*

SPORTS AND THE OUTDOORS

Miller State Park. About 3 mi east of town, an auto road takes you almost 2,300 feet up Pack Monadnock Mountain. The road is closed mid-November through mid-April. ✉ *Rte. 101* ☎ *603/924–3672* 🌐 *www.nhstateparks.com/miller.html* 🎟 *$4.*

GOLF At the Donald Ross–designed **Crotched Mountain Golf Club** (✉ *740 Francestown Rd., Francestown* ☎ *603/588–2923*), you'll find a hilly, rolling 18-hole layout with nice view of the Monadnocks. Green fees are $60 (weekends).

SKI AREA **Crotched Mountain.** New Hampshire's southernmost skiing and snowboarding facility has 17 trails, half of them intermediate, and the rest divided pretty evenly between beginner and expert. There's an 875-foot vertical drop. The slopes have ample snowmaking capacity, ensuring good skiing all winter long. Crotched is famous for its night skiing and a Midnight Madness lift ticket (9 PM–3 AM). Other facilities include a 40,000-square-foot lodge with a couple of restaurants, a ski school, and a snow camp for youngsters. ✉ *615 Francestown Rd. (Rte. 47), Bennington* ☎ *603/588–3668* 🌐 *www.crotchedmountain.com.*

SHOPPING

The corporate headquarters and retail outlet of **Eastern Mountain Sports** (✉ *1 Vose Farm Rd., off of Rte. 124* ☎ *603/924–7231* 🌐 *www.ems.com*) sells everything from tents to skis to hiking boots, offers hiking and camping classes, and conducts kayaking and canoeing demonstrations.

Harrisville Designs (✉ *43 Main St., Harrisville* ☎ *603/827–3996* 🌐 *www.harrisville.com*) sells hand-spun and hand-dyed yarn as well as looms. The shop also conducts classes in knitting and weaving. **Sharon Arts Center** (✉ *20–40 Depot Sq.* ☎ *603/924–2787* 🌐 *www.sharonarts.org*) exhibits locally made pottery, fabric, and woodwork and other crafts.

THE ARTS

From early July to late August **Monadnock Music** (✉ *2A Concord St.* ☎ *603/924–7610 or 800/868–9613* 🌐 *www.monadnockmusic.org*) produces a series of solo recitals, chamber music concerts, and orchestra and opera performances by renowned musicians. Events take place throughout the area on Wednesday through Saturday evenings at 8 and on Sunday at 4; many are free. The **Peterborough Folk Music Society** (☎ *603/827–2905* 🌐 *pfmsconcerts.org*) presents folk music concerts by artists such as John Gorka, Greg Brown, and Cheryl Wheeler. The **Peterborough Players** (✉ *55 Hadley Rd.* ☎ *603/924–7585* 🌐 *www.peterboroughplayers.org*) have performed since 1933. Productions are staged in a converted barn.

WHERE TO EAT AND STAY

$$ BISTRO ✕ **Acqua Bistro.** Start your meal with the wonderful ginger-crusted scallops or a lovely house salad with cilantro-orange dressing. The tea-smoked duck breast is a wonder as is the subtle margherita (tomato sauce and cheese) pizza. The white chocolate crème brûlée is an excellent way to finish your dinner at this café, which features patio dining next to the waters of the Nubanusit River. ✉ *18 Depot St.* ☎ *603/924–9905* 🌐 *www.acquabistro.com* 💳 *MC, V* ⊙ *Closed Mon. No lunch.*

$$–$$$ ★ **Hancock Inn.** This Federal-style 1789 inn is the real Colonial deal—the oldest in the state and the pride of this idyllic town 8 mi north of Peterborough. Common areas possess fireplaces, big wing chairs, couches, and dark-wood paneling. A tavern is painted with Rufus Porter murals from 1825. Colonial rooms have antique four-poster beds over original wood floors. Because the inn is in the heart of Hancock, just over from the green, you're right in the middle of a perfect hamlet. You don't need to go far to eat—the Inn's restaurant ($$) serves an excellent Shaker cranberry pot roast, and across the street is the town market and a very popular café. **Pros:** quintessential Colonial inn in a perfect New England town; cozy rooms. **Cons:** remote location. ✉ *33 Main St., Box 96, Hancock* ☎ *603/525–3318 or 800/525–1789* 🌐 *www.hancockinn.com* *14 rooms* *In-room: DVD (some), Wi-Fi. In-hotel: restaurant, bar, Internet terminal, Wi-Fi hotspot, some pets allowed* 💳 *AE, D, DC, MC, V* *BP.*

$ **Inn at Crotched Mountain.** Three of the nine fireplaces in this 1822 inn are in Colonial-style guest rooms. The property, with stunning views of the Monadnocks, was once a stop on the Underground Railroad. At the inn's restaurant ($$), where Singapore native Rose Perry is at the helm, you can sample both American and Asian-inspired fare, such as cranberry-port pot roast and Indonesian charbroiled swordfish with a sauce of ginger, green pepper, onion, and lemon. Weekend rates include breakfast and dinner. **Pros:** spectacular country setting. **Cons:** too remote for some. ✉ *534 Mountain Rd., 12 mi northeast of Peterborough, Francestown* ☎ *603/588–6840* 🌐 *www.innatcrotchedmt.*

com 13 rooms, 8 with private baths ♧ *In-hotel: restaurant, bar, tennis courts, pool, some pets allowed (fee)* ▭ *No credit cards* ⊙ *Closed Apr. and Nov.* 🍽 *BP, MAP.*

$ ★ **Jack Daniels Motor Inn.** With so many dowdy motels in southwestern New Hampshire, it's a pleasure to find one as bright and clean as the Jack Daniels, just ½ mi north of downtown Peterborough. The rooms are large and furnished with attractive reproduction antiques. Try to get one of two rooms looking out on the Contoocook River; otherwise, second-floor rooms have chairs on the hallway overlooking the river. **Pros:** affordable rooms; low-key atmosphere. **Cons:** basic motel-style rooms; have to drive or walk into town. ✉ *80 Concord St. (U.S. 202)* ☎ *603/924–7548 www.jackdanielsmotorinn.com* ⇨ *17 rooms* ♧ *In-room: refrigerator (some), DVD (some), Wi-Fi. In-hotel: Wi-Fi hotspot, some pets allowed* ▭ *AE, D, DC, MC, V.*

4

Inland Maine

WORD OF MOUTH

"The best foliage . . . is inland not on the coast. I drive up to Greenville and then up the west side of Moosehead Lake. At Greenville you [can] take a ride on the Katahdin steamship . . . the leaves are extra gorgeous when viewed on a sunny day from water."

—Virginia

WELCOME TO INLAND MAINE

TOP REASONS TO GO

★ **Baxter State Park:** Mt. Katahdin stands as a sentry over Baxter's forestland in its "natural wild state." Climbing the state's highest peak takes all day, but you can choose from many outstanding outdoor adventures.

★ **Moosehead Lake:** Surrounded by mountains, Maine's largest lake—dotted with islands and chiseled with inlets and coves—retains the rugged beauty that so captivated author Henry David Thoreau in the mid-1800s.

★ **Water sports:** It's easy to get out on the water with scheduled cruises on large inland lakes; marinas and outfitters renting boats, canoes, and kayaks throughout the region; and white-water rafting trips on several rivers.

★ **Winter pastimes:** For downhill skiing, choose from large mountain resorts with spa services, shopping, and condos or smaller ones that are family-friendly and less crowded. Maine's dense woods are perfect for snowmobiling, snowshoeing, cross-country skiing, and dogsledding.

1 Western Lakes and Mountains. Lakes both quiet and busy, classic New England villages, and ski resorts fit perfectly in the forested landscape. In winter, this is ski country; snowmobiling and snowshoeing are also popular. In summer, the woods and water draw vacationers for a cool escape. In fall, foliage drives invite exploration of the region's national forest and state parks. In spring, there are no crowds, but fishermen, white-water rafters, and canoeists make their way here.

2 The North Woods. Much of the North Woods' private forestland is open for public recreation and best experienced by paddling a canoe or raft, hiking, snowshoeing, snowmobiling, or fishing. Some great destinations are mostly undeveloped Moosehead Lake, Baxter State Park, and Allagash Wilderness Waterway. Greenville, a laidback and woodsy resort town, is a good base for day trips—take a drive (go slow!) down a "moose alley."

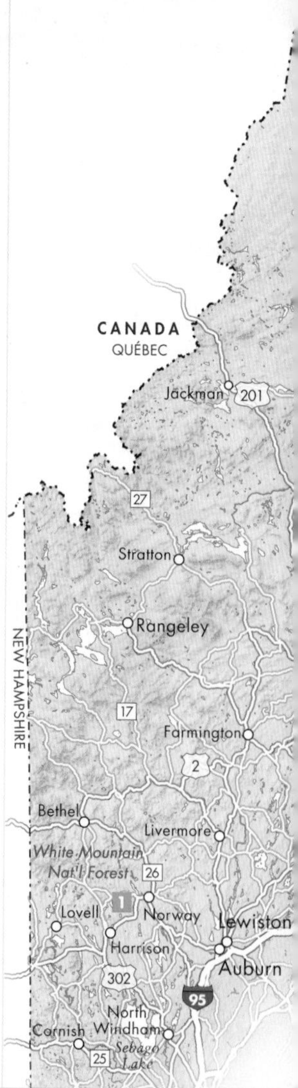

Madawaska
Fort Kent
1
Van Buren
161
161
Allagash
CANADA
11
Caribou
Allagash Wilderness Waterway
Fort Fairfield
Presque Isle
Ashland
163
NEW BRUNSWICK
11
1
2
Houlton
Baxter State Park
Mt. Katahdin
Sherman
Grindstone
95
Rockwood
Kokadjo
Millinocket
Moosehead Lake
Medway
2
11
Greenville
0
20 mi
Brownville Junction
0
20 km
Dover-Foxcroft
11
Passadumkeag
7
15
Old Town
Newport
Skowhegan
Bangor
95
Waterville
Augusta
Gardiner

GETTING ORIENTED

Though Maine is well known for its miles of craggy coastline, the inland part of the state is surprisingly vast and much less populated. Less than an hour's drive from the bays and ocean, huge swaths of forestland are dotted with lakes (sometimes called "ponds" despite their size). Summer camps, ski areas, and small villages populate the western part of the state, which stretches north along the New Hampshire border to Qu bec. Quiet waters are easy to find in the more remote inland areas, but busier Sebago Lake is just north of coastal Portland, Maine's largest city. The northwest area is more rugged and remote while in the north-central part of the state, wilderness areas beckon outdoor lovers to the North Woods, which extend north and west to Canada.

4

INLAND MAINE PLANNER

When to Go

Inland's Maine's most popular hiking trails and beaches may get busy in warm weather, but if splendid isolation is what you crave, you can easily find it. In summer, traffic picks up but rarely creates jams, except in a few spots. Peak lodging rates apply, but moderate weather makes this a great time to visit. Inland Maine gets hotter than the coast, though less so along lakes and at higher elevations. July and August are warmest; September is less busy.

Western Maine is the state's premier destination for leaf-peepers—hardwoods are more abundant here than on the coast. Late September through mid-October is peak foliage season.

Maine's largest ski areas can make their own snow; they usually open in mid-November and often operate into April. Inland Maine typically has snow cover by Christmas, so cross-country skiing, snowshoeing, and snowmobiling are in full swing by the end of the year. In ski towns, many lodgings charge peak rates in the winter.

Snowmelt ushers in mud season in early spring. Mid-May to mid-June is black fly season; they're especially pesky in the woods but less bothersome in town. Spring is a prime time for canoeing and fishing.

Getting Here and Around

Two primary airports serve Maine: Portland International (PWM 🌐 *www.portlandjetport.org*) and Bangor International (BGR 🌐 *www.flybangor.com*). Portland is closer to the Western Lakes and Mountains area; Bangor is more convenient to the North Woods. Regional flying services, operating from regional and municipal airports, provide access to remote lakes and wilderness areas and offer scenic flights (see specific towns for more information).

Because Maine is large and rural, a car is essential. U.S. 2 is the major east–west thoroughfare in western Maine, winding from Bangor to New Hampshire. Interstate 95 is a departure point for many visitors to inland Maine, especially the North Woods. The highway heads inland at Brunswick and is a toll road, the Maine Turnpike, from the New Hampshire border to Augusta. Because of the hilly terrain and abundant lakes and rivers, inland Maine roads are often curvy. Traffic rarely gets heavy, though highways often pass right through instead of around the larger towns, which can slow your trip a bit.

There are few public roads in Maine's North Woods, though private logging roads there are often open to the public (sometimes by permit and fee). When driving these roads, always give lumber-company trucks the right of way; loggers must drive in the middle of the road and often can't move over or slow down for cars. Be sure to have a full tank of gas before heading onto the many private roads in the region.

Planning Your Time

Inland Maine locales are often destinations where visitors stay their entire trip. That's certainly true of those who come to ski at a resort, fish at a remote sporting camp, or just relax at a lakeside cabin. After a day hike on a mountain trail reached by driving gravel logging roads, visitors are unlikely to hurry on to another town. Vacation rental homes and cottages often require a week's stay, as do lakeside cottage resorts. Generally speaking, the farther inland you go, the farther it is between destinations.

About the Restaurants

Fear not, lobster lovers: this succulent, emblematic Maine food is on the menu at many inland restaurants, from fancier establishments to roadside places. Lobster dishes are more common than boiled lobster dinners, but look for daily specials. Shrimp, scallops, and other seafood are also menu mainstays, and you may find surprises like bison burgers or steaks from a nearby farm. Organic growers and natural foods producers are planted throughout the state and often sell their food to finer restaurants nearby. Seasonal foods like pumpkins, blackberries, and strawberries make their way into homemade desserts, as do Maine's famed blueberries. Many lakeside resorts and sporting camps have a reputation for good food; some of the latter will cook the fish you catch.

About the Hotels

Although there is a higher concentration of upscale inns on the coast than inland, Bethel, Bridgton, the Kingfield area, and Rangeley have sophisticated hotels and inns. At lodgings near ski resorts, peak-season rates may apply in winter and summer. Both Sebago and Kezar lakes have full-service cottage resorts (usually a week's stay is required). The two largest ski resorts, Sunday River and Sugarloaf, offer a choice of hotels and condos. Greenville has the largest selection of lodgings in the North Woods region, with a nice mix of fine and homey inns. Lakeside sporting camps, from the primitive to the upscale, are popular around Rangeley and the North Woods. Many have cozy cabins heated with woodstoves and serve three hearty meals a day.

For information on state park campsites contact the **Maine State Parks Campground Reservation Program** (☎ *207/624–9950, 800/332–1501 in Maine* 🌐 *www.campwithme.com*).

WHAT IT COSTS

	¢	$	$$	$$$	$$$$
Restaurants	under $8	$8–$12	$13–$20	$21–$28	over $28
Hotels	under $80	$80–$120	$121–$170	$171–$220	over $220
Campgrounds	under $10	$10–$17	$18–$35	$36–$50	over $50

Restaurant prices are per person, for a main course at dinner. Hotel prices are for a standard double room during peak season and not including tax or gratuities. Some inns add a 15% service charge.

Outdoor Activities

People visit inland Maine year-round for hiking, biking (mountain biking is big at ski resorts off-season), camping, fishing, boating, canoeing, kayaking, white-water rafting, downhill and cross-country skiing, snowshoeing, and snowmobiling.

Bicycling: For information on bicycling in Maine, contact the **Bicycle Coalition of Maine** (☎ *207/623–4511* 🌐 *www.bikemaine.org*).

Boating: Raft Maine (🌐 *www.raftmaine.com*) provides information on white-water rafting on the Kennebec, Penobscot, and Dead rivers.

Fishing: For information about licenses, contact the **Maine Department of Inland Fisheries and Wildlife** (☎ *207/287–8000* 🌐 *www.mefishwildlife.com*). For assistance in finding a fishing guide, contact the **Maine Professional Guides Association** (🌐 *www.maineguides.org*), which represents Registered Maine Guides. These guides are also available through most wilderness camps, sporting goods stores, and outfitters.

Skiing: For alpine and cross-country skiing information, contact **Ski Maine** (☎ *207/773–7669* 🌐 *www.skimaine.com*).

Snowmobiling: The **Maine Snowmobile Association** (☎ *207/622–6983* 🌐 *www.mesnow.com*) distributes an excellent statewide trail map of about 3,500 mi of trails.

4

INLAND MAINE FALL FOLIAGE DRIVE

Throughout Maine, pine, spruce, and fir trees offset the fall foliage, seeming to deepen the orange, red, and yellow hues. But hardwoods, like the vibrant sugar maples, are more common inland. This route follows Western Maine's mountains, passing stunning overlooks, waterfalls, hiking trails, and a lakeside state park.

From Houghton and Mexico, Route 17 winds as it ascends, the countryside splashed with rich reds and oranges. The drive's literal pinnacle is **Height of Land**—where mountain vistas are reflected in the many (and often connected) lakes, ponds, rivers, and streams. On a clear day you can see west to New Hampshire and Canada. **Mooselookmeguntic Lake** and **Upper Richardson Lake** seem to float in the sea of forestland below. A few miles north of here at the Rangeley overlook, observe how the east end of town forms a small isthmus between Rangeley Lake and Haley Pond.

BEST TIME TO GO

Fall color usually peaks in the Rangeley area in mid-October. Learn more and get weekly foliage updates in season (🌐 *www.mainefoliage.com*).

PLANNING YOUR TIME

The Rangeley Lakes National Scenic Byway (🌐 *www.byways.org*) makes up most of this 52-mi drive (1½ hours without stops), but plan for a relaxed full day of exploring.

In tiny, welcoming Oquossoc, where Routes 17 and 4 meet, **The Farmer's Daughter** welcomes passersby with displays of pumpkins and mums during autumn. You can pick up apple cider and picnic items at this specialty foods store. Or stop for the **Gingerbread House Restaurant** for a meal, or just ice cream or baked goods. After a snack break, you can learn more about the outdoor enthusiasts that have been coming to this area since the mid-1800s at the **Rangeley Outdoor Sporting Heritage Museum**, which is expected to open in summer 2010.

Rangeley, 7 mi along Route 4, has restaurants, inns, waterfront parks, and outdoorsy shops. The countryside sweeps into view along public hiking trails at both **Saddleback Maine** ski resort and the 175-acre **Wilhelm Rich Museum.**

Also along or near this scenic drive are **Rangeley Lake State Park** and the **Appalachian Trail**, both accessible from Routes 4 and 17. Overhanging foliage frames waterfalls at the scenic rest areas at or near each end of the drive that are perfect for picnics: Smalls Falls on Route 4, the byway's eastern terminus, and Coos Canyon on Route 17.

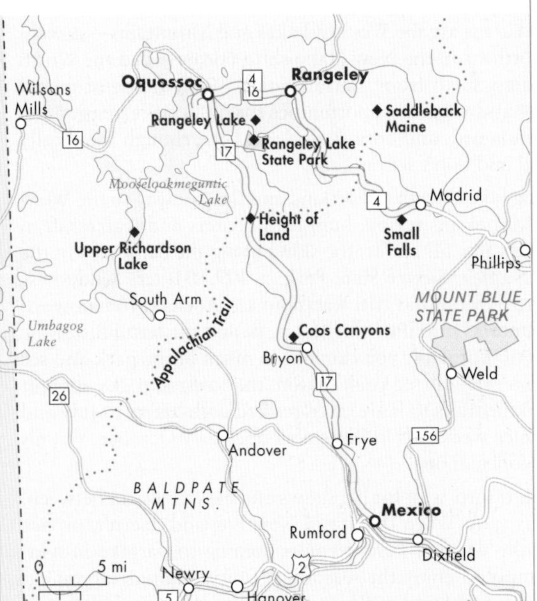

NEED A BREAK?

At The Farmer's Daughter (✉ *13 Rumford Rd. [Rte. 17], Oquossoc* ☎ *207/864–2492* 🌐 *www.thefarmersdaughteronline.com*) specialty food store, produce comes from the family farm. At the bakery counter, you can buy a cup of coffee, or apple cider in season.

Wilhelm Reich Museum (✉ *19 Orgonon Circle, Rangeley* ☎ *207/864–3443* 🌐 *www.wilhelmreichmuseum.org* 🎫 *Museum $6, grounds free* ⏲ *Museum July and Aug., Wed.–Sun. 1–5, Sept., Sun. 1–5. Grounds daily 8–sunset*) showcases the life and work of controversial physician-scientist Wilhelm Reich (1897–1957). There are magnificent views from the observatory and the many trails on the 175-acre grounds.

Rangeley Lakes Heritage Trust (✉ *52 Carry Rd. [Rte. 4], Oquossoc* ☎ *207/864–7311* 🌐 *www.rlht.org*) protects 13,000 acres of area land. Contact them for trail maps and more information about local activities.

Updated by Mary Ruoff

Unlike Maine's more famous, more populated, and more visited coast, inland Maine is a four-season destination. With strings of lakes and rivers framed by mountainous terrain, hilly pastoral stretches, classic New England villages with restaurants and shops that entice but don't overwhelm, and the region's most extensive wilderness areas, Maine's interior lures visitors in summer, fall, winter, and spring (yes, the slow season, but canoeists, fishermen, and white-water rafters venture inland).

The most visited areas are the Western Lakes and Mountains—stretching west and north from the New Hampshire border—and the North Woods—extending north from central Maine. While much of inland Maine is remote and rugged, opportunities for outdoor recreation are plentiful and renowned, and crowds do form here, though thankfully they're scattered and don't set the tone.

Sebago and Long lakes, north of Portland and the gateway to the Western Lakes and Mountains region, hum with boaters and watercraft in the summer. Sidewalks fill and traffic slows along the causeway in the tourist hub of Naples. Baxter State Park, a 209,501-acre wilderness park in the North Woods has Mt. Katahdin (an Abenaki Indian word for "Great Mountain"), Maine's highest peak and the terminus of the Appalachian Trail. But while you can hike in much of the park and see few other visitors even during peak season, the treeless, rocky summit of Katahdin and the trails to it are often packed with hikers in July and August and on nice weekends in September and early October. Yes, it's a crowd, but a collegial one.

Come winter, ski resorts wait for big snows and make snow in between. Maine often gets snow when the rest of New England doesn't, or vice versa, so track the weather here if you're coming to partake in winter sports or simply to enjoy the season's serenity. Maine's largest ski resorts, Sugarloaf and Sunday River, are in the Western Lakes and

Mountains region. Saddleback Mountain in Rangeley is an up-and-coming family-friendly resort, as is Shawnee Peak in Bridgton. But not to worry, the lift lines don't get too long.

Though they didn't come in the winter, "rusticators" began flocking to Maine to vacation in the mid-1800s, arriving at inland destinations by train or steamship, just as they did on Maine's coast. Escaping the summer heat and city pollution, these wealthy urbanites headed to the mountains to hike, swim, canoe, fish, hunt, and relax, staying at rustic sporting camps or at the grand hotels that cropped up in some of the most scenic spots. Moosehead Lake's Mt. Kineo—a walled outcropping north of Greenville where Indian tribes from throughout the Northeast came for flint—gave rise to one of the nation's largest and fanciest hotels. Rangeley was discovered for its sport fishing in the mid-1800s and is still a haven for anglers, who come to fish for "world-class" brook trout and landlocked salmon. Modern fly-fishing was born in the Rangeley region, and many of the local waters are restricted to fly-fishing.

The legacy of the rusticators and the locals who catered to them lives on at the sporting camps still found on inland Maine's remote lakes and rivers, albeit in fewer numbers. It also survives through Maine's unique system of licensed outdoor guides, known as Registered Maine Guides. These days they may lead kayak trips, hiking expeditions, white-water rafting excursions, and moose safaris as well as fishing and canoe trips. Guides are happy to show you their license—it's the law that they have one, and some also opt to wear a badge.

WESTERN LAKES AND MOUNTAINS

From Sebago Lake, less than 20 mi northwest of Portland, the sparsely populated Western Lakes and Mountains stretch north along the New Hampshire border to Québec. Each season offers different outdoor highlights: you can choose from snow sports, hiking, mountain biking, leaf-peeping, fishing, and paddling. The Sebago Lake area bustles with activity in summer. Harrison and the Waterfords are quieter, Center Lovell is a dreamy escape, and Bridgton is a classic New England town. So is Bethel, in the valley of the Androscoggin River; Sunday River, one of Maine's two major ski resorts, is nearby. The more rural Rangeley Lake area brings long stretches of pine, beech, spruce, and sky and more classic inns. Carrabassett Valley, just north of Kingfield, is home to Sugarloaf, a major ski resort with a challenging golf course.

SEBAGO LAKE AREA

17 mi northwest of Portland.

Sebago Lake is Maine's second largest lake after Moosehead and provides all the drinking water for Greater Portland. Many wilderness camps and year-round homes surround Sebago, which is popular with water-sports enthusiasts. Naples occupies an enviable location between Long and Sebago lakes. The town swells with seasonal residents and visitors in summer and, though winter is the slow season, things heat up in February with a winter carnival and ice-fishing derby. On clear

Western Lakes and Mountains
Moxie Pond
Monson
Stratton
Bingham
Oquossoc
Rangeley
Saddleback Maine
Kingfield
Solon
Wilsons Mills
Rangeley Lake State Park
New Portland
Height of Land
Phillips
New Vineyard
Skowhegan
Weld
Andover
Farmington
Grafton Notch State Park
South Arm
NEW HAMPSHIRE
Wilton
Mexico
Rumford
Waterville
Hanover
Dixfield
Sunday River
Newry
Chisholm
Livermore Falls
Bethel
Locke Mills
Mt. Abram Ski Resort
Bryant Pond
Livermore
White Mountain Nat'l Forest
AUGUSTA
Greenwood
Buckfield
Turner
Center Lovell
South Paris
Norway
Greene
Waterford
Lovell
Harrison
Lewiston
Mechanic Falls
Auburn
Bridgton
Fryeburg
Casco
Newcastle
Naples
Sabbathday Lake Shaker Museum
Brownfield
South Casco
Brunswick
Bath
Hiram
Sebago Lake State Park
Raymond
Freeport
Boothbay
Kezar Falls
Yarmouth
Georgetown
Sebago Lake
Standish
Falmouth
Casco Bay
Gorham
Portland
Atlantic Ocean
0
10 mi
10 km

days, the view up Long Lake takes in snowcapped Mt. Washington. The causeway separating Long Lake from Brandy Pond in the center of Naples pulses with activity in the summer. Open-air cafés overflow, boats and watercraft ply the water, and throngs of families parade along the sidewalk edging Long Lake.

GETTING HERE AND AROUND

Sebago Lake, gateway to Maine's Western Lakes and Mountains, is about 20 mi from Portland on U.S. Route 302.

ESSENTIALS

Vacation Rentals **Krainin Real Estate** (*1539 Roosevelt Tr. [Rte. 302], Raymond 800/332–1806 www.krainin.com*).

Visitor Information **Sebago Lakes Region Chamber of Commerce** (*747 Roosevelt Tr. [U.S. 302], Windham 207/892–8265 www.sebagolakeschamber.com*).

OFF THE BEATEN PATH

Sabbathday Lake Shaker Museum. Established in the late 18th century, this is the last active Shaker community in the United States, with fewer than 10 members. Open for guided tours are four buildings with rooms of Shaker furniture, folk art, tools, farm implements, and crafts from the 18th to the early 20th century: the 1794 Meetinghouse; the 1839 Ministry's Shop, where the elders and eldresses lived until the early 1900s; the 1821 Sister's Shop, where household goods and candies were made for sale and still are on a smaller scale; and the 1816 Spinhouse, where changing exhibits are housed. A store sells herbs and goods handcrafted by the Shakers. *707 Shaker Rd. (turn off Rte. 26), New Gloucester 207/926–4597 www.shaker.lib.me.us/ Tour $6.50 Late May–early Oct., Mon.–Sat. 10–4:30*

SPORTS AND THE OUTDOORS

U.S. 302 cuts through Naples, and in the center at the Naples causeway you'll find rental craft for fishing or cruising. Sebago, Long, and Rangeley lakes are popular areas for sailing, fishing, and motorboating.

Departing from the Naples causeway, ***Songo River Queen II***, a 93-foot sternwheeler, takes passengers on hour and two-hour cruises on Long Lake and longer voyages down the Songo River and through Songo Lock. *841 Roosevelt Tr. (U.S. 302) 207/693–6861 www.songoriverqueen.net Long Lake cruises $12 (one-hour) and $20 (two-hour), Songo River ride $25 Early-Apr.–mid-June and Sept., 1 cruise daily on weekends; mid-June–early Sept., 4 cruises daily.*

Sebago Lake State Park. This 1,300-acre park on the north shore of the lake provides swimming, picnicking, camping (250 sites), boating, and fishing (salmon and togue). Come winter, the 6 mi of hiking trails are groomed for cross-country skiing. *11 Park Access Rd., Casco 207/693–6231, 207/693–6613 May–mid-Oct. only www.parksandlands.com $4.50 mid-May–mid-Oct., $1.50 mid-Oct.–mid-May Late May–early Sept., daily 9–8; mid-Sept.–Oct., daily 9–6; Nov.–mid-May, daily 9–4.*

WHERE TO STAY

$$$$ **Migis Lodge.** The pine-paneled cottages scattered under canopied pines along the ½ mi of shorefront at this 125-acre resort have fieldstone fireplaces and porches and are handsomely furnished with colorful rugs and handmade quilts. A warm, woodsy feeling pervades the main lodge. The long front porch and the terrace below have views—marvelous at sunset—of Sebago Lake. All kinds of outdoor and indoor activities are included in the room rate, and canoes, kayaks, waterskiing, and sailboats are available. Three meals (guests dress for dinner) are served daily in the dining room (you can also lunch lakeside). **Pros:** exclusive woodsy resort with access to private island; daily outdoor cocktail hour with complimentary drinks on Monday and Friday; fresh flowers from the gardens in lodgings. **Cons:** week minimum in July and August (unless shorter openings occur). *30 Migis Lodge Rd., off U.S. 302, South Casco 207/655–4524 www.migis.com 35 cottages, 6 rooms In-room: no a/c (some), refrigerator, Wi-Fi. In-hotel: restaurant, tennis courts, gym, beachfront, water sports, bicycles, children's programs (ages infant–12), Internet terminal, Wi-Fi hotspot No credit cards Closed mid-Oct.–mid-June AI.*

BRIDGTON

8 mi north of Naples, 30 mi south of Bethel.

Bridgton's winding Main Street (U.S. 302) reveals picturesque New England townscapes at every curve. On steamy summer days, kids dive off the dock at the town beach tucked at the end of Highland Lake, just past storefronts with restaurants, galleries, and shops. The town has 10 lakes that are popular for boating and fishing. Come winter, people arrive to ski at Shawnee Peak.

The combination of woods, lakes, and views makes the surrounding countryside a good choice for leaf-peepers and outdoor lovers. A few miles north, Harrison anchors the northern end of Long Lake and is less commercial than Naples, its southern terminus. Tiny Waterford is a National Historic District. Come fall, Fryeburg, on the New Hampshire border, is home to the famed Fryeburg Fair (*www.fryeburgfair.com*), New England's largest agricultural fair.

GETTING HERE AND AROUND

U.S. 302 runs from Portland, along the east side of Sebago Lake to Naples, then up the west side of Long Lake to Bridgton.

ESSENTIALS

Vacation Rentals **Maine Lakeside Getaways** (*12 Hawk Ridge Rd., 207/647–4000 or 866/647–8557 www.mainelakesidegetaways.com*).

Visitor Information **Greater Bridgton Lakes Region Chamber of Commerce** (*101 Portland Rd. [U.S. 302], Bridgton 207/647–3472 www.mainelakeschamber.com*).

EXPLORING

Rufus Porter Museum and Cultural Heritage Center. Local youth Rufus Porter became a leading folk artist, painting landscape and harbor murals on the walls of New England homes in the early 1800s, including those in this red, Cape Cod–style house. For an additional fee, visitors can also view 10 signed Porter murals from a Massachusetts home that are displayed in a local gallery. Also an inventor, Porter founded *Scientific American* magazine. Early issues are showcased, as are some of his inventions and miniature portraits. ✉ *67 N. High St.* ☎ *207/647–2828* 🌐 *www.rufusportermuseum.org* 🎫 *$5* ⏲ *Late June–early Oct., Wed.–Sat. noon–5.*

SPORTS AND THE OUTDOORS

Just an hour's drive from Portland and a few miles from Bridgton's downtown, **Shawnee Peak** (✉ *119 Mountain Rd., turn off U.S. 302* ☎ *207/647–8444* 🌐 *www.shawneepeak.com*) appeals to families and those who enjoy nighttime skiing—beginner, intermediate, and expert trails are lit most evenings. Three lifts serve 40 trails, four glades, and two terrain parks. There are slope-side condominiums, and the base lodge has a deck-fronted restaurant, two cafeterias, babysitting, ski school and rentals, and a ski shop.

4

WHERE TO STAY

$$ ★ **Bear Mountain Inn.** On 25 acres above Bear Lake, this 1825 homestead has been meticulously decorated with country furnishings and bear decor. The luxurious Great Grizzly room has mesmerizing views and, like the other larger rooms, a fireplace, whirlpool bath for two, and wet bar. Cozy Sugar Bear Cottage is a romantic retreat with kitchenette; the two-bedroom suites attract families. Breakfast is served in the dining room, which has a fieldstone fireplace and lake views. **Pros:** sweeping lawn has lake-view deck with fireplace; benches and hammocks along riverside trail; guest-only dinners (reservations required). **Cons:** one suite is considerably smaller; some shared bathrooms. ✉ *364 Waterford Rd. (Route 35), Waterford 04088* ☎ *207/583–4404* 🌐 *www.bearmtninn.com* *9 rooms, 5 with bath; 2 suites, 1 cabin* *In-room: no phone, no a/c (some), refrigerator (some), DVD (some), no TV (some), Wi-Fi. In-hotel: beachfront, water sports, Wi-Fi hotspot, some pets allowed* *MC, V* *BP.*

CENTER LOVELL

17 mi northwest of Harrison, 28 mi south of Bethel.

At Center Lovell you can glimpse secluded Kezar Lake to the west, the retreat of wealthy and very private people. Only town residents and property owners can use the town beaches, but there is a public boat launch. Sabattus Mountain, which rises behind Center Lovell, has a public hiking trail.

WHERE TO EAT AND STAY

$$–$$$ ✕ **Center Lovell Inn Restaurant.** The eclectic furnishings in this eye-catching cupola-topped property from 1805 blend the mid-19th and mid-20th centuries in a pleasing, homey style. In summer the best tables for dining are on the wraparound porch, which has sunset views of the White Mountains. Inside, one dining room has mountain views and the other an original iron fireplace. Entrées may include pan-seared Muscovy duck, fillet of bison, or fresh swordfish. Breakfast is by reservation only (no lunch). Nine lodging rooms (some shared baths; some rooms can be combined as

suites) are upstairs and in the adjacent Harmon House. ✉ *1107 Main St. (Rte. 5)* ☎ *207/925–1575 or 800/777–2698* 🌐 *www.centerlovellinn.com* ▭ *D, MC, V* ⊗ *Closed Nov.–late Dec. and Apr.–mid-May.*

$$$$ **Quisisana.** This delightful summer-only cottage resort on Kezar Lake makes music a focus. The staff—students and graduates of the country's finer music schools—perform everything from Broadway tunes to concert-piano pieces throughout your stay. All of the white clapboard cottages (one-to–three-bedroom) have screened porches and simple wicker and country furnishings; some have fireplaces and pine-paneled living areas. **Pros:** unique musical theme; regular activities like Tuesday cocktail party and dinner-hour children's program. **Cons:** one-week minimum in peak season; no Wi-Fi in cottages; cash or check only. ✉ *42 Quisisana Dr., off Pleasant Point Rd.* ☎ *207/925–3500* 🌐 *www.quisisanaresort.com* *11 rooms in 2 lodges, 46 cottage units* *In-room: no phone, no a/c, no TV. In-hotel: restaurant, bar, tennis courts, beachfront, water sports, Internet terminal, Wi-Fi hotspot* ▭ *No credit cards* ⊗ *Closed Sept.–mid-June* *AI.*

BETHEL

28 mi north of Lovell; 66 mi north of Portland.

Bethel is pure New England, a town with white clapboard houses, white-steeple churches, and a mountain vista at the end of every street. In winter, this is ski country: Sunday River ski area in Newry is only a few miles north.

GETTING HERE AND AROUND

From the south, Route 35 winds along the east side of Long Lake to Harrison, through the Waterfords, and on to Bethel. Route 5 leads to Bethel from Center Lovell. The two roads overlap en route to Bethel, then split off from each other several miles south of town. Either road will get you there, but Route 5 is a little shorter and especially pretty come fall, with lots of overhanging trees. From the west, U.S. 2 passes through the White Mountain National Forest as it enters Maine from New Hampshire and continues to Bethel and nearby Newry, home of Sunday River ski resort.

ESSENTIALS

Vacation Rentals **Four Seasons Property Management & Rentals** (✉ *832 Parkway Plaza, Suite 1* ☎ *207/824–3776* 🌐 *www.fourseasonsrealtymaine.com).*

Visitor Information **Bethel Area Chamber of Commerce** (✉ *8 Station Pl.,* ☎ *207/824–2282 or 800/442–5826* 🌐 *www.bethelmaine.com).*

EXPLORING

Bethel Historical Society Regional History Center. Start your stroll in Bethel here, across from the Village Common. The center's campus comprises two buildings: the 1821 O'Neil Robinson House and the 1813 Dr. Moses Mason House, both of which are listed on the National Register of Historic Places. The Robinson House has changing exhibits pertaining to the region's history; the Moses Mason House has nine period rooms and a front hall and stairway wall decorated with murals by folk artist Rufus Porter. Pick up materials here for a walking tour of Bethel Hill

NORTH WOODS OUTFITTERS

BOATING

Allagash Canoe Trips (✉ *8 Bigelow, Carrabassett Valley* ☎ *207/237–3077* 🌐 *www.allagashcanoetrips.com*) operates guided trips on the Allagash Waterway, plus the Moose, Penobscot, and St. John rivers. **Beaver Cove Marina** (✉ *16 Coveside Rd., Beaver Cove* ☎ *207/695–3526* 🌐 *www.beavercovemarina.com*) rents power boats, fishing skiffs, and canoes and kayaks. **Katahdin Outfitters** (✉ *Less than 1 mi outside Millinocket on Baxter State Park Rd.* ☎ *207/723–5700 or 800/862–2663* 🌐 *www.katahdinoutfitters.com*) outfits canoeing and kayaking expeditions. **North Woods Ways** (✉ *2293 Elliottsville Rd., Willimantic* ☎ *207/997–3723* 🌐 *www.northwoodsways.com*) leads overnight canoe and snowshoe trips where gear is hauled on toboggans.

If requested, most canoe-rental operations will also arrange transportation, help plan your route, and provide a guide. Transportation to wilderness lakes can be handled through various regional flying services.

MULTI-SPORT

Moose Country Safaris (☎ *207/876–4907* 🌐 *www.moosecountrysafaris.com*) leads moose safaris and canoe, Jeep, snowshoe, and hiking trips in the Greenville area. **New England Outdoor Center** (☎ *207/723–5438 or 800/766–7238* 🌐 *www.neoc.com*) rents snowmobiles, canoes, and kayaks; offers lessons; and leads guided snowmobile, white-water-rafting, fishing, canoe, hiking, and moose-watching trips in the Millinocket area—some within Baxter State Park. It also has campgrounds and a dinner-only restaurant and rents cabins and "green" guest houses on Millinocket Lake. **Northwoods Outfitters** (✉ *5 Lilly Bay Rd.* ☎ *207/695–3288* 🌐 *www.maineoutfitter.com*) outfits for moose watching, biking, skiing, snowmobiling, snowboarding, canoeing, kayaking, and fishing; leads trips for many of these activities; and rents canoes, kayaks, bikes, snowmobiles, snowshoes, and more. Shop, get trail advice, and kick back in the Internet café at its downtown outfitters store.

RAFTING

Raft Maine (🌐 *www.raftmaine.com*) is an association of white-water outfitters licensed to lead trips down the Kennebec and Dead rivers and the west branch of the Penobscot River. Most outfitters offer lodging packages. Rafting season runs mid-April through mid-October.

Village. ✉ *10–14 Broad St.* ☎ *207/824–2908 or 800/824–2910* 🌐 *www.bethelhistorical.org* 🎫 *$3* 🕒 *O'Neil Robinson House Tues.–Fri. 10–noon and 1–4; July and Aug. also weekends 1–4. Dr. Moses Mason House July–early Sept., Tues.–Sun. 1–4 and by appointment year-round.*

SPORTS AND THE OUTDOORS

Grafton Notch State Park. Route 26 runs through this park, which stretches along the Bear River Valley 14 mi north of Bethel and is a favorite foliage drive. It's an easy walk from the roadside parking areas to Mother Walker Falls, Moose Cave, and the spectacular Screw Auger Falls. You can also hike to the summit of Old Speck Mountain, the state's third-highest peak.

If you have the stamina and the equipment, you can pick up the Appalachian Trail here, hike over Saddleback Mountain, and continue on to Mt. Katahdin. The **Maine Appalachian Trail Club** (*Box 283, Augusta 04332 www.matc.org*) publishes seven Appalachian Trail maps and a Maine trail guide. *Rte. 26 207/624–6080, 207/824–2912 mid-May–mid-Oct. www.parksandlands.com Mid-May–mid-Oct. $3 Daily.*

White Mountain National Forest. This forest straddles New Hampshire and Maine, with the highest peaks on the New Hampshire side. The Maine section, though smaller, has magnificent rugged terrain, camping and picnic areas, and hiking, from hour-long nature loops to a day hike up Speckled Mountain. Highway 113 through the forest is closed in the winter. Its **New Hampshire Visitor Center** (*Androscoggin Ranger Station Visitor Center, 300 Glen Rd. [Rte. 16], Gorham Late May–mid-Oct., daily 8–4:30; late Oct.–mid-May, weekdays 8–4:30*) has interactive exhibits for kids and displays on the forest's history and natural setting. *603/466–2713 www.fs.fed.us/r9/white Day pass $5 per car, week pass $10 per car Daily.*

CANOEING AND KAYAKING

Bethel Outdoor Adventure and Campground (*121 Mayville Rd. [U.S. Rte. 2] 207/824–4224 or 800/533–3607 www.betheloutdooradventure.com*) rents canoes, kayaks, and bikes; guides fishing, kayak, and canoe trips; and operates a hostel and riverside campground.

DOG SLEDDING

Mahoosuc Guide Service (*1513 Bear River Rd. [Rte. 26], Newry 207/824–2073 www.mahoosuc.com*) leads day and multiday dogsledding expeditions on the Maine–New Hampshire border, as well as canoeing trips. Its **Mahoosuc Mountain Lodge** (*www.mahoosucmountainlodge.com*) has dorm and B&B lodging.

MULTI-SPORT OUTFITTERS

Sun Valley Sports (*129 Sunday River Rd. 207/824–7533 or 877/851–7533 www.sunvalleysports.com*) has snowmobile rentals and guided tours. It also operates fly-fishing trips, canoe and kayak rentals, guided ATV tours, and moose and wildlife safaris.

Carter's Cross-Country Ski Center (*786 Intervale Rd. 207/824–3880 or 207/539–4848 www.cartersxcski.com*) has 33 mi of trails for all levels of skiers, lessons, and rentals—snowshoes, skis, and sleds to pull children are available. It also rents rooms and ski-in cabins.

What was once a sleepy little ski area with minimal facilities has evolved into a sprawling resort that attracts skiers from as far away as Europe. Spread throughout the valley at **Sunday River** (*15 S. Ridge Rd., turn on Sunday River Rd. from U.S. 2, Newry 207/824–3000 main number, 207/824–5200 snow conditions, 800/543–2754 reservations www.sundayriver.com*) are three base areas, two condominium hotels, trailside condominiums, town houses, and a ski dorm. Sunday River is home to the Maine Handicapped Skiing program, which provides lessons and services for skiers with disabilities. Rentals, lessons, children's programs, day care, and slope-side dining are all here, too; 16 lifts service 132 trails and four terrain parks. There's plenty else to do, including cross-country skiing, ice-skating, tubing, and, come summer and fall, hiking, mountain biking, and scenic lift rides.

Family-friendly **Mt. Abram Ski Resort** (*308 Howe Hill Rd., turn off Route 26 Greenwood 207/875–5000 www.skimtabram.com*), south of

One of the Rangetey Lakes, Mooselookmeguntic is said mean "portage to the moose feeding place" in the Abenaki language.

Bethel, has 44 trails, five lifts, two base lodges, glade areas, and night skiing on the first Saturday of the month.

WHERE TO STAY

$–$$ **Victoria Inn.** It's hard to miss this turreted inn in downtown Bethel, with its teal, mauve, and beige exterior and attached carriage house topped with a cupola. Inside, Victorian details include ceiling rosettes, stained-glass windows, elaborate fireplace mantels, and gleaming oak trim. Guest rooms vary in size (suites sleep three to eight); most are furnished with reproductions of antiques. The dinner-only restaurant ($–$$) has won acclaim with entrées like rack of lamb with basil and mint pesto and duck with pomegranate sauce. **Pros:** lots of breakfast choices; homemade cookies in your room; 10% discount on dinner. **Cons:** some rooms are dated; lofts in suites lack decor. ✉ *32 Main St.* ☎ *207/824–8060 or 888/774–1235* 🌐 *www.thevictoria-inn.com* *9 rooms, 4 suites* *In-room: Wi-Fi (some). In-hotel: restaurant, Wi-Fi hotspot* *AE, D, MC, V* *BP.*

EN ROUTE

The routes north from Bethel to the Rangeley district are all scenic, particularly in autumn when the maples are aflame with color. In the town of Newry, make a short detour to the **Artist's Bridge** (turn off Highway 26 onto Sunday River Road and drive about 4 mi), the most painted and photographed of Maine's eight covered bridges. Highway 26 continues north to the gorges and waterfalls of **Grafton Notch State Park.** Continue to Upton, but drive carefully and keep a lookout: this 10-mi stretch is one of Maine's moose alleys. At Errol, New Hampshire Highway 16 will return you east around the north shore of Mooselookmeguntic Lake, through Oquossoc, and into Rangeley.

RANGELEY

67 mi north of Bethel.

Rangeley, on the north side of Rangeley Lake on Highways 4 and 16, has long lured anglers and winter-sports enthusiasts to its more than 40 lakes and ponds and 450 square mi of woodlands. Equally popular in summer or winter, Rangeley has a rough, wilderness feel to it.

GETTING HERE AND AROUND

To reach Rangeley on a scenic drive, take Route 17 north from U.S. 2 to Route 16/Route 4, then head east. Route 16 continues east to Kingfield and Sugarloaf ski resort.

ESSENTIALS

Vacation Rentals **Morton & Furbish Vacation Rentals** (✉ *2478 Main St., Rangeley* ☎ *207/864–9065 or 888/218–4882* 🌐 *www.rangeleyrentals.com*)

Visitor Information **Rangeley Lakes Region Chamber of Commerce** (✉ *6 Park Dr.* ☎ *207/864–5571 or 800/685–2537* 🌐 *www.rangeleymaine.com*).

SPORTS AND THE OUTDOORS

Rangeley Lake State Park. On the south shore of Rangeley Lake, this park has superb lakeside scenery, swimming, picnic tables, a boat ramp, showers, and 50 campsites. ✉ *S. Shore Dr., off Rte. 17 or Rte. 4, Rangeley Plantation* ☎ *207/624–6080, 207/864–3858 May 15–Oct. 1 only* 🌐 *www.state.me.us/doc/parks* 🎫 *$4.50* ⏲ *May 15–Oct. 1, daily 8–8 or dusk, if earlier.*

BOATING AND FISHING

Rangeley and Mooselookmeguntic lakes are good for canoeing, sailing, fishing, and motorboating. Several outfits rent equipment and provide guide service if needed. Fishing for brook trout and salmon is at its best in May, June, and September; the Rangeley area is especially popular with fly-fishers.

GOLF

Mingo Springs Golf Course (✉ *Country Club Rd.* ☎ *207/864–5021* 🌐 *www.mingosprings.com*) is known for its mountain and water views as well as challenging play on its 18-hole course. Green fees start at $32.

SEAPLANES

Acadian Seaplanes (✉ *2640 Main St.* ☎ *207/864–5307 or 207/252–6630* 🌐 *www.acadianseaplane.com*) provides transportation to remote lodges as well as scenic flights above Rangeley and environs. It also does fly-ins to watch moose in the wild and dine-and-flys to a sporting lodge.

SKI AREAS

Rangeley Lakes Trail Center (✉ *524 Saddleback Mountain Rd., Dallas* ☎ *207/864–4309* 🌐 *www.xcskirangeley.com*) rents cross-country skis and snowshoes and has about 30 mi of groomed trails surrounding Saddleback Mountain. The snack bar is open in the winter, and you can hike, mountain bike, and run on the trails in warmer weather.

A family atmosphere prevails at **Saddleback Maine** (✉ *976 Saddleback Mountain Rd., follow signs from Rte. 4, Dallas* ☎ *207/864–5671 or 866/918–2225; 207/864–5441 or 877/864–5441 reservations* 🌐 *www.saddlebackmaine.com*), where the quiet, lack of crowds, and spectacularly wide valley views draw return visitors. The 66 trails and glades, accessed by five lifts, are divided among 38% novice, 29% intermediate, and 33% advanced. A fieldstone fireplace anchors the post-and-beam base lodge. You can also find a day-care center, ski school, rental and retail shop, and trailside condominium lodging on-site. Hiking (the Appalachian Trail crosses Saddleback's summit ridge), mountain biking, canoeing, kayaking, fly-fishing, moose tours, and birding are big draws in warm weather, as are music concerts, which continue in winter.

WHERE TO EAT AND STAY

$–$$ AMERICAN **Gingerbread House Restaurant.** A big fieldstone fireplace, well-spaced tables, wrap-around deck, and antique marble soda fountain, all with views of the woods beyond, make for comfortable surroundings inside what really looks like a giant gingerbread house. Breakfast, lunch, and dinner are served; you can also get baked goods to go. Soups, salads, and sandwiches at lunch give way to entrées such as Maine crab cakes and barbecued ribs with blueberry chipotle sauce and maple syrup. ✉ *55 Carry Rd. (Rte. 4), Oquossoc* ☎ *207/864–3602* 🌐 *gingerbreadhouserestaurant.net* ▭ *AE, D, MC, V* ⏲ *Closed Nov. and Apr.; and Mon. and Tues., Dec.–Mar. No lunch or dinner Sun., mid-Sept.–mid-June (except on holiday weeks and weekends).*

$–$$ **Country Club Inn.** Built in 1920 as the country club for the adjacent Mingo Springs Golf Course, this secluded hilltop retreat has sweeping lake and mountain views. Two fireplaces anchor the lodge-like living room, which has a cathedral ceiling. The cozy, low-ceilinged wood-paneled bar opens to a room with a pool table and lake-view deck. Rooms downstairs in the main building and in the adjacent 1950s motel are cheerfully, if minimally, decorated. The glassed-in dining room serves burgers and salads—as well as entrées like veal Gruyère and roast duck Montmorency. **Pros:** loads of lawn and board games; lots of photos of Rangeley's long-gone resorts. **Cons:** smallish rooms in main building. ✉ *56 Country Club Rd.* ☎ *207/864–3831* 🌐 *www.countryclubinnrangeley.com* *19 rooms* *In-room: no a/c, no TV, refrigerator (some), Wi-Fi (some). In-hotel: restaurant, bar, pool, Internet terminal, Wi-Fi hotspot, some pets allowed* ▭ *AE, D, MC, V* ⏲ *Closed Nov. and Apr.* *EP, BP, MAP.*

¢–$ **Rangeley Inn and Motor Lodge.** From Main Street you see only the large three-story blue inn, built in the early 1900s for wealthy urbanites on vacation. Set back behind it is a motel with decks or terraces on most rooms and views of Haley Pond, the large lawn, and a garden. No two rooms are alike in the main inn, where the many antique furnishings include brass beds and oak dressers and headboards. Some of the larger rooms have a queen bed and two twins. Some baths are marble, some have claw-foot tubs, and some have whirlpool tubs. **Pros:** historic hotel last of its kind in the region; in motel, all rooms have refrigerators, some have woodstoves, and some have microwaves. **Cons:** dining room breakfast buffet only on weekends. ✉ *2443 Main St., 04970* ☎ *207/864–3341 or 800/666–3687* 🌐 *www.rangeleyinn.com* *35 inn rooms, 15 motel rooms (including 1 suite)* *In-room: no a/c (some), refrigerator (some). In-hotel: restaurant, some pets allowed* ▭ *D, MC, V* ⏲ *Closed Apr., May, Nov., and Dec.*

CLOSE UP

Whoopie Pies

"The whoopie pie would probably be Maine's state dessert, if the state had one," said the *New York Times*, and funny enough, there's actually a movement to put that official stamp on this regional confection. Spend a few days anywhere in Maine and you'll notice just how popular the treat is. Whoopie pies can be found in groceries, bakeries, cafés, and convenience stores, often and piled high near the cash register.

The name is misleading: it's a pie only in the sense of a having a filling between two "crusts"—namely, a thick layer of sugary frosting sandwiched between two saucers of rich chocolate cake. It's said to have Pennsylvania Dutch roots and may have acquired its distinctive moniker from the jubilant yelp farmers emitted after discovering it in their lunchboxes, and it has been satisfying Maine's sweet tooth for decades. **Labadies Bakery** (✉ *161 Lincoln St.* ☎ *207/784–7042* 🌐 *www.labadiesbakery.com*) in Lewiston boasts 85 years of baking whoopie pies (which, over time, have grown from whoopie to whopping: they top out at 16 inches in diameter!).

Typically, the filling is buttercream, but some places still make it with shortening, and others scoop a dollop of marshmallow fluff between the layers of cake. Many bakers have indulged the temptation to experiment with flavors and ingredients, particularly in the filling, yielding pumpkin, raspberry, oatmeal cream, red velvet, peanut butter, and more different kinds of whoopie pies.

Where to find the best classic whoopie pies in Maine is, perhaps predictably, a point of contention. The bigger producers certainly have devotees and include Labadies, which ships its pies of all sizes across the country. The treats from **Wicked Whoopies** (✉ *621 Maine Ave., Farmingdale* ☎ *207/622–8860* ✉ *32 Main St., Freeport* ☎ *207/865–3100* 🌐 *www.wickedwhoopies.com*) are stocked in supermarkets and Rite Aid stores. **Cranberry Island Kitchen** (✉ *7 Corey Rd., Cumberland Center* ☎ *207/829–5200* 🌐 *www.cranberryislandkitchen.com*) supplies Williams-Sonoma with the confections.

Smaller, more eccentric bakers have received accolades for their whoopie pies, too: **Friars' Bakehouse** (✉ *21 Central St.* ☎ *207/947–3770*) was voted to have the best in the Bangor area by respondents to a *Bangor Daily News* poll. The bakery, run by two Franciscan friars, one of whom spent time in highly regarded culinary programs. **Moody's Diner** (✉ *1885 Atlantic Hwy., Waldoboro* ☎ *207/832–7785*) makes pies of considerable size, prized for their filling above all. **Two Fat Cats Bakery** (✉ *47 India St., Portland* ☎ *207/347–5144* 🌐 *www.twofatcatsbakery.com*) has whoopie pies that are more delicately proportioned, with a smooth and light filling reminiscent of Italian buttercream, and a conservative hand with flavors—no peanut-butter-mint-chocolate-chip pies to be found here. The old family-friendly standby **Governor's Restaurant Old Town** (✉ *963 Stillwater Ave, Old Town* ☎ *207/827–7630* 🌐 *governorsrestaurant.com*) is famed for its peanut butter pies as well as the old reliable standard and can accommodate special flavor combinations by request.

—Michael de Zayas

KINGFIELD

33 mi east of Rangeley, 15 mi west of Phillips.

In the shadows of Mt. Abram and Sugarloaf Mountain, Kingfield has everything a "real" New England town should have: a general store, historic inns, and white clapboard churches. Sugarloaf has golf and tennis in summer.

ESSENTIALS

Visitor Information **Sugarloaf Area Chamber of Commerce** (🌐 *www.sugarloafchamber.org*).

SPORTS AND THE OUTDOORS

SKI AREAS ★ Abundant natural snow, a huge mountain, and the only above-tree-line lift-service skiing in the East have made **Sugarloaf** (✉ *5092 Access Rd., Carrabassett Valley* ☎ *207/237–2000, 207/237–6808 snow conditions, 800/843–5623 reservations* 🌐 *www.sugarloaf.com)* one of Maine's best-known ski areas with 16 lifts and 138 trails and glades. Two slope-side hotels and hundreds of slope-side condominiums provide ski-in, ski-out access, and the base village has restaurants and shops. The Outdoor Center has more than 60 mi of cross-country ski trails as well as snowshoeing, snow tubing, and ice-skating. There's also plenty for the kids, from day care to special events. Once you are here, a car is unnecessary—a shuttle connects all mountain operations. Summer is much quieter than winter, but you can bike, fish, and hike, plus golf at the superb 18-hole, Robert Trent Jones Jr.–designed golf course ($69–$79 with cart, cost varies by season).

THE NORTH WOODS

Moosehead Lake, the four-season resort town of Greenville, Baxter State Park, and the Allagash Wilderness Waterway are dispersed within Maine's remote North Woods. This vast area in the north-central section of the state is best experienced by canoe or raft; via hiking, snowshoe, or snowmobile; or on a fishing trip. Maine's largest lake, Moosehead supplies more in the way of rustic camps, guides, and outfitters than any other northern locale. Its 420 mi of shorefront, three-quarters of which is owned by lumber companies or the state, is virtually uninhabited.

GREENVILLE

160 mi northeast of Portland; 71 mi northwest of Bangor.

Greenville, the largest town on Moosehead Lake, is an outdoors lover's paradise. Boating, fishing, and hiking are popular in summer, while snowmobiling, skiing, and ice fishing reign in winter. The town also has the greatest selection of shops, restaurants, and inns in the region—note that some are closed mid-October to mid-May.

GETTING HERE AND AROUND

To reach Greenville from Interstate 95, get off at Exit 157 in Newport and head north, successively, on Routes 7, 23, and 15.

DID YOU KNOW?

Mount Katahdin's summit—the end of the Appalachian Trail—can be reached by several routes, including the white-blazed Hunt Trail (officially part of the AT), the rocky Cathedral Trail, or the precarious Knife Edge Trail.

The North Woods
CANADA
QUÉBEC
CANADA
NEW BRUNSWICK
Madawaska
Fort Kent
Van Buren
Allagash
Dirt
Allagash River
Allagash Wilderness Waterway
Umsakis Lake
Saint John River
Caribou
Fort Fairfield
Presque Isle
Ashland
Squapan
Sebois
Priestly Lake
Churchill Lake
Allagash Lake
Eagle Lake
Munsungan Lake
Millinocket Lake
Grand Lake Sebois
Chamberlain Lake
Round Lake
Knowles Corner
Grand Lake Matagamon
Loon Lake
Gero Island
Baxter State Park
Smyrna Mills
Houlton
Chesuncook Lake
Patten
Island Falls
Mt. Katahdin
Ripogenus Dam
Sherman
Penobscot R.
Lobster Lake
Grindstone
Pemadumcook Lake
Rockwood
Kokadjo
Appalachian Trail
Millinocket
Danforth
Ragged Lake
Medway
Macwahoc
Moosehead Lake
Indian Pond
Gulf Hagas
Greenville
Big Squaw Mountain Resort
Seboeis Lake
Springfield
Brownville Junction
Lincoln
Moxie Pond
Sebec Lake
Monson
Milo
West Endfield
Dover-Foxcroft
Guilford
Lagrange
Passadumkeag
0 10 km

ESSENTIALS

Vacation Rentals Northwoods Camp Rentals (✉ *14 Lakeview St.,* ☎ *800/251–8042* 🌐 *www.mooseheadrentals.com).*

Visitor Information Moosehead Lake Region Chamber of Commerce (✉ *Indian Hills Plaza, 156 Moosehead Lake Rd., Greenville* ☎ *207/695–2702 or 888/876–2778* 🌐 *www.mooseheadlake.org).*

OFF THE BEATEN PATH

Mt. Kineo. Once a thriving summer resort for the wealthy, the Mount Kineo House was accessed primarily by steamship. The resort was torn down around 1940, but Kineo still makes a pleasant day trip. You can take the Kineo Shuttle, which departs from the State Dock in **Rockwood,** or rent a motorboat in Rockwood and make the journey across the lake in about 15 minutes. It's an easy hike to Kineo's summit for awesome views down the lake. A map is available at the Moosehead Lake Region Chamber of Commerce.

4

SPORTS AND THE OUTDOORS

Lily Bay State Park. Nine miles northeast of Greenville on Moosehead Lake, this park has a good swimming beach, a 2-mi walking trail with water views, two boat-launching ramps, and two campgrounds with 90 sites. ✉ *13 Myrle's Way, off Lily Bay Rd., Beaver Cove* ☎ *207/941–4014, 207/695–2700 mid-May–mid-Oct. only* 🌐 *www.parksandlands.com* 🎫 *$4.50* ⏲ *May 15–Oct. 15, daily 9–sunset.*

BIKING Mountain biking is popular in the Greenville area, but bikes are not allowed on some logging roads. Expect to pay about $25 per day to rent a bicycle. **Northwoods Outfitters** (✉ *5 Lily Bay Rd., Greenville* ☎ *207/695–3288* 🌐 *www.maineoutfitter.com*) rents mountain bikes, kids' bikes, and more.

FISHING Togue (lake trout), landlocked salmon, smallmouth bass, and brook trout lure thousands of anglers to the region from ice-out in mid-May until September; the hardiest return in winter to ice fish.

SEAPLANES **Currier's Flying Service** (✉ *Greenville Junction* ☎ *207/695–2778* 🌐 *www.curriersflyingservice.com*) offers sightseeing flights over the Moosehead Lake region.

RAFTING The Kennebec and Dead rivers and the west branch of the Penobscot River provide thrilling white-water rafting. These rivers are dam-controlled, so day and multiday guided trips run rain or shine daily from mid-April to mid-October. Many rafting outfitters operate resort facilities in their base towns. *See the Outdoor Activities section for more information.*

TOURS ★ ***Katahdin.*** The Moosehead Marine Museum runs three- and five-hour trips on Moosehead Lake aboard the *Katahdin,* a 115-foot 1914 steamship converted to diesel. Also called *The Kate,* the ship carried passengers to Mt. Kineo until 1938 and then was used in the logging industry until 1975. Trips range in price from $32 to $37. The boat and the free shore-side museum have displays about the steamships that transported people and cargo on the lake more than 100 years ago. ✉ *12 Lily Bay Rd.* ☞ *Board on shoreline by museum* ☎ *207/695–2716* 🌐 *www.katahdincruises.com* ⏲ *June–early Oct.*

OFF THE BEATEN PATH

Gulf Hagas. In a *very* remote area accessed by gravel roads, a hiking trail leads from Katahdin Iron Works Road to the east end of Gulf Hagas, a National Natural Landmark with chasms, cliffs, six large waterfalls, pools, exotic flora, and rock formations. Slippery rocks make for difficult hiking along the gorge rim. Hiking from either of the two parking areas to the gorge and around a loop that includes the rim trail is an 8-mi, all-day affair. Or you can hike to the first waterfall en route and then back to the parking lot. It's about 3 mi roundtrip from the Upper Gulf Parking Area (set to open in spring 2010) to Stairs Falls on the gorge's west end. You must ford the Pleasant River near the outset of the trail from the Gulf Hagas Parking Area, which leads to the gorge's east end. This is easily done in summer when the water (about 150 feet wide) is knee-deep, but use extra caution in spring or after heavy rains, when the river is swifter and deeper. The Hermitage, a rare patch of old-growth pine, rises beyond the waterway. It's a 3-mi roundtrip from this parking area to Screw Auger Falls, Gulf Hagas's most spectacular drop. **North Maine Woods** (☎ *207/435–6213* 🌐 *www.northmainewoods.org*) manages the private gravel roads to this very isolated area—yield to logging trucks. Fees are charged at checkpoints (sometimes closed in April, late October, and November), where you can buy trail maps. From Greenville, take Pleasant Street east (road becomes gravel) 11 mi to the Hedgehog checkpoint, follow signs to the Upper Gulf Parking Area (2½ mi) or the Gulf Hagas Parking Area (about 6½ mi). From Millinocket, take Route 11 south about 32 mi to the Katahdin Iron Works Road sign, continue 7 mi on dirt road to the Katahdin Iron Works checkpoint, follow signs to the Gulf Hagas Parking Area (about 7 mi) or the Upper Gulf Parking Area (about 12 mi).

WHERE TO STAY

$$$$ ★ **Blair Hill Inn.** Beautiful gardens and a hilltop location with marvelous views over the lake distinguish this 1891 estate, as do fine antiques, plush bedding, and elegant baths, some with oversize or claw-foot tubs. Guest rooms are spacious; all have sitting areas and four have fireplaces. A restaurant (reservations required) serves a prix-fixe five-course dinner ($$$$) Thursday through Saturday from mid-June to mid-October. Arrive early to enjoy cocktails on the wraparound porch or the swank bar area connected to it. The inn hosts a music series in July and August. **Pros:** third-floor deck the length of the inn; 15 acres with stone paths, wooded picnic area, and trout pond; flowers from gardens in rooms. **Cons:** no direct lake access; long, steep drive. ✉ *351 Lily Bay Rd., Box 1288 04441* ☎ *207/695–0224* 🌐 *www.blairhill.com* *7 rooms, 1 suite* *In-room: no phone, a/c (some), Wi-Fi. In-hotel: restaurant, Internet terminal, Wi-Fi hotspot* *D, MC, V* *Closed Apr. and Nov.* *BP.*

$$$ **Little Lyford Lodge and Cabins.** When you want to get away from everything, head to this rustic wilderness retreat on 37,000 acres of conservation land, part of the Appalachian Mountain Club's lodging network. Moose are abundant, and the fly-fishing, snowshoeing, hiking (Gulf Hagas is nearby), and backcountry skiing are excellent. Well-maintained cabins from an 1870s logging camp that was later a sporting camp have woodstoves and gas lights. Home-cooked fare is served family-style in the main lodge. The 1980s addition, like the bathhouse, has

mostly solar-powered lighting. **Pros:** woodsy getaway; family adventure camps in summer; cedar sauna in winter. **Cons:** winter access is by cross-country ski or snowmobile transport (for a fee); few indoor amenities. ✉ *About 16 mi east of Greenville, access via logging roads* ☎ *603/466-2727* 🌐 *www.outdoors.org/mainelodges* *10 cabins, 8-bed bunkhouse* *In-room: no phone, no a/c, no TV. In-hotel: water sports* *AE, MC, V* *Closed Apr.–early May and Nov.–late Dec.* *FAP.*

MILLINOCKET

67 mi north of Bangor, 88 mi northwest of Greenville via Routes 6 and 11.

Millinocket, a paper-mill town with a population of about 4,000, is a gateway to Baxter State Park and Maine's North Woods. Although it has a smattering of motels and restaurants, Millinocket is the place to stock up on supplies, fill your gas tank, or grab a hot meal or shower before heading into the wilderness. Numerous rafting and canoeing outfitters and guides are based here.

GETTING HERE AND AROUND

From Interstate 95, take Route 157 (Exit 244) northwest to Millinocket and nearby Baxter State Park.

ESSENTIALS

Vacation Rentals **Baxter's 4 Season Vacation Rentals** (✉ *973 Central St.* ☎ *207/723-9746* 🌐 *www.baxtersedge.com*).

Visitor Information **Katahdin Area Chamber of Commerce** (✉ *1029 Central St., Millinocket* ☎ *207/723-4443* 🌐 *www.katahdinmaine.com*).

SPORTS AND THE OUTDOORS

★ **Allagash Wilderness Waterway.** A spectacular 92-mi corridor of lakes and rivers, the waterway cuts across 170,000 acres of wilderness beginning at the northwest corner of Baxter State Park and running north to the town of Allagash, 10 mi from the Canadian border. From mid-May to October, this is prime canoeing and camping country, but it should not be undertaken lightly. The complete 92-mi course requires 7 to 10 days. The best bet for a novice is to go with a guide; a good outfitter will help plan your route and provide your craft and transportation. This waterway is just part of the 740-mi **Northern Forest Canoe Trail** (🌐 *www.northernforestcanoetrail.org*), which runs from New York to Québec. ✉ *Maine Bureau of Parks and Lands, 106 Hogan Rd., Bangor* ☎ *207/941-4014* 🌐 *www.parksandlands.com.*

Fodor's Choice ★ **Baxter State Park.** A gift from Governor Percival Baxter, this is the jewel in the crown of northern Maine, a 209,501-acre wilderness area that surrounds **Mt. Katahdin,** Maine's highest mountain (5,267 feet at Baxter Peak) and the terminus of the Appalachian Trail. Katahdin draws thousands of hikers every year for the daylong climb to the summit and the stunning views of woods, mountains, and lakes. Three trailheads lead to its peak; some routes include the hair-raising Knife Edge Ridge. The crowds climbing Katahdin can be formidable on clear summer days, so if you crave solitude, tackle one of the 45 other mountains in the park, 17 of which exceed an elevation of 3,000 feet and all of which are accessible from an extensive network of trails. South Turner can be climbed in a morning (if you're fit), and its summit has a great view of Katahdin across the valley. On the way you'll pass Sandy Stream Pond, where moose are often seen at dusk. The Owl, the Brothers, and Doubletop Mountain are good day hikes. **TIP→ Reserve a day-use parking space at the Katahdin trailheads if you plan to hike the mountain between May 15 and October 15.** Check the park Web site for information about this new system; without a reservation you may have to hike elsewhere in the park. Call the hiking hotline (☎ *207/723–4636*) for next-day weather and other seasonal hiking information. No pets, domestic animals, oversize vehicles, radios, all-terrain vehicles, motorboats, or motorcycles are allowed in the park, and there are no pay phones, gas stations, stores, running water, or electricity. The camping is primitive, and sites typically fill up well ahead for peak season. The visitor center is at the southern entrance outside Millinocket. You can also get information about Baxter in town at park headquarters. ✉ *Headquarters: 64 Balsam Dr., Millinocket Togue Pond Gate (southern entrance): Rte. 157, 18 mi northwest of Millinocket; Matagamon Gate (northern entrance): Grand Lake Rd., 26 mi northwest of Patten via Rte. 159 and Grand Lake Rd.* ☎ *207/723–5140* 🌐 *www.baxterstateparkauthority.com* *$13 per vehicle (free to Maine residents)* ⏲ *Daily, sunrise to sunset.*

SEAPLANES **Katahdin Air Service** (✉ *Millinocket* ☎ *207/723–8378* 🌐 *www.katahdinair.com*). Katahdin Air Service offers charter flights by seaplane from points throughout Maine to smaller towns and remote lake and forest areas. It can help you find a guide and also does scenic flights over the Katahdin area.

WHERE TO STAY

CAMPING **$$–$$$** **Baxter State Park Authority.** Camping spaces at the park's 10 primitive campgrounds must be reserved by mail or in person (check or cash) within four months of your trip or by phone (MC or V only) two weeks prior. Phone reservations are much harder to come by for July, August, and fall weekends, but cancellations do open up spots. There are also additional primitive backcountry sites. **Pros:** cabins at Daicey Pond and Kidney Pond campgrounds; great base for hiking. **Cons:** must reserve far ahead; winter access is by ski or snowshoe; no electricity or running water. ✉ *Headquarters: 64 Balsam Dr., Millinocket Togue Pond Gate (southern entrance): Hwy. 157, 18 mi northwest of Millinocket; Matagamon Gate (northern entrance): Grand Lake Rd., 26 mi northwest of Patten via Rte. 159 and Grand Lake Rd.* ☎ *207/723–5140* 🌐 *www.baxterstateparkauthority.com* *22 cabins, 4 bunkhouses, 57 lean-tos, 75 tent sites, 13 group tent sites* *Pit toilets, fire grates, fire rings, picnic tables, ranger stations, swimming (pond, lake, stream)* *MC, V* ⏲ *Closed mid-Oct.–Nov. and Apr.–mid-May.*

5

Maine Coast

WORD OF MOUTH

"Rent bikes in Bar Harbor and plan your route to include popovers at [Acadia National Park's] Jordan Pond. It's a beautiful ride."

—cindyj

"We finally got to Monhegan [Island]. . . . We just enjoyed taking a picnic lunch and binoculars and finding a place to sit on the rocks."

—dfrostnh

WELCOME TO MAINE COAST

TOP REASONS TO GO

★ **Perfection on a Bun:** It's not a Maine vacation without sampling the "lobster roll," lobster with a touch of mayo nestled in a buttery grilled hot-dog bun.

★ **Boating:** The coastline of Maine was made for boaters. Whether it's your own boat, a friend's or a charter, make sure you get out on the water.

★ **Wild Maine Blueberries:** They may be tiny, but the wild blueberries pack a flavorful punch in season (late July to early September).

★ **Cadillac Mountain:** Drive the winding 3½-mi road to the 1,530-foot summit in Acadia National Park for the sunrise.

★ **Perfect Souvenir:** Buy a watercolor, hand-painted pottery, or a handcrafted jewelry—artists and craftspeople abound.

★ **Ice Cream:** Summer in Maine means ice cream. Dig into a pint of Gifford's or stop by a homemade ice cream stand: you can't go wrong.

1 The Southern Coast. Stretching north from Kittery to just outside Portland, this is Maine's most-visited region. The towns along the shore and miles of sandy expanses cater to summer visitors. Old Orchard Beach and York Beach feature Coney Island–like amusements, while Kittery, the Yorks, and the Kennebunks are more low key getaways.

2 Portland. Maine's largest and most cosmopolitan city, Portland balances its historic role as a working harbor with its newer identity as a center of sophisticated arts and shopping, and innovative restaurants.

3 The Mid-Coast Region. North of Portland, from Brunswick to Monhegan Island, the craggy coastline winds its way around pastoral peninsulas. Its villages boast maritime museums, antiques shops, and beautiful architecture.

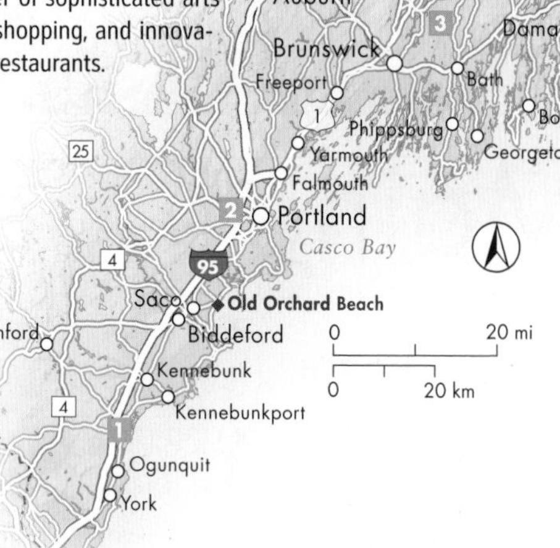

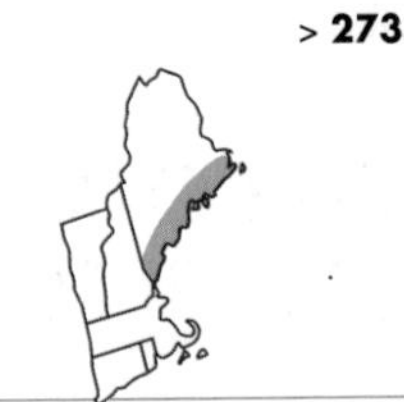

Old Town
Newport
Bangor
9
179
193
182
191
1
Lubec
7
Columbia Falls
Machias
Cherryfield
Jonesport
Hancock
Beals Island
Ellsworth
West Gouldsboro
Belfast
Searsport
Bar Harbor
5
6
Cadillac Mtn.
Islesboro
Blue Hill Peninsula
Mt. Desert Island
Frenchman Bay
Atlantic Ocean
4
Deer Isle Village
ACADIA NAT'L PARK
Camden
Stonington
Rockland
Thomaston
Isle au Haut
Penobscot Bay

GETTING ORIENTED

Much of the appeal of the Maine Coast lies in its geographical contrasts, from its long stretches of swimming and walking beaches in the south to the cliff-edged, rugged rocky coasts in the north. And not unlike the physical differences of the coast, each town along the way reveals a slightly different character.

4 Penobscot Bay. This region combines lively coastal towns with dramatic natural scenery. Camden is one of Maine's most picture-perfect towns, with its pointed church steeples, antique homes, and historic windjammer fleet.

5 Blue Hill Peninsula. Art galleries are plentiful here, and the entire region is ideal for biking, hiking, kayaking, and boating. For many, the peninsula defines the silent beauty of the Maine Coast.

6 Acadia National Park and Mount Desert Island. Millions come to enjoy Acadia National Park's stunning peaks and vistas of the island's mountains. Bar Harbor is more of a visitor's haven, while Southwest Harbor and Bass Harbor offer quieter retreats.

7 Way Down East. This is the "real" Maine, some say, and it unfurls in thousands of acres of wild blueberry barrens, congestion-free coastlines, and a tangible sense of rugged endurance.

MAINE COAST PLANNER

When to Go

Maine's dramatic coastline and pure natural beauty welcome visitors year-round, but note that many smaller museums and attractions are open only for high season—from Memorial Day to mid-October—as are many of the waterside attractions and eateries.

Summer begins in earnest on July 4, and many smaller inns and hotels from Kittery on up to the Bar Harbor region fill up early on weekends. Fall, with its fiery foliage, is when many inns and hotels are booked months in advance by leaf-peeping visitors. After Halloween, hotel rates drop significantly until ski season begins around Thanksgiving. Along the coast, bed-and-breakfasts that remain open will often rent rooms at far lower prices than in summer.

In spring, the third Sunday in March is designated as Maine Maple Sunday, and farms throughout the state open their doors to visitors not only to watch sap turn into golden syrup but to sample the sweet results.

Getting Here and Around

Maine has two major international airports, Portland International Jetport and Bangor International Airport, to get you to or close to your coastal destination. Manchester-Boston Regional Airport in New Hampshire is about 45 minutes away from the southern end of the Maine coastline. Boston's Logan Airport is the only truly international airport in the region; it's about 90 minutes south of the Maine border.

Amtrak offers regional service from Boston to Portland via its Downeaster line that originates at Boston's North Station and makes four stops in Maine: Wells, Saco, Old Orchard Beach (seasonal), and finally Portland. Greyhound and Concord Trailways also offer bus service from Boston to many towns along the Maine coast.

All that said, once you are here the best way to experience the winding back roads of the craggy Maine coast is in a car. There are miles and miles of roads far from the larger towns that no bus services, and you won't want to miss discovering your own favorite ocean vista while on a scenic drive.

Planning Your Time

You could easily spend a lifetime's worth of vacations along the Maine Coast and never truly see it all. But if you are determined to travel the coast from end to end, allot at least two weeks to travel comfortably.

Driving in Coastal Maine

	MILES	TIME
Boston–Portland	108	2 hours
Kittery–Portland	50	50 minutes
Portland–Freeport	17	20 minutes
Portland–Camden	80	2 hours
Portland–Bar Harbor	175	3 hours, 20 minutes

About the Restaurants

Many breakfast spots along the coast open as early as 6 AM to serve the going-to-work crowd. Lunch generally runs 11–2:30; dinner is usually served 5–9. Only in the larger cities will you find full dinners being offered much later than 9, although you can usually find a bar or bistro serving a limited menu late into the evening.

Many restaurants in Maine are closed Monday, though this isn't true in resort areas in high season. However, resort-town eateries often shut down completely in the off-season. Unless otherwise noted, restaurants in this guide are open daily for lunch and dinner.

Credit cards are accepted for meals throughout Maine, even in some of the most modest establishments.

The one signature dinner on the Maine Coast is, of course, the lobster dinner. It generally includes boiled lobster, a clam or seafood chowder, corn on the cob, and coleslaw or perhaps a salad. Lobster prices vary from day to day, but generally a full lobster dinner should cost around $25; without all the add-ons, about $18.

About the Hotels

Beachfront and roadside motels and historic-home B&Bs make up the majority of accommodation options along the Maine Coast. There are a few large luxury resorts, such as the Samoset Resort in Rockport or the Bar Harbor Inn in Bar Harbor, but most accommodations are simple and relatively inexpensive. Many properties close during the off-season—mid-October until mid-May; some that stay open drop their rates dramatically. There is a 7% state hospitality tax on all room rates.

WHAT IT COSTS

	¢	$	$$	$$$	$$$$
Restaurants	under $8	$8–$12	$13–$20	$21–$28	over $28
Hotels	under $80	$80–$120	$121–$170	$171–$220	over $220
Campgrounds	under $10	$10–$17	$18–$35	$36–$50	over $50

Restaurant prices are per person, for a main course at dinner. Hotel prices are for a standard double room during peak season and not including tax or gratuities. Some inns add a 15% service charge.

Outdoor Activities

No visit to the Maine Coast is complete without some outdoor activity—be it generated by two wheels, two feet, two paddles, or pulling a bag full of clubs.

Bicycling: The Bicycle Coalition of Maine (☎ *207/623–4511* 🌐 *www.bikemaine.org*) and **Explore Maine by Bike** (☎ *207/624–3300* 🌐 *www.exploremaine.org/bike*) are both excellent sources for trail maps and other riding information, including where to rent bikes.

Hiking: Exploring the Maine coast on foot is a quick way to acclimate to the relaxed pace of life here. **Healthy Maine Walks** (🌐 *www.healthymainewalks.com*) has comprehensive listings for quick jaunts as well as more involved hikes.

Kayaking: Nothing gets you literally off the beaten path like plying the salt waters in a graceful sea kayak. **Members of the Maine Association of Sea Kayaking Guides and Instructors** (🌐 *www.maineseakayakguides.com*) offer instructional classes and guided tours, plan trips, and rent equipment. More seasoned paddlers can get maps of Maine's famous sea trails system at the **Maine Island Trails Association** (☎ *207/761–8225* 🌐 *www.mita.org*).

5

As you drive across the border into Maine, a sign announces: THE WAY LIFE SHOULD BE. Romantics luxuriate in the feeling of a down comforter on a yellow pine bed or in the sensation of the wind and salt spray on their faces while cruising in a historic windjammer. Families love the unspoiled beaches and safe inlets dotting the shoreline. Hikers are revived while roaming the trails of Acadia National Park, and adventure seekers kayak along the coast.

The Maine Coast is several places in one. Portland may be Maine's largest metropolitan area, but its attitude is decidedly more big town than small city. South of Portland, Ogunquit, Kennebunkport, Old Orchard Beach, and other resort towns predominate along a reasonably smooth shoreline. North of Portland and Casco Bay, secondary roads turn south off U.S. 1 onto so many oddly chiseled peninsulas that it's possible to drive for days without retracing your route. Slow down to explore the museums, galleries, and shops in the larger towns and the antiques and curio shops and harborside lobster shacks in the smaller fishing villages. Freeport is an entity unto itself, a place where numerous name-brand outlets and specialty stores have sprung up around the retail outpost of famous outfitter L. L. Bean. And no description of the coast would be complete without mention of popular Acadia National Park, with its majestic mountains that are often shrouded in mist.

If you come to Maine seeking an untouched fishing village with locals gathered around a potbellied stove in the general store, you'll likely come away disappointed; that innocent age has passed in all but the most remote spots like Way Down East. Tourism has supplanted fishing, logging, and potato farming as Maine's number-one industry, and most areas are well equipped to receive the annual onslaught of visitors. But whether you are stepping outside a cabin for a walk in the woods or watching a boat rock at its anchor, you can sense the wilderness nearby, even on the edges of the most urbanized spots.

THE SOUTHERN COAST

Updated by Laura V. Scheel

Maine's southernmost coastal towns—Kittery, the Yorks, Ogunquit, the Kennebunks, and the Old Orchard Beach area—reveal a few of the stunning faces of the state's coast, from the miles and miles of inviting sandy beaches to the beautifully kept historic towns and carnival-like attractions. There is something for every taste, whether you seek solitude in a kayak or prefer being caught up in the infectious spirit of fellow vacationers.

North of Kittery, long stretches of hard-packed white-sand beach are closely crowded by nearly unbroken ranks of beach cottages, motels, and oceanfront restaurants. The summer colonies of York Beach and Wells brim with crowds and ticky-tacky shorefront overdevelopment, but nearby quiet wildlife refuges and land reserves promise an easy escape. York evokes yesteryear sentiment with its acclaimed historic district, while upscale Ogunquit tantalizes visitors with its array of shops and a cliffside walk.

More than any other region south of Portland, the Kennebunks—and especially Kennebunkport—provide the complete Maine Coast experience: classic townscapes where white-clapboard houses rise from manicured lawns and gardens; rocky shorelines punctuated by sandy beaches; quaint downtown districts packed with gift shops, ice-cream stands, and visitors; harbors with lobster boats bobbing alongside yachts; rustic, picnic-tabled restaurants serving lobster and fried seafood; and well-appointed dining rooms. As you continue north, the scents of friend dough and cotton candy mean you've arrived at Maine's version of Coney Island, Old Orchard Beach.

KITTERY

55 mi north of Boston; 5 mi north of Portsmouth, New Hampshire.

One of the earliest settlements in the state of Maine, Kittery suffered its share of British, French, and Native American attacks throughout the 17th and 18th centuries, yet rose to prominence as a vital shipbuilding center. The tradition continues; despite its New Hampshire name, the Portsmouth Naval Shipyard is part of Maine and has been one of the leading researchers and builders of U.S. submarines since its inception in 1800. It's not open to the public, but those on boats can pass by and get a glimpse.

Known as the "Gateway to Maine," Kittery has come to more recent light as a major shopping destination thanks to its complex of factory outlets. Flanked on either side of U.S. 1 are more than 120 stores, which attract hordes of shoppers year-round. For something a little less commercial, head east on Route 103 to the hidden Kittery most people miss: the lands around **Kittery Point.** Here you can find hiking and biking trails and great views of the water. With Portsmouth, New Hampshire, across the water, Whaleback Ledge Lighthouse, and the nearby Isles of Shoals, Kittery is a picturesque place to pass some time. Also along this winding stretch of Route 103 are two forts, both open in summer.

DID YOU KNOW?

Maine may not have many sandy beaches or warm water, but the rocky shoreline, powerful ocean, and contrasting evergreens have inspired photographers and artists for years.

ESSENTIALS

Visitor Information **Maine Tourism Association & Visitor Information Center** (✉ *U.S. 1 and I–95, Kittery* ☎ *207/439–1319* 🌐 *www.mainetourism.com*).

WHERE TO EAT

$–$$ SEAFOOD ★ ✕ **Chauncey Creek Lobster Pound.** From the road you can barely see this restaurant's red roof hovering below the trees, but chances are you can see the cars parked at this popular spot along the high banks of the tidal river. The menu has lots of fresh lobster choices and a raw bar with locally harvested offerings like clams and oysters. Bring your own beer or wine if you desire alcohol. In season, it's open daily for lunch and dinner. ✉ *16 Chauncey Creek Rd., Kittery Point* ☎ *207/439–1030* 🌐 *www.chaunceycreek.com* ▭ *MC, V* ⊗ *Closed mid-Oct.–Mother's Day.*

$$–$$$ SEAFOOD ✕ **Warren's Lobster House.** A local institution, this waterfront restaurant specializes in seafood and has a huge salad bar. The pine-sided dining room leaves the impression that little has changed since Warren's opened in 1940. Dine outside overlooking the water when the weather is nice. ✉ *11 Water St.* ☎ *207/439–1630* 🌐 *www.lobsterhouse.com* ▭ *AE, MC, V.*

5

YORK VILLAGE

About 6 mi north of Kittery on Route 103 or Route 1A via U.S. 1.

As subdued as the town may feel today, the history of York Village reveals a far different character. One of the first permanently settled areas in the state of Maine, it was once witness to great destruction and fierce fighting during the French, Indian, and British wars; towns and fortunes were sacked, yet the potential for prosperity encouraged the area's citizens continually to rebuild and start anew. Colonial York citizens enjoyed great wealth and success from fishing and lumber as well as a penchant for politics. Angered by the British-imposed taxes, York held its own little-known tea party in 1775 in protest.

The actual village of York is quite small, housing the town's basic components of post office, town hall, a few shops, and a stretch of antique homes. You may notice something amiss with York's Civil War Monument. After the war it was common for towns to erect a statue of a Civil War soldier. The statue sent to York, however, was most likely meant to be shipped much farther south—the figure is a Confederate soldier.

GETTING HERE AND AROUND

The York Trolley Company makes daily loops through York Village, York Harbor, out to Nubble Lighthouse, and all the way to Short Sands Beach in York Beach. Route maps can be picked up nearly everywhere in York and at the chamber of commerce; fares are $1.50 one-way and $3 for the loop.

ESSENTIALS

Transportation Information **York Trolley Company** (☎ *207/363–9600* 🌐 *www.yorktrolley.com*).

EXPLORING

York Village Historic District. Most of the 18th- and 19th-century buildings here are clustered along York Street and Lindsay Road; seven are owned by the Old York Historical Society and charge admission. You can buy tickets for all the buildings at the **Jefferds Tavern** (✉ *Rte. 1A at Lindsay Rd.*), a restored late-18th-century inn. The **Old York Gaol** (1720) was once the King's Prison for the Province of Maine; inside are dungeons, cells, and the jailer's quarters. Several times a week, costumed reenactors spin tales—based on real 18th-century prisoners—of why they're behind bars. The 1731 **Elizabeth Perkins House** reflects the Victorian style of its last occupants, the prominent Perkins family. The Historical Society also gives guided walking tours (or take the self-guided tour through each of the seven buildings; admission is valid for two consecutive days). ☎ *207/363–4974* 🌐 *www.oldyork.org* *All buildings $10; $5 for one building* ⏲ *Mid-June–mid-Oct., Mon.–Sat. 10–5.*

Stonewall Kitchen. You've probably seen the kitchen's smartly labeled jars of gourmet chutneys, jams, jellies, salsas, and sauces in specialty stores back home. York is the headquarters and processing center for them. The company's complex houses the company store, a bustling café and take-out restaurant, a viewing area of the cooking and bottling processes, and stunning gardens. Sample all the mustards, salsas, and dressings that you can stand, or have lunch at the café. Takeout is available during store hours. Lunch is served daily 11–3; Sunday is brunch day. The venture's latest addition is the cooking school, where participants can join in evening or luncheon courses. Reservations are recommended, though walk-ins are accepted if space allows; most classes cost $35–$50 and are shorter than two hours. ✉ *Stonewall La. just off U.S. 1, next to information center* ☎ *207/351–2712* 🌐 *www.stonewallkitchen.com* ⏲ *Mon.–Sat. 8–8, Sun. 9–6.*

SHOPPING

Bring a basket for Saturday morning shopping at the **Gateway Farmers' Market** (✉ *1 Stonewall La., just off U.S. Rte. 1*), held at the Greater York Region Chamber of Commerce visitor center from early June until Columbus Day. Beginning at 9 AM, you'll find fresh local produce as well as flowers, artisan bread, homemade soaps, and specialty foods. It's a good place to gather the makings for a beach picnic. The market also opens up on Tuesday afternoons from 2 to 5:30 June 30 until September 1. Guess the theme at **Gravestone Artwear** (✉ *250 York St. [Rte. 1A]* ☎ *800/564–4310* 🌐 *www.gravestoneartwear.com*), where you'll find items adorned with Colonial, Victorian, and Celtic gravestone carving designs. There are also crystals, gravestone-rubbing supplies, books, and candles. Watercolors, mixed media, oils, and photography can be had at **Village Gallery** (✉ *244 York St. [Rte. 1A]* ☎ *207/351–3110* 🌐 *www.yorkvillagegallery.com*), where many local artists are represented.

WHERE TO EAT

$$$$ SEAFOOD ✕ **Foster's Downeast Clambake.** Save your appetite for this one. Specializing in the traditional Maine clambake—a feast consisting of rich clam chowder, a pile of mussels and steamers, Maine lobster, corn on the cob, roasted potatoes and onions, bread, butter, and Maine blueberry crumb

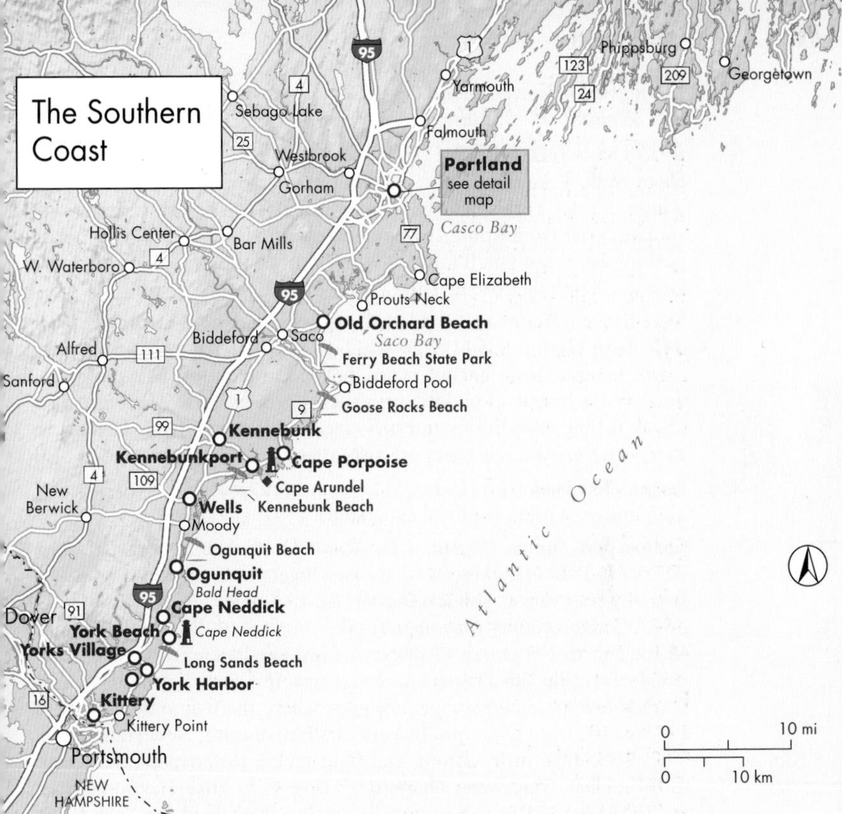

cake (phew!)—this massive complex provides entertainment as well as belly-busting meals. You can also opt to have clambake fixings shipped to your home. ✉ *5 Axholme Rd.* ☎ *207/363–3255 or 800/552–0242* 🌐 *www.fostersclambake.com* ▭ *AE, MC, V.*

YORK HARBOR

Approximately 3 mi north of York Village via Route 1A.

Just a few miles from the village proper, York Harbor opens up to the water and offers many places to linger and explore. The harbor is busy with boats of all kinds, while the harbor beach is a good stretch of sand for swimming. Much more formal than the northward York Beach and much quieter, the area retains a somewhat more exclusive air.

EXPLORING

Sayward-Wheeler House. Built in 1718, the waterfront home was remodeled in the 1760s by Jonathan Sayward, a local merchant who had prospered in the West Indies trade. By 1860 his descendants had opened the house to the public to share the story of their Colonial ancestors. The house, accessible only by guided tour, reveals both the simple 18th-century decor and the more elaborate (and opulent) furnishings of the 19th century. ✉ *9 Barrell La. Extension, York Harbor* ☎ *207/384–2454* *www.historicnewengland.org* *$5* *June–mid-Oct., 2nd and 4th Sat. of month 11–5; tours on the hr. 11–4.*

SPORTS AND THE OUTDOORS

Shore Walk. Take the stroll for a good beachcombing exploration and a jaunt across York's beloved Wiggly Bridge. You can start at various spots—either from Route 103 alongside York Harbor (there is minimal parking here, but you'll know it when you see the bridge) or from the George Marshall Store in York Village (140 Lindsay Road).

KAYAKING Take to the water in a guided kayak trip with **Harbor Adventures** (*Box 345, York Harbor 03911* *207/363–8466* *www.harboradventures.com*). Choose from harbor tours, full-moon paddles, half-day trips, and even a luncheon paddle; prices start around $45. There are also kayak fishing expeditions and surf kayaking trips available. Departure locations vary. Bicycle tours are also offered.

BIKING **Berger's Bike Shop** (*241 York St., No. 1, York* *207/363–4070*) rents all manner of bikes for local excursions.

FISHING **Captain Tom Farnon** (*Rte. 103, Town Dock No. 2, York Harbor* *207/363–3234*) takes up to six passengers at a time on lobstering trips, by reservation. **Fish Tale Charters** (*85 Bog Rd., York* *207/363–3874* *www.maineflyfishing.net*) takes anglers on fly-fishing or light tackle charters in search of stripers or juvenile bluefin tuna; departure points vary. **Rip Tide Charters** (*1 Georgia St., York* *207/363–2536* *www.mainestriperfishing.com*) goes where the fish are—departure points vary, from Ogunquit to York and Portsmouth, New Hampshire. They specialize in fly-fishing and light tackle for stripers, mackerel, and bluefish. **Shearwater Charters** (*Box 472, York Harbor 03911* *207/363–5324*) offers spin or fly-casting charters in the York River and along the shoreline from Kittery to Ogunquit. Bait-fishing trips are also available. Departure spots depend on time and tides.

HIKING AND WALKING For a peek into the Rachel Carson National Wildlife Refuge, take the 2-mi **Brave Boat Harbor Trail,** which is one of the few walking trails in the refuge. It's a prime bird-watching area. Look for Brave Boat Harbor Road just off Route 103 for trail access and parking.

WHERE TO EAT

$$$–$$$$ SEAFOOD **Dockside Restaurant.** On an island overlooking York Harbor, this restaurant has plenty of seafood on the menu, which also includes such treats as beef tenderloin and duckling. Start with the rich lobster and scallop crepe or an order of local oysters. *22 Harris Island Rd., just off Rte. 103* *207/363–2722* *www.docksidegq.com* *D, MC, V* *Closed Mon. (except July and Aug.) and late Oct.–May.*

$$$–$$$$ AMERICAN **Harbor Porches.** Eating here is very much like sitting on someone's porch—assuming that someone has a lot of money and can afford extravagant views over York Harbor. Wicker chairs at linen-covered tables fill the space and are surrounded by large windows. Local seafood is on the menu, as well as rack of lamb and steak. For lunch, try one of the hearty sandwiches or specialty pizzas. The Maine crab cake appetizer is worth a try, as is the lobster bisque. Jeans and sneakers

are not allowed at dinner. The restaurant is open for breakfast, lunch, Sunday brunch, and dinner. ✉ *Stage Neck Rd.* ☎ *207/363–3850* ▭ *AE, D, DC, MC, V* ⊙ *Closed 2 wks. in Jan.*

WHERE TO STAY

$$$–$$$$ Fodor's Choice ★ **Chapman Cottage.** This impeccably restored inn, named for the woman who had it built as her summer cottage in 1899, sits proudly atop a swath of lawn. The luxuriant bedspreads, fresh flowers, antiques, and beautiful rugs only hint at the indulgence found here. Innkeepers Donna and Paul Archibald spoil their guests with sumptuous breakfasts, afternoon hors d'oeuvres, port, sherry, and homemade chocolate truffles, all prepared by Paul, a professionally trained chef. Most rooms have fireplaces and whirlpool tubs; all are spacious and bright. It's a five-minute walk to either York Village or the harbor. **Pros:** beautifully restored historic lodging; luxury appointments; attention to detail. **Cons:** no water views; most rooms on upper floors. ✉ *370 York St.* ☎ *207/363–2059 or 877/363–2059* 🌐 *www.chapmancottagebandb.com* *6 rooms* *In-room: no phone, Wi-Fi. In-hotel: restaurant, bar, no kids under 12, no elevator* ▭ *AE, D, MC, V* *BP.*

$$$–$$$$ ★ **Inn at Tanglewood Hall.** The inn's artfully painted floors, lush wallpapers, and meticulous attention to detail are the fruits of a former designation as a designers' showcase home. This 1880s Victorian "cottage," as these mansions were humbly called back in the day, is a haven of elegance and comfort, set back among trees and stunning perennial gardens. Rooms are individually decorated, though all share decadently rich coloring and fabrics, high ceilings, and many large windows; some have fireplaces. **Pros:** elegant and authentic historic lodging; serene setting amid gardens and grand trees; short walk to beaches and nature trails. **Cons:** no water views. ✉ *611 York St.* ☎ *207/351–1075* 🌐 *www.tanglewoodhall.com* *6 rooms* *In-room: no phone, refrigerator (some), no TV, Wi-Fi. In-hotel: no kids under 12, no elevator* ▭ *AE, MC, V* *BP.*

$$–$$$$ ★ **York Harbor Inn.** A mid-17th-century fishing cabin with dark timbers and a fieldstone fireplace forms the heart of this inn, while several wings and outbuildings have been added over the years, making for a complex with a great variety of styles and appointments. The rooms are furnished with antiques and country pieces; many have decks overlooking the water, and some have whirlpool tubs or fireplaces. The nicest rooms are in two adjacent buildings, Harbor Cliffs and Harbor Hill. The dining room ($$$–$$$$; no lunch off-season) has great ocean views. **Pros:** many rooms have harbor views; close to beaches and scenic walking trails. **Cons:** rooms vary greatly in style and appeal. ✉ *480 York St., Coastal Route 1A, York Harbor* ☎ *207/363–5119 or 800/343–3869* 🌐 *www.yorkharborinn.com* *54 rooms, 2 suites* *In-room: Wi-Fi. In-hotel: 2 restaurants, bar, no elevator* ▭ *AE, DC, MC, V* *CP.*

5

YORK BEACH

6 mi north of York Harbor via Route 1A.

Like many shorefront towns in Maine, York Beach has a long history of entertaining summer visitors. Take away today's bikinis and iPods and it's easy to imagine squealing tourists adorned in the full-length bathing garb of the late 19th century. Just as they did back then, visitors today come here to eat ice cream, enjoy carnival-like novelties, and indulge in the sun and sea air.

York Beach is a real family destination, devoid of all things staid and stuffy—children are meant to be seen and heard here. Just beyond the sands of Short Sand Beach are a host of amusements, from bowling to indoor minigolf and the Fun-O-Rama arcade.

ESSENTIALS

Visitor Information The **Greater York Region Chamber of Commerce** (✉ *1 Stonewall La., off U.S. 1* ☎ *207/363–4422* 🌐 *www.gatewaytomaine.org*).

EXPLORING

Nubble Light. Head out a couple of miles on the peninsula to see one of the most photographed lighthouses on the globe. Direct access is prohibited, but an information center shares the 1879 light's history. Find parking at Sohier Park, at the end of Nubble Road, as well as restrooms and benches. ✉ *End of Nubble Rd., off Rte. 1A.*

York's Wild Kingdom. Between the zoo and the carnival rides, it's sometimes hard to distinguish the wild animals from the kids here. The zoo has an impressive variety of exotic animals and is home to the state's only white Bengal tiger. Combination tickets can be purchased to visit the zoo and the amusement park, and discounts are available for kids under 10. ✉ *U.S. 1 (about 2 mi from Exit 7, look for the 40-foot sign), also entrance at 23 Railroad Ave. at York Beach, York* ☎ *207/363–4911* 🌐 *www.yorkzoo.com* 🎟 *$14.50 zoo only; $19.50 zoo and rides (adults)* ⏲ *Late May–Sept.*

NIGHTLIFE

Inn on the Blues (✉ *7 Ocean Ave., York Beach* ☎ *207/351–3221*) is a hopping blues club that attracts national bands.

WHERE TO EAT AND STAY

$$$–$$$$ AMERICAN Fodor's Choice ★

✕ **Blue Sky on York Beach.** Making its home on the second floor of the grandly restored Atlantic House Hotel, this wide-open and inviting restaurant adds a keen sense of swanky sophistication to this casual beach town. A massive stone fireplace anchors the great room of high ceilings, exposed ductwork, and warm wood floors; unusual hanging light fixtures attract the eye and cast a gentle glow. The menu, executed by well-known chef and owner Lydia Shire, takes regional New England fare to new heights. Memorable choices include the lamb pizza appetizer and the lobster stew; the deep-fried short ribs are painfully delicious, as is the charcoaled duck breast with sugar pumpkin. For a closer look at what happens in the kitchen, you can sit at the curved food bar, with full views of the wood-fired oven and the chefs at work. There's an additional bar menu for the lounge. In good weather, sit out on the large deck with views of the town below. Sunday jazz brunch is also a winner here. ✉ 2 Beach St., York Beach ☎ 207/363–0050 🌐 www.blueskyonyorkbeach.com ✍ Reservations recommended ▭ AE, D, MC, V ⏲ No lunch Sept.–June.

$–$$ AMERICAN ✕ **The Goldenrod.** If you wanted to—and you are on vacation—you could eat nothing but the famous taffy here, made just about the same way today as it was back in 1896. The famous Goldenrod Kisses, some 65 tons of which are made per year, are a great attraction, and people line the windows to watch the taffy being made. Aside from the famous candy, this eating place is family oriented, very reasonably priced, and a great place to get ice cream from the old-fashioned soda fountain. Breakfast is served all day, while the simple lunch menu doubles as dinner; choose from sandwiches and burgers. ✉ *2 Railroad Ave.* ☎ *207/363–2621* 🌐 *www.thegoldenrod.com* ▭ *AE, MC, V* ⏲ *Closed Columbus Day–late May.*

$$$$ ★ **Atlantic House Hotel.** For years, this aged beauty sat weary and neglected in the middle of York Beach, caught in the mire of area zoning laws. An eyesore no longer, this 1888 hotel has returned to its former splendor. The standard hotel rooms are awash in calming blues, greens, and creams, accented with designer fabrics, gas fireplaces, and Jacuzzi tubs. For more space, there are one- and two-bedroom suites (with surprisingly reasonable weekly rates), complete with full kitchens, laundry, and separate living and dining rooms. All spaces are uncluttered, have gleaming hardwood floors, and are blessed with ample windows to allow for plenty of natural light. Several suites have private decks. Many conveniences are also housed within the hotel: the elegant Blue Sky at York Beach ($$$) restaurant, a full-service spa, Clara's Cupcake Café (¢), a wine and specialty food shop, a children's apparel store, and a women's boutique with clothing, jewelry, cosmetics, and accessories. **Pros:** elegant, sophisticated lodging; walk to beach/town; great on-site amenities; good choice for weekly stay. **Cons:** not a beachfront location (fourth floor has partial water views); not for budget travelers. ✉ *2 Beach St., York Beach* ☎ *207/363–0051* 🌐 *www.atlantichouseyorkbeach.com* *7 rooms, 8 suites* *In-room: safe, kitchen (some), refrigerator (some), DVD, Wi-Fi. In-hotel: 2 restaurants, bar, spa, laundry facilities, Wi-Fi hotspot, parking* ▭ *AE, D, DC, MC, V.*

CAPE NEDDICK

4 mi north of York Beach via Rte. 1A, just north of York on U.S. 1.

Cape Neddick is one of the less developed of York's villages, running from the water (and Route 1A), along U.S. 1 between York and Ogunquit. The town has many modest residential homes, with a sprinkling of businesses catering to both locals and visitors. There are a few restaurants and inns but no distinct downtown hub.

EXPLORING

Mount Agamenticus Park. Maintained by the York Parks and Recreation Department, this humble summit of 692 feet is said to be the highest peak along the Atlantic seaboard. That may not seem like much, but if you choose to hike to the top, you will be rewarded with incredible views all the way to the White Mountains in New Hampshire. If you don't want to hoof it (though it's not very steep), there is parking at the top. To get here, take Mountain Road just off U.S. 1 in Cape Neddick (just after Flo's Steamed Hot Dogs) and follow the signs. The area is open daily, with no charge. It's popular with equestrians and cyclists as well as families and hikers. *York Parks and Recreation Department, 200 U.S. Rte. 1 S, York 03909 207/363–1040.*

WHERE TO EAT AND STAY

¢ AMERICAN ★ **Flo's Steamed Hot Dogs.** Yes, it seems crazy to highlight a hot-dog stand, but this is no ordinary place. Who would guess that a hot dog could make it into *Saveur* and *Gourmet* magazines? There is something grand about this shabby, red-shingle shack that has been dealing dogs since 1959. The line is out the door most days, but the operation is so efficient that the wait is not long. Flo has passed on, but her granddaughter keeps the business going, selling countless thousands of hot dogs each year. Be sure to ask for the special sauce—consisting of, among other things, hot sauce and mayo (you can take a bottle home, and you'll want to). *1359 U.S. 1 No phone www.floshotdogs.com No credit cards Closed Wed.*

$$$–$$$$ VEGETARIAN **Frankie & Johnny's Natural Food Restaurant.** If you've had about all the fried seafood you can stand for one day, try this casual little spot that focuses on healthy but tasty meals. Choose from a variety of vegetarian dishes as well as seafood, poultry, and meat options. The toasted peppercorn seared sushi-grade tuna, served with coconut risotto on gingered vegetables, is excellent. You're welcome to bring your own libations. *1594 U.S. 1, Cape Neddick 207/363–1909 www.frankie-johnnys.com No credit cards No dinner Mon.–Wed. No lunch.*

$–$$$ **Country View Motel & Guesthouse.** Set back along one of U.S. 1's less hectic sections is this appealing little motel that looks more like an inn. There are a few rooms in the main house, and the rest are in the adjacent motel complex. It's clean, pretty, and in a good central location for exploring the Yorks and Ogunquit, which are just a few miles away. Suites sleep up to four people and have full kitchens. Guests with well-behaved dogs will appreciate the on-site pet park for exercise and play. **Pros:** convenient to both Ogunquit and Yorks; ample grounds provide picnic areas and gas grills. **Cons:** not an in-town location; no water views or beachfront. *1521 U.S. 1 207/363–7160 or 800/258–6598 www.countryviewmotel.com 19 rooms, 3 suites In-room: kitchen (some), refrigerator, Wi-Fi. In-hotel: pool, some pets allowed MC, V CP Closed Jan.–mid-Apr.*

SHOPPING

Home furnishings with an antique feel are the specialty of **Jeremiah Campbell & Company** (*1537 U.S. 1 207/363–8499*). Everything here is handcrafted, from rugs, decoys, furniture, and lighting to glassware. The shop is closed Wednesday.

Ogunquit's Perkins Cove is a pleasant place to admire the boats—and wonder at the origin of their names.

SPORTS AND THE OUTDOORS

FISHING Offering various guided fishing trips, private casting lessons, and a summer "striper school" is **Eldredge Bros. Fly Shop** (✉ *1480 U.S. 1* ☎ *207/363–9269 or 207/363–9279* 🌐 *www.eldredgeflyshop.com*). Kayak rentals and rod-and-reel rentals are also available.

KAYAKING Hop on one of the regularly scheduled guided kayak trips with **Excursions/Coastal Maine Outfitting Co.** (✉ *1740 U.S. 1* ☎ *207/363–0181* 🌐 *www.excursionsinmaine.com*). You can cruise along the shoreline or sign up for an overnight paddle. Reservations are recommended; trips start at $60. Kayaks and other boats are available for rental.

OGUNQUIT

10 mi north of the Yorks via Rtes. 1A and 1 or Shore Rd.

A resort village in the 1880s, stylish Ogunquit gained fame as an artists' colony. Today it has become a mini Provincetown, with a gay population that swells in summer. Many inns and small clubs cater to a primarily gay and lesbian clientele. The nightlife in Ogunquit revolves around the precincts of Ogunquit Square and Perkins Cove, where people stroll, often enjoying an after-dinner ice-cream cone or espresso. For a scenic drive, take Shore Road through downtown toward the 100-foot Bald Head Cliff; you'll be treated to views up and down the coast. On a stormy day the surf can be quite wild here.

GETTING HERE AND AROUND

The Ogunquit Trolley is one of the best things that has happened to this area. Parking in the village is troublesome and expensive, beach parking is costly and limited, and it's often easier to leave your car parked at the hotel. The trolley runs from May until Columbus Day. The route begins at Perkins Cove and follows Shore Road through town, down to Ogunquit Beach, and out along U.S. 1 up to Wells (where a connecting Wells trolley takes over for northern travel). Maps are available wherever you find brochures and at the chamber of commerce Welcome Center on U.S. 1, just as you enter Ogunquit from the south.

ESSENTIALS

Transportation Information Ogunquit Trolley (*Box 2368, Ogunquit 03907 207/646–1411 www.ogunquittrolley.com $1.50 [at each boarding]; kids under 10 ride free with an adult*).

Visitor Information Ogunquit Chamber of Commerce (*36 Main St. [U.S. 1] 207/646–2939 www.ogunquit.org*).

EXPLORING

★ **Perkins Cove.** This neck of land, connected to the mainland by Oarweed Road and a pedestrian drawbridge, has a jumble of sea-beaten fish houses. These have largely been transformed by the tide of tourism to shops and restaurants. When you've had your fill of browsing, stroll out along **Marginal Way,** a mile-long footpath between Ogunquit and Perkins Cove that hugs the shore of a rocky promontory known as Israel's Head. Benches allow you to appreciate the open sea vistas, flowering bushes, and million-dollar homes.

WHERE TO EAT AND STAY

¢–$ AMERICAN ★ **Amore Breakfast.** One could hardly find a more-satisfying, full-bodied breakfast than at this smart and busy joint just shy of the entrance to Perkins Cove. A lighthearted mix of retro advertising signs adorns the walls of this bright, open, and very bustling dining room. You won't find tired standards here—the only pancakes are German potato. The Oscar Madison omelet combines crabmeat with asparagus and Swiss, topped with a dill hollandaise. For a real decadent start, opt for the Banana Foster: pecan-coated, cream-cheese–stuffed French toast with a side of sautéed bananas in rum syrup. To ease the wait for a morning table, a self-serve coffee bar is next door at the Café Amore. You can also pick up sandwiches, baked goods, and gift items here. *309 Shore Rd. 207/646–6661 www.amorebreakfast.com D, MC, V Closed mid-Dec.–Mar., and Wed. and Thurs. in spring and fall. No lunch and dinner.*

$$$$ ECLECTIC Fodor's Choice ★ **Arrows.** Elegant simplicity is the hallmark of this restaurant in an 18th-century farmhouse 2 mi up a back road. You'll likely find delicacies such as wild sturgeon caviar paired with vodka-cured salmon on the daily-changing menu—much of what appears depends on what is ready for harvest in the restaurant's abundant garden. The appetizers of roasted quail with fried noodles and of escargots with summer herb-butter are also beautifully executed. Try the "Indulgence Menu," a 10-course tasting menu prepared "at the whim of the chef," for $135. Guests are encouraged to dress up; no jeans or shorts. *41 Berwick*

Rd. ☎ 207/361–1100 ⊕ www.arrowsrestaurant.com ✍ Reservations essential ▭ MC, V ⊗ Closed Mon. and mid-Dec.–mid-Apr. No lunch.

$$–$$$$ **Ogunquit Resort Motel.** Right along U.S. 1 about 2 mi north of Ogunquit Village, this large complex is great for families and for those who prefer larger hotels over B&Bs. Boasting the largest pool in Ogunquit, the resort also has an outdoor hot tub. Beachgoers can walk to Footbridge Beach just about ½ mi away. Choose from deluxe, superior, and luxury rooms; luxury suites have fireplaces and Jacuzzi tubs. You can leave your car here and hop on the trolley to get around, saving yourself the agony (and expense) of trying to park in town or at the beach. Ask about Internet specials. **Pros:** on the Ogunquit Trolley route; good for families; good-size rooms. **Cons:** not an in-town location. ✉ *719 Main St. (U.S. 1) ☎ 877/646–8336 ⊕ www.ogunquitresort.com ⇁ 85 rooms, 8 suites ♘ In-room: refrigerator, Wi-Fi. In-hotel: pool, gym ▭ AE, D, MC, V ⟨CP⟩ CP.*

5

WELLS

5 mi north of Ogunquit on U.S. 1.

Lacking any kind of noticeable village center, Wells could be easily overlooked as nothing more than a commercial stretch on U.S. 1 between Ogunquit and the Kennebunks. But look more closely—this is a place where people come to enjoy some of the best beaches on the coast. Part of Ogunquit until 1980, this family-oriented beach community has 7 mi of densely populated shoreline, along with nature preserves where you can explore salt marshes and tidal pools.

GETTING HERE AND AROUND

Leave your car at your hotel and take the Wells Trolley to the beach or to the shops on U.S. 1. The seasonal trolley makes pickups at the Wells Transportation Center when the *Downeaster* (the Amtrak train with service from Boston to Portland) pulls in. If you want to continue south toward Ogunquit, the two town trolleys meet at the Wells Chamber of Commerce on U.S. 1; get a route map here.

ESSENTIALS

Transportation Information Wells Trolley (☎ *207/646–2451* ⊕ *www.wellschamber.org* 🎫 *$2*).

Visitor Information Wells Chamber of Commerce (📫 *Box 356, 04090* ☎ *207/646–2451* ⊕ *www.wellschamber.org*).

QUICK BITES

How would you like a really superior doughnut that the same family has been making since 1955? Congdon's (✉ *1090 Post Rd.* ☎ *207/646–4219* ⊕ *www.congdons.com*) makes about 30 different varieties, though the plain one really gives you an idea of just how good these doughnuts are. There's a drive-through window, or you can sit inside and have breakfast or lunch.

KENNEBUNK WALKING TOURS

To take a little walking tour of Kennebunk's most notable structures, begin from the Federal-style Brick Store Museum, on Main Street. Head south on Main Street (turn left out of the museum) to see several extraordinary 18th-century homes, including the Nathaniel Frost House at 99 Main Street (1799) and the Benjamin Brown House at 85 Main Street (1788).

When you've had your fill of historic homes, head back up toward the museum, pass the 1773 First Parish Unitarian Church (its Asher Benjamin–style steeple contains the original Paul Revere bell), and turn right onto Summer Street. This street is an architectural showcase, revealing an array of styles from Colonial to Federal. Walking past these grand beauties will give you a real sense of the economic prowess and glamour of the long-gone shipbuilding industry.

For a guided architectural walking tour of Summer Street, contact the Brick Store Museum at 207/985–4802.

For a dramatic walk along the rocky coastline and beneath the views of Ocean Avenue's grand mansions, head out on the **Parson's Way Shore Walk**, a paved, 4.8-mi round-trip. Begin at Dock Square and follow Ocean Avenue along the river, passing the Colony Hotel and St. Ann's Church, all the way to Walker's Point. You can simply turn back from here or take a left onto Wildes District Road for a walk amid more luxury homes and trees.

SPORTS AND THE OUTDOORS

BEACHES With its thousands of acres of marsh and preserved land, Wells is a great place to spend a lot of time outdoors. Nearly 7 mi of sand stretch along the boundaries of Wells, making beach-going a prime occupation. Tidal pools sheltered by rocks are filled with all manner of creatures awaiting discovery. Parking is available for a fee (take the trolley!) at **Crescent Beach**, along Webhannet Drive; **Wells Beach** (at the end of Mile Road off U.S. 1) has public restrooms and two parking areas. There is another lot at the far end of Wells Beach, at the end of Atlantic Avenue. Across the jetty from Wells Harbor is **Drakes Island Beach** (end of Drakes Island Road off U.S. 1), which also has parking and public restrooms. Lifeguards are on hand at all the beaches. Rent bikes, surfboards, wet suits, boogie boards, and probably a few other things at **Wheels and Waves** (✉ *578 U.S. 1* ☎ *207/646–5774*).

STATE PARKS AND REFUGES The **Rachel Carson National Wildlife Refuge** (✉ *321 Port Rd. [Rte. 9]* ☎ *207/646–9226* 🌐 *www.fws.gov/northeast/rachelcarson*) has a mile-long-loop nature trail through a salt marsh. The trail borders the Little River and a white-pine forest where migrating birds and waterfowl of many varieties are regularly spotted.

WHERE TO EAT AND STAY

$–$$$ SEAFOOD ✕ **Billy's Chowder House.** Locals head to this simple restaurant in a salt marsh for the generous lobster rolls, haddock sandwiches, and chowders. Big windows in the bright dining rooms overlook the marsh.

✉216 Mile Rd. ☎207/646–7558 🌐www.billyschowderhouse.com ▭AE, D, MC, V ⏲Closed mid-Dec.–mid-Jan.

$$ AMERICAN ✕ **Maine Diner.** One look at the 1953 exterior and you start craving good diner food. You'll get a little more than you're expecting; how many greasy spoons make an award-winning lobster pie? That's the house favorite, as well as a heavenly seafood chowder. There's plenty of fried seafood in addition to the usual diner fare, and breakfast is served all day. Check out the adjacent gift shop, Remember the Maine. *✉2265 U.S. 1. ☎207/646–4441 🌐www.mainediner.com ▭D, MC, V ⏲Closed 1 wk in Jan.*

$$–$$$$ Fodor's Choice ★ **Haven by the Sea.** Once the summer mission of St. Martha's Church in Kennebunkport, this exquisite inn has retained many of the original details from its former life as a seaside church. The cathedral ceilings and stained-glass windows remain. The guest rooms are spacious, some with serene marsh views. Four common areas, including one with a fireplace, are perfect spots for afternoon refreshments. The inn is one block from the beach. **Pros:** unusual structure with elegant appointments; nightly happy hour; walk to beach. **Cons:** not an in-town location. *✉59 Church St. ☎207/646–4194 🌐www.havenbythesea.com 6 rooms, 2 suites, 1 apartment In-room: Wi-Fi. In-hotel: no kids under 12 ▭AE, MC, V BP.*

KENNEBUNK

Approximately 6 mi north of Wells via U.S. 1; 23 mi south of Portland via Maine Tpke.

Sometimes bypassed on the way to its sister town of Kennebunkport, Kennebunk has its own appeal. In the 19th century the town was a major shipbuilding center; docks lined the river with hundreds of workers busily crafting the vessels that would bring immense fortune to some of the area's residents. Although the trade is long gone, the evidence that remains of this great wealth exists in Kennebunk's mansions. Kennebunk is a classic small New England town, with an inviting shopping district, steepled churches, and fine examples of 18th- and 19th-century brick and clapboard homes. There are also plenty of natural spaces for walking, swimming, birding, and biking.

The town of Kennebunk is divided between two villages; the upper one extends around the Mousam River on Route 9, while the lower one is several miles down Route 35, just shy of Kennebunkport proper. The drive down Route 35 keeps visitors agog with the splendor of the area's mansions, spread out on both sides of the road. To get to the grand and gentle beaches of Kennebunk, go straight on Beach Avenue from the intersection of Routes 9 and 35 in the lower village.

GETTING HERE AND AROUND

Get a good overview of the sights with an Intown Trolley tour. The narrated 45-minute jaunts leave every hour starting at 10 AM at the designated stop on Ocean Avenue, around the corner of Dock Square. The fare is valid for the day, so you can hop on and off at your leisure.

ESSENTIALS

Transportation Information **Intown Trolley** (✉ *Ocean Ave., Kennebunkport* ☎ *207/967–3686* 🌐 *www.intowntrolley.com* 🎫 *$15 all-day fare* ⏲ *Late May–mid-Oct., daily 10–5*).

Visitor Information **Kennebunk-Kennebunkport Chamber of Commerce** (📫 *17 Western Ave.* ☎ *207/967–0857* 🌐 *www.visitthekennebunks.com*).

EXPLORING

Brick Store Museum. The cornerstone of this block-long preservation of early-19th-century commercial buildings is **William Lord's Brick Store.** Built as a dry-goods store in 1825 in the Federal style, the building has an openwork balustrade across the roof line, granite lintels over the windows, and paired chimneys. Exhibits chronicle Kennebunk's relationship with the sea. The museum leads architectural walking tours of Kennebunk's National Register Historic District on Wednesday and Friday, typically from May to October. ✉ *117 Main St., Kennebunk* ☎ *207/985–4802* 🌐 *www.brickstoremuseum.org* 🎫 *Donations accepted; walking tours $5* ⏲ *Tues.–Fri. 10–4:30, Sat. 10–1.*

First Parish Unitarian Church. Built in 1773, just before the American Revolution, this stunning church is a marvel. The 1804 Asher Benjamin–style steeple stands proudly atop the village, and the sounds of the original Paul Revere bell can be heard for miles. It holds Sunday services, and on Tuesdays in summer tours of the sanctuary take place at 10 AM. ✉ *114 Main St.* ☎ *207/985–3700* 🌐 *www.uukennebunk.org.*

SHOPPING

The **Gallery on Chase Hill** (✉ *10 Chase Hill Rd.* ☎ *207/967–0049* 🌐 *www.maine-art.com*) presents original artwork by Maine and New England artists. **Tom's of Maine Natural Living Store** (✉ *52 Main St.* ☎ *207/467–4005*) sells all-natural personal-care products.

SPORTS AND THE OUTDOORS

Kennebunk Beach has three parts: Gooch's Beach, Mother's Beach, and Kennebunk Beach. Beach Road, with its cottages and old Victorian boardinghouses, runs right behind them. Gooch's and Kennebunk attract teenagers; Mother's Beach, which has a small playground and tidal puddles for splashing, is popular with families. For parking permits (a fee is charged in summer), go to the **Kennebunk Town Office** (✉ *1 Summer St. [Rte. 35]* ☎ *207/985–2102* 🌐 *www.kennebunkmaine.us* ⏲ *Mon., Tues., Thurs., and Fri. 8–4:30; Wed. 1–4:30*).

For an unusual exploring treat, visit the **Kennebunk Plains** (✉ *Rte. 99 W, a few miles out of Kennebunk* ☎ *207/729–5181*), a 135-acre protected grasslands habitat that is home to several rare and endangered species of vegetation and wildlife. Locally known as the blueberry plains, a good portion of the area is abloom with the hues of ripening wild blueberries in late July; after August 1 visitors are welcome to pick and eat all the berries they can find. The roads take you through vast grasslands and scrub-oak woods and by ponds. The area is maintained by the Nature Conservancy and is open daily from sunrise to sunset.

Three-mile-long **Goose Rocks,** a few minutes' drive north of town off Route 9, has plenty of shallow pools for exploring and a good long stretch of smooth sand; it's a favorite of families with small children. You can pick up a parking permit ($12 a day, $50 a week) at the **Kennebunkport Town Hall** (✉ *6 Elm St., Kennebunkport* ☎ *207/967–4243* ⏲ *Weekdays 8–4:30*) or at the Police Department on Route 9 on the way to the beach.

WHERE TO EAT

$ AMERICAN ✕ **Duffy's Tavern & Grill.** Every small town needs its own lively and friendly tavern, and this bustling spot is Kennebunk's favorite, housed in a former shoe factory with exposed brick, soaring ceilings, and hardwood floors. Right outside are the tumbling waters of the Mousam River as it flows from the dam. There's a large bar with several overhead televisions and plenty of seating in the main room, plus more tables in the less-captivating back section. Prices are reasonable for these parts; you'll find plenty of comfortable standards here, including burgers, sandwiches, pizza, and salads, as well as an appetizer menu with lots of chicken wings and fried items. Breakfast is served on Saturday and Sunday mornings, and there's live entertainment on weekend evenings. ✉ *4 Main St., Kennebunk* ☎ *207/985–0050* 🌐 *www.duffyskennebunk.com* 💳 *AE, MC, V.*

$$ AMERICAN ✕ **Federal Jack's.** Run by the Kennebunkport Brewing Company, this complex is housed in an old shipbuilding warehouse on the water. Many beers are handcrafted on-site, including Blue Fin Stout and Goat Island Light—try the sampler if you can't decide. The food is American pub style, with lots of seafood elements; the clam chowder is rich and satisfying. There's also Sunday brunch buffet and a late-night menu for those who get hungry playing pool in the back room. Brew tours are available. You can find the restaurant and brewery just before the bridge into Kennebunkport. ✉ *8 Western Ave., Lower Village* ☎ *207/967–4322* 🌐 *www.federaljacks.com* 💳 *AE, MC, V.*

$$$$ AMERICAN ★ ✕ **White Barn Inn.** Formally attired waiters, meticulous service, and exquisite food have earned this restaurant accolades as one of the best in New England. Regional fare is served in a rustic but elegant dining room. The three-course, prix-fixe menu ($95), which changes weekly, might include steamed Maine lobster nestled on fresh fettuccine with carrots, ginger, and snow peas. ✉ *37 Beach Ave., Kennebunk* ☎ *207/967–2321* 🌐 *www.whitebarninn.com* ✍ *Reservations essential* 👔 *Jacket required* 💳 *AE, MC, V* ⏲ *Closed 3 wks. in Jan. No lunch.*

WHERE TO STAY

$$$–$$$$ 🏨 **Bufflehead Cove Inn.** On the Kennebunk River at the end of a winding dirt road, this gray-shingle B&B sits amid fields and apple trees. Surprisingly it's only five minutes from Dock Square. Rooms in the main house are outfitted with a funky mix of antiques and Far Eastern and eclectic art. The Hideaway Suite, with a two-sided gas fireplace, king-size bed, and large whirlpool tub, overlooks the river. The Garden Studio has a fireplace and offers the most privacy. It's a great place to bring your kayak or canoe for paddling trips right from the dock, or you can opt to gaze upon the river from the expansive wraparound porch. The roomy cottage, set back from the main house, has a large private deck with water views, a wood-burning fireplace, and a two-person whirlpool tub; a two-night minimum stay is required. **Pros:** beautiful and

Kennebunk is a classic riverfront New England town, while Kennebunkport (pictured) is a more upscale resort area.

peaceful pastoral setting; ideal riverfront location; perfect for a serene getaway. **Cons:** a short drive from town. ✉ *18 Bufflehead Cove Rd., Kennebunk* ☎ *207/967–3879* 🌐 *www.buffleheadcove.com* *2 rooms, 3 suites, 1 cottage* *In-room: no phone, refrigerator (some), Wi-Fi. In-hotel: Internet terminal, no kids under 1* ▭ *D, MC, V* ⊗ *Closed Dec.–Apr.* *BP.*

$$$$ **The Seaside.** This handsome seaside property has been in the hands of the Severance family since 1667. The modern hotel units, all with sliding-glass doors that open onto private decks or patios (half with ocean views), are appropriate for families; so are the cottages with one to four bedrooms. You can't get much closer to Gooch's Beach. The inn supplies beach chairs; take a dip in the outdoor shower to wash off the salt and the sand. **Pros:** beachfront location; great ocean views from upper-floor rooms. **Cons:** rooms are hotel standard and a little outdated; not an in-town location. ✉ *80 Beach Ave., Kennebunk* ☎ *207/967–4461 or 800/967–4461* 🌐 *www.kennebunkbeachmaine.com* *22 rooms, 11 cottages* *In-room: refrigerator, Wi-Fi. In-hotel: beachfront, laundry service* ▭ *AE, MC, V* ⊗ *Cottages closed Nov.–May* *CP.*

$$ **Waldo Emerson House.** The home itself is a historical gold mine, made grand with unusual maritime architectural touches by a shipbuilder in 1784 and later home to the great-uncle of beloved writer Ralph Waldo Emerson (who spent many youthful summers in the house). It's believed that the house was also a stop on the famed Underground Railroad. Notice the sliding wooden panels in the windows, said to keep inhabitants safe from the soaring arrows of irate Native Americans. The elegance of the wide-plank pine floors remains, as does some remarkable original tile work around the many fireplaces. Rooms are

spacious and filled with antiques and colorful quilts, and all of them have working fireplaces. Innkeepers Kathy and John Daamen provide a shuttle to area beaches and operate the Mainely Quilts gift shop next door. **Pros:** good base for exploring Kennebunk and Kennebunkport; authentic historic lodging; complimentary afternoon tea. **Cons:** most rooms accessed via steep stairs; no water views or beachfront; not in town. ✉ *108 Summer St. (Rte. 35), Kennebunk* ☎ *207/985–4250* or *877/521–8776* 🌐 *www.waldoemersoninn.com* *4 rooms* *In-room: no phone, no TV (some), Wi-Fi. In-hotel: bicycles, Internet terminal, no kids under 6* ▭ *AE, D, MC, V* *BP.*

$$$$ ★ **White Barn Inn.** For a romantic overnight stay, you need look no further than the exclusive White Barn Inn, known for its attentive, pampering service. No detail has been overlooked in the meticulously appointed rooms, from plush bedding and reading lamps to robes and slippers. Rooms are in the main inn and adjacent buildings. Some have fireplaces, hot tubs, and luxurious baths with steam showers. The inn is within walking distance (10–15 minutes) of Dock Square and the beach. **Pros:** elegant, luxurious lodging; full-service; in a historic building. **Cons:** no water views or beachfront; overly steep lodging prices; not in town. ✉ *37 Beach Ave., Kennebunk* ☎ *207/967–2321* 🌐 *www.whitebarninn.com* *16 rooms, 9 suites* *In-room: DVD, Wi-Fi. In-hotel: restaurant, bar, pool, spa, bicycles, laundry service, Internet terminal, no kids under 12* ▭ *AE, MC, V* *CP.*

KENNEBUNKPORT

Approximately 6 mi north of Wells via U.S. 1; approximately 22 mi south of Portland.

Kennebunkport has been a resort area since the 19th century, but its most famous residents have made it even more popular—the presidential Bush family is often in residence in their immense home, which sits dramatically out on Walker's Point. The amount of wealth here is as tangible as the sharp sea breezes and the sounds of seagulls overhead. Newer mansions have sprung up alongside the old; a great way to see them is to take a slow drive out along Ocean Avenue. The area focused around the water and Dock Square in Kennebunkport is where you can find the most activity (and crowds) in the Kennebunks. Winding alleys disclose shops and restaurants geared to the tourist trade, right in the midst of a hardworking harbor.

GETTING HERE AND AROUND

The Intown Trolley covers Kennebunk and Kennebunkport. The narrated 45-minute jaunts leave every hour starting at 10 AM at the designated stop on Ocean Avenue, around the corner of Dock Square. The fare is valid for the day, so you can hop on and off at your leisure.

ESSENTIALS

Transportation Information Intown Trolley (✉ *Ocean Ave., Kennebunkport* ☎ *207/967–3686* 🌐 *www.intowntrolley.com* *$15 all-day fare* *Late May–mid-Oct., daily 10–5*).

EXPLORING

Dock Square. The heart and pulse of busy little Kennebunkport is this town center. Boutiques, T-shirt shops, art galleries, crafts stores, and restaurants encircle the square and spread out alongside streets and alleys. Walk onto the drawbridge to admire the tidal Kennebunk River.

Nott House. Also known as White Columns, the imposing Greek Revival mansion with Doric columns is furnished with the belongings of four generations of the Perkins-Nott family. The 1853 house is open for guided tours and serves as a gathering place for village walking tours, offered Thursday and Saturday at 11. It is maintained by the Kennebunkport Historical Society, which also runs the **History Center of Kennebunkport,** a mile away on North Street; the year-round center includes several exhibit buildings containing an old schoolhouse and jail cells. ✉ *8 Maine St., Kennebunkport* ☎ *207/967–2751* 🌐 *www.kporthistory.org* 🎟 *$7 for house tours; $7 for walking tours* ⏲ *July–mid-Oct., Thur. 10–4 and 7–9, Fri. 1–4, Sat. 10–1.*

★ **Seashore Trolley Museum.** Here streetcars built from 1872 to 1972, including trolleys from major metropolitan areas and world capitals (Boston to Budapest, New York to Nagasaki, San Francisco to Sydney), are all beautifully restored and displayed. Best of all, you can take a trolley ride for nearly 4 mi on the tracks of the former Atlantic Shoreline trolley line, with a stop along the way at the museum restoration shop, where trolleys are transformed from junk into gems. Both guided and self-guided tours are available. ✉ *195 Log Cabin Rd., Kennebunkport* ☎ *207/967–2712* 🌐 *www.trolleymuseum.org* 🎟 *$8.50* ⏲ *Early May–mid-Oct., daily 10–5; reduced hrs in spring and fall, call ahead.*

SHOPPING

Abacus (✉ *2 Ocean Ave., Dock Sq., Kennebunkport* ☎ *207/967–0111* 🌐 *www.abacusgallery.com*) sells eclectic crafts and furniture. **Mast Cove Galleries** (✉ *Mast Cove La., Kennebunkport* ☎ *207/967–3453* 🌐 *www.mastcove.com*) sells graphics, paintings, and sculpture by 105 artists.

SPORTS AND THE OUTDOORS

BIKING **Cape-Able Bike Shop** (✉ *83 Arundel Rd., Kennebunkport* ☎ *207/967–4382* 🌐 *www.capeablebikes.com*) rents bicycles of all types, including trailer bikes and tandems. Guided bike and kayak tours are also available.

BOATING AND FISHING To reserve a private sail for up to six people, contact Captain Jim Jannetti of the ***Bellatrix*** (✉ *Kennebunkport* ☎ *207/590–1125* 🌐 *www.sailingtrips.com*), a vintage racing yacht. Find and catch fish with **Cast Away Fishing Charters** (📫 *Box 245, Kennebunkport 04046* ☎ *207/284–1740* 🌐 *www.castawayfishingcharters.com*). **First Chance** (✉ *4-A Western Ave., Kennebunk 04043* ☎ *207/967–5507 or 800/767–2628* 🌐 *www.firstchancewhalewatch.com*) leads whale-watching cruises and guarantees sightings in season. Daily scenic lobster cruises are also offered aboard *Kylie's Chance*. For half- or full-day fishing trips as well as discovery trips for kids, book some time with **Lady J Sportfishing Charters** (✉ *Arundel Wharf, Ocean Ave.04046* ☎ *207/985–7304* 🌐 *www.ladyjcharters.com*).

Several scenic cruises and lobster-trap hauling trips run daily aboard the **Rugosa** (*Depart from Nonantum Resort, Ocean Ave. 207/967–5595 www.rugosacharters.com*) .

WHERE TO EAT

$$–$$$$ SEAFOOD **Mabel's Lobster Claw.** Mabel's has long been serving lobsters, homemade pies, and lots of seafood for lunch and dinner in this tiny dwelling out on Ocean Avenue. Decor includes paneled walls, wooden booths, autographed photos of various TV stars (plus members of the Bush family), and paper place mats that illustrate how to eat a Maine lobster. The house favorite is the Lobster Savannah—split and filled with scallops, shrimp, and mushrooms in a Newburg sauce. Save room for the peanut-butter ice-cream pie. Reservations are recommended. *124 Ocean Ave., Kennebunkport 207/967–2562 AE, D, MC, V Closed Nov.–Apr.*

$$$ SEAFOOD **Pier 77 Restaurant & the Ramp Bar & Grille.** The view takes center stage at this dual establishment, consisting of a fine-dining portion and a more casual and boisterous section. Pier 77 serves up more sophisticated fare, focusing on meats and seafood; the tiny, tiny Ramp pays homage to a really good burger, fried seafood, and other pub-style choices. The place is vibrant with live music most nights in summer and a great place for cocktails on the water. *77 Pier Rd., Cape Porpoise 207/967–8500 www.pier77restaurant.com AE, MC, V Closed Jan.–mid-Mar.*

WHERE TO STAY

$$$$ AMERICAN **Cape Arundel Inn.** This shingle-style inn commands a magnificent ocean view that takes in the Bush estate at Walker's Point. The spacious rooms are furnished with country-style furniture and antiques, and most have sitting areas with ocean views. You can relax on the front porch or by the fireplace. The Rockbound complex, a later addition (1950s), doesn't have the 19th-century charm of the main house, but the rooms are large, many have fireplaces, and all have private balconies from which to take in the views. In the candlelit dining room ($$$–$$$$), open to the public for dinner, every table has a view of the surf. The menu changes seasonally. **Pros:** extraordinary views from most rooms; close to town and attractions. **Cons:** not for the budget-minded. *208 Ocean Ave., Kennebunkport 207/967–2125 www.capearundelinn.com 19 rooms, 1 suite In-room: no phone, no a/c, no TV (some), Wi-Fi. In-hotel: restaurant, bicycles AE, D, MC, V Closed Jan. and Feb. CP.*

$$$$ Fodor's Choice ★ **Captain Lord Mansion.** Of all the mansions in Kennebunkport's historic district that have been converted to inns, the 1812 Captain Lord Mansion is the stateliest and most sumptuously appointed. Distinctive architecture, including a suspended elliptical staircase, gas fireplaces in all rooms, and near-museum-quality accoutrements make for a formal but not stuffy setting. Six rooms have whirlpool tubs. The extravagant suite has two fireplaces, a double whirlpool, a hydro-massage body spa, a TV/DVD and stereo system, and a king-size canopy bed. Day-spa services are available for added luxury. **Pros:** elegant and luxurious historic lodging; in-town location; beautiful landscaped grounds. **Cons:** expensive; not a beachfront location. *Pleasant and Green Sts., Kennebunkport*

5

☎ 207/967–3141 or 800/522–3141 🌐 *www.captainlord.com* 15 *rooms, 1 suite* *In-room: Wi-Fi. In-hotel: bicycles, Internet terminal, no kids under 12* *D, MC, V* *BP.*

$$$–$$$$ Fodor's Choice ★ **The Colony.** You can't miss this place—it's grand, white, and incredibly large, set majestically atop a rise overlooking the ocean. The hotel was built in 1914 (after its predecessor caught fire in 1898), and much of the splendid glamour of the earlier era remains. Many of the rooms in the main hotel (there are two other outbuildings) have ocean views from private or semiprivate balconies. All are outfitted with antiques and hardwood floors; the bright white bed linens nicely set off the colors of the Waverly wallpaper. The restaurant ($$–$$$$) features New England fare, with plenty of seafood and steaks. **Pros:** lodging in the tradition of grand old hotels; many ocean views; plenty of activities and entertainment for all ages. **Cons:** not intimate; rooms with ocean views come at steep prices. ✉ *Ocean Ave.* ☎ *207/967–3331 or 800/552–2363* 🌐 *www.thecolonyhotel.com/maine* *124 rooms* *In-room: no a/c (some), no TV (some), Wi-Fi. In-hotel: restaurant, room service, bar, pool, beachfront, bicycles, some pets allowed* *AE, MC, V* *Closed Nov.–mid-May* *BP.*

EN ROUTE

For a rewarding drive that goes into the reaches of the coastline on the way to Old Orchard Beach, head out of Kennebunkport on Route 9. Plan to do some beach walking at Goose Rocks Beach or Fortunes Rocks Beach, both ideal for stretching your legs or just looking for shells or critters in the tide pools. Route 9 continues to wind through wooded areas, then heads through the slightly weary-looking old mill town of Biddeford, across the Saco River, and into Saco, a busy town with commerce and its accompanying traffic. Once you get past Saco, Route 9 returns to its peaceful curves and gentle scenery, leaving crowded civilization behind and winding through the charming resort villages of Camp Ellis and Ocean Park. You could pack a picnic and spend some time at Ferry Beach State Park (look for the entrance just off Route 9 on Bayview Road). The varied landscapes in the park include forested sections, swamp, beach, and lots of dunes, all of which have miles of marked trails to hike.

OLD ORCHARD BEACH AREA

15 mi north of Kennebunkport; 18 mi south of Portland.

Back in the late 19th century Old Orchard Beach was a classic, upscale, place-to-be-seen resort area. The railroad brought wealthy families looking for entertainment and the benefits of the fresh sea air. Although a good bit of this aristocratic hue has dulled in more recent times—admittedly, the place is more than a little pleasantly tacky these days—Old Orchard Beach remains a good place for those looking for entertainment by the sea.

The center of the action is a 7-mi strip of sand beach and its accompanying amusement park. Despite the summertime crowds and fried-food odors, the atmosphere can be captivating. During the 1940s and '50s, the pier had a dance hall where stars of the time performed. Fire claimed the end of the pier—at one time it jutted out nearly 1,800 feet into the sea—but booths with games and candy concessions still line both sides. In summer the town sponsors fireworks (on Thursday night). Places to stay run the gamut from cheap motels to cottage colonies to full-service seasonal hotels. You won't find free parking in town, but there are ample lots. Amtrak has a seasonal stop here.

ESSENTIALS

Visitor Information Old Orchard Beach Chamber of Commerce (*✉ 1st St.* *Box 600, 04064* *☎ 207/934–2500 or 800/365–9386* *www.oldorchardbeachmaine.com*).

EXPLORING

Ocean Park. A world away from the beach scene lies Ocean Park, on the southwestern edge of town. Locals and visitors like to keep the separation distinct, touting their area as a more peaceful and wholesome family-style village (to that end, there are no alcohol or tobacco sales in this little haven). This vacation community was founded in 1881 by Free Will Baptist leaders as an interdenominational retreat with both religious and educational purposes, following the example of Chautauqua, New York. Today the community hosts an impressive variety of cultural happenings, including movies, concerts, recreation, workshops, and religious services. Most are presented in the Temple, which is on the National Register of Historic Places. Although the religious nature of the place is apparent in its worship schedule and some of its cultural offerings, visitors need not be members of any denomination; all are welcome. There's even a public shuffleboard area for vacationers not interested in the neon carnival attractions several miles up the road. Get an old-fashioned raspberry lime rickey at the Ocean Park Soda Fountain (near the library, at Furber Park); it's also a good place for breakfast or a light lunch. (*☎ 207/934–9068 Ocean Park Association*)

SPORTS AND THE OUTDOORS

Not far from Old Orchard Beach is the Maine Audubon–run **Scarborough Marsh Nature Center** (*✉ Pine Point Rd. [Rte. 9], Scarborough* *☎ 207/883–5100* *www.maineaudubon.org* *Free guided tours begin at $5* *Memorial Day–Sept.*). You can rent a canoe and explore this natural haven on your own or sign up for a guided trip. The salt marsh is Maine's largest and is an excellent place for bird-watching and peaceful paddling along its winding ways. The Nature Center has a discovery room for kids, programs for all ages ranging from basket making to astronomy, birding and canoe tours, and a good gift shop.

WHERE TO EAT

$$–$$$ ECLECTIC ★

The Landmark. This restaurant almost feels as if it doesn't belong here. Tables are set either on the glassed-in porch or within high, tin-ceiling rooms. Candles and a collection of giant fringed Art Nouveau lamps provide a gentle light. The menu has a good selection of seafood and meats, many treated with flavors from various parts of the globe. It's the kind of menu that encourages you to try new things, and you definitely won't be disappointed. Outside on the stone patio and sheltered by umbrellas is the "in the rough" dinner menu, with everything cooked on the adjacent grill. Choose from clambake-style meals, charbroiled and marinated skewers, and BBQ ribs. Coffee and pastries are served out here in the morning. ✉ *25 E. Grand Ave., Old Orchard Beach* ☎ *207/934–0156* 🌐 *www.landmarkfinedining.com* ▭ *AE, D, MC, V* ⊙ *Closed late Nov.–Mar.*

$$$ SEAFOOD ✕ **Yellowfin's.** Inside this diminutive restaurant housed in an impeccably kept yellow Victorian, it is fresh, bright, and appropriately beachy. A giant tank bubbles quietly in the background while its resident colorful fish in the tank survey the landscape of white linen–covered tables adorned with sand and shell centerpieces. White cloth panels draped along the ceiling add an enveloping sense of comfort to the lively space. Not surprisingly, the house specialty is ahi yellowfin tuna, pan seared and treated with a wasabi ginger sauce; other choices include seared scallops, lamb, and a savory seafood fra diavolo (with a spicy tomato sauce). Brunch is offered weekends in July and August. In Ocean Park it's BYOB—you'll have to stock up in nearby Old Orchard Beach. ✉ *5 Temple Ave., Ocean Park* ☎ *207/934–1100* ▭ *D, MC, V* ⊙ *No lunch.*

PORTLAND

Maine's largest city is considered small by national standards—its population is just 64,000—but its character, spirit, and appeal make it feel much larger. In fact, it is a cultural and economic center for a metropolitan area of 230,000 residents—one-quarter of Maine's entire population. Portland and its environs are well worth at least a day or two of exploration.

A city of many names throughout its history, including Casco and Falmouth, Portland has survived many dramatic transformations. Sheltered by the nearby Casco Bay Islands and blessed with a deep port, Portland was a significant settlement right from its start in the early 17th century. Settlers thrived on fishing and lumbering, repeatedly building up the area while the British, French, and Native Americans continually sacked it. Many considered the region a somewhat dangerous frontier, but its potential for prosperity was so apparent that settlers came anyway to tap its rich natural resources.

Portland's first home was built on the peninsula now known as Munjoy Hill in 1632. The British burned the city in 1775, when residents refused to surrender arms, but it was rebuilt and became a major trading center. Much of Portland was destroyed again in the Great Fire on July 4, 1866, when a boy threw a celebratory firecracker into a pile of wood shavings; 1,500 buildings burned to the ground.

Today, there is an excellent restaurant scene and a great art museum, and the waterfront is a lively area to walk around.

ESSENTIALS

Contacts Greater Portland Convention and Visitors Bureau (✉ *14 Ocean Gateway Pier, off Commercial St.* ☎ *207/772–5800 or 877/833–1374* 🌐 *www.visitportland.com*). **Portland Regional Chamber of Commerce** (✉ *60 Pearl St.* ☎ *207/772–2811* 🌐 *www.portlandregion.com*). **Portland's Downtown District** (✉ *549 Congress St.* ☎ *207/772–6828* 🌐 *www.portlandmaine.com*).

Portland's busy harbor is full of working boats, pleasure craft, and ferries headed to the Casco Bay Islands.

THE OLD PORT

Numbers in the margin correspond to numbers on the Portland map.

Fodor's Choice ★ A major international port and a working harbor since the early 17th century, the Old Port bridges the gap between the city's historical commercial activities and those of today. It is home to fishing boats docked alongside whale-watching charters, luxury yachts, cruise ships, and oil tankers from around the globe. Commercial Street parallels the water and is lined with brick buildings and warehouses that were built following the Great Fire of 1866. In the 19th century candle makers and sail stitchers plied their trades here; today specialty shops, art galleries, and restaurants have taken up residence.

As with much of the city, it's best to park your car and explore the Old Port on foot. You can park at the city garage on Fore Street (between Exchange and Union streets) or opposite the U.S. Custom House at the corner of Fore and Pearl streets. A helpful hint: look for the PARK & SHOP sign on garages and parking lots and get one hour of free parking for each stamp collected at participating shops. Allow a couple of hours to wander at leisure on Market, Exchange, Middle, and Fore streets. The city is very pedestrian-friendly. Maine state law requires vehicles to stop for walkers in crosswalks.

1 **Maine Narrow Gauge Railroad Co. & Museum.** Whether you're crazy about old trains or just want to see the sights from a different perspective, the railroad museum has an extensive collection of locomotives and rail coaches and tours on narrow-gauge railcars. The 3-mi jaunt takes you along Casco Bay, at the foot of the Eastern Promenade. Theme trips

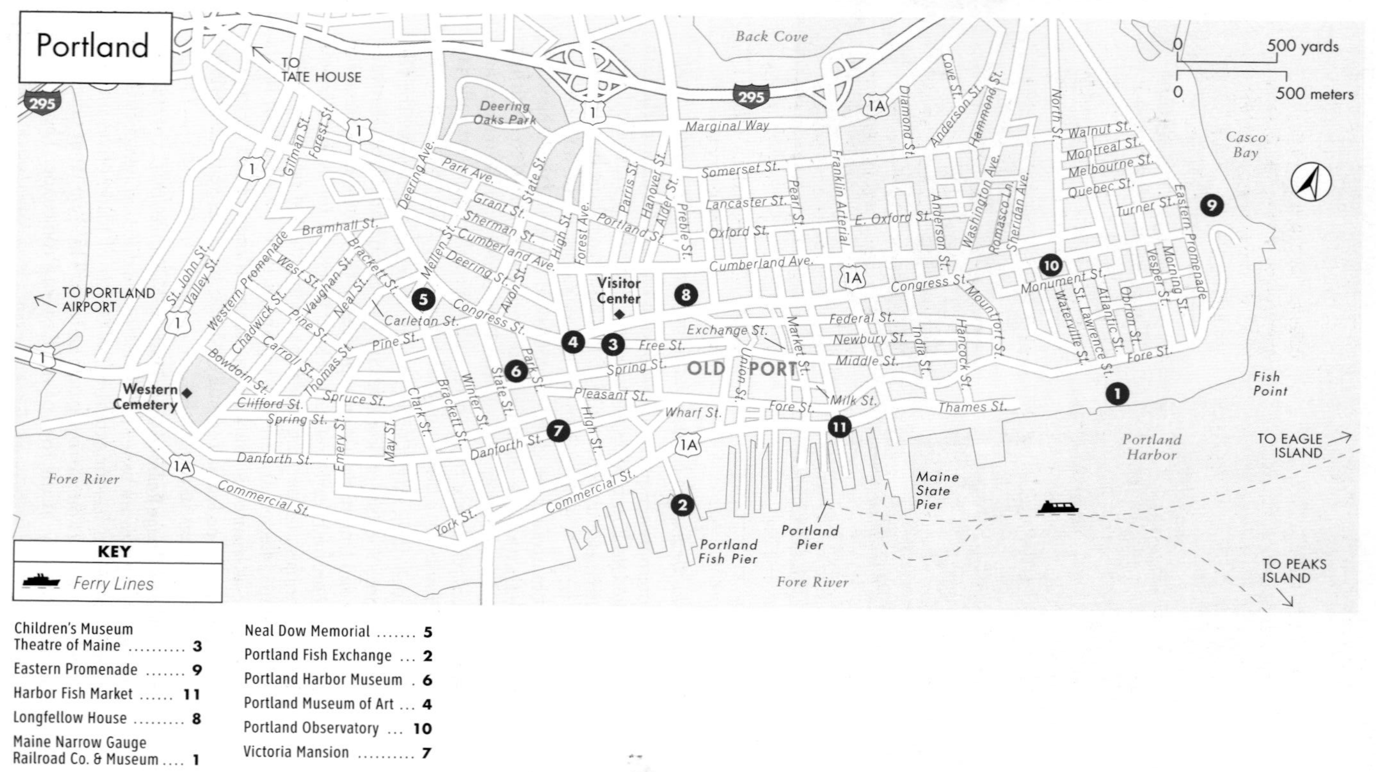
Portland
TO TATE HOUSE
Back Cove
0 500 yards
0 500 meters
Deering Oaks Park
Marginal Way
Casco Bay
TO PORTLAND AIRPORT
Visitor Center
OLD PORT
Western Cemetery
Fish Point
Portland Harbor
TO EAGLE ISLAND
Maine State Pier
Portland Pier
Portland Fish Pier
Fore River
TO PEAKS ISLAND
Gilman St.
Forest St.
Park Ave.
Deering Ave.
Grant St.
Sherman St.
Cumberland Ave.
Deering St.
Mellen St.
State St.
High St.
Forest Ave.
Parris St.
Hanover St.
Alder St.
Portland St.
Preble St.
Somerset St.
Lancaster St.
Oxford St.
Pearl St.
Franklin Arterial
E. Oxford St.
Diamond St.
Cove St.
Anderson St.
Hammond St.
Washington Ave.
Romasco Ln.
Sheridan Ave.
North St.
Walnut St.
Montreal St.
Melbourne St.
Quebec St.
Turner St.
Eastern Promenade
Morning St.
Vesper St.
Obrion St.
Atlantic St.
St. Lawrence St.
Waterville St.
Monument St.
Congress St.
Mountfort St.
Hancock St.
India St.
Federal St.
Newbury St.
Middle St.
Exchange St.
Market St.
Union St.
Free St.
Spring St.
Fore St.
Milk St.
Thames St.
Wharf St.
Pleasant St.
Bramhall St.
Western Promenade
West St.
Vaughan St.
Brackett St.
Neal St.
Chadwick St.
Pine St.
Carroll St.
Thomas St.
Carleton St.
Avon St.
Park St.
Bowdoin St.
Clifford St.
Spruce St.
Spring St.
Emery St.
May St.
Clark St.
Brackett St.
Winter St.
State St.
Danforth St.
High St.
St. John St.
Valley St.
Commercial St.
York St.
1
1A
295
KEY
Ferry Lines
Children's Museum Theatre of Maine 3
Eastern Promenade 9
Harbor Fish Market 11
Longfellow House 8
Maine Narrow Gauge Railroad Co. & Museum 1
Neal Dow Memorial 5
Portland Fish Exchange 2
Portland Harbor Museum 6
Portland Museum of Art 4
Portland Observatory 10
Victoria Mansion 7

PORTLAND TOURS

AUTO TOURS

The informative trolley tours of **Portland Discovery Land & Sea Tours** (✉ *Long Wharf, 170 Commercial St.* ☎ *207/774–0808* 🌐 *www.portlanddiscovery.com*) detail Portland's historical and architectural highlights from Memorial Day through October. Options include combining a city tour with a bay cruise or a trip to four lighthouses.

WALKING TOURS

Learn about Portland's culinary history and sample local delights like lobster hors d'oeuvres, organic cheese, and the famous Maine whoopie pie with **Maine Foodie Tours** (✉ *Kiosk at 10 Moulton St.* ☎ *207/233–7485* 🌐 *www.mainefoodietours.com*). You also can sign up for a pub crawl, a tour of microbreweries, or a "destination" trip to nearby farms and bakeries. Tours operate year-round; prices start at $29. **Greater Portland Landmarks** (✉ *93 High St.* ☎ *207/774–5561* 🌐 *www.portlandlandmarks.org*) conducts 1½-hour walking tours of the Old Port from July through September; tours begin at the visitor's kiosk at **Tommy's Park** (✉ *Corner of Middle and Exchange St.*) and cost $10. The group also offers self-guided tours of the Old Port, Congress Street, historic churches, the West End, and other spots. Pick up maps and itineraries at their offices (a small fee is charged) or download them for free online. **Portland Freedom Trail** (☎ *207/591–9980* 🌐 *www.portlandfreedomtrail.org*) provides a self-guided tour, available for free download online, of sites associated with the Underground Railroad and the anti-slavery movement.

5

include the Polar Express ride, based on the popular children's book, a Halloween ride (wear your costumes), and a July 4 fireworks ride. ✉ *58 Fore St.* ☎ *207/828–0814* 🌐 *www.mngrr.org* 🎫 *Train $10, museum $2* ⏲ *Trains mid-May–mid-Oct., daily on the hr 11–4; mid-Feb.–mid-May and mid-Oct.–mid-Nov., weekends on the hr 11–3. Museum late-Oct.–mid May, weekdays 10–4; late May–late Oct., daily 10–4.*

❷ **Portland Fish Exchange.** You may want to hold your nose for this glimpse into the Old Port's active fish business when you drop by the 30,000-square-foot Portland Fish Exchange. Peek inside coolers teeming with cod, flounder, and monkfish and watch fishermen repairing their nets and prices being settled through an auction process. It's a great behind-the-scenes view of this dynamic market. Auctions take place Sunday at 11 AM and Monday through Thursday at noon. ✉ *6 Portland Fish Pier* ☎ *207/773–0017* 🌐 *www.pfex.org* 🎫 *Free.*

⓫ **Harbor Fish Market.** A Portland favorite for more than 40 years, this freshest-of-the-fresh seafood market ships lobsters and other Maine delectables almost anywhere in the country. A bright-red facade on a working wharf opens into a bustling space with bubbling lobster pens and fish, clams, and other shellfish on ice; employees are as skilled with a fillet knife as sushi chefs. ✉ *9 Custom House Wharf* ☎ *207/775–0251 or 800/370–1790* 🌐 *www.harborfish.com* 🎫 *Free.*

THE ARTS DISTRICT

This district starts at the top of Exchange Street, near the upper end of the Old Port, and extends west past the Portland Museum of Art. Congress Street is the district's central artery. Art galleries, specialty stores, and a score of restaurants line Congress Street. Parking is tricky; two-hour meters dot the sidewalks, but there are several nearby parking garages.

TOP ATTRACTIONS

3 **Children's Museum & Theatre of Maine.** Touching is okay at Portland's small but fun Children's Museum, where kids can pretend they are lobstermen, veterinarians, shopkeepers, or actors in a play. The majority of the museum's exhibits, many of which have a Maine theme, are best for children 10 and younger. Camera Obscura, an exhibit about optics, provides fascinating panoramic views of the city. The museum's newest addition, Have a Ball! teaches about the science of motion, letting kids build ramps that make balls speed up, slow down and leap across tracks. *142 Free St.* *207/828–1234* *www.kitetails.org* *Museum $8; Camera Obscura only, $4* *Memorial Day–Labor Day, Mon.–Sat. 10–5, Sun. noon–5; day after Labor Day–day before Memorial Day, Tues.–Sat. 10–5, Sun. noon–5.*

8 **Longfellow House.** The boyhood home of the famous American poet is one of the first brick houses in Portland. It's particularly interesting because most of the furnishings, including French Rococo–Revival wallpaper, a vibrant painted carpet, and the young Longfellow's writing desk, are original. The Colonial Revival structure, built in 1785, sits back from the street and has a small portico over its entrance and four chimneys surmounting the roof. The house is part of the Maine Historical Society, which includes an adjacent museum with exhibits about Maine life and a research library. After your guided tour of the home, stay for a picnic in the Longfellow Garden, designed from period sketches. *489 Congress St.* *207/774–1822* *www.mainehistory.org* *House and Maine Historical Society Museum $8; museum only, $5; garden, free* *House and Maine Historical Society Museum May–Oct., Mon.–Sat. 10–5, Sun. noon–5; last tour at 4. Nov. and Dec., call for hrs. Library: year-round, Tues.–Sat. 10–4.*

6 **Portland Harbor Museum.** Immerse yourself in Portland's maritime history at this thoughtfully executed museum. An exhibit features Rosie the Riveter types, women who went to work as mechanics, crane operators, and electricians in the Portland shipyard during World War II. Another exhibit is devoted to the steamship known as New England's Titanic, which sank in an 1898 storm, taking 175 people with it. You'll also find vintage postcards depicting coastal scenes, with their inscriptions transcribed on the wall, photography by local artists, model ships, historical maps, and marine artifacts. *510 Congress St.* *207/773–3800* *www.portlandharbormuseum.org* *$3* *Mid-May–mid-Oct, daily 10–4; after mid-Oct, call for hours.*

4 ★ **Portland Museum of Art.** Maine's largest public art institution has a number of strong collections, including fine seascapes and landscapes by Winslow Homer, John Marin, Andrew Wyeth, Edward Hopper, Marsden

Hartley, and other painters. Homer's *Weatherbeaten*, a quintessential Maine Coast image, is here, and the museum owns and displays more than 20 of his other works. The Joan Whitney Payson Collection of Impressionist and Post-Impressionist art includes works by Monet, Picasso, and Renoir. Harry N. Cobb designed the strikingly modern Charles Shipman Payson building. The nearby L. D. M. Sweat Galleries house the museum's collection of 19th-century American art, and the 1801 McLellan House has gorgeous Federal design and interactive educational stations. ✉ *7 Congress Sq.* ☎ *207/775–6148* 🌐 *www.portlandmuseum.org* 🎫 *$10, free Fri. 5–9* ⏲ *Memorial Day–Columbus Day, Mon.–Thurs. and weekends 10–5, Fri. 10–9; Columbus Day–Memorial Day, Tues.–Thurs. and weekends 10–5, Fri. 10–9.*

WHAT'S ON TAP: MICROBREWERIES

Maine is home to more than 20 breweries, and several of the larger ones—Allagash, Geary's, Shipyard, and Casco Bay (try their summer ale!)—are around Portland. These breweries are open for tours and tastings, but beer lovers may prefer the smaller brewpubs that make their own beer and serve it fresh from their own taps in neighborhood taverns. In the Old Port you'll find Gritty McDuff's and Sebago Brewing Company. In South Portland there's Sea Dog Brewing Company. If you're in town in November, check out the Maine Brewer's Festival (🌐 *www.mainebrew.com*).

5

7 ★ **Victoria Mansion.** Built between 1858 and 1860, this Italianate mansion is widely regarded as the most sumptuously ornamented dwelling of its period remaining in the country. Architect Henry Austin designed the house for hotelier Ruggles Morse and his wife, Olive. The interior design—everything from the plasterwork to the furniture (much of it original)—is the only surviving commission of New York designer Gustave Herter. Behind the elegant brownstone exterior of this National Historic Landmark are colorful frescoed walls and ceilings, ornate marble mantelpieces, gilded gas chandeliers, a magnificent 6-foot-by-25-foot stained-glass ceiling window, and a freestanding mahogany staircase. Guided tours run about 45 minutes and cover all the architectural highlights. ✉ *109 Danforth St.* ☎ *207/772–4841* 🌐 *www.victoriamansion.org* 🎫 *$15* ⏲ *May–Oct., Mon.–Sat. 10–4, Sun. 1–5; Christmas tours day after Thanksgiving–Jan. 3, daily 11–5.*

WORTH NOTING

9 **Eastern Promenade.** Of the two promenades, this one, often overlooked by tourists, has by far the best view. Gracious Victorian homes border one side of the street; on the other is a 68-acre hillside park that slopes down to the water. At the base of the hill are the Eastern Prom Trail, a great place for walking or cycling, and the tiny East End Beach. On a sunny day the park is a lovely spot for picnicking and people-watching. ✉ *Congress St. and Eastern Promenade.*

5 **Neal Dow Memorial.** Now the headquarters of the Maine Women's Christian Temperance Union, this majestic 1829 Federal-style home is open for tours. The mansion, once a stop on the Underground Railroad, is

filled with the Civil War general's original antiques, books, and papers on Prohibition—he was responsible for Maine's adoption of the anti-alcohol bill in 1851. ✉ *714 Congress St.* ☎ *207/773–7773* 🎫 *Free* ⏲ *Weekdays 11–4 or by appointment.*

10 **Portland Observatory.** This octagonal observatory on Munjoy Hill was built in 1807 by Captain Lemuel Moody, a retired sea captain, as a signal tower. Moody used a telescope to identify incoming ships and flags to signal to merchants where to unload their cargo. Held in place by 122 tons of ballast, it's the last remaining signal tower in the country. After visiting the small museum at the base, climb to the Orb deck and take in views of Portland, the islands, and inland to the White Mountains. ✉ *138 Congress St.* ☎ *207/774–5561* 🌐 *www.portlandlandmarks.org* 🎫 *$7* ⏲ *Memorial Day weekend–Columbus Day, daily 10–5.*

OFF THE BEATEN PATH

★ **Tate House.** Built astride rose granite steps and a period herb garden overlooking the Stroudwater River on the outskirts of Portland, this magnificent 1755 house was built by Captain George Tate. Tate had been commissioned by the English Crown to organize "the King's Broad Arrow"—the marking and cutting down of gigantic forest trees, which were shipped to England to be fashioned as masts for the British Royal Navy. The house has several period rooms, including a sitting room with some fine English Restoration chairs. With its clapboard still gloriously unpainted, its impressive Palladian doorway, dogleg stairway, unusual clerestory, and gambrel roof, this house will delight all lovers of Early American decorative arts. Guided tours of the gardens are held once a week from mid-June to mid-October. House tours are offered five days a week in season. Call or visit the Web site for special holiday programs during December. ✉ *1267 Westbrook St.* ☎ *207/774–6177* 🌐 *www.tatehouse.org* 🎫 *$7* ⏲ *Mid-June–mid-Oct., call for hrs.*

THE WEST END

A leisurely walk through Portland's West End, beginning at the top of the Arts District, offers a real treat to historic architecture buffs. The neighborhood, on the National Register of Historic Places, reveals an extraordinary display of architectural splendor, from High Victorian Gothic to lush Italianate, Queen Anne, and Colonial Revival.

A good place to start is at the head of the Western Promenade, which has parking, benches, and a nice view. From the Old Port, take Danforth Street all the way up to Vaughn Street; take a right on Vaughn and then an immediate left onto Western Promenade. Pass by the Western Cemetery, Portland's second official burial ground, laid out in 1829 (inside is the ancestral plot of famous poet Henry Wadsworth Longfellow) and just beyond is the parking area.

You could easily spend an hour or two wandering the backstreets of the West End; longer if you bring a picnic to enjoy in the grassy park alongside the Promenade. If you're interested in the particular history of individual homes, download or pick up a brochure from **Greater Portland Landmarks.** A map is included, as well as the stories of some of the more prominent homes. The group also offers a guided house tour on Fri-

Exchange Street, in the Arts District, is a popular place to explore for art, shopping, and summer treats.

day mornings July through September. ✉ *93 High St.* ☎ *207/774–5561* ⏲ *Weekdays 9–5* 🌐 *www.portlandlandmarks.org.*

WHERE TO EAT

Portland is blessed with exceptional restaurants rivaling those of a far larger city. Fresh seafood, including the famous Maine lobster, is still popular and prevalent, but there are plenty more cuisines to be enjoyed. More and more restaurants are using local meats, seafood, and produce as much as possible; changing menus reflect what is available in the region at the moment. As sophisticated as many of these establishments have become, the atmosphere is generally casual; with a few exceptions, you can leave your jacket and tie at home.

Smoking is banned in all restaurants, taverns, and bars in Portland. As always, reservations are recommended and allowed unless we state otherwise.

$ AMERICAN ✕ **Becky's.** You won't find a more local or unfussy place—or one that is more abuzz with conversation at 4 AM—than this waterfront institution, way down on the end of Commercial Street. Sitting next to you at the counter or in a neighboring booth could be rubber-booted fishermen back from sea, college students soothing a hangover, or suited business folks with Blackberries. The food is cheap, generous in proportion, and has that satisfying, old-time diner quality. Breakfast and lunch are served from 4 AM to 9 PM; dinner is available from 4 PM until closing. Nightly specials add to the large menu of fried seafood platters, salads, and sandwiches. Get a pie, cake, or pudding to go. ✉ *390 Commercial St.* ☎ *207/773–7070* 🌐 *www.beckysdiner.com* 💳 *AE, D, MC, V.*

$ MEXICAN ★ ✕ **El Rayo Taqueria.** For the best Mexican food in town, head slightly out of your way to this hip joint housed in a former gas station on an industrial stretch above Commercial Street. The flavors are as vibrant as the turquoise, yellow, and fuchsia decor. All of the salsas and guacamole are made fresh daily. Pull up a stool at the counter, sit at a table inside, or grab a bright, oilcloth-covered picnic table out front. Wash down achiote-seasoned fish tacos or a citrus-and cumin-marinated chicken burrito with a virgin lemon-hibiscus *refresco* (cold drink) or house margarita. There's plenty of parking in the old filling-station lot. ✉ *101 York St. (at High St.)* ☎ *207/780–8226* 🌐 *www.elrayotaqueria.com* 💳 *AE, D, MC, V* ⏲ *Closed Mon.*

$$$–$$$$ AMERICAN Fodor's Choice ★ ✕ **Five Fifty-Five.** Classic dishes are cleverly updated at this cozy Congress Street spot. The ubiquitous lobster roll, dubbed a "knuckle sandwich," consists of meat tossed with basil aioli and sandwiched between two slices of fried green tomato; the mac and cheese boasts artisanal cheeses and shaved black truffle. The menu changes seasonally (and sometimes daily) to reflect ingredients available within a 30-mi radius, but the seared local diver scallops, served in a buttery carrot-vanilla emulsion, are an exquisite mainstay. The space, which features exposed brick and copper accents, is a former 19th-century firehouse. ✉ *555 Congress St.* ☎ *207/761–0555* 🌐 *www.fivefifty-five.com* 💳 *AE, MC, V* ⏲ *No lunch Mon.–Sat.*

$$ PIZZA ★ ✕ **Flatbread Company.** Families, students, and bohemian types gather at this popular pizza place, known locally as Flatbread's. A giant wood-fire oven, where the pies are cooked, is the heart of the soaring, warehouse-like space; in summer you can escape the heat by dining on the deck overlooking the harbor. The simple menu has eight signature pizzas plus weekly veggie and meat specials; everything is homemade, organic, and nitrate-free. Be sure to order the delicious house salad with toasted sesame seeds, seaweed, blue or goat cheese, and ginger-tamarind vinaigrette. ✉ *72 Commercial St.* ☎ *207/772–8777* 🌐 *www.flatbreadcompany.com* 💳 *AE, MC, V* ✍ *Reservations not accepted for parties smaller than 10.*

$$$–$$$$ AMERICAN ★ ✕ **Fore Street.** One of Maine's best chefs, Sam Hayward, opened this restaurant in a renovated warehouse on the edge of the Old Port. The menu changes daily to reflect the freshest local ingredients. Every copper-top table in the main dining room has a view of the enormous brick oven and hearth and the open kitchen, where sous-chefs seem to dance as they create entrées such as three cuts of Maine island lamb, Atlantic monkfish fillet, and breast of Moulad duckling. Desserts include artisanal cheeses. Reservations are strongly recommended—in fact, if you want to dine in July or August, book two months in advance, and a week or more at other times. But last-minute planners take heart: each night a third of the tables are reserved for walk-in diners. ✉ *288 Fore St.* ☎ *207/775–2717* 🌐 *www.forestreet.biz* 💳 *AE, MC, V* ⏲ *No lunch.*

$$–$$$ SEAFOOD ★ ✕ **Gilbert's Chowder House.** This is the real deal, as quintessential as Maine dining can be. Clam rakes and nautical charts hang from the walls of this unpretentious waterfront diner. The flavors are from the

CLOSE UP

The Eastern Prom Trail

To experience the city's busy shoreline and grand views of Casco Bay, walkers, runners, and cyclists head out on the Eastern Prom Trail.

Beginning at the intersection of Commercial and India streets, this paved trail follows the old railroad tracks of the Maine Narrow Gauge Railroad Co. & Museum. There are plenty of places with benches and tables for a picnic break along the way. From the trailhead, it's about 1¼ mi to the small East End Beach.

You can continue along the trail, pass underneath busy Interstate 295, and reemerge at Back Cove, a popular 3½-mi loop; or you can return to the Old Port by backtracking along the trail or heading up a grassy hill to the Eastern Promenade, a lovely picnic spot and playground.

Take a left back toward the Old Port. Starting down the hill, a gazebo and several old cannons to your left indicate the small Fort Allen Park. Use one of the coin-operated viewing scopes to view Ft. Gorges, a Civil War–era military garrison that was never used.

Where the Eastern Prom becomes Fore Street, either head straight back into the Old Port or take a left on India Street, which will bring you just about back to where you started.

Plan an hour to walk to East End Beach and back; add an hour or two if you continue along the Back Cove Trail.

5

depths of the North Atlantic, prepared and presented simply: fish, clam, corn, and seafood chowders; fried shrimp; haddock; clam strips; and extraordinary clam cakes. A chalkboard of daily specials often features Alaskan king crab legs and various entrée and chowder combinations. Don't miss out on the lobster roll—a toasted hot-dog bun bursting with claw and tail meat lightly dressed with mayo but otherwise unadulterated. It's classic Maine, fuss-free and presented on a paper plate. ✉ 92 *Commercial St.* ☎ *207/871–5636* 🌐 *www.gilbertschowderhouse.com* 💳 *D, MC, V.*

$$$$ ECLECTIC ★ ✕ **Hugo's.** James Beard Award–winning chef-owner Rob Evans has turned Hugo's into one of the city's best restaurants. If you're adventurous, the six-course "blind-tasting" ($85 per person) is a lot of fun—if you don't mind not knowing what you're going to be served. You also can mix and match $10 to $20 items from the à la carte menu, such as roasted rib eye and crispy arctic char with seaweed slaw. Portions are small, as they're meant to be part of a four- to six-course meal. Serving the freshest local organic foods is a high priority here, so the menu changes almost every day. ✉ *88 Middle St.* ☎ *207/774–8538* 🌐 *www.hugos.net* 💳 *AE, MC, V* ⏲ *Closed Sun. and Mon. No lunch.*

$$ SPANISH ✕ **Local 188.** At this funky Arts District eatery many diners don't bother with the menu, which is deliberately vague, and instead wait for their server to explain what just-caught seafood will decorate the paella and which fresh veggies are starring in the tortilla tapas. The vibe inside the 3,000-square-foot space, with its lofty tin ceilings and worn maple

floors, is relaxed and quirky—mismatched chandeliers dangle over the dining area, and a pair of antlers crowns the open kitchen. This is also a popular spot to come for a drink. Sink into a comfy couch in the bar area and choose from 150 mostly European wines. ✉ *685 Congress St.* ☎ *207/761–7909* 🌐 *www.local188.com* ▭ *AE, D, MC, V* ⊙ *No lunch weekdays.*

$$–$$$ AMERICAN ✕ **Walter's Cafe.** A fixture in the Old Port for more than 20 years, this casual, busy place is popular with suits and tourists alike. The menu manages a good balance of local seafood and meats with Asian and more eclectic flavors. Begin with calamari dressed with lemon–cherry pepper aioli; then move on to salmon marinated in miso sake or grilled duck breast with green-chile--corn fritters. ✉ *2 Portland Sq.* ☎ *207/871–9258* 🌐 *www.walterscafe.com* ▭ *AE, MC, V* ⊙ *No lunch Sun.*

WHERE TO STAY

As Portland's popularity as a vacation destination has increased, so have its options for overnight visitors. Though several large hotels—geared toward high-tech, amenity-obsessed guests—have been built in the Old Port, they have in no way diminished the success of smaller, more intimate lodgings. Inns and B&Bs have taken up residence throughout the city, often giving new life to the grand mansions of Portland's 19th-century wealthy businessmen. For the least expensive accommodations, investigate the chain hotels near the Interstate and the airport.

Expect to pay from about $140 a night for a pleasant room (often with complimentary breakfast) within walking distance of the Old Port during high season, and more than $400 for the most luxurious of suites. In the height of the summer season many places are booked; make reservations well in advance, and ask about off-season specials.

$$$$ **Danforth Inn.** New ownership and extensive redecorating have transformed a once-shabby 1823 inn with grandmotherly decor into a stunning showpiece. It stands on a block known in the early 19th century as "Social Corners" for the elaborate parties the owners hosted in what is now the downstairs lounge area. Updated with modern furnishings, the space has a glamorous, Old Hollywood feel: you almost expect a young Elizabeth Taylor to come waltzing through the double doors. The guest rooms are individually decorated with vibrant patterns and original artwork; most have working fireplaces. Room 3, with its semicircle design, bank of windows, and crystal chandelier over the bed, is exquisite. **Pros:** boutique hotel experience minutes from downtown. **Cons:** some third-floor rooms have very small windows. ✉ *163 Danforth St.* ☎ *207/879–8755 or 800/991–6557* 🌐 *www.danforthmaine.com* *9 rooms, 1 suite* *In-room: no phone, DVD (some), Wi-Fi. In-hotel: Wi-Fi hotspot, parking (free), no kids under 16* ▭ *AE, MC, V* *BP.*

$$–$$$ **The Inn at Park Spring.** The husband and wife who own this small, comfortable town-house inn pride themselves on the fact that many of their guests have been returning for more than 30 years. They come for the reasonable rates, delicious and satisfying breakfast (think stuffed ham-and-cheese croissant or savory French toast with poached egg), and fabulous location: it's less than five minutes on foot to the Arts

District and 10 minutes to Exchange Street. You can also spend a pleasant evening right here. Pick up a bottle of wine at the West End Deli downstairs and head a few doors down to **Miyake** (✉ *129 Spring St.* ☎ *207/871–9170*), a tiny BYOB, for inventive, phenomenally fresh sushi. **Pros:** fenced-in courtyard is lovely on a sunny day. **Cons:** no-frills decor; some rooms need updating. ✉ *135 Spring St.* ☎ *207/774–1059 or 800/437–8511* 🌐 *www.innatparkspring.com* *6 rooms* *In-room: no TV, Wi-Fi. In-hotel: Internet terminal, Wi-Fi hotspot, parking (free)* *AE, D, DC, MC, V* *BP.*

$$$–$$$$ Fodor'sChoice ★ **Pomegranate Inn.** The classic facade of this handsome 1884 inn in the architecturally rich Western Promenade area gives no hint of the surprises within. The common spaces have who-would-have-thunk-it combinations like bright, faux marble walls, a painted checkerboard floor, and a leopard-print runner; most of the guest rooms are hand-painted with splashy florals or polka dots. The inn feels like a gallery, with almost every available surface covered by contemporary art. (The paintings on the second floor are on loan from Portland's Cygnet Gallery and for sale.) Somehow it all comes together, creating a whimsical, outrageous, and wonderful effect. **Pros:** heaven for art lovers; close to Western Promenade. **Cons:** not within easy walking distance of Old Port. ✉ *49 Neal St.* ☎ *207/772–1006 or 800/356–0408* 🌐 *www.pomegranateinn.com* *8 rooms* *In-room: no phone, Wi-Fi. In-hotel: Wi-Fi hotspot, parking (free), some pets allowed, no kids under 16* *AE, MC, V* *BP.*

$$$$ **Portland Harbor Hotel.** Making luxury its primary focus, the Harbor Hotel has become a favorite with business travelers seeking meetings on a more intimate scale and vacationing guests who want high-quality service and amenities. Book a massage or pedicure at the on-site Nine Stones spa. In season, eat on the enclosed garden patio. **Pros:** luxurious extras; amid the action of the Old Port and waterfront. **Cons:** not for the quaint of heart. ✉ *468 Fore St.* ☎ *207/775–9090 or 888/798–9090* 🌐 *www.portlandharborhotel.com* *88 rooms, 18 suites* *In-room: Wi-Fi. In-hotel: restaurant, bar, gym, spa, bicycles, laundry service, Internet terminal, Wi-Fi hotspot, parking (paid), some pets allowed* *AE, D, MC, V.*

$$$$ **Portland Regency Hotel and Spa.** One of just a handful of major hotels in the center of the Old Port, the brick Regency building was Portland's armory in the late 19th century. Some of the traditionally furnished rooms have four-poster beds, and all have tall standing mirrors, desks, flat-screen TVs, and terry robes. You can walk to shops, restaurants, and museums from the hotel. The full-service spa offers a variety of massage treatments, a sea-salt body polish, a seaweed wrap, an herb-and-fruit-infused facial, and even eyelash tinting! **Pros:** convenient to town; has all the amenities you'd want. **Cons:** some rooms on the third and fourth floors have low ceilings and no windows (there are skylights, however). ✉ *20 Milk St.* ☎ *207/774–4200 or 800/727–3436* 🌐 *www.theregency.com* *84 rooms, 11 suites* *In-room: Wi-Fi. In-hotel: restaurant, bar, gym, spa, laundry service, Wi-Fi hotspot, parking (paid)* *AE, D, DC, MC, V.*

$$$–$$$$ **West End Inn.** Set among the glorious aged homes of the Western Promenade, this 1871 house displays much of the era's Victorian grandeur, with high tin ceilings, intricate moldings and ceiling medallions, and a dramatic ruby-red foyer. Spacious rooms are either brightly painted or papered with traditional Waverly prints, and all have private baths and alarm clocks with MP3 player docks. For breakfast, innkeeper Beth Oliver often whips up a French toast casserole with blueberries and cream cheese; or sausage and herb quiche with a hash brown crust. Oliver is also a fountain of Portland knowledge and will cheerfully field questions, make reservations, and gently remind you to wear your walking shoes—it's a 20-minute stroll to the action downtown. **Pros:** elegant library with fireplace is a cozy place to relax. **Cons:** one room uses a bathroom across the hall. ✉ *146 Pine St.* ☎ *207/772–1377 or 800/338–1377* 🌐 *www.westendbb.com* *6 rooms* *In-room: no phone, Wi-Fi. In-hotel: Wi-Fi hotspot, parking (free), no kids under 16* *AE, MC, V* *BP.*

NIGHTLIFE

Portland's nightlife scene is largely centered around the bustling Old Port and a few smaller, artsy spots on Congress Street. There's a great emphasis on local, live music and pubs serving award-winning local microbrews. Several hip wine bars have cropped up, serving appetizers along with a full array of specialty wines and whimsical cocktails. It's a fairly youthful scene in Portland, in some spots even rowdy and rough-around-the-edges, but there are plenty of places where you don't have to shout over the din to be heard.

To see live local and national acts any night of the week, try **The Big Easy** (✉ *55 Market St.* ☎ *207/775–2266* 🌐 *www.bigeasyportland.com*). For nightly themed brew specials, plenty of Guinness, and live entertainment, head to **Bull Feeney's** (✉ *375 Fore St.* ☎ *207/773–7210* 🌐 *www.bullfeeneys.com*), a lively two-story Irish pub and restaurant. **Gritty McDuff's** (✉ *396 Fore St.* ☎ *207/772–2739* 🌐 *www.grittys.com*) brews fine ales and serves British pub fare and seafood dishes. At **Novare Res Bier Café** (✉ *4 Canal Plaza, Exchange St. between Middle St. and Fore St.* ☎ *207/761–2437* 🌐 *www.novareresbiercafe.com*), choose from 25 rotating drafts and more than 300 bottled brews, relax on an expansive deck, and munch on antipasti. Happening Irish pub and restaurant **Rí Rá** (✉ *72 Commercial St.* ☎ *207/761–4446* 🌐 *www.rira.com*) has live music Thursday through Saturday nights; for a mellower experience, settle into a couch at the upstairs bar. **Space Gallery** (✉ *538 Congress St.* ☎ *207/828–5600* 🌐 *www.space538.org*) sparkles as a contemporary art gallery and alternative arts venue, opening its doors to everything from poetry readings to live music and documentary film showings.

THE ARTS

Art galleries and studios have spread throughout the city, infusing with new life many abandoned yet beautiful old buildings and shops. Many are concentrated along the Congress Street downtown corridor; others are hidden amid the boutiques and restaurants of the Old Port and the

East End. A great way to get acquainted with the city's artists is to participate in the First Friday Art Walk, a self-guided, free tour of galleries, museums, and alternative art venues that happens—you guessed it—on the first Friday of each month. Brochures and maps are available on the organization's Web site: *www.firstfridayartwalk.com.*

Merrill Auditorium (✉ *20 Myrtle St.* ☎ *207/842–0800* 🌐 *www.porttix.com*) has numerous theatrical and musical events, including performances by the Portland Symphony Orchestra, Portland Ovations (performing arts), and Portland Opera Repertory Theatre. Every other Tuesday from mid-June to the end of August, organ recitals (suggested $15 donation) are given on the auditorium's huge 1912 Kotzschmar Memorial Organ. **Portland Stage** (✉ *25-A Forest Ave.* ☎ *207/774–0465* 🌐 *www.portlandstage.com*) mounts theatrical productions from September to May on its two stages.

SHOPPING

Exchange Street is great for arts and crafts and boutique browsing, while Commercial Street caters to the souvenir hound—gift shops are packed with nautical items, and lobster and moose emblems are emblazoned on everything from T-shirts to shot glasses.

ART AND ANTIQUES

Abacus (✉ *44 Exchange St.* ☎ *207/772–4880* 🌐 *www.abacusgallery.com*), an appealing crafts gallery, has unusual gift items in glass, wood, and textiles, plus fine modern jewelry. **Foundry Lane Contemporary Crafts** (✉ *221 Commercial St.* ☎ *207/773–2722* 🌐 *www.foundrylane.com*) sells beautiful, limited-edition jewelry, as well as glass and ceramic home accessories by 20 Maine artists. **Gleason Fine Art** (✉ *545 Congress St.* ☎ *207/699–5599* 🌐 *www.gleasonfineart.com*) exhibits paintings by Maine artists from the 19th to 21st centuries. **Greenhut Galleries** (✉ *146 Middle St.* ☎ *207/772–2693 or 888/772–2693* 🌐 *www.greenhutgalleries.com*) shows contemporary art and sculpture by Maine artists. An antiques junkie's dream, **Portland Architectural Salvage** (✉ *131 Preble St.* ☎ *207/780–0634* 🌐 *www.portlandsalvage.com*) has four floors of unusual reclaimed finds, including furniture, fixtures, hardware, and stained-glass windows.

BOOKS

Cunningham Books (✉ *188 State St.* ☎ *207/775–2246*) is a grand browsing (and buying) experience for book lovers. The owner knows in a moment whether your request is present amid the estimated 70,000 titles lining the walls. **Longfellow Books** (✉ *1 Monument Way* ☎ *207/772–4045* 🌐 *www.longfellowbooks.com*) is known for its good service and thoughtful literary collection. Auhor readings are scheduled regularly.

CLOTHING

Hip boutique **Bliss** (✉ *58 Exchange St.* ☎ *207/879–7125* 🌐 *www.blissboutiques.com*) stocks T-shirts, dresses, jewelry, and lingerie by cutting-edge designers, plus jeans by big names like 7 For All Mankind.

Photos of style icon Audrey Hepburn grace the walls of **Hélène M.** (✉ *425 Fore St.* ☎ *207/772–2564*), where you'll find classic, fashion-

CLOSE UP

Lobster Shacks

If it's your first time to the Maine Coast, it won't be long before you stumble upon the famous and quintessential seaside eatery, the lobster shack. Also known as a lobster "pound," especially in other parts of New England, this humble establishment serves only two kinds of fresh seafood—lobster and clams.

Lobster shacks are essentially wooden huts with picnic tables set around the waterfront. The menu is simplicity itself: steamed lobster or clams by the pound, or a lobster roll. Sides may include potato chips, cole slaw, or corn on the cob. Some pounds are even BYOB—no, not bring your own bib; those are usually provided—but bring your own beer or refreshments.

A signature item at a lobster shack is the lobster dinner. Although this can vary from pound to pound, it generally means the works: a whole steamed lobster, steamed clams, corn on the cob and potato chips. If the lobster dinner sounds like a bit much, then go for the classic lobster roll, a buttered hot dog roll filled with chunks of lobster meat and a bit of mayo. Some pounds will serve it with lemon, some will serve it with butter, and some with even a touch of lettuce or herbs. Purists will serve no toppings at all (and why bother when the unadulterated taste of fresh, sweet lobster meat can't be beat). Most shacks will have even have a tank with live lobsters; few will let you pick your own.

We can say this much: the best place to get a lobster dinner or lobster roll is at a shack, and the only authentic ones are right next to the water. There's a general sense that the "purest" pounds are the one's that are the simplest: a wooden shack,

A lobster roll: perfection on a bun.

right on the water with wooden picnic tables, and perhaps most important of all, a beautiful unobstructed view of working lobster boats in a scenic Maine harbor.

A few of our favorites sit on side-by-side piers right on Moscungus Bay: **Round Pond Fisherman's Coop** (✉ *Town Landing Rd., Round Pond* ☎ *207/529–5725*) and **Moscungus Bay Lobster Company** (✉ *Town Landing Rd., Round Pond* 🌐 *www.mainefreshlobster.com*).

Waterman's Beach Lobster (✉ *359 Waterman Beach Rd.* ☎ *207/596–7819 or 207/594–7518* 🌐 *www.watermansbeachrestaurant.com*)in South Thomaston is authentic, inexpensive and scenic. You can eat lunch or dinner right on a pier overlooking the Atlantic. In addition to the seafood favorites, Waterman's also sells freshly baked pies and locally made ice cream.

You can find out more about Maine lobster from the **The Maine Lobster Council** (🌐 *www.lobsterfrommaine.com*).

—Michael de Zayas

A traditional clambake may also include lobsters and corn. It's best enjoyed outside—just add drawn butter.

able pieces by designers like Tory Burch, Diane von Furstenberg, and Rebecca Taylor.

With a funky combination of good-quality consignment and new jewelry and clothing for both men and women, **Material Objects** (✉ *500 Congress St.* ☎ *207/774–1241*) makes for an affordable and unusual shopping spree. At **Sea Bags** (✉ *25 Custom House Wharf* ☎ *888/210–4244* 🌐 *www.seabags.com*), totes made from recycled sailcloth and decorated with bright, graphic patterns are sewn right in the store.

HOUSEHOLD ITEMS/FURNITURE

Maine islander **Angela Adams** (✉ *273 Congress St.* ☎ *207/774–3523 or 800/255–9454* 🌐 *www.angelaadams.com*) specializes in simple but bold geometric motifs parlayed into dramatic rugs, handbags, trays, pillows, and paper goods.

For reproduction and antique furnishings with a Far East feel, head to one of the two locations of **Asia West** (✉ *219 Commercial St.* ☎ *888/775–0066* ✉ *125 Kennebec St.* ☎ *207/774–9300* 🌐 *www.asiawest.net.*) The former has mostly accessories; the latter is a furniture showroom. The handsome cherrywood pieces at **Green Design Furniture** (✉ *267 Commercial St.* ☎ *207/775–4234 or 800/853–4234* 🌐 *www.greendesigns.com*) are made locally with sustainable harvested wood and eco-friendly finishes. A unique system of joinery enables easy assembly after shipping.

SPORTS AND THE OUTDOORS

When the weather's good, everyone in Portland heads outside. There are also many green spaces nearby Portland, including Fort Williams Park, home to Portland Head Light; Crescent Beach State Park; and Two Lights State Park. All offer biking and walking trails, picnic facilities, and water access. Bradbury Mountain State Park, in Pownal, has incredible vistas from its easily climbed peak. In Freeport is Wolfe's Neck Woods State Park, where you can take a guided nature walk and see nesting ospreys.

BICYCLING

For state bike trail maps, club and tour listings, or hints on safety, contact the **Bicycle Coalition of Maine** (✉ *341 Water St., No. 10, Augusta* ☎ *207/623–4511* 🌐 *www.bikemaine.org*). Rent bikes downtown at **Cycle Mania** (✉ *59 Federal St.* ☎ *207/774–2933* 🌐 *www.cyclemania1.com*) or **Gorham Bike and Ski** (✉ *693 Congress St.* ☎ *207/773–1700* 🌐 *www.gorhambike.com*). For local biking information, contact **Portland Trails** (✉ *305 Commercial St.* ☎ *207/775–2411* 🌐 *www.trails.org*). They can tell you about designated paved routes that wind along the water, through parks, and beyond. For a map, call or get one online.

BOATING

Various Portland-based skippers offer whale-, dolphin-, and seal-watching cruises; excursions to lighthouses and islands; and fishing and lobstering trips. Board the ferry to see the nearby islands. Self-navigators can rent kayaks or canoes.

Casco Bay Lines (✉ *Maine State Pier, 56 Commercial St.* ☎ *207/774–7871* 🌐 *www.cascobaylines.com*) provides narrated cruises and transportation to the Casco Bay Islands. **Lucky Catch Cruises** (✉ *Long Wharf, 170 Commercial St.* ☎ *207/761–0941* 🌐 *www.luckycatch.com*) sets out to sea in a real lobster boat so passengers can get the genuine experience, which includes hauling traps and the chance to purchase the catch. **Odyssey Whale Watch** (✉ *Long Wharf, 170 Commercial St.* ☎ *207/775–0727* 🌐 *www.odysseywhalewatch.com*) leads whale-watching and deep-sea–fishing trips.For tours of the harbor and Casco Bay, including a trip to Eagle Island and an up-close look at several lighthouses, try **Portland Discovery Land & Sea Tours** (✉ *Long Wharf, 170 Commercial St.* ☎ *207/774–0808* 🌐 *www.portlanddiscovery.com*).

Portland Schooner Co. (✉ *Maine State Pier, 56 Commercial St.* ☎ *207/766–2500 or 877/246–6637* 🌐 *www.portlandschooner.com*) offers daily sails aboard vintage schooners from 1912 and 1924.

HOT-AIR BALLOON RIDES

Hot Fun First Class Balloon Flights (☎ *207/799–0193* 🌐 *www.hotfunballoons.com*) flies mainly sunrise trips and can accommodate up to three people. The price of $300 per person includes a post-flight champagne toast, snacks, and shuttle to the lift-off site.

CASCO BAY ISLANDS

The islands of Casco Bay are also known as the Calendar Islands because an early explorer mistakenly thought there was one for each day of the year (in reality there are only 140). These islands range from ledges visible only at low tide to populous Peaks Island, a suburb of Portland. Some are uninhabited; others support year-round communities as well as stores and restaurants. Fort Gorges commands Hog Island Ledge, and Eagle Island is the site of Arctic explorer Admiral Robert Peary's home. The brightly painted ferries of Casco Bay Lines are the islands' lifeline. There is frequent service to the most populated ones, including Peaks, Long, Little Diamond, and Great Diamond.

There is little in the way of overnight lodging on the islands; the population swells during the warmer months due to summer residents. There are few restaurants or organized attractions other than the natural beauty of the islands themselves. Meandering about by bike or on foot is a good way to explore on a day trip.

5

GETTING HERE AND AROUND

Casco Bay Lines provides ferry service from Portland to the islands of Casco Bay. The CAT, a stunning, modern high-speed ferry, travels between Portland and Yarmouth, Nova Scotia.

ESSENTIALS

Transportation Information Casco Bay Lines (☎ *207/774–7871* ⊕ *www.cascobaylines.com*). **The CAT** (☎ *877/359–3760* ⊕ *www.catferry.com*).

CAPE ELIZABETH TO PROUTS NECK

EXPLORING

Fodor's Choice ★ **Portland Head Light.** Familiar to many from photographs and the Edward Hopper's painting *Portland Head-Light* (1927), this lighthouse was commissioned by George Washington in 1790. The towering white stone structure stands over the keeper's quarters, a white home with a blazing red roof, now the Museum at Portland Head Light. The lighthouse is in 90-acre Fort Williams Park, a sprawling green space with walking paths, picnic facilities, a beach and—you guessed it—a cool old fort. *Museum* ✉ *1000 Shore Rd., Cape Elizabeth* ☎ *207/799–2661* ⊕ *www.portlandheadlight.com* 🎫 *$2* ⏲ *Memorial Day–mid-Oct., daily 10–4; Apr., May, Nov., and Dec., weekends 10–4.*

WHERE TO EAT AND STAY

$$$ SEAFOOD ✕ **Joe's Boathouse.** The two simple dining rooms of this dockside establishment are finished in sea-foam green, with large windows looking out to a marina. Dinner specials include tuna steak and lobster fettuccine; for lunch try the grilled-crab and avocado club or Asian-inspired crispy salmon salad. In summer, eat out on the patio. ✉ *1 Spring Point Dr., South Portland* ☎ *207/741–2780* ⊕ *www.joesboathouse.com* 💳 *AE, MC, V.*

$$ SEAFOOD ✕ **The Lobster Shack at Two Lights.** You can't beat the location—right on the water, below the lighthouse pair that gives Two Lights State Park its name—and the food's not bad either. Enjoy fresh lobster whole or piled into a hot-dog bun with a dollop of mayo. Other menu must-

haves include chowder, fried clams, and fish-and-chips. It's been a classic spot since the 1920s. Eat inside or out. ✉ *225 Two Lights Rd., Cape Elizabeth* ☎ *207/799–1677* 🌐 *www.lobstershacktwolights.com* ▭ *MC, V* ⏲ *Closed Nov.–late Mar.*

$$$$ **Black Point Inn.** Toward the tip of the peninsula that juts into the ocean at Prouts Neck stands this stylish, tastefully updated historic resort with spectacular views up and down the coast. Guests have access to beaches, trails, kayaking equipment, a country club with tennis courts and a golf course, and a yacht club. Finer touches abound, such as Frette linens and in-room terry-cloth robes. The Cliff Walk, a pebbled path that wanders past Winslow Homer's former studio, runs along the Atlantic headlands that Homer often painted. Rates include breakfast, dinner, and gratuities (they're tacked on for you). The inn is 12 mi south of Portland and about 10 mi north of Old Orchard Beach. **Pros:** stunning water views; set amid scenery that inspired Winslow Homer. **Cons:** 18% "guest service charge" is tacked on to room rate. ✉ *510 Black Point Rd., Scarborough* ☎ *207/883–2500* 🌐 *www.blackpointinn.com* *25 rooms* ⏲ *Closed late Oct.–early May* *In-room: DVD (some), Wi-Fi. In-hotel: 2 restaurants, bar, pool, gym, bicycles, laundry service, Internet terminal, Wi-Fi hotspot, parking (free)* ▭ *AE, D, MC, V* *MAP.*

FREEPORT

17 mi northeast of Portland; 10 mi southwest of Brunswick.

Those who flock straight to L.L. Bean and see nothing else of Freeport are missing out. The city's charming backstreets are lined with historic buildings and old clapboard houses, and there's a pretty little harbor on the south side of the Harraseeket River. It's true, many who come to the area do so simply to shop—L.L. Bean is the store that put Freeport on the map, and plenty of outlets and some specialty stores have settled here. Still, if you choose, you can stay a while and experience more than fabulous bargains; beyond the shops are bucolic nature preserves with miles of walking trails and plenty of places for leisurely ambling that don't require the overuse of your credit cards.

GETTING AROUND

Pick up a village walking map, sign up for a tour, and check out historical exhibits at the **Freeport Historical Society** (✉ *45 Main St.* ☎ *207/865–3170* 🌐 *www.freeporthistoricalsociety.com* ⏲ *Mon., Thurs., and Fri. 10–5, Sat. 10–2).*

SPORTS AND THE OUTDOORS

CLASSES It shouldn't come as a surprise that one of the world's largest outdoor outfitters also provides its customers with instructional adventures to go with its products. L.L. Bean's year-round **Outdoor Discovery Schools** (☎ *888/552–3261* 🌐 *www.llbean.com/ods*) include half- and full-day classes, trips, and tours that encompass canoeing, shooting, biking, kayaking, fly-fishing, cross-country skiing, and other outdoor sports. Classes are for all skill levels; it's best to sign up several months in advance.

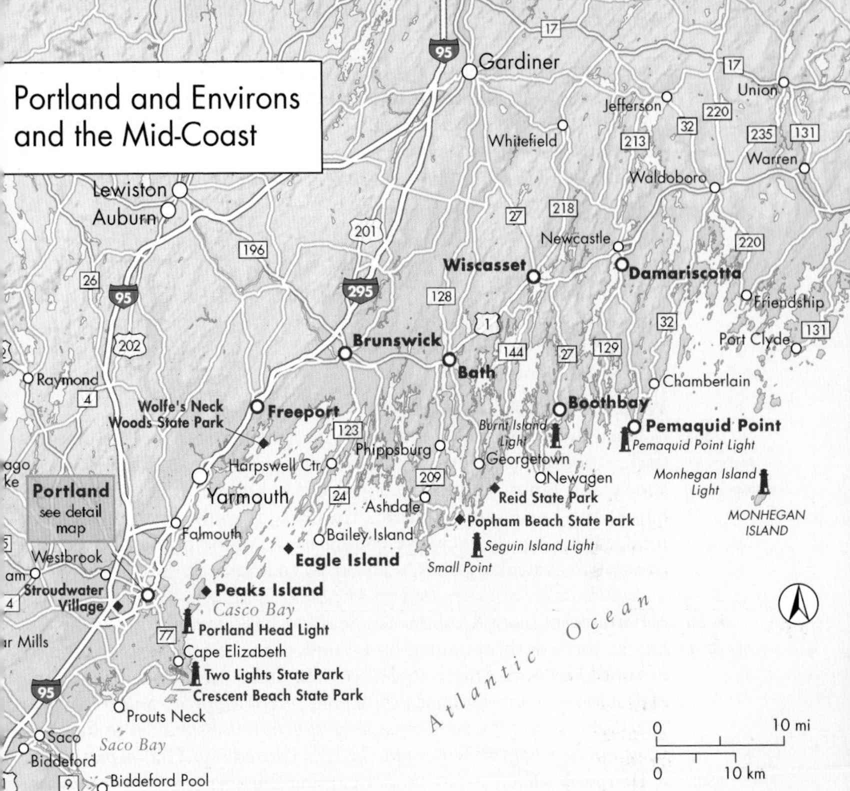

SHOPPING

The **Freeport Visitors Guide** (☎ *207/865–1212, 800/865–1994 or* 🌐 *www.freeportusa.com for a copy*) lists the more than 200 stores on Main Street, Bow Street, and elsewhere, including Patagonia, Coach, Brooks Brothers, Banana Republic, J. Crew, and Cole-Haan.

Edgecomb Potters (✉ *8 School St.* ☎ *207/865–1705* 🌐 *www.edgecombpotters.com*) showcases vibrant, hand-thrown porcelain tableware finished with an unusual crystalline glaze. **R. D. Allen Freeport Jewelers** (✉ *13 Middle St.* ☎ *207/865–1818 or 877/837–3835* 🌐 *www.rdallen.com*) specializes in brightly colored tourmaline and other locally mined gemstones. Famed local furniture company **Thos. Moser Cabinetmakers** (✉ *149 Main St.* ☎ *207/865–4519* 🌐 *www.thosmoser.com*) sells artful, handmade wood pieces with clean, classic lines.

Fodor's Choice ★ Founded in 1912 as a mail-order merchandiser of products for hunters, guides, and anglers, **L.L. Bean** (✉ *95 Main St. [U.S. 1]* ☎ *877/755–2326* 🌐 *www.llbean.com*) attracts more than 3 million shoppers a year to its giant store (open 24 hours a day) in the heart of Freeport's shopping district. You can still find the original hunting boots, along with cotton and wool sweaters, outerwear, camping and ski equipment, comforters, and hundreds of other things for the home, car, boat, and campsite. For items related to specific activities and the home, as well as discounted merchandise (available at the L. L. Bean Outlet), head to the following nearby stores. **L. L. Bean Bike, Boat & Ski Store** (✉ *57 Main St.* ☎ *877/755–2326*). **L. L. Bean Home Store** (✉ *12 Nathan Nye St.* ☎ *877/755–2326*). **L. L. Bean Hunting & Fishing Store** (✉ *95 Main St.* ☎ *877/755–2326*). **L. L. Bean Outlet** (✉ *One Freeport Village Station [Depot St.]* ☎ *207/552–7772*).

NIGHTLIFE AND THE ARTS

Every Saturday from late June to early September, sit under the stars for the **L. L. Bean Summer Concert Series** (✉ *Morse St.* ☎ *877/755–2326* 🌐 *www.llbean.com/events*). The free concerts start at 7:30 PM in downtown Freeport at L. L. Bean's Discovery Park. The entertainment ranges from folk, jazz, and country to rock and bluegrass. Bring a blanket and refreshments.

WHERE TO EAT AND STAY

$$$ AMERICAN Fodor's Choice ★ ✕ **Broad Arrow Tavern.** On the main floor of the Harraseeket Inn, this dark, wood-paneled tavern with mounted moose heads, decoys, snowshoes, and other outdoor sporty decor is known for both its casual nature and its sumptuous menu. The chefs use only organically grown food, with a nearly exclusive emphasis on Maine products, to create treats such as steaks, pizzas, seafood. ✉ *162 Main St.* ☎ *207/865–9377* *Reservations not accepted* ▭ *AE, D, DC, MC, V.*

$–$$ SEAFOOD ✕ **Harraseeket Lunch & Lobster Co.** Seafood baskets and lobster dinners are the focus at this popular, bare-bones place beside the town landing in South Freeport. Order at the counter, find a seat inside or out, and expect long lines in summer. ✉ *On pier, end of Main St., South Freeport* ☎ *207/865–4888* 🌐 *www.harraseeketlunchandlobster.com* *Reservations not accepted* ▭ *No credit cards* ⊙ *Closed mid-Oct.–Apr.*

$$$$ Fodor's Choice ★ **Harraseeket Inn.** Despite modern appointments such as elevators and whirlpool baths in some rooms, this 1850 Greek Revival home provides a pleasantly old-fashioned, country-inn experience just a few minutes' walk from L. L. Bean. Guest rooms have print fabrics and reproductions of Federal quarter-canopy beds. Ask for a second-floor, garden-facing room. The formal Maine Dining Room ($$$–$$$$) specializes in contemporary American regional (and organic) cuisine such as whole poached lobster and all-natural filet mignon. The casual yet excellent Broad Arrow Tavern ($$$) serves heartier fare and has a charming seasonal patio. Inn rates include a full buffet breakfast and afternoon tea. **Pros:** excellent on-site dining; walk to shopping district. **Cons:** building updates have diminished some authenticity. ✉ *162 Main St.* ☎ *207/865–9377 or 800/342–6423* 🌐 *www.harraseeketinn.com* *82 rooms, 2 suites* *In-room: refrigerator (some), Wi-Fi. In-hotel: 2 restaurants, bars, pool, gym, laundry service, parking (free), some pets allowed* ▭ *AE, D, DC, MC, V* *BP.*

THE MID-COAST REGION

Updated by Michael de Zayas

Lighthouses dot the headlands of Maine's Mid-Coast region, where thousands of miles of coastline wait to be explored. Defined by chiseled peninsulas stretching south from U.S. 1, this area has everything from the sandy beaches and sandbars of Popham Beach to the jutting cliffs

Boardwalks help protect the dunes—and therefore the beach—at Popham Beach State Park.

of Monhegan Island. If you are intent on hooking a trophy-size fish or catching a glimpse of a whale, there are plenty of cruises available. If you want to explore deserted beaches and secluded coves, kayaks are your best bet. Put in at the Harpswells, or on the Cushing and Saint George peninsulas or simply paddle among the lobster boats and other vessels that ply these waters.

Tall ships often visit Maine, sometimes sailing up the Kennebec River for a stopover at Bath's Maine Maritime Museum, on the site of the old Percy and Small Shipyard. Next door to the museum, the Bath Iron Works still builds the U.S. Navy's Aegis-class destroyers.

Along U.S. 1, charming towns, each unique, have an array of attractions. Brunswick, while a bigger, commercial city, has rows of historic wood and clapboard homes and is home to Bowdoin College. Bath is known for its maritime heritage. Wiscasset has arguably the best antiques shopping in the state. On its waterfront you can choose from a variety of seafood shacks competing for the best lobster rolls. Damariscotta, too, is worth a stop for its lively main street and good seafood restaurants.

South along the peninsulas the scenery opens to glorious vistas of working lobster harbors and marinas. It's here you find the authentic lobster pounds where you can watch your catch come in off the traps. Boothbay Harbor is the quaintest town in the Mid-Coast, and has lots of little stores that are perfect for window-shopping. It's one of three towns where you can take a ferry to Monhegan Island, which seems to be inhabited exclusively by painters at their easels, depicting the cliffs and weathered homes with colorful gardens.

At the Maine Maritime Museum, a boatbuilder works on a yacht tender, used to ferry people to shore.

ESSENTIALS

Visitor Information **Maine Tourism Association** (*✉ 1100 U.S. 1 [I–95 Exit 17], Yarmouth ☎ 207/846–0833 or 888/624–6345 🌐 www.mainetourism.com*). **Southern Midcoast Maine Chamber** (*✉ Border Trust Business Center, 2 Main St., Topsham ☎ 877/725–8797 🌐 www.midcoastmaine.com*).

BRUNSWICK

10 mi north of Freeport; 30 mi northeast of Portland.

Lovely brick-and-clapboard buildings are the highlight of Brunswick's Federal Street Historic District, which includes Federal Street and Park Row and the stately campus of Bowdoin College. From the intersection of Pleasant and Maine streets, in the center of town, you can walk in any direction and discover an impressive array of restaurants. Seafood? German cuisine? A Chinese buffet that beats out all the competition? It's all here. So are bookstores, gift shops, boutiques, and jewelers.

From Brunswick, Routes 123 and 24 take you south to Harpswell Neck peninsula and the more than 40 islands that make up the town of Harpswell, known collectively as the Harpswells. Small coves along Harpswell Neck shelter lobster boats, and summer cottages are tucked away among birch and spruce trees. On your way down from Cook's Corner to Land's End at the end of Route 24, you cross Sebascodegan Island. Heading east here leads to East Harpswell and Cundy's Harbor. Continuing straight south down 24 leads to Orr's Island. Stop at Mackerel Cove to see a real fishing harbor; there are a few parking spaces where you can stop to picnic and look for beach glass or put in your kayaks. Inhale the salt breeze as you cross the world's only cribstone bridge (designed so that water flows freely through gaps between the granite blocks) on your way to Bailey Island, home to a lobster pound made famous thanks in part to a Visa commercial.

SPORTS AND THE OUTDOORS

★ The coast near Brunswick is full of hidden nooks and crannies waiting to be explored by kayak. **H2Outfitters** (✉ *1894 Rte. 24, Orr's Island* ☎ *207/833–5257 or 800/205–2925* 🌐 *www.h2outfitters.com*) is the place in Harpswells to get on the water. It's at the end of Orr's Island just before the Cribstone Bridge and provides top-notch kayaking instruction and gear for people of all skill levels.

WHERE TO EAT

$$ SEAFOOD Fodor's Choice ★ ✕ **Cook's Lobster House.** What began as a lobster shack on Bailey's Island in 1955 has grown into this huge, internationally famous family-style restaurant, complete with its own gift shop. The restaurant still catches its own fish and seafood, so you can count on the lobster casserole and the haddock sandwich to be delectable. But along with fame come prices; the shore dinner—the most expensive menu option—is $43, and includes a 1¼-lb lobster with steamed or fried clams or mussels, a choice of sides, and a bowl of chowder or lobster stew. Whether you choose inside or deck seating, you can watch the activity on the water: men checking lobster pots and kayakers fanning across the bay. ✉ *68 Garrison Cove Rd., Bailey Island* ☎ *207/833–2818* 🌐 *www.cookslobster.com* *Reservations not accepted* 💳 *D, MC, V* ⊙ *Closed New Year's Day–mid-Feb.*

BATH

11 mi northeast of Brunswick; 38 mi northeast of Portland.

Bath has been a shipbuilding center since 1607. The result of its prosperity can be seen in its handsome mix of Federal, Greek Revival, and Italianate homes along Front, Centre, and Washington streets. In the heart of Bath's historic district are some charming 19th-century homes, including the 1820 Federal-style home at 360 Front St., the 1810 Greek Revival–style mansion at 969 Washington St., covered with gleaming white clapboards, and the Victorian gem at 1009 Washington St., painted a distinctive shade of raspberry. All three operate as inns. An easily overlooked site is the town's City Hall. The bell in its tower was cast by Paul Revere in 1805.

The venerable Bath Iron Works completed its first passenger ship in 1890. During World War II BIW—as it's locally known—launched a new ship every 17 days. It is still building today, turning out destroyers for the U.S. Navy. BIW is one of the state's largest employers, with about 5,600 workers. It's a good idea to avoid U.S. 1 on weekdays from 3:15 PM to 4:30 PM, when a major shift change takes place. You can tour BIW through the Maine Maritime Museum.

Continued on page 332

MAINE'S LIGHTHOUSES

GUARDIANS OF THE COAST

By John Blodgett

Perched high on rocky ledges, on the tips of wayward islands, and sometimes seemingly on the ocean itself are the more than five dozen lighthouses standing watch along Maine's craggy and ship-busting coastline.

Marshall Point Light

LIGHTING THE WAY: A BIT OF HISTORY

Portland Head Light

Most lighthouses were built in the first half of the 19th century to protect the vessels from running aground at night or when the shoreline was shrouded in fog. Along with the mournful siren of the foghorn and maritime lore, these practical structures have come to symbolize Maine throughout the world.

SHIPWRECKS AND SAFETY

These alluring sentinels of the eastern seaboard today have more form than function, but that certainly was not always the case. Safety was a strong motivating factor in the erection of the lighthouses. Commerce also played a critical role. For example, in 1791 Portland Head light was completed, partially as a response to local merchants' concerns about the rocky entrance to Portland Harbor and the varying depths of the shipping channel, but approval wasn't given until a terrible accident in 1787 in which a 90-ton sloop wrecked. Beginning in 1790, the federal government was the owner of these towers of light, with the U.S. Lighthouse Service (later the U.S. Coast Guard) managing them.

Some lighthouses in Maine were built in a much-needed venue, but the points and islands upon which they sat eventually eroded into the ocean. This meant that over the years many lighthouses had to be rebuilt or replaced.

LIGHTHOUSES TODAY

In modern times, many of the structures still serve a purpose. Technological advances, such as GPS and radar, augment a ship's navigation through the choppy waters, but they don't replace a lighthouse or its foghorns. The numerous channel-marking buoys still in existence also are testament to the old tried-and-true methods.

Of the 61 lighthouses along this far northeastern state, 55 are still working, alerting ships (and even small aircraft) of the shoreline's rocky edge. Towns, historical organizations, the National Park Service, and a few private individuals own the decomissioned lights.

KEEPERS OF THE LIGHT

Some keepers also used bells and sirens, like this Fog Signal Station on Manana Island in 1898.

Pemaquid Point's fourth-order Fresnel lens

LIFE OF A LIGHTKEEPER

One thing that has changed with the modern era is the disappearance of the lighthouse keeper. In the 20th century, lighthouses began the conversion from oil-based lighting to electricity. A few decades later, the U.S. Coast Guard switched to automation, phasing out the need for an on-site keeper.

While the keepers of tradition were no longer needed, the traditions of these stalwart, 24/7 employees live on through museum exhibits and retellings of Maine's maritime history, legends, and lore. The tales of a lighthouse keeper's life are the stuff romance novels are made of: adventure, rugged but lonely men, and a beautiful setting along an unpredictable coastline.

The lighthouse keepers of yesterday probably didn't see their own lives so romantically. Their daily narrative was one of hard work and, in some cases, exceptional solitude. A keeper's primary job was to ensure that the lamp was illuminated all day, every day. This meant that oil (whale oil or coal oil) had to be carried about and wicks trimmed on a regular basis. When fog shrouded the coast, they sounded the solemn horn to pierce through the damp darkness that hid their light. Their quarters were generally small and often attached to the light tower itself. The remote locations of the lights added to the isolation a keeper felt, especially before the advent of radio and telephone, let alone the Internet. Though some brought families with them, the keepers tended to be men who lived alone.

THE LIGHTS 101

Over the years, Fresnel (fray-NELL) lenses were developed in different shapes and sizes so that ship captains could distinguish one lighthouse from another. Invented by Frenchman Augustin Fresnel in the early 19th century, the lens design allows for a greater transmission of light perfectly suited for lighthouse use. Knowing which lighthouse they were near helped captains know which danger was present, such as a submerged ledge or shallow channel. Some lights, such as those at Seguin Island Light, are fixed and don't flash. Other lights are colored red.

DID YOU KNOW?

A lighthouse's personality shines through its flash pattern. For example, Bass Harbor Light (pictured) blinks red every four seconds. Some lights, such as Seguin Island Light, are fixed and don't flash.

LIGHTHOUSE FINDER

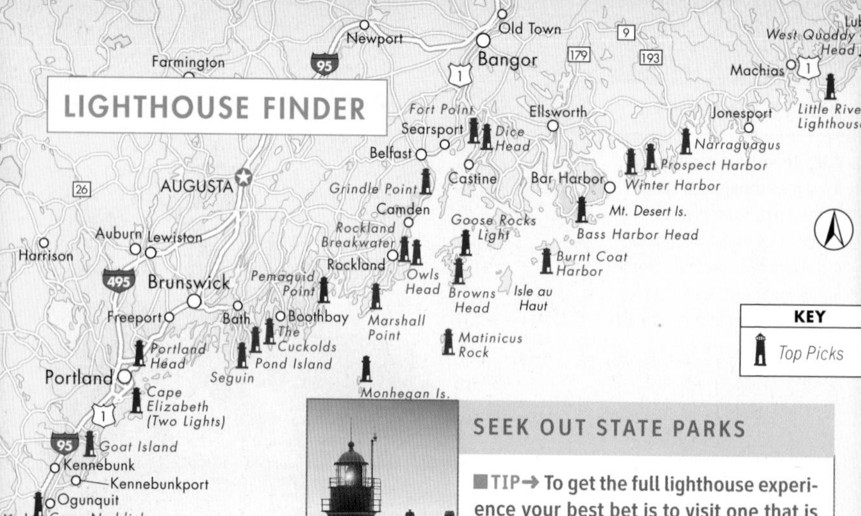

West Quoddy Head

SEEK OUT STATE PARKS

■ TIP→ **To get the full lighthouse experience your best bet is to visit one that is part of a state park.** These are generally well kept and tend to allow up-close approach, though typically only outside. While you're at the parks you can picnic or stroll on the trails. Wildlife is often abundant in and near the water; you might spot sea birds and even whales in certain locations (try West Quoddy Head, Portland Head, or Two Lights).

VISITING MAINE'S LIGHTHOUSES

As you travel along the Maine Coast, you won't see lighthouses by watching your odometer—there were no rules about the spacing of lighthouses. The decision as to where to place a lighthouse was a balance between a region's geography and its commercial prosperity and maritime traffic.

Lighthouses line the shore from as far south as York to the country's easternmost tip at Lubec. Accessibility varies according to location and other factors. A handful are so remote as to be outright impossible to reach (except perhaps by kayaking and rock climbing). Some don't allow visitors according to Coast Guard policies, though you can enjoy them through the zoom lens of a camera. Others you can walk right up to and, occasionally, even climb to the top. Lighthouse enthusiasts and preservation groups restore and maintain many of them. All told, approximately 30 lighthouses allow some sort of public access.

MUSEUMS, TOURS, AND MORE

Most keeper's quarters are closed to the public, but some of the homes have been converted to museums, full of intriguing exhibits on lighthouses, the famous Fresnel lenses used in them, and artifacts of Maine maritime life in general. Talk to the librarians at the **Maine Maritime Museum** in Bath (🌐 *www.mainemaritime-museum.org*) or sign up for one of the museum's daily lighthouse cruises to pass by no fewer than ten on the Lighthouse Lovers Cruise. In Rockland, the **Maine Lighthouse Museum** (🌐 *www.mainelighthousemuseum.com*) has the country's largest display of Fresnel lenses. The museum also displays keepers' memorabilia, foghorns, brassware, and more.

For more information, check out the lighthouse page at Maine's official tourism site: 🌐 *www.visitmaine.com/attractions/sightseeing_tours/lighthouse*.

SLEEPING LIGHT: STAYING OVERNIGHT

Goose Rock, where you can play lighthouse keeper for a week.

Want to stay overnight in a lighthouse? There are several options to do so. ■ **TIP→ Book lighthouse lodgings as far in advance as possible, up to one year ahead.**

Our top pick is **Pemaquid Point Light** (*Newcastle Square Vacation Rentals ☎ 207/563–6500*) because it has one of the most dramatic settings on the Maine coast. Four miles south of **New Harbor**, the second floor of the lighthouse keeper's house is rented out on a weekly basis early May through mid-November to support upkeep of the grounds. When you aren't enjoying the interior, head outdoors: the covered front porch has a rocking-chair view of the ocean. The one-bedroom, one-bath rental sleeps up to a family of four.

Situated smack dab in the middle of a major maritime thoroughfare between two Penobscot Bay islands, **Goose Rocks Light** (*☎ 207/867–4747*) offers lodging for the adventuresome—the 51-foot cast-iron lighthouse is completely surrounded by water. Getting there requires a ferry ride from Rockland to nearby **North Haven**, a ten-minute ride by motorboat, and then a climb up an iron-rung ladder from the pitching boat—all based on high tide and winds, of course. There's room for up to eight people. It's a bit more cushy experience than it was for the original keepers: there's a flat-screen TV with DVD player and a selection of music and videos for entertainment. In addition, a hammock hangs on the small deck that encircles the operational light; it's a great place from which to watch the majestic windjammers and the fishing fleet pass by.

Little River Lighthouse (*☎ 207/259–3833*), along the far northeastern reaches of the coast in **Cutler**, has three rooms available for rent from July through September. You're responsible for food and beverages, linens, towels, and other personal items (don't forget the bug spray), but kitchen and other basics are provided. The lighthouse operators will provide a boat ride to the island upon which the lighthouse sits.

TOP LIGHTHOUSES TO VISIT

BASS HARBOR LIGHT

One Maine lighthouse familiar to many because it is the subject of countless photographs is Bass Harbor Light, at the southern end of **Mount Desert Island.** It is a short drive from Acadia National Park and the town of Bar Harbor. The station grounds are open year-round, but the former keeper's house is now a private home for a Coast Guard family. This lighthouse is so close to the water it seems as if a blustery wind could tip it over the rocks right into the North Atlantic. **■TIP→ To photograph Bass Harbor, get up close, or walk a short trail for a horizontal shot of the lighthouse and its outbuildings. Also use a tripod or stand firm in the salted wind.**

Bass Harbor

CAPE ELIZABETH LIGHT

Two Lights State Park, as the name suggests, is home to two lighthouses. Both of these **Cape Elizabeth** structures were built in 1828, the first twin lighthouses to be erected on the Maine coast. The western light was converted into a private residence in 1924; the eastern light still projects its automated cylinder of light 17 mi out to sea, from a height of 129 feet, and is the subject of Edward Hopper's *Lighthouse at Two Lights* (1929). The grounds immediately surrounding the building and the lighthouse itself are closed to the public, but the structure is easily viewed and photographed from the nearby parking lot. Explore the tidal pools for the small snails known as periwinkles. **■TIP→ If it's foggy, don't stand too close to the foghorn, and in season (late March through late October) be sure to eat a lobster roll at the Lobster Shack Restaurant—but do not feed the seagulls; you will be publicly chastised on the restaurant's loudspeaker if you do.**

Cape Elizabeth

CAPE NEDDICK LIGHT

More commonly known as Nubble Light for the smallish offshore expanse of rock it rests upon, Cape Neddick Light sits a few hundred feet off **York Beach.** With such a precarious location, its grounds are inaccessible to visitors, but close enough to be exceptionally photogenic, especially during the Christmas season when the Town of York hangs Christmas lights and wreaths from the lighthouse and its surrounding buildings (Santa Claus makes an appearance via lobster boat at the annual lighting celebration). You also can view it from Sohier Park. Notice that it emits a red light.

Cape Neddick

MONHEGAN ISLAND LIGHT

Only the adventuresome and the artistic see this light, because **Monhegan Island**, known both for its fishing and artistic communities, is accessible by a 90-minute ferry ride. To reach the lighthouse, you have an additional half-mile walk uphill from the ferry dock. But it's well worth the effort, especially if you enjoy island life—it's nothing but the rugged North Atlantic out here. The light was automated back in 1959, and since the early 1960s the former keeper's quarters has been home to the Monhegan Museum, which has exhibits about the island more so than the lighthouse. The tower itself is closed to the public. ■ **TIP→ If you've made it this far, stay a quiet night at one of a handful of lodging options on the island, lulled to sleep by muffled waves and the distance from the mainland.**

Monhegan Island

PORTLAND HEAD LIGHT

The subject of Edward Hopper's painting *Portland Head-Light* (1927) and one of Maine's most photographed lighthouses (and its oldest), the famous Portland Head Light was completed in January 1791. Its first keeper, Revolutionary War veteran Captain Joseph Greenleaf, was appointed by George Washington. At the edge of Fort Williams Park, in **Cape Elizabeth**, the towering white stone lighthouse stands 101 feet above the sea. The United States Coast Guard operates it and it is not open for tours. However the adjacent keeper's dwelling, built in 1891, is now a museum, where you can inspect various lenses used in lighthouses. Visitors can also explore the numerous trails within the park, as well as its grassy areas, popular for picnics, kite flying, and watching ships from around the globe enter Portland Harbor.

Portland Head

WEST QUODDY HEAD LIGHT

Originally built in 1808 by mandate of President Thomas Jefferson, West Quoddy Head Light sits in **Lubec** on the easternmost tip of land in the mainland United States—so far east that at certain times of the year it's the first object in the country to be touched by the rising sun's rays. The 49-foot-high lighthouse, now famously painted with distinctive red and white candy stripes, is part of 541-acre Quoddy Head State Park, which has some of the state's best wildlife watching, including humpback, minke, and finback whales. Learn more in the lightkeeper's house-turned-visitor center. You also can climb the 50 steps to the top of the tower.

West Quoddy Head

EXPLORING

Fodor's Choice ★ **Maine Maritime Museum.** No trip to Bath is complete without a visit to this cluster of buildings that once made up the historic Percy & Small Shipyard. Plan on half a day at the museum, which examines the world of shipbuilding and is the only way to tour the Bath Iron Works. In summer, boat tours cruise the scenic Kennebec River. A particular favorite is the lighthouse tour that covers the area of the Kennebec from Bath down to Fort Popham at the mouth of the river. A number of impressive ships, including the 142-foot Grand Banks fishing schooner *Sherman Zwicker,* are on display in summer. Inside the main museum building, exhibits use ship models, paintings, photographs, and historical artifacts to tell the maritime history of the region. From May to November, hour-long tours of the shipyard show how these massive wooden ships were built. You can watch boatbuilders wield their tools in the boat shop. A separate historic building houses a fascinating lobstering exhibit. It's worth coming here just to watch the 18-minute video on lobstering written and narrated by E. B. White. A gift shop and bookstore are on the premises, and you can grab a bite to eat in the café or bring a picnic to eat on the grounds. Kids ages 4 and younger get in free. ✉ *243 Washington St.* ☎ *207/442–0961* 🌐 *www.mainemaritimemuseum.org* *$12* ⏲ *Daily 9:30–5.*

OFF THE BEATEN PATH

Popham Beach State Park (✉ *Rte. 209, Phippsburg* ☎ *207/389–1335*) has bathhouses and picnic tables. There are no restaurants at this end of the beach, so pack a picnic or get takeout from Spinney's Restaurant near the Civil War–era Fort Popham or **Percy's Store** (✉ *6 Sea St.* ☎ *207/389–2010*) behind Spinney's. At low tide you can walk miles of tidal flats and also out to a nearby island, where you can explore tide pools or fish off the ledges. Drive past the entrance to the park, and on the right you can see a vista often described as "Million Dollar View." The confluence of the Kennebec and Morse rivers creates an ever-shifting pattern of sandbars.

WHERE TO EAT AND STAY

$$ AMERICAN ✕ **Beale Street Barbecue.** Ribs are the thing at this barbecue joint. Hearty eaters should ask for one of the platters piled high with pulled pork, pulled chicken, or shredded beef. Jalapeño popovers and chili served with corn bread are terrific appetizers. Enjoy a beer at the bar while waiting for your table. ✉ *215 Water St.* ☎ *207/442–9514* 🌐 *www.mainebbq.com* 💳 *MC, V.*

$$$–$$$$ AMERICAN ✕ **Robinhood Free Meetinghouse.** This 1855 church and meetinghouse is a remarkable setting for a meal. On occasion you can even eat upstairs among the pews. Though owned by acclaimed chef and owner Michael Gagné—whose multilayer cream-cheese biscuits are shipped all over the country—this meetinghouse serves meals that are primarily made by chef de cuisine Troy Mains. The menu changes daily but always has a variety of seafood, vegetables, and dairy products purchased locally. You might begin with the lobster and crab cakes, then move on to grilled fillet of beef stuffed with crab or the duck confit. Finish up with the signature Obsession in Three Chocolates. The wine list is quite good

as well. ✉ *210 Robinhood Rd., Georgetown* ☎ *207/371–2188* 🌐 *www.robinhood-meetinghouse.com* ▭ *AE, D, MC, V* ⊗ *No lunch.*

$$$–$$$$ Fodor's Choice ★ **Sebasco Harbor Resort.** This destination family resort spread across 575 acres at the foot of the Phippsburg Peninsula has an exceptional range of accommodations and services. Comfortable guest rooms in the clapboard-covered main building have antique furnishings and new bathrooms, while rooms in a building designed to resemble a lighthouse have wicker furniture, paintings by local artists, and rooftop access. The Fairwinds Spa Suites are corporate luxury units next to the resort's spa; prices for combo room and treatment packages range from $369 to $399. The recently added Harbor Village Suites are set in exquisitely landscaped grounds and include 18 spacious and air-conditioned rooms that rent for $319–$459. The resort's Pilot House restaurant ($$–$$$) is known for its innovative take on classic dishes and is a wonderful spot for watching sunsets. In summer there are outdoor lobster and clambakes. **Pros:** ocean location; excellent food and service; kids' activities; airport shuttle. **Cons:** pricey. ✉ *29 Kenyon Rd., off Rte. 217, Sebasco Estates* ☎ *207/389–1161 or 800/225–3819* 🌐 *www.sebasco.com* *115 rooms, 23 cottages* *In-room: Wi-Fi (some). In-hotel: 3 restaurants, bar, golf course, tennis courts, pool, gym, bicycles, children's programs, Wi-Fi hotspot* ▭ *AE, D, MC, V* ⊗ *Closed Nov.–mid-May* *MAP.*

5

WISCASSET

10 mi north of Bath; 46 mi northeast of Portland.

Settled in 1663, Wiscasset sits on the banks of the Sheepscot River. It bills itself "Maine's Prettiest Village," and it's easy to see why: it has graceful churches, old cemeteries, and elegant sea captains' homes (many converted into antiques shops or galleries), and a good wine and specialty foods shop called Treats (stock up here if you're heading north).

Pack a picnic and take it down to the dock, where you can watch the fishing boats or grab a lobster roll from Red's Eats or the lobster shack nearby. Wiscasset has expanded its wharf, and this is a great place to catch a breeze on a hot day. U.S. 1 becomes Main Street, and traffic often slows to a crawl. You can walk to all galleries, shops, restaurants, and other attractions. **TIP→ You'll likely have success if you try to park on Water Street rather than Main.**

SHOPPING

Not to be missed is **Edgecomb Potters** (✉ *727 Boothbay Rd., Edgecomb* ☎ *207/882–9493* 🌐 *www.edgecombpotters.com*), which specializes in pricey, exquisitely glazed porcelain and has one of the best selections in the area. It also carries jewelry. **Sheepscot River Pottery** (✉ *34 U.S. 1, Edgecomb* ☎ *207/882–9410* 🌐 *www.sheepscot.com*) boasts beautifully glazed kitchen tiles as well as kitchenware and home accessories.

WHERE TO EAT

¢ FAST FOOD ✕ **Red's Eats.** You've probably driven right past this little red shack on the Wiscasset side of the bridge if you've visited this area and seen the long line of hungry customers. Red's is a local landmark famous for its hot dogs, burgers, crisp onion rings, lobster and crab rolls, and even its ice cream (try black raspberry or pistachio). There are a few picnic tables, but you can get your food to go and walk down to the dock to enjoy the view. Watch out for the seagulls; they like lobster rolls, too. ✉ *41 Water St.* ☎ *207/882–6128* *Reservations not accepted* *No credit cards* *Closed mid-Oct.–mid-Apr.*

OFF THE BEATEN PATH

The Boothbay region is made up of Boothbay proper, East Boothbay, and Boothbay Harbor. This part of the shoreline is a craggy stretch of inlets where pleasure craft anchor alongside trawlers and lobster boats. Boothbay Harbor is like a smaller version of Bar Harbor—touristy but friendly and fun—with pretty, winding streets and lots to explore. Commercial Street, Wharf Street, Townsend Avenue, and the By-Way are lined with shops and ice-cream parlors. You can browse for hours in the trinket shops, crafts galleries, clothing stores, and boutiques around the harbor or take a walk around the 248-acre **Coastal Maine Botanical Garden** (✉ *Barters Island Rd.* ☎ *207/633–4333* *www.mainegardens.org*).

Excursion boats and ferries to Monhegan Island leave from the piers off Commercial Street. Drive out to Ocean Point in East Boothbay for some incredible scenery. Boothbay is 13 mi southeast of Wiscasset via U.S. 1 to Rte. 27.

DAMARISCOTTA

8 mi north of Wiscasset via U.S. 1.

The Damariscotta region comprises several communities along the rocky coast. The town itself sits on the water and is a lively place filled with attractive shops and several good restaurants.

A few minutes' walk across the bridge over the Damariscotta River is the town of Newcastle, between the Sheepscot and Damariscotta rivers. Newcastle was settled in the early 1600s. The earliest inhabitants planted apple trees, but the town later became an industrial center, home to several shipyards and a couple of mills. The oldest Catholic church in New England, St. Patrick's, is here, and it still rings its original Paul Revere bell.

Bremen, which encompasses more than a dozen islands and countless rocky outcrops, offers numerous sporting activities. Nobleboro was settled in the 1720s by Colonel David Dunbar, sent by the British to build the fort at Pemaquid. Neighboring Waldoboro is situated on the Medomak River and was settled largely by Germans in the early 1770s. You can still visit the old German Meeting House, built in 1772. The peninsula stretches south to include Bristol, Round Pond, South Bristol, New Harbor, and Pemaquid.

ESSENTIALS

Visitor Information **Damariscotta Region Chamber of Commerce** (*Box 13, Damariscotta 04543* ☎ *207/563–8340* *www.damariscottaregion.com*).

WHERE TO EAT AND STAY

$$–$$$ AMERICAN ★ **King Eider's Pub & Restaurant.** The classic pub bills itself as having the finest crab cakes in New England. Other specialties of the house include lobster Courvoisier and house-made ravioli (e.g., stuffed with crabmeat)

Lobster pot buoys are popular decorations in Maine; the markings represent a particular lobsterman's claim.

that vary day to day. Penne pasta in a creamy dill sauce with a mound of sea scallops is out of this world. With exposed brick walls and low wooden beams, it's a cozy place to enjoy your favorite ale. There is also seating on the deck. Stop by in the evening for live entertainment. ✉ 2 *Elm St.* ☎ *207/563–6008* 🌐 *www.kingeiderspub.com* ✍ *Reservations essential* 💳 *D, MC, V.*

$$$–$$$$ 🏨 **Newcastle Inn.** A riverside location and an excellent dining room make this country inn a classic. All the guest rooms are filled with antiques and decorated with sumptuous fabrics; some rooms have fireplaces and whirlpool baths. There are two rooms designated pet-friendly, with private entrances. On pleasant mornings breakfast is served on the back deck overlooking the river. The dining room ($$$$), which is open to the public by reservation, serves six-course meals with an emphasis on local seafood and is open Tuesday through Saturday in season. **Pros:** innkeepers' reception evenings with cocktails and hors d'oeuvres. **Cons:** away from town. ✉ *60 River Rd. Newcastle* ☎ *207/563–5685 or 800/832–8669* 🌐 *www.newcastleinn.com* *14 rooms, 3 suites* *In-room: no phone, no TV (some). In-hotel: no kids under 12* 💳 *AE, MC, V* 🍴 *BP.*

PEMAQUID POINT

17 mi south of Damariscotta via U.S. 1 to Rte. 129 to Rte. 130.

Route 130 brings you to Pemaquid Point, home of the famous lighthouse and its attendant fog bell and tiny museum. If you are going to New Harbor or Round Pond, take a left onto Route 32 where it intersects Route 130 just before Pemaquid Point. New Harbor is about

4 mi away, and Round Pond about 6 mi beyond that. Just north of New Harbor on Route 32 is the Rachel Carson Salt Pond Preserve.

EXPLORING

★ **Pemaquid Point Light.** At the terminus of Route 130, this lighthouse looks as though it sprouted from the ragged, tilted chunk of granite that it commands. The former keeper's cottage is now the Fishermen's Museum, which displays historic photographs, scale models, and artifacts that explore commercial fishing in Maine. Also here are the original fog bell and bell house built in 1897 for the two original Shipman engines. Pemaquid Art Gallery, on-site, mounts exhibitions by area artists in July and August, and admission, once you have paid your fee to be on the lighthouse property, is free. Restrooms, picnic tables, and barbecue grills are all available on-site. Next door is the Sea Gull Shop, with a dining room, gift shop, and ice-cream parlor. The museum onsite is adjacent to the lighthouse. ✉ *Rte. 130 (Bristol Rd.), Pemaquid* ☎ *207/677–2494* *$1* *Memorial Day–Columbus Day, Mon.–Sat. 10–5, Sun. 11–5* *$5.*

SPORTS AND THE OUTDOORS

CRUISES You can take a cruise to Monhegan with **Hardy Boat Cruises** (✉ *Shaw's Wharf, New Harbor* ☎ *207/677–6026*).

WHERE TO STAY

$$ **Unique Yankee Bed & Breakfast.** If you are traveling with a dog, you'll find few more accommodating spots in Maine than this out-of-the way place on Rutherford Island. One room even has its own fenced-in dog play yard. Though it's a 6-minute drive to the water, the inn has a tower where, if you have a clear day, you might see all the way to Monhegan Island. The 2.3-acre property is surrounded by a 2-acre greenbelt, so it's quite private. The main house has rooms with four-season electric fireplace, microwave, coffee pot, and two-person jetted bath (plus separate shower). A newer annex has very large rooms with modern amenities. **Pros:** great if you're traveling with dogs; long views of Pemaquid on clear days from lookout. **Cons:** dogs on premises. ✉ *53 Coveside Rd., South Bristol* ☎ *207/644–1502 or 866/644–1502* *www.uniqueyankeeofmaine.com* *6 rooms* *In-room: Wi-Fi, refrigerator, DVD. In-hotel: some pets allowed* *MC, V* *BP.*

THOMASTON

10 mi northeast of Waldoboro, 72 mi northeast of Portland.

Thomaston is a delightful town, full of beautiful sea captains' homes and dotted with antiques and specialty shops. A National Historic District encompasses parts of High, Main, and Knox streets. The town is the gateway to the two peninsulas, so you will see water on both sides as you arrive.

WHERE TO EAT

$$–$$$ AMERICAN **Thomaston Café & Bakery.** A must-stop on the long, slow drive up Route 1. Works by local artists adorns the walls of this small café, and it's next door to an independent bookstore. Entrées, prepared with

locally grown ingredients, include seared fresh tuna on soba noodles, lobster ravioli with lobster sauce, and filet mignon with béarnaise sauce. They serve an excellent breakfast, including homemade corned beef hash, as well as delicious sandwiches for lunch. ✉ *154 Main St.* ☎ *207/354–8589* 🌐 *www.harborviewrestaurant.com* ▭ *MC, V* ⏲ *No dinner Sun.–Thurs.*

TENANTS HARBOR

10 mi south of Thomaston.

Tenants Harbor is a quintessential coastal harbor—dominated by lobster boats, its shores are rocky and slippery, and its downtown streets are lined with clapboard houses, a church, and a general store. It's a favorite with artists, and galleries and studios welcome browsers.

WHERE TO STAY

$$$ Fodor's Choice ★ **Craignair Inn.** It's tough to find a better waterfront location than Craignair, which overlooks Wheeler's Bay and Clark Island on 4 waterfront acres. It was originally built to house granite workers from nearby quarries. The annex house was the chapel where the stonecutters and their families worshipped. Rooms aren't as wonderful as the views but are clean and functional. You can easily explore Clark Island by walking over a narrow isthmus. Another perk is the excellent food. Chef Seiler, most recently from the Samoset Resort, wins awards for his creative cuisine served in the inn's dining room ($$$). You might want to start with the Caribbean jerk grilled shrimp brochettes or the steamed Great Eastern mussels and move on to pecan-crusted salmon, bacon-wrapped tenderloin, or baked stuffed haddock. **Pros:** stellar food; waterfront location. **Cons:** pets allowed in some rooms can be troublesome to those with allergies. ✉ *5 3rd St., Spruce Head* ☎ *207/594–7644 or 800/320–9997* 🌐 *www.craignair.com* *21 rooms, 13 with bath* *In-room: no a/c, Wi-Fi. In-hotel: Wi-Fi hotspot, some pets allowed* ▭ *D, MC, V* *BP.*

PORT CLYDE

2 mi south of Tenants Harbor via Rte. 131.

The fishing village of Port Clyde sits at the end of the St. George Peninsula. The road leading to Port Clyde meanders along the St. George River, passing meadows and farmhouses. Shipbuilding was the first commercial enterprise here, followed by the catching and canning of seafood. You can still buy Port Clyde sardines. Its boat landing is home to the *Elizabeth Ann* and the *Laura B*, the mail boats that serve nearby Monhegan Island and are operated by the **Monhegan Boat Line** (☎ *207/372/8848* 🌐 *www.monheganboat.com*). Several artists make their homes in Port Clyde, so check to see if their studios are open while you are visiting. From here you can also visit Owls Head Light and the Marshall Point Lighthouse, the latter of which has inspired artists like Jamie Wyeth.

MONHEGAN ISLAND

Fodor's Choice ★ *East of Pemaquid Peninsula, 10 mi south of Port Clyde.*

Simple and artful living is the order of the day on remote Monhegan Island. To get here you'll need to take a ferry. A tiny hamlet greets you at the harbor. There are no paved roads, and everywhere you look artists stand before their canvases, rendering the landscape of serene gardened cottages and rugged coast.

The island was known to Basque, Portuguese, and Breton fishermen well before Christopher Columbus discovered America. About a century ago, Monhegan was discovered again by some of the finest American painters, including Rockwell Kent, Robert Henri, A. J. Hammond, and Edward Hopper, who sailed out to paint its open meadows, savage cliffs, wild ocean views, and fishermen's shacks. Tourists followed, and now three excursion boats dock here for a few hours each day in the warm months when harbor shops and artist studios bustle with activity.

You can escape the crowds on the island's 17 mi of hiking trails, which lead to the lighthouse and to the cliffs, or spend a night and feel some of the privacy that the island can afford. Note that if you're the kind of traveler who likes lots of activities, skip Monhegan. (Actually, you should probably skipped Maine altogether.) A day trip is typified by a little shopping and a hike across the island to view the bluffs. If the weather's bad, there's little to do. But if you enjoy a good hike, nature, or the concept of an island that's home to just artists and fishermen, the silence and serenity of the high cliffs at White Head, Black Head, and Burnt Head and the serendipitous pleasures that the island creates will be unforgettable.

PENOBSCOT BAY

Updated by Stephen and Neva Allen

Few could deny that Penobscot Bay is one of Maine's most dramatically beautiful regions. Its 1,000-mi-long coastline is made up of rocky granite boulders, wild and often undeveloped shore, a sprinkling of colorful towns, and views of the sea and shore that are a photographer's dream.

The second-largest estuary in New England, Penobscot Bay stretches 37 mi from Port Clyde in the south to Stonington, the little fishing village at the tip of Deer Isle, in the north. The bay begins where the Penobscot River ends, near Stockton Springs, and terminates in the Gulf of Maine, where it is 47 mi wide. It covers an estimated 1,070 square mi and is home to hundreds of islands.

Initially, shipbuilding was the primary moneymaker here. In the 1800s, during the days of the great tall ships (or Down Easters, as they were often called), more wooden ships were built along Penobscot Bay than in any other place in the United States. This golden age of billowing sails and wooden sailing ships came to an end with the development of the steam engine. By 1900, sailing ships were no longer a viable commercial venture in Maine. However, as you will see when traveling the coast, the tall ships have not disappeared—they have simply been

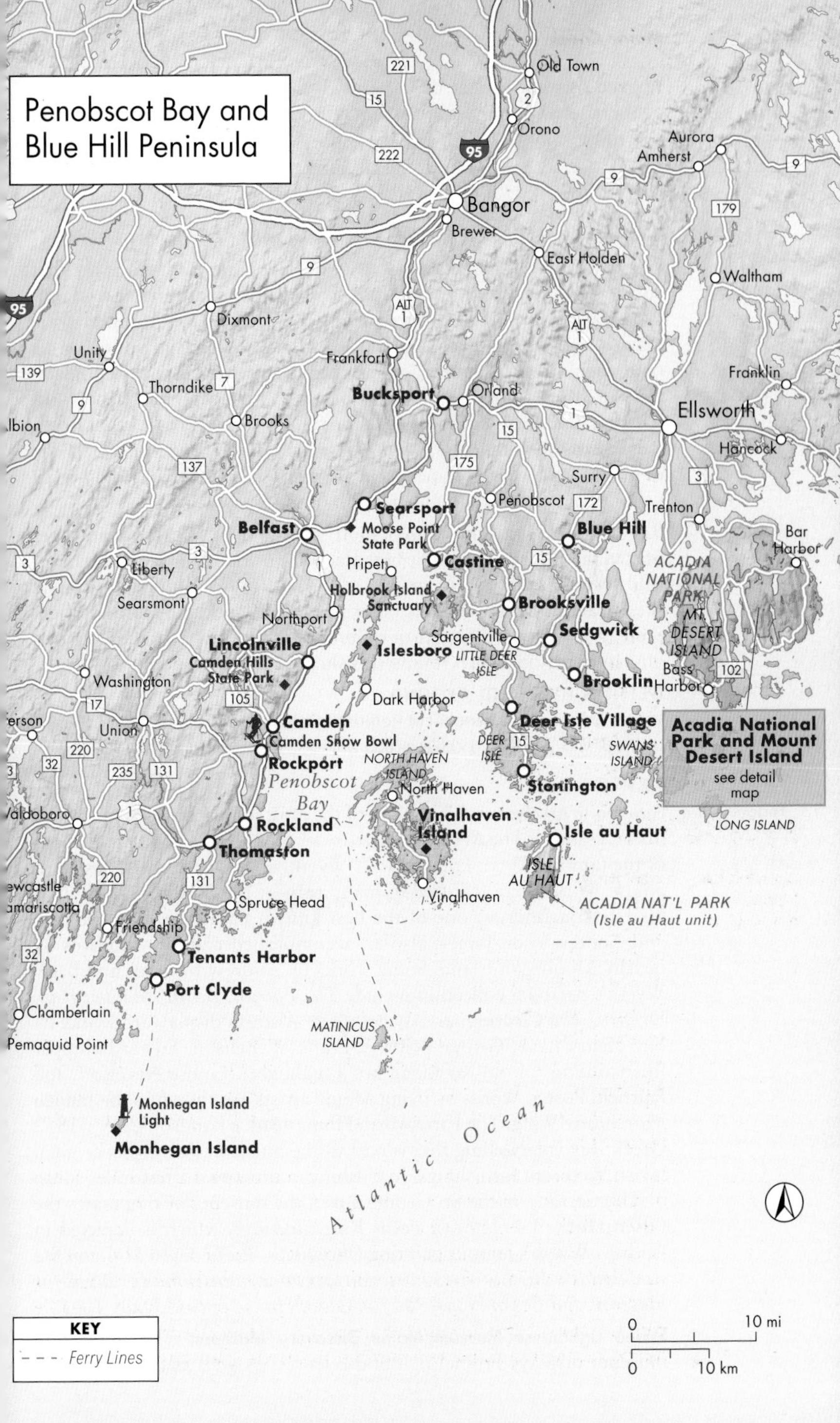

Penobscot Bay and Blue Hill Peninsula
Old Town
Orono
Bangor
Brewer
Aurora
Amherst
East Holden
Waltham
Dixmont
Unity
Frankfort
Thorndike
Brooks
Bucksport
Orland
Franklin
Ellsworth
Hancock
Surry
Penobscot
Trenton
Searsport
Moose Point State Park
Belfast
Blue Hill
Bar Harbor
Liberty
Searsmont
Pripet
Castine
Holbrook Island Sanctuary
Northport
Brooksville
ACADIA NATIONAL PARK
MT. DESERT ISLAND
Sargentville
Sedgwick
Lincolnville
Camden Hills State Park
Islesboro
LITTLE DEER ISLE
Washington
Brooklin
Bass Harbor
Dark Harbor
Camden
Camden Snow Bowl
Union
Deer Isle Village
DEER ISLE
SWANS ISLAND
Acadia National Park and Mount Desert Island
see detail map
Rockport
NORTH HAVEN ISLAND
North Haven
Penobscot Bay
Stonington
Vinalhaven Island
Rockland
Thomaston
Isle au Haut
LONG ISLAND
ISLE AU HAUT
ACADIA NAT'L PARK
(Isle au Haut unit)
Vinalhaven
Spruce Head
Friendship
Tenants Harbor
Port Clyde
Chamberlain
Pemaquid Point
MATINICUS ISLAND
Monhegan Island Light
Monhegan Island
Atlantic Ocean
KEY
Ferry Lines
0 10 mi
0 10 km

revived as recreational boats, known as windjammers. Today, once again, there are more tall ships along Penobscot Bay than anywhere else in the country.

ROCKLAND

4 mi northeast of Thomaston; 14 mi northeast of Tenants Harbor.

The town is considered the gateway to Penobscot Bay and is the first stop on U.S. 1 offering a glimpse of the often sparkling and island-dotted blue bay. Though once merely a place to pass through on the way to tonier ports like Camden, Rockland now gets attention on its own, thanks to a trio of attractions: the renowned Farnsworth Museum, the increasingly popular summer Lobster Festival, and the lively North Atlantic Blues Festival. Specialty shops and galleries line the main street, and one of the restaurants, Primo (between Camden and the little village of Owls Head), has become nationally famous. The town is still a large fishing port and the commercial hub of this coastal area.

Rockland Harbor is the berth of more windjammer ships than any other port in the United States. The best place in Rockland to view these beautiful vessels as they sail in and out of the harbor is the mile-long granite breakwater, which bisects the outer portion of Rockland Harbor. To get there, go north on U.S. 1, turn right on Waldo Avenue, and right again on Samoset Road, then follow this short road to its end.

GETTING HERE AND AROUND

Visitor Information **Penobscot Regional Chamber of Commerce** (✉ *1 Park Dr., Rockland* ☎ *207/596–0376 or 800/562–2529* 🌐 *www.therealmaine.com*).

EXPLORING

Fodor's Choice ★ **Farnsworth Art Museum.** This is one of the most important small museums in the country. The **Wyeth Center** is devoted to Maine-related works of the famous Wyeth family: N. C. Wyeth, an accomplished illustrator whose works were featured in many turn-of-the-20th-century books; his late son Andrew, one of the best-known painters in the country; and Andrew's son James, also an accomplished painter, who lives on nearby Monhegan Island. Some works by Andrew from his and Betsy Wyeth's personal collection include *The Patriot, Adrift, Maiden Hair, Dr. Syn, The Clearing,* and *Watch Cap*. Also on display are works by Fitz Henry Lane, George Bellows, Frank W. Benson, Edward Hopper (his paintings of old Rockland are a highlight), Louise Nevelson, and Fairfield Porter. Works by living Maine artists are shown in the **Jamien Morehouse Wing.** The **Farnsworth Homestead,** a handsome circa-1852 Greek Revival dwelling that is part of the museum, retains its original lavish Victorian furnishings. In Cushing, a tiny town a few miles south of Thomaston, on the St. George River, the museum also operates the **Olsen House** (✉ *Hathorn Point Rd., Cushing*), which is depicted in Andrew Wyeth's famous painting *Christina's World.* ✉ *16 Museum St., Rockland* ☎ *207/596–6457* 🌐 *www.farnsworthmuseum.org* 🎟 *$12 for museum and Olsen House; $4 for Olsen House only* ⏲ *Daily 10–5.*

★ **Maine Lighthouse Museum/Maine Discovery Museum.** The lighthouse museum displays Fresnel lighthouse lenses, as well as a collection of lighthouse artifacts and Coast Guard memorabilia. Sharing the same building are the Maine Discovery Museum, which is great for kids, and the Penobscot Bay Regional Chamber of Commerce, where visitors can pick up maps and area information. ✉ *1 Park Dr.* ☎ *207/594–3301* 🌐 *www.mainelighthousemuseum.com* 🎫 *$5* ⏲ *Weekdays 9–5, weekends 10–4.*

NIGHTLIFE AND THE ARTS

FESTIVALS ★ More than a dozen well-known artists gather for the **North Atlantic Blues Festival** (☎ *207/593–1189* 🌐 *www.northatlanticbluesfestival.com*), a two-day weekend affair held every July. The show officially takes place at Harbor Park, but it also includes a Blues Club Crawl Saturday night through downtown Rockland. Admission is $25 in advance, $30 at the gate. Rockland's annual **Maine Lobster Festival** (☎ *207/596–0376 or 800/562–2529* 🌐 *www.mainelobsterfestival.com*), in early August, is more than 60 years old and has become the biggest local event of the year. People come from all over the country to sample lobster in every possible form. During the few days of the festival about 10 tons of lobsters are steamed in the world's largest lobster cooker—you have to see it to believe it. The festival, held in Harbor Park, includes a parade, entertainment, craft and marine exhibits, food booths—and, of course, the crowning of the Maine Sea Goddess.

WHERE TO EAT

$$$–$$$$ CONTINENTAL Fodor's Choice ★ ✕ **Primo.** Owner-chef Melissa Kelley and her world-class gourmet restaurant in a restored Victorian home have won many awards and been written about favorably in *Vanity Fair, Town and Country,* and *Food and Wine*. The cuisine combines fresh Maine ingredients with Mediterranean influences. The menu, which changes daily, may include wood-roasted black sea bass, local crab–stuffed turbot, or diver-harvested scallop and basil ravioli. Pastry chef and co-owner Price Kushner creates unusual and delectable desserts such as Cannoli Siciliana, featuring crushed pistachios and amarena cherries. ✉ *2 S. Main St., Rockland (on the border between Rockland and the little village of Owls Head; if you see the sign that reads "Welcome to Owls Head," you've passed Primo by 100 feet)* ☎ *207/596–0770* 🌐 *www.primorestaurant.com* 💳 *AE, D, MC, V* ⏲ *Open Wed.–Sun. No lunch. Closed mid-Jan.–mid-Apr.*

$$ SEAFOOD ★ ✕ **Rockland Café.** It may not look like much from the outside, but the Rockland Café is probably the most popular eating establishment in town. It's famous for the size of its breakfasts (get the fishcakes) and is also open for lunch and dinner. At dinner, the seafood combo of shrimp, scallops, clams, and fish is excellent, or there's the classic liver and onions. ✉ *441 S. Main St., Rockland* ☎ *207/596–7556* 🌐 *www.rocklandcafe.com* 💳 *AE, D, MC, V.*

WHERE TO STAY

$$$–$$$$ ★ **Berry Manor Inn.** Originally the residence of Rockland merchant Charles H. Berry, this 1898 inn is in a historic residential neighborhood. The large guest rooms of this B&B are elegantly furnished with antiques and reproduction pieces. All rooms have fireplaces; TVs are available upon request, and some rooms have whirlpools. A guest pantry is stocked with sweets. **Pros:** in a nice, quiet neighborhood; within walking distance of

CLOSE UP

Windjammer Excursions

A windjammer cruise gives you a chance to admire Maine's dramatic coast from the water.

Nothing defines the Maine coastal experience more than a sailing trip on a windjammer. Windjammers were built all along the East Coast in the 19th and early 20th centuries. Designed primarily to carry cargo, these iron- or steel-hulled beauties have a rich past—the *Nathaniel Bowditch* served in World War II, while others plied the waters in the lumbering and oystering trades. They vary in size but could be as small as 40 feet and hold 6 passengers (plus a couple of crew members) or more than 130 feet and hold 40 passengers and 10 crew members. During a windjammer excursion passengers are usually able to participate in the navigation, be it hoisting a sail or playing captain at the wheel.

The majority of windjammers are berthed in Rockland, Rockport, or Camden. You can get information on the fleets by contacting one of two windjammer organizations: **Maine Windjammer Association** (☎ *800/807-9463* 🌐 *www.sailmainecoast.com*) or **Maine Windjammer Cruises** (☎ *207/236-2938* or *800/736-7981* 🌐 *www.mainewindjammercruises.com*) . Cruises can be anywhere from one to eight days. The price, ranging from nearly $200 to $900, depending on length of trip, includes all meals. Trips leave from Camden, Rockland, and Rockport.

Here is a selection of some of the best windjammer cruises in the area.

CAMDEN–ROCKPORT: Angelique (☎ *207/785-6036*). *Appledore*, which can take you out for just a day sail (☎ *207/236-8353*). *Mary Day*, Coastal Cruises (☎ *207/785-5670*). *Olad*, Downeast Windjammer Packet Co. (☎ *207/236-2323*); *Schooner Heron* (☎ *207/236-8605* or *800/599-8605*).

★ ROCKLAND: *American Eagle* and *Schooner Heritage*, North End Shipyard (☎ *207/594-8007* 🌐 *www.schoonerheritage.com*). *Nathaniel Bowditch* (☎ *800/288-4098*). *Summertime* (☎ *207/563-1605* or *800/562-8290*).

downtown and the harbor. **Con:** not much of a view. ✉ *81 Talbot Ave.* ☎ *207/596–7696 or 800/774–5692* 🌐 *www.berrymanorinn.com* *12 rooms* *In-room: no TV, Wi-Fi* *AE, MC, V* *BP.*

$$–$$$$ ★ **LimeRock Inn.** This inn is in the center of town, so you can easily walk to the Farnsworth Museum or any of the other downtown attractions and restaurants. The house is built in the Queen Anne–Victorian style, and among the meticulously decorated rooms is one called Island Cottage, which features a whirlpool tub and doors that open onto a private deck overlooking a garden. The Grand Manan room has a fireplace, a whirlpool tub, and a four-poster king-size bed. TVs are available upon request. **Pros:** this is like living in an old New England house; free Wi-Fi. **Cons:** not much of a view. ✉ *96 Limerock St.* ☎ *207/594–2257 or 800/546–3762* 🌐 *www.limerockinn.com* *8 rooms* *In-room: no TV, Wi-Fi. In-hotel: Internet terminal* *AE, D, MC, V* *BP.*

ROCKPORT

5

4 mi north of Rockland on U.S. 1.

Heading north on U.S. 1, you come to Rockport before you reach the tourist mecca of Camden. The most interesting part of Rockport—the harbor—is not right on U.S. 1. You can get here by following the first ROCKPORT sign you see off U.S. 1 at Pascal Road.

Originally called Goose River, the town was part of Camden until 1891. The cutting and burning of limestone was once a major industry in this area. The stone was cut in nearby quarries and then burned in hot kilns, and the resulting lime powder was used to create mortar. Some of the massive kilns are still here.

One of the most famous sights in Rockport is the **Rockport Arch,** which crosses Union Street at the town line. It was constructed of wood and mortar in 1926, demolished in 1984, then rebuilt by popular demand in 1985. The arch has been displayed in a number of movies, including *Peyton Place* and *In the Bedroom.*

ESSENTIALS

Visitor Information Camden-Rockport-Lincolnville Chamber of Commerce (✉ *2 Public Landing, Camden* ☎ *207/236–4404 www.visitcamden.com*).

WHERE TO EAT AND STAY

$$$–$$$$ FRENCH Fodor's Choice ★ **Marcel's.** If you're a serious gourmet and only have time to sample one dining experience in the Rockport-Rockland-Camden area, this lavish restaurant in the big Samoset Resort ought to be the one. Marcel's offers a fine array of Continental cuisine. Enjoy table-side preparation of a classic rack of lamb, chateaubriand, or steak Diane while admiring the bay view. The menu includes a variety of Maine seafood and a fine wine list. The Sunday brunch buffet has some of the finest seafood along the coast. ✉ *220 Warrenton St., off U.S. 1* ☎ *207/594–2511* 🌐 *www.samoset.com* *Reservations essential* *Jacket required* *AE, D, MC, V* *No lunch.*

$$–$$$$ Fodor's Choice ★ **Samoset Resort.** This 230-acre, all-encompassing oceanside resort on the Rockland–Rockport town line offers luxurious rooms and suites, all with a private balcony or patio and an ocean or garden view. The

THE PRETTIEST WALK IN THE WORLD

A few years ago *Yankee*, the quintessential magazine of New England, did a cover story on what it called "The Prettiest Walk in the World." The two-lane paved road, which winds up and down, with occasional views of the ocean, connects Rockport to Camden. To judge the merits of this approximately 2-mi journey for yourself, you can travel on foot or by car. Begin at the intersection of U.S. 1 and Pascal Road. Take a right off U.S. 1 toward Rockport Harbor, then cross the bridge and go up the hill. On your left is Russell Avenue. Take that all the way to Camden. Lining the way are some of the most beautiful homes in Maine, surrounded by an abundance of flora and fauna. Keep an eye out for Aldermere Farm and its Belted Galloway cows, as well as views of the sparkling ocean. For those who may not know, these rare cows get their name from the foot-wide white "belt" around their middles. The walk or drive is beautiful at any time of the year, but in fall it's breathtaking. Like the rest of New England, the coast of Maine gets a large number of fall-foliage "leaf peepers," and the reds and golds of the chestnut, birch, and elm trees along this winding route are especially beautiful.

spacious rooms are decorated in deep green and burgundy tones. The resort has three dining options: Marcel's, the Breakwater Café, and the Clubhouse Grille. The flagship restaurant Marcel's ($$$–$$$$) features French and American cuisine, as well as seafood specials. Reservations are essential, and men must wear a jacket. For a less-formal affair, try the Breakwater Café ($$), featuring basic New England fare such as homemade chowder and lobster rolls; there's outdoor seating when the weather is nice. The Clubhouse Grille ($), catering to the golf crowd, serves casual food, which you can enjoy inside or on the porch. *Golf Digest* called the resort's 18-hole championship course the "Top Ranked Resort Course in New England," and the "Seventh Most Beautiful Course in America." Green fees range from $70 to $140. **Pros:** a resort property that seems to meet every need; airport shuttle. **Cons:** not within walking distance of Rockland or Camden shops. ✉ *220 Warrenton St., Rockport* ☎ *207/594–2511 or 800/341–1650* 🌐 *www.samoset.com* *156 rooms, 22 suites* *In-room: Internet, Wi-Fi. In-hotel: 3 restaurants, bar, golf course, tennis courts, pools, gym, children's programs (ages 3–12), laundry service, Internet terminal* ▭ *AE, D, MC, V* *CP.*

CAMDEN

★ *2 mi north of Rockport.*

More than any other town along Penobscot Bay, Camden is the perfect picture-postcard of a Maine coastal village. It is one of the most popular destinations on the Maine Coast, so June through September the town is crowded with visitors, but don't let that scare you away; Camden is worth it. Just come prepared for busy traffic on the town's Main Street (U.S. 1) and make reservations for lodging and restaurants well in advance.

The view from Camden Hills is a great way to see Penobscot Bay and the town of Camden.

Camden is famous not only for its geography, but also for its large fleet of windjammers—relics and replicas from the age of sailing—with their romantic histories and great billowing sails. At just about any hour during the warm months you're likely to see at least one windjammer tied up in the harbor. The excursions, whether for an afternoon or a week, are best from June through September.

The town's compact size makes it perfect for exploring on foot: shops, restaurants, and galleries line Main Street, as well as side streets and alleys around the harbor. Especially worth inclusion on your walking tour is Camden's residential area. It is quite charming and filled with many fascinating old period houses from the time when Federal, Greek Revival, and Victorian architecture were the rage among the wealthy. Many of them are now B&Bs. The chamber of commerce, at the Public Landing, can provide you with a walking map.

WHEN TO GO

FESTIVAL ★ One of the biggest and most colorful events of the year in Camden is **Windjammer Weekend**, which usually takes place at the beginning of September and includes the single largest gathering of windjammer ships in the world, plus lots of good eats. ☎ *207/374–2993 or 800/807–9463* *www.sailmainecoast.com.*

SHOPPING

Camden's downtown area is a shopper's paradise with lots of interesting places to spend money. Most of the shops and galleries are along Camden's main drag. Start at the Camden Harbor, turn right on Bay View, and walk to Main/High Street. **TIP→ U.S. 1 has three different**

names within the town limits—it starts as Elm Street, changes to Main Street, then becomes High Street.

Bayview Gallery (✉ *33 Bay View St.* ☎ *207/236–4534* 🌐 *www.bayviewgallery.com*) specializes in original art, prints, and posters, most with Maine themes. **Lili, Lupine & Fern** (✉ *44 Bayview St.* ☎ *207/236–9600*) offers a wonderful array of gourmet foods, wines, and cheeses. **Planet Toys** (✉ *10 Main St.* ☎ *207/236–4410*) has unusual gifts—including books, toys, and clothing—from Maine and other parts of the world.

WHERE TO EAT

$$$–$$$$ SEAFOOD ✕ **Atlantica.** Right on the water's edge, the Atlantica is in a historic clapboard building. Its lower deck is cantilevered over the water, offering a romantic setting with great views, and the interior decor is a mix of red walls and contemporary paintings. Fresh seafood with French and Asian accents is the specialty here. Favorites include pan-roasted split lobster tails with lemon butter, lobster stuffed with scallops, and pan-roasted king salmon. ✉ *Bayview Landing* ☎ *207/236–6011 or 888/507–8514* 🌐 *www.atlanticarestaurant.com* *Reservations essential* *AE, MC, V* *No lunch.*

$–$$ SEAFOOD ★ ✕ **Cappy's Chowder House.** As you would expect from the name, Cappy's "chowdah" is the thing to order here—it's been written up in the *New York Times* and in *Bon Appétit* magazine—but there are plenty of other seafood specials on the menu. Don't be afraid to bring the kids—this place has many bargain meals. ✉ *1 Main St.* ☎ *207/236–2254* 🌐 *www.cappyschowder.com* *Reservations not accepted* *MC, V.*

$$–$$$ FRENCH-AMERICAN Fodor's Choice ★ ✕ **Natalie's.** This restaurant may be the most sought-after dining spot in Camden. It's the creation of Dutch owners Raymond Brunyanszki and Oscar Verest, and is in the Camden Harbour Inn. The restaurant is fine dining with a French-American flair and offers a variety of prix-fixe menus, such as "The Menu Saisonnier," which showcases fresh, seasonal ingredients, and the "Homard Grand Cru," a cascade of lobster dishes (lobster gazpacho, lobster with squid ink, lobster with fiddleheads, lobster with beef cheek and foie-gras ravioli). In the lounge enjoy a pre-dinner cocktail in front of the big fireplace. ✉ *83 Bay View St.* ☎ *207/236–7008* 🌐 *www.camdenharbourinn.com* *AE, D, MC, V.*

WHERE TO STAY

$$–$$$$ ★ **Camden Hartstone Inn.** This downtown 1835 mansard-roofed Victorian home has been turned into an elegant and sophisticated retreat and a fine culinary destination. No detail has been overlooked, from soft robes, down comforters, and chocolate truffles in the guest rooms to china, crystal, and silver in the elegantly decorated dining room ($$$$). The inn hosts seasonal food festivals. **Pros:** excellent on-site restaurant. **Cons:** no water views, but the harbor and the downtown are not far away. ✉ *41 Elm St. (U.S. 1)* ☎ *207/236–4259 or 800/788–4823* 🌐 *www.hartstoneinn.com* *6 rooms, 6 suites* *In-room: Internet. In-hotel: restaurant* *MC, V* *BP.*

$$$–$$$$ ★ **Lord Camden Inn.** If you want in the center of Camden and near the harbor, this is the place. The exterior of the building is red brick with bright blue-and-white awnings. The colorful interior is furnished with restored antiques and paintings by local artists. Despite being downtown, the inn

offers plenty of ocean views from the upstairs rooms, and some rooms have lovely old-fashioned four-poster beds. There's no on-site restaurant, but plenty of dining options are within walking distance. **Pros:** central location. **Cons:** in the front rooms the U.S. 1 traffic may keep you awake. ✉ *24 Main St. (U.S. 1)* ☎ *207/236–4325 or 800/336–4325* 🌐 *www.lordcamdeninn.com* *37 rooms* *In-room: refrigerator (some), DVD, Wi-Fi. In-hotel: gym, some pets allowed* ▭ *AE, MC, V* *BP.*

$$$–$$$$ Fodor's Choice ★ **Norumbega Inn.** This is the most photographed piece of real estate in the state of Maine, and once you take a look at it, you'll understand why. This castle B&B looks as if it were created by Stephen King (a Maine resident) or Count Dracula. It's easy to find, as it's right on U.S. 1, just a little north of downtown Camden. The outside consists of gray stone walls covered with ivy, but inside it's cheerier and elegant, with many of the antique-filled rooms offering fireplaces and private balconies overlooking the bay. The inn was built in 1886 by local businessman and inventor (of duplex telegraphy) Joseph Stearns. Before erecting his home, he spent a year visiting the castles of Europe and adapted the best ideas he found. He named the castle after what Maine was called in the 17th century, "Norumbega," and the home was converted into a B&B in 1984. **Pros:** beautiful views; close to town. **Cons:** guests who have difficulty climbing stairs will not find it comfortable ✉ *63 High St. (U.S. 1)* ☎ *207/236–4646 or 877/363–4646* 🌐 *www.norumbegainn.com* *12 rooms* *In-room: no a/c, DVD (some), Wi-Fi. In-hotel: concierge service* ▭ *AE, MC, V* *BP.*

$$–$$$ ★ **Whitehall Inn.** One of Camden's best-known inns, the Whitehall is an 1834 white-clapboard sea captain's home just north of town. The Millay Room, off the lobby, preserves memorabilia of the poet Edna St. Vincent Millay, who grew up in the area and read her poetry here. The inn is a delightful blend of the old and the new. The telephones are antiques, but the electronics are brand new. The rooms, remodeled in 2007, have dark-wood bedsteads, white bedspreads, and claw-foot tubs. The dining room serves traditional and creative American cuisine as well as many seafood specialties, and the popular prix-fixe dinner is $36 a person. **Pros:** connection to local poetess Edna St. Vincent Millay. **Cons:** only some rooms have water views. ✉ *52 High St.* ☎ *207/236–3391 or 800/789–6565* 🌐 *www.whitehall-inn.com* *50 rooms, 45 with bath* *In-room: no a/c, Wi-Fi. In-hotel: restaurant, tennis court, Internet terminals* ▭ *AE, D, MC, V* ⊗ *Closed mid-Oct.–mid-May* *BP.*

LINCOLNVILLE

6 mi north of Camden via U.S. 1.

Looking at a map, you may notice there are two parts to Lincolnville: Lincolnville Beach on U.S. 1 and the town of Lincolnville Center a little inland on Route 73. The area of most interest—where you can find the restaurants and the ferry to Islesboro—is Lincolnville Beach, which is tiny; you could be through it in less than a minute. Still, it has a history going back to the Revolution, and you can see a few small cannons on the beach that were intended to repel the British in the War of 1812 (they were never used).

WHERE TO EAT AND STAY

$$–$$$ SEAFOOD ★ ✕ **Lobster Pound Restaurant.** If you're looking for an authentic place to have your Maine lobster dinner, this is it. This simple restaurant looks more like a cannery, with rustic wooden picnic tables and hundreds of live lobsters swimming in tanks—if you want, you can pick out your own, which will be served to you with clam chowder and corn. Forget about ordering a pre-dinner cocktail or wine with dinner (sorry, no bar service); have an iced tea instead. On U.S. 1, right on the edge of the sea, the restaurant provides beautiful views from both its indoor and outdoor seating. The menu includes the classic "Shore Dinner," which consists of lobster stew or fish chowder, steamed or fried clams, 1½-pound lobster, potato, and dessert. There is seating for nearly 300, so even if it's a busy time, you won't have to wait long. There's also a 70-seat picnic area if you want to take your food to go. ✉ *2521 Atlantic Hwy. (U.S. 1)* ☏ *207/789–5550* 🌐 *www.lobsterpoundmaine.com* 💳 *AE, D, MC, V* ⏲ *Closed Nov.–Apr.*

ISLESBORO

★ *3 mi east of Lincolnville via Islesboro Ferry (terminal on U.S. 1).*

Islesboro is only a 20-minute ferry ride off the mainland, and you can take your car with you. The drive from one end of the island to the other (on the island's only road) is lovely. It takes you through Warren State Park, a nice place to stop for a picnic and the only public camping area on the island. There are two stores on the island where you can buy supplies for your picnic: the Island Market is a short distance from the ferry terminal on the main road, and Durkee's General Store is 5 mi farther north at 863 Main Road. Next to the island's ferry terminal are the Sailor's Memorial Museum and the Grindle Point Lighthouse, both worth a brief look.

The permanent year-round population of Islesboro is about 625, but it swells to around 3,000 in summer. Most of the people who live on the island full time earn their living in one way or another from the sea.

The **Islesboro Ferry,** operated by the Maine State Ferry Service, departs from Lincolnville Harbor, a few hundred feet from the Lobster Pound Restaurant. Try to head out on one of the early ferries so you have enough time to drive around and get back. If you miss the last ferry, you'll have to stay on the island overnight. The ferry runs back and forth nine times a day from April through October and seven times a day from November through March. There are fewer trips on Sunday. The round-trip cost for a vehicle and one passenger is $22.25, slightly more with additional passengers, less if you leave the vehicle behind. Call *207/789–5611* for schedules.

⚠ **If you are just visiting the island and don't have friends there to stay with, make sure that you don't miss the last ferry. There are NO public accommodations on the island. You would have to sleep in your car.**

BELFAST

10 mi north of Lincolnville, 46 mi northeast of Augusta.

A number of Maine coastal towns, such as Wiscasset and Damariscotta, like to think of themselves as the prettiest little town in Maine, but Belfast (originally to be named Londonderry) may be the true winner of this title. It has a full variety of charms: a beautiful waterfront; an old and interesting main street climbing up from the harbor; a delightful array of B&Bs, restaurants, and shops; and a friendly population. The downtown even has old-fashioned streetlamps, which set the streets aglow at night. If you like looking at old houses, many of which go all the way back to the American Revolution and are in the Federal and Colonial style, just drive up and down some of the side streets.

EXPLORING

In the mid-1800s Belfast was home to a number of wealthy business magnates. Their mansions still stand along High Street, offering some excellent examples of Greek Revival and Federal architecture. The **Belfast Chamber of Commerce Visitor Center** (✉ *14 Main St.[a block from the harbor]* ☎ *207/338–5900* 🌐 *www.belfastmaine.org*) has a large array of magazines, guidebooks, maps, and brochures that cover the entire Mid-Coast. It also can provide you with a free walking-tour brochure that describes the various historic homes and buildings, as well as the old business section in the harbor area. Ask the staff to tell you about the Museum in the Streets signage.

5

NIGHTLIFE AND THE ARTS

★ **Rollie's Bar & Grill** (✉ *37 Main St.* ☎ *207/338–4502* 🌐 *www.rollies.me.com* 💳 *MC, V*) looks like it's been here 100 years, but actually it's only since 1972. The tavern is right in the heart of town, and at first glance it might look like a biker bar. It is that—and a lot more. The vintage bar is from an 1800s sailing ship. Rollie's is the most popular watering spot in town with the locals, and it just may serve the best hamburgers in the state of Maine. It also has a sister site in nearby Searsport with the same name and fare, on U.S. 1.

WHERE TO EAT AND STAY

$–$$ CONTINENTAL ★ ✕ **Darby's Restaurant and Pub.** Darby's, a charming old-fashioned restaurant and bar, is very popular with locals. The building, with pressed-tin ceilings, was constructed in 1865 and has been a bar or a restaurant ever since. The antique bar is original. Artwork on the walls is by locals and may be purchased. A lot of the regular items on the menu, such as the pad thai and the Seafood à la Greque, are quite unusual for a small-town restaurant. It also has hearty homemade soups and sandwiches, as well as dishes with an international flavor. ✉ *155 High St.* ☎ *207/338–2339* 🌐 *www.darbysrestaurant.com* 💳 *AE, D, MC, V.*

$$–$$$ SEAFOOD ★ ✕ **Young's Lobster Pound.** The place looks more like a corrugated-steel fish cannery than a restaurant, but it is one of the best places to have an authentic Maine lobster dinner. Young's sits right on the edge of the water, across the river from Belfast Harbor (cross Veterans Bridge and turn right on Mitchell Avenue). When you first walk in, you'll see tanks and tanks of live lobsters of varying size. The traditional

Learn about Maine's seafaring heritage at the Penobscot Marine Museum.

meal here is the Shore Dinner: fish or clam chowder; steamed clams or mussels; a 1½-pound boiled lobster; corn on the cob; and rolls and butter. Order your dinner at the counter, then find a table inside or on the deck. ■ **TIP→ If you are enjoying your lobster at one of the outside tables, don't leave the table with no one to watch it. Seagulls are notorious thieves—and they LOVE lobster.** ✉ *2 Fairview St.* ☎ *207/338–1160* 🌐 *www.youngslobsterpound.com* ▭ *AE, D, MC, V* ⏲ *Closed Labor Day–Easter.*

$–$$$ **Fodor's Choice** ★ **Penobscot Bay Inn & Restaurant.** This lovely accommodation is on 5 meadowed acres overlooking Penobscot Bay and is owned and managed by Kristina and Valentinas Kurapka. The rooms are bright and decorated in pastel shades, with old-fashioned New England quilts on the beds. Some rooms even have their own fireplaces. The inn's Continental gourmet restaurant ($$–$$$$) is one of the best in the area. **Pros:** you don't have to go out for dinner. **Cons:** no special views from the restaurant; a drive to Belfast's colorful downtown. ✉ *192 Northport Ave.* ☎ *207/338–5715 or 800/335–2370* 🌐 *www.penobscotbayinn.com* *19 rooms* *In-room: refrigerator (some). In-hotel: restaurant*, bar ▭ *AE, D, MC, V* *BP.*

SEARSPORT

6 mi northeast of Belfast; 57 mi northeast of Augusta.

Searsport is well known as the antiques and flea-market capital of Maine and with good reason: the Antique Mall alone, on U.S. 1 just north of town, contains the offerings of 70 dealers, and flea markets during the visitor season line both sides of U.S. 1.

Searsport also has a rich history of shipbuilding and seafaring. In the early to mid-1800s there were 10 shipbuilding facilities in Searsport, and the population of the town was about 1,000 people more than it is today because of the ready availability of jobs. By the mid-1800s Searsport was home to more than 200 sailing-ship captains.

ESSENTIALS

Visitor Information **Searsport Chamber of Commerce** (✉ *1 Union St., Searsport* ☎ *207/548-0173* 🌐 *www.searsportme.com*).

EXPLORING

Penobscot Marine Museum. This museum is dedicated to the history of Penobscot Bay and Maine's maritime history. Exhibits, artifacts, souvenirs, and paintings are displayed in a unique setting of seven historic buildings, including two sea captains' houses and five other buildings in an original seaside village. The museum's outstanding collection of marine art includes the largest gathering in the country of works by Thomas and James Buttersworth. Also of note are photos of local sea captains; a collection of China-trade merchandise; artifacts of life at sea (including lots of scrimshaw); navigational instruments; tools from the area's history of logging, granite cutting, fishing, and ice cutting; treasures collected by seafarers from around the globe; and models of famous ships. ✉ *5 E. Main St. (U.S. 1)* ☎ *207/548-2529* 🌐 *www.penobscotmarinemuseum.org* *$8* *Memorial Day–mid-Oct., Mon.–Sat. 10–5, Sun. noon–5.*

Fodor's Choice ★

SHOPPING

ANTIQUES

All Small Antiques (✉ *357 W. Main St.* ☎ *207/338-1613*) has just what the name implies. In the very heart of town, **Captain Tinkham's Emporium** (✉ *34 E. Main St.* ☎ *207/548-6465*) offers antiques, collectibles, old books, magazines, records, paintings, and prints. The biggest collection of antiques is in the **Searsport Antique Mall** (✉ *149 E. Main St. [U.S. 1]* ☎ *207/548-2640*), which has more than 70 dealers.

BUCKSPORT

9 mi north of Searsport via U.S. 1.

The new Penobscot Narrows Bridge, spanning the Penobscot River, welcomes visitors to Bucksport, a town founded in 1763 by Jonathan Buck. Bucksport was the site of the second worst naval defeat in American history (the first was Pearl Harbor), in 1779, when a British Armada defeated the fledgling American Navy. It became known as "the disaster on the Penobscot." You can learn more about it at the museum in Bucksport or at the Penobscot Marine Museum in Searsport.

EXPLORING

Penobscot Narrows Bridge & Observatory Tower/Fort Knox Historic Site. These two attractions, which previously were considered separate, have been combined into one—with one admission—as they are right next to each other. The 2,120-foot-long Penobscot Narrows Bridge, opened at the end of 2006, has been declared an engineering marvel. It is certainly beautiful to look at or to drive over (no toll). Spanning the Penobscot

Fodor's Choice ★

River at Bucksport, the bridge replaced the old Waldo-Hancock Bridge, built in 1931. The best part is the observation tower at the top of the western pylon, the first bridge observation tower in the country and, at 420 feet above the river, the highest in the world. An elevator shoots you to the top for $5, which includes a visit to the nearby Fort Knox Historic Site. Don't miss it—the view, which encompasses the river, the bay, and the sea beyond, is breathtaking.

Fort Knox is the largest fort in Maine and was built between 1844 and 1869, when the British were disputing the border between Maine and New Brunswick. It was intended to protect the Penobscot River valley from a British naval attack. The fort never saw any actual fighting, but it was used for troop training and a garrison during the Civil War and the Spanish-American War. Visitors are welcome to explore the fort's passageways and many rooms. Guided tours are available during the summer season. ✉ *711 Ft. Knox Rd., at U.S. 1, Prospect* ☎ *207/469–6553* 🌐 *www.maine.gov/observatory* ⏲ *Open Sept.–June 9–5, July and Aug. 9–6.*

BANGOR

133 mi northeast of Portland, 20 mi northwest of Bucksport, 46 mi west of Bar Harbor.

The second-largest city in the state (Portland being the largest), Bangor is about 20 mi from the coast and is the unofficial capital of northern Maine. Back in the 19th century the "Queen City's" most important product and export was lumber from the state's vast North Woods. Now, because of its airport, Bangor has become a gateway to Mount Desert Island, Bar Harbor, and Acadia National Park.

ESSENTIALS

Visitor Information Greater Bangor Convention & Visitors Bureau (✉ *40 Harlow St., Bangor* ☎ *207/947–5205 or 800/91–MOOSE [916–6673]* 🌐 *www.bangorcvb.org*).

EXPLORING

Maine Discovery Museum. The largest children's museum north of Boston, the Maine Discovery Museum has three floors with more than 60 interactive exhibits. Kids can explore Maine's ecosystem in Nature Trails, travel to foreign countries in Passport to the World, and walk through Maine's literary classics in Booktown. ✉ *74 Main St.* ☎ *207/262–7200* 🌐 *www.mainediscoverymuseum.org* 🎟 *$7.50* ⏲ *Tues.–Sat. 9:30–5, Sun. 11–5.*

WHERE TO STAY

$$–$$$ Fodor's Choice ★ **Lucerne Inn.** This is one of the most famous and respected inns in New England. Nestled in the mountains, the Lucerne overlooks beautiful Phillips Lake. The inn was established in 1814, and in keeping with that history every room is furnished with antiques. The rooms all have a view of the lake, gas-burning fireplaces, and a whirlpool tub; some have wet bars, refrigerators, and balconies as well. There's a golf course directly across the street. The inn's restaurant ($$–$$$$) is nearly as famous as the inn itself and draws many locals for its lavish Sunday

brunch buffet. The traditional dinner is the boiled Maine lobster. The inn is about 15 mi from Bangor. **Pros:** some rooms have lovely views of Phillips Lake (you can request one). **Cons:** some rooms are a little on the shabby side. ✉ *2517 Main St. (Rte. 1A), Dedham* ☎ *207/843–5123 or 800/325–5123* 🌐 *www.lucerneinn.com* *31 rooms, 4 suites* *In-room: Wi-Fi. In-hotel: restaurant, bar, pool* *AE, D, MC, V* *CP.*

THE BLUE HILL PENINSULA

Updated by George Semler

If you want to see unspoiled Down East Maine land- and seascapes, explore art galleries, savor exquisite meals, or simply enjoy life at an unhurried pace, you should be quite content on the Blue Hill Peninsula.

The peninsula, approximately 16 mi wide and 20 mi long, juts south into Penobscot Bay. Not far from the mainland are the islands of Deer Isle, Little Deer Isle, and the picturesque fishing town of Stonington. A twisting labyrinth of roads winds through blueberry barrens and around picturesque coves, linking the towns of Blue Hill, Brooksville, Sedgwick, and Brooklin. Blue Hill and Castine are the area's primary business hubs.

5

Painters, photographers, sculptors, and other artists are drawn to the area. You can find more than 20 galleries on Deer Isle and in Stonington and at least half as many on the mainland. With its small inns, charming B&Bs, and outstanding restaurants scattered across the area, the Blue Hill Peninsula may just persuade you to leave the rest of the coastline to the tourists.

ESSENTIALS

Visitor Information Blue Hill Peninsula Chamber of Commerce (✉ *107 Main St., Blue Hill* ☎ *207/374–3242* 🌐 *www.bluehillpeninsula.org*). **Deer Isle–Stonington Chamber of Commerce** (✉ *Rte. 15, Deer Isle* ☎ *207/348–6124* 🌐 *www.deerisle.com*).

CASTINE

30 mi southeast of Searsport.

A summer destination for more than 100 years, Castine is a well-preserved seaside village rich in history. The French established a trading post here in 1613, naming the area Pentagoet. A year later Captain John Smith claimed the area for the British. The French regained control of the peninsula with the 1667 Breda Treaty, and Jean Vincent d'Abbadie de St. Castin obtained a land grant in the Pentagoet area, which would later bear his name. Castine's strategic position on Penobscot Bay and its importance as a trading post meant there were many battles for control until 1815. In the 19th century Castine was an important port for trading ships and fishing vessels. The Civil War and the advent of train travel brought its prominence as a port to an end, but by the late 1800s some of the nation's wealthier citizens had discovered Castine as a pleasant summer retreat.

EXPLORING

Federal- and Greek Revival–style architecture and spectacular views of Penobscot Bay make Castine an ideal spot to spend a day or two. Explore its lively harbor front, two small museums (the Wilson Museum and the Castine Historical Society), and the ruins of a British fort. For a nice stroll, park your car at the landing and walk up Main Street toward the white Trinitarian Federated Church. Among the white-clapboard buildings ringing the town common are the Ives House (once the summer home of poet Robert Lowell), the Abbott School, and the Unitarian Church, capped by a whimsical belfry.

SPORTS AND THE OUTDOORS

At Eaton's Wharf, **Castine Kayak Adventures** (✉ *17 Sea St.* ☎ *207/866–3506* 🌐 *www.castinekayak.com*) operates tours run by owner Karen Francoeur, a master Maine Sea Kayak Instructor and Registered Maine Guide. Sign up for a half-day of kayaking along the shore; a full day of kayaking by shipwrecks, reversing falls, and islands in Penobscot Bay; or an extended five-to-seven-day kayaking trip to the Outer Islands with the mothership *Wanderbird* (🌐 *www.wanderbirdcruises.com*), a refurbished 90-foot fishing boat, as base camp.

WHERE TO EAT

$$ AMERICAN ✕ **Dennett's Wharf.** Originally built as a sail-rigging loft in the early 1800s, this longtime favorite is a good place for oysters and fresh seafood of all kinds. The waterfront restaurant also serves burgers, sandwiches, and light fare. There are several microbrews on tap, including the tasty Dennett's Wharf Rat Ale. Eat in the dining room or outside on the deck. ✉ *15 Sea St.* ☎ *207/326–9045* 🌐 *www.dennettswharf.net* 💳 *MC, V* ⏲ *Closed Columbus Day–May.*

BLUE HILL

19 mi east of Castine.

Snuggled between 943-foot Blue Hill Mountain and Blue Hill Bay, the village of Blue Hill sits cozily beside its harbor. Originally known for its granite quarries, copper mines, and shipbuilding, today the town is known for its pottery and galleries, bookstores, antiques shops, and studios that line its streets. The Blue Hill Fair (🌐 *www.bluehillfair.com*), held Labor Day weekend, is a tradition in these parts, with agricultural exhibits, food, rides, and entertainment.

SHOPPING

ART GALLERIES ★ **Blue Hill Bay Gallery** (✉ *11 Tenny Hill* ☎ *207/374–5773* 🌐 *www.bluehillbaygallery.com* ⏲ *Memorial Day–Labor Day, daily; mid-May–Memorial Day and Labor Day–mid-October, weekends*) sells oil and watercolor paintings of the local landscape. Bird carvings and other items are also available. **Leighton Gallery** (✉ *24 Parker Point Rd.* ☎ *207/374–5001* 🌐 *www.leightongallery.com*) shows oil paintings, lithographs, watercolors, and other contemporary art. Outside, granite, bronze, and wood sculptures are displayed in a gardenlike setting under apple trees and white pines.

POTTERY **Rackliffe Pottery** (✉ *126 Ellsworth Rd.* ☎ *207/374–2297*) sells colorful pottery made with lead-free glazes. You can choose between water pitchers, tea-and-coffee sets, and sets of canisters. **Rowantrees Pottery** (✉ *9 Union St.* ☎ *207/374–5535*) has an extensive selection of dinnerware, tea sets, vases, and decorative items. The shop makes many of the same pieces it did 60 years ago, so if you break a favorite item, you can find a replacement.

WINE In what was once a barn out behind one of Blue Hill's earliest houses, the **Blue Hill Wine Shop** (✉ *138 Main St.* ✥ *halfway between intersection of Rtes. 172 and 176 and Rte. 15 in center of town* ☎ *207/374–2161*) carries more than 1,000 carefully selected wines. Wine tastings are held the last Saturday of every month.

WHERE TO EAT AND STAY

$$$ CONTINENTAL Fodor's Choice ★ ✕ **Arborvine.** Glowing (albeit ersatz) fireplaces, period antiques, exposed beams, and hardwood floors covered with Oriental rugs adorn each of the four candlelit dining rooms in this renovated Cape Cod–style house. Begin with a salad of mixed greens, sliced beets, and pears with blue cheese crumbled on top. For your entrée, choose from dishes such as medallions of beef and goat cheese with shoestring potatoes or pork tenderloin with sweet cherries in a port-wine reduction. The specials and fresh fish dishes are superb, as are the crab cakes. Save room for dessert; the lemon mousse and the creamy cheesecake are especially delicious. A take-out lunch menu is available at the adjacent Moveable Feasts deli, where the Vinery piano bar offers drinks, tapas, and live music in the evening. ✉ *33 Tenney Hill* ☎ *207/374–2119* 🌐 *www.arborvine.com* ▭ *AE, DC, MC, V* ⏲ *Closed Mon. and Tues. Sept.–June. No lunch.*

$$$–$$$$ ★ 🏨 **Blue Hill Inn.** This 1830 inn is a comfortable place to relax after climbing Blue Hill Mountain or exploring nearby shops and galleries. Original pumpkin pine and painted floors set the tone for the mix of Empire and early-Victorian pieces that fill the two parlors and the guest rooms, several of which have working fireplaces. One of the nicest rooms is No. 8, which has exposures on three sides and views of the flower gardens and apple trees. Two rooms have antique claw-foot tubs. The inn has a bar offering an ample selection of wines and whiskies where you can enjoy appetizers before you head out to dinner or try specialty coffees and liqueurs when you return. **Pros:** the bedroom fireplaces and the antique floorboards make you want to stay here forever. **Cons:** some rooms are on the small side; walls are thin. ✉ *40 Union St.* ☎ *207/374–2844 or 800/826–7415* 🌐 *www.bluehillinn.com* *11 rooms, 2 suites* *In-room: no phone, no TV. In-hotel: bar, Internet terminal, Wi-Fi hotspot* ▭ *AE, MC, V* 🍽 *BP.*

5

SEDGWICK, BROOKLIN, AND BROOKSVILLE

Winding through the hills, the roads leading to the villages of Sedgwick, Brooklin, and Brooksville take you past rambling farmhouses, beautiful coves, and blueberry barrens studded with occasional masses of granite. From the causeway at Sedgwick to the Deer Isle Bridge along Route

175 an anthology of typical Maine farmhouses lines the road, while the view from Caterpillar Hill merits a special detour.

Incorporated in 1798, **Sedgwick** runs along much of Eggemoggin Reach, the body of water that separates the mainland from Deer Isle, Little Deer Isle, and Stonington. The village of **Brooklin,** originally part of Sedgwick, established itself as an independent town in 1849. Today it is home to the world-famous Wooden Boat School, a 64-acre oceanfront campus offering courses in woodworking, boatbuilding, and seamanship. The town of **Brooksville,** incorporated in 1817, is almost completely surrounded by water, with Eggemoggin Reach, Walker Pond, and the Bagaduce River marking its boundaries.

WHERE TO EAT AND STAY

¢–$ AMERICAN Fodor's Choice ★ **Bagaduce Lunch.** Winner of a 2008 James Beard Award, this little fried-fish specialist next to the reversing falls on the Bagaduce River, 7 mi west of Blue Hill, is the perfect place for a lunch of clams, scallops, halibut, and onion rings. Seals, bald eagles, ospreys, and (sometimes) striped bass provide natural entertainment in this rich tidal estuary. *145 Franks Flat Rd., Brooksville 207/326–4197 No credit cards Closed Sept. 15–June 15.*

$–$$ ★ **Brooklin Inn.** This B&B in downtown Brooklin has plenty of homey touches like hardwood floors and an upstairs deck. The sunny rooms have attractive bureaus and beds piled with cozy quilts. The restaurant ($$–$$$$) specializes in fresh fish and locally raised beef, poultry, and lamb. It also has fine soups, salads, and desserts worth saving room for. In summer you can dine on the enclosed porch. An Irish pub downstairs showcases local musicians most Saturday nights. **Pros:** relaxing; on-site dining. **Cons:** rooms are small; walls are paper-thin. *Rte. 175, Brooklin 207/359–2777 www.brooklininn.com 5 rooms, 3 with bath In-room: no phone, no a/c, no TV. In-hotel: restaurant, Wi-Fi hotspot AE, D, DC, MC, V.*

DEER ISLE VILLAGE

16 mi south of Blue Hill.

Around Deer Isle Village, thick woods give way to tidal coves. Stacks of lobster traps populate the backyards of shingled houses, and dirt roads lead to secluded summer cottages. This region is prized by artists, and studios and galleries are plentiful.

EXPLORING

Haystack Mountain School of Crafts. Want to learn a new craft? This school offers two- and three-week courses for people of all skill levels in blacksmithing, basketry, printmaking, and weaving. Artisans from around the world present evening lectures throughout summer. Free tours of the facility are at 1 on Wednesdays, June through September. The school is 6 mi from Deer Isle Village, off Route 15. *89 Haystack School Dr. 207/348–2306 www.haystack-mtn.org Free (tours) Daily, June–Sept.*

Enjoying miles of woodland and shore trails at the **Edgar M. Tennis Preserve** (*Tennis Rd. off Sunshine Rd. No phone Free Daily* *dawn–dusk*). Look for hawks, eagles, and ospreys and wander among old apple trees, fields of wildflowers, and ocean-polished rocks.

SHOPPING

Purchase a handmade quilt from **Dockside Quilt Gallery** (✉ *928 Sunshine Rd.* ☎ *207/348–2849* 🌐 *www.docksidequiltgallery.com*). Call for an appointment to see quilts. **Nervous Nellie's Jams and Jellies** (✉ *598 Sunshine Rd.* ☎ *207/348–6182 or 800/777–6845* 🌐 *www.nervousnellies.com*) sells jams and jellies, operates the Mountainville Café, and has a woods and meadow sculpture park with more than 75 works by sculptor Peter Beerits.

STONINGTON

7 mi south of Deer Isle.

Stonington is at the southern end of Route 15, which has helped it retain its unspoiled small-town flavor. The boutiques and galleries lining Main Street cater mostly to out-of-towners, though the town remains a fishing community at heart. The principal activity is at the waterfront, where boats arrive overflowing with the day's catch. The sloped island that rises to the south is Isle au Haut, which contains a remote section of Acadia National Park; it's accessible by mail boat from Stonington.

5

EXPLORING

Deer Isle Granite Museum. This tiny museum documents Stonington's quarrying tradition. The museum's centerpiece is an 8-by-15-foot working model of quarrying operations on Crotch Island and the town of Stonington at the turn of the last century. ✉ *51 Main St.* ☎ *207/367–6331* *Free* *Memorial Day–Labor Day, Mon.–Sat. 10–5, Sun. 1–5.*

SPORTS AND THE OUTDOORS

Old Quarry Ocean Adventures (✉ *130 Settlement Rd.* ☎ *207/367–8977* 🌐 *www.oldquarry.com*) rents bicycles, canoes, and kayaks and offers guided tours of the bay. Captain Bill Baker's three-hour boat tours leave from Webb Cove and take you past Stonington Harbor on the way to the outer islands. You can see Crotch Island, which has one of the area's two active stone quarries, and Green Island, where you can take a dip in a water-filled quarry. Tours cover the region's natural history, the history of Stonington, and the history of the granite industry.

WHERE TO EAT AND STAY

$–$$ AMERICAN ★ **Lily's.** Homemade baked goods, delicious sandwiches, and fresh salads are on the menu at this cheerful café. Try the Italian turkey sandwich, which has slices of oven-roasted turkey and Jack cheese on homemade sourdough bread. ✉ *450 Airport Rd. (Corner of Rte. 15 and Airport Rd.)* ☎ *207/367–5936* *MC, V.*

CAMPING ¢ **Old Quarry Campground.** This oceanfront campground offers both open and wooded campsites with raised platforms for tents, tables, chairs, and fire rings. Carts are available to tote your gear to your site. Another property, Sunshine Campground, is on Deer Isle. **Pro:** campsites on the water have spectacular views. **Con:** somewhat uproarious in August. ✉ *130 Settlement Rd., off Oceanville Rd.* ☎ *207/367–8977* 🌐 *www.oldquarry.com* *10 tent sites* *Flush toilets, drinking water,* *guest laundry, showers, public telephone, Wi-Fi, general store, swimming* ▭ *MC, V* ⏲ *Closed Nov.–Apr.*

ISLE AU HAUT

14 mi south of Stonington.

Isle au Haut thrusts its steeply ridged back out of the sea south of Stonington. French explorer Samuel D. Champlain discovered Isle au Haut—or "High Island"—in 1604, but heaps of shells suggest that native populations lived on or visited the island prior to his arrival. The island is accessible only by mail boat, but the 45-minute journey is well worth the effort. The ferry makes two trips a day between Stonington and the Town Landing from Monday to Saturday and adds one Sunday from mid-May to mid-September. From mid-June to mid-September the ferry also stops at Duck Harbor, within Acadia National Park, where it will not unload bicycles, kayaks, or canoes.

Except for a grocery store, a chocolatier, the Sea Urchin gift shop, and a natural-foods store, Isle au Haut is not a shopping excursion. The island is ideal for day-trippers intent on exploring its miles of trails or those seeking a night or two of low-key accommodations and delicious homemade meals at the Inn at Isle au Haut.

WHERE TO STAY

$$$$ Fodor's Choice ★ **Inn at Isle au Haut.** This sea captain's home from 1897 retains its architectural charm. On the eastern side of the island, the seaside inn has views of sheep roaming around distant York Island and Cadillac Mountain. Comfortable wicker furniture is scattered around the porch, where appetizers are served when the weather is good. Downstairs, the dining room has original oil lamps and a model of the sea captain's boat (which sank just offshore). Breakfast includes granola and a hot dish like a spinach, tomato, and cheese frittata. Dinner is an elaborate five-course meal usually incorporating local seafood. The first-floor Captain's Quarters, the only room with a private bath, has an ocean view, as do two of the three upstairs rooms. All have colorful quilts and frilly canopies. **Pros:** nonpareil views; first-class dining. **Cons:** shared baths. ✉ *78 Atlantic Ave.* ☎ *207/335–5141* 🌐 *www.innatisleauhaut.com* *4 rooms, 1 with bath* *In-room: no phone, no a/c, no TV. In-hotel: bicycles* ▭ *No credit cards* ⏲ *Closed Oct.–May* 🍽 *MAP.*

ACADIA NATIONAL PARK AND MOUNT DESERT ISLAND

Updated by George Semler

With some of the most dramatic and varied scenery on the Maine Coast and home to Maine's only national park, Mount Desert Island (pronounced "Mount Dessert" by locals) is Maine's most popular tourist destination, attracting more than 2 million visitors a year. Much of the approximately 12-by-9-mi island belongs to Acadia National Park. The rocky coastline rises starkly from the ocean, appreciable along the scenic drives. Trails for hikers of all skill levels lead to the rounded tops of the mountains, providing views of Frenchman and Blue Hill bays and beyond. Ponds and lakes beckon you to swim, fish, or boat. Ferries and charter boats provide a different perspective on the island and a chance to explore the outer islands, all of which are part of Maine but not necessarily of Mount Desert. A network of old carriage roads lets you explore Acadia's wooded interior, filled with birds and other wildlife.

Mount Desert Island has four different townships, each with its own personality. The town of Bar Harbor is on the northeastern corner of the island and includes Bar Harbor and the little villages of Hulls Cove, Salisbury Cove, and Town Hill. The town of Mount Desert comprises the southeastern corner of the island and parts of the western edge and includes Mount Desert and the little villages of Somesville, Hall Quarry, Beech Hill, Pretty Marsh, Northeast Harbor, Seal Harbor, and Otter Creek. As its name suggests, the town of Southwest Harbor is on the southwestern corner of the island, although the town of Tremont is at the southernmost tip of the west side. This area includes the villages of Southwest Harbor, Manset, Bass Harbor, Bernard, and Seal Cove. The island's major tourist destination is Bar Harbor, which has plenty of accommodations, restaurants, and shops. Less congested are the smaller communities of Northeast Harbor, Southwest Harbor, and Bass Harbor. Mount Desert Island is a place with three personalities: the hustling, bustling tourist mecca of Bar Harbor; the "quiet side" of the island composed of the little villages; and the vast natural expanse that is Acadia National Park.

ESSENTIALS

Visitor Information Bar Harbor Chamber of Commerce (✉ *1201 Bar Harbor Rd., Bar Harbor* ☎ *207/288–5103* 🌐 *www.barharbormaine.com*). **Mount Desert Chamber of Commerce** (✉ *18 Harbor Rd., Northeast Harbor* ☎ *207/276–5040* 🌐 *www.mountdesertchamber.org*). **Mount Desert Island Chambers and Acadia National Park Information Center** (✉ *Rte. 3, Thompson Island* ☎ *207/288–3411* 🌐 *www.acadiachamber.com*).

BAR HARBOR

160 mi northeast of Portland; 22 mi southeast of Ellsworth.

A resort town since the 19th century, Bar Harbor is the artistic, culinary, and social center of Mount Desert Island. It also serves visitors to Acadia National Park with inns, motels, and restaurants. Around the turn of the last century the island was known as the summer haven of the very rich because of its cool breezes. The wealthy built lavish mansions throughout the island, many of which were destroyed in a great fire that devastated the island in 1947, but many of those that survived have been converted into businesses. Shops are clustered along Main, Mount Desert, and Cottage streets. Take a stroll down West Street, a National Historic District, where you can see some fine old houses.

The island and the surrounding Gulf of Maine are home to a great variety of wildlife: whales, seals, eagles, falcons, ospreys, puffins (very unusual-looking birds), and forest dwellers such as moose, deer, foxes, coyotes, and black bears.

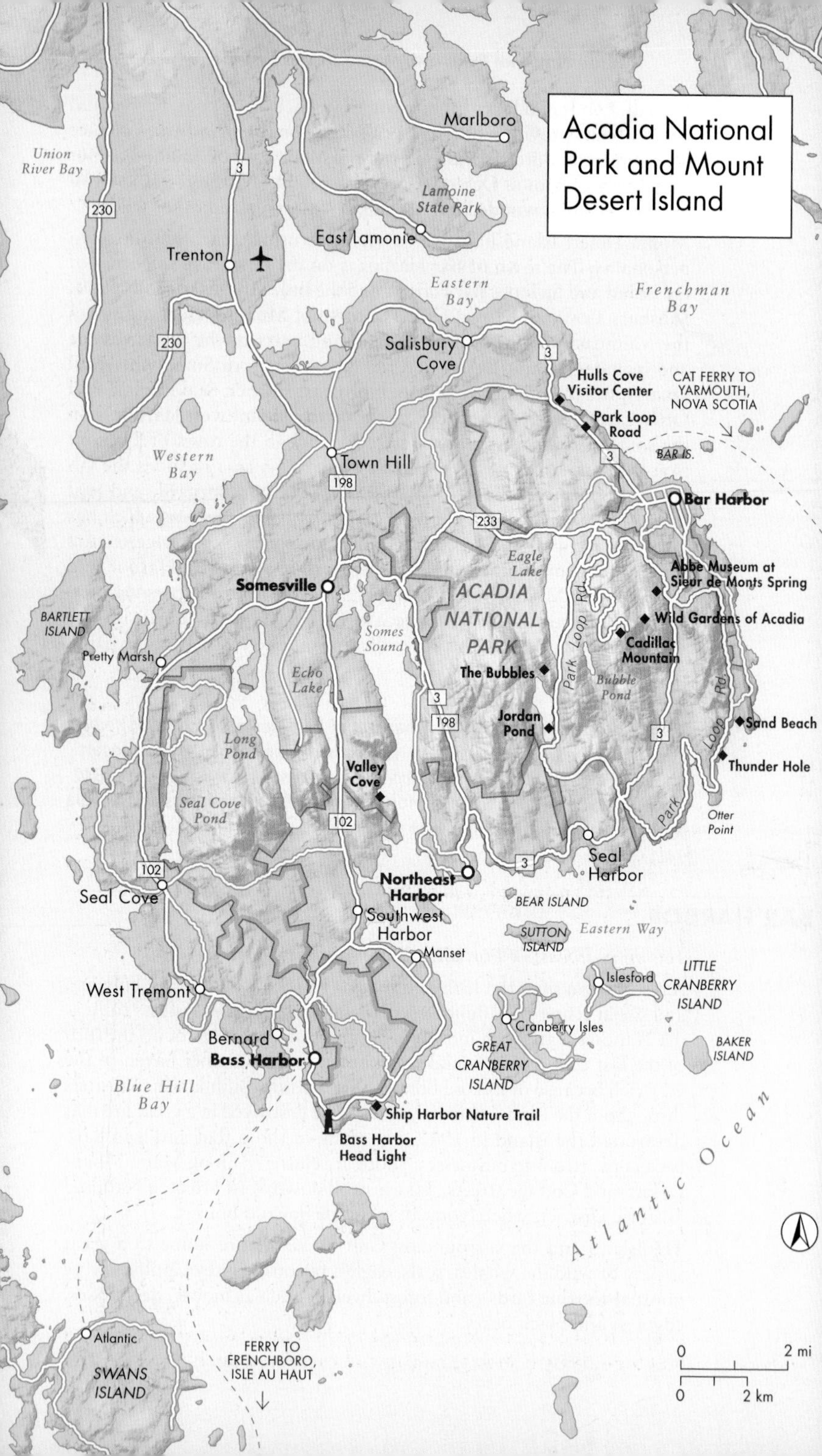
Acadia National Park and Mount Desert Island
Marlboro
Union River Bay
230
3
Lamoine State Park
East Lamonie
Trenton
Eastern Bay
Frenchman Bay
230
Salisbury Cove
3
Hulls Cove Visitor Center
CAT FERRY TO YARMOUTH, NOVA SCOTIA
Park Loop Road
3
BAR IS.
Western Bay
Town Hill
198
Bar Harbor
233
Eagle Lake
Abbe Museum at Sieur de Monts Spring
Somesville
ACADIA NATIONAL PARK
Wild Gardens of Acadia
BARTLETT ISLAND
Somes Sound
Cadillac Mountain
Pretty Marsh
The Bubbles
Park Loop Rd.
Bubble Pond
Echo Lake
3
198
Jordan Pond
3
Sand Beach
Loop Rd.
Long Pond
Thunder Hole
Valley Cove
Seal Cove Pond
102
Park
Otter Point
Seal Harbor
3
102
Northeast Harbor
Seal Cove
BEAR ISLAND
Southwest Harbor
SUTTON ISLAND
Eastern Way
Manset
LITTLE CRANBERRY ISLAND
Islesford
West Tremont
Cranberry Isles
Bernard
GREAT CRANBERRY ISLAND
BAKER ISLAND
Bass Harbor
Blue Hill Bay
Ship Harbor Nature Trail
Bass Harbor Head Light
Atlantic Ocean
Atlantic
SWANS ISLAND
FERRY TO FRENCHBORO, ISLE AU HAUT
0
2 mi
0
2 km

EXPLORING

Bar Harbor Whale Museum. Learn about the history of whaling, the anatomy of whales, and how biologists are working to gain more information about these massive creatures at this interesting museum. ✉ *52 West St.* ☎ *207/288–0288* 🌐 *www.barharborwhalemuseum.org* *Free* *June, daily 9–10; July and Aug., daily 9–9.*

SPORTS AND THE OUTDOORS

AIR TOURS

★ **Scenic Biplane & Glider Rides Over Bar Harbor** (✉ *968 Bar Harbor Rd. [Rte. 3], Trenton* ☎ *207/667–7627* 🌐 *www.acadiaairtours.com*) is a part of Acadia Air Tours and provides exactly what the name suggests: biplane and glider rides over Bar Harbor and Acadia National Park. Tours run from 25 minutes to an hour and range from $225 to $425 for two people. The sunset tour is $50 extra. Helicopter tours are also available on occasion.

BICYCLING

Acadia Bike Rentals & Coastal Kayaking Tours (✉ *48 Cottage St.* ☎ *207/288–9605 or 800/526–8615* 🌐 *www.acadianfun.com*) rents mountain bikes good for negotiating the trails in Acadia National Park. The **Bar Harbor Bicycle Shop** (✉ *141 Cottage St.* ☎ *207/288–3886 or 800/824–2453* 🌐 *www.barharborbike.com*) rents bikes by the half or full day.

★ The big 151-foot four-masted schooner **Margaret Todd** (✉ *Bar Harbor Inn Pier* ☎ *207/288–4585* 🌐 *www.downeastwindjammer.com*) operates 1½- to 2-hour trips three times a day among the islands of Frenchman's Bay from mid-May to October. The sunset sail is the most popular. The schooner **Rachel B. Jackson** (✉ *848 Eagle Lake Rd., Harborside Hotel & Marina* ☎ *207/288–2216* 🌐 *www.downeastsail.com*) offers two-hour and sunset cruises for $30.

WHALE-WATCHING

★ **Bar Harbor Whale Watch Co.** (✉ *1 West St.* ☎ *207/288–2386 or 800/942–5374* 🌐 *www.whalesrus.com*) merged with the Acadian Whale Watcher to make one big company with four boats, one of them a 138-foot jet-propelled catamaran with spacious decks. In season the outfit also offers lobster and seal cruises, a nature cruise, and puffin cruises.

SHOPPING

ART

Fodor's Choice ★

Paint your own pottery or piece together a mosaic at **All Fired Up** (✉ *101 Cottage St.* ☎ *207/288–3130* 🌐 *www.acadiaallfiredup.com*). The gallery also sells glass sculptures, pendants, paintings, and decorative pottery. The **Alone Moose Fine Crafts** (✉ *78 West St.* ☎ *207/288–4229* 🌐 *www.mainefinecrafts.com*) is the oldest made-in-Maine gallery on the island. It offers bronze wildlife sculpture, jewelry, pottery, and watercolors. The **Eclipse Gallery** (✉ *12 Mount Desert St.* ☎ *207/288–9048* 🌐 *www.eclipsegallery.us*) carries handblown glass, ceramics, and wood furniture. **Island Artisans** (✉ *99 Main St.* ☎ *207/288–4214* 🌐 *www.islandartisans.com*) sells basketry, pottery, fiber work, and jewelry created by more than 100 of Maine's artisans. **Native Arts Gallery** (✉ *99 Main St.* ☎ *207/288–4474* 🌐 *www.nativeartsgallery.com*) sells Native American silver and gold jewelry.

SPORTING GOODS

One of the best sporting-goods stores in the state, **Cadillac Mountain Sports** (✉ *28 Cottage St.* ☎ *207/288–4532* 🌐 *www.cadillacmountainsports.com*) has developed a following of locals and visitors alike. You can find top-quality climbing, hiking, and camping equipment. In winter

Long ramps on Maine's many docks make it easier to access boats at either high tide or low tide.

you can rent cross-country skis, ice skates, and snowshoes. **Michael H. Graves Antiques** (✉ *10 Albert Meadow* ☎ *207/288–3830*) specializes in maps and books focusing on Mount Desert Island.

WHERE TO EAT AND STAY

$$$–$$$$ SEAFOOD Fodor's Choice ★ ✕ **Burning Tree.** One of the top restaurants in Maine, this easy-to-miss gem is on Route 3 between Bar Harbor and Otter Creek. The ever-changing menu emphasizes freshly caught seafood, and seven species of fish are offered every day, all from the Gulf of Maine. Entrées include pan-sautéed monkfish, oven-poached cod, and gray sole. There are always two or three vegetarian options and an emphasis on organic produce (much of it from the owners' garden). ✉ *69 Otter Creek Drive (Rte. 3), Otter Creek* ☎ *207/288–9331* ▭ *DC, MC, V* ⊗ *Closed Tues. and mid-Oct.–mid-June.*

$$$–$$$$ CONTINENTAL Fodor's Choice ★ ✕ **Reading Room at the Bar Harbor Inn & Spa.** This elegant waterfront restaurant serves Continental fare along with Maine specialties such as lobster pie and Indian pudding. There's live music nightly. When the weather is nice, what could be more romantic than dining out under the stars at the inn's Terrace Grille with the ships of beautiful Bar Harbor right at your feet? The natural thing to order here would be the Maine lobster bake with all the fixings. The restaurant is also famous for its Sunday brunch. ✉ *7 Newport Dr.* ☎ *207/288–3351 or 800/248–3351* 🌐 *www.barharborinn.com* ⚠ *Reservations essential* ▭ *AE, DC, MC, V* ⊗ *Closed late Nov.–late Mar.*

$$$–$$$$ Fodor's Choice ★ 🏨 **Bar Harbor Inn & Spa.** Originally established in the late 1800s as a men's social club, this waterfront inn has rooms spread out over three buildings on well-landscaped grounds. Most rooms have gas fireplaces

and balconies with great views. Rooms in the Oceanfront Lodge have private decks overlooking the ocean. Many rooms in the main inn have balconies overlooking the harbor. There are also some two-level suites. A luxury spa offers everything from massages and mud wraps to aromatherapy and facials. The inn is a short walk from town, so you're close to all the sights, and a terrific restaurant, the Reading Room ($$$–$$$$), is on-site. **Pros:** seems to meet every need; right at the harbor. **Cons:** not as close to Acadia National Park as some Bar Harbor properties. ✉ *Newport Dr.* ☎ *207/288–3351 or 800/248–3351* 🌐 *www.barharborinn.com* *138 rooms, 15 suites* *In-room: safe, refrigerator, DVD, Wi-Fi. In-hotel: 2 restaurants, pool, gym, Wi-Fi hotspot* *AE, DC, MC, V* *Closed late Nov.–late Mar.* *CP.*

ACADIA LEAF PEEPING

The fall foliage in Maine can be spectacular. Because of the moisture, it comes later along the coast, around the middle of October, than it does in the interior of the state. The best way to catch the colors along the coast is travel on the Acadia National Park Loop Road. For up-to-date information, go online to 🌐 *www.mainefoliage.com.*

5

ACADIA NATIONAL PARK

4 mi northwest of Bar Harbor.

Fodor's Choice ★

With more than 30,000 acres of protected forests, beaches, mountains, and rocky coastline, Acadia National Park is the second-most-visited national park in America (the first is Great Smoky Mountains National Park). According to the National Park Service, more than 2.2 million people visit Acadia each year. The park holds some of the most spectacular scenery on the eastern seaboard: a rugged coastline of surf-pounded granite and an interior graced by sculpted mountains, quiet ponds, and lush deciduous forests. Cadillac Mountain (named after a Native American, not the car), the highest point of land on the East Coast, dominates the park. Although it's rugged, the park also has graceful stone bridges, horse-drawn carriages, and the Jordan Pond House restaurant (famous for its popovers).

The 27-mi Park Loop Road provides an excellent introduction, but to truly appreciate the park you must get off the main road and experience it by walking, biking, sea kayaking, or taking a carriage ride. If you get off the beaten path, you can find places you'll have practically to yourself. Mount Desert Island was once a preserve of summer homes for the very rich (and still is for some), and, because of this, Acadia is the only national park in the United States that was largely created by donations of private land. A small part of the park is on Isle au Haut, more than 10 mi away out in the ocean.

DID YOU KNOW?

Acadia was the first National Park established east of the Mississippi River, in 1916. Wealthy landowners donated parcels of Mount Desert Island to protect this unique place where mountains meet the sea.

PARK ESSENTIALS

ADMISSION FEE

A user fee is required if you are anywhere in the park. The fee is $20 per vehicle for a seven-consecutive-day pass, or use your National Park America the Beautiful Pass, which allows entrance to any national park in the United States. See 🌐 *www.nps.gov* for details.

ADMISSION HOURS

The park is open 24 hours a day, year-round, though the roads often are closed in winter because of snow. Visitor center hours are 8–4:30 April 15–June, September, and October and until 6 in July and August

PARK CONTACT INFORMATION

Acadia National Park (*Acadia National Park, Box 177, Bar Harbor 04609 ☎ 207/288–3338 🌐 www.nps.gov/acad*).

EXPLORING

HISTORIC SITES AND MUSEUMS

★ **Bass Harbor Head Light.** Built in 1858, this lighthouse is one of the most photographed lights in Maine. Now automated, it marks the entrance to Blue Hill Bay. The grounds and residence are Coast Guard property, but two trails around the facility provide excellent views. ■ **TIP→ The best place to take a picture of this small but beautiful lighthouse is from the rocks below—but watch your step; they can be slippery.** ✉ *Rte. 102, halfway between Tremont and Manset, Bass Harbor* *Free* ⏲ *Daily 9–sunset.*

SCENIC DRIVES AND STOPS

★ **Cadillac Mountain.** At 1,532 feet, this is one of the first places in the United States to see the sun's rays at break of day. It is the highest mountain on the eastern seaboard north of Brazil. Dozens of visitors make the trek to see the sunrise or, for those less inclined to get up so early, sunset. From the smooth summit you have an awesome 360-degree view of the jagged coastline that runs around the island. A small gift shop and some restrooms are the only structures at the top. The road up the mountain is generally closed from the end of October through March because of snow.

★ **Park Loop Road.** This 27-mi road provides a perfect introduction to the park. You can do it in an hour, but allow at least half a day for the drive so that you can explore the many sites along the way. Traveling south on Park Loop Road toward Sand Beach, you'll reach a small ticket booth, where, if you haven't already, you will need to pay the park's good-for-seven-consecutive-days $20 entrance fee (not charged from November through April). Traffic is one-way from the Route 233 entrance to the Stanley Brook Road entrance south of the Jordan Pond House. The section known as Ocean Drive is open year-round.

BOOK A CARRIAGE RIDE

If you would like to take a horse-drawn carriage ride down one of these roads, you can do so from mid-June to mid-October by making a reservation with Wildwood Stables (☎ 207/276–3622). Two of their carriages can accommodate two wheelchairs each.

VISITOR CENTER

At the Hulls Cove entrance to Acadia National Park, northwest of Bar Harbor on Route 3, the **Hulls Cove Visitor Center,** operated by the National Park Service, is a great spot to get your bearings. A large relief map of Mount Desert Island gives you the lay of the land, and you can watch a free 15-minute video about everything the park has to offer. Pick up guidebooks, maps of hiking trails and carriage roads, schedules for naturalist-led tours, and recordings for drive-it-yourself tours. Don't forget the *Acadia Beaver Log,* the park's free newspaper detailing guided hikes and other ranger-led events. Junior-ranger programs for kids, nature hikes, photography walks, tide-pool explorations, and evening talks are all popular. The visitor center is off Route 3 at Park Loop Road. ✉ *Park Loop Rd., Hulls Cove* ☎ *207/288–3338* 🌐 *www.nps.gov/acad* ⏲ *Mid-June–Aug., daily 8–6; mid-Apr.–mid-June, Sept., and Oct., daily 8–4:30.*

> **CAUTION**
>
> A couple of people a year fall off one of the park's trails or cliffs and are swept out to sea. There is a lot of loose, rocky gravel along the shoreline, and sea rocks can often be slippery—so watch your step. Don't bring a sudden end to your visit by trying to get that "impossible" photo op.

The **Acadia National Park Headquarters** is on Route 233 in the park not far from the north end of Eagle Lake and serves as the park's visitor center during the off-season.

SPORTS AND THE OUTDOORS

The best way to see Acadia National Park is to get out of your vehicle and explore on foot or by bicycle or boat. There are more than 40 mi of carriage roads that are perfect for walking and biking in the warmer months and for cross-country skiing and snowshoeing in winter. There are more than 120 mi of trails for hiking, numerous ponds and lakes for canoeing or kayaking, two beaches for swimming, and steep cliffs for rock climbing.

HIKING

Acadia National Park maintains more than 115 mi of hiking paths, from easy strolls around lakes and ponds to rigorous treks with climbs up rock faces and scrambles along cliffs. Although most hiking trails are on the east side of the island, the west side also has some scenic trails. For those wishing for a long climb, try the trails leading up Cadillac Mountain or Dorr Mountain. Another option is to climb Parkman, Sargeant, and Penobscot mountains. Most hiking is done from mid-May to mid-October. Snow falls early in Maine, so from late October to the end of March, cross-country skiing and snowshoeing replace hiking. ■ **TIP→ You can park at one end of any trail and use the free shuttle bus to get back to your starting point.** Distances for trails are given for the round-trip hike.

EASY ★ **Ocean Patch Trail.** This 3.6-mi, easily accessible trail runs parallel to the Loop Road from Sand Beach to Otter Point. It has some of the best scenery in Maine: cliffs and boulders of pink granite at the ocean's edge, twisted branches of dwarf jack pines, and ocean views that stretch to the horizon. ✉ *Sand Beach or Otter Point parking area.*

DIFFICULT ★ **Acadia Mountain Trail.** This is the king of the trails. The 2½-mi round-trip climb up Acadia Mountain is steep and strenuous, but the payoff is grand: views of Somes Sound and Southwest Harbor. If you want a guided trip, look into the ranger-led hikes for this trail. ✉ *Acadia Mountain parking area, on Rte. 102.*

THE EARLY BIRD GETS THE SUN

During your visit to Mount Desert, pick a day when you are willing to get up very early, such as 4:30 or 5 AM. Drive with a friend to the top of Cadillac Mountain in Acadia National Park. Stand on the highest rock you can find and wait for the sun to come up. When it does, have your friend take a photo of you looking at it and label the photo something like "The first person in the country to see the sun come up on June 1, 2010."

SWIMMING

The park has two swimming beaches, Sand Beach and Echo Lake Beach. Sand Beach, along Park Loop Road, has changing rooms, restrooms, and a lifeguard on duty from Memorial Day to Labor Day. The water temperature here rarely reaches above 55°F. Echo Lake Beach, on the western side of the island just north of Southwest Harbor, has much warmer water, as well as changing rooms, restrooms, and a lifeguard on duty throughout summer.

WHERE TO STAY

CAMPING ¢ **Blackwoods Campground.** One of only two campgrounds inside inland Acadia National Park, Blackwoods is open throughout the year (though restrictions apply for winter camping; call ahead for details). Reservations are handled by the National Recreation Reservation Service (☎ *877/444–6777*), not by the park. Reservations for high season (May–October) can be made up to six months in advance. During the off-season a limited number of campsites are available for primitive camping, and a camping permit must be obtained from the park headquarters. Rates drop by 50% for the shoulder season (April and November). ✉ *Rte. 3, 5 mi south of Bar Harbor, Otter Creek* ☎ *207/288–3274 or 800/365–2267* 🌐 *www.nps.gov* *35 RV sites; 198 tent sites* *No hookups or utilities; bathrooms, water, showers, picnic tables, fire pits, shuttle bus* 💳 *DC, MC, V.*

¢ **Seawall Campground.** On the "quiet side" of the island, this campground does not accept reservations but offers space on a first-come, first-served basis, starting at 8 AM. Seawall is open from late May to late September. Walk-in tent sites are $14 per night, while drive-in sites for tents and RVs are $20. ✉ *Rte. 102A, 4 mi south of Southwest Harbor, Manset* ☎ *207/244–3600* *www.nps.gov* *42 RV sites; 163 tent sites* *No hookups or utilities; bathrooms, showers, fire pits, picnic tables* 💳 *MC, V* ⊙ *Closed late Sept.–late May.*

NORTHEAST HARBOR

12 mi south of Bar Harbor via Rtes. 3 and 198 or Rtes. 233 and 198.

The summer community for some of the nation's wealthiest families, Northeast Harbor has one of the best harbors on the coast, which fills with yachts and powerboats during peak season. It's a great place to sign up for a cruise around Somes Sound or to the Cranberry Islands. Other than that, this quiet village has a handful of restaurants, boutiques, and art galleries.

SOMESVILLE

7 mi northwest of Northeast Harbor via Rtes. 198 and 102.

Most visitors pass through Somesville on their way to Southwest Harbor, but this well-preserved village, the oldest on the island, is more than a stop along the way. Originally settled by Abraham Somes in 1763, this was once a bustling commercial center with shingle, lumber, and wool mills; a tannery; a varnish factory; and a dye shop. Today Route 102, which passes through the center of town, takes you past a row of white-clapboard houses with black shutters and well-manicured lawns.

5

WHERE TO STAY

¢ **Mount Desert Campground.** Near the village of Somesville, this campground has one of the best locations imaginable. It lies at the head of Somes Sound, the only fjord on the East Coast of North America. The campground prefers tents, so vehicles longer than 20 feet are not allowed. Many sites are along the waterfront, and all are tucked into the woods for a sense of privacy. Restrooms and showers are placed sensibly throughout the campground and are kept meticulously clean. Canoes and kayaks are available for rent, and there's a dock with access to the ocean. The Gathering Place has baked goods in the morning and ice cream and coffee in the evening. **Pros:** a lovely location for sightseeing. **Cons:** fills up quickly during peak season. ✉ *516 Sound Dr.* ☎ *207/244–3710* 🌐 *www.mountdesertcampground.com* *150 sites* *Flush toilets, drinking water, showers, fire pits, food service, swimming (ocean)* ▭ *MC, V* ⏲ *Closed mid-Sept.–mid-June.*

BASS HARBOR

4 mi south of Southwest Harbor via Rte. 102 or Rte. 102A

Bass Harbor is a tiny lobstering village with a relaxed atmosphere and a few accommodations and restaurants. If you're looking to get away from the crowds, consider using this hardworking community as your base. Although Bass Harbor does not draw as many tourists as other villages, the Bass Harbor Head Light in Acadia National Park is one of the region's most popular attractions and is undoubtedly the most photographed lighthouse in Maine. From Bass Harbor you can hike on the Ship Harbor Nature Trail or take a ferry to Frenchboro.

GETTING HERE AND AROUND

The Maine State Ferry Service operates a ferry, the Captain Henry Lee, carrying both passengers and a maximum of 19 vehicles per voyage, to Swans Island (30 min., $17.50) and Frenchboro (50 min., $11.25).

ESSENTIALS

Transportation Information Maine State Ferry Service (✉ *114 Grandville Rd.* ☎ *207/244–3254*).

WHERE TO EAT

¢–$$ SEAFOOD **Thurston's Lobster Pound.** On the peninsula across from Bass Harbor, Thurston's is easy to spot because of its bright yellow awning. You can buy fresh lobsters to go or sit at outdoor tables. Order everything from a grilled-cheese sandwich to a boiled lobster served with clams or mussels. ✉ *1 Thurston Rd., at Steamboat Wharf, Bernard* ☎ *207/244–7600* *www.thurstonslobster.com* *MC, V* *Closed Columbus Day–Memorial Day.*

WAY DOWN EAST

By Mary Ruoff

Slogans such as "The Real Maine" ring truer Way Down East. The raw, mostly undeveloped coast in this remote region is more accessible than it is farther south. Even in summer here you're likely to have rocky beaches and shady hiking trails to yourself. The slower pace is as calming as a sea breeze.

One innkeeper relates that visitors who plan to stay a few days often opt for a week after learning more about the region's offerings, which include historic sites; museums on local history, culture, and art; national wildlife refuges; state parks and preserves; and increasingly, conservancy-owned public land. Cutler's Bold Coast, with its dramatic granite headlands, is protected from development. Waters near Eastport have some of the world's highest tides. Lakes perfect for canoeing and kayaking are sprinkled inland, and rivers snake through marshland as they near the many bays. Boulders are strewn on blueberry barrens. Rare plants thrive in coastal bogs and heaths, and dark-purple and pink lupines line the roads in late June.

VISITOR INFORMATION

Many chambers of commerce in the region distribute free copies of the pamphlet "Maine's Washington County: Just Off the Beaten Path," which is several cuts above the usual tourist promotion booklet.

Contacts DownEast & Acadia Regional Tourism (✉ *Box 4, Cherryfield* ☎ *207/546–3600 or 800/665–3278* *www.downeastacadia.com*).

SCHOODIC PENINSULA

25 mi east of Ellsworth via U.S. Rte. 1 and Rte. 186.

The landscape of Schoodic Peninsula's craggy coastline, towering evergreens, and views over Frenchman Bay are breathtaking year-round. A drive through the well-to-do summer community of Grindstone Neck shows what Bar Harbor might have been like before so many of its

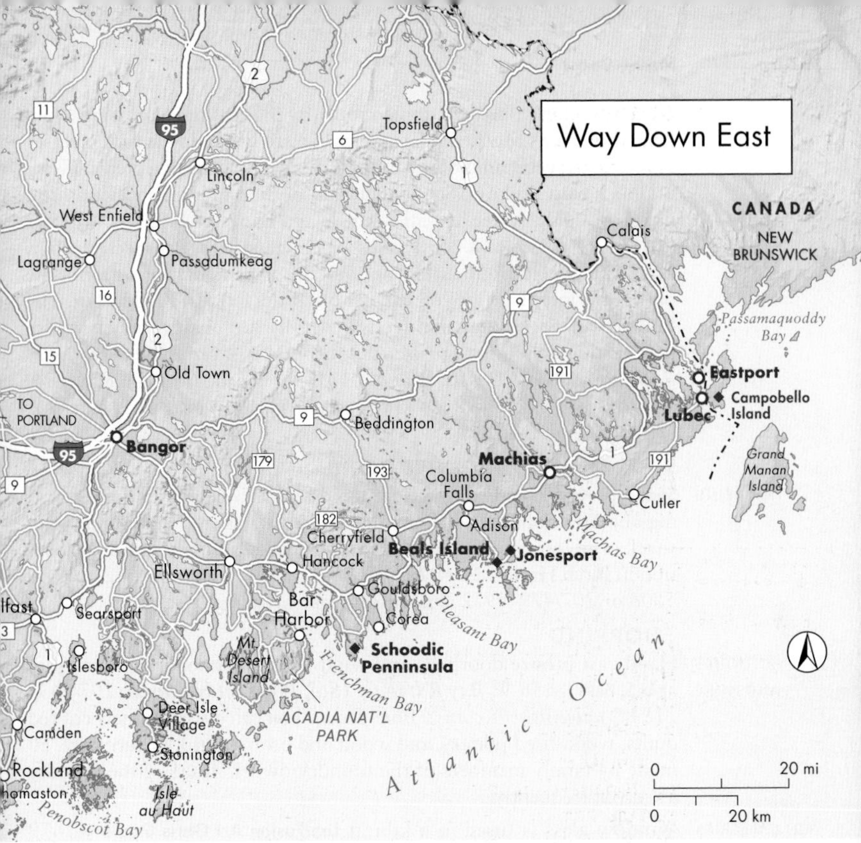

mansions were destroyed in the Great Fire of 1947. Artists and artisans have opened galleries in and around Winter Harbor. Anchored at the foot of the peninsula, Winter Harbor was once part of Gouldsboro, which wraps around it.

ESSENTIALS

Visitor Information **Schoodic Area Chamber of Commerce** (*Box 381, Winter Harbor 04693* *www.acadia-schoodic.org*).

EXPLORING

Coastal Villages. Within Gouldsboro on the Schoodic Peninsula are several small coastal villages. You drive through **Wonsqueak** and **Birch Harbor** after leaving the Schoodic section of Acadia National Park. Near Birch Harbor you can find **Prospect Harbor,** a small fishing village nearly untouched by tourism. In **Corea,** there's little to do besides watch the fishermen at work, wander along stone beaches, or gaze out to sea.

Fodor's Choice ★ **Acadia National Park.** The only section of Maine's national park that sits on the mainland is at the southern side of the Schoodic Peninsula in the town of Winter Harbor. The park has a scenic 6-mi one-way loop that edges along the coast and yields views of Grindstone Neck, Winter Harbor, Winter Harbor Lighthouse, and, across the water, Cadillac Mountain. At the tip of the point, huge slabs of pink granite lie jumbled along the shore, thrashed unmercifully by the crashing surf (stay away from the water's edge), and jack pines cling to life amid the rocks. Fraser Point, at the beginning of the loop, is an ideal place for a picnic. Work off lunch with a hike up Schoodic Head for the panoramic views up and down the coast. A free bus called the Island Explorer (☎ *207/288–4573* 🌐 *www.exploreacadia.com*) takes passengers from Prospect Harbor, Birch Harbor, and Winter Harbor and drops them off anywhere in the park. In Winter Harbor you can get off at the ferry to Bar Harbor. The $20-per-car park admission fee is generally not charged when you're just visiting Schoodic. *For more information ⇨ see Acadia National Park and Mount Desert Island.* ✉ *Moore Road, turn off Rte. 186, Winter Harbor* ☎ *207/288–3338* 🌐 *www.nps.gov/acad* *$20 per car* ⏲ *Year-round, 24/7.*

SPORTS AND THE OUTDOORS

KAYAKING **SeaScape Kayaking.** Led by a Registered Maine Guide, SeaScape's morning and afternoon kayak tours include an island stop and a blueberry snack. The company also rents canoes, kayaks, and bikes from its location in Birch Harbor. ✉ *18 E. Schoodic Dr., Birch Harbor* ☎ *207/963–5806 or 207/479–9912* 🌐 *www.seascapekayaking.com.*

SHOPPING

ANTIQUES AND MORE Hand-cast bronze doorbells and wind bells are among the items sold at **U.S. Bells** (✉ *56 W. Bay Rd. [Rte. 186], Prospect Harbor* ☎ *207/963–7184* 🌐 *www.usbells.com* ⏲ *June–Dec.*). You can also buy finely crafted quilts, wood-fired pottery, and wood and bronze outdoor furniture, all made by family members of the foundry owner. Tours of the foundry are given frequently.

ART GALLERIES Window glass is fused in a kiln at **Lee Fusion Art Glass Studio** (✉ *679 S. Gouldsboro Rd. [Rte. 186], Gouldsboro* ☎ *207/963–7280* 🌐 *www.leefusionartglass.com* ⏲ *June–Oct.*) to create unusual glass dishware. Colorful enamel accents depict birds, lighthouses, flowers, and designs made from doilies.

FOOD Along with mostly organic local produce, **Winter Harbor Farmers' Market** (✉ *10 Newman St. [Rte. 186], Winter Harbor* ☎ *207/537–5673* ⏲ *June–early Sept., Tues. 9–noon*) sells goat cheese, baked goods, beef and chicken, hand-spun yarn, knitted items, and maple syrup, chutney, and preserves.

WHERE TO EAT AND STAY

$$ SEAFOOD ✕ **Chase's Restaurant.** The orange booths may remind you of a fast-food joint, but this family restaurant has a reputation for serving good, basic fare. In this region that means a lot of fish. There are large and small fried seafood dinners and several more expensive seafood platters. Try the sweet-potato fries as a side. Lunch fare, sold all day, includes wraps and burgers. It's also open for breakfast. ✉ *193 Main St. (Rte. 186), Winter Harbor* ☎ *207/963–7171* 💳 *AE, D, MC, V.*

$–$$ CAFÉ ✕ **J. M. Gerrish Provisions.** The store that opened here in the early 1900s was the place where locals and visitors alike went for ice cream. The name remains, as well as part of the old marble counter, but today it is a deli and café where folks bustle in for light meals or linger over coffee at tables inside and on the porch. A simple menu has soups, salads, and savory sandwiches, such as turkey and cheddar topped with cranberry relish. The deli case offers salads, from potato to Mediterranean octopus, and dishes such as baby back ribs. Baked goods crowd the counter, ice cream is still sold, and you can buy wine and beer to go. ✉ *352 Main St., Winter Harbor* ☎ *207/963–6100* 🌐 *www.jmgerrish.com* ▭ *MC, V* ⏲ *Closed mid-Oct.–mid-May.*

$–$$ ★ **Bluff House Inn.** Combining the service of a hotel with the ambience of a cozy lodge, this modern two-story inn on a secluded hillside has expansive views of Frenchman Bay. You can see the bay's granite shores from the inn's partially screened wraparound porches. There's a picnic area with grill (a lobster pot is available for those who want to boil their own dinner), and a stone fireplace warms one of the knotty-pine lounge areas. The individually decorated guest rooms have furnishings from around the state. **Pros:** close to things yet secluded. **Cons:** path to water a bit steep. ✉ *57 Bluff House Rd., off Rte. 186, Gouldsboro* ☎ *207/963–7805* 🌐 *www.bluffinn.com* *8 rooms, 1 apartment* *In-room: no a/c, no TV (some), kitchen (some), DVD (some), Wi-Fi. In-hotel: Wi-Fi hotspot, some pets allowed* ▭ *MC, V* *CP.*

$$–$$$ Fodor's Choice ★ **Oceanside Meadows Inn.** This place is a must for nature lovers. Trail maps guide you through a 200-acre preserve dotted with woods, streams, salt marshes, and ponds. Inspired by the moose, eagles, and other wildlife that thrive here, the innkeepers created the Oceanside Meadows *Inn*stitute for the Arts & Sciences, which holds lectures, musical performances, art exhibits, and other events in the restored barn. Furnished with antiques, country pieces, and family treasures and scented with flowers from the extensive gardens, the inn has sunny, inviting living rooms with fireplaces and a separate guest kitchen. Guest rooms are spread between two white clapboard buildings fronting a private beach flanked by granite ledges. Breakfast is an extravagant multicourse affair that includes chilled fruit soup. **Pros:** one of the region's few sand beaches; many spacious rooms; packages include lobster dinner and boat tour. **Cons:** need to cross road to beach. ✉ *202 Corea Rd. (Rte. 195), Prospect Harbor* ☎ *207/963–5557* 🌐 *www.oceaninn.com* *13 rooms, 2 suites* *In-room: no a/c, no TV, Wi-Fi. In-hotel: beachfront, laundry services, Wi-Fi hotspot, some pets allowed* ▭ *AE, D, DC, MC, V* ⏲ *Closed Nov.–Apr.* *BP.*

JONESPORT AND BEALS ISLAND

48 mi northeast of Winter Harbor via Rte. 186, US Rte. 1, and Rte. 187; 20 mi southwest of Machias.

The birding is superb around Jonesport and Beals Island, a pair of fishing communities joined by a bridge over the harbor. A handful of stately homes ring Jonesport's Sawyer Square, where Sawyer Memorial Congregational Church's exquisite stained-glass windows are illuminated at night. But the towns are less geared to travelers than those on the Schoodic Peninsula. Lobster traps are still piled in the yards, and lobster-boat races near Moosabec Reach are the highlight of the community's annual Independence Day celebration.

CLOSE UP

Wild for Blueberries

There's no need to inquire about the cheesecake topping if you dine out in August when the wild blueberry crop comes in. Anything but blueberries would be unthinkable.

Way Down East, wild blueberries have long been a favorite food and a key ingredient in cultural and economic life. Maine produces about a third of the commercial harvest, which totals about 70 million pounds annually, Canada supplying virtually all the rest. Washington County yields 65% of Maine's total crop, which is why the state's largest blueberry processors are here: Jasper Wyman & Son and the predecessor of what is now Cherryfield Foods were founded shortly after the Civil War.

Wild blueberries, which bear fruit every other year, thrive in the region's cold climate and sandy, acidic soil. Undulating blueberry barrens stretch for miles in Deblois and Cherryfield ("the Blueberry Capital of the World") and are scattered throughout Washington County. Look for tufts among low-lying plants along the roadways. In spring the fields shimmer as the small-leaf plants turn myriad shades of mauve, honey-orange, and lemon-yellow. White flowers appear in June. Fall transforms the barrens into a sea of red.

Amid Cherryfield's barrens, a plaque on a boulder lauds the late J. Burleigh Crane for helping advance an industry that's not as wild as it used to be. Honeybees have been brought in to supplement native pollinators, fields are irrigated, and barrens are burned and mowed to rid plants of disease and insects, reducing the need for pesticides. Most of the barrens in and around Cherryfield are owned by the large blueberry processors.

About 80% of Maine's crop is now harvested with machinery. That requires moving boulders, so the rest continues to be harvested by hand with blueberry rakes, which resemble large forks and pull the berries off their stems. Years ago, year-round residents did the work. Today migrant workers make up 90% of this seasonal labor force.

Blueberries get their dark color from anthocyanins, believed to provide antioxidants. Wild blueberries have more of these antiaging, anticancer compounds than their cultivated cousins. Smaller and more flavorful than cultivated blueberries, wild ones are mostly used in packaged foods. Less than 1% of the state's crop—about 500,000 pints—is consumed fresh, mostly in Maine. Look for fresh berries (sometimes starting in late July and lasting until early September) at roadside stands, farmers' markets, and supermarkets.

Wild Blueberry Land in Columbia Falls sells everything blueberry, from muffins and candy to socks and books. Find farm stores, stands, and markets statewide, many selling blueberries and blueberry jams and syrups, at 🌐 *www.getrealgetmaine.com*, a Maine Department of Agriculture site that promotes Maine foods.

—Mary Ruoff

DID YOU KNOW?

Almost unrelated to the bloated berries at most grocery stores, Maine's small and flavor-packed wild blueberries are a must in season, from late July to early September. Try a handful fresh, in pancakes, or a pie.

SPORTS AND THE OUTDOORS

In business since circa 1940, **Norton of Jonesport** (☎ *207/497–5933* 🌐 *www.machiassealisland.com*) takes passengers on day trips to Machias Seal Island, where thousands of puffins nest. Arctic terns, razorbill auks, common murres, and many other seabirds also nest on the rocky island. Trips, which cost $100 per person, are offered from late May through August.

WHERE TO EAT

$$ SEAFOOD ✕ **Tall Barney's.** Salty accents add plenty of flavor at this down-home restaurant, which serves a late-morning breakfast (10 to 11 weekdays, 8 to 11 on Saturday), lunch, and dinner. A pamphlet tells the story of Tall Barney, a brawny fisherman who left truly tall tales in his wake. Your server may be among his multitudinous descendants. The menu includes five types of seafood stew; grilled, baked, and fried seafood; vegetarian dishes; and oversize desserts including seasonal pies. Call the night before to order a boxed lunch. ✉ *52 Main St.* ☎ *207/497–2403* 🌐 *www.tallbarneys.com* ▭ *MC, V* ⊙ *Closed Mon.; generally closed Mon. and Tues. late Sept.–mid-Nov., Sun.–Wed. late Nov.–mid-May.*

MACHIAS

20 mi northeast of Jonesport.

The Machias area—Machiasport, East Machias, and Machias, the Washington County seat—lays claim to being the site of the first naval battle of the Revolutionary War, which took place in what is now Machiasport. Despite being outnumbered and outarmed, a small group of Machias men under the leadership of Jeremiah O'Brien captured the armed British schooner *Margaretta.* That battle, fought on June 12, 1775, is now known as the "Lexington of the Sea." The town's other claim to fame is wild blueberries. On the third weekend in August the annual Machias Wild Blueberry Festival is a community celebration complete with parade, crafts fair, concerts, and plenty of blueberry dishes.

ESSENTIALS

Visitor Information Machias Bay Area Chamber of Commerce (✉ *85 Main St., Suite 2, Machias* ☎ *207/255–4402* 🌐 *www.machiaschamber.org*).

EXPLORING

★ **Burnham Tavern Museum.** It was in this gambrel-roofed tavern home that the men of Machias laid the plans that culminated in the capture of the *Margaretta* in 1775. After the Revolutionary War's first naval battle, wounded British sailors were brought here. Tour guides dressed in period garb highlight exhibits and tell colorful stories of early settlers. Period furnishings and household items show what life was like in Colonial times. On the National Register of Historic Places, the dwelling is among the 21 in the country deemed most important to the Revolution. ✉ *14 Colonial Way (Rte. 192)* ☎ *207/255–6930* 🌐 *www.burnhamtavern.com* 🎟 *$5* ⊙ *Mid-June–Sept., weekdays 9:30–4 (last tour at 3:30), or by appointment.*

WHERE TO EAT

$$$–$$$$ AMERICAN ★ **Riverside Inn & Restaurant.** A bright yellow exterior invites a stop at this delightful restaurant in a former sea captain's home perched on the bank of the Machias River. Ask for a table in the intimate sunroom, which has water views and opens to the other dining room. The chef-owner brings a special flair to traditional dishes, such as pork served with a pistachio crust. His signature dish is salmon stuffed with crabmeat and shrimp. In summer months the menu includes dressed-up dinner salads—try pairing one with standout appetizers like hake cakes and red-tuna wontons. Also a charming inn (open daily except in early winter) with Victorian touches, Riverside has two guest rooms in the main house and two suites in the coach house. ✉ *608 Main St. (U.S. 1) , East Machias* ☎ *207/255–4134 or 888/255–4344* 🌐 *www.riversideinn-maine.com* 💳 *MC, V* 🕐 *Closed Jan.–early Feb.; Mon.–Wed. mid-Feb.–mid-June, Nov., and Dec.; Mon. late June–Oct. No lunch.*

LOOK UP!

With no large cities, Way Down East offers great stargazing. But if you want a great show on a dark night, paddle a canoe on a lake and look down. Bioluminescent organisms in the water light up as you churn your paddle.

5

LUBEC

28 mi northeast of Machias via U.S. 1 and Rte. 189.

Lubec is one of the first places in the United States to see the sunrise. A popular destination for outdoor enthusiasts, it offers plenty of opportunities for hiking and biking, and the birding is renowned. It's a good base for day trips to New Brunswick's Campobello Island, reached by a bridge—the only one to the island—from downtown Lubec. The village is perched at the end of a narrow strip of land, so you often can see water in three directions.

SPORTS AND THE OUTDOORS

★ **Quoddy Head State Park.** The easternmost point of land in the United States is marked by candy-striped West Quoddy Head Light. In 1806 President Thomas Jefferson signed an order authorizing construction of a lighthouse on this site. You can't climb the tower, but the former light keeper's house has a museum with a video showing the interior. The museum also has displays on Lubec's maritime past and the region's marine life. A gallery displays lighthouse art by locals. A mystical 2-mi path along the cliffs here, one of four trails, yields magnificent views of Canada's cliff-clad Grand Manan Island. Whales can often be sighted offshore. The 540-acre park has a picnic area. ✉ *973 S. Lubec Rd., off Rte. 189* ☎ *207/733–0911 or 207/941–4014* 🌐 *www.parksandlands.com* 🎟 *$3* 🕐 *May 15–Oct. 15, 9–sunset.*

TAKE A TOUR

On educational tours by Tours of Lubec and Cobscook (✉ *135 Main St. [Rte. 189]* ☎ *207/733-2997 or 888/347-9302* 🌐 *www.toursoflubecandcobscook.com*) you can visit historic locales, view

DID YOU KNOW?

Atlantic puffin colonies were reintroduced to the Maine coast by the Maine Audubon Society and Project Puffin. Get a closer look at these seabirds and their distinctive beaks on a puffin cruise from Jonesport to Machias Seal Island.

lighthouses by boat, walk the shoreline to learn about the area's high tides and tide pools, tour a ninth-generation farm on Cobscook Bay, and explore a bog. Tours run from May through October and start at $10 per person. The tour office is at the tourism Info Stop, which shares a building with the Lubec Historical Society Museum.

WHERE TO EAT AND STAY

$$ SEAFOOD **Uncle Kippy's Restaurant.** There isn't much of a view from the picture windows, but locals don't mind—they come here for the satisfying seafood. There's one large dining room with a bar beside the main entrance. The menu includes seafood dinners and combo platters, and the fresh-dough pizza is popular. A take-out window and ice-cream bar are open June through September. ✉ *170 Main St.* ☎ *207/733–2400* 🌐 *www.unclekippys.com* ▭ *D, MC, V* ⏲ *Generally closed Mon. and Tues. Dec.–June.*

$–$$ ★ **Peacock House.** Five generations of the Peacock family lived in this white-clapboard house before it was converted into an inn. With a large foyer, library, and living room, the 1860 sea captain's home has plenty of places where you can relax. Minglers are drawn to the sunroom, which opens to the deck and has a handsome bar. The best of the rooms has a separate sitting area, wet bar, and gas fireplace. **Pros:** piano in living room; lovely garden off deck. **Cons:** only one off-street parking space. ✉ *27 Summer St.* ☎ *207/733–2403 or 888/305–0036* 🌐 *www.peacockhouse.com* *5 rooms, 2 suites* *In-room: no phone, no a/c, refrigerator (some), DVD (some), no TV (some), Wi-Fi. In hotel: Wi-Fi hotspot* ▭ *MC, V* ⏲ *Closed Nov.–Apr.* *BP.*

CAMPOBELLO ISLAND, CANADA

28 mi east of Machias.

A popular excursion from Lubec, New Brunswick's Campobello Island has two fishing villages, Welshpool and Wilson's Beach. The only bridge is from Lubec, but in summer a car ferry shuttles passengers from Campobello Island to Deer Island, where you can continue on to the Canadian mainland. (⇨ *See the Travel Smart section at the back of the book for information on passports or other documents U.S. citizens need when traveling between the United States and Canada.)*

EXPLORING

★ **Roosevelt Campobello International Park.** A joint project of the American and the Canadian governments, this park is crisscrossed with interesting hiking trails. Groomed dirt roads attract bikers. Eagle Hill Bog has a wooden walkway and signs identifying rare plants. Neatly manicured Campobello Island has always had a special appeal for the wealthy and famous. It was here that President Franklin Roosevelt and his family spent summers. The 34-room Roosevelt Cottage was presented to Eleanor and Franklin as a wedding gift, and the wicker-filled structure looks essentially as it did when the family was in residence. A visitor center has displays about the Roosevelts and Canadian-American relations. **■ TIP→ Note that the Islands are on Atlantic Time, which is an hour later than EST.** ✉ *459 Rte. 774, Welshpool, New Brunswick, Canada*

506/752–2922 www.fdr.net Free House, Memorial Day weekend–Columbus Day, daily 10–6; Grounds, year-round 24/7; Visitor center, Memorial Day weekend–Oct., 9–5.

WHERE TO EAT

$$–$$$ SEAFOOD ★ **Family Fisheries.** Seafood lovers know that fried fish doesn't have to be greasy. That's why people keep heading across the bridge to eat at this family restaurant in Wilson's Beach. The freshest seafood is delivered to the restaurant and the adjoining fish market. Order fried haddock, scallops, shrimps, or clams alone or as part of a seafood platter. Lobsters are cooked outside. Eat in the large dining room or near the playground at picnic tables or in a screened room. You can buy ice cream at the take-out window; the restaurant also serves breakfast. *1977 Rte. 774, Wilson's Beach 506/752–2470 MC, V Closed late Dec.–Mar. No dinner Sun.*

EASTPORT

39 mi northeast of Lubec via Rte. 189, U.S. 1, and Rte. 190; 109 mi north of Ellsworth via U.S. 1 and Rte. 190.

Connected by a granite causeway to the mainland at Pleasant Point Reservation, Eastport has wonderful views of the nearby islands, and you can sometimes spot whales from the waterfront because the harbor is so deep. Known for its diverse architecture, the island city was one of the nation's busiest seaports in the early 1800s. In the late 19th century 14 sardine canneries operated here. The industry's decline in the 20th century left the city economically depressed, but now the town has set its sights on salmon, shipping, tourism, and the arts—performing and visual arts are thriving here. The weekend after Labor Day the Maine Salmon Festival attracts large crowds with boat tours of salmon pens, an arts and crafts show, a historic-home walking tour, a wine tasting, and a dinner featuring the local delicacy and live music. On the same weekend the Eastport Pirate Festival brings folks out in pirate attire for a ship race, parade, and other events, including a children's breakfast and schooner ride with pirates.

Get downtown early to secure a viewing spot for Maine's largest July 4th parade. Canadian bagpipe bands make this an event not to be missed. The day culminates with fireworks over the bay. On the weekend of the second Sunday in August, locals celebrate Sipayik Indian Days at the Pleasant Point Reservation. This festival of Passamaquoddy culture includes canoe races, dancing, drumming, children's games, fireworks, and traditional dancing.

ESSENTIALS

Visitor Information **Eastport Area Chamber of Commerce** (*Box 254, Eastport 04631 207/853–4644 www.eastport.net*).

WHERE TO EAT

$$–$$$ SEAFOOD **Eastport Chowder House.** Just north of downtown Eastport, this expansive waterfront eatery sits on the pier next to where the ferry docks. Built atop an old cannery foundation, it has original details such as wood beams and a stone wall. Eat in the downstairs pub, upstairs in

the dining room, or on the large deck. The house specialties include a smoked fish appetizer and seafood pasta in a wine-and-cheese sauce. Lunch, served until 4, includes fried seafood plates, burgers, wraps, and sandwiches. ☒ *169 Water St.* ☎ *207/853–4700* ▭ *D, MC, V* ⊙ *Closed mid-Oct.–mid-May.*

$$–$$$ AMERICAN ★ ✕ **Pickled Herring.** Linger near the open kitchen and you may hear diners pay homage to the chef at the wood-fire grill as he prepares dishes like duck with a maple-peppercorn glaze, salmon with house pesto, and the popular strip sirloin (12, 14, or 16 ounces). Thin wood-fired pizza with toppings like caramelized onions, lobster, and blue cheese is a lighter choice. Housed in a landmark downtown storefront with soaring windows and ceilings, this restaurant's wonderful food and atmosphere have made it a destination. Pictures of Eastport's former sardine plants hang on a brick wall, and gas-burning lanterns and streetlamp-like lights throw a soft glow. Urbanites will feel at home, but locals do, too. A fun bar is hidden behind an interior wall. Specialty cocktails like the Foghorn (Tanqueray, fresh-squeezed lime juice, and ginger ale) have a Down East twist. ☒ *32 Water St.* ☎ *207/853–2323* 🌐 *www.thepickledherring.com* ▭ *AE, D, MC, V* ⊙ *Closed Jan. and Feb., and Mon.–Wed. late Sept.–Dec. and March–early June. No lunch.*

Travel Smart Maine, Vermont & New Hampshire

WORD OF MOUTH

"As far as [driving] times goes, you'll have a greater challenge in more northern areas like Vermont, western New Hampshire, and western or northern Maine. It gets much more rural in some of those parts and you do not always have a direct, major highway that cuts through them."
—Shandy1977

www.fodors.com/community

GETTING HERE AND AROUND

New England's largest city, Boston is the major transportation hub for reaching Maine, New Hampshire, and Vermont. Portland, Maine, is a secondary hub. How best to get around depends upon the extent of your itinerary—flying from one location to another once you reach the Maine, Vermont, and New Hampshire area can get expensive. Your best bet is to fly into Boston or Maine (or even Burlington, Vermont, or Manchester, New Hampshire), and then travel by car, planning your itinerary according to how much driving you're willing to do.

See the Getting Here and Around section at the beginning of each chapter for more transportation information.

AIR TRAVEL

It's costly and generally impractical to fly within Northern New England, so most travelers visiting the region head for a major gateway, such as Boston, Manchester, or Portland, and then rent a car to explore the region. Maine, New Hampshire, and Vermont form a fairly compact region, with few important destinations more than six hours apart by car.

Boston's Logan Airport is one of the nation's most important domestic and international airports, with direct flights arriving from all over North America and internationally. New England's other major airports receive few international flights (mostly from Canada) but do offer a wide range of direct domestic flights to East Coast and Midwest destinations and, to a lesser extent, to the western United States. Some sample flying times to Boston are: from Chicago (2½ hours), London (6½ hours), and Los Angeles (6 hours). It's more difficult to find direct flights from major airports into Northern New England.

AIRPORTS

The main gateway to Maine, Vermont, and New Hampshire is Boston's Logan International Airport (BOS), the region's largest. Manchester Boston Regional Airport (MHT) in New Hampshire is a rapidly growing, lower-cost alternative to Logan—it's about 50 mi north of Boston. Other regional airports are Portland International Jetport (PWM) and Bangor International Airport (BGR) in Maine; and Burlington International Airport (BTV) in Vermont. Albany International Airport (ALB) in Albany, New York, is also an option if your itinerary begins in Vermont.

Airport Information Albany International Airport (☎ *518/242–2200* ⊕ *www.albanyairport.com*). **Bangor International Airport** (☎ *207/992–4600* ⊕ *www.flybangor.com*). **Burlington International Airport** (☎ *802/863–1889* ⊕ *www.burlingtonintlairport.com*). **Logan International Airport–Boston** (☎ *800/235–6426* ⊕ *www.massport.com/logan*). **Manchester Boston Regional Airport** (☎ *603/624–6556* ⊕ *www.flymanchester.com*). **Portland International Jetport** (☎ *207/874–8877* ⊕ *www.portlandjetport.org*).

FLIGHTS

Numerous airlines fly to and from Boston; additionally, the discount carrier Southwest Airlines flies to Albany, Boston, and Manchester, New Hampshire. Smaller or discount airlines serving Boston include AirTran, Cape Air, and JetBlue. You can fly to Burlington from New York City on JetBlue, and you can fly to Boston from Atlantic City, Myrtle Beach, and Fort Lauderdale on Spirit Airlines.

Airline Contacts AirTran Airways (☎ *800/247–8726* ⊕ *www.airtran.com*). **American Airlines** (☎ *800/433–7300* ⊕ *www.aa.com*). **Cape Air** (☎ *866/227–3247* ⊕ *www.flycapeair.com*). **Continental Airlines** (☎ *800/523–3273* ⊕ *www.continental.com*). **Delta Airlines** (☎ *800/221–1212*

🌐 *www.delta.com*). **JetBlue** (☎ *800/538–2583* 🌐 *www.jetblue.com*). **Northwest Airlines** (☎ *800/225–2525* 🌐 *www.nwa.com*). **Southwest Airlines** (☎ *800/435–9792* 🌐 *www.southwest.com*). **Spirit Airlines** (☎ *800/772–7117* 🌐 *www.spiritair.com*). **United Airlines** (☎ *800/864–8331* 🌐 *www.united.com*). **USAirways** (☎ *800/428–4322* 🌐 *www.usairways.com*).

BOAT TRAVEL

Ferry routes provide access to many islands off the Maine coast. In addition, ferries cross Lake Champlain between Vermont and upstate New York. International service between Portland and Bar Harbor, Maine, and Yarmouth, Nova Scotia, is also available. With the exception of the Lake Champlain ferries, which are first-come, first-served, car reservations are always advisable.

BUS TRAVEL

Regional bus service is relatively plentiful throughout New England. It can be a handy and affordable means of getting around, as buses travel many routes that trains do not.

BoltBus offers cheap fares in new, Wi-Fi– and electrical-outlet–equipped buses between Boston, New York, Philadelphia, and Washington, D.C., starting at just $1 if you reserve early enough. Megabus also offers low fares, and its Wi-Fi–equipped buses serve New York City and many other points on the East Coast. BoltBus and Megabus use Boston's South Station. Major credit cards are accepted for all buses, and for BoltBus you can only purchase tickets online.

Bus Information BoltBus (☎ *877/265–8287* 🌐 *www.boltbus.com*). **Megabus** (☎ *877/462–6342* 🌐 *www.megabus.com*).

CAR TRAVEL

Northern New England is best explored by car. Areas in the interior are largely without heavy traffic and congestion. Public transportation options are limited in areas in the interior, however these areas are largely without heavy traffic and congestion, and parking is consistently easy to find. It is considerably more congested along the coast, and parking likewise can be hard to find or expensive. Morning and evening rush-hour traffic can also be a bit of a problem, especially along the coast. Note that Interstate 95 is a toll highway throughout New England, and Interstate 90 (the Massachusetts Turnpike) is a toll road throughout Massachusetts. If you rent a car at Logan International Airport, allow plenty of time to return it—as much as 60 minutes to be comfortable.

GASOLINE

Gas stations are easy to find along major highways and in most communities throughout the region. At this writing, the average price of a gallon of regular unleaded gas in Northern New England is $2.68. However, prices vary from station to station within any city. The majority of stations are self-serve with pumps that accept credit cards, though you may find a holdout full-service station on occasion. Tipping is not expected at these.

PARKING

Parking in Northern New England is a familiar situation. In Boston and other large cities, finding a spot on the street can be time- and quarter-consuming. The best bet is to park in a garage, which can cost upward of $20 a day. In smaller cities, street parking is usually simpler, though parking garages are always convenient and less expensive than their big-city counterparts. Enforcement varies; in Portland, Maine, meter readers might sooner give a warning (a friendly reminder, really) than a ticket.

FOR INTERNATIONAL TRAVELERS

CUSTOMS

Information U.S. Customs and Border Protection (*www.cbp.gov*).

CURRENCY

The dollar is the basic unit of U.S. currency. It has 100 cents. Coins are the penny (1¢); the nickel (5¢), dime (10¢), quarter (25¢), half-dollar (50¢), and the rare golden $1 coin and even rarer silver $1. Bills are denominated $1, $5, $10, $20, $50, and $100, all mostly green and identical in size; designs and background tints vary. You may come across a $2 bill, but the chances are slim.

DRIVING

Driving in the United States is on the right. Speed limits are posted in miles per hour (usually between 55 MPH and 70 MPH). Watch for lower limits in small towns and on back roads (usually 25 MPH to 40 MPH). Front-seat passengers and children in the backseat must wear seat belts. In cities rush hour is between 7 and 10 AM; afternoon rush hour is between 4 and 7 PM. Some freeways have special lanes, ordinarily marked with a diamond, for high-occupancy vehicles (HOV)—cars carrying two people or more.

Highways are well paved. Interstates—limited-access, multilane highways designated with an "I–" before the number—are fastest. Interstates with three-digit numbers circle urban areas, which may also have other limited-access expressways, freeways, and parkways. Tolls may be levied on limited-access highways. U.S. and state highways aren't necessarily limited-access, but may have several lanes. If you are on a toll road, be aware that some lanes are reserved for cars with toll transponder tags; if you don't have one, use a lane where cash is accepted.

Gas stations are plentiful, except in rural areas and city centers. Most stay open late (24 hours along major highways and in big cities) except in rural areas, where Sunday hours are limited and where you may drive for long stretches without a refueling opportunity. Along larger highways, roadside stops with restrooms, fast-food restaurants, and sundries stores are well spaced. State police and tow trucks patrol major highways. If your car breaks down on an interstate, pull onto the shoulder and wait for help, or have your passengers wait while you walk to an emergency phone (available in most states). If you carry a cell phone, dial *55, noting your location on the small green roadside mileage marker.

ELECTRICITY

The U.S. standard is AC, 110 volts/60 cycles. Plugs have two flat pins set parallel to each other.

EMBASSIES

Contacts Australia (*202/797–3000 www.austemb.org*). **Canada** (*202/682–1740 www.canadianembassy.org*). **United Kingdom** (*202/588–7800 www.britainusa.com*).

EMERGENCIES

For police, fire, or ambulance, dial 911 (0 in rural areas).

HOLIDAYS

New Year's Day (Jan. 1); Martin Luther King Day (3rd Mon. in Jan.); Presidents' Day (3rd Mon. in Feb.); Memorial Day (last Mon. in May); Independence Day (July 4); Labor Day (1st Mon. in Sept.); Columbus Day (2nd Mon. in Oct.); Thanksgiving Day (4th Thurs. in Nov.); Christmas Eve and Christmas Day (Dec. 24 and 25); and New Year's Eve (Dec. 31).

Expect banks and post offices to be closed on all national holidays. Restaurants and hotels, depending on location, may be even busier at holiday times. Public transportation schedules are also affected on major holidays; in general, schedules will be similar to those of a normal Sunday.

Patriots' Day (the Monday closest to April 19) is a state holiday in Massachusetts and Maine.

MAIL

You can buy stamps and aerograms and send letters and parcels in post offices. U.S. mailboxes are stout, dark blue steel bins. Parcels weighing more than a pound must be mailed at a post office or at a private mailing center.

Within the United States a first-class letter weighing 1 ounce or less costs 44¢; each additional ounce costs 17¢. Postcards cost 28¢. Postcards or 1-ounce airmail letters to most countries costs 98¢; postcards or 1-ounce letters to Canada or Mexico cost 79¢.

To receive mail on the road, have it sent c/o General Delivery at your destination's main post office. You must pick up mail in person within 30 days, with your driver's license or passport.

Contacts DHL (☎ *800/225–5345* 🌐 *www.dhl.com*). **FedEx** (☎ *800/463–3339* 🌐 *www.fedex.com*). **UPS (United Parcel Service)** (☎ *800/742–5877* 🌐 *www.ups.com*). **USPS (United States Postal Service)** (🌐 *www.usps.com*).

PASSPORTS AND VISAS

Visitor visas aren't necessary for citizens of Australia, the United Kingdom, or most citizens of European Union countries coming for tourism and staying for fewer than 90 days. If you require a visa, the cost is $131, and waiting time can be substantial, depending on where you live. Apply for a visa at the U.S. consulate in your place of residence; check the U.S. State Department's special Visa Web site for further information.

Visa Information U.S. Department of State (🌐 *travel.state.gov/visa*).

PHONES

Numbers consist of a three-digit area code and a seven-digit local number. Within many local calling areas you dial only the seven digits; in others you dial "1" first and all 10 digits—as you would for calls between area-code regions. The same is true for calls to numbers prefixed by "800," "888," "866," and "877"—all toll free.

For international calls, dial "011" followed by the country code and the local number. For help, dial "0" and ask for an overseas operator. The country code for Australia is 61, for New Zealand 64, for the United Kingdom 44. Calling Canada is the same as calling within the United States, whose country code is 1.

For operator assistance, dial "0." For directory assistance, call 555-1212 or 411 (free at many public phones). You can reverse long-distance charges by calling "collect"; dial "0" instead of "1" before the 10-digit number.

CELL PHONES

The United States has several GSM (Global System for Mobile Communications) networks, so multiband mobiles from most countries (except for Japan) work here. But it's very hard to buy a pay-as-you-go mobile SIM card in the United States without also buying a phone. Still, cell phones with pay-as-you-go plans are sold for well under $100. The cheapest ones with decent national coverage are the GoPhone from Cingular and Virgin Mobile, which only offers pay-as-you-go service.

Contacts Cingular (☎ *888/333–6651* 🌐 *www.cingular.com*). **Virgin Mobile** (☎ *888/322–1122* 🌐 *www.virginmobileusa.com*).

ROAD CONDITIONS

Major state and U.S. routes are generally well maintained, with snowplows at the ready during the winter to salt and plow road surfaces soon after the flakes begin to fall. Traffic is heaviest around Boston, especially during rush hour but pretty much any time of the day between sunrise and sunset. Secondary state routes and rural roads can be a mixed bag; generally, Route 1 is well maintained but with slower traffic that can get locally congested in even the smallest coastal towns.

Boston drivers are notorious for going all-for-broke, so only the adventurous should drive here. Once you're in Maine, New Hampshire, and Vermont it is far more relaxed. Rural drivers are known to stop to chat in the road.

ROADSIDE EMERGENCIES

Throughout Northern New England, call 911 for any travel emergency, such as an accident or a serious health concern. For automotive breakdowns, 911 is not appropriate. Instead, find a local directory and dial a towing service. When out on the open highway, call the nonemergency central administration phone number of the State Police for assistance.

RULES OF THE ROAD

On city streets the speed limit is 30 MPH unless otherwise posted; on rural roads, the speed limit ranges from 40 to 50 MPH unless otherwise posted. Interstate speeds range from 50 to 65 MPH, depending on how densely populated the area is. Throughout the region, you're permitted to make a right turn on red except where posted. Be alert for one-way streets in congested communities, such as Boston and Providence.

State law requires that drivers and all passengers wear seat belts at all times. Always strap children under age five or under 40 pounds into approved child-safety seats.

You will encounter many traffic circles/rotaries if you drive in New England (especially in the Boston area). Remember that cars entering traffic circles must yield to cars that are already in the circle. Some rotaries have two lanes, which complicates things. If you're leaving the rotary at the next possible exit, enter from the right lane. If you're leaving the rotary at any exit after the first possible exit, enter from the left lane (which becomes the inner lane of the circle); you can also exit the circle directly from this lane—though check your right side so you don't sideswipe a driver who's incorrectly in the right lane.

CAR RENTAL

Because a car is the most practical way to get around New England, it's wise to rent one if you're not bringing your own. The major airports serving the region all have on-site car-rental agencies. If you're traveling to the area by bus or train, you might consider renting a car once you arrive. A few train or bus stations have one or two major car-rental agencies on-site.

Rates at the area's major airport, Boston's Logan Airport, begin at around $75 a day and $350 a week for an economy car with air-conditioning, automatic transmission, and unlimited mileage. The same car might go for around $60 a day and $300 a week at a smaller airport such as Portland International Jetport. These rates do not include state tax on car rentals, which varies depending on the airport but generally runs 12% to 15%. Generally, it costs less to rent a car outside of an airport, but factor into the value whether it is easy or difficult to get there with all your luggage.

Most agencies won't rent to you if you're under the age of 21, and several major agencies will not rent to anyone under 25. When picking up a rental car, non-U.S. residents need a voucher for any prepaid reservations that were made in their home country, a passport, a driver's license, and a travel policy that covers each driver. Boston's Logan Airport is large, spread out, and usually congested, so if you will be returning a rental vehicle there make sure to allow plenty of time to take care of it before heading for your flight.

Major Rental Agencies
Alamo (☎ *877/222-9075* ⊕ *www.alamo.com*). **Avis** (☎ *800/331-1212* ⊕ *www.avis.com*). **Budget** (☎ *800/527-0700* ⊕ *www.budget.com*). **Hertz** (☎ *800/654-3131* ⊕ *www.hertz.com*). **National Car Rental** (☎ *877/222-9058* ⊕ *www.nationalcar.com*).

TRAIN TRAVEL

Amtrak's *Downeaster* connects Boston with Portland, Maine, with stops in coastal New Hampshire. Other Amtrak services include the *Vermonter* between Washington, D.C., and St. Albans, Vermont; and the *Ethan Allen Express* between New York and Rutland, Vermont. These trains run on a daily basis. To avoid last-minute confusion, allow 15 to 30 minutes to make train connections.

Private rail lines have scenic train trips throughout Northern New England, particularly during fall foliage season. Several use vintage steam equipment; the most notable is the Cog Railway to Mt. Washington in New Hampshire.

Information Amtrak (☎ 800/872-7245 ⊕ www.amtrak.com). **Mt. Washington Cog Railway** (☎ *603/278-5404 or 800/922-8825* ⊕ *www.thecog.com*). **Massachusetts Bay Transportation Authority** (*MBTA* ☎ *617/222-3200 or 800/392-6100* ⊕ *www.mbta.com*).

ESSENTIALS

ACCOMMODATIONS

Northern New England can be a bit expensive when it comes to accommodations. Many areas are seasonal. Coastal sections tend to have the highest rates in summer, mountains regions can be pricey during the ski season, and virtually all of Northern New England can be expensive during the peak fall foliage times. In fact, it can be down-right tough to find weekend hotel rooms in summer and fall, so if you're planning to visit during that time, try to book your stay several weeks ahead.

See the planner at the start of each chapter for lodging price ranges.

BED-AND-BREAKFASTS

Historic B&Bs and inns proliferate throughout Northern New England. In many rural or less-touristy areas, B&Bs offer an affordable alternative to chain properties, but in tourism-dependent communities (i.e., most of the major towns in this region), expect to pay about the same or more for a historic inn as for a full-service hotel. Many of the state's finest restaurants are also in country inns. Although many B&Bs and smaller establishments continue to offer a low-key, homey experience, in recent years many such properties have begun offering amenities like Wi-Fi, whirlpool tubs, and TVs with DVD players. Quite a few inns and B&Bs serve substantial breakfasts.

Reservation Services **Bed & Breakfast.com** (*512/322–2710 or 800/462–2632* *www.bedandbreakfast.com*). **Bed & Breakfast Inns Online** (*310/280–4363 or 800/215–7365* *www.bbonline.com*). **BnB Finder.com** (*888/469–6663* *www.bnbfinder.com*).

HOUSE AND APARTMENT RENTALS

In Northern New England, you are most likely to find a house, apartment, or condo rental in areas in which ownership of second homes is common, such as beach resorts and ski country. Home-exchange directories sometimes list rentals as well as exchanges. Another good bet is to contact real-estate agents in the area in which you are interested.

Contacts **Cyberrentals.com** (*512/684–1098* *www.cyberrentals.com*). **Forgetaway** (*www.forgetaway.weather.com*). **Home Away** (*512/493–0382* *www.homeaway.com*). **Interhome** (*800/882–6864* *www.interhome.us*). **Villas International** (*415/499–9490 or 800/221–2260* *www.villasintl.com*).

HOTELS

Major hotel and motel chains are amply represented in Northern New England. The region is also liberally supplied with small, independent motels, which run the gamut from the tired to the tidy. Don't overlook these mom-and-pop operations; they frequently offer cheerful, convenient accommodations at lower rates than the chains.

Reservations are always a good idea, particularly in summer and in winter resort areas; in college towns in September and at graduation time in spring; and at areas renowned for autumn foliage.

Most hotels and motels will hold your reservation until 6 PM; call ahead if you plan to arrive late. All will hold a late reservation for you if you guarantee your reservation with a credit-card number.

All hotels listed have a private bath unless otherwise noted.

CHILDREN IN NEW ENGLAND

Throughout Northern New England, you'll have no problem finding comparatively inexpensive child-friendly hotels and family-style restaurants—as well as some top children's museums, beaches, parks, planetariums, and lighthouses.

Just keep in mind that a number of fine, antiques-filled B&Bs and inns punctuate the landscape, and these places are not always suitable for kids—many flat-out refuse to accommodate children. Also, some of the quieter and more rural areas lack child-oriented attractions.

Favorite destinations for family vacations in Northern New England include the White Mountains and coastal Maine, but in general, the entire region has plenty to offer families. Places that are especially appealing to children are indicated by a rubber-duckie icon (🐤) in the margin.

LODGING

Chain hotels and motels welcome children, and Maine, Vermont, and New Hampshire have many family-oriented resorts with lively children's programs. You'll also find farms that accept guests and can be lots of fun for children. Rental houses and apartments abound, particularly around ski areas; off-season, these can be economical as well as comfortable touring bases. Some country inns, especially those with a quiet, romantic atmosphere and those furnished with antiques, are less enthusiastic about little ones. Many larger resorts and hotels will provide a babysitter at an additional cost. Others will provide a list of sitters in the area.

Most hotels in Northern New England allow children under a certain age to stay in their parents' room at no extra charge, but others charge for them as extra adults; find out the cutoff age for children's discounts. Note that in Maine, by state law, hotels and inns (unless they have five or fewer rooms) cannot put age restrictions on children.

Most lodgings that welcome infants and small children will provide a crib or cot, but remember to give advance notice so that one will be available for you (and ask about any additional charges). Many family resorts make special accommodations for small children during meals.

WORD OF MOUTH

Was the service stellar or not up to snuff? Did the food give you shivers of delight or leave you cold? Did the prices and portions make you happy or sad? Rate restaurants and write your own reviews in Travel Ratings or start a discussion about your favorite places in Travel Talk on www.fodors.com. Your comments might even appear in our books. Yes, you, too, can be a correspondent!

TRANSPORTATION

Each New England state has specific requirements regarding age and weight requirements for children in car seats. If you're renting a car, ask about the state(s) you're planning to drive in. If you will need a car seat, make sure the agency you select provides them and reserve well in advance.

COMMUNICATIONS

INTERNET

Most major chain hotels and many smaller motels throughout Northern New England now offer Wi-Fi or other Internet access, both from individual rooms and in lobbies (which usually have a desktop computer available for guest use); ask about access fees when you book. Many coffee shops provide Wi-Fi (some for free), as do most libraries; the latter also provide computers with free Internet access. Cybercafes lists more than 4,000 Internet cafés worldwide.

Contacts **Cybercafes** (🌐 *www.cybercafes.com*).

EATING OUT

Although certain ingredients and preparations are common to the region as a whole, Maine, Vermont, and New Hampshire's cuisine varies greatly from place to place. Especially in such urban areas as Portland and in upscale resort areas such as coastal Maine and Stowe, Vermont, you can expect to find stellar restaurants, many of them with culinary luminaries at the helm and a reputation for creative—and occasionally daring—menus.

Elsewhere, restaurant food tends more toward the simple, traditional, and conservative. Cities, collegiate communities, and other sophisticated New England areas also have a great variety of international restaurants, especially excellent Italian, French, Japanese, Indian, and Thai eateries. There are also quite a few diners, which typically present patrons with page after page of inexpensive, short-order cooking and often stay open until the wee hours.

The proximity to the ocean accounts for a number of restaurants, often tiny shacks, serving very fresh seafood, and the numerous boutique dairy, meat, and vegetable suppliers that have sprung up throughout New England account for other choice ingredients. In fact, menus in the more upscale and tourism-driven communities often note which Vermont dairy a particular goat cheese came from.

For information on food-related health issues, see Health below.

MEALS AND MEALTIMES

In general, the widest variety of mealtime options in Maine, Vermont, and New Hampshire is in larger cities and at resort areas, though you may be pleasantly surprised to hear about a creative café in a smaller town, especially along the Maine Coast.

For an early breakfast, pick places that cater to a working clientele. City, town, and roadside establishments specializing in breakfast for early workers often open their doors at 5 or 6 AM. At country inns and B&Bs, breakfast is seldom served before 8; if you need to get an earlier start, ask ahead of time if your host or hostess can accommodate you. Lunch in New England generally runs from around 11 to 2:30; dinner is usually served from 6 to 9 (many restaurants have early-bird specials beginning at 5). Only in the larger cities will you find full dinners being offered much later than 9. Many restaurants in Northern New England are closed Monday, and sometimes Sunday or Tuesday, although this is never true in resort areas in high season. However, resort-town eateries often shut down completely in the off-season.

Unless otherwise noted, the restaurants listed in this guide are open daily for lunch and dinner.

PAYING

For guidelines on tipping see chart below.

Credit cards are accepted for meals throughout New England in all but the most modest establishments. *See price chart at the beginning of each chapter for price categories for dining and lodging establishments.*

RESERVATIONS AND DRESS

It's a good idea to make a reservation if you can. We only mention them specifically when reservations are essential (there's no other way you'll ever get a table) or when they are not accepted. For popular restaurants, book as far ahead as you can (often 30 days) and reconfirm as soon as you arrive. (Large parties should always call ahead to check the reservations policy.) We mention dress only when men are required to wear a jacket or a jacket and tie.

WINES, BEER, AND SPIRITS

Maine, Vermont, and New Hampshire are no strangers to microbrews. The granddaddy of New England's independent beer makers is Boston's Samuel Adams, producing brews available throughout the region since 1985. Following the Sam Adams lead in offering hearty English-style ales and special seasonal brews are breweries such as Vermont's Long Trail, Maine's Shipyard, and New Hampshire's Smuttynose Brewing Co. Green Mountain Cidery makes Woodchuck hard cider in Middlebury, Vermont.

New England is beginning to earn some respect as a wine-producing region. Varieties capable of withstanding the region's harsh winters have been the basis of

TIPPING GUIDELINES FOR NEW ENGLAND	
Bartender	$1 to $5 per round of drinks, depending on the number of drinks
Bellhop	$1 to $2 per bag, depending on the level of the hotel
Hotel Concierge	$5 or more, if he or she performs a service for you
Hotel Doorman	$1 to $2 if he helps you get a cab
Hotel Maid	$1 to $3 a day (either daily or at the end of your stay, in cash)
Hotel Room-Service Waiter	$1 to $2 per delivery, even if a service charge has been added
Porter at Airport or Train Station	$1 per bag
Skycap at Airport	$1 to $3 per bag checked
Taxi Driver	15%–20%, but round up the fare to the next dollar amount
Tour Guide	10% of the cost of the tour
Valet Parking Attendant	$1 to $2, but only when you get your car
Waiter	15%–20%, with 20% being the norm at high-end restaurants; nothing additional if a service charge is added to the bill
Other Attendants	Restroom attendants in more expensive restaurants expect some small change or $1. Tip coat-check personnel at least $1 to $2 per item checked unless there is a fee, then nothing.

promising enterprises such as Snow Farm Vineyard in the Lake Champlain Islands.

Although a patchwork of state and local regulations affect the hours and locations of places that sell alcoholic beverages, Northern New England licensing laws are fairly liberal. State-owned or -franchised stores sell hard liquor in New Hampshire, Maine, and Vermont; many travelers have found that New Hampshire offers the region's lowest prices. Look for state-run liquor "supermarkets" on interstate highways in the southern part of New Hampshire; these also have good wine selections.

HEALTH

Lyme disease, so named for its having been first reported in the town of Lyme, Connecticut, is a potentially debilitating disease carried by deer ticks, which thrive in dry, brush-covered areas, particularly on the coast. Always use insect repellent; outbreaks of Lyme disease all over the East Coast make it imperative that you protect yourself from ticks from early spring through summer. To prevent bites, wear light-color clothing and tuck pant legs into socks. Look for black ticks about the size of a pinhead around hairlines and the warmest parts of the body. If you have been bitten, consult a physician, especially if you see the telltale bull's-eye bite pattern. Influenza-like symptoms often accompany a Lyme infection. Early treatment is imperative.

Maine, Vermont, and New Hampshire's two greatest insect pests are black flies and mosquitoes. The former are a phenomenon of late spring and early summer and are generally a problem only in the densely wooded areas of the far north. Mosquitoes, however, can be a nuisance just about everywhere in summer. The best protection against both pests is repellent containing DEET; if you're camping in the woods during black fly season, you'll also want to use fine mesh screening in eating and sleeping areas and even wear mesh headgear. A particular pest of coastal areas, especially salt marshes, is the greenhead fly. Their bite is nasty, they are hard to kill, and they are best repelled by a liberal application of Avon Skin So Soft or a similar product.

Coastal waters attract seafood lovers who enjoy harvesting their own clams, mussels, and even lobsters; permits are required, and casual harvesting of lobsters is strictly forbidden. Amateur clammers should be aware that New England shellfish beds are periodically visited by red tides, during which microorganisms can render shellfish poisonous. To keep abreast of the situation, inquire when you apply for a license (usually at town halls or police stations) and pay attention to red tide postings as you travel.

HOURS OF OPERATION

Hours in Maine, Vermont, and New Hampshire differ little from those in other parts of the United States. Within the region, shops and other businesses tend to keep slightly later hours in larger cities and along the coast, which is generally more populated than interior New England.

Most major museums and attractions are open daily or six days a week (with Monday being the most likely day of closing). Hours are often shorter on Saturday and especially Sunday, and some prominent museums stay open late one or two nights a week, usually Tuesday, Thursday, or Friday. Northern New England also has quite a few smaller museums—historical societies, small art galleries, highly specialized collections—that open only a few days a week and sometimes only by appointment in winter or slow periods.

MONEY

It costs a bit more to travel in most of Northern New England than it does in the rest of the country, with the most costly areas being Boston and the coastal resort areas. There are also a fair number of somewhat posh inns and restaurants in parts of Vermont and New Hampshire. ATMs are plentiful, and larger denomination bills (as well as credit cards) are readily accepted in tourist destinations during the high season.

Prices throughout this guide are given for adults. Substantially reduced fees are almost always available for children, students, and senior citizens.

CREDIT CARDS

Throughout this guide, the following abbreviations are used: **AE**, American Express; **D**, Discover; **DC**, Diners Club; **MC**, MasterCard; and **V**, Visa.

Major credit cards are readily accepted throughout New England, though in rural areas you may encounter difficulties or the acceptance of only MasterCard or Visa (also note that if you'll be making an excursion into Canada, many outlets there accept Visa but not MasterCard).

Reporting Lost Cards American Express (☎ *800/528–4800* 🌐 *www.americanexpress.com*). **Diners Club** (☎ *800/234–6377* 🌐 *www.dinersclub.com*). **Discover** (☎ *800/347–2683* 🌐 *www.discovercard.com*). **MasterCard** (☎ *800/627–8372* 🌐 *www.mastercard.com*). **Visa** (☎ *800/847–2911* 🌐 *www.visa.com*).

PACKING

The principal rule on weather in Northern New England is that there are no rules. A cold, foggy morning in spring can and often does become a bright, 60°F afternoon. A summer breeze can suddenly turn chilly, and rain often appears with little warning. Thus, the best advice on how to dress is to layer your clothing so that you can peel off or add garments as needed for comfort. Showers are frequent, so pack a raincoat and umbrella. Even in summer you should bring long pants, a sweater or two, and a waterproof windbreaker, for evenings are often chilly and sea spray can make things cool.

Casual sportswear—walking shoes and jeans or khakis—will take you almost everywhere, but swimsuits and bare feet will not: shirts and shoes are required attire at even the most casual venues. Dress in restaurants is generally casual, except at some of the distinguished restaurants in Vermont and Kennebunkport, Maine. Upscale resorts will, at the very least, require men to wear collared shirts at dinner, and jeans are often frowned upon.

In summer, bring a hat and sunscreen. Remember also to pack insect repellent; to prevent Lyme disease you'll need to guard against ticks from early spring through summer (⇨ *Health*).

SAFETY

Rural Northern New England is one of the country's safest regions, so much so that residents often leave their doors unlocked. In the cities, particularly in Boston, observe the usual precautions. You should avoid out-of-the-way or poorly lighted areas at night; clutch handbags close to your body and don't let them out of your sight; and be on your guard in subways and buses, not only during the deserted wee hours but in crowded rush hours, when pickpockets are at work. Keep your valuables in hotel safes. Try to use ATMs in busy, well-lighted places such as bank lobbies.

If your vehicle breaks down in a rural area, pull as far off the road as possible, tie a handkerchief to your radio antenna (or use flares at night—check if your rental agency can provide them), and stay in your car with the doors locked until help arrives. Don't pick up hitchhikers. If you're planning to leave a car overnight to make use of off-road trails or camping facilities, make arrangements for a supervised parking area if at all possible. Cars left at trailhead parking lots are subject to theft and vandalism.

The universal telephone number for crime and other emergencies throughout Northern New England is 911.

TAXES

See Restaurant and Hotel charts at the beginning of each chapter for information about taxes on restaurant meals and accommodations. Sales taxes in Northern New England are as follows: Maine 5% and Vermont 6%. No sales tax is charged in New Hampshire. Some states and municipalities levy an additional tax (from 1% to 10%) on lodging or restaurant meals. Alcoholic beverages are sometimes taxed at a higher rate than that applied to meals.

TIME

Northern New England operates on Eastern Standard Time and follows daylight saving time. When it is noon in Portland it is 9 AM in Los Angeles, 11 AM in Chicago, 5 PM in London, and 3 AM the following day in Sydney. When taking a ferry to Nova Scotia, remember that the province operates on Atlantic Standard Time and, therefore, is an hour ahead.

TOURS

Brennan Vacations and Insight Vacations both offer a selection of fall foliage tours. Contiki Holidays, specialists in vacations for 18- to 35-year-olds, has a few tours available that pass through parts of New England as well as the rest of the Northeast.

Recommended Companies
Brennan Vacations (☎ *800/237–7249* 🌐 *www.brennanvacations.com*). **Contiki Holidays** (☎ *866/266–8454* 🌐 *contiki.com*). **Insight Vacations** (☎ *888/680–1241* 🌐 *www.insightvacations.com/us*).

SPECIAL-INTEREST TOURS

BICYCLING AND HIKING

TIP→ Most airlines accommodate bikes as luggage, provided they're dismantled and boxed.

Contacts **Bike New England** (☎ *978/979–6598* 🌐 *www.bikenewengland.com*). **TrekAmerica** (☎ *800/873–5872* 🌐 *www.trekamerica.com*).

CULINARY

Contacts **Creative Culinary Tours** (☎ *888/889–8681* 🌐 *www.creativeculinarytours.com*).

CULTURE

Contacts **Northeast Unlimited Tours** (☎ *800/759–6820* 🌐 *www.newenglandtours.com*). **New England**

INSPIRATION

BOOKS

■ Get a feel for classic Maine coast life by checking out *Ralph Stanley: Tales of a Maine Boatbuilder.* Written by Craig Milner and coauthored by Stanley, it includes a summary of boats built by the man many consider the finest wooden boat builder around. In *Good Fences: A Pictorial History of New England's Stone Wall,* photographer William Hubbell assembled 192 color images he made of these highly functional yet charming barriers. In addition to photos, the book includes conversations with contemporary wall builders and a chronological history of styles. In *Wandering Home,* noted environmental author Bill McKibben walks for three weeks from his home in Vermont to his former home in the nearby Adirondack Mountains of New York via the Champlain Valley.

MOVIES

■ A winner in the 2005 Maine Documentary Film Competition, Red Door Media's *Closing the Circle* follows more than 100,000 of the tiny alewife—a type of herring—as they make their annual run up the Damariscotta River to Damariscotta Lake, their freshwater birthplace. In telling the tale, the filmmakers discuss the impact of the fish on the culture and livelihood of the village alongside the lake. Henry Fonda gives one of his last great performances in 1981's *On Golden Pond.* Written by a screenwriter who spent summers lakeside in Belgrade, Maine, and filmed at Squam Lake in New Hampshire, the film gives a good if fictionalized feel for New England lake life.

Vacation Tours (*800/742–7669 www.newenglandvacationtours.com*). **Wolfe Adventures & Tours** (*888/449–6533 www.wolfetours.com*).

SKIING

Contacts New England Action Sports (*800/477–7669 www.skitrip.net*). **New England Vacation Tours** (*800/742–7669 www.newenglandvacationtours.com*).

VISITOR INFORMATION

Each New England state provides a helpful free information kit, including a guidebook, map, and listings of attractions and events. All include listings and advertisements for lodging and dining establishments. Each state also has an official Web site with material on sights and lodgings; most of these sites have a calendar of events and other special features.

Contacts Maine Office of Tourism (*888/624–6345 www.visitmaine.com*). **State of New Hampshire Division of Travel and Tourism Development** (*800/386–4664 or 603/271–2665 www.visitnh.gov*). **Vermont Department of Tourism and Marketing** (*802/828–3237, 800/837–6668 brochures www.vermontvacation.com*).

ONLINE RESOURCES

Check out the official home page of each New England state for information on state government as well as links to state agencies with information on doing business, working, studying, living, and traveling in these areas. GORP is a terrific general resource for just about every kind of recreational activity; just click on the state link under "Destinations," and you'll be flooded with links to myriad topics, from wildlife refuges to ski trips to backpacking advice.

Yankee, New England's premier regional magazine, also publishes an informative travel Web site. Another great Web resource is Visit New England.

Online Info GORP (*www.gorp.com*). **Visit New England** (*www.visitnewengland.com*). ***Yankee Magazine*** (*www.yankeemagazine.com/travel*).

INDEX

A

B

PHOTO CREDITS

1, William Britten/iStockphoto. 2, Robert Plotz/iStockphoto. 5, Kindra Clineff. **Chapter 1: Experience Northern New England:** 8-9, Kindra Clineff. 10, Natalia Bratslavsky/iStockphoto. 11 (left), Denis Jr. Tangney/iStockphoto. 11 (right), William Britten/iStockphoto. 14 (left), Ken Canning/iStockphoto. 14 (top right), Kindra Clineff. 14 (bottom right), iStockphoto. 15 (left), drewthehobbit/Shutterstock. 15 (top center), Kindra Clineff. 15 (bottom center), Kindra Clineff. 15 (top right), T. Markley/Shutterstock. 15 (bottom right), Natalia Bratslavsky/iStockphoto. 16, Vermont Dept. of Tourism and Marketing/Dennis Curran. 17 (left) , Rod Kaye/iStockphoto. 17 (right), Ken Canning/Flickr. 18, Michael Czosnek/iStockphoto. 19 (left), Hnin Khine/iStockphoto. 19 (right), kworth30/wikipedia.org. 20, Eric Foltz/iStockphoto. 21, Chris Coe / age fotostock. 22, Christine Glade/iStockphoto. 23, Doug Schneider/iStockphoto. 26-27, Ken Canning/iStockphoto. 29 (top left), Michael Krakowiak/iStockphoto. 29 (bottom left), Steffen Foerster Photography/Shutterstock. 29 (top center), Lisa Thornberg/iStockphoto. 29 (bottom center), iStockphoto. 29 (top right), Scott Cramer/iStockphoto. 29 (bottom right), Paul Aniszewski/Shutterstock. **Chapter 2: Vermont:** 31, Kindra Clineff. 32 (top), Marcio Silva/iStockphoto. 32 (bottom), Denis Jr. Tangney/iStockphoto. 33, Denis Jr. Tangney/iStockphoto. 34, Thomas Lars Lichtman/iStockphoto. 36, Heeb Christian / age fotostock. 37, Sarah Kennedy/iStockphoto. 38, S. Greg Panosian/iStockphoto. 43, Kindra Clineff. 44, Kindra Clineff. 45, Kindra Clineff. 50, Kindra Clineff. 56, Hildene. 59, Lee Krohn Photography, Manchester, Vermont. 67, Kindra Clineff. 70, Kindra Clineff. 77, Kindra Clineff. 79, Dale Halbur/iStockphoto. 86 and 87, S. Greg Panosian/iStockphoto. 93, Kindra Clineff. 98, Fraser Hall / age fotostock. 103, Dennis Curran / age fotostock. 104, Skye Chalmers Photography, inc. 105 (left), Henryk T Kaiser / age fotostock. 105 (right), Hubert Schriebl. 106 (left), Marcio Silva/iStockphoto. 106 (right), Hubert Schriebl. 107, SMUGGLERS' NOTCH RESORT/Ski Vermont. 108, OkemoMountain Resort. 110, Ellen Rooney / age fotostock. 111 (left), Barry Winiker / age fotostock. 111 (right), Don Landwehrle. 112 (left), OKEMO MOUNTAIN RESORT/Ski Vermont. 112, Magic Mountain. 123, Kindra Clineff. 124, Skye Chalmers/State of Vermont. 127, Kindra Clineff. 133, Alan Copson / age fotostock. 134, Jack Sumberg. **Chapter 3: New Hampshire:** 137, Denis Jr. Tangney/iStockphoto. 138 (top), Denis Jr. Tangney/iStockphoto. 138 (bottom), Ken Canning/iStockphoto. 140, Rob Sylvan/iStockphoto. 142, Mary Ann Alwan / Alamy. 143, iStockphoto. 144, Sebastien Cote/iStockphoto. 149, Kindra Clineff. 150, Kindra Clineff. 154, Denis Jr. Tangney/iStockphoto. 160 and 161 , cyanocorax/Flickr. 162, NHDTTD/Dave Martsolf. 165, DAVID NOBLE PHOTOGRAPHY / Alamy. 171, Kindra Clineff. 173, Roy Rainford / age fotostock. 183 (top), Jerry and Marcy Monkman EcoPhotography.com/Alamy 183 (bottom), Liz Van Steenburgh/Shutterstock. 184, Kindra Clineff. 185, Mike Kautz/AMC. 186 left and bottom right, nialat/Shutterstock. 186 (top right), RestonImages/Shutterstock. 187 (top left), jadimages/Shutterstock. 187(bottom left), Ansgar Walk/wikipedia.org. 187 (bottom center), J. Carmichael/wikipedia.org. 187 (right), rebvt/Shutterstock. 189, Matty Symons/Shutterstock. 190, Danita Delimont / Alamy. 191, Frank Siteman / age fotostock. 199, Kindra Clineff. 200, Kindra Clineff. 206, First Light / Alamy. 211, Kenneth C. Zirkel/iStockphoto. 213, gailf548/Flicks. 220, Kindra Clineff. 223, Jet Low/Wikimedia Commons. 228, Currier Museum of Art./ 2005 Jose Martinez. 235, Franz Marc Frei / age fotostock. 238, Andre Jenny / Alamy. **Chapter 4: Inland Maine:** 243, Jeff Martone/Flickr. 244, Kenneth C. Zirkel/iStockphoto. 245, Stephen G Page/iStockphoto. 248, Denis Jr. Tangney/iStockphoto. 249, The Wilhelm Reich Infant Trust. 250, BrendanReals/Shutterstock. 259, D A Horchner / age fotostock. 264 and 265, Kazela/Shutterstock. **Chapter 5: Maine Coast:** 271, SuperStock/age fotostock. 272 (top), Denis Jr. Tangney/iStockphoto. 272 (bottom), Paul Tessier/iStockphoto. 273, Andrea Pelletier/iStockphoto. 276, Aimin Tang/iStockphoto. 278, ARCO/L Weyers / age fotostock. 287, Perry B. Johnson / age fotostock. 294, Lucid Images / age fotostock. 301, SuperStock/age fotostock. 307, Jeff Greenberg / age fotostock. 314, Lee Coursey/Flickr. 315, Kindra Clineff. 321, Jeff Greenberg / age fotostock. 322, Jeff Greenberg / Alamy. 324, Michael Czosnek/iStockphoto. 325, SuperStock / age fotostock. 326 (left), Maine State Museum. 326 (right), David Cannings-Bushell/iStockphoto. 327, Paul D. Lemke/iStockphoto. 328, Michael Rickard/Shutterstock. 329 (left), Dave Johnston. 329 (top right), Robert Campbell. 329 (bottom right), Casey Jordan. 330 (top), Doug Lemke/Shutterstock. 330 (center), Jason Grower/Shutterstock. 330 (bottom), Kenneth Keifer/Shutterstock. 331 (top), Pat & Chuck Blackley / Alamy. 331 (center), Doug Lemke/Shutterstock. 331 (bottom), liz west/wikipedia.org. 335, Raymond Forbes / age fotostock. 342, David Mathies/iStockphoto. 345, Kindra Clineff. 350, Kindra Clineff. 362, Kindra Clineff. 364 and 365, Alan Majchrowicz / age fotostock,. 375, Kindra Clineff. 378 and 379, Lyle Fink/iStockphoto